MSDE Bible

MSDE Bible

David C. Walls
Denise M. Gosnell

IDG Books Worldwide, Inc.
An International Data Group Company
Foster City, CA ✦ Chicago, IL ✦ Indianapolis, IN ✦ New York, NY

MSDE Bible

Published by
IDG Books Worldwide, Inc.
An International Data Group Company
919 E. Hillsdale Blvd., Suite 400
Foster City, CA 94404
www.idgbooks.com (IDG Books Worldwide Web site)

ISBN: 0-7645-4681-3

Printed in the United States of America

10 9 8 7 6 5 4 3 2 1

1B/QW/RS/QQ/FC

Distributed in the United States by IDG Books Worldwide, Inc.

Distributed by CDG Books Canada Inc. for Canada; by Transworld Publishers Limited in the United Kingdom; by IDG Norge Books for Norway; by IDG Sweden Books for Sweden; by IDG Books Australia Publishing Corporation Pty. Ltd. for Australia and New Zealand; by TransQuest Publishers Pte Ltd. for Singapore, Malaysia, Thailand, Indonesia, and Hong Kong; by Gotop Information Inc. for Taiwan; by ICG Muse, Inc. for Japan; by Intersoft for South Africa; by Eyrolles for France; by International Thomson Publishing for Germany, Austria, and Switzerland; by Distribuidora Cuspide for Argentina; by LR International for Brazil; by Galileo Libros for Chile; by Ediciones ZETA S.C.R. Ltda. for Peru; by WS Computer Publishing Corporation, Inc., for the Philippines; by Contemporanea de Ediciones for Venezuela; by Express Computer Distributors for the Caribbean and West Indies; by Micronesia Media Distributor, Inc. for Micronesia; by Chips Computadoras S.A. de C.V. for Mexico; by Editorial Norma de Panama S.A. for Panama; by American Bookshops for Finland.

For general information on IDG Books Worldwide's books in the U.S., please call our Consumer Customer Service department at 800-762-2974. For reseller information, including discounts and premium sales, please call our Reseller Customer Service department at 800-434-3422.

For information on where to purchase IDG Books Worldwide's books outside the U.S., please contact our International Sales department at 317-572-3993 or fax 317-572-4002.

For consumer information on foreign language translations, please contact our Customer Service department at 800-434-3422, fax 317-572-4002, or e-mail rights@idgbooks.com.

For information on licensing foreign or domestic rights, please phone +1-650-653-7098.

For sales inquiries and special prices for bulk quantities, please contact our Order Services department at 800-434-3422 or write to the address above.

For information on using IDG Books Worldwide's books in the classroom or for ordering examination copies, please contact our Educational Sales department at 800-434-2086 or fax 317-572-4005.

For press review copies, author interviews, or other publicity information, please contact our Public Relations department at 650-653-7000 or fax 650-653-7500.

For authorization to photocopy items for corporate, personal, or educational use, please contact Copyright Clearance Center, 222 Rosewood Drive, Danvers, MA 01923, or fax 978-750-4470.

Library of Congress Cataloging-in-Publication Data

Walls, David C. (David Charles), 1967-
MSDE bible / David C. Walls, Denise Gosnell, Mark Scott.
p. cm.
ISBN 0-7645-4681-3 (alk. paper)
1. Database design. 2. SQL server. I. Gosnell, Denise. II. Scott, Mark. III. Title
QA76.9.D26 W35 2000
005.75'85–dc21 00-063363

ABOUT IDG BOOKS WORLDWIDE

Welcome to the world of IDG Books Worldwide.

IDG Books Worldwide, Inc., is a subsidiary of International Data Group, the world's largest publisher of computer-related information and the leading global provider of information services on information technology. IDG was founded more than 30 years ago by Patrick J. McGovern and now employs more than 9,000 people worldwide. IDG publishes more than 290 computer publications in over 75 countries. More than 90 million people read one or more IDG publications each month.

Launched in 1990, IDG Books Worldwide is today the #1 publisher of best-selling computer books in the United States. We are proud to have received eight awards from the Computer Press Association in recognition of editorial excellence and three from Computer Currents' First Annual Readers' Choice Awards. Our best-selling *...For Dummies®* series has more than 50 million copies in print with translations in 31 languages. IDG Books Worldwide, through a joint venture with IDG's Hi-Tech Beijing, became the first U.S. publisher to publish a computer book in the People's Republic of China. In record time, IDG Books Worldwide has become the first choice for millions of readers around the world who want to learn how to better manage their businesses.

Our mission is simple: Every one of our books is designed to bring extra value and skill-building instructions to the reader. Our books are written by experts who understand and care about our readers. The knowledge base of our editorial staff comes from years of experience in publishing, education, and journalism — experience we use to produce books to carry us into the new millennium. In short, we care about books, so we attract the best people. We devote special attention to details such as audience, interior design, use of icons, and illustrations. And because we use an efficient process of authoring, editing, and desktop publishing our books electronically, we can spend more time ensuring superior content and less time on the technicalities of making books.

You can count on our commitment to deliver high-quality books at competitive prices on topics you want to read about. At IDG Books Worldwide, we continue in the IDG tradition of delivering quality for more than 30 years. You'll find no better book on a subject than one from IDG Books Worldwide.

John Kilcullen
Chairman and CEO
IDG Books Worldwide, Inc.

Eighth Annual Computer Press Awards 1992

Ninth Annual Computer Press Awards 1993

Tenth Annual Computer Press Awards 1994

Eleventh Annual Computer Press Awards 1995

IDG is the world's leading IT media, research and exposition company. Founded in 1964, IDG had 1997 revenues of $2.05 billion and has more than 9,000 employees worldwide. IDG offers the widest range of media options that reach IT buyers in 75 countries representing 95% of worldwide IT spending. IDG's diverse product and services portfolio spans six key areas including print publishing, online publishing, expositions and conferences, market research, education and training, and global marketing services. More than 90 million people read one or more of IDG's 290 magazines and newspapers, including IDG's leading global brands — Computerworld, PC World, Network World, Macworld and the Channel World family of publications. IDG Books Worldwide is one of the fastest-growing computer book publishers in the world, with more than 700 titles in 36 languages. The "...For Dummies®" series alone has more than 50 million copies in print. IDG offers online users the largest network of technology-specific Web sites around the world through IDG.net (http://www.idg.net), which comprises more than 225 targeted Web sites in 55 countries worldwide. International Data Corporation (IDC) is the world's largest provider of information technology data, analysis and consulting, with research centers in over 41 countries and more than 400 research analysts worldwide. IDG World Expo is a leading producer of more than 168 globally branded conferences and expositions in 35 countries including E3 (Electronic Entertainment Expo), Macworld Expo, ComNet, Windows World Expo, ICE (Internet Commerce Expo), Agenda, DEMO, and Spotlight. IDG's training subsidiary, ExecuTrain, is the world's largest computer training company, with more than 230 locations worldwide and 785 training courses. IDG Marketing Services helps industry-leading IT companies build international brand recognition by developing global integrated marketing programs via IDG's print, online and exposition products worldwide. Further information about the company can be found at www.idg.com.

1/26/00

Credits

Acquisitions Editor
Grace Buechlein

Contributing Writer
Mark D. Scott

Project Editors
Marcia Brochin
Eric Newman

Technical Editor
Jonathon Walsh

Copy Editor
Gabrielle Chosney

Project Coordinators
Marcos Vergara
Danette Nurse

Graphics and Production Specialists
Robert Bilhmayer
Jude Levinson
Michael Lewis
Ramses Ramirez
Victor Pérez-Varela

Quality Control Technician
Dina F Quan

Permissions Editor
Laura Moss

Media Development Specialist
Brock Bigard

Media Development Coordinator
Marisa Pearman

Book Designer
Drew R. Moore

Illustrators
Gabriele McCann
Rashell Smith
Shelley Norris

Proofreading and Indexing
York Production Services

Cover Image
Joann Vuong

About the Authors

David C. Walls is originally from Chester, Pennsylvania, and now makes his home in Springfield (Delaware County), which is also in the Keystone State. He began working with computers professionally in 1983 at Widener University. While there, he worked with the Pick database system in various forms, introduced the university to the Internet, and rolled out Novell NetWare-based networks to the campus computer labs. For four years he was the Manager of Engineering at FasPak, a communications cabling company. Since then, he has been teaching and consulting on a variety of topics, with emphasis on Microsoft's SQL Server. He has previously contributed to a book about SQL Server 7.0, has written several magazine articles, and has spoken at computer-oriented conferences.

Denise M. Gosnell is a Senior Programmer Consultant with Ambassador, Inc., a solutions firm headquartered in Indianapolis, Indiana. Her previous positions include Director of IS for CMG Worldwide, Inc., Programmer/Analyst for Key Benefit Administrators, Inc., and Systems Engineer for Electronic Data Systems (EDS). She obtained her Microsoft Certified Solution Developer (MCSD) status in 1997.

Denise has been involved in software development professionally for over 6 years, and has worked with computer programming as a hobby since she was 12 years old. She received her bachelor's degree in Computer Science-Business from Anderson University and recently received a Doctor of Jurisprudence from Indiana University. She plans to pursue a career in patent and intellectual property law.

Mark D. Scott is a consultant for RDA. He is a Microsoft Certified Database Administrator, System Engineer + Internet, Solution Developer and Trainer. He is a nationally recognized speaker and author. He holds a bachelor's degree in Computer Science.

This book is dedicated to the memory of

Glenn R. Miller

1962–1999

Preface

This book is about the SQL Server 2000 Desktop Engine. The Desktop Engine is a version of SQL Server that has a special licensing agreement, making it very appealing for use with database applications that are developed using Access or any of Microsoft's programming languages. If you have the right license, you can distribute the Desktop Engine to users of your application free of charge. The Desktop Engine has a few limitations relative to all other editions of SQL Server, and it does not include the graphical management tools that are included with other editions. The previous version of the Desktop Engine (the one that was an edition of SQL Server 7.0) was called the Microsoft Database Engine, or MSDE (an acronym that continues to be used for the current version).

While this book is written specifically for the Desktop Engine (MSDE), it will still be a useful reference for you when you eventually upgrade to the Standard or Enterprise edition of the software. The only differences you will find when moving from MSDE to another edition are the removal of some limitations and the addition of some advanced features. The limitations are covered completely in this book; the advanced features not present in MSDE have been left to other, more energetic authors.

Who Should Read This Book

> If you want a complete guide to working with MSDE and SQL, then the *MSDE Bible* is a necessary addition to your reference library. –Trevor Dwyer, Chief Database Architect, The iGroup and Microsoft SQL Server MVP

This book is intended to be used by anyone who needs to work with the Desktop Engine version of SQL Server 2000. If you develop applications with Access or any Visual Studio product, you are a good candidate for using the Desktop Engine. If you use an application that is based on the Desktop Engine, you will also find this book very helpful. No prior knowledge of SQL Server or the SQL language is required; introductory material is provided for all topics in addition to many intermediate and some advanced concepts.

This book makes extensive use of examples to show how to accomplish the tasks that are necessary for working with databases. Since the readers of this book may not have access to all the tools that ship with the full versions of SQL Server, instructions and examples are given using all available tools, including Access, Visual Studio, SQL Server Enterprise Manager, SQL statements, and programmatic interfaces such as the Data Management Objects. The examples for the programmatic interfaces are written in VBScript and are primarily given in short, working scripts that can be used as they are. You can also integrate the techniques that are used into other scripting languages or full-fledged programming languages, such as Visual Basic. Where it is necessary or helpful, examples have been provided in Visual Basic.

What You'll Find in This Book

This book consists of 33 chapters organized into 8 parts. In general, the difficulty of the material increases toward the end of the book, and the second half of the book relies on introductory material presented in the first half. A brief description of the topics covered in each part follows.

Part I: The MSDE Environment

The first part gives an overview of the purpose and function of the SQL Server Desktop Engine (MSDE). The differences in the various versions of SQL Server are explained, and MSDE is compared with the Jet database engine, to which it is an alternative. All of the tools that can be used to administer MSDE are fully described, including any inherent limitations. A chapter is included that covers the installation of the standard editions of SQL Server, since many developers will want to use these editions during the development process. This part is rounded out with an overview of all of Microsoft's object models that can be used with SQL Server.

Part II: Database Structures

The second part covers the structure, function, and administration of databases, tables, indexes, and other associated objects. It also includes an explanation of indexes (how and why they should be used) and locks.

Part III: Data Retrieval and Modification

The third part provides an introduction to the SQL language and how it can be used with SQL Server. Retrieving and updating data are both covered, as well as topics that allow for scripts with complicated program logic. This part will enable anyone unfamiliar with SQL to use it well enough for most day-to-day operations. While intermediate functions are covered, advanced users may wish to seek out one of the many books written exclusively on the topic of SQL.

Part IV: Advanced Database Structures

The fourth part builds on the material presented in the second and third parts. It covers the structure, function, and administration of more advanced components of databases, such as views, stored procedures, and triggers. Also covered in this part are cursors, which allow for programming techniques not possible with the basic SQL functions.

Part V: Working with External Data

The fifth part addresses issues that arise when it is necessary to integrate data stored in one MSDE installation with data stored on other computers. Importing and exporting data is covered using a variety of tools, including detailed information on the Data Transformation Services (DTS). The SQL Server replication services that are available for MSDE are covered using the Enterprise Manager interface (which provides the only current method for complete control of replication). Distributed transactions in a multiserver environment are also covered for programmers and developers who wish to create their own mechanisms for replicating data.

Part VI: Database Administration

The sixth part covers administration techniques that have not been included in previous parts. Some of the material in this part relies on an understanding of previous chapters. Topics include controlling MSDE services, backing up and restoring data, using the ActiveX Data Objects (ADO), and creating Web pages using data stored in MSDE. The new feature of SQL Server that allows for native use of XML is covered in this part as well.

Part VII: Database Monitoring, Maintenance, and Optimization

The seventh part presents the tools and techniques that can be used to monitor, maintain, and optimize an MSDE installation. All of the chapters in this part assume that you have either read the earlier chapters or have had some previous experience with SQL Server.

Part VIII: Database Deployment

The three chapters of the last part cover the deployment of MSDE into a production environment. A general description of how and why to deploy it is presented, including a discussion of the use of either scripts or the Windows Installer to perform the installation. Deploying MSDE with both Access projects and Visual Studio projects is covered in two separate chapters.

Acknowledgments

Thanks go first and foremost to my wife, Nancy, for being the light of my life, for showing enormous tolerance during the writing of this book, and for more reasons than I can put into words. Special thanks also go to Amy and Wendy. Life is worth living because of the people you love.

The following people have helped me when I needed it, and to each of them I am forever indebted: Peter Grimaldi pointed me in the right direction. Hope Lindauer told me I could teach, told me I could work for myself, and was generally very successful at predicting the future. Megan Poulson taught me everything I know about grace and professionalism through her example. Al Miller taught me the meaning of motivation and attention to detail. Laurent Bass introduced me to Cal Tjader. If you would like to read this book in the rhythm in which it was written, listen to *Latin Concert*. Cordell Sloan was my SQL teacher and is one of the most interesting people I know. He and Lonnie Moseley have always been truly inspirational.

Thanks to all of the people who have provided assistance on this book: Mark Scott put me in touch with the initial concept. Judy Brief at IDG Books got the ball rolling. Grace Buechlein, Marcia Brochin, Gabrielle Chosney, and Eric Newman, all at IDG Books, and freelancer, Jonathon Walsh, showed me the way through the maze of writing a technical book. Chuck Urwiler lent me software in my time of need.

Thanks to all of the contributors to the MCT SQL newsgroup. They have taught me a great deal and have helped me continue to realize that using and teaching SQL Server really is a lot of fun.

Thanks to my co-authors, without whom I could not have written this book: Denise Gosnell wrote Chapters 5, 12–17, 21, 24, and 27. Mark Scott wrote chapters 18 and 19. I wrote the rest, and if there are any errors anywhere, I am probably responsible for them, too.

Contents at a Glance

Contents

Part IV: Advanced Database Structures 265

PART I

The MSDE Environment

This part introduces the MSDE environment, explains the preparations and methods of communication necessary for working with MSDE, and describes the Microsoft mechanisms for accessing data from programs which can be used in conjunction with MSDE-specific object models to provide control over the MSDE database from external programs.

In This Part

What is MSDE?

✦ ✦ ✦ ✦

In This Chapter

The purpose of MSDE

Selecting a data engine

Comparing MSDE, Jet, and SQL Server

✦ ✦ ✦ ✦

The Microsoft SQL Server Desktop Engine, or MSDE, is a database management system that runs on Windows 95, 98, NT, and 2000. It provides data storage, retrieval, and maintenance; it also provides mechanisms that, when used correctly, guarantee data consistency. MSDE is tightly integrated with Microsoft Access 2000, as well as all of Microsoft's programming languages. It can easily be used to supply data services to any product that supports Microsoft's Component Object Model (COM), including all the MS Office 2000 products and many others from Microsoft and third-party software publishers.

The Purpose of MSDE

MSDE is the most recent product from Microsoft to provide database management services and was released in the summer of 1999 to round out the SQL Server product line and to fill the gap that existed between this product line and the low-end Jet database.

Jet is the database engine that has historically been included with Microsoft Access. Access and Jet are tightly integrated to provide a low-maintenance rapid application development environment for data-centric applications. Such applications can be distributed to, and run by, anyone who owns a copy of Access. Applications that are developed in Access using the Jet data engine sometimes need to be converted to SQL Server when the number of users expands, or conversion becomes mission critical. Unfortunately, the conversion from Jet to SQL Server can be very complex and time-consuming. MSDE provides a seamless upgrade path from Access to SQL Server.

MSDE, like Jet, is freely redistributable and 100 percent compatible with SQL Server. It is, in fact, a version of SQL Server, and it not only marries the high-end functionality of that product with low-cost distribution and ease of development provided by Access 2000, it integrates seamlessly with the Visual Studio products.

Benefits

MSDE benefits a wide variety of developers. Whether you decide to use MSDE for small, homegrown applications or high-end Internet products, MSDE makes good business sense. Microsoft has even published case studies of some high-end applications that were developed with MSDE.

Upsizing from Access to SQL Server

Many experts in the software industry specialize in upsizing applications that were developed in Access to function with SQL Server. The process can be aided by Microsoft's upsizing wizard, but additional changes to program code are often necessary. Applications developed in Access with MSDE can be converted to other editions of SQL Server by installing the new edition and allowing the setup program to migrate the database or copying a few files to a new SQL Server and running a single stored procedure. No code modifications are necessary.

Maintaining a single code base

According to one Microsoft case study, O'Reilly and Associates has used MSDE in their most recent version of WebBoard, software that supports Web-based collaboration, such as bulletin boards, newsgroups, and chat. WebBoard was previously available in two different versions: one that used Jet for the low-end market and one that used SQL Server for the high-end market. Having two versions increased the cost of development and maintenance. So, in release 4.0, WebBoard was developed solely for the SQL Server platform and is being distributed with MSDE for low-volume sites. Customers can more easily upgrade from the low end to the high end, and O'Reilly saves on development and support costs.

Easily distributing software demos

Two other companies described in Microsoft case studies are Telemate.Net and Valadeo. Telemate.Net, whose eponymous product gathers and reports on usage information for phone systems, firewalls, proxy servers, etc. has used MSDE to provide a low-cost, entry-level product. They also use this version as a bundled trial version, to make it easier and cheaper for companies to evaluate the software. Valadeo produces two products called LiveSite and LiveSite Server, which provide Web publishing for end users and tracking and account for Internet Service Providers (ISPs). Valadeo uses a strategy similar to Telemate.Net's in that it has a low-end version based on MSDE that can serve as a demonstration of the capabilities of its software. Both companies anticipate expanding their market by making their products available to companies that would not previously have been able to cost justify them, as well as creating easy-to-distribute demo versions.

Types of Users

MSDE is the data engine of choice for a variety of developers. It is available to users of any version of Microsoft Office 2000 that comes with Access 2000 and to users of the Visual Studio development products: Visual Studio 6.0 Professional or Enterprise and later versions, Visual Basic 6.0 Professional or Enterprise and later versions, Visual C++ Professional or Enterprise, Visual Interdev 6.0 Professional and later versions, Visual J++ Professional, and Visual FoxPro 6.0 Professional and later versions. The terms of the license agreement for MSDE vary depending upon which product is used. This book describes the general sense of the license agreement; however, the actual license agreement, which is provided with every copy of MSDE, is authoritative and should be read carefully before use or redistribution.

Access 2000 users

There are two different license agreements for Access 2000 users. The license agreement included with Office 2000 Premium allows MSDE to be used with all of the Office products for internal use. The license agreement for Office 2000 Developer allows internal use, but also redistribution.

For internal use

Access 2000 developers who develop applications for internal use can take advantage of MSDE. It allows them to keep the cost of their projects low while planning for the future. The historical problem with applications developed in Access is that the initial design often underestimates the ultimate demand that will be placed upon it. Such applications were often initially only required to support relatively small amounts of data and users. But as their use spreads and the size of the data grows, they become slower and less reliable. Eventually, one of two things usually happens: the application is completely scrapped and replaced or rewritten, or a major project is undertaken to upsize the application to SQL Server. MSDE will turn the upsizing project into a task that can be accomplished in a single morning.

For distribution

The ease of upsizing is also useful for Access 2000 developers who write applications for resale or distribution. These applications can have a lower initial purchase cost because there is no need to purchase SQL Server and its client access licenses. The end users who buy such applications can feel secure in the knowledge that if they ever decide to move to SQL Server, they can do so with minimal cost and effort. The considerations for upsizing will be:

- **The cost of the database server software.** There may also be a need for a server and operating system, such as Windows NT Server or Windows 2000 Server.
- **The client access licenses.** These are either sold as per-server or per-seat. Per-server determines a maximum number of simultaneous connections to the database server without regard to who the users are. If additional servers are added, additional licenses must be purchased. Per-seat licenses allow particular users to connect one or more servers.
- **Installation.** While the installation of SQL Server and the conversion of MSDE databases to SQL Server are relatively simple tasks, adequate planning is necessary to avoid interruptions of service and poor performance.

Visual Studio developers

Programmers who use the Visual Studio products will enjoy the same benefits as the Access 2000 developers. They will also find it easier to distribute demonstration copies of their programs. If a program is written to use SQL Server, its creators can certainly distribute copies of their own code freely, but they cannot freely distribute SQL Server. That places a burden on potential users of the software, in that they must acquire their own version of SQL Server. With the advent of MSDE, the developers can simply include this freely distributable version with demos, and then resell the full version of SQL Server to potential clients who decide to buy.

Microsoft Data Engines

Microsoft produces a variety of data engines that fill a variety of needs across its wide product line. Data engines are software components that provide for the storage and manipulation of data. They can appear in a database management system (DBMS), such as SQL Server, or they can be embedded in some other product which itself has data storage and manipulation needs, such as Windows 2000 Active Directory. A DBMS usually consists of the data engine and graphical management tools. Sometimes a specialized programming language, like FoxPro, is also included. A detailed discussion of MSDE and the two other data engines for which MSDE is most likely to be an alternative, Jet and SQL Server, follows this summary of Microsoft's data engines.

- ESE, the Extensible Storage Engine, was developed from Jet and was formerly known as Jet Blue. It is used by Exchange Server for storing e-mail and relating information, and by Windows 2000 Server for storing the Active Directory. Programmers can manipulate ESE through the interfaces provided with Exchange or Active Directory, but ESE is not intended to be used as a general-purpose database engine.

- ✦ Microsoft's OLAP Services, the data-warehousing component of SQL Server, has a data engine used to store multidimensional data in structures called MOLAP (Multidimensional OnLine Analytical Processing) cubes. This data engine provides high-speed storage and retrieval of large quantities of original (base) and aggregated data. It only interfaces with OLAP Services, which includes a client component called the PivotTable Service.
- ✦ The FoxPro data engine has many useful features. Although accessible from other programming languages through ODBC drivers, the FoxPro data engine is tightly tied into and used mainly with the FoxPro development environment. The FoxPro programming environment can also access data stored in Jet, MSDE, and SQL Server databases.
- ✦ Jet is the database that has historically been used with Access for small, primarily stand-alone applications. It is easy to work with, freely redistributable, and requires minimal resources to run. It can also be used with any of Microsoft's programming languages.
- ✦ SQL Server is Microsoft's high-end, server-based DBMS that is comparable with products from companies such as Oracle and Informix. It can be used from any programming language or Access and provides extensive capabilities for distributed data. SQL Server comes in three versions. The Enterprise Edition is used for very large-scale data operations, and the Standard Edition, which speaks for itself, run on Windows NT Server. The Desktop Edition is for very small-scale data operations and can be used on computers running Windows NT Workstation, Windows 95, or Windows 98.
- ✦ MSDE is the data engine of SQL Server Personal Edition without the graphical management tools. It functions exactly like the other editions of SQL Server, with some exceptions noted in the next two sections, but it has a licensing agreement similar to Jet, allowing for free redistribution in the right circumstances. MSDE sits squarely between Jet and SQL Server in terms of choosing a data engine for a new application.

MSDE and Jet

The primary factor to consider when choosing MSDE or Jet is scalability. Ultimately, MSDE scales better than Jet because upsizing to SQL Server is as simple as copying a file. Conversely, Jet can probably handle more users than MSDE on its own without upsizing. Microsoft's documentation indicates that MSDE is tuned to support five users, which is exactly the same as the desktop version of SQL Server 7.0. Jet requires fewer system resources than MSDE and can support up to 10 or 20 users comfortably.

The installation of MSDE is more complex than that of Jet's. MSDE runs as one or more services that must be installed in addition to the actual database. The installation of Jet simply requires that the database files be copied to the destination computer.

Jet supports cascading updates and deletes. These are not directly supported in MSDE, although their functionality can be reproduced with triggers. Cascading modifications happen when a change is made to a table that has a defined relationship with another table. For example, suppose an ice cream shop has a database of ice cream flavors. One table contains information about the manufacturer of ice creams, and another contains the details of all the flavors they produce. If a manufacturer goes out of business and its record is deleted from the manufacturer's table, all of the corresponding flavors should be deleted from the flavors table. Jet allows this relationship to be easily defined and automatically executed. In MSDE, this action could be accomplished by writing a trigger, which is a segment of SQL code that automatically runs when data is modified. Writing cascading delete triggers can be somewhat tricky in MSDE when they are used in combination with foreign key constraints.

Another major difference between Jet and MSDE is that MSDE uses client-server technology, whereas Jet is entirely controlled by the client. When a query is sent across the network to a computer running MSDE, the MSDE can process the query and return only a small result set. The developer can control how much processing is performed by MSDE and how much is performed by the client. Jet places the entire data processing load on the client and, typically, must send more data across the network. MSDE uses exactly the same version of Transact-SQL as SQL Server 7.0. The Jet version is slightly different in a number of subtle ways. For example, Jet requires that dates are indicated with # signs.

Jet does not support transaction logging, while MSDE does. Transaction logging provides superior fault tolerance for a transactional database. Every change to the database is first written to a transaction log, and only after the change is complete, or committed, can the change be written to the actual database table. In the event of a system failure, the transaction log is scanned and all committed transactions are rolled forward and stored in the database tables, while all uncommitted transactions are completely rolled back as though they never happened. This process, called recovery, guarantees that the database will always be in a consistent state, as long as programmers use transactions properly.

Transaction logging also allows MSDE to support point-in-time restoration. When a database is being restored from backup tape, transactions in the transaction log can be replayed to any arbitrary point in time. Jet databases can be restored only to the time at which the backup was actually made.

When MSDE is run on Windows NT or Windows 2000, it supports integrated security, allowing database permissions to be given to users defined by the network administrator. Jet does not support any integration with Windows NT/2000 security. When either Jet or MSDE is run on Windows 95 or 98, security is implemented in the form of users and groups created within the database.

Jet and MSDE both support pre-compiled queries. They are implemented slightly differently, but provide the same functionality. In Jet, they are QueryDefs; in MSDE, they are stored procedures or views. Converting QueryDefs to stored procedures and views is one of the major tasks involved in upsizing Jet databases to SQL Server.

MSDE and SQL Server

MSDE runs the same code as other editions of SQL Server and has all the same functionality, with the following exceptions:

- The maximum database size in MSDE is 2GB.
- MSDE cannot publish data using transactional or snapshot replication. Replication is an automated process in which data originates on one computer and is automatically transferred to one or more other computers. The computer on which the data originates is called the publisher; all the computers that receive the data are called subscribers. There are three basic types of replication: snapshot, merge, and transactional. MSDE can participate as the publisher or a subscriber in merge replication, but can only be a subscriber when using transactional or snapshot replication.
- The MSDE services cannot be started remotely on Windows 95 or 98. That is also true of the Desktop Edition of SQL Server. However, the Standard and Enterprise Editions require Windows NT Server or Windows 2000, which both support remote startup and shutdown of services. MSDE and SQL Server desktop allow remote service control if run on Windows NT Workstation.
- MSDE and the Desktop Edition of SQL Server require a Client Access License (CAL) in order to replicate with other SQL Servers. Neither SQL Server Standard nor Enterprise require such a license.

Summary

MSDE provides a new option for developers who must choose a data engine. It is particularly appropriate for applications that have the potential to be upsized to SQL Server, or that require functionality or stability beyond that provided by Jet. The license agreement for MSDE also makes it a good choice when the purchase of another edition of SQL cannot be justified for a small application or a demo version of an application.

✦ ✦ ✦

MSDE Architecture

In This Chapter

MSDE runs as a series of services, which, like Unix daemons, are programs that run on the computer independently of the logged-on user. Windows NT and Windows 2000 support true services that can be configured to start when the computer is booted. The services run whether or not a user is logged on. Windows 95 and Windows 98 do not support true services, so the MSDE services actually run as executable background processes.

The Services

Three services are installed by default with MSDE. The SQL Server service provides the main data access functions. The SQL Agent service provides automation capabilities. And the Distributed Transaction Coordinator service provides the ability to have a transaction span multiple computers.

The SQL Server service

The SQL Server service is the core component of MSDE, consisting of two primary parts: the query processor (also called the relational engine) and the storage engine. There are some other subcomponents, such as Net-Library, which handles communication with software on client computers, and Open Data Services (ODS), which provides non-network specific communication management and an interface between the Net-Library and the query processor. The query processor is responsible for receiving, optimizing, and executing SQL commands. The storage engine manages reading and writing data to and from database files on disk. It also handles automatic locking and transaction control to provide concurrency while assuring consistency.

Net-Library

Programs on client computers communicate with MSDE through the Net-Library. The Net-Library provides a layer of abstraction between the data services (which would be OLE DB or ODBC on a client) and the network protocol stack. This helps to make the details of the network implementation transparent to a programmer who needs to access the MSDE environment.

Although you have several options when deciding which Net-Library to use, you must choose one that is compatible with the underlying network protocol stack and the same on both client and server. The Multiprotocol and Named Pipes Net-Libraries (available only in Windows NT and Windows 2000) can operate over various network stacks: NetBEUI, IPX/SPX, and TCP/IP. Other, older Net-Libraries are designed to work with specific protocol stacks and are named appropriately, for example, the Banyan Vines Net-Library.

There is a Net-Library implemented on Windows 95 and Windows 98 that communicates directly through memory and does not use a network protocol stack. It is called the Shared Memory Net-Library and is used by default when the client software is running on the same computer with MSDE. This allows MSDE to be used on these operating systems without network support. The Named Pipes Net-Library provides similar functionality on Windows NT and Windows 2000.

On the server side, the Net-Library communicates with the SQL Server service through the Open Data Services, or ODS. The data format used for passing information back and forth between the client and server Net-Libraries is called Tabular Data Stream, or TDS. ODS can also provide communication with other software components that need to interact with the data engine. Some database gateways are written to use ODS to communicate with the SQL Server service.

ODS is responsible for setting up and breaking down client connections to the data engine. It is also responsible for noticing and cleaning up connections that have been abnormally terminated — by a network failure, for example.

Query processor

The query processor receives commands from a client via the Net-Library and runs those commands through several processes. Initially, it parses the commands, one batch at a time, breaking them up into constituent components that it analyzes for proper syntax. A batch is one or more SQL commands. The `Go` command in a SQL script separates series of commands into individual batches. The `Execute` command is always treated as an individual batch. The parser creates an internal representation of the batch called a query tree, which is then optimized and compiled into an execution plan.

Creating the execution plan

During compilation and optimization, choices are made about what indexes to use, if any, and in what order joins should be performed with what algorithm. Security checks and links are added to the execution plans for any triggers needing to be fired. Constraints defined in tables that are to be accessed are retrieved, and their code is ordered and added into the plan. These decisions are made by accessing statistics that are stored in the indexes. Choices are based on a comparison of the projected amount of CPU cycles, hard disk reads and writes, and memory usage. The execution plan created minimizes the impact on overall system performance.

In some database systems, the order in which items appear in a SQL statement has a large impact on the statement's ultimate performance. Because of the sophistication of the query optimization process in MSDE, the order of the SQL statements has no effect on the final execution plan. For the same reason, the order of the results set cannot be predicted without a specific `Order By` clause. Some control over the structure of the execution plan is available through query hints.

The execution plan itself consists of two parts: the query plan and the execution context. Multiple clients can use a single query plan simultaneously. Each client connection is assigned an execution context that keeps track of information specific to that connection. Query plans are retained in memory in a cache until they age out (just like the query plans for stored procedures). They are reused whenever an identical SQL batch is sent to the system. A query plan can also be reused for SQL batches that are very similar; to make this determination, the query processor auto-parameterizes each batch and then reuses the plan when a new batch is received that differs only in the discovered parameters. Programmers can make this task easier for the query processor by using stored procedures (which have explicitly defined parameters) and by using the `Execute` command with variables that will be interpreted as parameters.

Managing execution plans

When MSDE needs more memory, it will age old execution plans out of the cache. The plans are aged out based on two factors: the length of time since the plan was accessed and the number of resources originally required to compile the plan. A small and simple plan will be aged out before a large and complex plan, even if the small plan has been accessed more recently than the large plan, because it can be more easily re-created.

Certain changes to the database invalidate existing execution plans. The query processor marks existing plans invalid when:

- ✦ A table that is referenced by the plan is altered.
- ✦ The view that is referenced by the plan is altered.
- ✦ Statistics are regenerated on an object referenced by the plan.
- ✦ An index referenced by the plan is dropped.
- ✦ Large numbers of rows are inserted or deleted in a table referenced by the plan.
- ✦ The system's stored procedure, `sp_recompile`, is run against a table referenced by the plan.

When an execution plan is run, each step is sent to the storage engine, which returns any results. Whenever this involves retrieving or modifying data (as opposed to creating a new database, for example), OLE DB is used for the communication between query processor and storage engine.

Storage engine

The storage engine handles all disk access. It creates the files that are used to store databases, deletes those files when they are no longer necessary, and can dynamically expand and shrink those files if configured to do so (by default, databases automatically expand but do not shrink). The storage engine keeps statistics up-to-date and handles the retrieval and modification of data.

Database files

When a database is created, enough disk space is allocated to contain the database and its log. The storage engine then overwrites the entire file with zeroes to ensure that old data is not erroneously retained. A database always uses at least two files: one for all data objects and one for the transaction log. Additional files can be added, and the storage engine will track the usage of each file.

All data within a database is allocated in units of 8K pages. All disk I/O in MSDE is performed in pages. The pages themselves are organized into units called extents. Each extent contains eight pages. When the data within an extent is contiguous, performance gains can be realized because the storage engine Read Ahead Manager can read an entire extent in about the same amount of time that it takes to read a page. Over time, pages can become noncontiguous within extents, degrading performance. Therefore, periodic maintenance is required.

The performance gains that can be achieved with contiguous data, and the methods that can be used to maintain contiguity will be covered in more detail in Chapter 9 and Chapter 30.

If auto-grow is configured for a file, the storage engine will add additional space to the file whenever it tries and fails to allocate more space within the existing file. This can cause noticeable delays in the performance of MSDE, particularly during large data loads. The amount of additional space added during automatic growth is determined by the configuration of the database. This amount is originally set when the database is created but can be changed at any time. The growth can occur in units of megabytes or in a percentage of the current size. Growth can be regulated by an upper-limit placement or by available disk space.

Updating statistics

By default, the storage engine is configured to automatically regenerate distribution statistics. These are the statistics that the query processor uses to make decisions about index use. If they are not kept up-to-date, the overall performance of the server will suffer. The storage engine tracks the number of changes that are made to tables. When the number of changes passes a threshold, the storage engine uses statistical sampling to update the statistics. Updating occurs while a query is executing, causing the query to slow down. However, by making the statistics more accurate, there is an overall performance gain. This behavior can be turned off for each database, in which case the statistics must be manually updated.

Data access

When the storage engine receives requests from the query processor to either retrieve or change data, it must perform several functions. An appropriate lock must be placed on the data to ensure that multiple processes do not interfere with one another. Upon occasion, two connections hold locks on data that prevent each other from completing. This is called a deadlock, or deadly embrace. The storage engine attempts to detect this situation, chooses a victim process (the one that has processed for the least amount of time), and rolls back its transaction.

Data access can happen only if the data has first been read from disk into a memory cache. So the first thing the storage engine must do is determine if the requested data is already in cache. A hashing algorithm is used to track the data pages that are currently in cache in order to find them quickly. If a page is not in cache, it must be read from the disk into free space in memory. A component of the storage engine, the LazyWriter, periodically scans pages and ages them out to disk (this is the same process that ages out execution plans) to make free space available for incoming data.

Read-ahead

The MSDE storage engine also supports read-ahead. This process anticipates data that will be needed in the future and reads it into cache. Read-ahead is one of the features that differs somewhat depending on whether MSDE is installed on Windows 98 or Windows NT/2000. In the former, the read-ahead is not asynchronous; thus, it is not as beneficial to performance as it is on NT or 2000. Read-ahead is still used with Windows 98, and it is able to read larger amounts of data, but it can't take advantage of the advanced I/O techniques.

Data modification

Whenever data is to be changed, the changes are first made in the transaction log. Writes to the transaction log are buffered in memory to increase throughput, but the changes are flushed out to the transaction log file on disk when the transaction commits. After a transaction commits, it can be checkpointed. Checkpoint is a process that runs periodically and confirms that the changes from committed transactions are, in fact, written to the data pages in the database file on disk. Checkpoint plays a crucial role in system recovery, which runs whenever MSDE starts, rolling committed transactions forward and rolling uncommitted transactions back. The recovery process guarantees that the database will always be in a consistent state, although it does not absolutely prevent data loss.

Data change is not always as simple as just writing data onto the disk. If an update to data won't fit in an existing page, the storage engine will either split the page or write a forwarding pointer. A page split will occur if the table has a clustered index. A new page is allocated for half of the data from the old page. Because records are moved from one page to another, other changes may be required. Indexes, in particular, may have to be updated. If the table being modified does not have a clustered index and an existing row is modified in such a way that it no longer fits on the page, it will be replaced with a forwarding pointer that points to a location on another page where the data will be written. This method ensures that indexes will not have to be updated since they will continue to point to the same location, which now contains a forwarding pointer.

The SQL Agent service

The SQL Agent service provides automated administrative functionality to MSDE. While not necessary for the core functionality of MSDE, it provides the ability to schedule jobs (such as backups) and define alert conditions (such as nearly full transaction logs). It sends e-mail notifications about the status of these jobs and alerts.

Jobs

A job is a set of predefined steps that can be performed by the SQL Agent service at a certain point in the future. The steps can be SQL commands, operating system commands, an Active Script, or a replication step. An active script is a script written in a language that can be processed by the Windows Scripting Host (WSH). There are two WSH languages installed by default: VBScript and JavaScript. There are several types of steps available for advanced replication tasks.

Each step within a job can be of any type. For example, a SQL command could back up a database to a file, and upon successful completion of the backup, an operating system command could copy the file to another computer. Each step also allows control of flow and error handling: the next step to be performed can be defined based on whether the current step succeeds or fails or without regard to the completion status.

Jobs can be scheduled with one or more schedules. A schedule can cause a job to run whenever MSDE starts, when there is idle CPU time, on a single specified day and time, or on a recurring schedule. Recurring schedules can be set up to run daily, weekly, or monthly. For example, since multiple schedules can be defined for a single job, it is possible to have a job run on the last day of every week and on the last day of every month.

Alerts

An alert is a mechanism that causes a response when a set of predefined conditions is met. Alerts can be configured to be initiated by specific error messages. For example, an alert may be configured to run when the Log File Full error occurs for a database. In Windows NT or Windows 2000, alerts can also be configured to run when a Performance Monitor counter reaches a critical value. For example, an alert may be configured to run when the average wait time for a locked resource rises above 800 milliseconds. When an alert has been initiated by a condition, it responds by sending an e-mail, calling a pager, or running a predefined job.

Notifications

Notifications can be sent upon the completion of a job or the firing of an alert through MAPI-compliant e-mail or a NetBIOS net send. Before a notification can be sent, at least one operator must be defined. Operators are defined by configuring an e-mail address, a net send address, or an e-mail address that can be accessed via pager. The pager setup supports on-call configuration, which allows operators to be configured with the time and day of the week when they will be paged. A fail-safe operator of last resort can also be configured, in case no operators are on call.

The Distributed Transaction Coordinator service

The Distributed Transaction Coordinator service provides infrastructure that allows transactions to span multiple physical computers on a network. Such a distributed transaction has the same properties as a normal transaction in that every operation within the transaction must successfully complete or be rolled back as though it had never happened. This is accomplished with a mechanism known as the two-phase commit.

A distributed transaction proceeds like a local transaction — with commands being processed normally after they are sent to appropriate servers — until the application that controls the transaction requests a commit. At this point, the DTC begins the two-phase commit. The first of the two phases is the prepare phase, which begins when the DTC sends a `Prepare` command to each server. The servers are responsible for making the transaction durable (for example, for verifying that all commands in the transaction have been written to the transaction log on disk). The servers then respond to the controlling DTC indicating whether or not the prepare phase was successful. If all participants in the transaction were successful, the DTC enters the commit phase and sends a `Commit` command to each server indicating success of the entire distributed transaction to the calling application. If any servers indicate to the DTC that the prepare failed, then the DTC sends a `Rollback` command to all participants in the transaction and indicates failure to the calling application. This process guarantees that the transaction succeeds everywhere. In the event of a failure on a server or a network failure, the DTC will either process the error or time out. In either case, the DTC will roll the transaction back.

Distributed transactions can be initiated explicitly or implicitly. An application can initiate a distributed transaction explicitly by issuing the Begin Distributed Transaction command. It can begin a distributed transaction implicitly by referencing an object or stored procedure on a remote server.

Supported Platforms

MSDE can be installed on computers running Windows 98, Windows NT, or Windows 2000. The Windows 98 installation differs to some degree with Windows NT and Windows 2000 installations:

- SQL Server service, SQL Agent service, and the Distributed Transaction Coordinator all run as executables rather than services. Therefore, they can't be configured with their own security contexts or started and stopped remotely, and they are susceptible to being crashed by other programs that are running at the same time.
- Neither Performance Monitor, nor, consequently, the Performance Monitor alerts are available.
- Named Pipes, AppleTalk, and Banyan Vines Net-Libraries are not available, and the MSDE Multiprotocol Net-Library does not support encryption.
- MSDE cannot use the NT integrated security. Logins must be created within MSDE and cannot be associated with an NT Domain user.
- Read-ahead is synchronous rather than asynchronous and cannot use NT's scatter-gather I/O. This is a throughput issue rather than an issue of functionality.

The only feature that is not available on Windows NT and 2000 is the Shared Memory Net-Library. The architecture of these operating systems does not support the sharing of memory directly between applications for security reasons. The same functionality is available through the Named Pipes Net-Library, however.

Summary

MSDE runs as three services: SQL Server service, SQL Agent service, and the Distributed Transaction Coordinator (DTC). The SQL Server service provides the core functionality of MSDE and is the only required service. It consists of many components that work cooperatively to handle communications, query processing, and data storage. The SQL Agent service provides task automation and server monitoring. The DTC provides network infrastructure to allow transactions to span multiple computers while still guaranteeing data consistency.

There are few differences between MSDE running on the 98 platform and the NT/2000 platform. Most of these differences pose little difficulty on a small-scale system, which is the intended target for MSDE—larger-scale systems can easily be upgraded to SQL Server running on NT or 2000.

✦ ✦ ✦

Methods for Communicating with MSDE

In This Chapter

Osql

Access 2000

Visual Studio

Query Analyzer

Enterprise Manager

Controlling MSDE programmatically

MSDE can be used in many different environments with different configurations. This chapter describes various tools that are available to communicate with MSDE. The set of tools used to communicate with MSDE varies depending upon what other programs are installed on the computer being used.

Any computer on which MSDE has been installed will have the osql utility, which enables SQL statements and scripts to be sent to and processed by MSDE. Osql can be used to directly control MSDE and to create, modify, and delete tables, indexes, users, and so on, or it can be used to develop and test scripts that will be embedded within other applications.

Access 2000 can be installed alone or as part of the Office 2000 suite; it provides a graphical environment for developing data-centric Windows applications that are based around either the Jet engine or MSDE. Access 2000 has graphical tools for working with objects within MSDE databases and is used during development and by end users of the Access application.

Visual Studio is the integrated development environment used for Microsoft programming languages. It has a set of graphical tools much like those available with Access 2000 and is used only during application development. Any manipulation of MSDE that is to be performed by users must be done through custom-built tools.

The Query Analyzer and Enterprise Manager are tools that are available with all versions of SQL Server except for MSDE. The editions that ship with the graphical tools include the developer's edition that is part of Visual Studio. Query

Analyzer provides a Windows interface with all of the functionality of osql and a number of advanced tools and features. As with osql, the developer can use Query Analyzer to control MSDE and to write and test scripts. Enterprise Manager is the graphical management environment component to SQL Server that can be used to control MSDE; however, it is not licensed as part of MSDE.

Finally, any COM-compliant programming language, including scripting languages, can control MSDE using various interfaces supplied by Microsoft.

Access 2000

Access 2000 is a component in Microsoft's Office suite of programs that provides a quick and easy mechanism for developing data-based applications, including graphical front ends for users to interact with the data, use menus, and create hard copy reports. The current version is designed to use either SQL Server/MSDE or Jet as the primary data engine for an application.

When creating a new application, an Access developer can choose either to create an Access database (using Jet) or to create a project. A project is an application that stores information in a local configuration file (for example, form and report definitions), but that is linked to an MSDE or SQL Server database. During project creation, an Access developer can, for the first time, create a SQL database from within Access.

Figure 3-1 shows the main screen in Access 2000. A project has been created and focused on the pubs database in MSDE. The primary database objects — tables, views, and stored procedures — can all be accessed from this screen, as well as Access objects such as forms, data access pages, and reports. Any of these objects can be created, modified, or deleted. Figure 3-2 shows the stored procedure window, along with the details of the reptq2 stored procedure in the pubs database. Access provides automatic syntax checking for stored procedures. Keywords, functions, and required punctuation are all color coded as you type to make spotting mistakes quicker and easier.

The table designer presents a grid in which each row represents a column in the table, and dialog boxes are available for advanced features, as shown in Figure 3-3. This figure shows the table window for the pubs database, the designer window for the publishers table, and the Properties dialog box. The Properties dialog box is accessed by right-clicking anywhere in the table designer and choosing Properties as shown in the figure. The Properties dialog box controls table constraints, indexes, and the allocation of objects to filegroups. To manage triggers on a table, right-click on the table in the table window and choose Triggers from the menu.

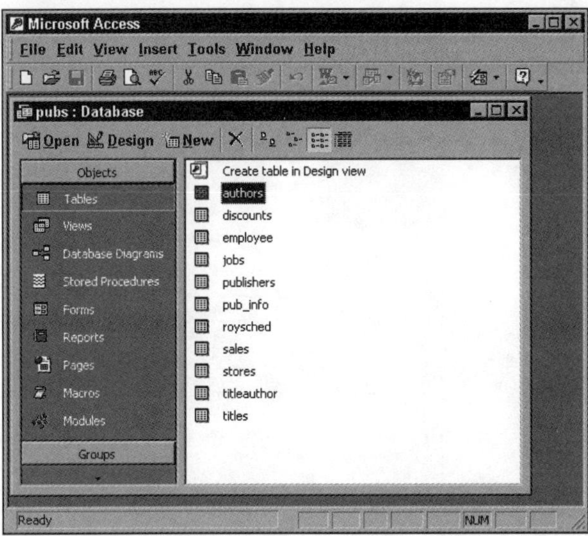

Figure 3-1: Access 2000

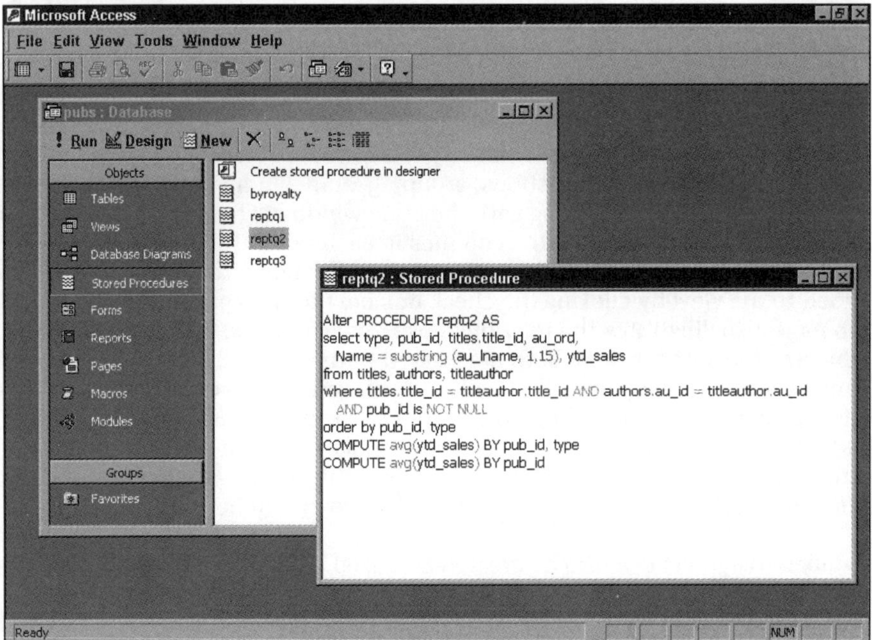

Figure 3-2: A stored procedure in Access 2000

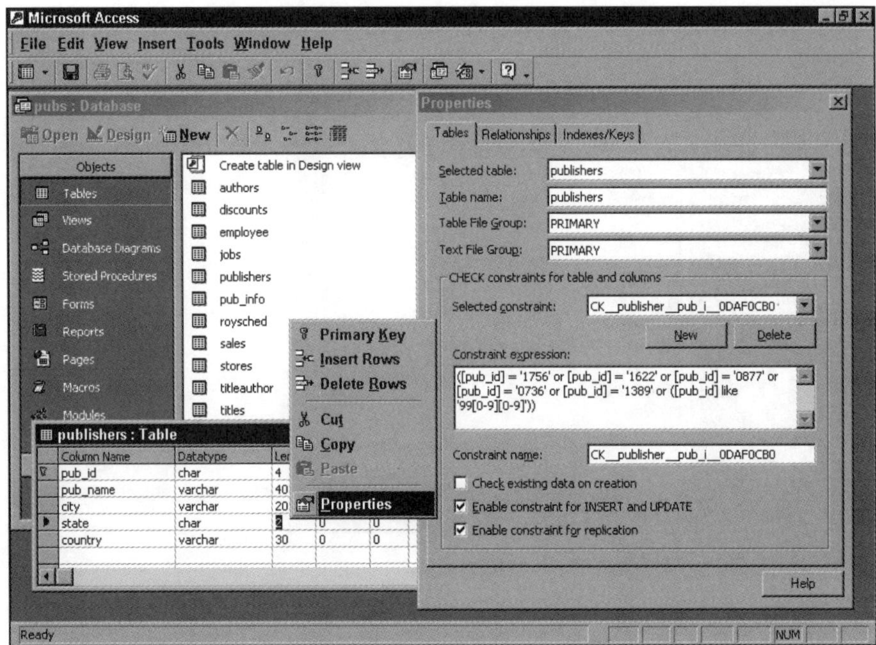

Figure 3-3: The table designer and Properties dialog box in Access 2000

The interface for creating views is very sophisticated with drag-and-drop functionality for specifying the tables, columns, and rows that should be included in the view as well as aggregate functions, grouping, and column headings. Figure 3-4 shows the view designer along with the table window. The top pane in the view designer displays tables and the columns in each table. Tables can be added to this pane by dragging them from the table window. Columns from the tables can be added to the view by clicking the check box next to the appropriate column. The top pane also illustrates the relationships between tables; in Figure 3-4, the titles table and the authors table both are related to the titleauthor table. The center pane lists all of the columns that will be displayed in the view. Criteria are entered into this pane to restrict which rows should be retrieved. For example, if the criteria >49 were entered in the price row, only books that cost more than $49 would be returned in this view. The bottom pane shows the SQL query that was generated by the graphical tools in the top two panes. The query can be manually edited as well.

Database diagrams can also be created and used to display and manipulate the relationships between tables. The database diagram designer works much like the top pane in the view designer. Indexes, constraints, and triggers can all be accessed from the Properties dialog box on any table. There is a database security item on the Tools menu that can control MSDE logins, database users, roles, and permissions (although the Permissions dialog box is buried inside the properties of the database users). In short, nearly anything that can be done within the context of an MSDE database can be done within Access 2000 using the graphical user interface (GUI).

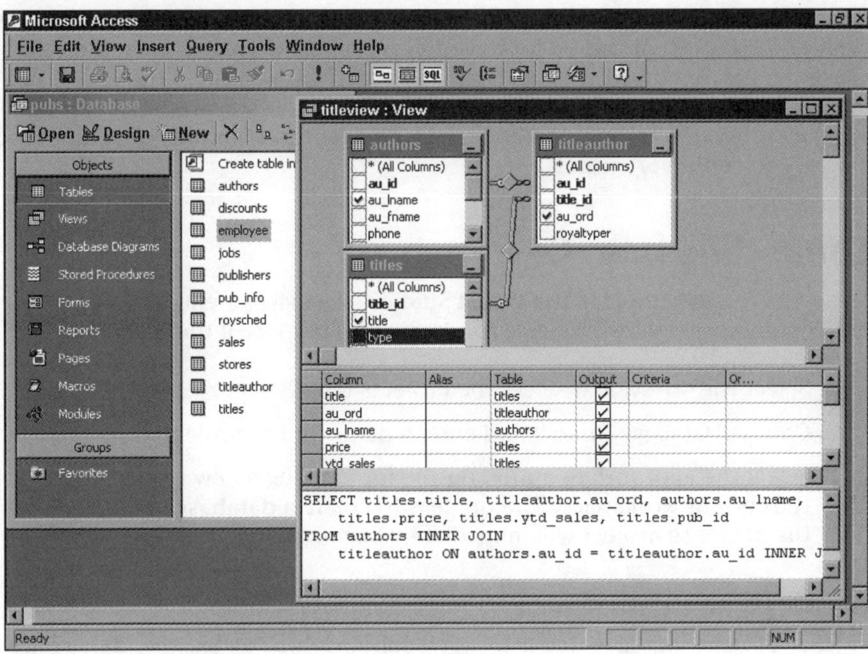

Figure 3-4: The view designer in Access 2000

Visual Studio

Visual Studio is Microsoft's suite of development products that includes and supports its programming languages: Visual Basic, Visual C++, Visual J++, and Visual FoxPro. It also includes Visual Interdev, which is an environment for developing Web sites using Active Server Pages (ASPs). Visual Studio comes with graphical tools, very similar to those included with Access 2000, for manipulating databases, including MSDE. The procedures for accessing these tools vary somewhat depending on which language is being used. Like Access, they allow for control of tables, views, stored procedures, and database diagrams.

The window that is used to view, create, modify, and delete database objects in Visual Studio is called the Data View window. The method for accessing the Data View window varies slightly depending on which language is being used. In all cases, a data connection must first be created that contains information allowing Visual Studio to connect to the database and authenticate properly. After a data connection is established, the Data View window displays the objects that are stored in the database.

The Visual Studio data tools also provide shortcut methods for adding data access to programs. For example, in Visual Basic, after a data connection has been established, it is only a matter of using drag and drop to create a data input and display screen for the database. Naturally, the code produced by this method is not as efficient as the code that can be produced by a proficient programmer, but it provides a fast and easy method for prototyping designs. The section at the end of this chapter briefly describes methods of controlling data and data structures with code; other chapters throughout the book provide details and examples of how to include data access within programs.

Connecting from C++

To access the data tools in the Visual Studio C++ environment, add a database project to the current workspace (or create a workspace if there is none).

1. Select File ⇨ New and select the Projects tab.
2. Choose Database Project and enter a name for the project.
3. Select the appropriate option button for creating a new workspace or using the current workspace. The process to create a database connection within the database project will immediately begin.

Creating a new data source

The Select Data Source dialog is displayed, from which an existing data source can be selected or a new data source can be created. To create a new data source that points to the pubs database:

1. Select the Machine Data Source tab and then click New. The Create New Data Source dialog displays.
2. Choose an option button for a user or system data source, depending on whether the data source will be shared with other users on the computer. Click Next.
3. A list of installed drivers is displayed. The SQL Server driver works well with MSDE and can be selected from this list, followed by clicking Next and Finish.
4. Assign a name to the new data source. An optional description may also be added.
5. The server name should then be entered. Although there is a drop-down list of servers that may list the local server as (local), it is preferable to type the server name because some applications do not support a nonexplicit reference to the local server.
6. Select an authentication method. Windows NT authentication is supported only if MSDE is installed on Windows NT or 2000. If SQL authentication is chosen, enter a valid login and password and click Next.
7. On the subsequent screen, choose a database from the drop-down list. If the databases are not listed, there may have been an error on a previous screen, which can be checked by using the Back button. Connection settings can be changed if necessary; then click Finish.

8. The new data source can be tested, and when the summary dialog is dismissed, the Select Data Source dialog will be redisplayed with the new data source available in the list. Select the new data source and click OK.

9. A login and password must be entered again — C++ will use this login for the data connection. A new item should appear in the File View pane that represents the data connection.

Using the data connection

To manipulate MSDE objects, click the Data View tab that appears in the bottom of the workspace explorer, which is the pane along the left side if the screen is in the default C++ environment configuration. A hierarchy is displayed that contains the database and, within it, database diagrams, tables, views, and stored procedures. This screen is shown in Figure 3-5. In this figure, the authors table has been expanded to show its columns. The structure of the database cannot be modified with these tools, although individual tables or views can be opened and the data stored in them can be modified. The figure also shows the contents of the authors table, which has been opened with the query builder. This SQL query builder is the same tool that is available in Access and is invoked in C++ by opening either a table or a view. It provides some graphical assistance in creating SQL statements, allowing tables and views to be dragged from the data view pane and dropped into the query builder. After a table is in the query builder, its column can be added to the query with a click.

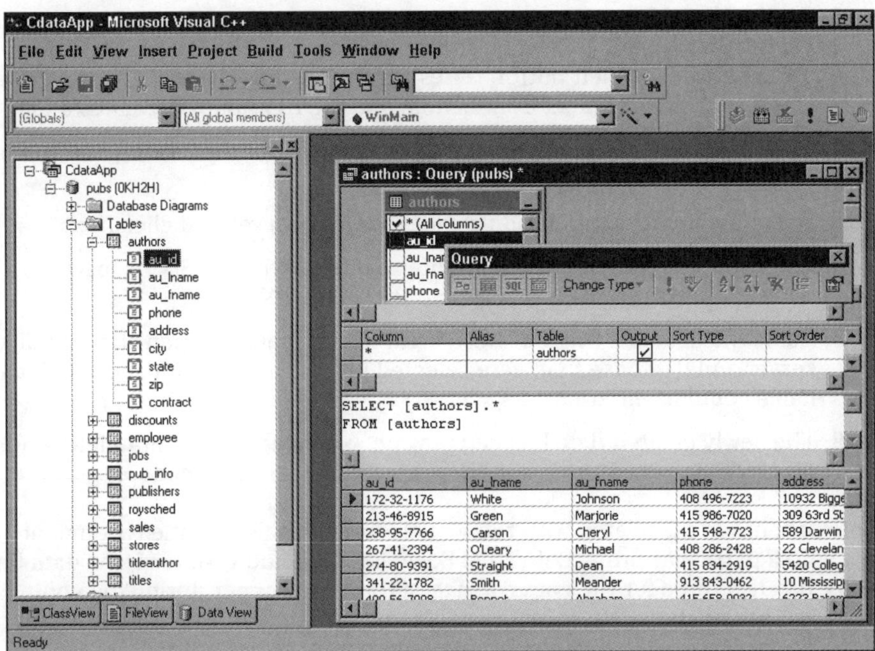

Figure 3-5: Visual Studio C++ environment showing the data view and query builder

Connecting from Visual Basic

The data tools in Visual Basic are available from the Data View window which can be displayed with View ➪ Data View Window. Two items are displayed in this window: the data links and the Data Environment Connections. The data links are used to create a connection to MSDE for displaying the structure and contents of a database, much like the data view in C++. The Data Environment Connections are used to create a connection to MSDE that will be embedded as one or more objects in a Visual Basic project. These objects can be used to quickly generate visual elements and the underlying code necessary for a program to manipulate the contents of a database. Buttons at the top of this dialog box create new data links and Data Environment Connections.

Using a data link

The screens presented when creating a new data link require the same information that is required when creating a new data source for C++, although the layout of the dialog boxes may differ somewhat. After a data link is created, it presents a hierarchy nearly identical to that available in C++, although in Visual Basic each container can be right-clicked to choose whether or not system objects (tables and views) should be displayed. There is also an option to filter the objects that are shown by the owner of the objects.

To create a data link:

1. Open a Visual Basic project and display the Data View window by selecting View ➪ Data View Window. As shown in Figure 3-6, the Data View window has three buttons: the left button refreshes the windows, the middle button creates a Data Environment Connection, and the right button creates a data link.
2. Click the Data Link button, and the Data Link Properties dialog box will be displayed, as shown in Figure 3-6.
3. Select the Microsoft OLE DB provider for SQL Server and click Next.
4. Enter the server name (the computer name on which MSDE is installed), login name, password, and database, and then click OK.
5. Name the data link that has been created. The name chosen should reflect the server and database that were selected in the previous step, although any name could be entered.
6. The newly created data link can now be expanded in the Data View window to display database diagrams, table, views, and stored procedures.

This data link is associated with the Visual Studio development environment and not with a particular project. If Visual Basic is exited and restarted, the data link will still exist. It is there for the convenience of the programmer during the coding process, but has no direct effect on the program. If a data connection that will become part of a program is desired, use a Data Environment Connection.

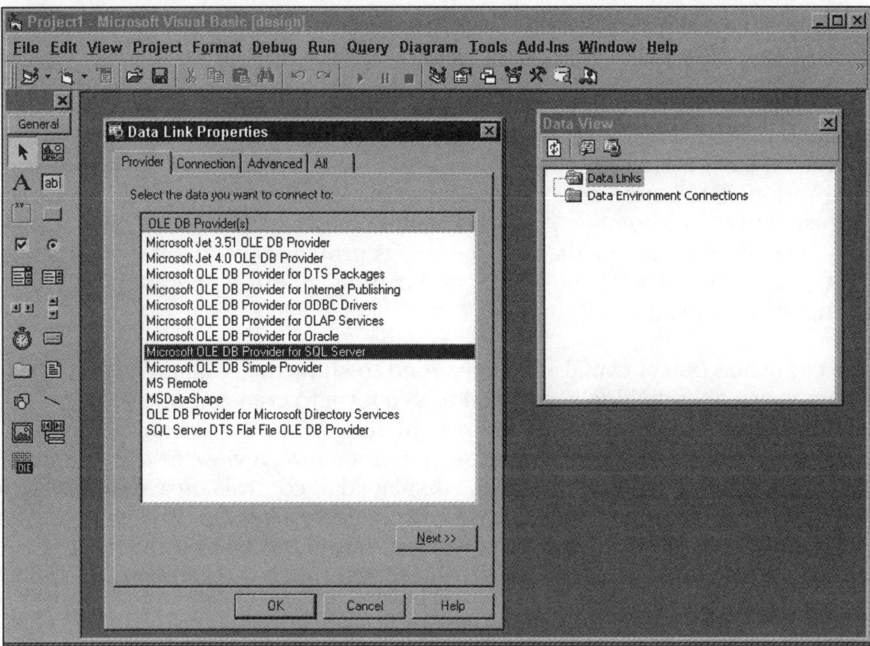

Figure 3-6: Visual Basic environment with Data View

Using a Data Environment Connection

To create a new Data Environment Connection:

1. Click the center button in the Data View window. The Data Environment window (which is shown on the right side of Figure 3-7) is displayed, showing the newly created, but as yet unconnected Data Environment Connection.
2. Right-click the Data Environment Connection and select Properties. The Data Link properties dialog box displays.
3. Select the Microsoft OLE DB provider for SQL Server and click Next.
4. Enter the server name (the computer name on which MSDE is installed), login name, password, and database, and then click OK. The connection object is now actively connected to the database and is displayed in the Data View window, where it can be expanded to display database diagrams, tables, views, and stored procedures.

The newly created Data Environment Connection has become a part of the Visual Basic project. If Visual Basic is exited and restarted, the Data Environment Connection will not appear again until the project is reloaded. Information about the connection will be compiled into the final program when the project is built into an executable.

Additional features are available through the Data Environment Connection. For example, clicking the second button from the left in the Data Environment window creates an ADO command object. Choose a database object type of table, select a table from the list, and then click OK. The command you just created is displayed in the Data Environment window, as shown by cmdAuthors in Figure 3-7. This command can be dragged onto a form, and Visual Basic will automatically create appropriate data-bound controls on the form for each of the columns in the table represented by the command. A data-bound control is any control that automatically displays data from a data source that is provided by an ActiveX Data Objects (ADO) command object. The results of this drag-and-drop operation are shown in the upper left of Figure 3-7.

The command object can also be expanded to show the columns. Any of these columns can be individually dragged onto a form to create controls. ADO commands can also represent other sources of data, in addition to an entire table. A command can be configured with a stored procedure, a view, or a SQL statement, and the results of any of these can be displayed in controls on a Visual Basic form. Additional controls must be added to any form that uses automatically created data-bound controls. The additional controls are required to provide navigation, that is, movement from one record to another through the database.

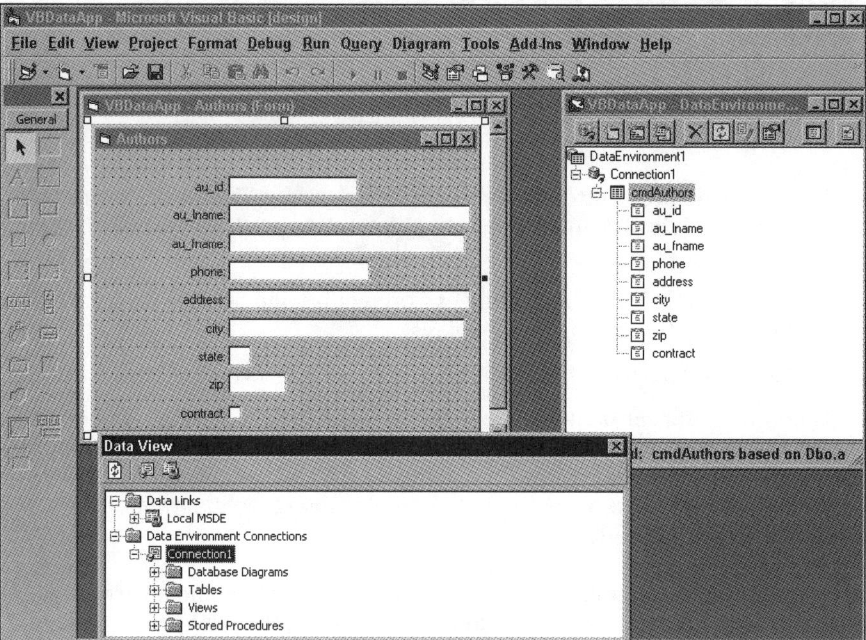

Figure 3-7: Visual Basic environment with Data Environment and an automatically created data entry form

Tip

Data Environment Connections and command objects provide extremely quick prototyping. They do not provide efficient code. After the design of a prototype has been approved, ADO objects that were created with the visual interface should be replaced with personally hand-coded ADO objects. Doing so can provide significant performance improvements.

Enterprise Manager

Enterprise Manager is the primary tool for managing SQL Server. It uses the Microsoft Management Console (MMC) as a graphical framework. The MMC is used as the basis for all of Microsoft's management tools, including all of those with Windows 2000, SMS 2.0, and the Internet Information Server. The MMC uses Internet Explorer as a graphical engine and provides a standardized look and feel across all of Microsoft's management platforms.

Figure 3-8 is a screen shot of Enterprise Manager using a standard two-pane display. The left pane contains a collapsible hierarchy, and the right pane displays the contents or details of whatever object is selected in the left pane.

The hierarchy for the MMC always begins with the Console Root. The next level is the root of the MMC application, or snap-in, which, in this case, is called Microsoft SQL Servers. The snap-in can contain one or more groups, which are containers to organize SQL Servers (or MSDE servers). Within the group, the name of the server is displayed (in this figure there are two servers: 0KH2H and AS7500), along with the operating system that the server is running and an icon that displays the state of the SQL Server service. A green arrow on a white background as shown in Figure 3-8 for server 0KH2H indicates that the server is running, but Enterprise Manager is not connected to it. Server AS7500 shows a white arrow on a green background that means that the server is running and Enterprise Manager has an open connection to it.

Within the server there are seven containers.

- ✦ The **Databases container** enables any databases on the server to be displayed, manipulated, or created.
- ✦ The **Data Transformation Services container** includes DTS packages that enable sophisticated movement and processing of data. DTS packages are described fully in Chapter 19.
- ✦ The **Management container** is home to the SQL Server Agent, with its automated jobs and alerts, as well as mechanisms for accessing the system logs and viewing current activity.
- ✦ The **Replication container** controls most of the replication activities for the server. If a server is configured as a replication distributor and additional container, the Replication Monitor is shown in Enterprise Manager.

- ✦ The **Security container** controls who has access to the MSDE server and what other servers the MSDE server can itself access. Within the Security container are Logins and Server Roles containers, which control who can connect to the server and what kind of access they will have, and Linked Servers and Remote Servers containers, which control server-to-server communication.
- ✦ The **Support Services container** has an icon for the Distributed Transaction Coordinator and enables it to be started and stopped.
- ✦ The **Meta Data Services container** controls the meta data repository, a standardized mechanism for storing and retrieving data about data.

For a server to be displayed in Enterprise Manager, it must be registered. If Enterprise Manager is installed on the same computer as MSDE, it will automatically register the local server. Registration consists of providing Enterprise Manager with the security context so that it can connect to the server. Right-clicking on the server and choosing Edit SQL Server Registration properties displays the current registration information. This dialog box also has some settings that affect the way Enterprise Manager runs. There is a check box called Display SQL Server state in console, which, when turned on, polls the SQL Server service to find out whether it's running and displays an icon accordingly. There is a useful check box called Show systems databases and system objects that is turned on by default and that can access system tables when performing maintenance or debugging tasks on the server. However, most of the time system tables just get in the way, so it is helpful to be able to hide them. Finally, there is a check box to automatically start SQL Server whenever Enterprise Manager attempts to connect to it.

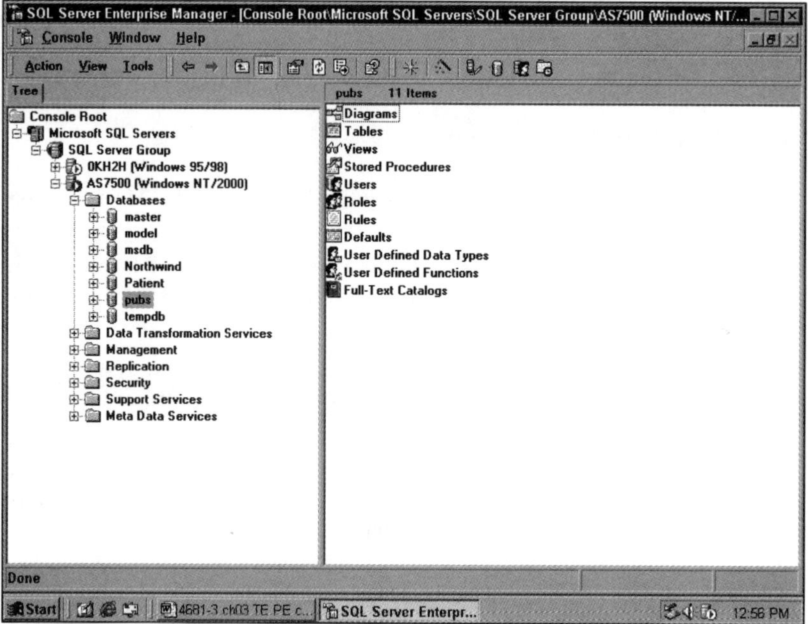

Figure 3-8: Enterprise Manager

In addition to providing a centralized, graphical environment for managing MSDE, Enterprise Manager includes the script generator, a tool useful for development. By right-clicking on any object within a database or the database itself and selecting All Tasks ➪ Generate Scripts, a SQL script can be generated that will recreate any or all objects. So a test database can be created, modified over time, and scripts can be generated that will provide an easy mechanism for recreating the database on other computers. Figure 3-9 shows the script generator that was invoked by right-clicking on the authors table. There are many options available that allow control over how the script is created. For example, in this screenshot, the option has been set to script table constraints. The preview of the script is shown in the foreground in the lower left. Notice that the table constraints are added to the table with an `Alter Table` command at the end of the script (part of the end of the script is not displayed).

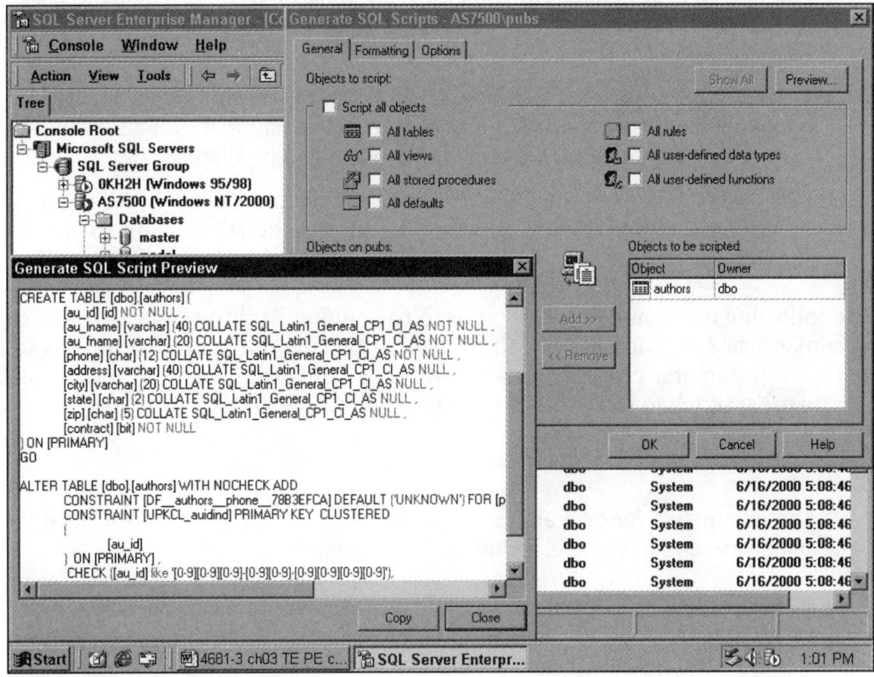

Figure 3-9: Enterprise Manager and the Script Generator with sample script

Enterprise Manager and the Script Generator with Sample Script Command Line – osql

The osql command line is available on any MSDE installation. Osql.exe is a program that can be run interactively from the command line or in a batch file in any version of Windows. It enables any SQL command or series of commands to be sent to the MSDE query processor.

Osql is very similar to the older program isql, which was used with SQL Server before version 7.0. The main difference between isql and osql is the connection mechanism used to communicate with data engines. Isql used db-Library, whereas osql uses ODBC. The behavior of isql can be simulated in osql by using the `-O` parameter.

Osql has many parameters; the three most commonly used are `-U`, `-P`, and `-S`. This book uses the same convention as the help returned from osql `-?`, which is to enclose the parameters in square brackets with a short name for better readability. When the parameter is actually used, it is entered with a hyphen followed by a single letter parameter, which is followed by the value for the parameter. See the examples for clarification.

- ✦ `[-U` *`login id`*`]` is used for the MSDE login name that is to be used for the connection. If this parameter is not supplied, an attempt will be made to connect as a null login.
- ✦ `[-P` *`password`*`]` is used for the password. If this parameter is not supplied, osql will use the value of the environmental variable, `OSQLPASSWORD`. If this variable does not exist, a password prompt will be displayed.
- ✦ `[-S` *`server`*`]` is used for the server name. This parameter is the name of the computer hosting MSDE. If it is not supplied, osql will attempt to connect to the local computer.

The following command line can be used to connect osql to MSDE as the system administrator (sa) immediately after installation (the initial password for sa is null, so the `-P` parameter can be supplied with no value as the example shows, or Enter can be pressed when the prompt for a password appears):

```
Osql -Usa -P
```

The parameters for osql are case sensitive and some have different meanings in uppercase and lowercase, including `-U`, `-S`, and `-P`.

Typing this command will connect to MSDE and present a numbered prompt. SQL commands can be typed at the prompt, and when the `GO` command is entered, they will be sent to the query processor and executed. The prompt displays the line number of the current batch. A batch is a series of SQL commands delineated by the `GO` command. All commands in a batch are compiled together, and a syntax error in a batch will abort the entire batch. A runtime error will abort only the current transaction, not the entire batch.

In the following example, osql is run in interactive mode from the C: prompt. A numbered prompt with the number 1 is displayed, indicating the start of a batch. The command to use the Finance database is entered, followed by a `select` command. The `select` command is typed on three lines only for readability. This batch would have run with exactly the same results if the `select` command had been typed on a single line. Finally, the `GO` command is issued. `GO` is interpreted by osql, causing all previous lines in the batch to be sent to MSDE. In this example, MSDE responds by returning the firstname and lastname of the one row in the People table that matches the criteria in the select statement. The last line is again a numbered prompt with the number 1, indicating that osql has begun a new batch and is awaiting input.

```
C:\>osql -Usa -P
1> use Finance
2> select firstname, lastname
3> from People
4> where lastname = 'Turing'
5> go
 firstname            lastname
 -------------------- ------------
 Alan                 Turing

(1 row affected)
1>
```

There must not be a space between any parameter and its value. For example, '`-Usa`' is valid; '`-U sa`' would produce an error.

The other parameters for osql are as follows:

- ✦ [`-H` *`hostname`*] provides information to applications and administrators about who is connected to the database. This information is stored in the master database, sysprocesses system table, hostname column. It is also visible in Enterprise Manager in the Current Activity under Process Info. If not supplied, the value of hostname is the computer name at which the user sits.
- ✦ [`-E`] sets the authentication to a trusted connection. It can only be used with MSDE installed on Windows NT or Windows 2000. Supplying this parameter indicates that neither a login nor password will be supplied. MSDE will retrieve user information about the currently logged-on user from the operating system. This Windows NT domain user must have been added to MSDE as a valid login. If this parameter is not supplied, then osql assumes that a non-trusted (sometimes called standard) connection will be used and will require a login name and password.
- ✦ [`-d` *`database name`*] sets the initial database to be used by the connection. This parameter is used in exactly the same way as typing the `USE` command as the first command after osql has been invoked. If this parameter is not supplied, the default database defined for the login within MSDE is used.
- ✦ [`-l` *`login time out`*] is the amount of time osql will wait for a successful connection to MSDE. Supplying this parameter with no value disables time out. If the parameter is not supplied, 15 seconds will be used for the time out.

✦ [-t *query time out*] is the amount of time osql will wait for any query to complete. Supplying this parameter with no value disables time out, and queries will wait indefinitely to complete. If this parameter is not supplied, 8 seconds will be used.

✦ [-h *lines between headers*] controls printing of column headings in a query. Column headings are printed once at the beginning of the output by default. They can also be printed periodically by specifying a number. The headers will reprint after that many lines of output, for example, `-h66` would cause the headers to be printed on the first line of a report, the 67th line, the 133rd line, and so forth. This parameter would normally be set to the page length if the output were to be redirected to a printer. Headers can also be suppressed entirely by supplying this parameter with a value of –1 (negative one); confusingly, doing so looks like this:

```
osql -Usa -P -h-1
```

✦ [-s *colseparator*] specifies the character that will be printed between every column in the output. If not specified, a single space will be used. If specified without a value, there will be no separation between columns. To specify characters that might otherwise be misinterpreted by the operating system, such as the redirect or pipe symbols (<, >, |), enclose the character in double quotes. For example,

```
osql -Usa -P -s"|"
```

✦ [-w *columnwidth*] specifies the number of characters that will be printed on a single line of output. If the output exceeds this value, it will be broken into multiple lines. If not supplied, the columnwidth is 80. If the parameter is supplied, a value must be supplied and must be greater than 8.

✦ [-a *packetsize*] controls the amount of data that will be sent at one time across the network to the MSDE server. The default is 4096. For most queries, the default works well. Fine-tuning this value can sometimes improve performance on bulk loads of data.

✦ [-e] does not require any value. If it is provided, any commands that are entered will be printed along with the output.

✦ [-I] turns on the quoted identifiers connection setting. When the quoted identifiers setting is turned on, MSDE differentiates between single and double quotes such that double quotes are used to delimit the names of objects. Turning on the quoted identifiers enables nonstandard naming conventions for objects to be used, such as spaces within the names.

When the quoted identifier setting is turned off, single and double quotes act in exactly the same manner: they delimit literals, that is, strings. When the setting is turned on, single quotes delimit literals, while double quotes delimit identifiers, that is, object names. To see the difference, the following code sample is run with quoted identifiers turned off:

```
1> set quoted_identifier off
2> go
```

```
1> select "lastname" from People
2> go
 --------
 lastname
 lastname
 lastname
 lastname
 lastname
 lastname
 lastname
```

MSDE interprets lastname not as a column name, but as an actual literal value that should be included in the output. The same behavior would be produced by using single quotes, without regard to the quoted identifiers setting. The next code sample runs the same command, but this time with quoted identifiers turned on:

```
1> set quoted_identifier on
2> go
1> select "lastname" from People
2> go
 lastname
 --------------------
 Walls
 Shaftoe
 Turing
 Rendell
 Franklin
 Penn
 Smith
```

In this case, lastname is interpreted as a column name, and the values from that column are returned in the output. This behavior can be produced by using square brackets instead of quotes, without regard to the quoted identifiers setting (for example, [lastname] instead of "lastname").

As demonstrated by the examples, the quoted identifiers setting can be changed with the `set` command, as well as with a command line parameter. In addition, the default setting for all connections to MSDE can be sent at the server level. Any confusion can be avoided by using single quotes and square brackets and avoiding double quotes altogether.

✦ [`-L`] can be issued with no other parameters and a list of known servers will be returned. The list of known servers varies depending upon the configuration of the computer on which the command is run. The list can also vary depending on how long the computer has been running because one of the processes that builds the list listens to broadcasts from other servers.

- [-c *cmdend*] Normally, a batch of commands is sent from osql to MSDE when the GO command is entered. This command terminator property can be changed from GO to some other string or character with this parameter. The value must be enclosed in quotes if the OS could misinterpret it. The command terminator is interpreted by osql; it is not sent to MSDE.
- [-q "*cmdline query*"] executes any string that is passed with it as a command immediately when osql starts. The results of the command will be returned, and the osql command prompt will be displayed again, awaiting additional batches.
- [-Q "*cmdline query*"] is similar to the lowercase q parameter, except that as soon as the command completes, osql terminates. This parameter is useful for including SQL batches within operating system batch files. It enables osql to be used as a single-line mechanism for running SQL statements from the operating system.
- [-n] suppresses the osql prompt. When osql starts and whenever a command completes, a blank line is displayed. The functionality of osql is otherwise unchanged.
- [-m *errorlevel*] displays any errors generated with a severity higher than the value passed with it with extended information. Extended information includes the error number, severity level, state, server name, and so on. Any errors that are generated with a severity equal to or less than this value will display only the error message. The default error level value is 10.
- [-r *0 or 1*] accepts a 1 or 0 as a value. 0 is the default. It allows certain messages to be sent to the screen even if output is redirected by the command line. If a parameter is not specified or if 0 is specified, only error messages with a severity level of 17 or higher are redirected. If 1 is specified, all message output, including that generated by the PRINT command, is redirected. For example, the following command starts osql, immediately runs a select that returns a list of lastnames from a table called People in a database called test, and redirects this output to a file called people.txt:

  ```
  osql -Usa -P -dtest -Q"select lastname from People" >
  people.txt
  ```

  If an error message with a severity of 17 or higher were generated during the execution of this command, it would be displayed on the screen rather than being added to people.txt. Any error with a severity less than 17 (or the output of a print statement) would be written to people.txt. Controlling this behavior is particularly important when the osql command is being used within a batch file and subsequent commands must act on the output of osql.

  The effect of this parameter is easily demonstrated:

  ```
  osql -Usa -P -Q"Print 'This message goes to a file'" >
  file.txt

  osql -Usa -P -Q"Print 'This one goes to the screen'" -r1 >
  file.txt
  ```

- [-i *inputfile*] redirects input from a file. The commands of a SQL batch can be entered into a file and run using the osql command with this parameter. The standard operating system redirect input (<) performs a similar function.
- [-o *outputfile*] redirects output from the osql command to a file. The standard operating system redirect output (>) performs a similar function.
- [-p] prints statistics along with the output at the end of each batch. The statistics provided are the network packet size, the number of transactions involved in the batch, the total number of milliseconds required to process the batch, and the average number of milliseconds per transaction within the batch.
- [-b] causes osql to terminate in the event of an error caused by a SQL command. Controlling this behavior can be particularly important when using osql within an operating system batch file.
- [-O] causes osql to behave like older (pre-SQL Server 6.5) isql, allowing older scripts to be run without modification.
- [-?] displays all available parameters for the osql command.

There are a few subtle differences between osql and the most recent version of isql. To run old isql script, the connection settings must be considered. As mentioned previously, connection setting defaults can be determined at the server level or at the connection level, and they can also be reset with a script. To completely duplicate the default setting of isql, the following commands can be issued to set the appropriate connection settings:

```
SET QUOTED_IDENTIFIER OFF
SET ANSI_WARNINGS OFF
SET ANSI_PADDING OFF
SET ANSI_NULLS OFF
SET CONCAT_NULL_YIELDS_NULL OFF
```

Most of the commands that are typed into osql are passed through to MSDE for processing. However, there are a few commands that are processed by osql itself. Any commands that are to be processed by osql must appear alone at the beginning of a line.

- The GO command indicates the end of a batch. Commands that are typed into osql are stored in a cache until the end of batch indicator is reached. Then the batch is sent to MSDE. Before the end of batch indicator, the contents of the cache can be manipulated with several other commands. The GO command also accepts an integer parameter. The batch will be executed multiple times, according to the number supplied as a parameter. All of the executions are submitted in a single batch to MSDE.

Tip

Care should be taken with the use of block comments /*...*/ to debug osql scripts that involve more than one batch. The `GO` command is interpreted by osql and sends everything in the previous batch to MSDE. If block quotes are used and span a `GO` command, the opening /* will be sent to the data engine with the batch in which it is contained, which will generate a syntax error. Subsequent batches from inside the block comment will be sent to the data engine and processed until the batch is reached which contains the close block quote. This last batch will include the */ and will generate a syntax error. This problem can be overcome by commenting any `GO` commands within the block quote using a double dash: -- `GO`

- ✦ The `RESET` command clears the current batch cache without sending any commands to MSDE.
- ✦ The `ED` command invokes an editor and passes the current contents of batch cache to the editor. The default editor is edit.exe. When the `ED` command is executed, osql saves the current contents of the batch cache to a unique file name with no extension in the system root directory (c:\windows in Windows 98, for example). It then invokes the editor and passes it the name of this file. After the file has been edited, it too must be saved so that osql can read it back into the cache. Other editors can be used by setting an environmental variable, `EDITOR`, equal to the executable name of the editor. However, the editor must accept the name of a file as a parameter. An example of an editor that does not work particularly well is Notepad. Notepad assumes a txt extension on any file it edits. When used with osql, it attempts to create a new file using the name that osql has created, but adding the txt extension. For this to function successfully, the user would have to decline to have a new file created and open the temporary file created by osql.

Note

The `EDITOR` environmental variable is read only when osql is started. Changing this variable while osql is running will have no effect until osql is terminated and restarted.

- ✦ A running batch can be terminated with the Ctrl+C key sequence.
- ✦ `QUIT` terminates osql without executing the current batch.
- ✦ `EXIT` also terminates osql; however, it can be used to pass a return value to the operating system. Passing a return value can be useful when osql is used within the batch file and other statements in the batch file must take action based upon the results of the osql query. To pass a return value, a user must enter a query within parentheses immediately following the `EXIT` command. Any commands currently in the batch cache will be executed followed by the query in parentheses. The first column of the first row of the results of this query is sent as a return value. The `EXIT` command with empty parentheses will execute the current contents of the batch cache, but not set a return value for the operating system. The `EXIT` command with no parentheses acts identically to the `QUIT` command and terminates osql without executing the current batch.

Operating system commands can be executed from within osql by preceding them with two exclamation marks.

If any error with a state of 127 is raised within a batch, osql will terminate at the end of the batch. The error message will be returned to the user.

Query Analyzer

Query Analyzer is a graphical tool that serves a similar function to osql. It accepts input from the keyboard or from a file and passes the input to MSDE for processing. It is shown in Figure 3-10 with the results of a simple query it has just had processed by MSDE. Query Analyzer has a number of advanced features that make it ideal for writing SQL scripts. These include the ability to parse syntax, to automatically color code reserved words, to include an index usage analyzer, and so on.

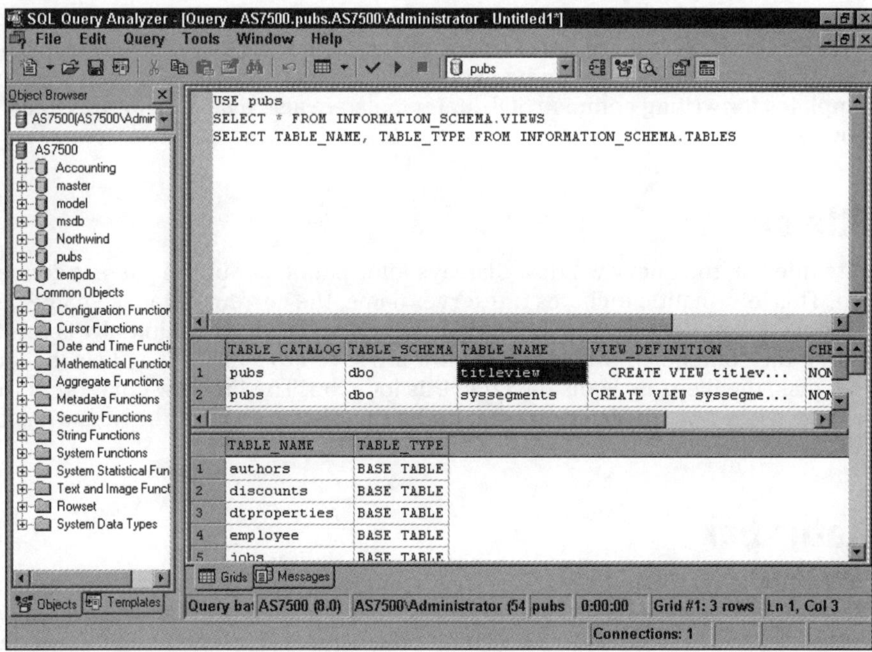

Figure 3-10: Query Analyzer with query and results in a grid

Connection dialog

When Query Analyzer is started it presents a Connect to SQL Server dialog box. This dialog box is used to set up the initial connection to MSDE. It provides a drop-down list box of all known MSDE and SQL Servers, which defaults to the local computer. It also has two option buttons that enable selection of a security mode: Windows NT authentication or SQL Server authentication (which, of course, also means MSDE authentication). If the Windows NT authentication button is chosen, the security credentials of the currently logged-on user will be used to connect to the server. MSDE supports this kind of connection only when it is run on a Windows NT or Windows 2000 platform. If the SQL Server authentication button is chosen, a login name and password must be entered. After the user has been properly authenticated, a blank query window displays.

Object Browser

By default, Query Analyzer displays the Object Browser on the left side of the screen, as shown in Figure 3-10. The Object Browser displays all of the objects on an MSDE server in a hierarchical tree similar to Windows Explorer. The top-level objects are databases that can be expanded to display the objects they contain. Templates for writing common SQL statements are also available in the Object Browser.

Title bar

In its title bar, the query window displays information about the current connection. This information includes the server name, the current database name, and the login name. The name of the query is also displayed, which initially is (untitled). If the contents of the query window are saved to a file or if a file is loaded from disk, the filename is displayed in this location. The first few characters from the query window are also displayed in the title bar as soon as the query has been run for the first time.

Status bar

The status bar at the bottom of the query window consists of several sections. The left-most section contains a general status that indicates whether the system is ready, is executing a query, or has completed a query. The center sections contain the server name and version, the user name and process ID, the current database, the execution time of the most recently executed query, and the number of rows returned along with a grid number if multiple result sets are displayed in grids. The right-most section contains a line and column counter indicating the current location of the cursor.

Toolbar

There is a toolbar at the top of the query window. Many buttons have key sequence shortcuts, and when they do, the shortcut is listed in parentheses when the mouse pointer hovers over the button. The first button (Ctrl+N) creates a new query window that represents a new connection to MSDE using the same security credentials that were used for the current window. A drop-down list is available next to the New button that lists available templates. When a template is chosen, the new query window is preloaded with sample code. The second button enables a file containing the SQL script to be opened and loaded into the query window. The third button (Ctrl+S) enables the current contents of the query window to be saved to a text file. The fourth button inserts template code into the current window.

The second set of buttons provides standard cut (Ctrl+X), copy (Ctrl+C), and paste (Ctrl+V) functions, along with a button that clears the contents of the current query but keeps the connection open (Ctrl+Shift+Del), a button that invokes the Find dialog box (Ctrl+F), and an Undo button (Ctrl+Z). Following these is the execute mode button. There are two mutually exclusive execute modes: results in text (Ctrl+T) and results in grid (Ctrl+D). Either of these two modes also enables the additional selection of the button to show the execution plan (Ctrl+K). When the results are returned in text, they appear in the lower pane as a single group in much the same way that results are returned with osql. Each column is displayed according to the column width specified in the table definition. Any messages are displayed along with the batch that created them, such as the number of rows returned. If more than one result set is returned, they are displayed one after the other in the order in which they were created. Such a display can be so wide and long as to be unwieldy. In cases such as these, returning the results to a grid can be more workable because it displays the results in a format much like a spreadsheet with dynamically resizable columns. Each result set is displayed individually in grids that follow one another in the lower pane and that can be individually scrolled. In Figure 3-10, there are two result sets, each in its own grid, and there are two vertical scroll bars: one for the entire lower pane and one for the currently selected result grid. There is also a tab that displays all messages, which is important because some commands, such as `DBCC`, return only messages and no result set. Selecting the Show Execution Plan button causes an additional tab to be added after execution of the query. This tab will display both a text and graphical representation of the execution plan.

The set of buttons with a blue check mark, a green triangle, and a (usually) gray or (occasionally) red square, corresponds to the parse query (Ctrl+F5), execute query (F5), and cancel query (Alt+Break) functions. The parse query button scans the query for syntax errors but does not execute it, which is extremely useful when writing long queries having multiple parts that cannot be executed multiple times. If the syntax scan is successful, the message “The command(s) completed successfully” is returned. If it fails, a syntax error is displayed along with the location at which it was detected (not necessarily the exact location of the error). Execute query parses and executes the query. Cancel query is available, and thus red, only while a query is actually executing.

Parsing a query checks only the syntax; it does not verify object names. If a query parses correctly, but generates an invalid object name error when it runs, the object name should be checked for a misspelling.

The database drop-down list allows a database to be selected as current. Selecting a database from this list performs the same function as the `USE` command. After a database is selected, all commands are executed against the database unless otherwise specified. Any `USE` command in the query overrides and modifies the database selected in the drop-down list.

The button that looks like a tiny, multicolored organizational chart displays the estimated execution plan (Ctrl+L). It parses the query and generates and displays an execution plan, but does not execute the plan. If a syntax error occurs, the error message is displayed and no plan is generated. It will produce and display a plan even if the query governor has been set and has prevented a particular query from running because it is too long and resource intensive.

Generating an estimated execution plan is useful when attempting to fine-tune or better understand long running queries, because it places almost no load on the server. A user must be aware, however, that the plan is estimated. It will occasionally vary from the plan that is actually used to run the query.

Following the estimated execution plan are two buttons that display and hide the Object Browser and the Object Search dialog box.

The last two buttons are the current connection options button and the show/hide results pane (Ctrl+R) button. The current connection options button displays a dialog box that allows the inspection and modification of connection options. These options are described below. The show/hide results pane button is a toggle that when clicked will change the state of the results pane; if it is currently hidden it will be displayed, and if it is currently displayed it will be hidden.

Menu

Most of the agents on the menu are also found on the toolbar and are explained above. There are a few exceptions, the most interesting of which is Perform Index Analysis (Ctrl+I) in the Query menu. This item analyzes the current query and determines whether adding or modifying indexes in the database could improve its performance. It is sometimes unable to make recommendations, for example, if the tables involved are very small.

Several items in the File menu allow both queries and result sets to be saved to files. To save the text of the query, a user can click the upper pane and choose Save. Query Analyzer will save the query to a file with an extension of .sql. Saving while the lower pane is selected varies depending upon whether the results are formatted in text or a grid. Results in text are written to a file with an extension of .rpt and formatted just as they are seen on the screen. Results in a grid are written to a comma-delimited file with an extension of .csv. If there is more than one results set, only the currently selected set is saved unless Save All is chosen. If the Message tab is selected, then the results are saved as plain text in a .rpt file.

A Goto item in the View menu allows instant access to a particular line specified by its number, which is particularly useful during debugging when an error message has specified the line in the script that generated the error. The Advanced item in the view menu enables the currently selected text to be set to all uppercase or all lowercase letters.

The Help menu enables access to two different help files. Contents and Index provides help on the Query Analyzer itself. Transact SQL help provides syntax and examples for SQL commands. These are both very specific help files and are distinct from the main books online help.

Connection properties

Figure 3-11 shows the Connection Properties tab. All of the settings available in this dialog box can also be set with the SQL `Set` command. If a connection setting is modified within a script, that setting overrides the settings made in this dialog box.

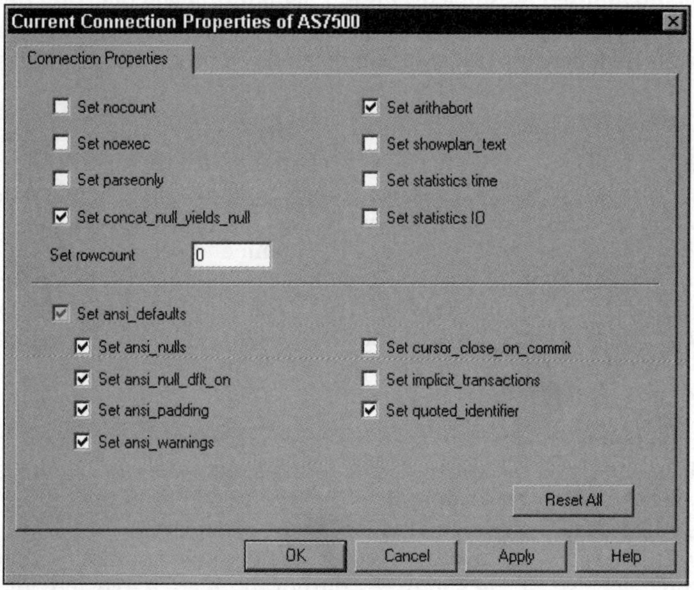

Figure 3-11: Connection Properties tab

The query settings function as follows:

- **Set nocount** — suppresses the row count that is normally returned after every batch; for example, "(7 row(s) affected)."
- **Set noexec** — prevents the query from executing. The MSDE query processor compiles all batches in the query, and all object names are checked. Selecting this option disables all other query setting options.

A user should use the No Execute option, rather than the Parse Query button, for more exhaustive checking of the Query. No Execute will verify that all object names in the query refer to valid objects, thereby preventing one of the most common syntax errors.

- **Set parseonly** — causes the Execute button (or any other method of executing) to perform a parse only, exactly like the Parse query button.
- **Set concat_null_yields_null** — determines the results of string concatenation when one of the operands is a null. If the setting is turned on, then the result of any operation with a null will be a null.
- **Set arithabort** — causes the entire query to end when an arithmetic error is encountered.
- **Set showplan_text** — causes the text of the query plan to be displayed instead of executing the query. The Show execution plan button will override this setting and cause the query to be executed and the results and graphical query plan to be returned. Selecting this option disables all other query-setting options.
- **Set statistics time** — displays the number of milliseconds required to parse and compile, as well as to execute each batch along with the results of the batch. When connection options are set, Query Analyzer must send commands to MSDE to enforce those options. In the case of Show stats time, Query Analyzer sends a batch containing the command set statistics time on before the query and another batch containing the command set statistics time off. These batches also generate statistics, although they are usually less than 1 millisecond and show up as zeroes. The parse and compile statistics for the query itself appear immediately preceding the result set, and the execution time immediately follows the result set.

  In the example below, the elapsed time for parsing and compiling the query was 55 milliseconds, and the elapsed time for its execution was 15 milliseconds. The execution time that appears in the first two lines of the output reflects the batch that turned on statistics. There are no stats for parse and compile for this batch because at the time it was compiled statistics were not yet turned on. Likewise, at the end of the output there are parse and compile stats for the batch that turned statistics off, but none for the execution of this batch.

```
SQL Server Execution Times:
   CPU time = 0 ms,  elapsed time = 0 ms.
SQL Server parse and compile time:
   CPU time = 0 ms, elapsed time = 55 ms.
lastname
--------------------
Turing

(1 row(s) affected)


SQL Server Execution Times:
   CPU time = 0 ms,  elapsed time = 15 ms.
SQL Server parse and compile time:
   CPU time = 0 ms, elapsed time = 0 ms.
```

✦ **Set statistics I/O**—turns on statistics reporting for the I/O associated with the query. Showing statistics will display the following:

- The table name that is being accessed
- The number of scans that are performed
- The number of logical reads, that is, the number of pages that have already been placed in cache and can be read directly from RAM
- The number of physical reads, that is, the number of pages that must be retrieved from disk because they are not in cache at the time they are needed
- The number of read-ahead reads, that is, the number of pages that are read from disk into cache by the read-ahead manager as a result of the query, but which are actually located in cache at the time they are needed

✦ **Set rowcount**—allows the number of returned rows to be limited. The choice of rows that are returned should be considered arbitrary. To return only the first or last rows, the `Top` function in the query should be used. This option can be useful for testing the reasonableness of the results of a query that would run for a long period of time and return a large number of rows. A value of zero for this option returns all rows.

✦ **Set ansi_defaults**—turns on all of the following settings in order to comply with ANSI standards.

✦ **Set ansi_nulls**—controls the results of comparisons that are performed on a null value. When turned on, the equal and not equal comparison will return a null (rather than true or false) whenever either or both of the compared values are null. Using ANSI nulls is in keeping with the idea that null is used as an unknown value rather than as a specific value. The question, "Does null equal null?" could be rephrased as, "Does something whose value is unknown equal the value of some other thing whose value is also unknown?"

The answer must be, "I don't know," at least according to ANSI SQL. If the equals or not equals comparisons are used in a query's logic, it can be crucial to know the value of this setting. When this option is turned on, there are special operators, `is null` and `is not null`. These operators always work without regard to the setting of the ANSI nulls option.

- **Set ansi_null_dflt_on** — controls the default setting for nullability in newly created columns.
- **Set ansi_padding** — determines whether trailing blanks and zeroes are added or taken away when data is inserted. There are three cases to consider when understanding the effect of this setting on the database: a fixed-length char or binary column that does not allow nulls; a fixed-length char or binary column that does allow nulls; and a variable-length varchar or varbinary column. With fixed-length data that does not allow nulls, character data is always padded with spaces, and binary data is always padded with zeroes so that the inserted data is equal to the defined length of the column. The same behavior will be seen with fixed length data that does allow nulls when the ANSI padding setting is turned on. When it is turned off, the data will be inserted with whatever length it has coming from the client. Data inserted into a variable length column will be entered as is if ANSI padding is turned on. If it is turned off, trailing spaces or zeroes will be trimmed and discarded.
- **Set ansi_warnings** — will issue a warning anytime an attempt is made to enter data that must be truncated in order to fit into a column. For example, if a name that is 35 characters is being inserted into a column defined as char(30), the last five characters will be truncated. If the ANSI warnings option is turned on, a warning will be issued; if it is not, the data will be truncated and saved with the user none the wiser.
- **Set cursor_close_on_commit** — automatically closes all cursors when a transaction commits.
- **Set implicit_transactions** — causes any data modification statement to automatically begin a transaction, which must be ended with a commit or rollback command.
- **Set quoted_identifier** — determines whether double quotes perform the same function as single quotes or square brackets. See the `-I` parameter example in the section on osql earlier in this chapter for more explanation.

Other settings that were in the Connection options dialog box in previous versions can be accessed from the Tools ⇨ Options menu.

Executing a query

Any number of SQL commands can be typed into the query window. They can be divided into batches with the `GO` command; however, unlike osql, the `GO` command does not cause execution of the current batch. All of the batches in the query window can be executed by clicking on the green right arrow, by using the Ctrl+E key combination, by using the F5 key, or by selecting Query ⇨ Execute from the menu. After a query has been executed, the query window will split horizontally into two panes. The upper pane contains the original query while the lower pane contains any results. Subsets of the query can be executed individually by selecting the subset and initiating execution. Only the selected text will be executed.

Controlling MSDE Programmatically

In addition to the tools mentioned above, a user will doubtless have needs that are better met by writing one's own program. A program that a user writes can be used to access the data stored by MSDE or to provide management functions such as creating tables, rebuilding indexes, or initiating replication. A user can write a program that will have access to MSDE in any language that supports Microsoft's COM specification. Typical examples of languages that support COM are Visual Basic, VBScript, and Visual C++. After the user has mastered the techniques for programmatic access, it can sometimes be easier to write a quick program or script, rather than trying to figure out which tool can be used to do what is needed. Whatever language the user chooses to use (or combination of languages), one or more of the programmatic interfaces to MSDE, collectively called the Application Programming Interfaces (APIs), must be understood.

A number of APIs can be used to programmatically manipulate MSDE. The APIs that can be used with MSDE are described in detail in Chapter 5. In particular, there is an object model called the Distributed Management Objects (DMO) that provides mechanisms for creating, modifying, and deleting objects within MSDE, and another object model called the ActiveX Data Objects (ADO) that provides access to the data stored in MSDE. ADO is discussed in more detail in Chapter 24, including accessing data from a Visual Basic program, a Web Page, and a script. Examples are also included in other chapters for using the APIs to perform tasks with MSDE. The code examples that are provided are written primarily in VBScript. Any code example can be saved to a file and run on any Windows platform that is running the Windows Scripting Host. The syntax for using the object models can easily be adapted to any other COM-compliant language.

Summary

The methods used to access MSDE will depend on a variety of factors: who is performing the access, what licenses do they have, what are their preferences, what role do they play (that is, developer or end user), and what functionality has been built into custom applications. Access 2000 developers will most likely use a combination of Access and osql, and maybe some script. Access 2000 end users will probably not use osql, but will rely on the native features of Access and any scripts that might be provided by the developer. Visual Studio developers have an array of choices. They can use the tools bundled in the IDE or osql, but they also have access to Enterprise Manager and Query Analyzer in the developer's edition of SQL Server. They will have to create tools for the end users of the applications because there are no graphical tools automatically provided as with Access. Whatever the development environment, the developers must ensure that end users will have properly licensed tools to perform their jobs. Either developers or administrators must ensure that controls are in place to secure data. The limitations of tools provided to users are never sufficient to protect data because it is easy to acquire other tools that can leave unprotected systems open to accidental or malicious damage.

✦ ✦ ✦

Preparing to Use MSDE

In This Chapter

MSDE installation requirements

Installing SQL Server and MSDE

Choosing the collation

Choosing the network libraries

Understanding character sets and sort order

Understanding Unicode

Because MSDE does not include graphical management tools, developers will benefit by creating their applications with another version of SQL Server and then distributing the application with MSDE to the end users of the application. Occasionally, using another version of SQL Server is not practical, so the developer will use MSDE for development and production. No matter what edition of SQL Server is used for development, a number of issues must be addressed prior to or during installation. This chapter covers those issues and outlines the installation process for both MSDE and the other editions of SQL Server; this chapter also provides enough information for developers to begin creating an application with MSDE or SQL Server.

Chapters 31, 32, and 33 cover the issues associated with distributing MSDE to end users.

Installation Requirements

The system requirements for MSDE are as follows:

- **Operating System** — Windows 98, Windows Me, Windows NT 4.0, or Windows 2000.
- **System Memory** — 64MB for Windows 2000, 32MB for all other operating systems.
- **Hard Drive** — 44MB of free space. This is for the data engine itself; it does not include space for the data contained therein. The actual amount of space consumed will vary depending on the file system and total drive size. FAT, FAT32, and NTFS are all supported file systems.
- **Client Software** — Access 2000 requires the Office 2000 or Access 2000 Service Release 1. The Visual Studio Service Pack 4 is recommended when using any of the Visual Studio 6.0 products.

At the time of publication, both Access and Visual Studio had functional limitations with MSDE 2000. Neither is able to create a new MSDE database, nor can they save changes to database diagrams, stored procedures, tables, or views. A future service pack or service release should restore some of this functionality. The instructions provided in this book reflect the intended functionality of Access and Visual Studio. Alternative methods of accomplishing all tasks are provided throughout this book. For example, instructions are provided for creating databases using Enterprise Manager, osql, and scripting languages.

Installation Procedures

The setup for any edition of SQL Server except for MSDE is initiated by inserting the CD; the Autorun feature displays a menu offering to install SQL Server components or to display a variety of information about installation. Setup can also be initiated manually by running setupsql.exe, which is found in the \x86\setup directory. The following screens are displayed during setup:

1. **Welcome** — No information is requested on this screen.
2. **Computer Name** — Select the type of installation. A local installation installs SQL Server on the computer at which you are working. A remote installation allows you to install SQL Server on another computer across the network. When performing a remote installation, you must supply the name of the remote computer on which the software is to be installed. A virtual server is used for installing SQL Server in a cluster. Clusters are supported only by the Enterprise Edition; this option is disabled (grayed out) in this dialog box for other editions.
3. **Installation Selection** — Choose to install a new instance of SQL Server, modify an existing instance, or work with advanced options. The advanced options are used to create scripts for unattended installation, manage clusters, and rebuild the SQL Server items in the system registry.
4. **User Information** — Enter your name and company. The information entered in this screen does not affect the functionality of SQL Server.
5. **Software License Agreement** — Read the license agreement. You can continue with the installation only if you click the button that indicates that you accept the license agreement.
6. **Installation Definition** — Choose to install client tools, server services, or connectivity components. Client tools include the programs that are used to manage and interact with SQL Server, such as Enterprise Manager and Query Analyzer. The server consists of the three services: SQL Server service, SQL Server Agent service, and the Distributed Transaction Coordinator service. Connectivity includes the low-level software that is necessary to communicate with SQL Server. These components are also referred to as the Microsoft Data Access Components (MDAC).

7. **Instance Name**—Choose whether the installations should be the default instance or a named instance. If you clear the check box for default instance, you must enter the instance name. Multiple instances of MSDE or SQL Server can run on a single computer. Each instance behaves like an entirely independent installation, and each can support thousands of databases. Multiple instances can be useful in a development environment to maintain multiple versions of the same database on a single computer.
8. **Setup Type**—Select a typical, minimal, or custom installation and choose the directories for the program files and the data files. The default installation directory is \Program Files\Microsoft SQL Server on the same drive as the operating system. This screen also gives you the statistics about how much space is required and how much space is available on each drive. If you choose a custom installation, you will later have the opportunity to configure the collation settings and network libraries.
9. **Services Accounts**—When installing SQL Server on Windows NT or 2000, an account must be specified that will be used by the services to provide a security context. The security context that is used for the services must have administrative authority on the computer. The local security context has administrative privilege on the local computer, but none on any computer on the network, so it cannot be used if MSDE needs to communicate with other computers, for example, using replication. A selected user account should be a member of the local administrators' group or something similar, and it should have appropriate permissions on any remote computers with which it might need to communicate. Services accounts are covered in detail in Chapter 25.
10. **Authentication Mode**—Choose Windows authentication or mixed mode. Both modes allow the use of Windows NT user accounts; mixed mode also allows the use of logins that are entirely defined within SQL Server. Authentication is covered in Chapter 25.
11. **Collation Settings**—Choose the collation, which specifies the character set, sort order, and Unicode collation. The collation can either be a Windows collation, which is based on the Windows locale setting, or a SQL collation, which provides backward compatibility with earlier versions of SQL Server and is not dependent on the localization configuration of Windows. The default collation cannot be changed without reinstalling the SQL Server; however, different collations can be specified for each column in a table. See the sections on collations later in this chapter for a more complete discussion of this topic.
12. **Network Libraries**—Choose the protocols on which the server will listen for connection from clients. The settings can be reconfigured later using the server network utility. The default settings work well for most installations.
13. **Start Copying Files**—No information is requested on this screen.
14. **Choose Licensing Mode**—Select Per Seat or Processor License mode.

Configuring Network Protocols

In a client/server environment, the computers must share common protocols (for example, Named Pipes, TCP/IP, or IPX) in order to communicate. The client and server network utilities provide a means for configuring the protocols that will be used for database communication. On the client side, you can set the protocol that will be used by default when a client connects to a database server. You can also specify server aliases that allow the client to use a particular protocol and configuration on a server-by-server basis. With the server network utility, you can configure multiple protocols on which the server will listen for client connections, perhaps using different protocols for different groups of clients. The configuration of protocols will often be determined by other network and security considerations. Such considerations might include the use of a nonstandard TCP/IP port, which would require explicit configuration on both the server and all clients.

MSDE requires the same configuration choices as the other editions of SQL Server; however, the setup program for MSDE is not interactive. The configuration settings must be entered at the command line or in a configuration file.

See Chapter 31 for instructions on how to run the MSDE setup from the command line.

On Windows 98 and Me, MSDE must be manually started after each reboot of the computer. This can be changed with the Service Manager by checking the box "Auto-start service when OS starts."

Uninstalling

Upon occasion it will be necessary to uninstall an instance of SQL Server. For example, if multiple instances are running on a computer that is used for development and testing, an instance can be removed when the development or testing process is complete. To remove an instance, use the Add/Remove Programs utility in Control Panel. Select the appropriate instance of MSDE or SQL Server from the list and click the Add/Remove button. An instance of MSDE is identified in the Add/Remove Programs list as 'Microsoft SQL Server Desktop Engine.' All other editions of SQL Server are identified as 'Microsoft SQL Server 2000.' If an instance is named, the name is shown in parentheses after the product name.

Understanding Collations

One of the settings that cannot be changed without either reinstalling or rebuilding the master database (which amounts to the same thing) is the collation. The collation specifies three things: the character set, or code page; the sort order for the code page; and the sort order for Unicode data.

Character sets

Any computer program that manipulates characters, including MSDE, has to represent those characters internally with numbers. The alphabets used for business communication in the Western Hemisphere and most European countries use one byte, or eight bits, to represent each character. Eight bits can be arranged in 256 possible combinations, and each combination can represent a single character. The set of characters that can be represented at any one time is sometimes called a code page. A code page that contains 256 characters can adequately represent many languages, like English, Spanish, and French. A 256-character code page can also represent a language that uses an entirely different character set, like Russian, which uses Cyrillic characters. However, it is unable to represent both English and Russian, because there are simply too many characters when you take into consideration uppercase and lowercase letters, accent marks, punctuation, numerals, and so on.

Database designers must choose the single, most appropriate character set at the time the database manager is installed. Many choices are available in addition to English, such as Greek, Turkish, Hebrew, or Arabic. For some languages, like Chinese, Korean, Japanese, or Thai, 256 characters are insufficient for all the characters needed to communicate effectively. The character sets for these languages include the notation DBCS, for double byte character set. These character sets use two bytes for each character, which the database designer must take into account. For example, when creating a column designed to support 15 characters from the double byte character set, the data type for the column would be CHAR(30). The number of characters that can be represented with two bytes, 65,536, is far in excess of the number needed to represent any single business language. From this observation, a relatively recent innovation has developed: the Unicode character set.

Unicode is a character set that uses two bytes to represent each character, and as the name implies, it is designed to be a single character set that can be used for all languages. MSDE does not directly support Unicode for native data storage; however, Unicode is supported by three data types for individual columns in tables in the database. These data types are NCHAR, NVARCHAR, and NTEXT. They take into account the fact that Unicode requires two bytes per character, so a Unicode column designed to support 15 characters would be specified as NCHAR(15). Using Unicode for all storage would double the amount of space required for all character data; therefore, the installation of MSDE requires that a standard code page be specified.

Sort order

In addition to the character set, the collation specifies the sort orders for the two kinds of character data that can be stored in MSDE tables: characters from the code page and characters from Unicode. Different sort orders are available based on which character set is selected. As their name implies, sort orders dictate the order in which sorted lists will be created, but they also dictate the outcome of comparisons. It is important that MSDE has a collation that is compatible with any client software so that data is presented correctly to users. Sort order has multiple aspects: the order, the case sensitivity, the accent sensitivity, and possibly kana- and width-sensitivity for some double byte code pages.

Order

There are two general types of order: binary order and dictionary order. Binary order is the most restrictive of the possible sort orders. It uses the underlying numerical representation of a character for both sorting and comparison and is always both case and accent sensitive. That means that uppercase characters are considered completely distinct from lowercase, and both are likewise distinct from characters with diacritical marks. So, a sorted list would display all words that begin with capital letters first, A-Z, then all words that begin with lowercase letters, a-z, and finally all words that begin with letters with diacritical marks (for example, ä, ç, ó). Table 4-1 shows an example of two different sort orders. The left column shows a series of five words sorted in binary order, and the right column shows them in case insensitive dictionary order. The difference in the two columns can be seen by examining the location of the words that begin with lowercase letters. In the binary sort order, the lowercase letters follow all uppercase letters. In the case insensitive order, the words beginning with lowercase letters are treated exactly the same as the words beginning with uppercase letters.

Table 4-1
Comparison of Sort Orders

Binary Order	*Case Insensitive Order*
Deadlock	Deadlock
Debug	deadly
Deep	Debug
deadly	decimal
decimal	Deep

Dictionary order sorts words in the order they are found in the dictionary. Of course, words are found in different orders in different dictionaries, so the dictionary orders are also available with localizations. For example, in the default 1252 ISO character set, there is a general dictionary order that works well with languages like English, Spanish, German, or French. Within the same character set, there is also a Danish/Norwegian dictionary order, Swedish/Finnish dictionary order, and Icelandic dictionary order. Other character sets offer their own dictionary orders; for example, the 1250 Central European character set has dictionary orders for Slovak, Czech, Hungarian, Polish, Romanian, Croatian, and Slovenian.

Case sensitivity

Sort orders that are in dictionary order can be either sensitive or insensitive to case. A case sensitive sort order will distinguish between words if they use letters of different case. This means that all references to objects in MSDE must use the same case that was used to define the object. A table created as "Orders" will not be found if a command uses the form "orders" or "ORDERS". To add to the confusion, MSDE allows objects with each of those spellings (and any other combination of uppercase and lowercase) to exist simultaneously.

Accent sensitivity

Accent sensitivity is similar to case sensitivity. It determines whether an accented and unaccented character should be treated the same. This can make finding words that are spelled with diacritical marks much easier, particularly when a user does not know an easy way to type the accented character. For example, a user searching for the name "Björn" could simply type "Bjorn" in a search on a database configured with accent insensitivity.

Mixed collations

MSDE supports the ability to have more than one collation in use within a single database. The collation that is specified during installation is the default collation that will be used for the system databases any user database created without specifying a collation. Within a database, the columns of a table will use the database default collation unless specified otherwise. So, different databases can have different collations, and the columns with the database can have different collations. Using more than one collation on an instance of MSDE is inadvisable unless there is a specific and overriding need. In general, when there is a need to store data that is not in the default code page, Unicode is the best choice since there can be no ambiguity about the meaning of a Unicode character. Storing characters in multiple code pages creates an opportunity for incorrect translation from one code page to another.

Summary

In order to begin developing an application that uses MSDE, MSDE or another edition of SQL Server must be installed on the computer that will be used for the development. The choice of collation that is made for this initial installation is particularly important because any client programs must be compatible with it. The same collation should be used on all subsequent installations of MSDE that will run the application. Other configuration choices, such as the network library and installation directory, can vary from one computer to another to accommodate local conditions.

✦ ✦ ✦

Understanding Microsoft Object Models

In This Chapter

ODBC defined

OLE DB defined

Accessing data from programs using DAO

Accessing data from programs using RDO

Accessing data from programs using ADO

Manipulating MSDE databases using DMO

Manipulating MSDE databases using SQL NS

Manipulating MSDE databases using DTS

Microsoft provides a wide variety of mechanisms for accessing data from programs, including: OLE DB, ODBC, ADO, RDO, and DAO. This chapter describes each of these mechanisms and identifies what they do and when they should be used. After addressing these data access mechanisms, the SQL Server/MSDE-specific object models are described. MSDE object models refer to the DMO, SQL NS, and DTS object models. These object models can be used in conjunction with the data access models to provide complete control over your MSDE database from external programs, such as those written in Visual Basic.

Low-Level Data Access

The data access mechanisms can be divided into two groups: low-level and high-level. The low-level mechanisms, ODBC and OLE DB, provide extensive libraries of functions that can be called from a program to access data. Using low-level mechanisms efficiently requires extensive training and practice. The low-level mechanisms also limit the choice of programming languages. The high-level mechanisms — DAO, RDO, and ADO — provide a simpler and easier way to access data from a wider range of programming languages.

ODBC

Open Database Connectivity (ODBC) provides a standard application programming interface (API) to access data in relational databases. ODBC is widely used and supported by many database and application vendors. There is an ODBC driver available for almost any relational database format. Thus, programs can access large amounts of data through ODBC.

There are several advantages to using ODBC: it is fast, widely supported, and generally enables programmers to write code that is database-independent. Many ODBC drivers have extended functionality that is specific to that particular database. This is both good and bad. It is good because it provides expanded functionality within that specific database platform. On the other hand, if that specific functionality is not supported by the ODBC drivers of other databases, then the code will not work with those ODBC sources. This means that if ultimate portability is desired, a user should avoid using any of the extended functions of a given ODBC driver. If portability is not a concern, then the user should make use of the extended functions available with the ODBC driver to fully leverage the database being worked with.

The primary disadvantage to ODBC is that it only supports relational databases. If a user has nonrelational data that cannot be manipulated with SQL, such as files on the network or an ISAM file, then ODBC is not a practical solution. It is extremely difficult and slow to access data in a nonrelational database through ODBC because a relational structure has to be written on top of the nonrelational structure first. This was less of a drawback in the past, but today, there is an increasing need for accessing data across multiple platforms, locations, and technologies. Such information may exist in both relational and nonrelational formats. Unfortunately, ODBC does not provide such flexibility. However, a low-level access method was developed in response to such an increasing need: OLE DB.

OLE DB

Object Linking and Embedding-Database (OLE DB) was developed in response to the growing need for more diverse data access strategies. OLE DB picks up where ODBC leaves off. OLE DB can access data from a variety of sources together, such as from relational and nonrelational databases. For example, a user may have files on the file server, e-mails on the e-mail server, and an MSDE database with information, all of which relate to each other in some way. OLE DB harnesses the information the user has access to in the most powerful way. A statement can be written to join those three sources together to retrieve a certain set of information. OLE DB enables the user to take full advantage of both relational and nonrelational sources.

Developers access OLE DB through ADO, which is a high-level model. ADO provides a much simpler method for communicating with OLE DB objects and exposes almost all of OLE DB's functionality.

OLE DB leverages the COM object model, and can be accessed from any application that can access COM object functionality, such as Visual Basic and C++. An example of accessing an MSDE database with OLE DB is described in the ADO section later in this chapter.

High-Level Data Access

High-level data access object models provide developers with a more user-friendly way to access the lower-level models such as ODBC and OLE DB. OLE DB, for example, is not intended to be accessed directly from Visual Basic programs because of its complexities. ODBC can be accessed directly from programs such as Visual Basic, but to do so requires some very complex API declarations and calls. Using a high-level data access method such as ADO is the only practical solution. If a programmer has worked with RDO, transitioning to ADO is straightforward. This is because those models can be referenced in similar ways. The Data Access Objects (DAO), Remote Data Objects (RDO), and ADO data access object models are described in the following sections.

DAO

DAO was originally developed as an object-oriented interface that enabled programmers to connect to the Jet data engine (the same data engine used by Access). DAO can still be used in programs written in languages such as Visual Basic, but is no longer the best solution for new applications that are being developed. It is still included in Visual Basic so that the older programs written with it will still work. DAO has an option that allows it to be used with types of databases other than Jet by using the ODBCDirect option. ODBCDirect loads a subset of RDO to access ODBC data sources and bypasses the Jet engine.

The following code enables a user to connect to an MSDE database using ODBCDirect:

```
Dim wrkMain As Workspace
Dim oConn As Connection
Dim rsSample As Recordset

Set wrkMain = CreateWorkspace("ODBCWorkspace", _
   "sa", "", dbUseODBC)

Set oConn = wrkMain.OpenConnection("MSDESample", _
   dbDriverNoPrompt, False, _
   "ODBC;DATABASE=MSDESample;UID=sa;PWD=;DSN=MSDESample")

Set rsSample = oConn.OpenRecordset("SELECT * FROM contacts
   WHERE PatientId = 1", dbOpenDynaset)

If not rsSample.EOF then
    MsgBox rsSample.Fields("Email").Value
End If
```

This example assumes that the user has an ODBC data source called MSDESample on the computer running the code and that the database has a Contacts table. It further assumes that the Visual Basic project has a reference to the Microsoft DAO 3.6 Object Library. This example uses DAO to connect to the MSDESample database and retrieve the e-mail address of Patient 1 from the Contacts table. It then displays the e-mail address for that patient in a message box. The workspace, connection, and recordset objects were used to access this data in the MSDE database.

RDO

RDO was developed as an object-oriented wrapper (that is, a simplified interface) for ODBC. As such, it provides better performance in ODBC data access over DAO. RDO, using ODBC, provides the user with many powerful ways to retrieve data from queries and stored procedures. RDO is widely used in many business applications today, but it is not the recommended solution for new applications. RDO is powerful and stable, but because it is based on ODBC technology, it cannot access data in nonrelational databases or files.

To take advantage of RDO in Visual Basic programs, a reference to Microsoft Remote Data Object 2.0 must first be added into the project. The code that follows can be used to establish a connection to an ODBC data source:

```
Dim oConn as New rdoConnection
oConn.Connect = "uid=sa;pwd=;dsn=MSDESample;"
oConn.CursorDriver = rsUseODBC
oConn.EstablishConnection
```

The code uses the ODBC data source MSDESample to connect to the database. Assuming that the user has an open connection and a table called Patient in the database, the code below can be used to retrieve data from the Patient table:

```
Dim rsPatients as rdoResultset
Set rsPatients = oConn.OpenResultset ("select * from patient")
```

The `openresultset` method of RDO is used to retrieve the patient records from the database. A resultset is really the same concept as a recordset.

RDO can be used to execute an MSDE stored procedure:

```
Dim oQuery as New rdoQuery
Dim rsResults as rdoResultset

Set oQuery.ActiveConnection = oConn
oQuery.sql = "{ ? = retrieve_patient_records (?)}"
oQuery.rdoParameters(0).Direction = rdParamReturnValue
oQuery(1) = "Doe"

set rsResults = oQuery.OpenResultset()
```

```
rdoGridResults.ShowData rsResults
ShowRows = rsResults.RowCount

rsResults.close
set rsResults = nothing
```

In the example above, RDO calls a stored procedure called `retrieve_patient_records` and passes Doe as the parameter so that the stored procedure can return the Doe patient records. The `openresultset` method is executed to run the stored procedure, and the results are displayed in an RDO data grid. The examples shown in this section are just a few of the many possible ways in which you can connect to MSDE through RDO to retrieve data, execute stored procedures, and so on.

ADO

ADO is a high-level data access model that can be used to communicate with OLE DB or ODBC via an OLE DB provider that essentially translates from OLE DB to ODBC. The ADO/OLE DB combination is the recommended solution for new development because of the power it gives the user to fully access both relational and nonrelational data. The ADO object model follows:

- ✦ Connection
  - Error
  - Property
- ✦ Command
  - Parameter
  - Property
- ✦ Recordset
  - Field
  - Property

There are three primary objects in the ADO object model: connection, command, and recordset. The other objects contain extended information about their parent object. Here are some helpful definitions:

- ✦ The **connection** object maintains the information about the database connection, such as the connection string and default database.
- ✦ The **command** object maintains information about a command, such as the SQL query string to be executed and parameters being passed. SQL statements can be executed without using the command object. The command object is most appropriate when a user needs to execute an SQL statement or stored procedure that does not return any records.

✦ The **recordset** object should be used to execute the SQL statement and retrieve the records when needed.

✦ The **error** object contains information about any errors that occur when using the connection object.

✦ The **property** object can be used with the connection, command, or recordset object to retrieve additional information about them. It is important to mention that ADO has several built-in properties that can be used with any data source, but also allows for data providers to provide their own dynamic properties. These dynamic properties allow each data provider (such as SQL Server/MSDE engine) to provide their own special features.

A connection to the database must be made from a user's code before data can be accessed. There are a couple of ways to connect to the database: one way is through ODBC and the other way is through OLE DB. In either case, the user must begin by declaring a new ADO connection object, which will be used to connect to the MSDE database:

```
Dim oConn as New ADODB.Connection
```

After declaring the new connection, connection properties can be set and a connection to the database can be established. To connect to the MSDE database through ODBC, assuming there is an existing ODBC data source called MSDESample, execute the `open` method of the connection object and pass the DSN name, followed by the user ID and password, as shown below:

```
'connect to MSDE using the MSDESample Data Source
oConn.Open "MSDESample", "sa", ""
```

Another way to connect through ODBC is to specify the entire connection string together instead of the user ID and password separately as shown above.

```
oConn.Open "DSN=MSDESample;User Id=sa;Password=;"
```

In this alternative, to connect through OLE DB, the user must specify more details about the data provider, database, and so forth. Here is an example:

```
Dim strConnect as string
StrConnect = "Provider=SQLOLEDB;Server=MSDEServer;" & _
     "Database=MSDESample;User Id=sa;Password=;"
oConn.Open strConnect
```

The example above assumes that the MSDE server is called MSDEServer and that the MSDE database is called MSDESample. In this case, the OLE DB provider is connecting to the database.

Once there is a connection to the database, the user can employ the command or recordset objects to execute SQL statements and/or retrieve records. The example in Listing 5-1 connects to the database and then retrieves all records in the hypothetical Patient table from the database. The results are displayed in a data grid control that is on the form.

Listing 5-1: Visual Basic Code Using ADO Recordsets

```
'Use ODBC to connect to MSDE and retrieve all
'records in the patient table.  Then, display
'those records in a data grid.

'In order for this example to work, you must
'have a Data Source called MSDESample set up and
'you must have a patient table in your database.
'You can replace MSDESample with any valid DSN
'and the patient table in the SQL for any table
'name.

Dim oConn As New ADODB.Connection
Dim rsPatients As New ADODB.Recordset

'connect to MSDE using the MSDESample Data Source
oConn.Open "MSDESample", "sa", ""

'retrieve the results from the database and then
'disconnect the recordset from the active connection
'so that it can be used locally
rsPatients.CursorLocation = adUseClient
rsPatients.Open "select * from patient", oConn, adOpenKeyset,
      adLockBatchOptimistic
Set rsPatients.ActiveConnection = Nothing

'display the results in the data grid
Set DataGridResults.DataSource = rsPatients

Set rsPatients = Nothing
```

The code in this listing can be found in the file named `Ch 5\ADORecordset.txt`.

The example in Listing 5-1 uses the recordset object and the `open` method of the recordset object to retrieve all patient records from the database. The lines that surround the Open statement, the one where the CursorLocation is set to client and the ActiveConnection is set to nothing, "disconnect" the recordset from the database. When the cursor is set to client and the connection is disconnected, the records remain in the local memory but no longer have any association with the source. This is often a helpful and necessary feature to use, especially when a user wants to retrieve the results and move on without keeping an open connection. The results are then displayed in the data grid on the form.

ADO is a very powerful and flexible data access object. The examples presented in this section are just a small glimpse at the functionality ADO provides. For more information about ADO, please consult Microsoft's Web site or other technical resources on ADO.

Administering Databases

MSDE objects provide a great deal of power over controlling MSDE programmatically from programs such as Visual Basic. Distributed Management Objects (DMO) enables the user to create, delete, and modify database objects. SQL Namespace (NS) enables the user to take advantage of many Enterprise Manager user interface elements, and Data Transformation Services (DTS) enables the user to transform data. Each of these concepts will be discussed in the sections that follow.

DMO – creating, deleting, and modifying database objects

SQL DMO is a COM object that can be accessed from Visual Basic, C++, or any other development package that can utilize COM components. The DMO object enables the user to manipulate MSDE databases from their programs. For example, a user can employ the DMO object to create or modify database structures, create indexes, or automate administrative tasks.

The DLL that implements DMO is sqldmo.dll. It is installed in the MSDE BINN directory by default as part of the MSDE install. Programs created utilizing DMO need to have this DLL installed and registered on the client machine as well as the sqldmo.rll resource file that is located in the \binn\resources\ directory. SQL DMO clients must have Windows 95, 98, or NT 4.0 or later. They also must have the SQL Server ODBC Driver. Although the ODBC driver must be on the client machine, it should be noted that DMO does not actually use an ODBC data source for connecting; instead, it locates instances of MSDE using the instance name. Thus, an ODBC data source does not need to be created on the client machine.

The first step in using DMO in a Visual Basic program is to add a reference to it in the project by selecting Project, References, and then selecting Microsoft SQLDMO Object Library from the list.

After a reference has been added to the project, the user can access the DMO object. Listing 5-2 demonstrates how to create a new table on an existing database using the DMO object. For this code to work, the project needs a reference to the DMO object and the MSDE database server (or local machine, if that is where MSDE is running) needs to have a database called MSDESample. The MSDESample database name can be changed in the set oDatabase line to any MSDE database that exists on the MSDE database server. Here's the VB code to create a new table called Contacts:

Listing 5-2: Visual Basic Code Using DMO to Create a New Table

```
'This example creates a new table called Contacts
'with PatientId, HPhone, WPhone, Email, RelativeName,
'and RelativePhone fields.  This table gets created
'on an existing database called MSDESample

'declare the server object
Dim oMSDEServer As SQLDMO.SQLServer
Set oMSDEServer = New SQLDMO.SQLServer
oMSDEServer.LoginTimeout = 15
oMSDEServer.ODBCPrefix = False

'declare the database object
Dim oDatabase As SQLDMO.Database

'declare the table object
Dim oTable As New SQLDMO.Table

'declare the columns that will be added to the
'new database table
Dim ColPatientId As New SQLDMO.Column
Dim ColHPhone As New SQLDMO.Column
Dim ColWPhone As New SQLDMO.Column
Dim ColEmail As New SQLDMO.Column
Dim ColRelativeName As New SQLDMO.Column
Dim ColRelativePhone As New SQLDMO.Column
```

Continued

Listing 5-2 *(continued)*

```
'Declare and populate the server, userid, and
'password variables here...(Typically, you would
'pass them in to a routine such as this or declare
'them in a module versus declaring them here.  This
'is done for simplicity here.)
Dim strServerName As String
Dim strUserId As String
Dim strPassword As String

'In our example the server is (local).  This would
'be different if the database is on a server
'separate from the machine where you're running this
'code
strServerName = "(local)"
strUserId = "sa"
strPassword = ""

'log in and connect to the MSDESample database
oMSDEServer.Connect strServerName, strUserId, strPassword
Set oDatabase = oMSDEServer.Databases("MSDESample")

'Populate the PatientId column object
ColPatientId.Name = "PatientId"
ColPatientId.Datatype = "int"
ColPatientId.AllowNulls = False

'Populate the HPhone column object
ColHPhone.Name = "HPhone"
ColHPhone.Datatype = "varchar"
ColHPhone.Length = "13"
ColHPhone.AllowNulls = True

'Populate the WPhone column object
ColWPhone.Name = "WPhone"
ColWPhone.Datatype = "varchar"
ColWPhone.Length = "13"
ColWPhone.AllowNulls = True

'Populate the Email column object
ColEmail.Name = "Email"
ColEmail.Datatype = "varchar"
ColEmail.Length = "50"
ColEmail.AllowNulls = True

'Populate the RelativeName column object
ColRelativeName.Name = "RelativeName"
ColRelativeName.Datatype = "varchar"
ColRelativeName.Length = "75"
```

```
ColRelativeName.AllowNulls = True

'Populate the RelativePhone column object
ColRelativePhone.Name = "RelativePhone"
ColRelativePhone.Datatype = "varchar"
ColRelativePhone.Length = "13"
ColRelativePhone.AllowNulls = True

'Assign the table a name
oTable.Name = "Contacts"

'Add the columns that were defined above to this
'table object
oTable.Columns.Add ColPatientId
oTable.Columns.Add ColHPhone
oTable.Columns.Add ColWPhone
oTable.Columns.Add ColEmail
oTable.Columns.Add ColRelativeName
oTable.Columns.Add ColRelativePhone

'Create the table on the database
oDatabase.Tables.Add oTable

'disconnect from the database
oMSDEServer.DisConnect

Set oMSDEServer = Nothing
Set oDatabase = Nothing
Set oTable = Nothing
```

The code in this listing can be found in the file named `Ch 5\CreateTable.txt`.

Because the objective of Listing 5-2 is to add a new table to the database, the server, database, and table DMO objects first have to be declared. After connecting to the database with the `connect` method of the server object, the `databases` property of the database object is set to the correct database. Then columns are added to the column object. Column by column, the attributes for PatientId, HPhone, WPhone, Email, RelativeName, and RelativePhone are defined. After defining all of the columns for the new table, the columns are added to the Column collection of the table object using the `add` method. Finally, with the table object populated with the structure of the new table, the table is added to the database object, which physically adds the table to the database.

Now that the Contacts table has been successfully created on the MSDE database, the table can be altered to add a Primary Key constraint, as shown in Listing 5-3.

Listing 5-3: Visual Basic Code Using DMO to Add a Primary Key Constraint

```
'declare the server object
Dim oMSDEServer As sqldmo.SQLServer
Set oMSDEServer = New sqldmo.SQLServer
oMSDEServer.LoginTimeout = 15
oMSDEServer.ODBCPrefix = False

'declare the database object
Dim oDatabase As sqldmo.Database

'declare the table object
Dim oTable As sqldmo.Table

'declare the Key object
Dim oPrimaryKey As New sqldmo.Key

'declare the Names object
Dim oPrimaryKeyNames As sqldmo.Names

'Declare and populate the server, userid, and
'password variables here...(Typically, you would
'pass them in to a routine such as this or declare
'them in a module versus declaring them here.  This
'is done for simplicity here.)
Dim strServerName As String
Dim strUserId As String
Dim strPassword As String

'In our example the server is (local).  This would
'be different if the database is on an NT server
'separate from the machine where you're running this
'code
strServerName = "(local)"
strUserId = "sa"
strPassword = ""

'log in and connect to the Contacts table in the
'MSDESample database
oMSDEServer.Connect strServerName, strUserId, strPassword
Set oTable =
oMSDEServer.Databases("MSDESample").Tables("Contacts")

'Create a primary, clustered key on PatientId
oPrimaryKey.Clustered = True
oPrimaryKey.Type = SQLDMOKey_Primary
Set oPrimaryKeyNames = oPrimaryKey.KeyColumns
```

```
oPrimaryKeyNames.Add "PatientId"

'Start the modification to the table
oTable.BeginAlter

'Add the Key object to the Keys collection of the table
'object
oTable.Keys.Add oPrimaryKey

'End the modification and commit the changes to the
'database
oTable.DoAlter

'disconnect from the database
oMSDEServer.DisConnect

Set oMSDEServer = Nothing
Set oDatabase = Nothing
Set oTable = Nothing
```

The code in this listing can be found in the file named `Ch 5\AddPK.txt`.

In Listing 5-3, the server, database, and table DMO objects are declared first. Then, the database is opened and a connection is made to the Contacts table. In this example, `oTable` is set equal to the specific table to be opened because changes must be made at the table level.

The core part of the above code has to do with creating the clustered key on PatientId. The `oPrimaryKey` clustered property is set to true and its type property is set to Primary. After the key object has been defined, the next step is to give the key a name by using the names object. After setting the oPrimaryKeyNames object equal to the oPrimaryKey keycolumns, the `add` method of the names object is invoked to give the primary key a name: PatientId. After the key is defined, the `BeginAlter` method is invoked on the table to let the database know that a change is going to be made. Next, the primary key is added to the table object. After the key is added to the table object, the `DoAlter` method is invoked to commit the change to the database.

As was demonstrated in the examples shown in Listings 5-2 and 5-3, the DMO object model provides the user with a great deal of flexibility in controlling the MSDE database from programs such as Visual Basic. In this section, we have just looked at two of the many possible uses of DMO in programs. Other examples of using DMO are provided in all of the chapters in this book that cover objects that can be managed by DMO.

SQL NS – using Enterprise Manager within a program

The SQL NS object model is a COM object that enables access to the SQL Server Enterprise Manager user interface components. The DLL that implements SQL NS is sqlns.dll. It is installed in the MSDE BINN directory by default as part of the MSDE install. When creating programs that utilize SQL NS, this DLL needs to be installed and registered on the client machine as well as the SQLNS.rll resource file that is in the \binn\resources directory. SQL NS clients must have Windows 95, 98, or NT 4.0 or later.

SQL NS enables the user to invoke dialog boxes, property sheets, wizards, and other Enterprise Manager user interface components. A good example of when a user might want to use SQL NS is to display the properties of an MSDE database from a program, such as Visual Basic. SQL NS can be used from Visual Basic or other programs that support COM to display the same Database Properties dialog box that appears in the Database Properties in Enterprise Manager.

SQL NS has four objects that are exposed: SQLNamespace, SQLNamespaceObject, SQLNamespaceCommands, and SQLNamespaceCommand. These objects are listed below in hierarchical order with their respective properties and methods:

SQLNamespace

- Methods
  - GetChildrenCount
  - GetFirstChildItem
  - GetName
  - GetNextSiblingItem
  - GetParentItem
  - GetPreviousSiblingItem
  - GetRootItem
  - GetSQLDMOObject
  - GetSQLNamespaceObject
  - GetType
  - Initialize
  - Refresh
  - SetLCID

SQLNamespaceObject

✦ Properties
    - Handle
    - Name
    - Type
    - Methods
    - ExecuteCommandByID
    - ExecuteCommandByName

SQLNamespaceCommands

✦ Properties
    - Count
    - Methods
    - tem

SQLNamespaceCommand

✦ Properties
    - CommandGroup
    - CommandID
    - HelpString
    - Name
    - Methods
    - Execute

The first step to making use of the SQL NS object model in Visual Basic is to add a reference to it. To do so, a user can select Project, References, and then select Microsoft SQL Namespace Object Library from the list to add it to the project. After adding SQL NS as a reference to the project, the VB code shown in Listing 5-4 can be run to display the Properties dialog box of the MSDESample database. MSDESample can be changed to any valid MSDE database name on the MSDE database server.

Listing 5-4: Visual Basic Code Using SQL NS to Display Database Properties

```
'Declare the sql namespace
Dim oSQLNS As SQLNamespace

'Declare the sql namespace object
Dim oSQLNSObject As SQLNamespaceObject

'declare long variables that will hold the values
'of the namespace tree structure
Dim lngServerGroup As Long
Dim lngServer as long
Dim lngDatabase as long

'initialize the sql namespace
Set oSQLNS = New SQLNamespace
oSQLNS.Initialize "MSDE Bible Test", SQLNSRootType_Server,
"Server=(local);UID=sa;PWD="

'use the namespace object to get the values from the
'namespace tree (the root value for server groups,
'then the first child item which is the server, and
'then the next child item which is the specific database
lngServerGroup = oSQLNS.GetRootItem
lngServer = oSQLNS.GetFirstChildItem(lngServerGroup,
SQLNSOBJECTTYPE_DATABASES)
lngDatabase = oSQLNS.GetFirstChildItem(lngServer,
SQLNSOBJECTTYPE_DATABASE, "MSDESample")

'use the value of the specific database that is stored in the
'lngDatabase variable to open the NS Object and execute the
'properties command to display the Properties dialog
'box
Set oSQLNSObject = oSQLNS.GetSQLNamespaceObject(lngDatabase)
oSQLNSObject.ExecuteCommandByName "Properties", hWnd,
    SQLNamespace_PreferModal

Set oSQLNSObject = Nothing
Set oSQLNS = Nothing
```

The code in this listing can be found in the file named `Ch 5\SQLNS.txt`.

In Listing 5-4, the SQLNamespace and SQLNamespaceObject objects are used to display the Properties dialog box of the MSDESample database. The SQLNamespace is used to retrieve the server ID's so that the MSDESample database can be accessed. The `GetRootItem` method is used to obtain the unique identifier for the server group. Then, using the information returned from the `GetRootItem` method, the `GetFirstChildItem` method is used to obtain the unique identifier for the server itself. After the server identifier has been returned, the GetFirstChildItem method can be executed against the Server to retrieve the identifier for the MSDESample database. After the identifier for the MSDESample database is returned, the SQLNamespaceObject ExecuteCommandByName method is executed to display the Properties dialog box in a modal format.

DTS – importing, exporting, and transforming data

The DTS object model is a COM object that can be accessed from Visual Basic, C++, or any other development package that can use COM components. The DTS object model can be used to manipulate the Data Transformation Services from one's own applications instead of using Enterprise Manager to do so. For example, a user can write a Visual Basic program to copy data from one table to another or to create and run a package that imports and exports data. The user can employ the DTS object model to programmatically perform nearly any of the tasks that can be done interactively in Enterprise Manager's DTS module.

Suppose that the Contacts table created using SQL DMO earlier in this chapter was heavily populated with data, and that a user wants to use DTS to copy the entire table into a new table in the same database. A new project must first be created and a reference added to DTS in the project. Select Project, References, and then choose Microsoft DTSPackage Object Library from the list to add a reference to the project. After the reference has been added, the code in Listing 5-5 can be executed to copy the data from the Contacts table to a ContactsNew table:

Listing 5-5: Visual Basic Code Using DTS to Copy a Table

```
'This example creates and executes a DTS Package that
'copies the entire contents of the Contacts table
'in the MSDESample database to a ContactsNew table
'in the same MSDESample database.  The source and
'destination databases did not have to be the same,
'but for simplicity, we used the same for both.
'For this example to work, you need to have an
'MSDE database called MSDESample with the Contacts
'table already populated with data.  You also need
'to have set up an ODBC data source called MSDESample
'that points to the MSDESample database.
```

Continued

Listing 5-5 *(continued)*

```
Dim oPackage As New DTS.Package

Dim oConn As DTS.Connection
Dim oTask As DTS.Task
Dim oStep As DTS.Step

Dim oTransformation As DTS.Transformation
Dim oDataPumpTask As DTS.DataPumpTask
Dim oProperties As DTS.Properties

oPackage.Name = "MSDE Bible Sample DTS Transformation"
oPackage.Description = "example in MSDE Bible to demonstrate
example use of DTS object"

'set up the connection for the source of the data
Set oConn = oPackage.Connections.New
oConn.ID = 1
oConn.DataSource = "MSDESample"
oConn.UserID = "sa"
oConn.Password = ""
oPackage.Connections.Add oConn
Set oConn = Nothing

'set up the connection for the destination of the data
Set oConn = oPackage.Connections.New
oConn.ID = 2
oConn.DataSource = "MSDESample"
oConn.UserID = "sa"
oConn.Password = ""
oPackage.Connections.Add oConn
Set oConn = Nothing

'create a task to retrieve the data from the contacts table
Set oTask = oPackage.Tasks.New("DTSDataPumpTask")
oTask.Name = "Task1"
Set oDataPumpTask = oTask.CustomTask

'set the task to retrieve from the Source database (1)
oDataPumpTask.SourceConnectionID = 1

'assign the SQl statement to the task to have it select
'everything from the contacts table
oDataPumpTask.SourceSQLStatement = "SELECT * from Contacts"

'set the destination of the task to be the destination database
'and name the desination table that the results are
'to be put into (ContactsNew)...
```

```
oDataPumpTask.DestinationConnectionID = 2
oDataPumpTask.DestinationObjectName = "ContactsNew"

'now that the task has been created, create the package
'steps, add it to the package, and then execute the
'package against the database (i.e. run the
'transformation).
Set oTransformation =
oDataPumpTask.Transformations.New("DTS.DataPumpTransformCopy")
oTransformation.Name = "Transform"
oTransformation.TransformFlags = 1
oDataPumpTask.Transformations.Add oTransformation
oPackage.Tasks.Add oTask
Set oTask = Nothing

Set oStep = oPackage.Steps.New
oStep.Name = "Step1"
oStep.TaskName = "Task1"
oPackage.Steps.Add oStep
Set oStep = Nothing

oPackage.Execute

Set oStep = Nothing
Set oTask = Nothing
Set oDataPumpTask = Nothing
Set oTransformation = Nothing
Set oPackage = Nothing
Set oConn = Nothing
```

The code in this listing can be found in the file named `Ch 5\DTSCopy.txt`.

The code in Listing 5-5 declares a new package, sets up the source and destination databases, and then creates the steps to be executed in the package. All of the records in the Contacts table are copied and inserted into a new table called ContactsNew. The task to do this is set up, and the step is added to the package that will run this task. After the step is added to the package, the package is executed and the transformation takes place. This is just one example of many other possible uses of the DTS object model.

Chapter 19 provides extensive coverage of DTS, including a complete Visual Basic project that builds DTS packages.

Summary

There are numerous ways to communicate with MSDE from external programs such as Visual Basic. The DAO, RDO, and ADO data access object models provide the user with a high-level data access method to the low-level models: ODBC and OLE DB. ODBC is widely available and supported, but limits the ability to access nonrelational data. OLE DB opens a whole new way of accessing relational and nonrelational data. In addition to data access methods, there are also object models available as part of the standard MSDE install that allow the user to manage MSDE programmatically. DMO manages objects such as tables, views, and stored procedures programmatically. With SQL SCM, you can start and stop database services. SQL NS enables the user to tap into the majority of the Enterprise Manager user interface elements. DTS enables the user to import, export, and transform data programmatically. Understanding how to use these objects is critical in taking full advantage of the MSDE database from external programs.

✦ ✦ ✦

P A R T

II

Database Structures

This part explores how data is organized in databases, how to efficiently use tables and indexes for storing data, how to ensure data consistency with constraints, triggers, and objects, and delves into the importance of using locks in a multiuser system.

✦ ✦ ✦ ✦

In This Part

✦ ✦ ✦ ✦

Databases

In This Chapter

MSDE stores its data in a database. The primary type of object in a database is a table, which contains the data organized into columns and rows. Other objects in a database are generally used in support of the data tables. Views, for example, are virtual tables, stored procedures provide predefined mechanisms for manipulating data, and users are used to organize security. Other objects, such as constraints and indexes, enhance consistency and performance.

Multiple instances of MSDE can run on a single computer, and each of these instances can support multiple databases. However, there are limitations on the interactions of objects between databases. For example, tables that are related to one another with foreign key constraints must be in the same database. Also, each database has its own independent system of users and permissions. To access objects in multiple databases requires having created multiple users and having assigned each of those users appropriate permissions.

Users and permissions are described in detail in Chapter 25.

An MSDE database is generally associated with an end-user application, or a set of related applications. It also defines the units of work for the recovery process, which runs whenever the SQL Server service starts and guarantees the consistency of the database. The primary tool of the recovery process is the transaction log, one of which is associated with each database on the server. When a row from any table in a database is modified, the instructions for modification are written to the database's transaction log. The instructions are read on system restarts to ensure that all completed transactions are written in the tables of the database and that any incomplete transactions are completely undone.

MSDE enforces a maximum size for a single database of 2GB (unlike the other editions of SQL Server, which have a virtually unlimited maximum size). Aside from the size limitation, the databases used by MSDE are exactly the same as those used by other editions of SQL Server. They can be disconnected from MSDE and moved and reconnected to another SQL Server without modification.

Logical Structure

There are two general types of database: system and user. On MSDE, four system databases are installed by default:

- master
- model
- msdb
- tempdb

Another system database, distribution, is created under some circumstances when replication is enabled. User databases are any databases created by a system administrator for use by applications. There are two sample user databases installed on SQL Server by default: Northwind and pubs. Although these are not installed on MSDE, there are scripts on the SQL Server CD that can create them.

The master database contains system information that is used for the entire server. Information about the server itself is stored there, as are all logins and information about any other databases that have been created. Every MSDE installation must have a master database. Without a fully functional master, there is no server. There is a command, `rebuildm.exe`, that can be used to recreate a master database in the event the master database has been destroyed. A backup of the master database should be created anytime a user database is created or deleted, since that information is stored in the master database's system tables.

The model database is a template for any new database created. It contains a number of system tables that are used to store administrative information that applies only to a single database. The information stored in these system tables includes the definitions of all user tables, the columns within tables, user information, permissions, and so on. All of the model's contents are copied into any new database upon creation. If any modifications are made to the model database, they will be included in any database that is subsequently created, although they will not affect any existing databases.

The msdb database is used by the SQL Agent service. It stores information about jobs, alerts, operators, and backups. Both msdb and model are recreated anytime master is recreated, and they should therefore be backed up at the same time.

The tempdb database stores temporary data. MSDE itself will use tempdb during complex operations, and applications may also create temporary tables that are stored there. Tempdb is recreated every time the SQL Server service is started. There is a transaction log associated with tempdb; however, it is used only to roll back transactions. It is not used for recoverability, since tempdb is recreated during startup, the time when databases would otherwise be recovered.

Like any other new database, tempdb is created at startup as a copy of model and will inherit any changes that are made to model, including permissions. Resetting the permissions for model is the only way to make permissions changes to tempdb that will persist through a restart.

The distribution database is created when an MSDE server is configured as a distribution server for replication. The distribution server is responsible for synchronizing data from the publishing server, where data originates, to the subscriber servers.

Each database has a number of database options that control its behavior. These options control the transaction logging behavior, as well as the default connection settings. They can also be used to put the database in a mode appropriate for maintenance. Database options can be set only after a database has been created and can be changed at any subsequent time.

Physical Structure

A database is stored on disk in at least two operating system files: one for data and the other for the transaction log. The files used by a database are created as part of the act of creating the database, although additional files can be added later, and the files can be resized dynamically.

Files and filegroups

When a database is created, at least one file must be specified for the data portion of the database. This file must be given a logical name that can be used to refer to the file within MSDE, and its physical name and location must be specified. The default location for data files is in the \MSSQL7\data subdirectory on the drive that was selected during installation. However, any location can be specified. The default extension for the first file in a database is `.mdf`. This file is called the primary file and is special in that it contains the system tables for the database. Any additional files used for the data part of the database will have a default extension of `.ndf`. These default extensions are not required, but they make future administration tasks easier. When a file is created, it must have an initial size and a filegroup name.

All files that are part of the data portion of a database belong to a filegroup. The filegroup to which the primary file belongs is called PRIMARY. As additional files are added to the database, they can be made members of the PRIMARY filegroup, or new filegroups can be created. New filegroups are created by giving a new filegroup name to one or more files. For example, a database could be created with three data files: file1, file2, and file3. File1 is the primary file and belongs to the PRIMARY filegroup. File2 and file3 could be made part of the PRIMARY filegroup, or they could be made part of another filegroup, perhaps one called Fgrp2. Another option could be to put each into its own filegroup, Frgp2 and Fgrp3. The names of filegroups are arbitrary and are assigned by the database administrator when they are created.

The system of files and filegroups was developed as part of SQL Server 7.0. It serves several purposes particularly advantageous for very large databases, which cannot exist in MSDE because of the 2GB database size limit. The system allows larger databases to be created if the maximum size of a hard drive or (more likely) RAID array is reached. Dividing a database into multiple files allows for load balancing across multiple disk drives, controllers, and arrays, as well as future flexibility in file placement if the disk configuration of the server is changed. Planning for the future is an important consideration when designing databases that will initially run on MSDE but may scale up to much larger systems. Another consideration for systems that may scale toward the very large is the ability to perform backups and restores at the file level. Some databases become so large that there is not a sufficient window of time to perform a regular backup of the entire database. All of these factors should be taken into account when designing databases that will be evaluated on MSDE but put into production on SQL Server.

If a database consists of more than one file in the same filegroup, MSDE will allocate new extents from the files in proportion to their size. Two files of the same size will have extents allocated equally. If one is twice the size of the other, the larger will have two extents allocated for every one allocated from the other.

Filegroups allow the database administrator to select the location in which an object will be created rather than allow the system to allocate extents across all files. The following configurations of files and filegroups within a database are possible:

- There are multiple files all in a single filegroup. In this case, MSDE has total discretion about space allocation among the files. It allocates proportionally to file size and does so at the extent level, so objects may exist in multiple files.
- There are multiple filegroups, each having a single file. In this case, the administrator has complete control over the allocation of space to objects, and the granularity is at the object level. The filegroup in which an object is to be created can be specified as a parameter when creating the object.
- There are multiple filegroups, each having multiple files. In this case, the administrator selects the filegroup for the creation of each object, and then MSDE allocates the extents for the object across the files within the filegroup. Objects will not span multiple filegroups, but may span multiple files within a group.

Pages and extents

Within the data files, MSDE manages space in units of extents and pages. A page is 8K, which is a basic unit of I/O in MSDE. Whenever data is read from or written to a disk, it is done one or more pages at a time. Each page has a 96-byte page header that contains information about the page, including a page ID, the ID of whatever object the page is a part of, the amount of free space on the page, and the sequence number from the transaction log that records the most recent change that has taken place on the page. An individual page can be allocated to only a single object. Each page also contains an array at the end of the page that stores the location of each row on the page, which is particularly helpful when the page is part of an index whose rows are in sorted order. If a new row needs to be added to the page, the rows that are already on the page don't have to be shuffled around to make room for the new one. The new row is added on the end, and the entries in the row-offset array are rearranged. So, when a process wants the third row on a page, it reads the third entry in the row-offset array, which specifies the byte location of the beginning of the third row.

Pages are organized on disk in groups of eight, called extents. Extents are the basic unit of allocation for objects in the database. They are used in the read-ahead process to make data available in memory in a timely fashion. They are also the unit of I/O used in backups and restores.

There are two kinds of extents: mixed and uniform. Mixed extents are not dedicated to an individual object, so the pages in a mixed extent can belong to as many as eight different objects. The pages in a uniform extent are all allocated to the same object. When an object is initially created, its pages will be drawn from mixed extents. Once it grows larger than eight pages, all future pages will be allocated from uniform extents. The use of mixed extents prevents small objects from occupying too much space; if all extents were uniform, then a 1K table would occupy an entire extent, or 64K, leaving 63K of unused space.

MSDE allocates pages to objects from existing extents whenever possible. If there is no free space available in existing extents, then new extents will be allocated from one of the database files. If all files are full, MSDE checks to see if the `autogrow` property is set. If so, the file will be expanded by the configured increment, and the extent will be allocated. If `autogrow` is turned off, a system error will occur and the transaction that caused the failed attempt at space allocation will be rolled back.

Allocation maps

MSDE maintains information about what extents in the database file have been allocated in a bitmap structure called the Global Allocation Map (GAM). Within this map, there is a bit that represents every extent in the file that is set to 1 if the extent is unallocated and available for use. For MSDE databases, the GAM is always a single page per file, since there are fewer 64K pages in a maximum sized 2GB database (about 32,000) than there are bits in an 8K page (about 64,000). SQL Server database files that exceed 4GB will use additional GAM pages.

Pages that are allocated to objects fall into one of three categories:

- ✦ If an object is larger than eight pages, it will come from a uniform extent with free space that is already allocated to the object.
- ✦ If the object is small or newly created, it will come from a mixed extent with free space.
- ✦ If no free space exists, it will come from an as yet unallocated extent.

To allocate a page, MSDE must first decide if the object is small enough to call for a mixed extent. If so, MSDE will look for a mixed extent with free space. If not, MSDE will look for a uniform extent that is already allocated to the object that has free space. If it cannot find either of these, it must allocate a new extent, located by scanning the GAM.

Information about which mixed extents have available free space is stored in Secondary Global Allocation Map (SGAM) pages. These are also bitmaps similar to the GAM, except that the bit is turned on only if the extent it represents is a mixed extent with free pages. The bit will be zero if it represents a uniform extent, or if it is mixed but full.

Information about free space in extents that are allocated to an object is kept in an Index Allocation Map (IAM). Each index and table has an associated IAM. The IAM records the location of the first eight pages of the object (these are located in mixed extents) and records which uniform extents in the file are allocated to the object. Aside from the first eight page pointers, the IAM is a bitmap, with each bit representing an extent in the file. If the bit is turned on, the extent is allocated to the object.

Transaction log files

MSDE uses transaction log files to protect the consistency of the database by recording data modifications as complete and indivisible units called transactions. Application software usually controls which commands are part of a transaction by indicating `Begin Transaction` before the commands and `Commit Transaction` after all the commands in the transaction have been sent to the server. As MSDE receives these commands, they are written to the transaction log. Until the transaction is committed, it exists in a state that can be rolled back, that is, undone in such a way that it never happened. A rollback can be invoked by the application if an error occurs, by the system (if, for example, the transaction is the chosen victim in a deadlock), or during recovery if the system halted before the transaction committed. Once the `commit` command is written in the log, the entire transaction becomes permanent in the database even if the system crashes before the results of the command are written to the data portion of the database. Every time the SQL Server service starts, it runs a process called recovery, which reads the transaction log and rolls forward any committed transactions and rolls back any uncommitted transactions. The recovery process works to ensure that no transaction is ever partially completed. It is either entirely completed, or it never happened. Using this technique, work that was in progress might be undone during a system crash, but the state of the database is always consistent.

A partially-completed transaction is undesirable. For example, if a bank customer using an automated teller machine attempts to transfer money from a savings account to a checking account, and the machine fails partway through the transaction, the money might be transferred out of savings, but never arrive in checking. Such a shortfall would certainly make the customer unhappy. Alternatively, if the money were added to checking but never deleted from savings, the bank would be in a bad situation. The solution is to include in a single transaction: the withdrawal from one account and the deposit into the other account. Then withdrawal and deposit happen together or not at all. If the machine fails while processing the transaction, the customer knows that the money is still in one account or the other.

A transaction begins in one of two ways: implicitly or explicitly. An implicit transaction begins when MSDE receives a command from a client application that modifies data in the form of an `Insert`, `Update`, or `Delete` command. A transaction that is started implicitly ends as soon as the command that initiated the transaction finishes. An explicit transaction begins when MSDE receives the `Begin Transaction` command from a client application. Explicit transactions include the work of all commands subsequent to the `Begin Transaction` until a `Commit Transaction` or `Rollback` is received. MSDE assigns a log sequence number (LSN) to every transaction. LSNs are used by MSDE for a number of purposes, including tracking the most recent change on a page, synchronizing transactional backups, and coordinating the checkpoint and recovery processes. After an LSN is assigned, all of the work specified by the commands in the transaction is written to the log cache and the data cache in memory. The log cache is structured as a queue, with each incoming command added to the end of the list. The log cache queue is simply an area of memory with free space. The data cache, on the other hand, is an in-memory copy of the data pages from disk. The appropriate data page must be in memory for the modification to take place. Usually, the data page will be in memory already, because MSDE has a very efficient read-ahead manager that predicts pages that will be needed in the near future. If the page is not already in memory, it is read from disk; there must be enough memory available to do this. When the transaction commits, its portion of the log cache is written, or flushed, to the transaction log file on disk. The transaction is not considered committed until it has been completely written in the transaction log file. For this reason, the disk subsystem on which the transaction log file is stored should have the best possible performance. Otherwise, it can severely impact the overall performance of MSDE. The changes made to the data pages in memory do not have to be written to disk immediately for the transaction to be completed. There are two processes responsible for writing these changes to the data files on disk: the LazyWriter and the checkpoint process.

The LazyWriter is a process that attempts to spread out I/O and make buffers available in memory for incoming pages. Its activity is primarily controlled by two settings: the max async I/O (set and controlled by the database administrator), which regulates the maximum number of processes that can simultaneously access the disk, and the number of free buffers (dynamically configured by MSDE) that MSDE needs to keep in memory in order to keep up with the demand for pages being read in from disk. The LazyWriter will run only when the number of simultaneous processes accessing the disk has exceeded the maximum level set by the administrator or where there is a demand for free buffers. When it does run, the LazyWriter writes dirty pages to disk and reinitializes them, thereby freeing the space they occupied in memory. A dirty page is one that has had changes made to it, but has not yet been written to disk. By running during periods of low I/O, the LazyWriter helps to spread out the load on the disk subsystem and improve overall performance.

The checkpoint process, which runs periodically, either verifies that dirty pages associated with committed transactions have been written to disk or writes them to disk itself. The frequency at which checkpoint runs is determined by the recovery period, which can be set by the database administrator or self-configured by MSDE. The recovery period is the length of time the system predicts it will take to run the recovery process on an individual database. Since recovery needs to read only that portion of the transaction log that has not yet been processed by checkpoint, the system can decrease recovery time by running checkpoint more frequently. So, the frequency at which checkpoint runs is determined less by elapsed time than by the number of elapsed transactions. Unlike the LazyWriter, the checkpoint process does not reinitialize the data pages in memory and delete their contents. The contents are left available in memory and can still be read or updated by any process.

Checkpoint is itself a transaction. When run, checkpoint is assigned an LSN and recorded in the transaction log. It saves a list of all active transactions, those transactions that have not yet been committed, and the minimum recovery LSN (minLSN). The minLSN corresponds to either the oldest uncommitted transaction, the oldest transaction whose modified data pages have not yet been flushed to disk, or the checkpoint transaction itself, if all prior transactions in the log have been committed and flushed to disk. As its name suggests, the minimum recovery LSN is the starting point for the recovery process. By recording the minLSN, checkpoint has guaranteed that all transactions prior to the minLSN have been committed and written to the disk, and thus do not need to be either rolled forward or rolled back.

Rather than being structured in pages like data files, log files are organized in units called virtual log files (VLF). The size of a VLF is not fixed like a page; when the system creates a VLF, it chooses the size based on the size of the transaction log file (if the file is being created) or the size of the growth increment (if the file is being expanded). Truncation, the process of deleting old transactions that have been committed and checkpointed and are no longer needed, works on one VLF at a time. Any VLF that contains an active transaction will not be truncated. The same is true when shrinking the log file. The system can remove VLFs only from the end of the file and only if they are not active.

Creating, Modifying, and Deleting Databases

Managing databases consists of several tasks, some of which are performed only once and some of which are ongoing. Every database must naturally be created, and possibly deleted, one time. Over the course of a database's lifetime, it may have to be expanded if the data it contains grows too large. Occasionally, it may need to be shrunk, usually when some process like a large import has caused it to be expanded beyond a reasonable size for daily operations. The database files and filegroups may also need to be modified as server hardware configuration changes. For example, if new disk drives are added to the server, database files could be added or moved to the new drives.

Managing databases with Enterprise Manager

Figure 6-1 shows the Data Files tab of the General Properties dialog box for the pubs database in Enterprise Manager. This dialog box is the same as the one that is displayed when a new database is created, except that the Options and Permissions tabs are not available during creation.

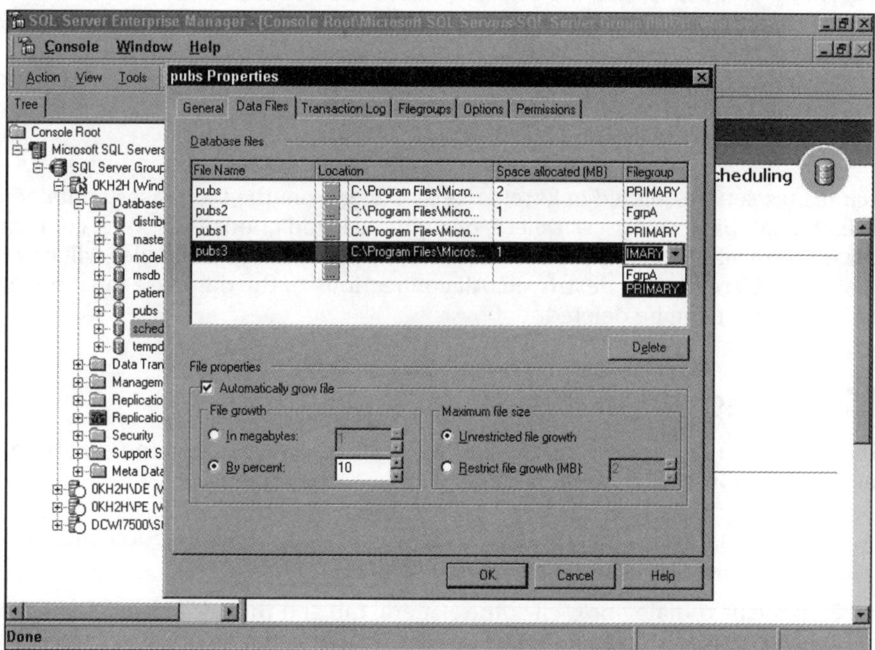

Figure 6-1: Database General Properties dialog box, Data Files tab in Enterprise Manager

In Figure 6-1, the pubs database consists of four data files. Two of these are in the PRIMARY filegroup, one is in the Fgrp A filegroup, and the last has the filegroup drop-down list displayed, from which either PRIMARY or FgrpA could be selected. Entering a new name into the filegroup field would create a new filegroup. Each file has a logical name: pubs, pubs1, pubs2, and pubs3.Each file also has a location (the operating system path and file name) and a size specified in megabytes (2, 1, 1, and 1, respectively). The ellipsis button (with three dots) in the location column displays a dialog box that allows the administrator to browse for a file location.

This dialog box can be used to add additional files to a database by filling in the fields for a new file. Files can be expanded by typing in a new, larger size in the Space Allocated field. Files can be deleted if they are empty by selecting the appropriate file and clicking the Delete button.

To shrink a database, right-click on it and choose All Tasks ➪ Shrink Database. The dialog box that appears has a check box that can be used to schedule shrinking the database. Otherwise, the database will be shrunk when the OK button is clicked. The process that shrinks the database operates in a slightly different way on the data files and the transaction log files. In either case, the files can have only empty space removed from the end. In the data files, pages are reorganized toward the beginning of the files, and the empty space at the end of the files is truncated. The transaction log simply marks inactive VLFs for deletion. If the marked VLFs are at the end of the file, they will be removed. If, however, there is even one active VLF at the end of the file, its size cannot be reduced until all transactions at the end of the file are committed and checkpointed. Shrinking the database does not reorganize the VLFs within the transaction log.

Databases can be deleted in Enterprise Manager from the Databases container. Select a database and press Delete, or right-click and choose Delete. A confirmation dialog box will be displayed, after which the database and all its files will be completely and irrevocably destroyed. All connections to the database must be terminated before it can be deleted.

Managing databases with Access

Databases can be created and deleted with Access 2000. To create a database, a new project must be created.

1. Select the Access database wizards, pages, and projects option button from the top section of the opening dialog box.
2. In the next dialog box, click the General tab and then double-click the icon for Project (New database). The File New Database dialog box is displayed. This same dialog box is also available at any time from the File ➪ New menu item.
3. Choose a file name and location for the Access project file, which will store Access-specific information about the project.

4. Click the Create button, and the Microsoft SQL Server Database Wizard begins.
5. Enter the name of the MSDE server, a valid login and password that have permissions to create a database, and a name for the new database.
6. Click Next, then click Finish, and the database will be created with a 2MB data file, with a 2MB log file, and with all other settings set to their default values.

The size of the database cannot be changed directly from Access; however, the default settings will allow automatic growth as needed.

To delete a database from Access, choose Tools ➪ Database Utilities ➪ Drop SQL Database from the menu. A dialog box is displayed with a warning that the database cannot be dropped while users are connected and the opportunity to back out of the delete. Click the Yes button, and the database will be deleted from MSDE. The Access project is not deleted, but is disconnected from any database. The project can be connected to another database by clicking File ➪ Connection from the menu and entering the server, login, and database name into the Data Link Properties dialog box.

Managing databases with SQL

A database can be created with SQL using the `Create Database` command:

```
CREATE DATABASE database_name
[ ON [PRIMARY]
        [ <filespec> [,...n] ]
        [, <filegroup> [,...n] ]
]
[ LOG ON { <filespec> [,...n]} ]
[ FOR LOAD | FOR ATTACH ]
```

The `database_name` is any valid identifier chosen by the database administrator. It is the only required parameter. If no other parameters are specified, the database will be created on a 1MB data file and a .5MB log file. The logical name for the data files will be the same as the database name, and the logical name for the log file will be the database name followed by an underscore and the word *log*. All other settings and options will take their default values.

The `On` clause allows the files and filegroups that are to make up the database to be individually specified. The keyword `PRIMARY` is used to indicate the primary file, which contains the system tables for the database. The `filespec` allows one or more files to be defined, as shown in the following syntax diagram:

```
<filespec> ::=
  ( [ NAME = logical_file_name, ]
  FILENAME = 'os_file_name'
```

```
[, SIZE = size]
[, MAXSIZE = { max_size | UNLIMITED } ]
[, FILEGROWTH = growth_increment] ) [,...n]
```

The only required parameter for the filespec is the file name, which includes the full operating system path. The size is specified in megabytes, as is the max-size. The growth-increment can be specified in megabytes (MB), kilobytes (KB), or percent (%) following a number. Unspecified units will default to megabytes. All files specified without a filegroup are added to the primary filegroup. To add files to specific filegroups, use the filegroup specifier as follows:

```
<filegroup> ::=
FILEGROUP filegroup_name <filespec> [,...n]
```

The LOG ON clause specifies the file(s) that will be used for the transaction log. It uses the same filespec as defined above.

The FOR LOAD option is available primarily for backward compatibility with SQL Server versions prior to 7.0. It creates the database and prepares it to be immediately loaded from a backup. In the current version, the Restore command can be used to create a database during the restore process, so manually creating with the FOR LOAD option isn't necessary.

The FOR ATTACH option attaches a database from a series of files that have previously been detached from another MSDE server or SQL Server. Using Create Database with the FOR ATTACH option works similarly to the sp_attach_db stored procedure, but is more complex. Create Database is necessary only if the database to be attached consists of more than 16 files.

Databases can be modified using SQL with the Alter Database command. The syntax is as follows:

```
ALTER DATABASE database
{    ADD FILE <filespec> [,...n] [TO FILEGROUP filegroup_name]
     | ADD LOG FILE <filespec> [,...n]
     | REMOVE FILE logical_file_name
     | ADD FILEGROUP filegroup_name
     | REMOVE FILEGROUP filegroup_name
     | MODIFY FILE <filespec>
     | MODIFY FILEGROUP filegroup_name filegroup_property
}
```

Using this command, files and filegroups can be added, removed, or modified. Log files can only be added. To remove log files, the database can either be detached and reattached or backed up and restored.

Only a single file property can be changed within a single `Alter Database` command. File names can be changed only for files in the tempdb database. The size of files can be increased only using `Alter Database`. Files can be made smaller using the `dbcc shrinkfile` command. The entire database can be made smaller with `dbcc shrinkdatabase`.

The filegroup properties can be set to read-only, read/write, and default. The primary filegroup cannot be set to read-only. Setting a filegroup as the default will cause it to be used as the location for objects that do not specify a particular filegroup when they are created. Some graphical tools like Enterprise Manager always use the primary filegroup as the default, without regard to the default filegroup properties setting.

The name of the database can be changed using the stored procedure `sp_renamedb`.

Databases can be deleted using SQL with the command `Drop Database`. This command must be issued within the context of the master database, and it is not reversible. The syntax is as follows:

```
DROP DATABASE databasename
```

All connections to the database must be terminated before it can be dropped.

Managing databases with DMO

The DMO hierarchy for the physical structure of a database is as follows:

```
Server
    Databases
        Database
            Filegroups
                Filegroup
                    DBFiles
                        DBFile
            TransactionLog
                LogFiles
                    LogFile
```

The absolute minimum requirements for creating a database with DMO are to instantiate a database object, set the `name` property for that object, connect to the MSDE server, and use the `add` method of the Databases collection to add the database object. A database created in this way will have all default properties.

More commonly, a database will be created with one or more DBFile and LogFile objects to set the size and location of the database files, as shown in the following code:

```
dim oMSDEserver
dim oDatabase
```

```
3    dim oDataFile
4    dim oLogFile
5
6    set oMSDEserver = CreateObject("SQLDMO.SQLServer")
7    set oDatabase = CreateObject("SQLDMO.Database")
8    set oDataFile = CreateObject("SQLDMO.DBFile")
9    set oLogFile = CreateObject("SQLDMO.LogFile")
10
11    oDatabase.Name = "scheduling"
12
13    oDataFile.Name = "sched_data"
14    oDataFile.PhysicalName = "c:\mssql7\data\sched_data.mdf"
15    oDataFile.Size = 5
16
17    oLogFile.Name = "sched_log"
18    oLogFile.PhysicalName = "c:\mssql7\data\sched_log.ldf"
19    oLogFile.Size = 3
20    oLogFile.MaximumSize = 50
21
22    oDatabase.Filegroups("PRIMARY").DBFiles.add(oDataFile)
23    oDatabase.TransactionLog.LogFiles.add(oLogFile)
24
25    oMSDEserver.connect "Okh2h","sa",""
26    oMSDEserver.databases.add(oDatabase)
27    oMSDEserver.disconnect
```

You can find this code on the CD-ROM in the file named `Ch 6\createdb.vbs`.

Lines 1–4 declare variables to represent the MSDE server, the database that will be created, the data file, and the log file. Lines 6–9 instantiate each of those objects. Line 11 sets the database name, which is the only required property. Lines 13–15 set the logical name, operating system name and path, and size (in megabytes) of the data file. Lines 17–20 set similar properties for the log file. In addition, the log file has a maximum size limit set to 50MB. Lines 22 and 23 add the data and log files to the appropriate collections of the database object. Note that the PRIMARY filegroup was automatically created and had only to be referenced by name. Having set all the properties, lines 25–27 create the connection to the server, add the database object to the Databases collection (which actually creates the database on the server), and finally disconnect.

It is generally a good idea to place a maximum limit on files that can automatically grow, especially log files. Doing so limits the problems that can occur in case a runaway process should cause the file to grow until it fills the hard drive.

Modifying databases with DMO involves getting a reference to the appropriate object and setting properties or adding new objects to collections, for example, adding a new file to a filegroup. The following code adds an additional 5MB data file to the PRIMARY filegroup in the scheduling database on Drive D:

```
dim oMSDEserver
dim oDataFile

set oMSDEserver = CreateObject("SQLDMO.SQLServer")
set oDataFile = CreateObject("SQLDMO.DBFile")

oDataFile.Name = "sched_data2"
oDataFile.PhysicalName = "d:\mssql7\data\sched_data2.ndf"
oDataFile.Size = 5

oMSDEserver.connect "Okh2h","sa",""
oMSDEserver.databases("scheduling").FileGroups("PRIMARY")_
.DBFiles.add(oDataFile)
oMSDEserver.disconnect
```

This code can be found on the CD-ROM in the file named `Ch 6\modifydb.vbs`.

Dropping a database with DMO is a matter of calling the `remove` method of the databases collection and referencing the correct database by name or ordinal number.

```
dim oMSDEserver
set oMSDEserver = CreateObject("SQLDMO.SQLServer")

oMSDEserver.connect "Okh2h","sa",""
oMSDEserver.databases.remove("scheduling")
oMSDEserver.disconnect
```

This code can be found on the CD-ROM in the file named `Ch 6\dropdb.vbs`.

Controlling the Behavior of MSDE with Database Options

The following options are available for databases in MSDE:

✦ **ANSI null default**—Determines whether the default behavior of columns in the database is to allow nulls or not. If a column's definition does not explicitly specify Null or Not Null, the default will be used during table creation. The default allows nulls. This setting can be overridden by the connection level settings.

✦ **ANSI nulls**—Determines the outcome of comparing to null values. When this setting is turned on, the result will be null for any expression that compares a value to see if it is equal to null. When this setting is turned off, two null values are considered equal to each other. This setting can be overridden by the connection level settings.

✦ **ANSI warnings**—Determines whether MSDE complies with the SQL-92 standard in certain error conditions. One such condition is the generation of a warning message when a null is encountered as an input value to an aggregate function. The other condition occurs when an arithmetic overflow or divide-by-zero error is encountered. In this case, when this setting is turned on, the current transaction is rolled back. When this setting is turned off, a null value is returned. This setting will also cause transactions to be rolled back when they include an insert or update into a character column and the new values exceed the length in the column definition.

✦ **Auto create statistics**—Allows MSDE to automatically create statistics on columns when they are included in a `Where` clause. The statistics allow the query optimizer to make better choices when compiling an execution plan.

✦ **Auto update statistics**—The statistics compiled about indexed columns are automatically updated when MSDE determines that they have become out-of-date due to too much data modification in the table. Having up-to-date statistics allows the query optimizer to make the best possible choices in creating an execution plan. If this setting is turned off, statistics are not automatically generated and must be manually generated periodically, or the system performance will degrade.

✦ **Autoclose**—When this setting is turned off, all files associated with databases in MSDE are kept open as long as the SQL Server service is running. When this setting is turned on, the files associated with a particular database are closed whenever there are no connections using that database. On a single-user machine, such as a laptop, turning on the autoclose setting is a reasonable choice. It would not be a reasonable choice on a server handling multiple users because of the overhead associated with opening and closing files. This option is turned on by default when MSDE is installed on Windows 98.

✦ **Autoshrink**—When this option is turned on, a background process periodically checks for free space in the database and, using that free space, reduces the size of the operating system files. This option is also more appropriate on a single-user system than on a multiuser server. It is turned on by default when MSDE is installed on Windows 95 or 98.

✦ **Concat null yields null**—Determines whether combining a null and a string will return the string itself or just a null. When this option is turned on, concatenating a null with any string will return only a null.

✦ **Cursor close on commit**—Determines whether MSDE complies with the SQL-92 standard. When turned on, a transaction commit will cause any open cursors to be closed.

✦ **Dbo use only**—Prevents any users other than the database owner from accessing the database. This option does not set the database to single-user mode. Multiple connections can have the database open as long as the connections are running within the security context of dbo.

✦ **Default to local cursor**—Determines the default scope of cursors. When this option is turned on, the default scope is local so that cursors can be accessed only within the trigger, batch, or stored procedure in which they are created. Stored procedures can work around locally scoped cursors by passing them through an output parameter to a calling procedure. When default to local cursor is turned off, the scope of the cursor is, by default, the entire connection. Cursors are automatically deallocated when they go out of scope.

✦ **Merge publish**—Allows databases to be published through merge replication and is set automatically by the system during replication configuration.

✦ **Offline**—Closes the database and makes it completely inaccessible to MSDE connections. It is commonly used when preparing to copy a database to another server with the assistance of `sp_detach_db` and so on or when preparing a database for copying to removable media.

✦ **Published**—Allows databases to be published through snapshot replication and is set automatically by the system during replication configuration.

✦ **Quoted identifier**—Determines whether single and double quotes are treated the same, or whether double quotes are treated identically to square brackets.

✦ **Read-only**—prevents modifications to the database, disables locking, and can improve performance when only reads are necessary.

✦ **Recursive triggers**—When this option is turned off, a trigger can never cause itself to be fired, even indirectly by firing a trigger in another table that ultimately attempts to fire the original trigger.

✦ **Select into/bulkcopy**—Allows certain nonlogged operations to be performed.

  • **Writetext** and **Updatetext** allow modifications to be performed on the large object data type columns: text, ntext, and image. Both of these commands provide an option for either logged or nonlogged operation. The default for both commands is nonlogged. In order to be run in their nonlogged form, the Select into/bulkcopy option must be turned on. Because these commands are normally used with very large amounts of data, using them when transaction logging is turned on quickly fills up the transaction log. Therefore, operations that use these commands are usually performed in batches; the Select into/bulkcopy option is turned on immediately prior to each operation and then turned off immediately after, and a backup is performed.

- Whenever **Select Into** is used to save a result set into a permanent table, the Select into/bulkcopy option must be turned on, and the operation will not be recorded in the transaction log.
- The **bcp** command has a logged and a nonlogged form. The nonlogged form is sometimes called a fast bulk copy. In order to use this form, the Select into/bulkcopy option must be set, the table into or out of which the data is to be copied must not be replicated, and the `Tablock` parameter must be specified.

✦ **Single user**—Allows only a single connection to use the database. Care must be taken when using this option since a number of programs like Enterprise Manager for Query Analyzer can easily open multiple connections to the database. There is also nothing to prevent an end user from acquiring the one allowable connection to the database. For this reason, this option is often used in combination with the dbo use only option.

✦ **Subscribed**—Is controlled by the Replication Setup Wizard and indicates that the database is receiving replicated information from another database.

✦ **Torn page detection**—Allows MSDE to detect pages that have been only partially updated due to a system failure. Since the 8KB size of a page in the database is relatively large compared to a typical sector size used by the operating system on disk (for example, 512 bytes), several I/O requests at the physical level are required to fulfill a single I/O request at the database level. There is a possibility that MSDE will believe a write operation has successfully completed when in fact it has not. The torn page detection option sets 1 bit for every 512 bytes and inverts the bit for every write operation on the page. If the system failure happens partway through a write operation, the bits at the beginning of the page will be set to a different value compared to the bits at the end of the page. When a torn page is detected during database recovery, the database is marked suspect and must be restored for a backup. Making the database immediately unusable is preferable to allowing the system to be operational when there may be inconsistency in the database. If such a database were to remain operational, the inconsistency could, over time, cause more errors and inconsistencies and eventually lead to even more lost production than would occur by restoring the database.

✦ **Trunc. Log on Chkpt. (Truncate log on checkpoint)**—Allows any checkpointed transaction to be automatically truncated, or deleted, from the transaction log. Setting this option will prevent transactional backups and allow only full database backups. Turning this option on does not interfere with the checkpoint and recovery mechanisms that guarantee database consistency. It is useful for a database that either does not need to be backed up at all or is small enough to be fully backed up on a frequent basis.

Setting database options with Enterprise Manager

Some of the most commonly set database options can be displayed and set with Enterprise Manager from the Properties dialog box of a database. Right-click on any database, choose Properties, and select the Options tab. The dialog box shown in Figure 6-2 will be displayed. The options that do not appear in this dialog box are either set by the system or accessed with stored procedures.

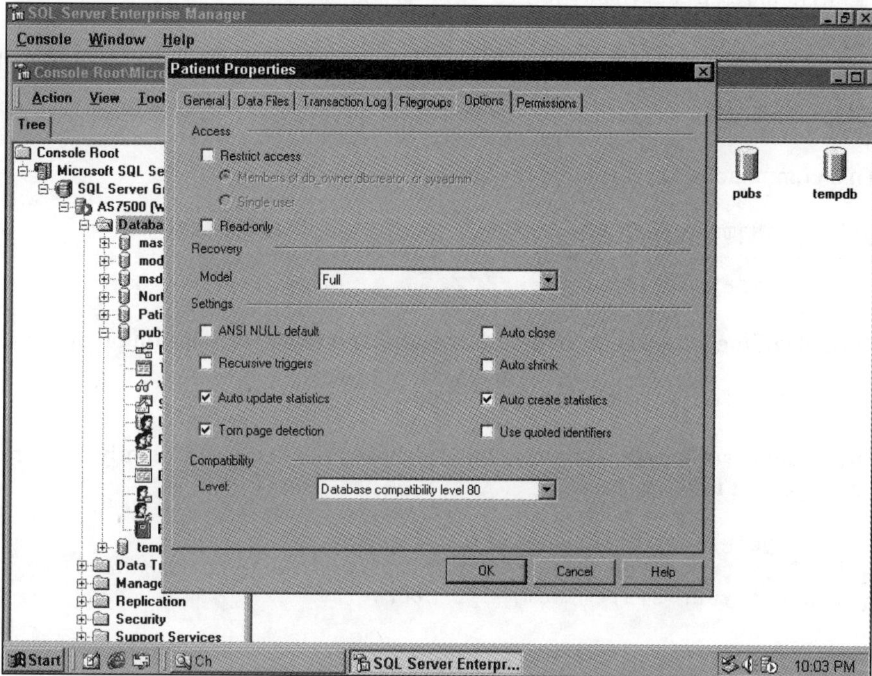

Figure 6-2: Database Options dialog box in Enterprise Manager

Setting database options with SQL

The stored procedure `sp_dboption` sets and views database options. There are three parameters that can be passed to this procedure: `database name`, `option name`, and `value`. If only the `database name` is passed, a list of options that are turned on (set) is displayed:

```
sp_dboption 'scheduling'
```

This command returns the following:

```
The following options are set:
-----------------------------------
autoclose
select into/bulkcopy
trunc. log on chkpt.
autoshrink
auto create statistics
auto update statistics
```

Using the `database name` and `option name` reports on the value of that one option:

```
sp_dboption 'scheduling', 'auto update statistics'
```

This command returns the following:

```
OptionName                          CurrentSetting
----------------------------------- --------------
auto update statistics              ON
```

And, of course, all three parameters are supplied to turn an option on or off:

```
sp_dboption 'scheduling', 'trunc. log on chkpt.', 'false'
```

Successfully setting any database option always results in the slightly obscure message that follows:

```
Checkpointing database that was changed.
DBCC execution completed. If DBCC printed error messages,
contact your system administrator.
```

Setting database options with DMO

The DMO hierarchy for database options is:

```
Server
    Databases
        Database
            DBOption
```

The database option is a property of the DBOption object, except for the following (which are controlled by replication processes):

- ✦ Merge Published
- ✦ Published
- ✦ Subscribed

The names of the DBOption properties in DMO are the following (the standard database option name is included in parentheses where the DMO name does not have an obvious mapping to the standard name):

- AssignmentDiag (ANSI warnings option)
- AutoClose
- AutoCreateStat
- AutoShrink
- AutoUpdateStat
- ColumnsNullByDefault (ANSI Null Default)
- CompareNull (ANSI Nulls)
- ContactNull (Concat Null Yields Null) (It should be spelled ContactNull. Go figure.)
- CursorCloseOnCommit
- DBOUseOnly
- DefaultCursor (Default to Local Cursor)
- Offline
- QuoteDelimiter (Quoted Identifier)
- ReadOnly
- RecursiveTriggers
- SelectIntoBulkCopy
- SingleUser
- TornPageDetection
- TruncateLogOnCheckpoint

The following sample code sets dbo use only and single user, which would be typical of a script about to perform maintenance.

```
dim oMSDEserver

set oMSDEserver = CreateObject("SQLDMO.SQLServer")

oMSDEserver.connect "Okh2h","sa",""
oMSDEserver.databases("scheduling").DBOption.dboUseOnly = true

oMSDEserver.disconnect
```

This code can be found on the CD-ROM in the file named `Ch 6\dboption.vbs`.

Summary

MSDE databases are made up of two or more files: at least one for the transaction log and one for data. The size of these files can be controlled by the database administrator or automatically increased and/or decreased by MSDE. The transaction logs provide a mechanism for guaranteeing database consistency and, when necessary, for performing incremental backups of the database. Databases can be created and deleted with Enterprise Manager, Access, SQL, or DMO. However, Access provides only very primitive control over the physical structure of the database. There are also a number of database options that provide control over how the database operates. Again, these can not be set through Access.

✦ ✦ ✦

CHAPTER 7

Using Tables to Store Data

In This Chapter

The structure of tables

Creating tables

Managing tables

Deleting tables

Tables are the most important objects in an MSDE database. Tables store all user data, which is the primary function of a database. They also store system data (metadata); all objects that exist in a database are defined in a system table. In fact, the only data structure in the ANSI SQL standard is the table, which may be categorized as a temporary table; permanent, or base, table; or virtual table (implemented as a view in MSDE).

Tables are extremely versatile. They store data that represents facts or objects in the real world. The data stored in the tables can be structured using system-defined data types, and if these are insufficiently detailed, new, user-defined data types can be created. There are many optional controls that can be placed on tables to provide rigid control over the data that is entered into them. Alternatively, tables can be created to accept just about any kind of data someone might choose to enter.

Exploring the Structure of Tables

Tables can be understood from two perspectives: the logical and the physical. The logical structure of tables is how they appear to someone writing SQL statements that retrieve or modify data. The physical structure consists of the mechanisms MSDE uses to implement tables. Understanding the logical structure of tables is a requirement for using MSDE. Understanding the physical structure is useful for debugging and optimizing processes that use MSDE.

Logical structure: rows, columns, and so on

All MSDE tables have the same basic structure. Data is organized in the table in columns and rows. Unlike a spreadsheet, the columns and rows in MSDE tables serve different functions and cannot be exchanged one for the other. A row is generally thought of as representing an individual fact or object. A column divides each row into individual attributes or properties of the fact or object. Additional structure can be added to the table by setting the properties of the columns and adding additional, supporting objects to the table, such as triggers and constraints.

Rows

Because MSDE is set-oriented, the rows in a table are usually treated as a set and thus have no intrinsic logical ordering. Just because they have no intrinsic logical ordering, however, does not mean that the rows must not have some physical ordering when they are stored on disk. Physical ordering (which can be controlled) and indexing are conveniences that allow for enhanced performance. Even a table with no rows is still a set; it is referred to as the Null, or empty, set.

By default, MSDE allows duplicate rows within a table. In other words, there can be any number of rows in a table with exactly the same value. Normally, it is undesirable to have duplicate rows because of the set-oriented nature of SQL, but mechanisms such as primary keys, unique constraints, and unique indexes can be used to prevent this situation. Writing code to handle duplicate rows is complex, time-consuming, and prone to error. However, in some situations (for example, when data is imported from outside sources) duplicate rows must be allowed in tables.

Columns

Columns in a table are used to define the attributes or properties of each row. Like rows, they are considered to be a set, and according to the ANSI SQL standard, they have no defined order. In its implementation of SQL, MSDE does have an ordering of columns, and even allows that ordering to be changed. However, it is considered bad practice to write code that relies on the ordering of columns within a table. Such code runs flawlessly if it refers to all columns only by name, but can be broken if column ordering changes for any reason.

There are a number of properties associated with each column. For example, a column must have a name, a data type, and a setting that allows or disallows null values to be entered into the column. Other optional properties may be set on a column, such as the `identity` property and the `unique ID` property.

Nulls

Every column has a property that determines whether or not null values will be allowed. Nulls are generally considered to represent the absence of a value. Despite this simple sounding definition, different people, applications, and database management systems handle nulls differently. Even within MSDE, database and connection options settings may cause nulls to be handled differently depending on the circumstances. For example, the Concat Null Yields Null setting, when turned on, causes any string that is concatenated with a null to result in null. If that setting is turned off, a string concatenated with null will return the original string. Not only must this option be set properly in accordance with the application that is running on the database, but it must also be well understood by the database administrator. Take the case of middle names and initials. If nulls are allowed in a column that stores middle initials and some application code attempts to concatenate first name, middle initial, and last name, the Concat Null Yields Null setting must be turned off. Otherwise, anyone without a middle initial (assuming a null was entered into the column) will have no name whatsoever. There are other ways to handle this specific problem. For example, MSDE allows the use of zero-length strings, which would work well in this situation. However, some programming languages and other databases consider a zero-length string to be equivalent to a null.

If a column does not allow nulls and a row is inserted that does not include a value for this column, MSDE will attempt to insert a default value. If no default value exists, an error will be generated and the insert will fail.

Identity

Another property available for a single column within any table is the `identity` property. The `identity` property causes MSDE to supply an incrementing value whenever a new row is inserted. The starting value (called the seed) and the increment can both be specified during table definition. User applications cannot provide a value for the identity column or an error will be generated.

`Identity` provides a convenient way of creating a unique value to identify each round in a table and is often used as a primary key. An `identity` value is unique only within the scope of an individual table. For this reason, the `identity` property is not sufficient for some distributed applications.

GUID

The Global Unique Identifier (GUID) value, also called a Universally Unique Identifier (UUID), provides statistical uniqueness across time and space. The column property `ROWGUIDCOL` is used to identify a column that will contain a GUID. This property may be set for only one column per table. Setting the `ROWGUIDCOL` property does not automatically cause the assignment of values to that column, as the `identity` property does. The preferred method for creating the GUID is to set the default constraint value to be the `NEWID()` function. Every time `NEWID()` is called, a new and statistically unique value is created. It is also possible to create a value that is formatted properly for the ROWGUIDCOL column by converting a string to a unique identifier.

Unique identifiers have no intrinsic order and support only the equality comparison operators (= and <>) and the IS NULL and IS NOT NULL operators. The following is an example of a unique identifier: BED035E1-F81E-11D3-8010-0050049957C4

Constraints

Constraints are mechanisms that restrict the possible values that can be entered into columns. Constraints can test an input value against a pattern, like a phone number or a zip code, or they can verify that a value being entered exists in another table. Constraints are considered to be a part of declarative data integrity (DDI), which is intended to improve the quality of data through the definition of a table, thus providing consistency across all applications that might use that table. There are a variety of different constraints, all of which are covered in detail in Chapter 8.

Triggers

Triggers are procedures that run anytime data in a table is modified. MSDE defines three different types of triggers: insert, update, and delete. There can be any number of triggers defined for each one of these three events. All insert triggers will be run anytime data is inserted into the table on which the trigger is defined. The same is true of update and delete triggers. Triggers are covered in detail in Chapter 16.

Indexes

Indexes can be created on tables to improve performance in finding and retrieving data from the table. Without indexes, any process that needs to find a row in a table must scan every row in the table until it finds the data it is looking for. With an index, the requesting process can look up the data in the index and find all occurrences, just as a person would look up a word in the index of a book. Indexes are covered in detail in Chapter 9.

Temporary tables

Most tables exist as permanent structures in the database in which they are defined, but temporary tables can be created either by the system or by a user process. These are stored in the tempdb database. The system will create temporary tables as holding areas when performing complex processes, typically sorts. The user process can create temporary tables for any reason whatsoever by using a # or a ## as the initial character(s) in the table name.

A table created with a single # as its first character is a local temporary table. A local temporary table can be accessed only by the connection that created it. As soon as the connection is disconnected, the table is destroyed.

A table created with a ## as its first two characters is a global temporary table. A global temporary table can be accessed by connections other than the one that created it. If any connections are accessing a global temporary table when the creating connection ends, the table is not immediately destroyed. The table cannot be opened by any new connections and can be destroyed only when all existing connections have ended.

MSDE normally handles the destruction of temporary tables, both those created by the system and those created by user connections. In the event that a temporary table is not properly destroyed when its creating connection ends, it will automatically be destroyed the next time the SQL Server service restarts because the entire tempdb database is automatically dropped and re-created.

Physical structure

MSDE hides most of the physical details of table storage from users and administrators. Understanding the details can be useful when designing tables (particularly if they are large), managing system maintenance, optimizing performance, and debugging problems. All data is stored in 8K pages, the contents of which can be directly examined with the `dbcc page` command, which will be covered in Chapter 29.

How tables are stored

The organization of the pages that make up a table can follow one of two structures: a heap, which is an agglomeration of pages, or a B-Tree, which has a particular order. Every page within either one of these structures has its own internal organization, including the page header, a series of rows, and a row-offset array (as described in Chapter 6). Each row also has its own internal structure that varies depending on whether or not there are any variable-length columns defined for the table.

Heap

A table is stored as a heap if there is no clustered index defined for the table. MSDE can identify which pages are assigned to a heap by looking up an entry in the sysindexes system table, which has an entry for every table and index. The entry for the heap table points to an Index Allocation Map (IAM) page. The IAM page is a bitmap in which each bit represents one extent in the current database file. If a bit is turned on, the corresponding extent belongs to the table. So, MSDE can quickly scan through the IAM and find all of the extents that belong to the file. There are individual entries in the IAM for each of the first eight pages in the table because these may be on mixed extents. No other connection exists between the pages and the heap other than the association through the IAM, as opposed to some other databases that link all the pages in a chain.

Index

When a clustered index is created on a table, the pages of the table are reorganized and become the leaf-level pages of the clustered index. Because these pages are in an index, they are linked together with forward and backward pointers, and there is also a B-Tree (balanced tree) structure that allows for fast access to any individual page entry. When MSDE needs to find a page in a table with a clustered index, it looks up the entry in the sysindexes system table and finds a pointer to the root page of the clustered index B-Tree. It must then navigate through the B-Tree structure to the particular page in which it is interested. Indexes are described in more detail in Chapter 9.

Temporary table

The physical structure of a temporary table is exactly the same as a normal table, except that it is stored in the tempdb database and can automatically be referenced from other databases.

How rows are structured

Row structure is the same whether the rows are in a heap or in a B-Tree, although the structure does varies slightly depending on whether or not there are any variable-length columns in the table. Every row begins with a 4-byte header that includes information about the type of row, the size of the fixed-length portion of the row, and the indicator for the presence of variable-length columns. All fixed-length columns immediately follow the header; their sizes are listed under data types discussed later in this chapter. Following the fixed-length fields is the Null block. The Null block is a bitmap containing one bit for every column in the row. If any column contains a null, the corresponding bit is set in the Null block. Using a bitmap to represent nulls allows MSDE to distinguish nulls from other similar values, like zero-length strings. If there are any variable-length columns, a variable block follows the Null block. The variable block contains a count of the number of variable columns. The location of the beginning of each of these columns is stored in an array that comes after the variable block. This array requires two bytes for every variable-length column. The rest of the row is used by the data from the variable-length column.

Rows cannot span multiple pages, so the maximum possible size of a row is 8060 bytes (8K, or 8192 bytes, minus 96 bytes for the page header and a little extra reserved for future use by Microsoft). If a row contains only a single column, the column's maximum size is 8000 bytes. Remember to subtract the row overhead from the figures when calculating the amount of data that will fit on a page.

Storing large amounts of text or binary data

The large object data types (text, ntext, and image) allow data that exceeds the storage capacity of a single data page to be stored. When a column in a table is defined with one of these data types, a 16-byte pointer is placed within the data row. This pointer contains the address of the 84-byte root node of a B-Tree that contains the value of the field.

Large object pages are managed as a single group for each table, even if the table contains more than one large object column. If a large object is less than 64 bytes, it is stored entirely in the root node. If it is between 64 bytes and 32K, the root node will contain pointers directly to the leaf nodes, which will be chunks of data spread throughout the large object pages. If the large object is more than 32K, additional nodes will be created between the root and the leaves. These nodes will be stored in large object pages dedicated to a single object.

Data types

MSDE provides a number of data types used to define what kind of data can be entered into a column. It also allows database administrators to create new data types, although the new types must be based on existing system data types. An administrator can create a data type that is more specific than the system data types, but not one that is less specific.

All data types have a length associated with them. In some data types, the length is implicitly defined as part of the data type. For example, the integer data type (int) is always stored as a four-byte value. Other data types, like the character data type (char), must have their lengths explicitly defined by the database designer.

System-defined data types

The system-defined data types can be grouped into several categories. There are character data types for storing small amounts of textual information, and there are two kinds of numeric data types: those that store exact numeric information, which are the most common in relational databases, and those that store approximate numeric data. Approximate numeric data types are used most often in scientific applications. There are also data types for storing large amounts of text or binary data. These are called large objects, or binary large objects (BLOBs). Other data types are available for storing time information, others for storing money, and a few others have miscellaneous functions. Several data types have fixed-length and variable-length alternatives. Using a fixed-length data type can provide space savings over a variable-length data type when the data to be stored is of a consistent length. This is because the variable-length columns require additional overhead in every row in the table, as described in the *Physical Structure* section earlier in this chapter. In the following descriptions, the space required for each data type is presented. This number does not include the overhead.

The character data types are as follows:

✦ **char** — a fixed number of characters from MSDE's configured code page. One byte is allocated for each character specified in the length. For example, char(10) allocates 10 bytes in every row without regard to how many characters are actually stored in each row.

✦ **varchar** — a variable number of characters from MSDE's configured code page. This data type uses one byte for each character, up to the maximum specified. If the configured code page is a DBCS (for example, code page 932 Japanese), some characters require two bytes.

✦ **nchar** — a fixed number of characters from the Unicode character set. Two bytes are allocated in every row for each character specified in the length. For example, nchar(10) allocates 20 bytes in every row.

✦ **nvarchar** — a variable number of characters from the Unicode character set. Two bytes are used for every character stored up to the maximum specified. For example, nvarchar(15) allows up to 15 characters to be stored, which would use 30 bytes in the row.

The exact numeric data types are as follows:

✦ **bit** — can contain a 1 or a 0. An entire byte is allocated when the first bit column is added to a row. Up to 7 additional bit columns can also be stored in this byte. If a 9th bit column is added, a second byte will be allocated.

✦ **int**—stores integer values from approximately –2 billion to +2 billion. The exact range is negative (2^{31} – 1) through positive 2^{31} and requires 4 bytes.

✦ **smallint**—stores integer values from –32K to +32K (negative (2^{15} – 1) through positive 2^{15}) and requires two bytes.

✦ **tinyint**—stores integer values from 0 to 255. Requires one byte.

✦ **decimal**—can store a fractional number. When using this data type, both precision and scale must be specified. Precision is the total number of digits that can be stored, with a maximum of 38. A precision of 5 would allow 1.2345, or 123.45 or 12,345. Scale is the total number of digits allowed to the right of the decimal and must be less than or equal to the precision. Using the same precision = 5 used previously, example 1.2345 requires a scale of four, example 123.45 requires a scale of two, and example 12,345 requires a scale of zero. Storage for this data type varies with the precision, from 5 bytes up to 17 bytes.

✦ **numeric**—is a synonym for decimal.

The approximate numeric data types are as follows:

✦ **real**—stores numbers with a precision up to 7 digits with varying scale. Any number stored in a real column is an approximation. Because these values are approximate, the equality comparison often does not work as expected. For columns whose values must be compared with other values for equality, consider using the decimal data type. The real data type requires four bytes of storage.

✦ **float**—similar to real, but with a precision up to 15 digits. It requires eight bytes.

The data types for storing dates and times are as follows:

✦ **datetime**—used for both dates and times (simultaneously), this data type can store dates from the first day of the year 1753 to the last day of the year 9999. Times stored in datetime can have up to millisecond precision. Datetime requires eight bytes.

✦ **smalldatetime**—similar to datetime, but stores dates from 1900 to 2079. Times have precision only to the minute. Smalldatetime requires four bytes.

The timestamp data type does not store dates or times! It is defined at the end of this section with other miscellaneous data types.

The data types for storing money are as follows:

✦ **money**—similar to decimal, but has fixed precision and scale. It stores fractional values to four decimal places and can store numbers up to approximately 922 trillion (positive or negative). Money requires eight bytes.

✦ **smallmoney**—also stores four places to the right of the decimal, but can store numbers only as large as 214,000 (positive or negative). Smallmoney requires four bytes.

The data types for storing large objects are as follows:

✦ **image** — can store up to 2GB of binary data. A pointer is placed in the row, but the data is kept in its own storage area. Only enough space for the data stored is required.

✦ **text** — can store up to 2GB of text data. Text is stored in the same way as image. One byte per character is required, except when using DBCSs.

✦ **ntext** — can store up to 1GB of Unicode text data. Ntext is also stored like image data. Two bytes per character are required.

The remaining data types are as follows:

✦ **binary** — stores a fixed number of bytes that can contain any binary values. The number of bytes specified is allocated from every row. For example, binary(10) allocates 10 bytes.

✦ **varbinary** — stores a variable number of bytes up to the maximum specified. Storage is allocated only for actual data.

✦ **sysname** — used by MSDE in system tables. It is the equivalent to nvarchar(128).

✦ **timestamp** — stores a system-supplied value that is unique within the database. Every time a row anywhere in the database is updated, the timestamp counter is incremented and written to the row that was updated if it includes a timestamp column. A table can have only one timestamp column. Timestamp requires eight bytes.

✦ **uniqueidentifier** — this data type is used to store Global Unique Identifier (GUID) values that are generated by the `newid()` function. Such numbers are statistically unique values created with an industry standard algorithm. They can be used to uniquely identify rows even among different databases on different servers. Uniqueidentifier requires 16 bytes.

There is one other data type, cursor, which cannot be used for columns in tables. It is used by stored procedure parameters to pass references to cursors.

When you are writing programs that will store data using MSDE, make sure that you understand how the data types for the language you are using interact with the data types used by MSDE. For example, an integer in Visual Basic corresponds to a smallint in MSDE, that is, both of these data types can store a number up to 2^{15}. To store a larger number in Visual Basic requires the long data type, while MSDE uses integer.

User-defined data types

Additional data types can be created within a database. They must be based on an existing system data type. When defining a new data type, it must be given a name, a base data type, and a length, or precision and scale if appropriate. As part of the definition, nulls can be allowed or forbidden, although this setting can be overridden when the user-defined data type is applied to a column definition.

There are two primary reasons to create a user-defined data type: One, they provide easy identification, and two, they can be associated with rules and defaults. An example of using a user-defined data type to identify data of a specific type and length is a social security number. For example, if many tables in a database store social security numbers, a user-defined data type called SSN, defined as char(9), might help to make the database more consistent and self-documenting.

User-defined data types also support binding with rules and defaults (not to be confused with a default constraint). A rule is an independent database object that embodies data-verification logic. The logic in a rule is syntactically similar to the predicates of a `Where` clause except that it cannot reference other columns in a table. Once a rule has been created, it can be bound to a user-defined data type or a column in a table. If bound to a user-defined data type, it will be operational for all columns in which that data type is used. Rules are not ANSI standard and, in general, are less flexible than check constraints, which can perform similar functions but can also refer to other columns within a table.

Defaults are also independent database objects that provide a value that can be inserted into a column if a row is created and no value is supplied for that column. Defaults can also be bound to columns or user-defined data types. In the latter case, they are made operational for all columns in which the data type is used. Defaults are not ANSI standard and are being largely replaced with default constraints.

Type conversion

Data types can be used to define columns in a table, and they can also be used within SQL scripts to define variables. Data of one type can be used in a variable or stored in a column of another type. When data types don't match exactly, MSDE will usually convert the data implicitly and automatically, although some conversions require the use of an explicit conversion function and a few others (mostly with the large object data types) are not allowed at all. In general, if a conversion makes sense, it will work. For example, any date that can be stored in a smalldatetime column can also be stored in a datetime column and can automatically be converted. When going the other way, from datetime to smalldatetime, MSDE will perform the conversion, but an error will occur if there is a loss of data. For example, the date "December 31st, 1899" is not a valid smalldatetime.

Note The SQL Server books online have a chart in the topic "Cast and Convert (T-SQL)" that shows all possible conversions and whether they will happen implicitly, require explicit conversion, or are not permitted.

Creating, Modifying, and Deleting Tables

Tables can be managed in Enterprise Manager, Access, the Data View in the Enterprise Edition of Visual Studio, SQL, and DMO. Tables can be examined but not modified with the Data View in the Professional Edition of Visual Studio.

Managing tables with Enterprise Manager, Access, and Visual Studio

Enterprise Manager, Access, and the Visual Studio Data View window each have two ways to manage tables. First, they have a Tables container, which displays a list of tables and allows the properties of any of the tables to be examined or modified, created, and deleted. Second, they have the ability to create database diagrams, which present a graphical representation of sets of tables, including the relationship of one table to another. The database diagrams can be used to perform all the same functions as the Tables container.

Tables container

To display the Tables container in Enterprise Manager, expand the server group, the server, and the database, and click the item called Tables. A list of all tables in the database, along with their type, owner, and creation date, will be displayed in the right pane, as shown in Figure 7-1. This list of tables may or may not include the system tables, depending upon the registration information for the server. To change the registration information for the server, right-click on the server and choose Edit Server Registration Properties. There is a check box near the bottom of this dialog box that allows system tables and system objects to be displayed or hidden.

To display the Tables container in Access, open a project that references the desired database and click on the item in the left pane called Tables. A list of user tables will be displayed in the right pane. There is no way to display system tables in Access.

If some tables seem to be missing from Tables container in the Data View window, right-click the Tables container and select the Filter By Owner, then delete any owner name, and click OK.

To display the Tables container in Visual Studio, open the Data View window and expand the Data Links or Data Environment Connection that is configured for the database in which you are interested. Expand the Tables container and the tables from the database are displayed. System tables can be displayed by right-clicking the Tables container and selecting Show System Objects.

See Chapter 3 for more information about creating and configuring Data Links and Data Environment Connections.

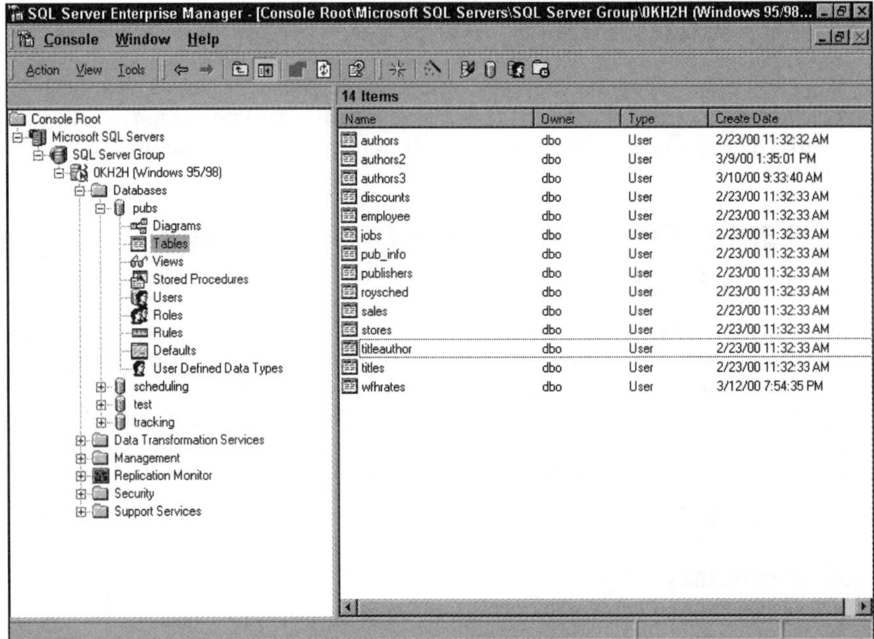

Figure 7-1: The Tables container in Enterprise Manager

Table properties in Enterprise Manager

The properties of a table can be displayed in Enterprise Manager for an overview of the table's structure. Figure 7-2 shows the properties of the Employee table in the pubs database. The top section shows the table name and contains a button that invokes the dialog box for managing permissions on the table. The middle section lists the owner; creation date; filegroup, if it is a filegroup other than primary—Employee is located in the primary filegroup so nothing is displayed; and the number of rows in the table. The bottom section summarizes the information about each column in the table. This section usually has scroll bars that can be used to see all of the table's columns. For each column, an icon of a key will be displayed if the column is part of the primary key. A check will be displayed under ID if the column has the `identity` property. The column name is displayed, along with the data type, the length (size), whether or not nulls are allowed, and the default value if one exists.

The Table Designer

To create a table in Enterprise Manager or Visual Studio, right-click on the Tables container and choose New Table. In Access, make sure the Tables container is displayed and click on the New button. A prompt will appear into which the name of the new table can be typed, and when it is dismissed, the Table Designer appears. The Table Designer from Enterprise Manager is shown in Figure 7-3. Each row in the top half of the Table Designer represents a column in the table, and each column in the Designer represents a property of the row. The bottom half of the Table Designer shows additional details about the item that is selected in the top half.

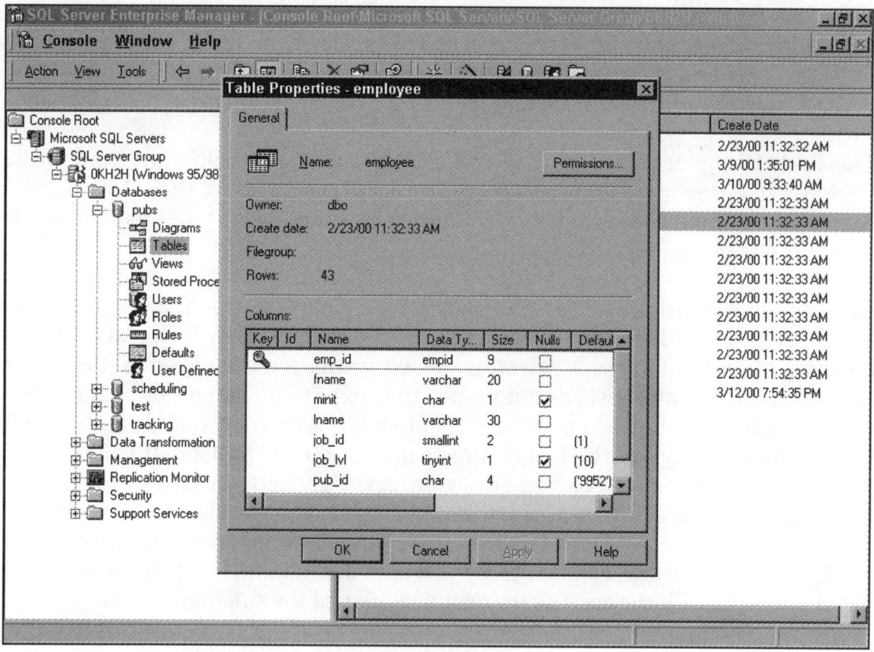

Figure 7-2: Table properties in Enterprise Manager

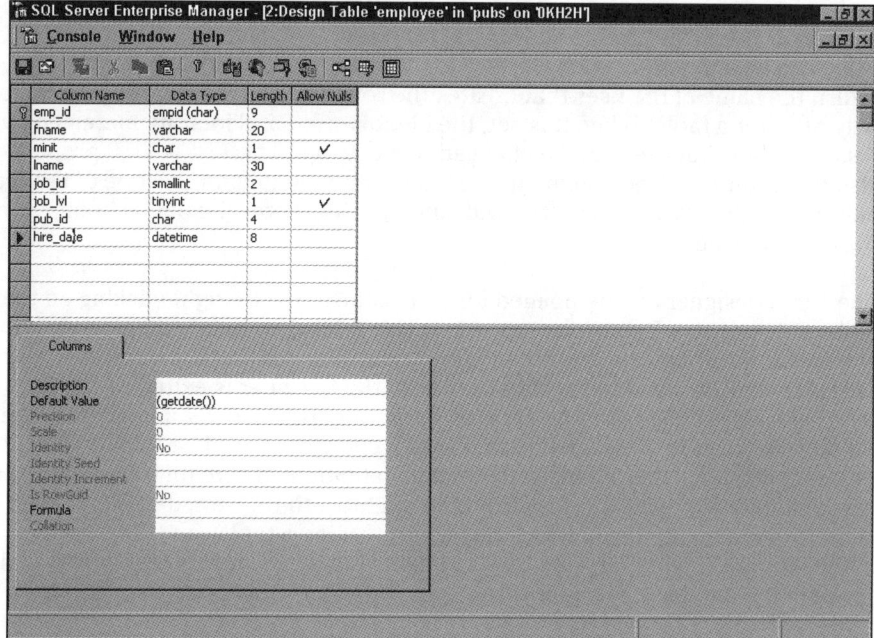

Figure 7-3: The Table Designer displaying the Employees table

You can create new objects in Enterprise Manager either by right-clicking the appropriate container—for example, tables, views, or stored procedures—in the left pane and choosing New or by selecting the container so that its contents are displayed in the right pane and then right-clicking anywhere in the right pane.

The Table Designer in Access and Visual Studio is slightly different than the Table Designer in Enterprise Manager. In Enterprise Manager, all of the information for each table column is presented in a single row; there is no detail pane in the bottom half of the screen.

Once you have started the Table Designer, type a name in the first column. The name must be unique in the table. Select a data type from the drop-down list in the second column. When a data type is selected, default values are displayed in the length, precision, and scale columns. For data types that require the length to be specified (for example, char, varchar, binary), the default length is displayed and can be modified. For all other data types, the length shows the number of bytes that will be allocated in each row. The `precision` and `scale` properties accept data entry for the decimal data type only. For all other numeric data types, scale is unused and precision displays the maximum number of numerals that the data type can store. For example, the largest number that can be stored in a smallint column is 32,767, which consists of five numerals. Therefore, the precision displayed for smallint is five.

The `allow nulls` property (it is a check box in Access and Visual Studio, and it is a drop-down list in Enterprise Manager) can be used to determine whether or not null values will be allowed in the column. Some other properties, such as `identity` and `primary key`, require that nulls be prohibited. Any valid expression can be entered as the default value and will be used as the default constraint. The default value can be a function, such as `newid()` for a uniqueidentifier or `user_name()` to return the name of the user that creates the row. The `identity` property can be set only once for a table. When it is set, the identity seed and identity increment will default to one, but they can be changed to any value. The `ISROWGUID` property can also be set for only one column in the table, and that column must be of the type uniqueidentifier. When it is set, it will automatically enter the `newid()` function as the default value.

The Table Designer can be opened for an existing table by right-clicking on the table and choosing Properties or Design. The Table Designer is displayed and changes can be made as described above. The changes that are entered into the Designer are not saved to the database until the Designer is exited or the Save button is clicked. Changes can be aborted by exiting the Designer and clicking the No button from the message box that asks if changes should be saved. The Table Designer accomplishes changes to column definitions by creating a table with the new definition, copying all rows from the old table to the new, deleting the old table, and renaming the new. Deleting and renaming a table can take a long period of time for tables with large amounts of data, and there must be enough available space in the database to support the copy.

A table can be deleted by selecting the table and pressing the Delete button or by right-clicking on the table and choosing Delete from the menu.

Database diagrams

The Database Diagrams container is initially empty, but diagrams can be created here which will provide a visual representation of a set of tables, including the relationships between tables defined by foreign key constraints.

To create a database diagram in Enterprise Manager or Visual Studio, right-click on the Database Diagrams container and choose New Database Diagram. In Access, click the New button. A dialog box is displayed from which tables can be selected to be included in the diagram. A check box allows related tables to be included automatically. If this check box is selected, any table that is related to a selected table will also be added to the diagram. In the "How many levels of related tables" box, a number can be entered to control how many links will be followed to add tables.

Database diagrams show each table's name and columns by default. Additional information is available by right-clicking on the name of a table and choosing Column properties. The Table Designer is also accessible by right-clicking and choosing Properties.

Tables can be deleted from the database or removed from the diagram without being deleted. Both of these functions are available from the right-click menu.

New tables can be created and existing tables can be added to the diagram by right-clicking on the background of the diagram.

User-defined data types

User-defined data types can be managed in Enterprise Manager by clicking on the container of the same name within the database. Any existing user-defined data types will be displayed in the right pane. To create a new user-defined data type, right-click in the right pane and choose New User-defined Data type. A dialog box is displayed into which a name is entered, a data type selected from the drop-down list, a length entered if appropriate, and the optional Allow Nulls box checked or left unchecked. There are also drop-down lists for rules and defaults. Selecting either of these will automatically bind it to the data type. For existing data types, the Where Used button is also available. This button will display a list of any tables in which this data type has been specified.

Managing tables with SQL

SQL has commands for creating, modifying, and deleting tables. There are stored procedures for having and deleting user-defined data types.

The Create Table statement

A partial syntax diagram for the Create Table statement is shown below. The syntax for table constraints and column constraints will be covered in a later chapter.

```
CREATE TABLE
[
    database_name.[owner].
    | owner.
] table_name
(
    {    <column_definition>
         | column_name AS computed_column_expression
         | <table_constraint>
    } [,...n]
)
[ON {filegroup | DEFAULT} ]
[TEXTIMAGE_ON {filegroup | DEFAULT} ]

<column_definition> ::= { column_name data_type }
[ [ DEFAULT constant_expression ]
| [ IDENTITY [(seed, increment ) [NOT FOR REPLICATION] ] ]
]
[ ROWGUIDCOL ]
[ <column_constraint>] [ ...n]
```

The command always begins with `CREATE TABLE`. The database name and/or owner may then optionally follow. If the database name is not included, the current database will be used. If the owner name is not included, the current user will be used. The table name must then be specified and followed, in parentheses, by a list of column definitions.

The column definition consists of the column name, a space, and the data type. The data type must include any required information, such as length, precision, or scale, according to the data type chosen. A default value for the column can optionally be specified by using the keyword default, followed by an expression, which could be a constant value or a function. The `identity` property can be set by using the identity keyword, optionally followed by a seed and increment. Both the seed and increment will be one by default if they are not included. The `identity` property can also be specified as Not For Replication, which means that any row that is inserted by the replication process will have to provide its own value for the identity column because an identity value will not be created by the system and the identity counter will not be incremented. Including the eponymous keyword will set the `ROWGUIDCOL` property.

After all of the columns have been defined, two additional optional clauses can be included. The `ON` clause allows specification of a filegroup on which the table should be created. The text image on clauses allows a filegroup to be specified for storage of any large object data type columns.

The following statement creates a table called Guide with four columns: ID, FirstName, LastName, and Specialty.

```
CREATE TABLE Guide (
    ID int IDENTITY (1, 1) NOT NULL ,
    FirstName char(15) NOT NULL ,
    LastName char(24) NOT NULL ,
    Specialty char(10) NOT NULL
)
```

The Alter Table command

Tables can be modified with the `Alter Table` command. Column properties such as `length` or `data type` can be changed. However, MSDE will verify that there will be no loss of data before executing the command. If loss of data may occur, MSDE will return an error. The syntax for `Alter Table` is as follows:

```
ALTER TABLE table
{    [ALTER COLUMN column_name
        {    new_data_type [ (precision[, scale] ) ]
                [ NULL | NOT NULL ]
            | {ADD | DROP} ROWGUIDCOL
        }
    ]
    | ADD
        {    [ <column_definition> ]
            |  column_name AS computed_column_expression
        }[,...n]
    | [WITH CHECK | WITH NOCHECK] ADD
        { <table_constraint> }[,...n]
    | DROP
        {    [CONSTRAINT] constraint_name
            | COLUMN column
        }[,...n]
    | {CHECK | NOCHECK} CONSTRAINT
        {ALL | constraint_name[,...n]}
    | {ENABLE | DISABLE} TRIGGER
        {ALL | trigger_name[,...n]}
}
```

The first section of the Alter Table statement allows existing columns to be altered. The data type can be changed as can the nullability and whether or not the column is the `ROWGUIDCOL`. The second section of the Alter Table statement allows additional columns to be added to the table. They use the same column definition used in the Create Table statement. The third section of the Alter Table statement allows table constraints to be added, a topic which will be covered in a later chapter. The fourth section allows existing constraints or columns to be dropped from the table. The last two sections of the statement allow column constraints and triggers to be enabled and disabled.

The following code modifies the specialty column on the table that was created above to allow nulls. The data type must be respecified at the same time that the Null setting is changed.

```
ALTER TABLE Guide
    ALTER COLUMN
    Specialty char(10) NULL
```

The Drop Table statement

The syntax of the Drop Table statement is `DROP TABLE` followed by the table name. The following code drops the Guide table created above.

```
DROP TABLE Guide
```

Sp_addtype

User-defined data types can be added to a database with the stored procedure, `sp_addtype`. The syntax is as follows:

```
Sp_addtype new_datatype_name, system_data_type, [nullability]
```

For example, the following code adds the type called SSN, which is based on the character data type of length ten and includes the requirement that nulls are not allowed.

```
sp_addtype SSN, 'char(10)', 'NOT NULL'
```

Any system data types that require a length or precision to be provided in parentheses must be included in single quotes. Quotes must also be used for the `'NOT NULL'` specifier.

Sp_droptype

To delete a user-defined data type, use `sp_droptype` followed by the name of the type. The following code deletes the data type that was added above.

```
sp_droptype SSN
```

Managing tables with DMO

The DMO hierarchy for tables is as follows:

```
Server
    Databases
        Database
            Tables
                Table
                    Columns
                        Column
```

The DMO hierarchy for user-defined data types is the following:

```
Server
    Databases
        Database
            UserDefinedDataTypes
                UserDefinedDataType
```

Creating tables

To create a table with DMO:

1. Instantiate a table object and set its `name` property.
2. Create column objects and add them to the Columns collection of the table object.
3. Make a connection to the MSDE server and add the table object to the Tables collection of the appropriate database.

The following VBScript creates a table called Guide with four columns: ID, which is integer, not null, and has the `identity` property; FirstName, which is char(15); LastName, which is char(24); and Specialty, which is char(24):

```
dim oMSDEserver
dim oTable
dim oColID
dim oColFirstName
dim oColLastName
dim oColSpecialty

set oMSDEserver = CreateObject("SQLDMO.SQLServer")
set oTable = CreateObject("SQLDMO.Table")
set oColID = CreateObject("SQLDMO.Column")
set oColFirstName = CreateObject("SQLDMO.Column")
set oColLastName = CreateObject("SQLDMO.Column")
set oColSpecialty = CreateObject("SQLDMO.Column")

oColID.Name = "ID"
oColID.DataType = "int"
oColID.Identity = true
oColID.AllowNulls = false

oColFirstName.Name = "FirstName"
oColFirstName.DataType = "char"
oColFirstName.Length = 15

oColLastName.Name = "LastName"
oColLastName.DataType = "char"
oColLastName.Length = 24
```

```
oColSpecialty.Name = "Specialty"
oColSpecialty.DataType = "char"
oColSpecialty.Length = 10

oTable.Name = "Guide"
oTable.Columns.add (oColID)
oTable.Columns.add (oColFirstName)
oTable.Columns.add (oColLastName)
oTable.Columns.add (oColSpecialty)

oMSDEserver.connect "Okh2h","sa",""
oMSDEserver.Databases("scheduling").Tables.add (oTable)
oMSDEserver.disconnect
```

You can find this code on the CD-ROM in the file named `Ch 25\createtab.vbs`.

The `DataType` property of the column object does not always fully specify the data type. When a length is required, for example, char(10), the `DataType` is just the string `"char"` (it must be all lowercase) and the `length` property must also be used, in this case 10.

Modifying tables

Modifications to tables can be made with DMO by opening a connection to the server, creating a reference to the table, and setting any appropriate properties. DMO does not allow changes to existing columns (like the `Alter Table` command), so they must be dropped and re-added. Changes to a table can be assembled into a unit of change, which is similar to a transactional unit of work. To create a unit of change, call the `BeginAlter` method on the table before changing its properties. When all changes have been submitted, call the `DoAlter` method, and the changes will be performed. A unit of change can be cancelled by calling the `CancelAlter` method of the table.

The following code adds a column to the Guide table:

```
dim oMSDEserver
dim oTable
dim oColHired

set oMSDEserver = CreateObject("SQLDMO.SQLServer")
set oColHired = CreateObject("SQLDMO.Column")

oColHired.Name = "Hired"
oColHired.DataType = "datetime"
oColHired.AllowNulls = true

oMSDEserver.connect "Okh2h","sa",""
set oTable = _
 oMSDEserver.Databases("scheduling").Tables("Guide")
oTable.BeginAlter
```

```
oTable.columns.add oColHired
oTable.DoAlter
oMSDEserver.disconnect
```

You can find this code on the CD-ROM in the file named `Ch 25\modifytab.vbs`.

Deleting tables

To delete a table with DMO, connect to the database, create a reference to the table that is to be deleted, and call the `remove` method.

```
dim oMSDEserver
set oMSDEserver = CreateObject("SQLDMO.SQLServer")

oMSDEserver.connect "0kh2h","sa",""
oMSDEserver.Databases("scheduling").Tables("Guide").remove
oMSDEserver.disconnect
```

You can find this code on the CD-ROM in the file named `Ch 25\deletetab.vbs`.

Creating user-defined data types

To create a user-defined data type (UDT) with DMO:

1. Instantiate a UserDefinedDataType object.
2. Set its `Name`, `BaseType`, `Length`, and `AllowNulls` properties. If the new type is derived from the Decimal base type, the `NumericPrecision` and `NumericScale` properties must also be set.
3. Connect to the server, obtain a reference to the appropriate database, and invoke the `add` method of the UserDefinedDatabases collection, passing the object that was created above.

The following code creates a user-defined data type called SpecialtyType that is based on the char data type. It has a length of five and allows nulls by default.

```
dim oMSDEserver
dim oUDDT
set oMSDEserver = CreateObject("SQLDMO.SQLServer")
set oUDDT = CreateObject("SQLDMO.UserDefinedDataType")

oUDDT.Name = "SpecialtyType"
oUDDT.BaseType = "char"
oUDDT.Length = 5
oUDDT.AllowNulls = true

oMSDEserver.connect "0kh2h","sa",""
```

```
oMSDEserver.Databases("scheduling") _
.UserDefinedDataTypes.add oUDDT
oMSDEserver.disconnect
```

You can find this code on the CD-ROM in the file named `Ch 25\createUDT.vbs`.

Deleting user-defined data types

To delete user-defined data types (UDTs), invoke the `remove` method of the UserDefinedDataType object that is to be deleted. Deletion can occur only if the data type is not in use. The `ListBoundColumns` method will identify any columns that are currently using the data type.

```
dim oMSDEserver
set oMSDEserver = CreateObject("SQLDMO.SQLServer")

oMSDEserver.connect "Okh2h","sa",""
oMSDEserver.Databases("scheduling")_
.UserDefinedDataTypes("SpecialtyType").remove
oMSDEserver.disconnect
```

You can find this code on the CD-ROM in the file named `Ch 25\deleteUDT.vbs`.

Summary

Tables are the most basic elements of a database. They store not only user data, but also system data that defines all other objects in the database. Tables are defined as a collection of columns that specify the type of data that can be added to the table. Other objects, such as triggers and constraints, can be added to a table to further restrict the manipulation of data. During normal operation, data is added to a table in the form of rows.

✦ ✦ ✦

CHAPTER 8

Ensuring Database Consistency

✦ ✦ ✦ ✦

In This Chapter

Keeping rows unique

Supplying default values

Creating relationships between tables

Using check constraints

✦ ✦ ✦ ✦

A major challenge for any database designer is to provide mechanisms for ensuring that all data in the database is always meaningful and consistent. Such a mechanism must monitor data anytime it is changed, whether new data is added or existing data modified or deleted. Programming these mechanisms into application software can be effective. However, there is always the danger that a user may find another way to access the database and thereby circumvent the controls. MSDE provides several methods of controlling data that can be defined as part of the database. These controls will always be enforced by MSDE without regard to the program being used to access the data or the user accessing it.

MSDE mechanisms fall into three categories: constraints, triggers, and objects. Constraints are part of the definition of a table. The two objects, the default object and the rule object, exist separately from the tables and must be bound to a table in order to be enforced for that table. Constraints are ANSI standard, while rule and default objects are not. Triggers, like constraints, are part of the definition of a table. Triggers are more flexible than constraints, rules, or defaults, but the additional flexibility comes at the expense of performance.

A discussion of the ANSI SQL standards can be found in Chapter 11, "Retrieving Data with SQL." Triggers are covered in Chapter 16, "Using Triggers to Enforce Data Integrity."

Constraints, rules, and defaults ensure data integrity in a variety of ways. They make certain that when data is entered into a table, it has an expected and meaningful value, for example, a person cannot be –21 years old. They guarantee that data that should be unique is unique, for example, there should be only one payroll check number 372. They can relate a row in one table to a row in another table in a meaningful way; for example, a dependent child must be dependent on someone, so the row representing the child should contain a value that identifies the responsible adult. They ensure that if a user fails to enter a value into a column, a reasonable default value is automatically entered, for example, a transaction date can default to the current day unless there is some reason for the user to change it. These are just a few of the ways that constraints, rules, and defaults can be used.

Understanding Constraints

Constraints are the ANSI standard mechanisms for controlling data entry and modification. In MSDE, they can be created at the same time as a table, or afterwards by modifying the table definition.

In MSDE, constraints are processed before a transaction begins. If an attempt is made to change data in a table that violates a constraint, the modification is aborted before the data is changed in the table. This can be of significant consequence. For example, if an inserted row violates constraints on a table, the insert triggers for the table will not fire because no data has been inserted. Also, application programs must be written with constraints in mind. If an application passes data to MSDE that violates a constraint, an error message will be passed back to the application program. The application must then provide the user with some kind of feedback to indicate why the transaction has not occurred.

Whenever possible, constraints should be given names to avoid MSDE's supplying a unique name that will be hard to read or remember. Naming and documenting constraints will significantly enhance future administration or modification of the database structure.

Using default constraints to provide values when the user doesn't

A default constraint is associated with a single column. It operates whenever a row is inserted and provides a value that will be automatically entered into the column if no value is provided.

Default constraints are particularly useful when nulls are not allowed in a column. They prevent users from having their data rejected and receiving an error message if they fail to supply a required value. Make sure that the default constraint supplies a reasonable value that won't surprise the user later.

The default constraint value inserted can be either a constant or a function. An example of a constant value would be a default constraint that automatically enters a zero if no value is provided for a numeric column. An example of a function would be the `User_Name()` function that provides the name of the user who inserted the row. This would be used in a char column.

Uniquely identifying rows with primary key constraint

The primary key constraint is used to identify the column or columns that uniquely identify the rows in a table. When a primary key constraint is added to a column, MSDE automatically creates an index on the column, which it uses to enforce uniqueness. If a user attempts to add a row to a table and the row has a value for its primary key that is already in use in the table, the insertion of the row will fail. The uniqueness of values in a primary key column is also enforced during modifications to the table. Any modification to a table that would cause a primary key value to become nonunique will fail.

The primary key constraint also identifies the primary key column in a table that is used by foreign key constraints, database diagrams, and in any other programs that must be able to identify the relationships between tables in a database.

There can be only a single primary key in a table, and a primary key does not allow any null values.

Some database management systems, particularly those that are file-based, use the primary key to determine the order of rows in the file or table. This is not true for MSDE. Logically, the rows in a table have no particular order, and physically, they are ordered only if a clustered index is created.

Relating tables with foreign key constraint

Foreign key constraints are used to create relationships between tables in the database. When a foreign key constraint is placed on a column, it must reference a specific column in another table. The column that it references must have either a primary key constraint or a unique constraint.

When an inserted row has a foreign key constraint, the value inserted into the column with the foreign key constraint will be compared to the reference column in another table. The insert will be able to proceed only if the value being inserted into the foreign key exists in the referenced table.

An example of a case in which a foreign key constraint might be used is a database that tracks purchase orders. In this database, one table, called Orders, contains the header information from the purchase order, including such information as the name and department of the person who created the purchase order, the date on which it was created, and the purchase order number.

Another table, called Line Items, contains rows corresponding to each of the line items from the purchase orders. In order to determine which line items correspond to which purchase orders, a column is included in the Line Items table that contains the purchase order number. Assuming that the purchase order number column in the Orders table is either a primary key or has a unique constraint, a foreign key constraint can be placed on the purchase order number column in the Line Items table. A purchase order line item can be entered into the Line Items table only if it has a valid, existing purchase order number that is already recorded in the Orders table.

When programs such as Enterprise Manager or Access create database diagrams, they determine the relationships between tables by examining which columns have foreign key constraints and which are primary keys. The program then draws a line between the table with the foreign key and the table with the referenced primary key.

Another program that uses this information is English Query, which comes with SQL Server. English Query converts normal English questions into SQL statements. In order to do this, it must understand the structure of the database, what kind of real-world objects are represented by the tables in the database, and the relationships between those objects. Using primary key and foreign key constraints is an easy way to document the relationships between these tables. For example, if the question, "What items were ordered on purchase order number 5275?" is being processed by English Query, it easily recognizes that the phrase "purchase order" refers to the Orders table, but it must also recognize the relationship between this table and the Line Items table in order to create a SQL statement that will bring back the appropriate line items.

Foreign key constraints, unlike primary key constraints and unique constraints, do not automatically create indexes. If a column with a foreign key constraint is frequently used to join tables, creating an index on the foreign key column can significantly improve the performance of the joins.

Providing built-in logic with check constraints

Check constraints allow values entered in a column to be verified with a logical expression. The logical expression used to check constraint is similar to the logical expression used in a `Where` clause of a `Select` statement. It can contain any number of conditions connected with Boolean operators (And, Or, or Not). A check constraint can contain a simple condition, such as a comparison with a constant to ensure that a column does not exceed a fixed maximum value. It can also contain a highly complex condition that involves multiple columns. For example, it could verify salary based on job description, seniority, and performance rating. Check constraints can even contain nested `Select` statements that will be executed for every value entered into the column. Multiple check constraints can affect the same column.

When using SQL to create check constraints, there is a slight (but crucial) difference in syntax for constraints that refer to a single column or multiple columns. The MSDE documentation calls a check constraint that refers to a single column a *column constraint* and a constraint that refers to multiple columns a *table constraint*.

Using unique constraints to prohibit duplicate values

The unique constraint enforces the uniqueness of values in a column or columns. For every unique constraint, MSDE automatically creates an index for the column or columns on which the constraint was placed. When any new row is inserted into a table with a unique constraint, the value provided for the column(s) that has the unique constraint will be compared to all other values to verify that it is not a duplicate. A duplicate will cause the insert to fail. The values in a column with a unique constraint are also monitored whenever a row is modified. If an attempt is made to modify a value in a column with a unique constraint such that the value would create a duplicate in the table, the modification will fail.

MSDE allows users to include nulls in columns with a unique constraint. However, the unique constraint recognizes the null as a value and will allow only a single row to have a null in the unique column. Normally, this behavior is not very helpful and can even be confusing, so careful consideration should be made before allowing nulls in a unique column.

Understanding Rules and Defaults

Rules and defaults are independent objects that are created within MSDE databases. They are associated with columns and, like constraints, evaluate changes that are made to data.

Neither rules nor defaults are ANSI standard. They are provided primarily to make MSDE compatible with earlier versions of Microsoft SQL Server. They can also provide additional flexibility if user-defined data types will be used extensively in a database.

Rules

A rule is an object that defines a condition using a single variable and any other expression syntax that is valid in the `Where` clause of a `Select` statement. These are similar to the expressions that are used in check constraints, except they are not as flexible because they cannot refer to other columns or tables. When rules are violated by an attempted data modification, the modification is aborted.

Default objects

Default objects consist of a name and a value that will be used when a row is inserted into a table. The `default` value is used when an inserted row does not supply a value for the column to which the default has been bound. The `default` value can be a constant, like the number zero, or a string, like 'Unknown' or 'None'. A `default` value can also be a system function, like `User_Name()`, which will provide the name of the user who is inserting the row.

Binding rules and defaults

Since rules and defaults are independent objects in the database, they must be associated with, or bound to, columns in tables before they can be enforced. This is done either directly, by binding the rule or default to the column, or indirectly, by binding the rule or default to a user-defined data type. When the latter course of action is chosen, the rule or default is enforced for all columns in which the data type is used.

Columns

When a rule or default is bound to a column, it remains bound until it is explicitly unbound or until the table is deleted. Rules and defaults that are bound cannot be deleted.

User-defined data types

A default or rule bound to a user-defined data type automatically affects all tables in which the data type is already in use, as well as any tables in which the data type is used in the future. A rule or default can be bound with the `futureonly` option such that it does not affect tables that have previously been defined with the data type, but only tables that are defined with the data type in the future.

Conversely, when a default or rule is unbound from a data type, it can automatically unbind from all tables in which that data type is in use or remain bound to tables to which it is already bound. In either case, when unbound from a data type, a rule or default is no longer enforced for tables to which the data type is bound in the future.

Adequate documentation of the use of rules and defaults is essential because of the complexity of the binding and unbinding behavior. In addition to thorough documentation, the behavior can be simplified by avoiding the use of the `futureonly` option.

Creating, Modifying, and Deleting Constraints, Rules, and Defaults

The full range of management tools is available for managing constraints: Enterprise Manager, Access, Visual Studio, SQL, and DMO. Access and Visual Studio have no mechanism for working with rules and defaults.

Managing constraints, rules, and defaults with Enterprise Manager, Visual Studio, and Access

The Table Designer tool is used to manage constraints in Enterprise Manager, Access, or Visual Studio. To display the Table Designer in Enterprise Manager, right-click on a table in the Tables container and choose Design Table. Figure 8-1 shows Enterprise Manager with the Table Designer at the bottom of the screen, as well as the menu that is displayed after right-clicking the Guide table.

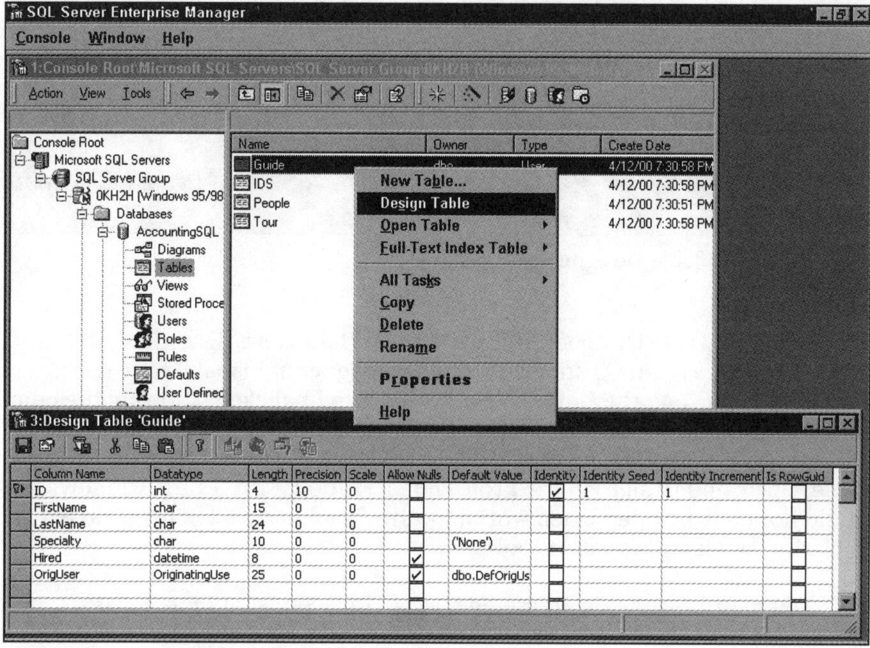

Figure 8-1: The Table Designer in Enterprise Manager

To display the Table Designer in Access, select a table and click Design — or right-click on the table and choose Design View. Figure 8-2 shows the Table Designer in Access, as well as the menu displayed by right-clicking the Guide table. Notice the Design item in the button bar.

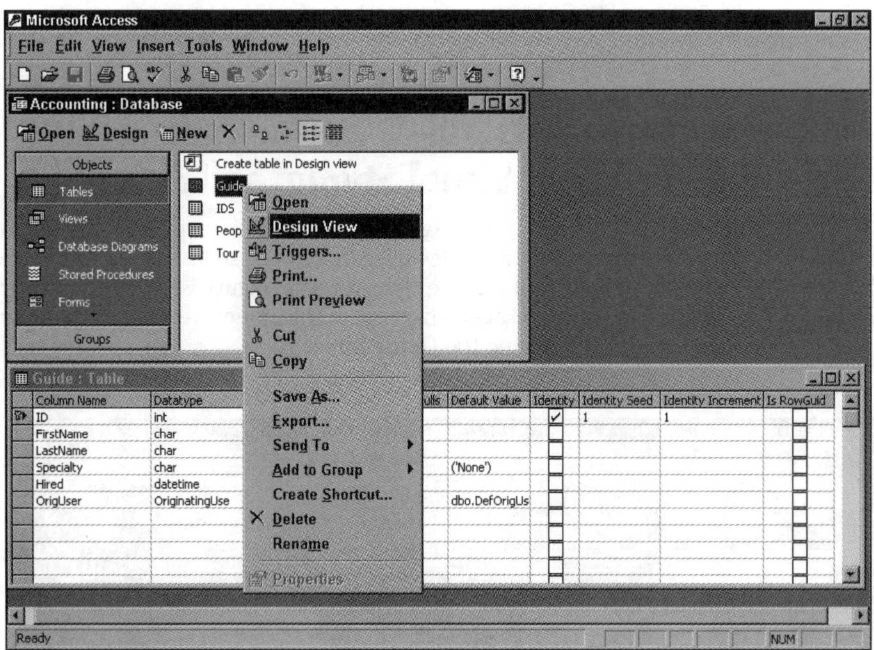

Figure 8-2: The Table Designer in Access

To display the Table Designer in Visual Studio Data View, right-click a table and choose Design. Figure 8-3 shows the Table Designer in Visual Basic. The Data View window is open, and the Guide table has been right-clicked, showing the context-sensitive menu with the Design item highlighted. Note that this figure shows the Enterprise Edition of Visual Basic; the menu would lack the first three items (New Table, Open, and Design) in the Professional Edition. Most of the windows that would normally be open when working with Visual Basic have been closed in order to clarify the view of the data tools.

You must have the Enterprise Edition of Visual Studio in order to view or modify constraints. The Professional Edition does not have a Design button.

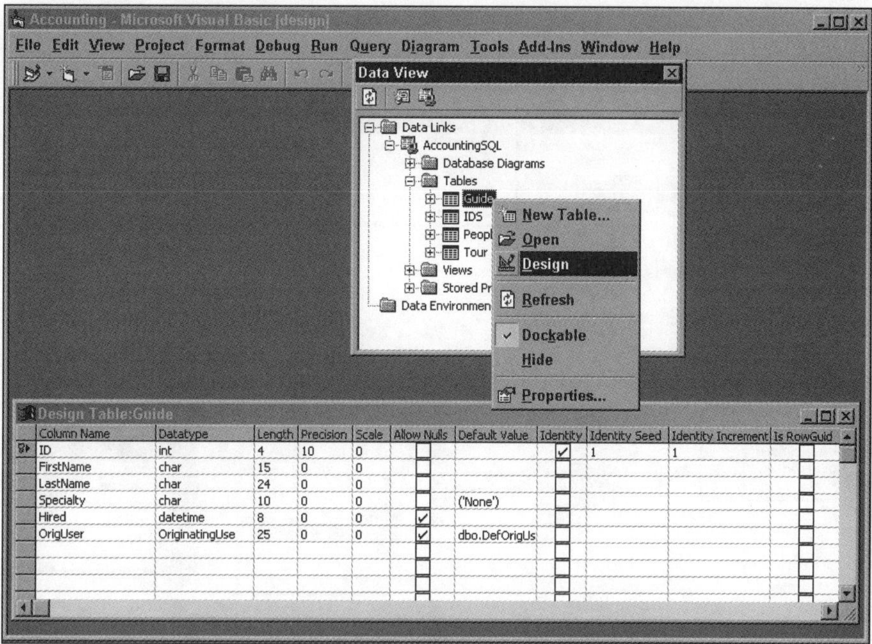

Figure 8-3: The Table Designer in Visual Studio (Visual Basic)

Constraints can also be managed from a database diagram that contains the tables of interest. Database diagrams can be opened or created from the Database Diagrams container in Access, Visual Studio Data View, or Enterprise Manager. Figure 8-4 shows a database diagram of the Northwind database. All of the tables are displayed with lines showing relationships among the tables. The graphical interface of the database diagram is identical in Enterprise Manager, Access, and Visual Studio.

Table Designer

To add a default constraint in the Table Designer, enter the desired constant or function in the `default` value column of the appropriate row.

To set the primary key constraint in the Table Designer:

1. Select the row or rows that are to become the primary key.
2. Verify that the Allow Nulls check box is closed.
3. Right-click the selected rows and choose primary key, or click the set primary key button on the button bar at the top of the dialog box.

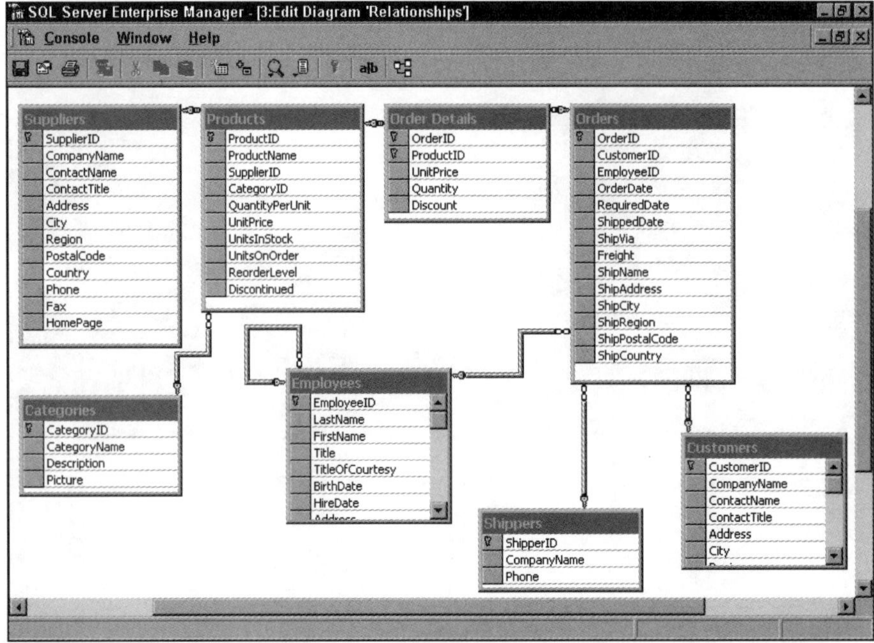

Figure 8-4: A database diagram of the Northwind database in Enterprise Manager

Both of these actions act as toggles, so removing a primary key can be accomplished by repeating the same procedure.

Foreign keys can be displayed from the Table and Index Properties dialog box (the second button from the left on the button bar of the Table Designer). Click the Relationships tab to display any foreign keys. The Table and Index Properties dialog box for the Guide table in the Accounting database is shown in Figure 8-5. Additional foreign keys may be added to tables with the following steps:

1. Click the New button.
2. Select a column from the primary key table.
3. Select a foreign key table.
4. Select a column in the foreign key table that has the same data type as the column selected in the primary key table.
5. Optionally modify the name of the relationship. A default name is automatically assigned that begins with FX, followed by the names of the foreign and primary key tables, separated with underscore characters.
6. Select any options including whether updates and deletes should be automatically cascaded.

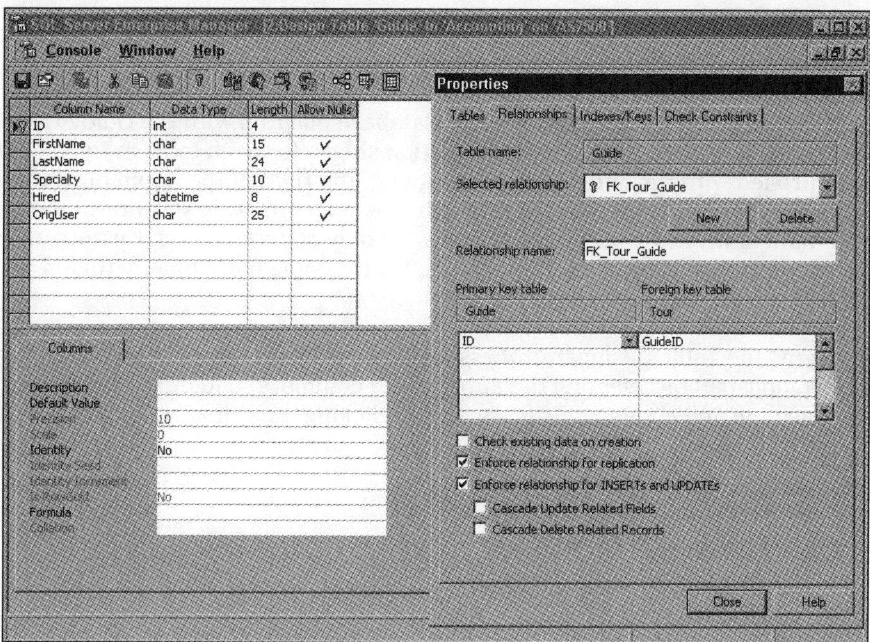

Figure 8-5: The Relationships tab of the Table and Index Properties dialog box

Check constraints are also controlled from the Table and Index Properties dialog box under the Check Constraints tab. This dialog box is shown in Figure 8-6. The following list provides instructions for managing constraints from the Table and Index Properties dialog box:

- ✦ **Create a new constraint.** Click the New button, type a valid expression (column names can be used), and name the constraint.
- ✦ **Delete a constraint.** Select it from the Selected Constraint drop-down list and click the Delete button.
- ✦ **Modify an existing constraint.** Select it from the drop-down list, make any changes to the expression, and click Close.
- ✦ **Add a unique constraint.** Click New, choose a column from the drop-down list, click the Create Unique check box (leaving the Constraint Option button selected), and click Close.

Changes that are made in any of the Table Designer dialog boxes are not actually made to the table until the Table Designer is closed or the Save button is clicked. Changes may be backed out by closing the Table Designer and choosing not to save changes.

Database diagrams

To set a default value for a column from a database diagram, right-click on the title of the table that must be changed, select Column Properties, and type a value in the Default column. Figure 8-6 shows a database diagram with the Guide table in the background. The amount of information shown for each table in the diagram is controlled with the Show button, located to the right of the Zoom button, which looks like a magnifying glass. The Guide table in Figure 8-6 is showing standard information, while the Tour table is showing only column names. Custom views can be defined, making it possible to display the same functionality that is available in the Table Designer.

Mirroring the Table Designer process, setting a primary key in a database diagram is accomplished by selecting the appropriate column(s) and either right-clicking the selection and choosing Primary Key or clicking the Primary Key button on the Database Diagram button bar.

To create a foreign key in a database diagram:

1. Click on the gray selection box to the left of the column that is to have the foreign key and, without releasing the mouse button, drag and drop over the table that is to be referenced.
2. A Create Relationship dialog box is displayed with the computer's estimation about the column to be referenced in the primary key table. Verify that the foreign key and primary key columns are correct.
3. Select any desired options and click OK.

To create a check constraint:

1. Right-click the appropriate table and select Properties.
2. Select the Table tab.
3. Fill in the expression and name for the desired constraint in the bottom section of the dialog box. (Modifications and deletions may also be made from this dialog box.)

Figure 8-6 shows the Check Constraints tab of the Table and Index Properties dialog box. The `CK_GuideSpec` check constraint is displayed, which allows only the values `Spinning`, `Weaving`, or `Ahusbandry` in the Specialty column.

To create a unique constraint:

1. Right-click the appropriate table and select Properties.
2. Choose the Indexes/Keys tab and click the New button.
3. Select the Create Unique check box and click Close.

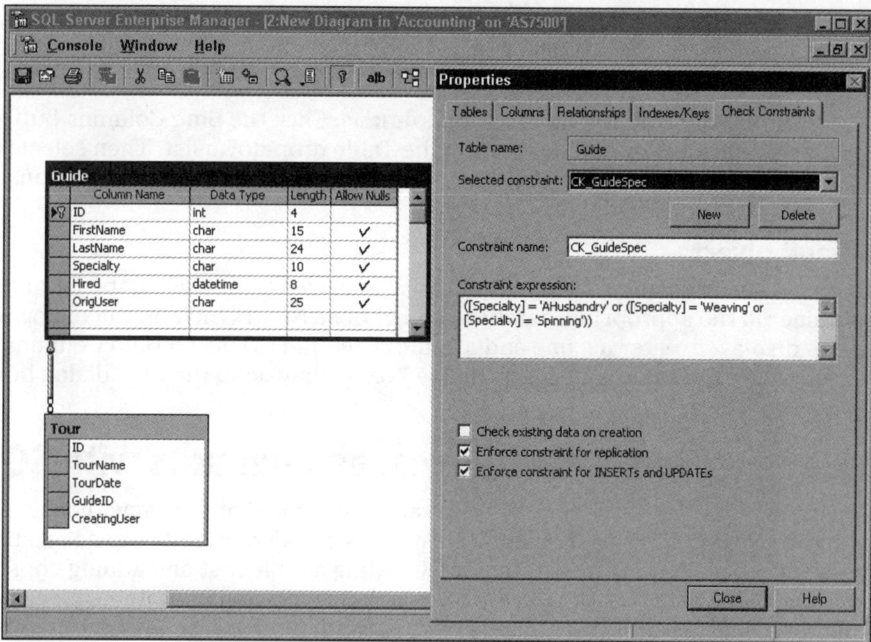

Figure 8-6: Database diagram with Table and Index Properties dialog box

Rule object

To create a rule object in Enterprise Manager:

1. Right-click the Rules container within a database and select New Rule.
2. Enter a new name for the rule.
3. Type the expression that defines the rule in the section labeled Text.

The expression used in step three can be any valid SQL expression that evaluates to `True` or `False`. It can contain a single variable in the form `@variablename`. This variable represents the value that is being tested by the rule.

Expressions can easily be written and tested for use in a rule by creating a `Select` statement and placing the expression in the `Where` clause. Instead of a variable name, use the appropriate column name from a table. When the `Select` works properly, copy the expression from the `Where` clause into the rule and replace the column name with a variable name.

When a rule is initially created, the Bind UDTs and Bind Columns buttons are not enabled.

- ✦ **Enabling Bind UDTs and Bind Columns.** Right-click on the rule that has just been created and select Properties. The same dialog box used to create the rule is displayed and the Bind buttons in question are enabled.

- **Binding the rule to a user-defined data type.** Click the Bind UDTs button and click in the check box next to any UDTs to which the rule should be bound. `Futureonly` may optionally be selected as well.
- **Binding the rule to one or more columns.** Click the Bind Columns button and select the appropriate table from the Table drop-down list. Then select the column(s) to which the rule should be bound and click the Add button.

Default object

To create a new default object in Enterprise Manager, right-click in the Defaults container in the appropriate database and choose New Default. In the dialog box that is displayed, enter a name and a value. The Bind UDTs and Bind Columns buttons work the same way in this dialog box as they do in the Rule dialog box.

Managing constraints, rules, and defaults with SQL

Constraints exist as properties of tables and are created at the same time as a table with the `Create Table` statement. Constraints can also be added to an existing table with the `Alter Table` statement. Creating a table first and adding constraints later can make the process of writing and debugging complex statements easier. Rules and defaults both have a `Create` command, but must be bound to a data type or column with a stored procedure.

Adding constraints during table creation (Create Table)

The basic syntax for the `Create Table` command was given in Chapter 7. That syntax diagram indicated that column constraints could appear as a component of a column definition and that a table constraint could appear in the list of columns (separated from column definitions by commas). The only difference between the two types of constraints is that a column constraint refers to a single column, while a table constraint refers to more than one. The syntax for each type of constraint follows.

```
<column_constraint> ::= [CONSTRAINT constraint_name]
{
     [ NULL | NOT NULL ]
     | [    { PRIMARY KEY | UNIQUE }
         [CLUSTERED | NONCLUSTERED]
         [WITH FILLFACTOR = fillfactor]
         [ON {filegroup | DEFAULT} ]]
      ]
     | [    [FOREIGN KEY]
         REFERENCES ref_table [(ref_column) ]
         [NOT FOR REPLICATION]
      ]
     | CHECK [NOT FOR REPLICATION]
         (logical_expression)
}
```

Null and Not Null prohibit and permit null values, respectively, and can be specified only as a column constraint, not a table constraint. Primary Key and Unique create the corresponding constraint, which creates an underlying index. The properties of the underlying index are controlled with the next three sets of parameters: clustered or nonclustered, fillfactor, and On. These are covered in Chapter 9. Foreign Key creates a link with the specified table and column. If no column is specified, the table's Primary Key is used. Check creates a check constraint with the specified logical expression. Foreign Key and check constraints can be created Not For Replication, which means that they will not be enabled for data that is received through the replication process (since it is presumably checked at its server of origin). These constraints will be enabled only for data received from a user connection.

```
<table_constraint> ::= [CONSTRAINT constraint_name]
{
    [ { PRIMARY KEY | UNIQUE }
        [ CLUSTERED | NONCLUSTERED]
        { ( column[,...n] ) }
        [ WITH FILLFACTOR = fillfactor]
        [ON {filegroup | DEFAULT} ]
    ]
    | FOREIGN KEY
            [(column[,...n])]
            REFERENCES ref_table [(ref_column[,...n])]
            [NOT FOR REPLICATION]
    | CHECK [NOT FOR REPLICATION]
        (search_conditions)
}
```

For each table constraint, the column(s) to which the constraint should apply must be specified.

Adding constraints to an existing table (Alter Table)

The Alter Table command uses the same syntax for constraints as the Create Table. Column constraints can be added with a new column. Table constraints can be added by themselves. Null and Not Null can be specified as part of the Alter Column clause.

Check and No Check parameters in the Alter Table statement can be used when a new constraint is added to an existing table. Specifying Check will enforce the constraint on data that exists in the table. If any data fails to comply with the constraint, the constraint creation will fail. If all data is known to comply with the constraint, it can be created with No Check, which will speed up the creation process.

Constraints can also be disabled and reenabled with the Alter Table command using Check and No Check and the constraint name or the keyword All, which will affect all constraints simultaneously.

Rules

The syntax to create a rule is as follows:

```
CREATE RULE rule_name AS expression
```

The rule_name can be any valid identifier. The expression can be any expression that could be used in the Where clause of a Select statement, except that it may not reference columns. A single variable can be used in the expression. This variable represents the value that is being tested, (for example, the value from the row that is being inserted or updated).

If the expression evaluates to True, the insert or update will be performed; otherwise, it will be aborted.

Once a rule has been created, it must be bound to a column or user-defined data type. To perform the binding, use the following syntax:

```
sp_bindrule rule_name, object, ['futureonly']
```

Use the rule_name that was assigned when the default was created. The object is either a column or a user-defined data type. Futureonly is a flag that can be used only when binding to a data type. If omitted, the rule will be used on all tables to which the data type has been or will be applied. If Futureonly is included, the rule will not be used on tables that have previously been defined with the data type.

Both Create Rule and sp_bindrule must be the first command in a batch.

The following example creates a rule and binds it to the Specialty column in the Guide table (the code to create this table was presented in Chapter 7):

```
Create Rule SpecialtyRule As @spec in
('Spinning', 'Weaving', 'AHusbandry')
go
sp_bindrule SpecialtyRule, [Guide.Specialty]
```

The syntax to delete a rule is as follows:

```
DROP RULE rule_name
```

Before a rule can be deleted, it must be unbound from any data types and columns. The syntax to unbind a rule is as follows:

```
sp_unbindrule object, ['futureonly']
```

Futureonly can be specified only if unbinding from a data type. If specified, the rule will be unbound from the data type but will remain bound to any tables in which that data type was in use. A rule that is left bound to a table in this way must be specifically unbound from the table before it can be deleted.

The following script unbinds and deletes the rule that was created in the previous example.

```
sp_unbindrule [Guide.Specialty]
drop rule Specialtyrule
```

Defaults

The syntax to create a default is as follows:

```
CREATE DEFAULT default_name AS expression
```

The `default_name` can be any valid identifier. The expression cannot contain the names of any database objects, such as tables or columns.

After a default is created, it must be bound to a column or user-defined data type. To perform the binding, use the following syntax:

```
sp_bindefault default_name, object, ['futureonly']
```

Use the `default_name` that was assigned when the default was created. The object is either a column or a user-defined data type. `Futureonly` is a flag that can be used only when binding to a data type. If it is omitted, then the default will be used on all tables to which the data type has been or will be used. If `Futureonly` is included, the default will not be used on tables that have previously been defined with the data type, only on those that are subsequently defined.

Both `Create Default` and `sp_bindefault` must be the first command in a batch.

The following example creates a user-defined data type, creates a default, and binds the default to the data type:

```
sp_addtype OriginatingUser, 'char(25)'
Go
CREATE DEFAULT DefOrigUser AS User_Name()
Go
sp_bindefault DefOrigUser, OriginatingUser
```

The `OriginatingUser` data type can be used in all tables in a database to record the user that originally inserted each row.

The syntax to delete a default is as follows:

```
DROP DEFAULT default_name
```

Before a default can be deleted, it must be unbound from any data types and columns. The syntax to unbind a default is as follows:

```
sp_unbindefault object, ['futureonly']
```

`Futureonly` works that same way with default as it does with rules in that a default can be unbound from a data type and left bound to table where the data type was in use.

The following script unbinds and deletes the default that was created in the previous example.

```
sp_unbindefault OriginatingUser
drop default DefOrigUser
```

Managing constraints, rules, and defaults with DMO

Constraints, rules, and defaults can all be managed with DMO. The constraints are not organized together in the object model; for example, default constraints are properties of a column, foreign and primary keys are contained in a collection that is a property of the table, and check constraints are direct properties of the table.

Default constraints

The DMO hierarchy for default constraints is as follows:

```
Server
    Databases
        Database
            Tables
                Table
                Columns
                        Column
                            DRIDefault
```

The DRIDefault object is automatically created as a property of each column. To set the default, acquire a reference to a column, and then set the text property of the DRIDefault object associated with the column. The value should be a string. In the following VBScript example, there are double quotes to indicate a string to VBScript and single quotes to indicate a string to MSDE. This code creates a default constraint of `'None'` for the Specialty column in the Guide table.

```
dim oMSDEserver
dim oTable
set oMSDEserver = CreateObject("SQLDMO.SQLServer")

oMSDEserver.connect "Okh2h","sa",""
set oTable = _ oMSDEserver.Databases("scheduling").Tables("Guide")
oTable.BeginAlter
oTable.columns("Specialty").DRIDefault.text = "'None'"
oTable.DoAlter
oMSDEserver.disconnect
```

You can find this code on the CD-ROM in the file named `Ch 8\DefConst.vbs`.

Primary and foreign keys

The DMO hierarchy for primary and foreign key constraints (omitting the top four levels) is as follows:

```
Table
    Keys
    Key
            KeyColumns
            ReferencedColumns
```

The next code sample sets the ID column as the primary key on the Guide table. It instantiates a Key object, sets the Type property to 1 (1 is used for primary key, 2 is used for unique constraint, and 3 is used for foreign keys), and adds the name of the column to the KeyColumns collection. Additional columns could have been added if the primary key were to have been multipart. In that case, the order in which they were added would have been critical: the first column added would have had the highest precedence. After any columns are added to the KeyColumns collection, a connection is opened to the server, a reference is acquired to the table, and the Key object is added to the Keys collection.

```
dim oMSDEserver
dim oTable
dim oPrimaryKey

set oMSDEserver = CreateObject("SQLDMO.SQLServer")
set oPrimaryKey = CreateObject("SQLDMO.Key")

oPrimaryKey.Type = 1
oPrimaryKey.KeyColumns.add ("ID")

oMSDEserver.connect "Okh2h","sa",""
set oTable = _ oMSDEserver.Databases("scheduling").Tables("Guide")
oTable.BeginAlter
oTable.keys.add (oPrimaryKey)
oTable.DoAlter
oMSDEserver.disconnect
```

You can find this code on the CD-ROM in the file named `Ch 8\SetPrimaryKey.vbs`.

Creating a foreign key requires at least two tables: one containing the foreign key column and one that has a primary key or unique constraint to which the foreign key refers. The following code creates a table called Tours in the scheduling database for the foreign key example that follows:

```
dim oMSDEserver
dim oTable
dim oColID
dim oColTourName
dim oColDate
dim oColGuideID
dim oCreatingUser

set oMSDEserver = CreateObject("SQLDMO.SQLServer")
set oTable = CreateObject("SQLDMO.Table")
set oColID = CreateObject("SQLDMO.Column")
set oColTourName = CreateObject("SQLDMO.Column")
set oColDate = CreateObject("SQLDMO.Column")
set oColGuideID = CreateObject("SQLDMO.Column")
set oCreatingUser = CreateObject("SQLDMO.Column")

oColID.Name = "ID"
oColID.DataType = "int"
oColID.Identity = true
oColID.AllowNulls = false

oColTourName.Name = "TourName"
oColTourName.DataType = "char"
oColTourName.Length = 15

oColDate.Name = "TourDate"
oColDate.DataType = "datetime"

oColGuideID.Name = "GuideID"
oColGuideID.DataType = "int"
oColGuideID.Length = 10

oCreatingUser.Name = "CreatingUser"
oCreatingUser.DataType = "char"
oCreatingUser.Length = 25

oTable.Name = "Tour"
oTable.Columns.add (oColID)
oTable.Columns.add (oColTourName)
oTable.Columns.add (oColDate)
oTable.Columns.add (oColGuideID)
oTable.Columns.add (oCreatingUser)

oMSDEserver.connect "0kh2h","sa",""
oMSDEserver.Databases("scheduling").Tables.add (oTable)
oMSDEserver.disconnect
```

You can find this code on the CD-ROM in the file named `Ch 8\CreateTourTab.vbs`.

A foreign key's `Type` property must be set to 3. The column to which the foreign key constraint will be applied must be added to the KeyColumns collection. The table that contains the primary key for the unique column that is being referenced by the foreign key must be set to a `ReferencedTable` property. And finally, the primary key or unique column in the reference table must be added to the Referenced Columns collection. The Key object can be added to the Keys collection of the appropriate table.

```
dim oMSDEserver
dim oTable
dim oForeignKey

set oMSDEserver = CreateObject("SQLDMO.SQLServer")
set oForeignKey = CreateObject("SQLDMO.Key")

oForeignKey.Type = 3
oForeignKey.KeyColumns.add ("GuideID")
oForeignKey.ReferencedTable = "Guide"
oForeignKey.ReferencedColumns.add ("ID")

oMSDEserver.connect "Okh2h","sa",""
set oTable = oMSDEserver.Databases("scheduling").Tables("Tour")
oTable.BeginAlter
oTable.keys.add (oForeignKey)
oTable.DoAlter
oMSDEserver.disconnect
```

You can find this code on the CD-ROM in the file named `Ch 8\SetForeignKey.vbs`.

Check constraints

The DMO hierarchy for check constraints (omitting the top four levels) is as follows:

```
Table
    Checks
        Check
```

To create a check constraint:

1. Instantiate a Check object.
2. Set its `Name` property to something recognizable.
3. Set its `Text` property to be a string that is the logical expression to be tested when data is changed.

The following sample tests the tour date to verify that a past date cannot be entered.

```
dim oMSDEserver
dim oTable
dim oCheck

set oMSDEserver = CreateObject("SQLDMO.SQLServer")
set oCheck = CreateObject("SQLDMO.Check")

oCheck.Name = "CurrentDate"
oCheck.Text = "TourDate >= GetDate()"

oMSDEserver.connect "Okh2h","sa",""
set oTable = oMSDEserver.Databases("scheduling").Tables("Tour")
oTable.BeginAlter
oTable.Checks.add (oCheck)
oTable.DoAlter
oMSDEserver.disconnect
```

You can find this code on the CD-ROM in the file named `Ch 8\CheckConst.vbs`.

Unique constraints

The DMO hierarchy for unique constraints is identical to that used for primary keys (omitting the top four levels):

```
Table
    Keys
    Key
            KeyColumns
```

Unique constraints are created in much the same way as primary key constraints except that the `Type` property of the Key object is set to 2.

```
dim oMSDEserver
dim oTable
dim oUniqueKey

set oMSDEserver = CreateObject("SQLDMO.SQLServer")
set oUniqueKey = CreateObject("SQLDMO.Key")

oUniqueKey.Type = 2
oUniqueKey.KeyColumns.add ("TourDate")

oMSDEserver.connect "Okh2h","sa",""
set oTable = oMSDEserver.Databases("scheduling").Tables("Tour")
oTable.BeginAlter
oTable.Keys.add (oUniqueKey)
oTable.DoAlter
oMSDEserver.disconnect
```

Rules

The DMO hierarchy for Rules is as follows:

```
Server
    Databases
        Database
            Rules
                Rule
```

To create a rule:

1. Instantiate a Rule object and set the `Name` property.
2. Set the `Text` property to a string representing the logical expression, using a single variable (any name will do) to represent the input value that is being checked.
3. Add the Rule object to the Rules collection of the database.
4. Call the `BindToColumn` method of the rule, passing the table and column to which it should be bound.

```
dim oMSDEserver
dim oDB
dim oRule

set oMSDEserver = CreateObject("SQLDMO.SQLServer")
set oRule = CreateObject("SQLDMO.Rule")

oRule.Name = "SpecRule"
oRule.Text = "@spec in ('Spinning', 'Weaving', 'AHusbandry')"

oMSDEserver.connect "Okh2h","sa",""
set oDB = oMSDEserver.Databases("scheduling")
oDB.Rules.add (oRule)
oDB.Rules("SpecRule").BindToColumn "Guide","Specialty"
oMSDEserver.disconnect
```

You can find this code on the CD-ROM in the file named `Ch 08\Script Rule.vbs`.

Defaults

The DMO hierarchy for defaults is as follows:

```
Server
    Databases
        Database
            Defaults
                Default
```

To create and bind a default:

1. Instantiate a Default object.
2. Set the Name property for the Default object.
3. Set the Text property for the Default object to a constant or system function to be used when a user inserts a null.
4. Call the Add method of the Defaults collection in the appropriate database, passing the Default object.
5. Call the BindToColumn method of the Default object in the Defaults collection.

```
dim oMSDEserver
dim oDB
dim oDefault

set oMSDEserver = CreateObject("SQLDMO.SQLServer")
set oDefault = CreateObject("SQLDMO.Default")

oDefault.Name = "DefOrigUser2"
oDefault.Text = "User_Name()"

oMSDEserver.connect "0kh2h","sa",""
set oDB = oMSDEserver.Databases("scheduling")
oDB.Defaults.add (oDefault)
oDB.Defaults("DefOrigUser2").BindToColumn "Tour","CreatingUser"
oMSDEserver.disconnect
```

You can find this code on the CD-ROM in the file named Ch 8\DefaultObj.vbs.

Summary

MSDE has extremely powerful built-in capabilities to ensure that the data in tables is good data. The definition of *good* will naturally vary, so the tools that enforce data quality are very flexible. Most of the available tools, the constraints, are ANSI standard. The other tools, rules, and defaults are specific to MSDE and SQL Server and can serve some purposes for which constraints are inadequate. Proper planning of constraints during database design can ease the burden of application design and provide a higher level of consistency for the database.

✦ ✦ ✦

CHAPTER 9

Improving Performance with Indexes

✦ ✦ ✦ ✦

In This Chapter

The effect of indexes on performance

Clustered indexes

Nonclustered indexes

Details of data modification

Managing indexes

✦ ✦ ✦ ✦

Indexes in MSDE serve to improve performance. A database with properly designed indexes can outperform a database without indexes by several orders of magnitude with no perceived functional difference between the two databases. Users of a database will often be unaware of an index's existence in a database. In fact, programmers who write database applications may not know if indexes will later be created to improve the performance of their application. Like any powerful tool, an index in the wrong hands can be deadly. If indexes are not carefully designed and maintained, they can ruin the performance of a database.

Disk access is one of the most important factors in determining overall performance for any database management system, so any mechanism that can reduce the number of disk reads will tend to increase throughput. Indexes reduce the number of pages that must be read from the disk by providing an efficient mechanism for locating a particular row or range of rows. They also significantly reduce the work that MSDE must perform when data is requested in sorted order. If an index exists that represents the requested order, the rows have only to be read; they don't have to be both read and sorted. Finally, indexes improve performance when they cover a query. Each index contains a sorted list of all of the values from the column it represents. If a query requests only values that exist in the index, the values can be read directly from the index, bypassing the data pages that store the entire rows.

How MSDE Locates Data

Chapter 7 described the structure of tables in MSDE. Data is stored in rows that are organized into 8K pages. The pages are identified as part of a particular table by a bitmap, the Index Allocation Map (called an IAM whether or not there is an index). So, MSDE knows which pages belong to which table, but how does it go about finding a particular row in the table? The process varies depending on whether or not MSDE uses an index.

Without an index: scanning a table

If a table has no index or if the query optimizer decides not to use an index, the table is scanned. MSDE scans by reading each table page individually. The order in which the pages are read is not related to the data contained on the pages. MSDE must read each page until it finds the page containing the pertinent data. If the requested data makes up a large percentage of the table, or if the table is small, then scanning all of its pages is efficient, and the query optimizer will choose not to use indexes even if they exist.

For example, if a table contains rows that represent people and the distribution of male and female is about even, then any query requesting all rows that represent females will have to access most or all of the pages in the table. The likelihood that any page needs to be read depends on the size of the rows, as each row has a 1-in-2 chance of representing a female. With smaller rows, more chances exist for a female to be represented on a page.

If a query is run requesting rows that make up only a small percentage of a table, then scanning every page becomes inefficient because the likelihood that a particular page has the requested data is low and most of the reads are wasted.

With an index: searching a B-Tree

In its essence, an index is an ordered list of values with pointers to the location of the information associated with those values. The pointers are the page numbers on which the words are located, and the order of the list is alphabetical. In an MSDE database, an index can be created on any column in a table, and an ordered list of all the distinct values from that column will be created with pointers to the database pages on which the values exist.

In MSDE 2000, an index can be created in either ascending or descending order. Select the order that will correspond to the primary anticipated use of the table. The order can always be changed later when the index is rebuilt as part of normal maintenance.

Once an ordered list of values exists, it is usually faster to look in that list than it is to scan through each individual row in a table. This is true both when retrieving information in a specific order and when searching for an individual row or group of rows. The ordered list of values will be smaller than the table itself because it contains only the values from the indexed column and pointers for each value to the location of the row or rows that contain that value. Less time will be spent on the scanning task.

Ordered list indexes save a significant amount of time and processing when processing queries that require a sorted order. For example, if a query is submitted to MSDE for a list of people ordered alphabetically by their last names, an index on the last name column will allow the system to look up each row in the index, find a pointer to the page on which the row exists, and retrieve the row. As the process moves through the index, sorted output is created.

A simple ordered list is not the most efficient structure when looking for a particular item, so MSDE uses an enhancement of an ordered list, called a Balanced Tree (B-Tree). A B-Tree consists of multiple levels. The lowest level (called the leaf level) is essentially a sorted list of values. The higher, nonleaf levels are sorted lists of the first value on each page in the next level down. Nonleaf levels act like the entries at the top of the page in a dictionary. When searching for an entry in the dictionary, determining what page a particular entry is on is easily accomplished by comparing it to the entries at the top of the pages. The query processor performs a similar process when searching for a value in an index.

Figure 9-1 shows a representation of part of an index. Each box in the figure represents a page in the database. Since every page in a database is numbered, there is an arbitrary number just above the left side of each page. The bottom row of pages (714–718) contains an ordered list of first names. This bottom row is the leaf level of the index. The ellipses next to each name in the leaf level represent some way to get to the rest of the information in each row of the table (presumably last names and other information about each person). The mechanism used to find the rest of the data varies depending on whether the index is clustered or nonclustered.

The row of pages just above the leaf level consists of an ordered list of the first entry from each page in the level below. So, page 719 contains the first entry for pages 714–716, as well as pointers to those pages. The pointers in this case are the page numbers. Page 720 finishes the second level with the first entries and pointers to pages 717 and 718. A B-Tree must always have a single node at the top (root) level. Nodes are a generic term for data containers in a B-Tree. In MSDE, nodes are always 8K pages. The root level in Figure 9-1 is page 721.

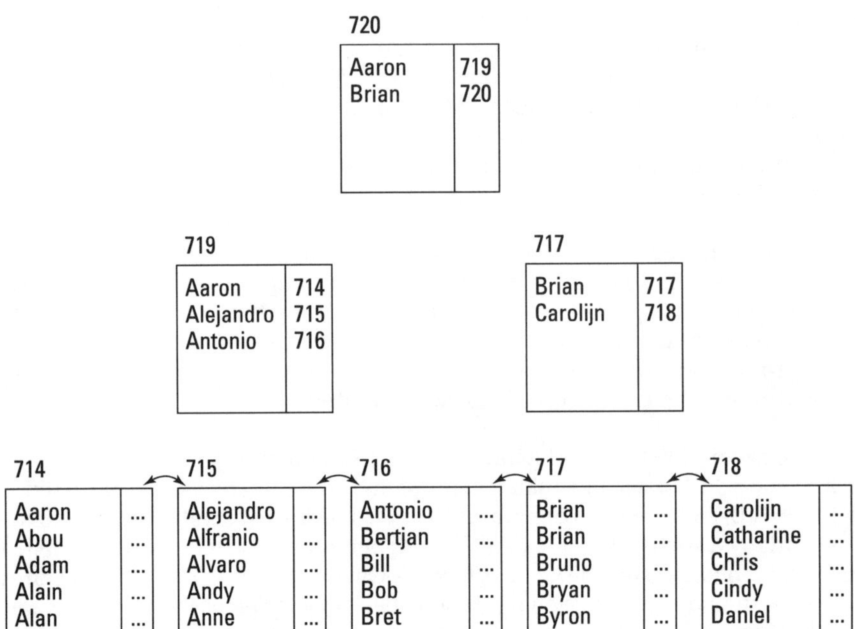

Figure 9-1: Generic representation of an index

Given the B-Tree structure in Figure 9-1, it is possible to find any individual name by reading exactly three pages: the root page, one page from the second level, and one page from the leaf level. For example, suppose a query requested the row that contains the name 'Bob.' MSDE will read the root page and begin comparing the requested value with each value in the page. When it finds a value that is greater than the requested value, it will follow the pointer from the previous value and repeat the process on the new page until it reaches the leaf level in the index.

In the example, the first value read from the root page is 'Aaron.' 'Bob' is greater than or equal to 'Aaron,' so the next value is read. 'Bob' is not greater than or equal to 'Brian,' so the previous pointer (the one associated with 'Aaron') is followed. This pointer contains the page number 719. Page 719 is read and the process begins again. 'Bob' is once again compared to 'Aaron,' to 'Alejandro,' and to 'Antonio.' It is greater than all of these values, so the query processor follows the last pointer on the page, which brings it to page 716. Since page 716 is a leaf level page, the value 'Bob' must be on that page. Examination of the figure confirms this.

The index shown in Figure 9-1 requires exactly three pages to be read to find any value in the ordered list. That doesn't seem like great performance considering that the leaf level contains only five pages. However, the figure contains only a fragment of any index and doesn't represent the true shape of a complete index. In an MSDE database, where each page is 8K, there would be many more values. For an index on a column that contains first names, a page could accommodate about 230 index entries (8060 bytes per page/35 bytes per value including overhead). So a two-level index would have one page at the root level and could have up to 230 pages at the leaf level. A three-level index would have one page at the root level, 230 pages at the intermediate level, and 52,900 pages at the leaf level. And this index would still require only three page reads in order to find any single value. That is a significant savings compared to searching each of 52,900 pages (or even half of this number).

Choosing the Right Type of Index

There are two types of indexes: clustered and nonclustered. Clustered indexes involve a fundamental change in the structure of a table, while nonclustered indexes are separate structures.

Indexes that don't affect a table's structure

Up to 249 nonclustered indexes can be created on a table. Each of these indexes can be associated with one or more columns, and a column can be used in more than one index if necessary.

A nonclustered index is structured as was shown in Figure 9-1. In addition to the pointers that are shown, the pages in the leaf level are forward and backward linked with their immediate neighbors. This allows the query processor to retrieve a range of values quickly from the index. When a range is requested in a query, the first value is found by searching through the index, starting with the root-level page and continuing down to the leaf level; then subsequent values can be read by following the leaf level page links. Forward and backward links allow the query processor to efficiently handle ordered requests whether they are in ascending or descending order.

The information represented by ellipses in the leaf level pages in Figure 9-1 varies depending on whether or not a clustered index exists for the table. If a clustered index does not exist, the table is a heap, and the information in the leaf level of the nonclustered index is a row identifier (RID). A RID consists of three pieces of information:

✦ **The file**. RIDs are usually written as three decimal numbers separated by colons. Since a database can consist of multiple files, the file information is necessary, although for small databases it will nearly always be 1, indicating the first file in the database.

✦ **The page**. The page number is the same sort of page number that was shown in Figure 9-1.

✦ **The slot**. The row position within a page is called a slot. By having the slot number, the query processor does not have to search the data page for the desired row, but can look up its position in the row-offset array that is at the end of every page.

Row-offset arrays are described in more detail in Chapter 7. Figure 9-2 is a modification of Figure 9-1 with more detail in the leaf level. It shows a nonclustered index that has been created on a table with no clustered index. The nonleaf levels of the index are unchanged, and the pointers in the leaf level nodes are RIDs — that is, they contain the file number (1 in each case in the figure), the page number (ranging from 605 to 632), and the slot within each page (ranging from 1 to 9). When the Storage Engine retrieves a row based on a value from this index, it first retrieves the root level page, compares values to retrieve a pointer to the next lower level index page, and so on until it reaches the leaf level. When it reaches the leaf level, the Storage Engine searches the leaf level page for the desired value. Finding this value, it retrieves the corresponding RID. Using the information in the RID, it reads the data page from the referenced file, looks up the referenced slot in the row-offset array, and immediately accesses the desired row from the data page.

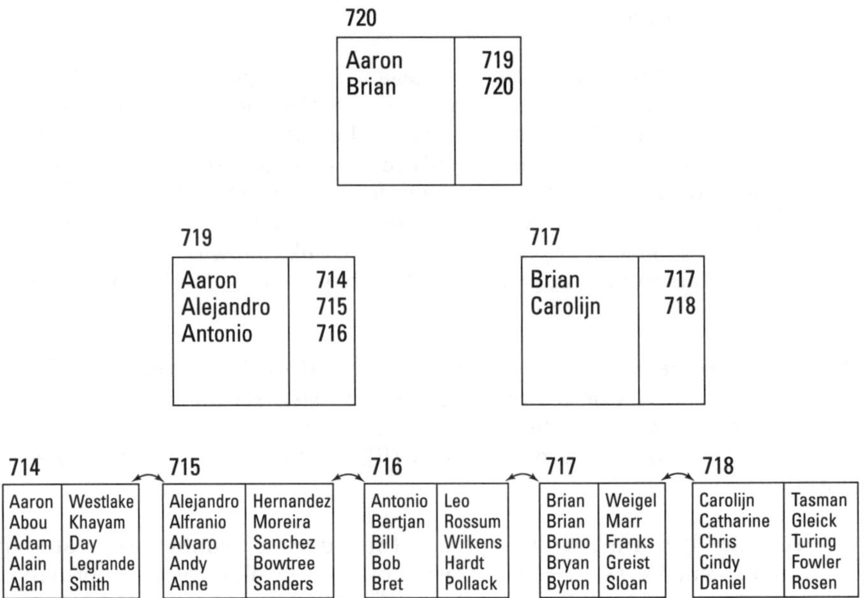

Figure 9-2: Nonclustered index on a heap table

If a clustered index exists for a table, then the leaf level of all nonclustered indexes stores the clustered key rather than a RID. For example, if the clustered index is on the LastName column, and a nonclustered index is created on FirstName, the leaf level entries will have the corresponding LastName values, as shown in Figure 9-3. Figure 9-3 shows a nonclustered index that has been created on a table with a clustered index. The nonleaf levels of the index are unchanged, but the pointers in the leaf level nodes are the values from the column on which a clustered index has been created (LastName). In order to locate a particular value given a first name, the query processor must seek through the nonclustered index, starting at the root page of the tree, and working its way down to the leaf level. At the leaf level, it can read the clustered key for the row with the first name for which it is searching. The query processor must then read the clustered index, starting at the root until the desired row is found in the leaf level, which is the data page.

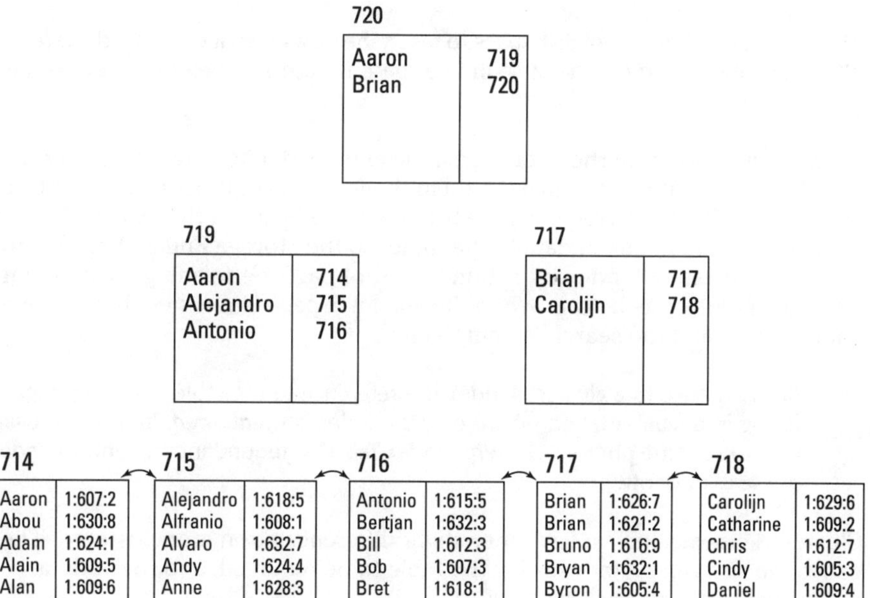

Figure 9-3: Nonclustered index on a clustered index table

While it may seem inefficient to have to read two indexes in order to find a row, there are some compensating efficiencies gained elsewhere. Whenever a table is modified, all indexes on the table must be modified to reflect the change. Sometimes when data is modified, rows are moved from one page to another. If all indexes on the table contain RIDs, then every index must be modified for any row that moves from one page to another. If the nonclustered indexes point to the clustered index, then the nonclustered indexes don't have to be modified just because the row has moved from one page to another.

Putting a table in sorted order: clustered indexes

When a clustered index is created on a table, the rows in the table are reordered according to the clustered index. For example, if the clustered index is on the LastName column, then the rows themselves will be sorted according to the values in LastName. Because clustered indexes sort the table, they are particularly effective when many queries retrieve clusters of rows based on small ranges of values from the column on which the clustered index was created. When such a query executes, the index is searched to find the first value in the range. Once that value is found, rows with subsequent values are immediately available, usually without reading more pages, because they are physically stored in the order of the clustered index column. If additional pages must be read, there is no need to traverse the B-Tree again because the leaf level pages are linked directly with the next and previous pages. The Storage Engine can simply follow these links until it finds a value that is outside the desired range.

MSDE needs plenty of disk space to resort the data when it creates a clustered index. 1.2 times the size of the table in free space is necessary before a clustered index is created.

In addition to ordering the data pages, the clustered index hierarchy is created directly on the data pages, making them the leaf level of the index. A clustered index looks like the B-Tree in Figure 9-1, and the ellipses in the leaf level represent the rest of the columns of data in the table. So the Storage Engine begins a row search in a clustered index by reading the root page, performing comparisons, and following pointers as before. When the leaf level page is reached, the entire row of data is found and the search is complete.

Any reference to a clustered index is a reference to the table. This may seem confusing in documentation where only the index is mentioned. In fact, the usage in this book of the phrase "Clustered Index Table" is redundant and only provided for the sake of clarity.

Clustered indexes have a few other slight differences from nonclustered. They cause the entry in sysindexes for the table to be removed, and they add a *uniqueifier* to any duplicate values.

When any index is created, a row is added to the sysindexes system table. Sysindexes tracks the metadata for indexes—that is, it contains the index's name, the location of the root page of the index, the original fillfactor, the number or rows currently contained in the index, and so on. When a table is a heap, there is an entry for the table in sysindexes with an indid (index ID) of 0. If a clustered index is created on a table, the indid 0 entry is removed from sysindexes, and a new entry is added with the name of the clustered index and an indid of 1. Nonclustered indexes are given numbers higher than 1 and do not affect the presence of the row representing the table.

If a clustered index is nonunique, then there is a possibility that duplicate clustered keys will exist. In this case, a four-byte value with a sequential counter is added to the duplicate keys to make them unique. This is necessary so that the pointers in the nonleaf levels of the index can locate all the pages on which these values exist. In earlier versions of SQL Server, other pages were chained on to the first leaf level pages, but this was found to be inefficient. Thus, the uniqueifier was born. With the uniqueifier, every value in the table is unique with regard to the B-Tree pointer structure. When a query is executed that uses a value that is nonunique, MSDE essentially does a pattern match and finds all rows that match the value, excluding the four bytes of the uniqueifier.

Clustered indexes also provide query coverage that is not immediately apparent. Every index contains all the values for the column on which they are created. A single column query, therefore, has to read only the index, and not the base table. If a clustered index is created on a table, then every nonclustered index also contains all the values from the clustered index (the clustering keys). That is because the clustering keys are used as pointers in the leaf level of the nonclustered indexes. The Storage Engine is clever enough to use these clustering key pointers to cover queries as well. For example, if there is a clustered index on the LastName column of a table and a nonclustered index on FirstName, a query that requests FirstName and LastName will be covered by the nonclustered index on FirstName. MSDE chooses to take advantage of this coverage when it improves the performance of a query.

What Happens to an Index When Data Changes?

When data in a table changes, any indexes that refer to the changed data are immediately updated by the system. The details of the update depend upon the type of index and on whether the modification is an insert, an update, or a delete.

Updating a heap: tables that don't have a clustered index

When a row is inserted into a table with no clustered index, the Storage Engine searches the Page Free Space bitmap, which indicates the location of any free space in the heap. If any sufficiently large free space is available, the new row will be placed there. Otherwise, a new page will be allocated to the table. If the table is smaller than eight pages, the new page will be allocated from a mixed extent—that is, an extent that can be shared with other objects. If the table is eight pages or larger, the new page will be allocated from a uniform extent used by only a single object. If there is a uniform extent with available free pages, one of these pages will be used. Otherwise, a new uniform extent will be allocated for the table.

When a row is updated in a table that has no clustered index, the Storage Engine will attempt to modify the row without moving it. For example, if a person changes their last name and the last name column in the table is a variable length data type, for instance, varchar(25), the Storage Engine will adjust the value in the column. If the new last name is longer than the previous last name, the Storage Engine will attempt to use existing free space on the current page. If there is insufficient space, a forwarding header will be inserted on the current page, and the row will be moved to a new page. Using the forwarding header means that no indexes will need to be modified except the index on the column that is being modified, if one exists. All indexes will still have a RID that points to the location of the forwarding header, and anytime the row is accessed, the pointer in the header is followed.

When a row is deleted from a table with no clustered index, the contents of the row are removed from the page, and the Page Free Space bitmap is updated.

Updating a clustered index

When a row is added to a table with a clustered index, the row must be inserted in the proper location with regard to the order of the index. If there is sufficient free space on the page to which the new row must be added, the row is inserted.

The rows on the page are not physically ordered according to the index order, since that would take a lot of movement of data within the page. The rows within the page are added in the most convenient order (wherever there is free space), and the row-offset array is updated. The row-offset array maintains a series of pointers in the correct order and records the correct starting byte location for each row on the page.

If a row is added to a page with insufficient free space to accommodate the new row, the Storage Engine performs a page split. A page split allocates a new page to the index, moving half of the rows from the full page to the new page and adding the inserted row in the appropriate location. When the new page is allocated, the forward and reverse pointers that connect all leaf level pages must be adjusted. Figures 9-4 and 9-5 illustrate a page split in a clustered index. Figure 9-4 represents the table with a clustered index. The leaf level consists of the data pages of the table stored in the order of first names. The ellipses in the leaf level represent the rest of the columns in the rows. There is an intermediate index level above the leaf level and a single-page root at the top of the B-Tree structure. Notice that the leaf level pages are all linked with the previous and next pages (this linkage is represented by little arrows, although the actual links are parts of the page header that stores the page number of the next and previous pages).

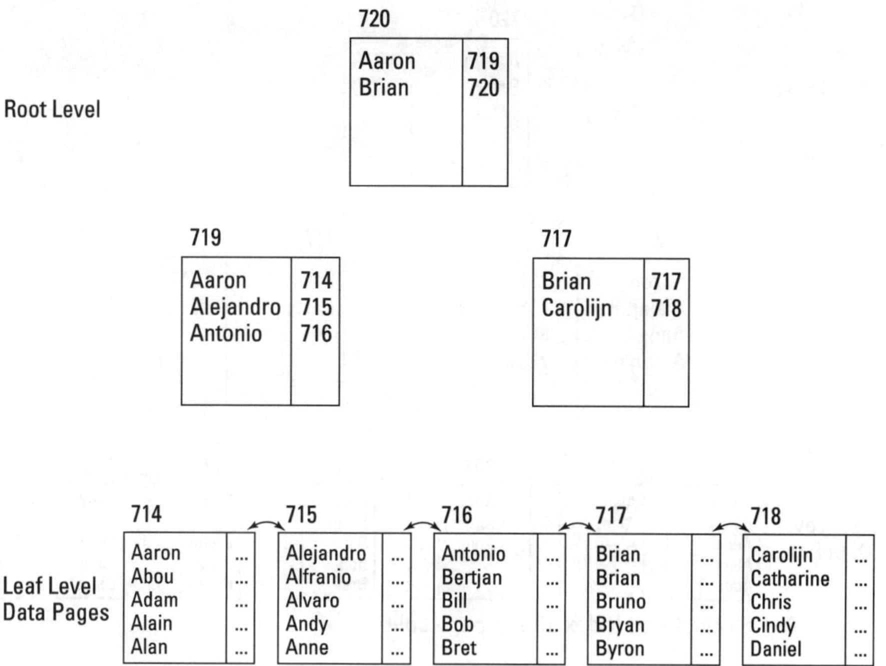

Figure 9-4: A clustered index before a page split

Figure 9-5 shows the results of inserting a record with the first name, 'Angus.' Alphabetically, 'Angus' falls between 'Andy' and 'Anne,' so the new record should be inserted into page 715. However, there is no available space on that page. The Storage Engine allocates a new page, 807. This new page will be inserted after page 715 and prior to page 716. The pointers for next and previous pages must be altered on 715, 807, and 716 so that they fall into the correct place within the ordered list. With the new page in place, half of the rows from the page being split (715) are moved to the new page. In this example, the rows that are moved are those containing 'Andy' and 'Anne' as first names. The 'Angus' row is then inserted into the appropriate position, which is now page 807.

Since a new page has been added at the leaf level, changes must be propagated up the B-Tree. A new pointer must be added that points to the new page and references the first value. As there is enough free space, an entry is made into page 719, with the value 'Andy' and the pointer to page 807. If page 719 had also been full, it would have been split as well. As a page split always requires a new entry in the level above, a new entry would also have been required in the root level page. Had that been full, it too would have been split, and since the root must always be a single page, a split at the root level generates an entirely new root level. In general, page splits are most common at the lowest level of the B-Tree. Once a split occurs, two pages are guaranteed to have 50 percent empty space, which reduces the possibility of another page split in the near future.

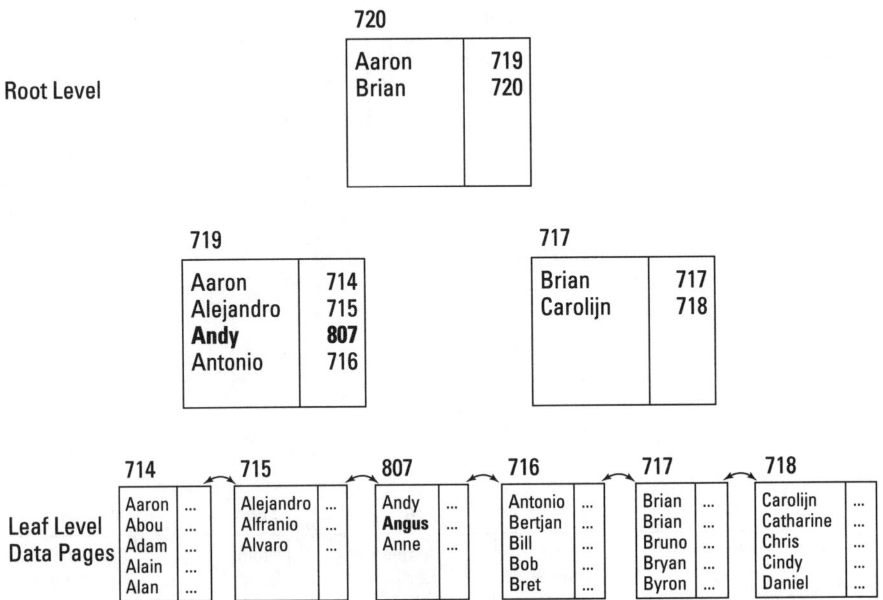

Figure 9-5: A clustered index after a page split

When a row is deleted from a table with a clustered index, the row is marked for deletion by a background process. The deleted row is called a ghost row and remains temporarily in the index to provide better concurrency for range locking. Range locking is described in Chapter 10.

Page splits and performance

Page splits are detrimental to performance in two ways: They hurt the performance of the query that caused the split, and they hurt the performance of future queries because they fragment the index. The performance of the query that causes the split is hurt because all of the modifications must happen synchronously with the transaction that causes them. That is, the insert that causes the split doesn't finish until the split is complete. Any other queries that are running at the same time are adversely affected because the system is performing additional work, and locks are placed on the table while the changes are made to the index, causing other transactions to wait.

Future performance suffers because the fragmentation of the index makes the Read Ahead Manager work less efficiently. Whenever a page is read from a disk, the Read Ahead Manager attempts to guess which pages will be required in the future and reads them before they are needed. The mechanism that the Read Ahead Manager uses is based on two factors: Data is often accessed in ranges, and the structure of disk hardware allows several pieces of contiguous data to be read in about the same time required to read a single piece of data. The first factor requires little explanation; if a query is requesting rows, it will often access other nearby rows. *Nearby* in this case means having a similar alphabetical value. The second factor requires a bit more explanation.

When a request is sent to a disk drive to retrieve data, three things happen:

1. The head is positioned over the correct cylinder, or track.
2. The disk must then spin until the requested data moves under the head.
3. Finally, the data is actually read from the disk, usually into a buffer on the disk controller and then into the computer's memory.

The speed at which the data is transferred off of the disk and into the computer is very high, relative to the time it takes to position the head and wait for the data to move under the head. Because of this, it costs very little extra time to read two pages from disk if they are located immediately adjacent to one another. The same is true of reading eight pages instead of one.

The Read Ahead Manager will read an entire extent whenever it can, instead of a single page. It will perform this expanded read if the odds are reasonably good that other pages in the extent will be needed in the future. This estimation is based on whether the pages within the extent are contiguous. Figure 9-4 showed leaf level pages that were contiguous. Following the order of the pages on disk (714, 715, 716, 717, and so on) also followed the order of the values in the index (Alan, Alejandro, Alfranio, and so on). After the pages split, however, they were no longer contiguous (as was shown in Figure 9-5), because reading values in the order of the index required jumping from page 715 to 807 and then back to 716.

To summarize the relevant aspect of the behavior of the Read Ahead Manager, before the page split if page 714 were read, the Read Ahead Manager would also read pages 715 through 721. 719 through 721 aren't shown in the diagram, but we will assume that they are also contiguous components of the same index. That would be a read of one extent, or eight pages, in only slightly more time than reading page 714 alone. If a query were generating a list sorted by first name or retrieving a group of names near the beginning of the alphabet, this would result in a great savings in I/O. After the page split, the Read Ahead Manager will no longer assume that the pages within the extent will be required in order. Since the extent has become noncontiguous, individual pages will be read instead of entire extents.

Only in environments that frequently call for ranges of data and sorted groups of data do page splits hurt performance. Such an environment would typically be found where the database is being used for decision support or other applications requiring many reports. Other environments are not hurt (and may even be helped a little) by fragmentation. An order-entry system, which requires many individual orders involving only newly inserted rows and access to a single row at any one time is one example. A customer service or help desk application might also rely mostly on the retrieval of individual rows. If only single rows are needed, then performing read-ahead on entire extents will not improve performance.

Environments that require good performance for both reporting/decision support and data entry can sometimes be better served with two servers. The data entry server can be configured to suit a highly transactional application, and the data can be copied to a decision support server using replication (see Chapter 20) or backup and restore with standby (see Chapter 23).

Fillfactor and pad_index

The administrator or designer of a database has some control over page splitting derived from the amount of free space that will be left on pages within indexes. There are two relevant settings in the `create index` command: fillfactor, and pad_index.

The fillfactor determines the amount of space in the leaf level of the index that will be filled with data when an index is created or rebuilt. It is specified as a number between 1 and 100, the number indicating the percentage of space that should be filled. For example, if a fillfactor of 70 is used, each page at the leaf level will have 30 percent free space, or about 2400 bytes. A lower fillfactor means fewer page splits. However, a lower fillfactor requires more pages to store the same amount of data. The more pages used to store a given amount of data, the more I/Os will have to be performed in order to read that data. And, of course, the more pages used to store data, the more total disk space required.

It is important to remember that fillfactors on a clustered index go on the data pages themselves because the data pages are the leaf level pages of a clustered index. Adding extra free space to the data pages can have a significant impact on the overall system requirements of the database.

Fillfactor is set only when an index is created or rebuilt. MSDE makes no effort to maintain a particular fillfactor. However, over the course of time, the amount of free space in any given index or table will tend to stabilize at some level that is determined by the relative number of inserts, updates, and deletes performed on the table. For example, the table with a roughly equal number of inserts, updates, and deletes will tend to stabilize with pages that are approximately 75 percent full. Naturally, any tables that are read-only do not require any free space, since rows won't be inserted and the pages will never split. The default fillfactor of 0 is functionally equivalent to a fillfactor of 100.

When designing a database, always look for tables that might be good candidates for 100 percent fillfactor, such as lookup tables that are downloaded from external sources like zip code files or tables that are periodically downloaded from a mainframe.

Setting fillfactor appropriately can significantly reduce the number of page splits at the leaf level. However, fillfactor itself only affects the leaf level pages; thus, on a table with a significantly heavy load of inserts, page splits can still occur on the nonleaf levels. In order to control the number of page splits of the nonleaf level, the `pad index` parameter is available. When `pad index` is specified, the fillfactor is applied to all pages in the index, not just the leaf level.

Rebuilding indexes

Since the MSDE does not maintain fillfactor over time, it may become desirable to eventually reset the fillfactor to its original value or perhaps set it to some new value based on experiences running a table with the original fillfactor. To do this, you have to rebuild the index, which is really nothing more than dropping it and recreating it with the new desired parameters to be implemented. There are several command shortcuts that can be used to perform the rebuild that don't require manually issued drop and rebuild commands for every index on a table.

One of the most important aspects of rebuilding indexes is the relationship between the existence of a clustered index and the structure of nonclustered indexes. Recall that a nonclustered index will use RIDs for pointers in the leaf level pages if there is no clustered index on a table, and it will use a clustered key as a pointer on the leaf of all pages if there is a clustered index. Because of this dependency, anytime a clustered index is dropped or created, the system will automatically rebuild any and all nonclustered indexes on the table. On large tables this can significantly impact the length of time it takes to drop and re-create a clustered index. Rebuilding a clustered index could take quite a long time if dropped and re-created manually. During the drop, the nonclustered indexes would have to be dropped and re-created with RIDs, and when the clustered index was re-created, all of the nonclustered indexes would have to, again, be dropped and created, this time with the clustered key as leaf level pointers.

The command used for rebuilding indexes is the `Create Index` command. It utilizes the `Drop_Existing` parameter, which is designed to facilitate rebuilding indexes, particularly clustered indexes, without causing all nonclustered indexes to be re-created twice. When `Create Index` is run with the `Drop_Existing` parameter, the rebuild of the nonclustered indexes is deferred until after the clustered index is dropped and completely rebuilt. At that time, all the nonclustered indexes will also be rebuilt.

Rebuilding indexes for unique and primary key constraints

Unique and primary key constraints automatically create indexes to support their functionality. These indexes cannot be dropped under normal circumstances without first dropping the constraints. The exceptions to this rule are the three commands that are used to perform maintenance on indexes: `DBCC DBReindex`, `DBCC Index Defrag`, and `Create Index With Drop_Existing`.

If you use the `Drop_Existing` parameter in the `Create Index` command, you must use exactly the same parameters that the system used initially to create the index.

Chapter 30 covers index maintenance in detail.

Indexes on Computed Columns

In MSDE 2000, indexes may be created on computed columns in tables. This capability has several restrictions. Normally, computed columns do not contain any data. They represent data derived from other columns. When an index is created on a computed column, the data represented by the column is stored in the index. The process of storing this derived data is sometimes called materialization.

The Enterprise and Developers' Editions of SQL Server 2000 have a similar feature that allows indexes to be created on Views.

The following conditions must be met to create an index on a computed column:

✦ Every function used in the definition of the column must be deterministic — that is, it must return a consistent value for consistent input value. An example of a nondeterministic function is `NewID`, which always returns a unique value, or `GetDate`, the value of which changes with the time of day.

✦ Any column referenced in the computed column must exist in the same table.

✦ No function in the computed column may refer to more than one row. For example, aggregate functions are not allowed.

✦ The computed column may not be any of the following datatypes: text, ntext, or image.

✦ The following connection settings must be on during creation of the computed column and during any query that accesses the column: ANSI_Nulls, ANSI_Padding, ANSI_Warnings, ArithAbort, Concat_Null_Yields_Null, and Quoted_Identifier. If any of these settings are not turned on when a query is executed, any index on the computed column is ignored.

✦ The Numeric_RoundAbort connection setting must be off during creation and access.

Creating, Deleting, and Modifying Indexes

Indexes can be managed in Enterprise Manager, Access, and Visual Studio from the Table and Index Properties dialog box. Enterprise Manager also has the Manage Indexes dialog box, DMO has two index objects, and SQL has several commands that can be used for the same purpose.

Managing indexes with Enterprise Manager, Access, and Visual Studio

To manage indexes from the Table and Indexes dialog box, open the Table Designer and right-click anywhere in the grid. Choose Properties from the menu and click the Indexes/Keys tab. From the dialog box that is displayed, indexes can be created, deleted, and modified.

In Enterprise Manager, the second button from the left on the button bar in the Table Designer provides a shortcut to the Table and Index Properties dialog box.

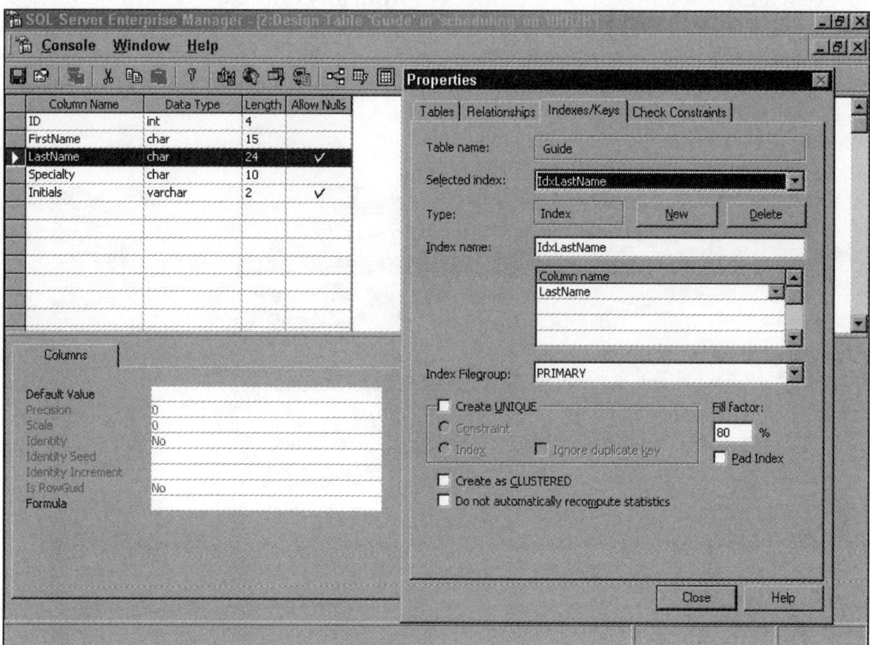

Figure 9-6: Table and Index Properties dialog box

Figure 9-6 shows the Table and Index Properties dialog box with the Indexes/Keys tab selected. A label at the top of the dialog box displays the name of the table that is currently selected. The drop-down list just below the table name allows access to any index for the table. The label below the index name displays the type of the currently selected index—a standard index created as part of a primary key or as part of a unique constraint. Next to this label are buttons that allow indexes to be created or deleted. At the midpoint of the dialog box is the list of columns that the index references. When creating a new index, any column from the table can be selected in this list by clicking the drop-down button. Additional columns can be added to the index by adding the appropriate column name in subsequent lines of this control. The list of columns in the index can also be scrolled should it become too long for all columns to be displayed simultaneously (rarely will there be that many columns in an index). Below the column list is a drop-down list that controls the physical location of the index. The index can be created in any existing filegroup. A check box is available for the index to enforce uniqueness in the column(s) it represents. The radio button just below this check box determines whether the index is created as a constraint or just as an index. In the bottom left of the dialog box is a check box to make the index a clustered index and a check box to defer the recalculation of statistics. On the bottom right is a text box for the index fillfactor and, if a value other than 0 or 100 is entered, the padindex check box becomes available to allow the fillfactor to be applied to all levels of the index rather than just the leaf level.

Enterprise Manager has a second, slightly different dialog box for managing indexes. It allows management of indexes from any database and table without leaving the dialog box. Right-click a table and then select All Tasks ➪ Manage Indexes. The Manage Indexes dialog box, shown in Figure 9-7, is displayed. The top two controls select the database and table. The grid in the center of the dialog box displays all indexes for the currently selected table.

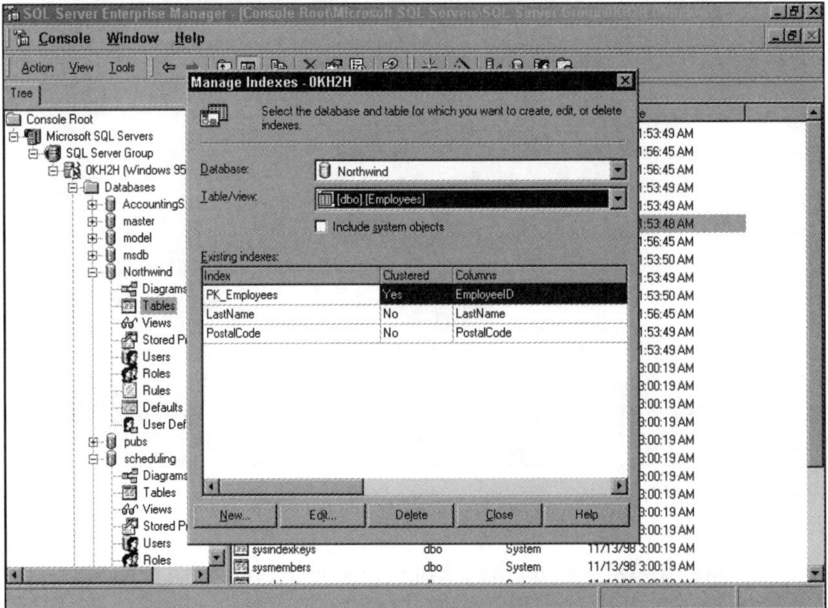

Figure 9-7: The Manage Indexes dialog box in Enterprise Manager

Managing indexes with SQL

Indexes are created in SQL with the `Create Index` command. The syntax for `Create Index` is as follows:

```
Create [Unique][Clustered | Nonclustered] Index indexname
    On tablename (col [ASC|DESC][...,])
[ WITH
        [ PAD_INDEX ]
        [ [ , ] FILLFACTOR = fillfactor ]
        [ [ , ] IGNORE_DUP_KEY ]
        [ [ , ] DROP_EXISTING ]
        [ [ , ] STATISTICS_NORECOMPUTE ]
        [ [ , ] SORT_IN_TEMPDB ]
]
[ ON filegroup ]
```

If `Unique` is not specified, duplicate values will be allowed.

If neither clustered nor nonclustered is specified, the index will be nonclustered.

Each index in a database must have a unique name.

One or more columns may be specified. For each column, the default sort order is ascending, but can be specified as descending.

Specifying the sort order provides an advantage for multicolumn indexes. If queries frequently access a particular set of columns in a particular combination of ascending and descending orders, create an index with orders that match the queries.

The following example creates a clustered index on the FirstName column of the Guide table. The `Fillfactor` clause causes the 20 percent free space to be added to the data pages of the table. The `On FILEGRP2` clause indicates that the table itself will be located on the Filegrp2 filegroup. The table is controlled because a clustered index is the table; so, moving the clustered index moves the table. To reference the Primary filegroup, the `On` clause must be omitted.

```
CREATE CLUSTERED
  INDEX IdxFirstName ON Guide (FirstName)
WITH FILLFACTOR = 80
ON FILEGRP2
```

The following command rebuilds (that is, drops and re-creates) the index that was created in the previous example. Note that the syntax is exactly the same as that used in creation, the only addition being the `Drop_Existing` clause:

```
CREATE CLUSTERED
  INDEX IdxFirstName ON Guide (FirstName)
WITH FILLFACTOR = 80, DROP_EXISTING
ON FILEGRP2
```

The following example deletes the clustered index created above. It turns the table back into a heap. It is necessary to specify the table name along with the index name:

```
DROP INDEX Guide.idxfirstname
```

The three preceding examples either create, delete, or both create and delete a clustered index. Since the structure of nonclustered indexes depends upon whether the table is a heap or a clustered index, any of these commands will cause an automatic rebuild (drop and re-create) of all nonclustered indexes.

If an index created by a unique or primary key constraint needs to be rebuilt, the parameters that were used to create it must first be found. The index associated with such a constraint will always be unique, but may be clustered or nonclustered. There are several ways to find the specifications for these indexes. Access, Enterprise Manager, or Visual Studio all provide graphical methods for viewing indexes.

Using SQL, information about index configuration is available through the following:

```
Sp_helpindex tablename
```

This returns a full description of all the indexes on the specified table. The following command shows the results of running `sp_helpindex` on the Employees table in the Northwind database:

```
Sp_helpindex employees

LastName     nonclustered located on PRIMARY    LastName
PK_Employees clustered, unique, primary key located on PRIMARY
EmployeeID
PostalCode nonclustered located on PRIMARY    PostalCode
```

So, there are three indexes: LastName, PK_Employees, and PostalCode. All three are located on the Primary filegroup, and they represent the LastName, EmployeeID, and PostalCode columns, respectively. The PK_Employees index is the clustered index for this table and was created as part of the primary key constraint. Based on the output of this stored procedure, all three indexes can be rebuilt with the following command:

```
CREATE UNIQUE CLUSTERED INDEX PK_Employees
    ON employees(employeeid)
WITH DROP_EXISTING
```

This command must be entered exactly. If `UNIQUE` is not specified, for example, MSDE responds with the following:

```
An explicit DROP INDEX is not allowed on index 'PK_Employees'.
It is being used for PRIMARY KEY constraint enforcement.
```

There is an alternative command provided in MSDE for backward compatibility: `DBCC DBREINDEX`. It can still be used for index maintenance, but is not recommended. The largest drawback to `DBCC DBREINDEX` is that it has no way to defer rebuilds of nonclustered indexes when used on a clustered index.

Managing indexes with DMO

The DMO hierarchy for tables is as follows:

```
Server
    Databases
        Database
            Tables
                Table
                    Indexes
                        Index
                        Index2
```

To create an index with DMO:

1. Instantiate an Index object. Set the name property to a descriptive string and set the `IndexedColumns` property to the appropriate column name or names.
2. Create a connection to the server.
3. Obtain a reference to the table on which the index is to be created.
4. Execute the `Add` method of the Indexes collection, passing the Index object as an argument.

The following code creates an index called IdxLastName on the Guide table in the Scheduling database. This database and table were created with the scripts in Chapters 6 and 7, respectively. In this code and other examples that follow, a variable is created and set for the table on which the indexes will be created, deleted, and rebuilt. There is no necessity for this variable. It is present here solely for the sake of readability.

```
dim oMSDEserver
dim oTable
dim oIndex

set oMSDEserver = CreateObject("SQLDMO.SQLServer")
set oIndex = CreateObject("SQLDMO.Index")

oIndex.Name = "IdxLastName"
oIndex.IndexedColumns = "LastName"

oMSDEserver.connect "Okh2h","sa",""
set oTable = oMSDEserver.Databases("scheduling").Tables("Guide")
oTable.Indexes.add (oIndex)
oMSDEserver.disconnect
```

You can find this code on the CD-ROM in the file named `Ch 9\Create Index.vbs`.

To drop an index, create a connection to the server, then create a reference to the table containing the server, and execute the `Remove` method of the index. In the following code, the index is referenced by name in the Indexes collection of the Guide table object.

```
dim oMSDEserver
dim oTable
dim oIndex

set oMSDEserver = CreateObject("SQLDMO.SQLServer")

oMSDEserver.connect "0kh2h","sa",""
set oTable =
oMSDEserver.Databases("scheduling").Tables("Guide")
oTable.Indexes("IdxLastName").remove
oMSDEserver.disconnect
```

You can find this code on the CD-ROM in the file named `Ch 9\DropIndex.vbs`.

To rebuild an index, create a connection to the server, obtain a reference to the index that is to be rebuilt, set the `Fillfactor` property if it needs to be changed from its previous value, and invoke the `Rebuild` method on the Index object.

```
dim oMSDEserver
dim oTable
dim oIndex

set oMSDEserver = CreateObject("SQLDMO.SQLServer")

oMSDEserver.connect "0kh2h","sa",""
set oTable =
oMSDEserver.Databases("scheduling").Tables("Guide")
set oIndex=oTable.Indexes("IdxLastName")
oIndex.Fillfactor=80
oIndex.Rebuild
oMSDEserver.disconnect
```

You can find this code on the CD-ROM in the file named `Ch 9\rebldIndex.vbs`.

The Rebuild method of the Index object uses DBCC DBREINDEX to rebuild the index. It is more efficient to use the SQL Create Index With Drop_Existing command than to use DMO if there is a clustered index on the table.

The Index object is compatible with MSDE 1.0, SQL Server 7.0, and SQL Server 2000. In addition, SQL Server 2000 has an Index2 object that inherits all of the properties and methods from the Index object, but also has properties and methods for the new features provided with the 2000 version. The features supported in Index2 that are not supported in Index allow the index to be created on a computed column or to specify that one or more columns in the index should be created in descending order rather than the default, ascending order.

```
dim oMSDEserver
dim oTable
dim oColInitials
dim oIndex

set oMSDEserver = CreateObject("SQLDMO.SQLServer")
set oColInitials = CreateObject("SQLDMO.Column")
set oIndex = CreateObject("SQLDMO.Index2")

oColInitials.Name = "Initials"
oColInitials.DataType = "Varchar"
oColInitials.Length = "2"
oColInitials.ComputedText="(left([FirstName],1) +
left([LastName],1))"
oColInitials.AllowNulls = True

oIndex.Name = "IdxSpecInit"
oIndex.IndexedColumns = "[Specialty] [Initials]"
oIndex.SetIndexedColumnDESC "Initials", True

oMSDEserver.connect "Okh2h","sa",""
set oTable =
oMSDEserver.Databases("Scheduling").Tables("Guide")
oTable.Columns.add (oColInitials)
oTable.Indexes.add (oIndex)
oMSDEserver.disconnect
```

You can find this code on the CD-ROM in the file named Ch 9\Index2.vbs.

The code above shows a few interesting features. The Index object that is created in the sixth line of code is an Index2. Using Index2 allows the use of all of the features of an Index and also allows the use of the features that were added in the 2000 version of MSDE. In particular, this code will create an index that specifies a descending sort order for one column and specifies that one of the columns in the index is a computed column.

The next block of code creates a computed column that will be added to the Guide table. This column uses the `Left` function to retrieve the initial letter of the first and last names and links them into the two-letter Initials column. This column allows nulls, which are required when adding a column to an existing table unless a default is specified.

In the next block of code, the Index2 object, called oIndex, is assigned properties. It is given the name, 'IdxSpecInit'. The columns on which it will be built are assigned as Specialty and Initials. These columns are both part of the same property, `IndexedColumns`. `IndexedColumns` is a property called a MultiString, which allows multiple values to be entered for a single property. In this code, the values are delimited by enclosing each value in square brackets. It is also possible to use commas or semicolons if these characters are not part of any of the column names; however, square brackets are the recommended mechanism.

If modifying an existing index, do not rely on the `IndexedColumns` property to provide a list of columns that are currently in the index. This property is designed only to set the columns. Use the mechanism `sp_helpindex` for retrieving the column names and completely respecify the columns.

The last line of code in the oIndex section is the `SetIndexedColumnDESC` method of the Index2 object. This method may be called only before an object has been created. It allows the sort order for each column to be configured. In this case, the Initials column will be sorted in descending order. The Specialty column will be sorted in ascending order, which is the default, and so does not need to be specified.

Once the new column and index objects have been created and configured, the code connects to the MSDE server and obtains a reference to the table on which the changes are to be made. The oColInitials object and oIndex object are added to the Columns and Indexes collections, respectively.

Summary

Indexes significantly improve the performance of MSDE. They do not change the functionality and can be added or removed without modifying applications that use the underlying table. MSDE automatically updates indexes whenever data is changed, and it makes decisions about using indexes based on statistics that are stored as part of index. Periodical maintenance is often necessary to keep the performance at high levels. Creating too many indexes can adversely affect performance, particularly in an environment that is dominated by writes to the database.

✦ ✦ ✦

CHAPTER 10

Locking: The Key to a Consistent Multiuser System

✦ ✦ ✦ ✦

In This Chapter

Consistency versus concurrency

Locking resources

The interaction of transactions and locks

The interaction of locks with other locks

Controlling locking

✦ ✦ ✦ ✦

Any computer system that allows multiple users to simultaneously access the same data runs certain risks with regard to the consistency of the data. MSDE is such a multiuser system; MSDE provides locks as a mechanism to prevent inconsistency in data. Locks enable one user to control or prevent access to data by other users. There is always a trade-off between consistency and concurrency. To have the most consistent data possible, only one user at a time should be able to access the data. To have the most concurrency possible, all users should be able to access any data at any time. MSDE takes an approach somewhere in the middle that allows a reasonable response time from the system, while providing some guarantees about the consistency of data. Applications developers must understand the trade-offs between consistency and concurrency, consider the methods that the database management system will use to provide these, and choose the most appropriate level of automatic locking to suit their applications.

A crucial aspect of locks is how long they are held. The longer locks are held, the poorer the overall throughput of the database, because one user's lock is another user's wait. MSDE uses a transaction mechanism to determine how long to hold a lock. A transaction is an atomic unit of change to data in a database. It is atomic in the sense that it cannot be divided. Either the entire change is made, or none of the change is made. Any data modification statement automatically creates its own transaction; however, a programmer can specify that a transaction should consist of more than one statement.

Locking is designed to prevent the four general types of risks that a multiuser system faces:

- **Lost updates** — A lost update problem occurs when two or more users read a row from a table more or less simultaneously and then update that row based on the value that was read without regard to the changes that have been made by other users. For example, suppose that a row contains the number of items in stock in a warehouse. User A physically removes two items from the warehouse, while User B physically removes one item from the warehouse. The software for User A and User B both read the current number of items in stock and find that it is four. User A's software subtracts two from the value it read in the table and writes the result back into the table: 2. User B's software subtracts one from the value it read in the table and writes the result back into the table: 3. In this way, the update made by User A has been lost, and the table no longer represents the reality of the warehouse. Lost updates are almost never acceptable in a production environment.
- **Dirty reads** — A dirty read, which is also called an uncommitted dependency, occurs when one user reads data that has been modified by another user in a transaction that is eventually rolled back and undone. The data read by the first user should never have existed because the transaction that created it never completed or committed. This is called a dirty read because a data page that has been modified but not committed is called dirty. Dirty reads can be acceptable, assuming the application developer and the users understand the ramifications. Dirty reads may be okay in a high-volume transactional environment assuming that most transactions will commit, and even if some small number of transactions don't, the characteristics of the application may allow a few rollbacks without altering the overall picture too much.
- **Nonrepeatable reads** — A nonrepeatable read, which is also sometimes called inconsistent analysis, occurs when a value upon which a transaction depends changes during the course of the transaction. For example, a particular transaction reads a value in a table and based upon that value takes some action. Later in the transaction, another action is taken based on the same value. If another user had changed the value during the course of the transaction, then the second choice of action may not have been made correctly. This is called a nonrepeatable read because the transaction reads the value in the table before the first decision point, but in reading it again before the second decision point, the transaction reads a value that may have changed. Thus, the read is not repeatable (at least not repeatable with the same results).

✦ **Phantoms—**Phantoms are rows that are not updated even though they appear to meet the criteria for an update that actually occurred. After an update occurs, phantom rows sometimes suddenly appear. This can occur when a modification is executed on a range of values and, during the modification, a row is changed by another user so that the altered row falls into the range being modified. For example, a retail sales company is making seasonal adjustments to the price of merchandise. The amount of the change is determined by the category of the items. Perhaps clothing prices increase by 2 percent and sporting goods increase by 4 percent. A transaction is begun to update the price of all clothing items and then to update the price of sporting goods. At the same time, another user modifies ice hockey jerseys so that they are no longer sporting goods and they become categorized as clothing. If the timing is just right, the ice hockey jerseys may be missed during the update of clothing, yet suddenly appear as clothing as soon as the update is finished. The effect is that the jerseys are never updated.

MSDE has mechanisms that can be used to prevent any or all of these possible problems. The default configuration prevents lost updates and dirty reads, but does not prevent nonrepeatable reads or phantoms. Nonrepeatable reads and phantoms can be prevented by specifying locking isolation levels, which are described later in the chapter.

Defining How Much Data is Locked: Lock Granularity

An MSDE database can lock several different types of objects. Some of these objects are used only for special purposes, such as extents, which are only locked when the Storage Engine is allocating new space for a database object like a table or index. The locks of primary interest to software designers and database administrators are those used for locking user data. The locks that control access to user data are the RID lock, the key lock (both the RID lock and the key lock are also referred to as row locks), the page lock, and the table lock. The database lock also restricts access to user data, but is used for special purposes, and is not normally invoked by user transactions.

Under normal circumstances, MSDE makes its own decisions about the proper granularity to be used for locking time, that is, whether locks are placed on rows, pages, or an entire table. It makes this decision based on the amount of system resources currently available, balanced against the amount of load being placed on the system by users. Programmers or system administrators can override the settings that MSDE chooses.

Locking a single row: RID locks and key locks

Whenever a user process accesses data, MSDE will attempt to lock individual rows in the table. If there are insufficient system resources to lock enough rows, then the system uses page or table locks. The type of lock that is used to control access to a row depends on whether or not the table has a clustered index. If a table is a heap, then row identifier (RID) locks are used. If a clustered index does exist on the table, then key locks are used.

The file number in a RID will always be one unless there are more than one data files in the database. All allocated pages in a database are numbered sequentially. This sequential number is used to identify a page in a RID. Within each page, there is a row-offset array that tracks the starting position of each row in the page as a byte offset from the beginning of the page. The slot indicator in a RID simply indicates the ordinal value (for example, first, second, third) of the row-offset array entry that corresponds to the row in question.

When a clustered index exists on a table, the data pages of the table are part of the index (see Chapter 9 for details on index structure). The key of a clustered index is the set of values that exists in the column(s) on which the index was created. In other words, if a clustered index was created on the LastName column, then the last name is the key value for the index. When a key lock is placed on a clustered index, it locks a particular key value. The uniqueifier mechanism in a clustered index ensures that a key lock affects only a single value.

A transaction can force the use of row locks with a table hint as in the following example, which updates every row in the Products table, adding 10 percent to the UnitPrice, and requires the system to use row locks:

```
UPDATE Products
    WITH (ROWLOCK)
    SET UnitPrice = UnitPrice * 1.1
```

It is usually a bad idea to specify the ROWLOCK table hint. MSDE always attempts to use row locks unless there are insufficient system resources. So, requiring the system to use row locks will not enhance performance and may starve the system of resources needed to service other users or transactions.

Locking multiple rows with page locks and range locks

When MSDE decides that there are insufficient system resources to lock all of the rows that will be accessed by a query and still maintain adequate performance for all users, it will place page locks. Page locks can also be placed if a query includes a table hint that specifies page locking. Page locks are very much like RID locks, except that they have only a file and page indicator. Page locks control access to all data on the page. The following example causes MSDE to place page locks rather than row locks. It updates every row in the Products table, adding 10 percent to the UnitPrice and uses the table hint WITH (PAGLOCK) to force the use of page locks:

```
UPDATE Products
    WITH (PAGLOCK)
    SET UnitPrice = UnitPrice * 1.1
```

Range locks can be placed on ranges of values within an index by setting the transaction isolation level to serializable (which is described later in the chapter). Locking a range of key values in an index helps to prevent the phantom problem. The idea is to prevent any value that falls within the range being modified. Ultimately, it is impossible to predict all the values that might be added to the range. When a range lock is set, all of the values in the index—from the first value in the range to the first value after the end of the range—are locked. Trying to modify any of the locked rows or to insert immediately before any of the locked rows, will result in a blocked attempt. This mechanism actually locks slightly more than the range; for example, a transaction with a serializable isolation level might have a `Where` clause like this:

```
WHERE Date BETWEEN '3/3/87' and '3/9/87'
```

And the values that exist in the index might be as follows:

```
.
.
.
2/25/87
3/4/87
3/5/87
3/7/87
3/12/87
.
.
.
```

In this case, the range locks would be placed on 3/4/87, 3/5/87, 3/7/87, and 3/12/87. No inserts would be permitted immediately prior to any of the values, which means that no insert would be permitted with a value greater than 2/25/87, because this is the value which immediately precedes the first locked value. In this case, all of the desired range is locked, from 3/3/87 to 3/9/87, but there are several additional dates locked at either end of the range. This approach is somewhat conservative, leaning toward consistency and away from concurrency. In most environments, this practice causes unnecessary contention on a few values.

Locking a whole table

In the same way that MSDE can decide to escalate locking from row or key locks to page locks in order to save resources, it can also decide to escalate the locking for a transaction to a table lock. A programmer can also specify table locks with table hints. The following code uses the table hint WITH (TABLOCK) to command MSDE to use a table lock on the Products table rather than individual row locks or page locks.

```
UPDATE Products
     WITH (TABLOCK)
     SET UnitPrice = UnitPrice * 1.1
```

MSDE tends to make good decisions about when to escalate locks and, in general, knows more about the system state at any moment in time than the programmer did at the time the code was written. Unless there is a specific reason for doing so, table hints should not be used to specify table locks. They can hurt the concurrency of the database, and no noticeable performance improvement will be gained.

Locking during space allocation: extent locks

When MSDE is allocating a new extent for an object, it places a special type of lock on the extent so that it cannot be accessed by any user process until it is fully allocated. Extent locks are always of very short duration and are rarely seen, even by an astute administrator.

Locking an entire database

Database locks are set only by the system. Anytime a user connection accesses a database, MSDE places a shared lock on the database, primarily to track when the database is in use.

If an administrator needs to prevent users from accessing a database, the database options Single User Mode or dbo Use Only can be used. These options must be turned on and off manually and are typically used for performing system maintenance, backups, and restores.

Choosing the Appropriate Lock Mode

Lock modes that determine how locks interact with each other can be set for each lock. The choice of locking, like the choice of which objects are locked, has a significant effect on the concurrency versus consistency equation.

Reading data with shared locks

The most common kind of lock is the shared lock. Shared locks are used when data is being read. Shared locks are similar to read locks that are used in other systems. A shared lock can coexist on any contract with any number of other shared locks, enabling many users to read data at the same time. While shared locks are placed on any object, exclusive locks that would enable changes to the object are prohibited. By default, shared locks are held only for the length of time that it takes to read the data.

There are no table hints that require a shared lock. Shared locks can, however, be held until the end of the transaction rather than releasing as soon as the Select is finished. Maintaining locks until the end of the transactions is done with the HOLDLOCK table hint, as shown in the following example:

```
BEGIN TRANSACTION
SELECT *
    FROM Guide
        WITH (HOLDLOCK)
    WHERE LastName = 'Carajuana'
.
.
.
COMMIT TRANSACTION
```

Shared locks will be placed on all rows containing the last name of Carajuana, and these locks will not be released until the Commit Transaction is executed or an error causes the entire transaction to be rolled back. Under some circumstances, MSDE may have decided to place page locks or a table lock for the previous example. Either of these locks would also have been held until the end of the transaction.

The HOLDLOCK table hint operates on any kind of lock, whether it is shared, update, or exclusive. Under normal circumstances, update and exclusive locks are held until the end of the transaction anyway, so a HOLDLOCK would be redundant.

There is also a table hint that allows reads of the database without placing or obeying any locks: NOLOCK. A Select statement containing the NOLOCK hint does not place any shared locks on the rows it reads, and it ignores exclusive locks and reads the protected data anyway. In reading data protected by an exclusive lock, the query may return uncommitted data. Uncommitted data is not durable and may simply disappear or revert to a former value. The disappearance of uncommitted data can happen if the transaction that created the data is rolled back, either due to an error or because of an unexpected stoppage of the server.

Preparing to modify data with an update lock

Exclusive locks may not be placed on any object that currently has a shared lock placed on it. Doing so can potentially cause a problem if multiple transactions are attempting to write to the same object while there are other transactions that periodically place shared locks on the object. Consider an example: Transaction A and Transaction B are both intending to write data on the same page. If Transaction A attempts to write to the page, but shared locks are present, Transaction A is unable to place the exclusive lock. Typically, the application running Transaction A now waits for a period of time and tries to place the lock again. While Transaction A waits for its opportunity, Transaction B could potentially gain an exclusive lock on the page and perform its write. In an environment that has many transactions using exclusive locks and trying to write to the database simultaneously, there is no way to predict how long it will take any individual transaction to place a lock. In order to prevent such chaos, the update lock mechanism is introduced to provide first-come, first-served precedence for transactions that are seeking to place exclusive locks on resources.

A single update lock is compatible with any number of shared locks on the same resource. After an update lock is placed on an object, no other update locks or exclusive locks can be placed on the object. The transaction that has placed an update lock on objects can later attempt to convert the lock to an exclusive lock. This process allows the first transaction that needs to write to an object to place the update lock, essentially reserving its place in the queue so it can be the first transaction to gain an exclusive lock on the object. Update locks are held until the end of the transaction that placed them by default; however, the lock is usually converted to an exclusive lock before the transaction ends.

To place an update lock, use the UPDLOCK table hint with a Select statement that accesses the data that will be updated later in the transaction. When an Insert, Update, or Delete is later executed on the same set of data, MSDE will attempt to convert the update lock to an exclusive lock. Here is an example of placing an update lock in a Select statement:

```
BEGIN TRANSACTION
SELECT *
    FROM Guide
    WITH (UPDLOCK)
    WHERE Specialty = 'AHusbandry'
.
.
.
UPDATE Guide
    SET Specialty = 'Horses'
    WHERE LastName = 'Griswold' AND Specialty = 'AHusbandry'
COMMIT TRANSACTION
```

When the Select statement runs, update locks are placed on all rows with a Specialty of AHusbandry. The ellipsis indicates that there would probably be more logic in production code. Finally, when the Update runs, all the rows with the LastName of Griswold and a Specialty of AHusbandry will have the Specialty changed to Horses. The conversion of the update locks to exclusive locks happens only on the rows with the LastName of Griswold. Any rows with an AHusbandry Specialty, but with a last name other than Griswold would continue to have update locks until the transaction ends.

Make sure that the statement that converts update locks to exclusive locks acts on a subset of the rows that have update locks. In the example, this was accomplished by including the predicate Specialty = 'AHusbandry'. If this had not been done and if any Griswolds had a Specialty other than AHusbandry, the whole transaction could have been blocked while waiting for an exclusive lock on those rows. Blocking is much less likely on a row with an update lock as opposed to no lock.

Modifying data using an exclusive lock

When a transaction wants to modify an object in the database, it places an exclusive lock on the object. Exclusive locks are not compatible with any other lock; no other transaction can read or write to the object while the exclusive lock is in place.

Whenever an exclusive lock is acquired, it is held until the end of the transaction that acquired it. In an explicit transaction in which the programmer has specified the Begin Transaction and Commit Transaction statements, any exclusive locks will be released when the Commit Transaction or Rollback statements are reached or if an error occurs that causes an automatic rollback. A transaction implicitly created by an Insert or Update statement that is executed without a Begin Transaction statement will release the exclusive lock at the end of the statement.

When a connection with the Implicit_Transactions setting turned on is used, any exclusive lock will be held until a Commit or Rollback is executed.

An exclusive table lock can be specified in a SQL statement with the TABLOCKX table hint as in the following example:

```
BEGIN TRANSACTION
SELECT *
    FROM GUIDE
    WITH (TABLOCKX)
.
.
.
COMMIT TRANSACTION
```

In this example, the ellipsis represents code that is expected to modify most of the data in the Guide table or to have some other reason to include an exclusive lock. There is little reason to place an exclusive table lock simply to read its rows. Placing such a lock degrades performance because the transaction has to wait until there are no other locks before the exclusive lock can be placed, and while the exclusive lock is held, no other transaction can access the table in any way.

XLOCK is a new locking hint available in the 2000 version. XLOCK can be used alone or in combination with ROWLOCK, PAGLOCK, or TABLOCK to ensure that whatever kind of lock is placed is an exclusive lock. The following example guarantees an exclusive lock, but allows MSDE to choose the granularity (row, page, or table):

```
BEGIN TRANSACTION
SELECT *
    FROM Guide
    WITH (XLOCK)
.
.
.
COMMIT TRANSACTION
```

The next example uses page-level exclusive locks (assuming that a table called Guide2 has been created with the same structure as Guide):

```
BEGIN TRANSACTION
INSERT
    INTO Guide2
        WITH (XLOCK, PAGLOCK)
    SELECT * FROM Guide
.
.
.
COMMIT TRANSACTION
```

It is not necessary that there be other code in this example where the ellipsis lies. Also, notice that the XLOCK is somewhat redundant in the example because an Insert statement will always place exclusive locks, with or without a table hint to that effect. The same table hint could also easily be used in a Select statement to prepare the appropriate exclusive locks for the rest of the transaction.

Using the XLOCK hint with the TABLOCK hint is equivalent to using the TABLOCKX hint.

Providing a lock hierarchy: intent locks

Because of the nature of lock interaction, MSDE must do a certain amount of work before placing a lock. It must ensure that no incompatible lock is placed on the object to be locked, and it must make sure that nothing contained within the object has an incompatible lock. If one transaction is reading a row in a table and has placed a shared lock on the row, then another transaction attempting to place an exclusive lock on the entire table to make modifications to every row should not be capable of doing so. The exclusive lock on the table is functionally equivalent to a row lock on every row in the table, including the row with a shared lock. MSDE must, therefore, have some mechanism to prevent lock conflicts among different types of objects (rows, pages, and tables) as well as among objects of the same type.

To reduce the amount of work that MSDE must perform as it places each lock, a hierarchical system of locks was created. The hierarchical system of locks consists of the lock that is placed on an object to be accessed and intent locks that are placed on any objects that contain the object that is to be read or written. For example, if a row is to have a shared lock (S) placed on it, then an intent-shared lock (IS) will be placed on the page containing the row and on the table containing the page. If a shared lock is placed on a page, then an intent-shared lock is placed on the table that contains the page. If an exclusive lock (X) is placed on a row, then an intent-exclusive lock (IX) is placed on the page and the table that contain the row.

When a new lock is to be placed on an object, MSDE can check that object for any intent locks. If there are no intent locks on the object, then there are no locks on any objects contained within the object, and it is safe to place the lock.

Figure 10-1 illustrates the concept of locking hierarchy. The largest horizontal rectangle represents a table. The four vertical rectangles within the table represent pages, and the smallest horizontal rectangles in each page represent rows. The first page contains a single row with an exclusive lock, and the page and the table have intent-exclusive locks. The second page has a shared page lock, and the table has an intent-shared lock. Every row within the second page is implicitly locked with a shared lock. The third page contains three rows with shared locks and one row with an exclusive lock; therefore, the page has three intent-shared locks and one intent-exclusive lock. By virtue of the locks on the third page, the table also must have intent-shared and intent-exclusive locks. The fourth page has no locks. Note that although there are no locks on the rows in the second page, lock compatibility still prevents exclusive locks from being placed on these rows. For an exclusive lock to be set on a row, an intent-exclusive lock must be set on the page containing the row. The second page already has an intent-shared lock that is not compatible with an intent-exclusive lock. An attempt to place an exclusive lock on a row in that page would be blocked.

In addition to the IS and IX intent locks, there is a shared intent-exclusive lock (SIX). A SIX is a combination of a shared lock and an intent-exclusive lock. The SIX lock is used when a transaction needs to be capable of reading all of the contents of an object and to be capable of modifying some, but not all of the objects contained in the larger object. For example, if a transaction needs to scan every row in a table and, based on the scan, needs to update several rows, it can place a SIX lock on the table and an IX on any pages that contain rows to be changed. The rows that are to be changed would, of course, have X locks placed on them.

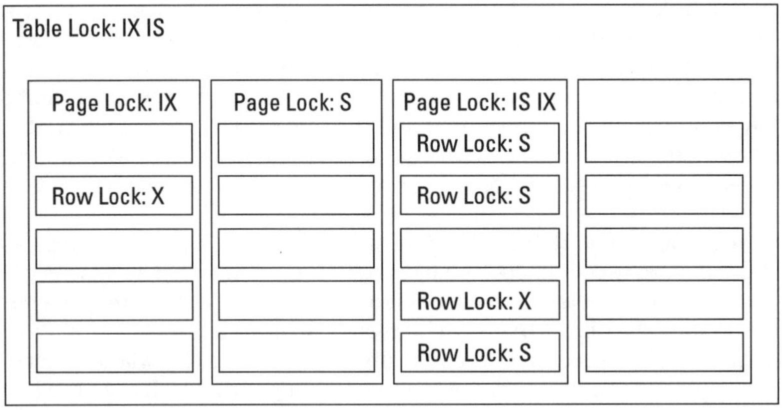

Table Lock: IX IS

Page Lock: IX	Page Lock: S	Page Lock: IS IX	
		Row Lock: S	
Row Lock: X		Row Lock: S	
		Row Lock: X	
		Row Lock: S	

Figure 10-1: Locking hierarchy

Changing metadata: schema locks

MSDE uses two other types of locks to control access to the database schema (the schema is the set of information that defines the structure of the database, including all tables, views, permissions, and so on). These locks are the schema-s and schema-m locks for schema stability and schema modification. The schema-s locks do not interact in any way with data locks. A schema-s lock will never prevent a data lock from being placed, and vice versa. The schema-m locks are incompatible with any other locks, both schema and data.

The schema-s is loosely equivalent to the shared lock for data and is used when query plans are being compiled to make sure the structure of the database remains stable during analysis. Schema-s locks are compatible with one another so that multiple plans accessing the same objects can be compiled at the same time.

The schema-m is loosely equivalent to the exclusive lock for data and is used when any of the structure of the database is being changed. Because schema-m locks are placed only when the structure is being changed, they do not allow any reads or writes of the data that resides in the structure being changed.

Programmers and administrators can ignore schema locks for the most part, except to realize how they are used and that they are tracked with the same mechanisms as data locks. It is also possible, although unlikely, that a transaction could be blocked while waiting to acquire a lock because a schema-m has been placed on an object the transaction needs. Such a conflict is rare because modifications to the schema are always short-lived.

Loading data in parallel with bulk update locks

A frequent task for database designers and administrators is the importation of data from outside sources such as mainframe databases. When there is a large amount of data to move, it can sometimes be helpful to performance to have multiple processes performing the load simultaneously, or in parallel. The bulk insert lock is designed for such an application. Bulk insert locks are compatible with one another, but not with any other kind of lock. They ensure that users are not accessing the data during the load.

Take care when using bulk insert locks to design a conflict avoidance strategy into the bulk insert operation. MSDE will not protect the data being loaded in one bulk load process from another bulk load process.

Bulk update locks can be invoked directly in the bulk copy command or by first setting the table lock on bulk load option. To set a bulk update lock in the `bcp` command that is run from the operating system command prompt or batch file, specify the TABLOCK table hint as the following example shows (this example is a single command that is too long to fit on one line):

```
bcp scheduling..Guide in c:\Guide.prn
    -SOkh2h -Usa -P -c -h "TABLOCK"
```

The next example shows the bulk insert SQL statement with the TABLOCK table hint (this could be run from Query Analyzer or some other tool that can execute a SQL script):

```
BULK INSERT Guide
    FROM 'c:\guide.prn'
    WITH (TABLOCK)
```

Setting the table lock on bulk load option causes any subsequent bulk copies to use bulk insert locks. Use the following command to set this option:

```
Sp_tableoption tablename, 'table lock on bulk load', true
```

The bulk update lock is always a table lock. So if either of the bulk copy/insert commands shown had been run without the TABLOCK hint and without the table lock on bulk load table option, the data transfer would have defaulted to normal locking behavior. MSDE would have attempted to use row-level locking and could have caused contention with other processes to lock the rows in the table. Because the bulk update lock is a table-level lock, it does not have to wait for any other locks once it is acquired. If multiple `bcp` or `bulk insert` commands are run at the same time with the TABLOCK hint, additional bulk update locks can be acquired immediately.

Understanding the Interaction of Locks

Locks have carefully designed interaction rules that must be considered to achieve the best possible performance from a database. Table 10-1 shows which locks can be blocked by other locks. B indicates that the corresponding locks are incompatible and either one will prevent (block) the other from being placed.

Table 10-1
Lock Compatibility

	S	U	X	IS	IX	SIX	Schema-S	Schema-M	Bulk Update
S			B		B	B		B	B
U		B	B		B	B		B	B
X	B	B	B	B	B	B		B	B
IS			B					B	B
IX	B	B	B			B		B	B
SIX	B	B	B		B	B		B	B
Schema-S								B	
Schema-M	B	B	B	B	B	B	B	B	B
Bulk Update	B	B	B	B	B	B		B	

It may seem that an intent-exclusive lock should be incompatible with other intent-exclusive locks; however, they can be compatible because an intent-exclusive indicates that some, but not all, of the resources contained in the locked object will have exclusive locks placed on them. For example, if one transaction places an exclusive page lock on the first page in a table, it will place an intent-exclusive lock on the table. If a second transaction wishes to place an exclusive page lock on the second page in the table, there is no reason why it cannot. Consequently, the second transaction can also place an intent-exclusive lock on the table.

For the same reason, intent-shared and intent-exclusive locks do not block each other. If a transaction attempts to place an intent-shared lock on a resource (a page, for example) already possessing an intent-exclusive lock, the transaction must check the row that it intends to lock to determine whether that row holds the exclusive lock that is responsible for the intent-exclusive lock on the entire page. If it does not hold the exclusive lock, the lock is placed, and the transaction proceeds. If the intended row is already locked exclusively, then the transaction is blocked and waits with the outstanding intent-shared at the higher level until the blocking lock is removed or until the application that controls the blocked transaction times out and rolls back to retry later.

Setting Automatic Locking with Isolation Levels

MSDE uses a configuration setting called the transaction isolation level to determine the automatic locking behavior. This setting can be controlled for a connection using the `Set Transaction Isolation Level` command. The behavior can also be controlled using table hints as mentioned previously. The possible settings for transaction isolation level are as follows:

- **Read Uncommitted** — Read Uncommitted is at the far end of the concurrency spectrum for transaction isolation levels. When the Read Uncommitted level is set, shared locks are not placed during reads, and exclusive locks do not block the transaction from accessing the data. With this level of transaction isolation, all of the possible problems listed at the beginning of this chapter are possible: lost updates, dirty reads, nonrepeatable reads, and phantoms. The advantage of this level is that transactions are completed rapidly. Because the level is not blocked and does not block, the transaction does not have to wait for a timeout and retry. For certain types of reporting, this can be an effective method for getting more performance out of your database. This isolation level is equivalent to including the NOLOCK table hint in every query.
- **Read Committed** — Read Committed is the default transaction isolation level. When this level is in effect, shared locks are held only until the system is done reading the data that caused the lock to be set. Update and exclusive locks are held until the end of the transaction. At this isolation level, only extremely poor programming can cause lost updates. Dirty reads are not permitted, so only durable data that was created by committed transactions can be seen. This isolation level does allow nonrepeatable reads because shared locks are immediately released. It also allows phantoms because it locks rows directly, not in ranges.
- **Repeatable Read** — Repeatable Read is less concurrent than Read Committed. It extends all shared locks so that they are not released until the end of the transactions. By doing so, any data that is touched in any way by a transaction is maintained in the same state from the time it is touched until the transaction is completed or rolled back. The same effect can be achieved by including the HOLDLOCK table hint in every Select statement. Including HOLDLOCK in only those Select statements that require it is often a good trade-off between Repeatable Read and Read Committed isolation levels.
- **Serializable** — Serializable is the least concurrent of the transaction isolation levels. In addition to all of the protections of Repeatable Read, any range that is accessed will have a range lock placed on the index. Serializable transaction isolation levels prevent all of the problems caused by multiuser systems.

In addition to the listed levels of transaction isolation, the read-only database option is another condition that can be considered analogous to an isolation level. The read-only database option must, of course, be set for the entire database, rather than for a single user connection as in the case of the other isolation levels. Setting a database to read-only allows MSDE to run that database with no locks. Because no data is permitted to change, it is impossible to have a lost update; there are no updates. It is impossible to have a dirty read; data can be dirty only after it has been written, and a read-only database allows no writes. Phantoms are impossible because they also involve changing data. Running a database with no locks means running a database with virtually no contention. The only limiting factor on the performance of the database is the hardware on which it runs and how fast that hardware can service requests for data. If a query-intensive application is required, it may be efficient to set up a read-only database to service it. Naturally, read-only can be used only in certain, very specific environments. However, an environment that supports read-only can sometimes be created by having two database servers, one that supports transactions and another that supports read-only queries and is bulk updated periodically.

Deadlocks

One condition that must be understood to design a well-performing application is deadlock. Deadlock is also known as deadly embrace. It can occur only when two or more transactions are attempting to lock the same resources in different orders.

Figure 10-2 illustrates deadlock between two user connections. User Connection A has an exclusive lock placed on page 472. User Connection B has an exclusive lock placed on page 590. Connection A needs to place a lock on page 590 to complete its work, and Connection B needs to place a lock on page 472 to complete its work. Neither connection can place the second lock that it needs to complete its transaction; because neither can complete their work, neither will release the lock that would allow the other connection to gain the required second lock—thus, deadlock.

This illustration is a relatively simple one. Deadlock can be much more complex and can involve many more connections.

MSDE evaluates locks periodically to try to determine whether any connections are in deadlock. Every few seconds, it checks to determine whether any processes are blocked. If any are blocked, the list of resources for which processes are waiting is examined. From this list, MSDE can usually detect any transactions that are in deadlock. If two or more transactions are in deadlock, the system will choose a victim based on criteria that includes the amount of process time that has been dedicated to a particular process. The victim is usually the process with the least amount of process time. In this way, the system tries to waste as little time as possible redoing work that was rolled back.

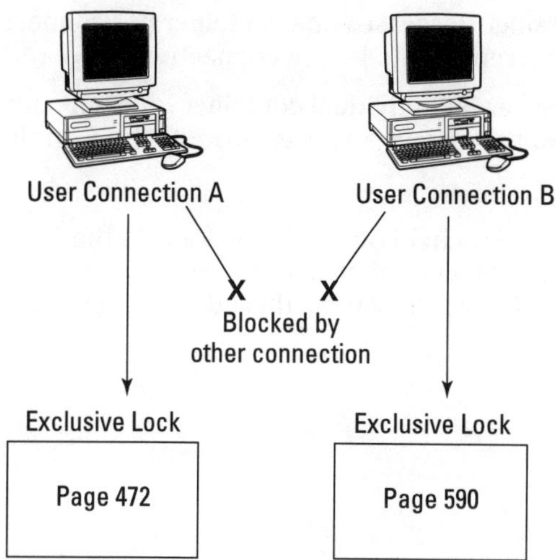

Figure 10-2: Deadlock between two connections

After a victim has been chosen, the transaction is aborted and rolled back, and error 1205 is sent to the client from which the transaction originated. In addition to the normal deadlock victimization algorithm, a connection can set its own Deadlock_Priority to low. The transaction on the low-priority connection will become the preferred victim.

Database programs should always contain error-handling code that looks for errors such as the 1205 deadlock error. When an error is encountered, the transaction should be retried once or twice and will normally succeed. Passing the error message back to the user is not usually very effective, although these errors should be logged in order to better assess system performance.

Viewing Locks

When designing or administering a database, it can be critical to be able to view the locks that are set on objects in the database. There are several methods of observing locking behavior in MSDE. Enterprise Manager has two ways of examining locks, and the stored procedure `sp_lock` provides a report showing all locks in the database.

In Enterprise Manager, open the server ➪ Management ➪ Current Activity. The three containers within Current Activity are as follows:

✦ **Process info** — This container displays all of the current connections to the MSDE server.

✦ **Locks/Process ID** — This container possesses one container per connection displaying any locks that are currently held by the connection.

✦ **Locks/Object** — This container has an individual container for each currently locked object, and each container displays all locks currently held on the object.

Figure 10-3 shows all of the locks currently held on the Guide table in the Scheduling database using the Locks/Object container. Connection 53 and connection 52 have locks open in the figure. Before displaying this container, connection 53 executed the following code:

```
BEGIN TRANSACTION
SELECT *
FROM Guide WITH (XLOCK)
WHERE LastName = 'Nichols'
```

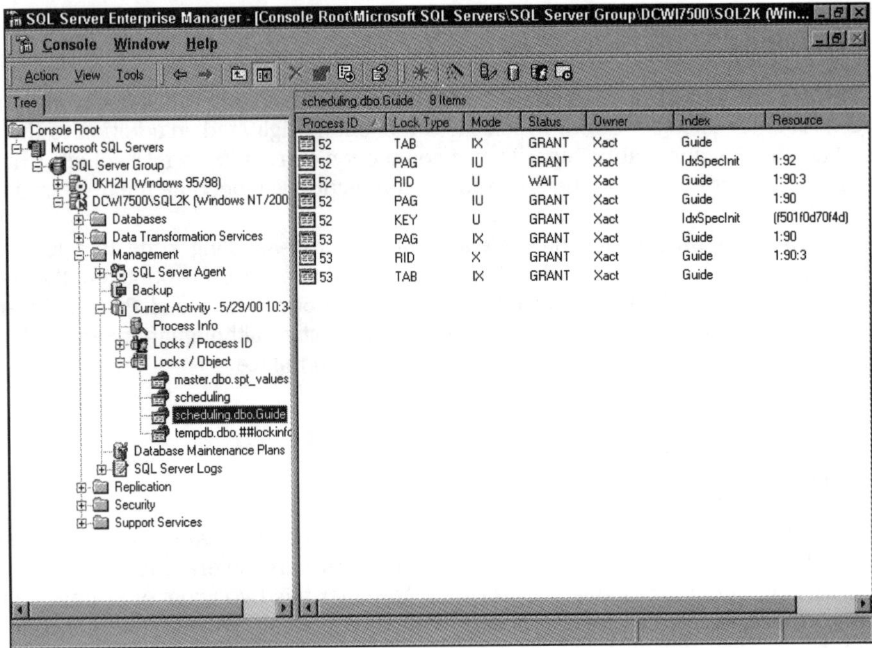

Figure 10-3: Displaying locks held on an object with Enterprise Manager

The Commit statement has not been executed, so the exclusive lock that has been set will not be released. As you can see in the figure, the last three lines in the display represent the locks held by connection 53. The Lock Type column indicates the granularity of the lock; there is one lock each for page (PAG), row (RID), and table (TAB). The Mode column indicates the intended use of the lock. The row lock is exclusive, and the page and table locks are intent-exclusive. The Index column indicates the name of the table or index being locked, and the Resource column shows the specifics of the particular resource that is locked. The table lock needs no specifics because it applies to the entire table, and the table is named in the Index column. The page lock shows a resource of 1:90, meaning that the locked page is the ninetieth page in the first file of the table. The row lock shows a fully qualified RID, indicating that the locked row is in the third slot on the ninetieth page in the first file of the table. Whenever an intent lock is acquired, it will correspond in the file and page number to a row lock.

After the lock is replaced by connection 53, connection 52 executes the following code:

```
BEGIN TRANSACTION
SELECT *
    FROM Guide
    WITH (UPDLOCK)
    WHERE Specialty = 'AHusbandry'
```

This code attempts to place an update lock on all values in a table with a specialty equal to AHusbandry. In this case, there are five lines representing locks in the display:

- ✦ The first line for connection 52 is an intent-exclusive table lock on the Guide table. This lock is intent-exclusive, rather than intent-update, in preparation for conversion to exclusive.
- ✦ The second line shows an intent-update page lock on the ninety-second page in the first file, which turns out to be part of the index IdxSpecInit. This lock gives us the expectation that an update lock will be found on a particular key value in the index further down in the display.
- ✦ The third line shows an update row lock on a RID in the Guide table. The status of this lock is wait, and the resource that is waiting for a lock is the third slot in the ninetieth page of the first file in the Guide table. This resource is the same resource that is already locked by connection 53 in the second from the last line on the display. Because another connection already has a lock on the resource, connection 52 is waiting to place the lock.
- ✦ The fourth line shows the intent-update lock on page ninety. This indicates that connection 52 has placed an update lock on a row within page ninety.
- ✦ The fifth line in the display is the key lock that connection 52 has placed on the value in the index. The resource in this case shows a hexadecimal value, which could be converted into the key value.

Tip

Enterprise Manager does not dynamically refresh its displays. When using Enterprise Manager to examine locks in MSDE, right-click the Current Activity container and choose refresh in order to get an updated list of locks and connections.

The SP_lock stored procedure displays essentially the same information available in Enterprise Manager. The output below was generated from the same system used in Figure 10-3.

```
spid  dbid  ObjId       IndId  Type Resource       Mode    Status
----- ----- ----------  ------ ---- -------------  ------- ------
52    7     0           0      DB                  S        GRANT
52    7     1977058079  0      TAB                 IX       GRANT
52    7     1977058079  0      RID  1:90:3         U        WAIT
52    7     1977058079  2      PAG  1:92           IU       GRANT
52    7     1977058079  0      PAG  1:90           IU       GRANT
52    7     1977058079  2      KEY  (f501f0d70f4d)U         GRANT
53    7     1977058079  0      PAG  1:90           IX       GRANT
53    7     1977058079  0      TAB                 IX       GRANT
53    7     1977058079  0      RID  1:90:3         X        GRANT
53    7     0           0      DB                  S        GRANT
54    5     0           0      DB                  S        GRANT
54    1     85575343    0      TAB                 IS       GRANT
```

This stored procedure displays all of the locks currently in the system. It displays the object identifiers for the locked object and the database, rather than displaying the names for the objects. The same is true for the index; the index id is displayed rather than the index name. The first line and the third line from the bottom show the shared lock that is placed by each connection on its current database to be used by the system to determine which databases are in use. The last two lines from connection 54 are the locks being used to run the SP_lock stored procedure.

The following output was generated by SP_lock after connection 53 committed the transaction that was holding an exclusive lock:

```
spid  dbid ObjId       IndId Type Resource       Mode     Status
----- ---- ----------  ----- ---- -------------  -------- ------
52    7    0           0     DB                  S        GRANT
52    7    1977058079  0     TAB                 IX       GRANT
52    7    1977058079  2     KEY  (f50137414e02) U        GRANT
52    7    1977058079  0     RID  1:90:4         U        GRANT
52    7    1977058079  0     RID  1:90:3         U        GRANT
52    7    1977058079  2     PAG  1:92           IU       GRANT
52    7    1977058079  0     PAG  1:90           IU       GRANT
52    7    1977058079  2     KEY  (f501f0d70f4d) U        GRANT
53    7    0           0     DB                  S        GRANT
54    5    0           0     DB                  S        GRANT
54    1    85575343    0     TAB                 IS       GRANT
```

Connection 53 has now released all locks except for the shared lock on the database that indicates that the database is in use. Connection 52 has been able to acquire the update lock on the third slot in page 90 and has additionally acquired a lock on the fourth slot, which also contains a row meeting the criteria of the `Where` clause. This lock had not been placed previously because the transaction had been unable to move forward because of the block situation with connection 53, so connection 52 had never gotten to the point of placing a lock on the fourth slot.

It can be useful to get to know the `SP_lock` stored procedure. The output is not hard to read and the `SP_lock` stored procedure doesn't require Enterprise Manager to run. It can be run from Query Analyzer or the osql command line. The object identifiers for tables, databases, and indexes can be translated into names by selecting the value from system tables.

To translate the database ID into the database name, run the following code, shown with its output:

```
USE Master
SELECT Name
FROM Sysdatabases
WHERE DBID = 7

Name
------------------------------------------------------
scheduling

(1 row(s) affected)
```

To translate the index ID into the index name, run the following code, shown with its output (note the use of the object ID and the index ID):

```
USE Scheduling
SELECT Name
FROM SysIndexes
WHERE ID = 1977058079 AND INDID = 2

Name
------------------------------------------------------
IdxSpecInit

(1 row(s) affected)
```

To translate the object ID into the object name, run the following code:

```
USE Scheduling
SELECT Name
FROM SysObjects
WHERE ID = 1977058079

Name
------------------------------------------------------
Guide

(1 row(s) affected)
```

Summary

MSDE provides a moderately conservative approach to balancing concurrency with consistency. Placing locks on resources protects the consistency of the database. These locks prevent access to the resources they protect. The default level of locking is called Read Committed, which places shared locks for any data read and exclusive locks for any data write. The shared locks are released as soon as the data has been read. Exclusive locks release when the transaction is complete. Other levels of locking are possible and can be controlled with session-level settings or with table hints that affect only the locks that are placed by a single statement. An option that can occasionally be used is to set a database to read-only, in which case locks are neither needed nor used.

✦ ✦ ✦

P A R T

Data Retrieval and Modification

This part explores the most commonly used command within SQL, the multi-faceted `Select` statement for retrieving data; the three basic types of SQL statements allowing data modification, `Insert`, `Update`, and `Delete`; and acts as a guide to programming with SQL's considerable list of commands.

✦ ✦ ✦ ✦

In This Part

✦ ✦ ✦ ✦

CHAPTER 11

Retrieving Data with the Structured Query Language

In This Chapter

A brief history of SQL

SQL standards

Using the `Select` statement

Sorting output

Joining tables

Using subqueries

Concatenating result sets

In whatever context MSDE is used, it is eventually necessary to use SQL. For example, it is much easier to perform complex and repetitive tasks by running a script than by using graphical tools in Access or Enterprise Manager. To have full control over data from within a program, SQL must be used (although there are graphical tools to assist in creating the SQL statement, they are useful only for relatively small and simple tasks). Finally, fine-tuning application performance and setting up maintenance tasks generally requires the use of SQL.

SQL appears at first to be a very simple language with only a few commands. These few commands turn out to have an enormous array of parameters that provide great functionality, but with it, great complexity. SQL is a subtle language. Its use is molded by the underlying data structures and by the experience of the person using it. The degree of difficulty in writing any given function in SQL is dictated in large part by the degree of normalization of the underlying tables or the ingenuity of the original designer.

A Cross-Platform Language

IBM developed SQL in the early 1970s. It was originally known as SEQUEL or Structured English Query Language. It became popular as part of a new, experimental database called System R in an attempt to make the database more readily accessible to nonprogrammers. System R was one of the first database systems to implement the ideas of E. F. Codd as published in his historic paper, "A Relational Model of Data for Large Shared Data Banks," in the June 1970 issue of the Association of Computer Machinery (ACM) journal *Communications of the ACM.* Other DBMS software manufacturers quickly adopted the relational model and SQL with it because it was a technically superior system and because they wanted to be as compatible as possible with IBM, which was the industry leader. As more and more products began to support it, SQL became the de facto standard and in 1989 was adopted as an official standard (the United States government adopted it as early as 1987 in a Federal Information Processing Standard, FIPS 127).

Standards: ANSI-89 and ANSI-92

The American National Standards Institute (ANSI) adopted SQL in 1989 as a vendor-independent database access language. Soon thereafter, a revised and now widely supported version of SQL was adopted. These two standards are generally referred to by year, that is, ANSI-89 and ANSI-92. Their official names are ANSI X3.135-1989 and ANSI X3.135-1992. ANSI works closely with the International Standards Organization, and the SQL defined in ANSI-92 is the same as that defined in ISO/IEC 9075:1992.

ANSI-92 SQL has four levels to which a particular implementation may adhere, and MSDE, like most other commercial products, adheres to the entry level. It also has full backward compatibility with ANSI-89 and supports the full set of Transact-SQL statements. Transact-SQL, or T-SQL, is the native language of Microsoft SQL Server. There are, therefore, several ways of performing the same action: the ANSI-89 method, the ANSI-92 method, and the T-SQL method. Examples are joins and transactions.

The importance of the ANSI standard is that if code is written according to the standard, it can be easily ported from one platform to another. It is not yet totally transparent because all major DBMS vendors support functionality that is outside the scope of the ANSI standard. When the features are used, the scripts that call them must be rewritten when moving to a different platform. The SQL that is used by Jet is not fully ANSI-92 compliant because it fails to support some features like locking, transactions, and granting security. MSDE and SQL Server use exactly the same, ANSI-compliant implementation of SQL.

The Organization of SQL Statements

SQL is composed of statements that can be organized into three groups:

- ✦ The Data Definition Language (DDL) is used to create, alter, or destroy the structures of a database, such as tables, views, and stored procedures.

✦ The Data Manipulation Language (DML) is used to access, create, modify, or delete the actual data that fills the tables of a database. The DML commands include SELECT, INSERT, UPDATE, and DELETE.

✦ The Data Control Language (DCL) is used to administer security for a database. The three DCL commands are GRANT, DENY, and REVOKE.

Using the Three Main Elements of a Query

Queries in SQL use the Select statement. The Select statement is the workhorse of SQL and is used whenever data is to be retrieved from a database. It can be used to view the contents of tables or views in a database. Additionally, because MSDE stores metadata in system tables, the Select statement can be used to view the structure and security setting of the database.

The Select statement has one required component—the select list—and two other components that are rarely omitted—the From clause and the Where clause. The Select list specifies the columns to be returned from the table or view that is being queried. The From clause lists the table(s) (or view(s)) that are to be queried. The Where clause defines a condition for which rows are to be returned. The following is a Select statement that lists the first and last name of all people whose last name is Turing, as defined in a database table called People:

```
Select firstname, lastname
From People
Where lastname = 'Turing'
```

The line breaks do not affect the function of the Select statement. There are a number of different styles used to format a Select statement; the particular style is less important than being sure that the statement is clear and easily read.

The select list

The Select statement begins with the select list. In its most basic form, the select list enumerates the columns from a table or view that is to be displayed. The syntax for the select list is as follows:

```
<select_list> ::=
    {    *
         | { table_name | view_name | table_alias }.*
         |     { column_name | expression | IDENTITYCOL |
ROWGUIDCOL }
             [ [AS] column_alias ]
         | column_alias = expression
    }    [,...n]
```

This syntax can be broken down as follows:

The first line indicates that a select list can be represented by any of the items as defined in the following lines.

The second line opens curly brackets that close on the last line. These brackets contain items separated by vertical bars which mean or. Following the open bracket is an asterisk, which indicates that allow columns should be returned. For example, the following `Select` statement would display all columns from all rows in the People table:

```
Select *
    From People
```

The third line indicates that the name of a table, view, or alias can be specified followed by a period and an asterisk. Using the table name acts differently than an asterisk alone only if more than one table or view is referenced in the `Select` statement (using more than one table or view in a `Select` statement is a join). It allows all of the columns from the specified table or view to be returned. Joins are discussed later in the chapter.

The fourth line is the heart of the select list; it enables any of the following to be specified:

✦ **A column name**. This will return the unaltered contents of a column.

✦ **An expression.** The expression can be any valid SQL expression. It can use any of the SQL operators, such as parentheses, addition, subtraction, multiplication, and division. It can refer to zero or more columns; that is, it could simply be a constant value that would appear in every row of the output. It can also include more complex constructs such as subqueries or the `Case` function. A simple example of an expression is a column that contains monthly salary multiplied by 12 to display yearly salary:

```
Select monthlysalary * 12
```

✦ **The keyword** `IDENTITYCOL`**.** MSDE allows a single column in each table to be defined as the identity column. This column acts as a counter which increments every time a new row is added to the table. `IDENTITYCOL` will return that column if it exists and an error if it does not.

✦ **The keyword** `ROWGUIDCOL`**.** MSDE allows a single column in each table to be defined as the Globally Unique Identifier column. `ROWGUIDCOL` will return that column if it exists and an error if it does not.

For any of the items in the preceding list, the table name may precede the column name or keyword to resolve ambiguity. For example, if a `Select` statement references two tables, table1 and table2, and there is a column called name in both tables, the column should be specified as either table1.name or table2.name. The same is true for IDENTITYCOL and ROWGUIDCOL. For example, if both table1 and table2 have a column with the IDENTITY property, they could be referenced as table1.IDENTITYCOL or table2.IDENTITYCOL.

When a column name is used, the output of the Select statement contains a column heading that is the column name. If an expression is used, no column name will appear. There are two methods for specifying a custom column name. The fifth line defines one method, which is to follow with the column name or expression with the keyword AS and the name that appears as the column heading. Using the monthly salary example from above:

```
Select monthlysalary * 12 AS 'Yearly Salary'
    From People
```

The other method for creating a column name in the output report is shown on line six of the syntax; that is to use the column name first, followed by =, and then any valid expression or column name as explained above. The next line of code is functionally equivalent to the previous line of code:

```
Select 'Yearly Salary' = monthlysalary * 12
    From People
```

The last line of the syntax indicates that any of the elements listed above can be repeated as many times as necessary if separated by commas. For example, the following code returns the first name, last name, and yearly salary of everyone defined in the table called People:

```
Select firstname, lastname, monthlysalary * 12 AS 'Yearly
Salary'
    From People
```

The From clause

The From clause must be included whenever a column name is referenced anywhere in the select list. There are only a few times when a From clause is not needed; for example, when examining the value of a variable or when assigning each value to a variable although a value can also be assigned to a variable with the SET command. The following code creates an integer variable, sets its value to 5, displays its value, sets its value to 7 using different syntax, and then displays its value again:

```
Declare @myvar int
Select @myvar = 5
Select @myvar
Set @myvar = 7
Select @myvar
```

Normally, the From clause is used to specify the tables from which data will be returned. The examples in the previous section illustrate how the table name can be listed in the From clause.

The tables listed in the From clause can be given aliases. The alias name is listed immediately following the table name, as in this example:

```
Select P.lastname
From People P
```

It is poor form to use aliases to save typing as in the previous example. However, aliases can make code more readable when table names are extremely long. Aliases also play a role in Self Joins and Correlated Subqueries, which are described later in this chapter.

If an alias is assigned to a table, only the alias can be used elsewhere in the query. If the original table name is used, a syntax error will be generated.

The Where clause

The Where clause primarily specifies which rows will be returned in a Select statement. It can also be used for old-style joins, although using old-style joins is not recommended. Joins of both types are discussed later in this chapter.

When using the Where clause to specify which rows should be returned, the keyword Where is followed by a search condition. The syntax for a search condition is:

```
<search_condition> ::=
    {    [ NOT ] <predicate> | ( <search_condition> ) }
        [ {AND | OR} [NOT] {<predicate> | ( <search_condition>
) } ]
    }    [,...n]
```

A search condition is a series of one or more predicates. Predicates are basically Boolean conditions or assertions; for example, lastname = 'Turing' or monthlysalary > 5000. Each predicate may be modified with the keyword NOT, and if there are more than one, they must be separated with either the keyword AND or the keyword OR. The syntax for a predicate is as follows:

```
<predicate> ::=
    {
        expression { = | <> | != | > | >= | !> | < | <= | !< }
expression
        | string_expression [NOT] LIKE string_expression
            [ESCAPE 'escape_character']
        | expression [NOT] BETWEEN expression AND expression
        | expression IS [NOT] NULL
```

```
          | CONTAINS
            (   {column | * }, '<contains_search_condition>' )
          | FREETEXT ( {column | * }, 'freetext_string' )
          | expression [NOT] IN (subquery | expression [,...n])
          | expression { = | <> | != | > | >= | !> | < | <= | !<
    }
            {ALL | SOME | ANY} (subquery)
          | EXISTS (subquery)
        }
```

A predicate consists of one expression related to another expression with a comparison operator or one expression related to a subquery. Table 11-1 lists the most common comparison operators. When two expressions are provided in the Where clause, they are often a column name and a constant or calculation, such as:

```
Select *
From People
Where monthlysalary >= 5000.
```

The functions CONTAINS and FREETEXT require the Full-Text Search Service, which requires SQL Server and is not available as part of MSDE.

Table 11-1
Common Comparison Operators

Operator	*Description*
=	Equal to
<> !=	Not equal to (these operators are interchangeable)
>	Greater than
>=	Greater than or equal to
!>	Not greater than
<	Less than
<=	Less than or equal to
!<	Not less than

Between

The Between operator provides a concise way to find a value that falls within a range. Between only makes sense when it is used with data that has an inherent order, such as dates. The following example returns the first and last name of all people who were born in 1952.

```
Select firstname, lastname
     From People
     Where birthdate between '01/01/52' and '12/31/52'
```

Is Null

Nulls are treated specially in MSDE. They represent an absence of a value or an unknown value, which is distinctly different from the data represented by 0 or an empty string. Because null represents an absence of data, it fails all comparisons; even the predicate Null = Null is always false. Therefore, in order to find a null value in the table, a special operator is needed; that operator is the `Is Null` operator. The following code returns the first name and last name of all people for whom the birthdate is null:

```
Select firstname, lastname
     From People
     Where birthdate is Null
```

In

It is sometimes necessary to find a value that matches one of several other values. Choosing a value if it is a member of a list can be accomplished using the equality comparison operator in a series of predicates strung together with `OR`s. However, there is an operator that provides a more concise way of writing code to perform this function: the `In` operator. The `In` operator must be followed by a list of values enclosed in parentheses and separated with commas. If the values are text strings, they must individually be enclosed in quotes. The following example returns the first and last name of all people who live in Lancaster, Devon, or Worcestershire:

```
Select firstname, lastname
     From People
     Where city in ('Lancaster', 'Devon', 'Worcestershire')
```

A subquery can also be used to provide values to the `In` operator.

All, Some, Any

Subqueries that provide a list of values can also be compared using the `all`, `some`, or `any` modifier. `Some` and `any` modifiers return true if a comparison is true for any of values returned by a subquery. The `all` modifier returns a true if the comparison is true for every value returned by the subquery.

Exists

`Exists` is similar to `all`, `some`, and `any`, except that it is not used with a common comparison operator. `Exists` must be followed by a subquery and returns a true if any values are returned by that subquery.

String expressions

String expressions can be used in the `Where` clause. They allow pattern matching to be performed against the column of a character-based type. String expressions can use the `LIKE` operator rather than one of the common comparison operators (in particular the = operator which can also be used with strings but will only find exact matches). The `LIKE` operator allows the use of wildcard characters in order to perform pattern matching. The wildcard characters are:

- _ The underscore matches any single character, so the predicate `col1 LIKE 'wing_'` would find wings (but not wing or winged).
- % The percent matches zero or more characters. The predicate `col1 LIKE 'wing%'` would find wing, winged, and wings.
- [] Square brackets match a single character from either a set or a range of characters. A set is specified by listing the characters within the square brackets, and a range is specified by listing the first character and last character separated with a hyphen. The predicate `col1 LIKE '[b-f]ig'` would find big, dig, and fig. The predicate `col1 LIKE '[bf]ig'` would find big and fig, but not dig.
- [^] The caret can be added within the square brackets to indicate that any character not included in the set or range will match. The predicate `col1 LIKE '[^b-f]ig'` would return rig, but not big, dig, or fig.

Wildcards can be used in any combination, making for some potentially difficult to interpret predicates. In addition, the wildcard characters themselves may sometimes need to be included in the string. For example, it may be necessary to match the string '5%' meaning five percent. To avoid matching any string that begins with the number 5, the percent character can be included in square brackets, which indicates that it is a literal: `col1 LIKE '5[%]'`. This trivial case can also be avoided by using the = operator: `col1 = '5%'`.

Sets and ranges can also be intermixed within square brackets. Intermixing appears as a construct similar to `col1 LIKE '[a-dhj]'`, which would match a, b, c, d, h, or j. Although it is sometimes confusing, the hyphen character can also be included in a set by making it the first character; thus, `col1 LIKE '[-dhj]'` would match -, d, h, or j.

Making results more meaningful

SQL provides a number of other elements to further control the output of the `Select` statement. These include methods for providing sorted output, aggregating values, and gathering data from more than one table.

Order By

The output of the Select statement can be sorted by using the Order By clause. Order By must follow the Where clause if it exists and takes as an argument one or more column names or aliases. If more than one column is specified, the column names must be separated with commas. For each column name, an additional parameter can be specified to determine whether a column should be sorted in ascending or descending order. The parameter is ASC for ascending and DESC for descending. The default order is ascending. The following example generates a report with the last name and monthly salary from the people table and orders first and by the monthly salary in ascending order. Any set of records that have the same monthly salary are sorted by last name in descending order.

```
Select lastname, monthlysalary
    From People
    Order By monthlysalary ASC, lastname DESC
```

Order By can use a column alias, so when using a calculation in the select list, give it an alias and use the alias in the Order By clause. Here is an example:

```
Select lastname, monthlysalary * 12 as 'Yearly Salary'
    From People
    Order By 'Yearly Salary' ASC, lastname DESC
```

Group By

SQL provides a number of aggregate functions that act on many inputs and return a single output. They are listed in Table 11-2.

Table 11-2
Aggregate Functions

Function	*Returned value*
AVG	Average of input values
COUNT	Number of input values
COUNT(*)	Total number of input rows and, unlike all other aggregate functions, does not ignore Null values
MAX	Single largest input value
MIN	Single smallest input value
SUM	Additive total of all inputs
STDEV	Standard deviation of all inputs
STDEVP	Standard deviation for the population of input values
VAR	Variance of all inputs
VARP	Variance for the population of input values

The aggregate functions are easy to use. For example, the following code returns the average monthly salary for all Philadelphians in the People table (an alias is provided for the average column because it is a calculation and therefore does not automatically get a column heading):

```
Select avg(monthlysalary) as 'Avg Salary'
    From People
    Where city = 'Philadelphia'
```

A `Select` statement that includes any aggregate functions can contain only aggregate functions. Because the aggregate functions summarize many values into one value and a nonaggregated column returns many values, the results would be incompatible.

Because aggregate functions only return a single value, to return the average monthly salary for each city in the People table, the `Group By` clause should be used to enable aggregates for each value at a column level to be returned with a single `Select` statement. For example, the following code returns the average monthly salary and city name for every distinct value in the city column; that is Philadelphia, Devon, and Manila.

```
Select avg(monthlysalary)as 'Avg Salary', city
    From People
    Group By city
```

When `Group By` its used, the select list can contain only columns that are included in the `Group By` clause and aggregate functions, for the same reason that `Select` statements with aggregate functions can contain only aggregate functions.

The `Group By` clause can also summarize according to unique combinations of values in multiple columns. The columns are listed after `Group By` separated by commas. The following code returns the average salary by city and by occupation within each city:

```
Select avg(monthlysalary)as 'Avg Salary', city, occupation
    From People
    Group By city, occupation
```

When used in this way, `Group By` returns the average for each occupation within the city. It is sometimes necessary to also return averages for the whole city and for the entire table. Returning averages (or any aggregate) for decreasing levels of granularity can be accomplished with the Rollup modifier.

```
Select avg(monthlysalary)as 'Avg Salary', city, occupation
    From People
    Group By city, occupation
    With Rollup
```

Rollup provides all of the same results that would be provided by the `Group By`. It also returns the results that would be provided by the city `Group By` without its last parameter, in this case the occupation column. That means that rows are returned with the average salary for each city. Because the rows that return these values do not rely on occupation, a null value is returned in the occupation column. The Rollup continues to nullify each of the parameters from the `Group By` clause until it provides the aggregate results for the entire set of rows, as defined in the `Where` clause. Output from the previous example is shown below:

```
Avg Salary  city                 occupation
----------- -------------------- ----------
900         Devon                Scientist
900         Devon                NULL
6000        Manila               Diver
6000        Manila               NULL
10000       Philadelphia         Actor
5000        Philadelphia         Author
5850        Philadelphia         Politician
4500        Philadelphia         Printer
6240        Philadelphia         NULL
5442        NULL                 NULL
```

In this case, the average salary for all occupations in Philadelphia is 6240. The average salary across all occupations and all cities is 5442. If the city column or the occupation column contained any null values, then this output would be difficult to interpret because there would be no way to differentiate between a null value that came from the table and a null value that was inserted by Rollup.

The Grouping function provides a way to make this distinction. An additional calculated column can be added to the select list passing as the parameter any column name that might be rolled up.

```
Select avg(monthlysalary)as 'Avg Salary',
       city, grouping(city) as 'City Rollup',
       occupation, grouping(occupation) as 'Occ. Rollup'
    From People
    Group By city, occupation
    With Rollup
```

The results are shown below:

```
Avg Salary  city          City Rollup occupation Occ. Rollup
----------- ------------- ----------- ---------- -----------
900         Devon         0           Scientist  0
900         Devon         0           NULL       1
6000        Manila        0           Diver      0
6000        Manila        0           NULL       1
10000       Philadelphia  0           Actor      0
```

```
5000        Philadelphia   0          Author     0
5850        Philadelphia   0          Politician 0
4500        Philadelphia   0          Printer    0
6240        Philadelphia   0          NULL       1
5442        NULL           1          NULL       1
```

The Grouping columns contain a one if they have been generated by the Rollup modifier and a zero if they have not.

Cube is another modifier related to Rollup. Cube returns all possible combinations of the `Group By` columns. If it had been used in the above example, average values for occupations regardless of city would have been generated. The output from Cube becomes rather difficult to read, and similar functionality is provided in data warehousing products.

If a `Where` clause is used in a `Select` statement, it is positioned before the `Group By` and is evaluated before the `Group By`. Rows that are excluded by a `Where` clause have no effect on the aggregates created by `Group By`. Because the `Where` clause is evaluated before the `Group By`, it does not have access to the aggregate values. In the example above, there is no way to exclude rows from the final report based on the average salary of a particular occupation. To do so requires the `Having` clause. `Having` functions very much like `Where`, except that it comes after the `Group By` and is able to access the aggregate values. The following code modifies the previous example so that only those occupations with an average salary higher than 5500 are returned.

```
Select avg(monthlysalary)as 'Avg Salary',
        city, grouping(city) as 'City Rollup',
        occupation, grouping(occupation) as 'Occ. Rollup'
    From People
    Group By city, occupation
    With Rollup
    Having avg(monthlysalary) > 5500
```

The results of this query are as follows:

```
Avg Salary  city            City Rollup occupation Occ. Rollup
----------- --------------- ----------- ---------- -----------
6000        Manila          0           Diver      0
6000        Manila          0           NULL       1
10000       Philadelphia    0           Actor      0
5850        Philadelphia    0           Politician 0
6240        Philadelphia    0           NULL       1
```

The row that represents the Rollup of city and occupation (the overall average) is no longer displayed because it fails to meet the condition of the `Having` clause.

Unlike the `Order By` clause, the `Having` clause cannot refer to an aggregate value by using a column alias. The aggregate calculation must be completely respecified in the `Having` clause.

Top

The `Top` function modifies a `Select` statement to return only a certain number of rows or a certain percentage of rows. This function accepts as a parameter either a number or a number and the word percent. Although it could be used without an `Order By` clause its results would not be particularly meaningful. The example below returns the two highest paying job/city combinations. The `Order By` clause is modified with a descending parameter in order to get the highest paying jobs. Without the descending parameter, the `Order By` would sort the results in ascending order, which would result in this statement returning the two lowest paying jobs.

```
Select top 2 avg(monthlysalary)as 'Avg Salary', city,
occupation
   From People
   Group By city, occupation
   order by 'Avg Salary' desc
```

Case

The `Case` function works likes a series of If statements. If evaluates an expression against one or more possible values and returns a result that corresponds to the matched value. In its simplest form, `Case` examines abbreviated values in a column and returns the full, unabbreviated version of those values. It can use a column containing state abbreviations, and when the value equals PA, it returns Pennsylvania; when it equals CA, it returns California and so on.

The `Case` function has two formats: the simple format and the searched format. The syntax for the simple format is:

```
CASE input_expression
    WHEN when_expression THEN result_expression
        [...n]
    [
        ELSE else_result_expression
    ]
END
```

The simple format compares an input expression to a series of other expressions (called when expressions in the syntax diagram). It then returns a specified value when a match is found. There is no limit to the number of When expressions that can be included. There is also an optional Else expression that is invoked if the input expression does not match any of the When expressions. As mentioned above, this simple form of `Case` can be used to expand abbreviations. To do so, it must contain code for all of the possible values or abbreviations. The following code examines a column called truth_value in a table called login and converts T to True, F to False, and anything else to Unknown.

```
Select
    Case truth_value
        When 'T' Then 'True'
        When 'F' Then 'False'
        Else 'Unknown'
    End
    From logic
```

Writing a similar `Case` function to expand state codes takes considerably more time, space, and server resources. Generally, when dealing with large numbers of values, a lookup table joined to the primary table makes more sense.

The searched format omits the input expression and includes a fully defined Boolean expression after each When:

```
CASE
    WHEN Boolean_expression THEN result_expression
        [...n]
    [
        ELSE else_result_expression
    ]
END
```

This format allows more flexibility than the simple format. The simple format can only evaluate the equality of expressions; the searched format allows any comparison operator (or any other expression that evaluates to either true or false). The searched format can be useful when categorizing ranges. For example, the following code might be used to generate reports for a warehouse in order to determine which products need to be ordered. It evaluates a column called units_in_stock and returns a descriptive phrase based on that value, along with a product name:

```
Select product_name,
    Case
        When units_in_stock = 0 Then 'Backordered'
        When units_in_stock < 15 Then 'Reorder now'
        Else 'In stock'
    End
    From inventory
```

Retrieving data from more than one table

Relational databases are organized as a set of tables that contain related information. Common examples of related objects are invoices, purchase orders, and bills of lading. In each of these cases, two (or more) tables can be created to represent a single form. One table contains a single row to represent the overall form, containing information such as shipping address, billing address, date, and other information that applies to all of the line items on the form. Another table uses a row to represent each line item and contains information such as description, quantity, price, and extended price. There must also be a column that contains information to link the two tables. This column is typically an integer value. There might be a column in the purchase order table containing the purchase order number, which would be unique for every row in that table. There is also a column in the purchase order line item table containing the purchase order number. Because there can be multiple line items on a single purchase order, there are multiple instances of the same purchase order number in the purchase order line item table. In this case, the purchase order number column in the purchase order table is that table's primary key, uniquely identifying each row. The purchase order column in the line item table is a foreign key, creating the relationship with a foreign table. A `Select` statement uses the two purchase order number columns to relate the rows in the two tables and to generate reports that have complete information about order. Combining information from more than one table in this way is called a Join.

In most cases, as in the purchase order example above, columns from two tables are compared, and equal values create a relation. It is possible to use any comparison when creating a join. That means rows from one table can be joined to any row from another table that has value that is greater than the value in its own column. Joining a value from one table with a different value in another table does not make sense in the purchase order example, but it is syntactically possible, and on rare occasions there is a call for it.

The syntax for a Join differs in the ANSI-89 standard and the ANSI-92 standard. MSDE supports them both, and the older syntax is still common in scripts on production servers. Therefore, both are discussed here; however, Microsoft strongly recommends that only the newer syntax be used.

Queries containing Joins are notoriously difficult to read. Using the new Join syntax makes it easier to read the code in the future.

Aside from the syntactic differences in Joins, there are three types of Joins: Inner, Outer, and Cross. Inner is by far the most common, closely followed by Outer. Cross Joins are generally used only in specialty applications, such as loading a fact table for a data warehouse.

Inner

An Inner Join relates only the rows in one table that have a matching row in the second table. In the purchase order example, all line item rows should have a matching row in the purchase order table; it does not make sense to have a line item that does not have a corresponding purchase order. In other situations, there may be rows that do not have corresponding entries in a related table. For example, if one table contains information about salespeople and another table contains information about the sales they have actually made, there may be salespeople who have not made a sale. An Inner Join does not return rows that correspond to the nonperforming salespeople.

The old-style for writing an Inner Join is to list all related tables in the `From` clause, to separate them by commas, and to list the criteria to be used to relate the rows in the `Where` clause:

```
Select salespeople.name, sales.quantity
    From salespeople, sales
    Where salespeople.id = sales.salesperson_id
```

This example returns the name of the salesperson and the quantity for each sale recorded in the sales table.

It may be noted that the older syntax varies from a standard, non-Join `Select` statement only in that there are multiple tables listed. It could be interpreted as returning all combinations of name and quantity from the two tables and then using the `Where` clause to weed out the undesirable combinations that do not make sense.

The newer and preferred syntax puts all of the information about the join in the `From` clause. After the keyword `From`, the first table is listed, followed by the keyword `Join`, followed by the second table. The second table name is followed by the keyword `On` and the condition that relates the first and second table (usually some column in the first table is equal to some column in the second table). If additional tables are to be included in the join, the keyword `Join` and the third table name follow the second table name. The Join shown above looks as follows in the new syntax:

```
Select salespeople.name, sales.quantity
    From salespeople Join sales
        On salespeople.id = sales.salesperson_id
```

Outer

Outer Joins are classified into three subtypes: Left Outer Joins, Right Outer Joins, and Full Outer Joins. The Left and Right Outer Joins solve the problem of the missing salespeople by returning all of the rows in one of the tables whether or not those rows have matching rows in the second table. Only matching rows are returned from the second table. A Full Outer Join returns all rows from both tables.

In the old syntax, Outer Joins are written just like Inner Joins, except that the Join criteria uses a `*=` or `=*` instead of an `=`. The `*=` indicates a Left Outer Join; the `=*` indicates a Right Outer Join. The following example returns all salespeople even if they have made no sales, in which case they show up in a single row in the output with a Null value under the Quantity column.

```
Select salespeople.name, sales.quantity
    From salespeople, sales
    Where salespeople.id *= sales.salesperson_id
```

The new syntax uses the words Left Outer Join or Right Outer Join and is otherwise the same as the Inner Join. It looks like this:

```
Select salespeople.name, sales.quantity
    From salespeople Left Outer Join sales
        On salespeople.id = sales.salesperson_id
```

Any Left Outer Join can be rewritten as a Right Outer Join. In the old syntax, a Left Outer Join is converted to a Right Outer Join by reversing the order of the Join criteria. Here is the previous example, rewritten as a Right Outer Join:

```
Select salespeople.name, sales.quantity
    From salespeople, sales
    Where sales.salesperson_id =* salespeople.id
```

To change a Left Outer Join to a Right Outer Join in the new syntax, reverse the order of the table names:

```
Select salespeople.name, sales.quantity
    From sales Right Outer Join salespeople
        On salespeople.id = sales.salesperson_id
```

Cross

Cross Joins, unlike Inner and Outer Joins, do not have criteria that define how rows from one table correspond to rows in the other table. Cross Joins return all combinations of rows from both tables; this return is called the Cartesian product. There is no specific old-style syntax for a Cross Join; any Join is a Cross Join until a predicate is added to the `Where` clause that restricts the rows in the result set. The new style syntax uses the words Cross Join in the `From` clause.

Self Joins

It is sometimes necessary to relate a row in a table to other rows in the same table. Joining a table to itself is called a Self Join. Self Joins require defining the table multiple times with a different alias each time. The aliases can be used as though there are multiple copies of the table. The following example gives the general flavor of Self Joins, although they can be extremely complex:

```
Select People1.lastname as Employee, People2.lastname as
Manager
    From People People1 Join People People2
        On People1.manager_ID = People2.ID
```

This query is based on a table that contains a unique employee ID for each person and a manager ID that is the employee ID of that person's manager. The report returned contains the last name of each employee and the manager's last name for every person who has a manager:

```
Employee             Manager
-------------------- --------------------
Walls                Turing
Shaftoe              Turing
Rendell              Franklin
Penn                 Franklin
Smith                Franklin
```

Those who do not have managers do not show up in the list because they do not meet the On criteria for this Inner Join. The following example returns all employees whether or not they have a manager by using an Outer Join:

```
Select People1.lastname as Employee, People2.lastname as
Manager
    From People People1 Left Outer Join People People2
        On People1.manager_ID = People2.ID
```

With the following result:

```
Employee             Manager
-------------------- --------------------
Walls                Turing
Shaftoe              Turing
Turing               NULL
Rendell              Franklin
Franklin             NULL
Penn                 Franklin
Smith                Franklin
```

Using a query within another query: subqueries

SQL allows the use of a `Select` statement imbedded within another `Select` statement. These are called Subqueries. Subqueries are expressions and are permitted anywhere in a `Select` statement that allows expressions. Subqueries are most often used in the select list or the `Where` clause. For example, the `In` operator enables comparison of a value with a list of values and returns true if the first value is contained in the list. The list itself can be a subquery. In this case, the subquery must return a single list of one or more values; it must contain only a single column in its select list.

The easiest way to remember how and where to use a subquery is to imagine using the possible results of the subquery in the outer query. If it is appropriate to have only a single value, make sure that the subquery only returns one column and one row. If a list of values is appropriate, make sure the subquery only returns one column.

There are Nested Subqueries and Correlated subqueries. Nested Subqueries execute once before the operation of the outer query. Correlated Subqueries operate once for every row that is evaluated by the outer query, which makes Correlated Subqueries very resource- intensive and normally not desirable. In general, anything that can be done with a subquery can also be done with a Join, and the Join is usually faster.

Nested Subqueries

A Nested Subquery is a completely self-contained `Select` statement that is enclosed in parentheses and used in place of an expression in another `Select` statement. The following example retrieves a list of all customers from French-speaking countries.

```
Select customer_name
    From customer
    Where customer_country_code In
     (Select country_code
            From country
            Where country_language = 'French')
```

This subquery could be rewritten as a Join:

```
Select customer_name
    From customer Join country
        On customer_country_code = country_code
    Where country_language = 'French'
```

Correlated Subqueries

A Correlated Subquery references a table that is defined in the outer query. As such, a Correlated Subquery executes outside the context of the outer query. The following example returns all people who have a lower-than-average salary for their city:

```
Select lastname, monthlysalary
    From People OuterPeople
    Where monthlysalary <
         (select avg(monthlysalary)
            From People
            Where People.city = OuterPeople.city)
```

In this case, a table alias is required because the subquery uses the same table as the outer query. By using an alias, the column OuterPeople.city is undefined, except in the context of a correlated subquery. The subquery determines the average monthly salary for city but for which city? The answer is that the subquery is run once for every row considered in the outer query, and the city from each row is inserted into the subquery. Correlated Subqueries require an enormous amount of system resources.

Combining results with the Union operator

The `Union` operator enables the result sets from multiple `Select` statements to be combined into a single result set. Combining result sets can be useful when information of a single type is distributed among several tables. For example, if a company does business with two different kinds of clients and keeps their information in two different tables, the `Union` operator can be used to create a report of all cities in which clients exist.

```
Select city from client1
Union
Select city from client2
```

Because the `Union` operator produces a result set that is indistinguishable from a result set generated by a `Select` statement, it follows that the result of a `Union` can itself be used in another `Union`:

```
Select city from client1
Union
Select city from client2
Union
Select city from client3
```

When using the `Union` operator, both `Select` statements must have the same number of expressions in their respective select list. Those expressions must also be of the same or compatible data types. Compatible data types are those that can be implicitly (automatically) converted by MSDE. The expressions in the select list must be in the same order; that is, if the first select list contains a char(10) column followed by an int column, the second select list must also have a char(10) column followed by an int.

If the result set of a `Union` is to be ordered, the `Order By` clause can be used after the last `Select` statement.

```
Select city from client1
Union
Select city from client2
Union
Select city from client3
    Order By city
```

The Union operator discards duplicate rows in the result set. If duplicates are to be retained, the All modifier can be used immediately after Union.

```
Select city from client1
Union
Select city from client2
Union All
Select city from client3
```

The placement of All is significant. In the example above, duplicates between client1 and client2 are eliminated, but duplicates between the resulting set and client3 are retained. Placing All after the first Union operator gives a different result set, assuming that duplicates did exist among the three tables.

Advanced examples

This section presents some additional examples of SQL statements for several types of situations.

Using a subquery to provide a derived table

A subquery can be used in the From clause as though it were a table. The results of the subquery are used as the source for the outer query; these results are called a Derived Table. Using a derived table lets the user break a problem up into multiple parts, which can simplify the logic needed to find the right answer.

The following example joins two derived tables as a way to aggregate two different kinds of information and to bring the results into a single report. This example is based on a hospital that tracks the meals are served to patients and the drugs that are administered to patients. The goal is to produce a report that shows the total cost for meals and for drugs for each patient.

There are three tables: Patient, Meals, and DrugAdmin. The Patient table is not actually used in this query, but both Meals and DrugAdmin have foreign key relationships to Patient. In that way, they can be joined to each other through the PatientID, which is recorded in all three tables.

The Meals table contains a row for each meal served to a patient and includes a column with PatientID, and a column labeled Cost for the cost of each meal served.

The DrugAdmin table contains a row for every administration of drugs to a patient and includes a column containing the PatientID and a column containing the cost of drugs that are administered.

```
Select MealsQ.PatientID, MealsQ.MealCost, DrugsQ.DrugCost
    From(
        Select PatientID, MealCost = Sum(Cost)
```

```
          From Meals
          Group By PatientID
      )
      As MealsQ
  Full Outer Join(
      Select PatientID, DrugCost = Sum(Cost)
          From DrugAdmin
          Group By PatientID
      )
      As DrugsQ
  On MealsQ.PatientID = DrugsQ.PatientID
```

Three columns are included in the select list: the PatientID, the MealCost, and the DrugCost. Both MealCost and DrugCost are calculated in the derived tables. PatientID is available from either derived table, so the choice of MealsQ.PatientID is arbitrary.

The `From` clause includes two derived tables named MealsQ and DrugsQ.

MealsQ is a query that calculates the sum of the cost column. This sum is performed for each unique value of PatientID by using a `Group By` clause. Using the `Group By` requires the inclusion of the PatientID in the select list.

DrugsQ also calculates the sum of cost for each patient, but it pulls its values from the DrugAdmin table.

The two queries that create the derived tables MealsQ and DrugsQ returns exactly one row for each patient that exists in their respective base table. These derived tables are then joined on equal PatientIDs. A Full Outer Join is used because there may be patients who receive meals but no drugs and vice versa.

The results of this query cannot be achieved by just joining the tables Meals and DrugAdmin. Because there can be many drug administrations and many meals for a particular patient, the aggregation must be performed before the join to ensure that no costs are counted more than once.

It is likely that in practice this query is significantly elaborated. Ordering the results is helpful, as is returning more information about the patients. Performing additional grouping on the results is also useful, perhaps by diagnosis or length of hospitalization, or by some other criterion. Nonetheless, this example shows the usefulness of derived tables.

Using the flexibility of expressions

When reading a syntax diagram for SQL statements, it is clear that there are many places where any valid expression is permitted. Keep in mind that there are an infinite number of valid expressions, so be creative. Consider that the IN function is usually written like this:

```
ColumnName IN (value1, value2, value3)
```

where value1 through value 3 are hard-coded values, like Zip codes, the names of states, or people. But IN is more flexible than that. It can be thought of as shorthand for writing multiple ORs, and it accepts expressions both as the left argument and as the list in parentheses. It is perfectly valid to write:

```
Value IN (Column1, Column2, Column3)
```

This can be used in a table that tallies votes or preferences and has three columns for first choice, second choice, and third choice. Say, for example, that a table records the three favorite composers of a sample of music lovers. This table has a column First, for their first choice, Second for their second choice, and Third for their third choice. To find out how many people vote for Schubert, a user can write:

```
Select count(*)
     From ComposerPreference
     Where 'Schubert' IN (First, Second, Third)
```

This saves the user from having to write three predicates connected with `OR` operators. This code is also very readable.

Summary

SQL provides a standardized way to access databases across many platforms. Originally developed at IBM, it has been adopted by U.S. and international standards organizations. The most commonly used command within SQL is the `Select` statement, which retrieves data.

`Select` appears initially to be quite simple, but it has many advanced features. It can join results from multiple tables into a single result set based on any number of criteria. It can calculate values on the fly with a staggering array of built-in functions and a full arsenal of mathematical operators. `Select` statements can sort, aggregate, group, and otherwise process and manipulate data. Multiple `Select` statements can work together either through concatenation with the `Union` operator or through nesting with subqueries. Understanding the `Select` statement is critical to working with MSDE.

✦ ✦ ✦

CHAPTER 12

Modifying Data with SQL

In This Chapter

Using the Insert statement

Using the Update statement

Using the Delete statement

Advanced SQL examples

There are three basic types of SQL statements that allow data modification in a database: `Insert`, `Update`, and `Delete`. A user can use the `Insert` statement to insert new rows into a table, the `Update` statement to modify information in existing rows, and the `Delete` statement to delete rows that are no longer needed.

Insert

There is more than one way to insert data into an MSDE database. One way to insert data is to use a graphical tool such as Access to open a table directly and fill in the data interactively, one row at a time. This method can be very time-consuming, especially when there are many records that need to be added. A more powerful and flexible way to insert data into MSDE tables is by using the `Insert` statement. The `Insert` statement allows the user to add a single row to a table, add the results from a select query into an existing table, or create a new table from the results of a select query.

Adding a row to a table

There will be times when it is necessary to add a single row to an existing table. Either a complete row or a partial row can be added. However, when adding a partial row, the user must at least include the fields that are required in the table, such as the primary keys (except Identity columns) and other fields that cannot contain null values.

Adding a complete row

The syntax for inserting a row into an existing table is as follows:

```
INSERT INTO tablename (fieldname1, fieldname2, ... .fieldnameN)
values (value1, value2,... .valueN)
```

Suppose a user wants to add a new record to the Patient table that has the following fields: LastName, FirstName, MiddleInitial, Address, City, State, Zip, Age, Gender, and DOB. The Name, Address, City, State, and Gender fields are character fields, the Zip and Age fields are numeric fields, and the DOB is a date field. Assume that the table was just created with the following SQL command:

```
CREATE TABLE patient (Patient_Id int IDENTITY (1,1) NOT NULL,
LastName char(40), FirstName char(40), MiddleInitial char(1),
Address char(100), City char(50), State char(2), Zip numeric,
Age integer, Gender char(1), DOB datetime)
```

The data types are essential to know because the values in the `Insert` statement will have to be delimited according to the data type. The `Insert` statement to add a new row to the Patient table will look something like this:

```
INSERT INTO patient (LastName, FirstName, MiddleInitial,
Address, City, State, Zip, Age, Gender, DOB) values ('Doe',
'John', 'A', '123 Anywhere Street', 'Anytown', 'IN', 46060, 25,
'M', '9/26/74')
```

In this example, the character and date values are delimited with single quotes, while the numeric values do not have the quote delimiter. Although not shown, it should also be noted that money data types do not need the quote delimiter. If the delimiters are not used properly in the `Insert` statement, an error will be raised and the row will not be inserted into the table.

The ordering of the fields in the `Insert` statement does not have to correspond with the order of the fields in the table. However, the field names and values must be listed in the corresponding order in the `Insert` statement.

Adding a partial row

Sometimes a partial row must be added to a table. This will commonly arise in situations where a user does not yet have information for each field in the table but wants to go ahead and add a new record with the information available. This also arises in situations where certain fields in a table are optional and not frequently filled in. In both of these scenarios, a partial row must be added that contains only the information that is available.

A user may only know the patient's LastName, FirstName, MiddleInitial, and Age, but want to go ahead and add the record to the Patient table. The patient will later be contacted to get the remaining information. The `Insert` statement will look something like this:

```
INSERT INTO patient (LastName, FirstName, MiddleInitial, Age)
values ('Doe', 'John', 'A', 25)
```

When adding a partial row to a table as in the example, the user must at least specify the required fields in the table. Required fields include those that are primary keys and other fields that cannot contain a null value. If the required fields are not included in the `Insert` statement, then an error will be generated and the row will not be added to the table. Identity columns that are system generated should not be included in this list.

Inserting the results of a Select into a table

Sometimes the results from a `Select` statement will need to be inserted into an existing table. Data from one or more tables can easily be inserted into another table, as long as the data types correspond with each other. The syntax for inserting the results of a `Select` statement into an existing table is as follows:

```
INSERT INTO destination_tablename (fieldname1, fieldname2,
   ... .fieldnameN)
SELECT fieldname1, fieldname2, ... .fieldnameN
FROM source_tablename
[WHERE CRITERIA]
```

If a user wants to insert the entire contents of the Patient table into the Temp_patient table that has already been created, there are two ways to accomplish this. The first way is as follows:

```
INSERT INTO temp_patient
SELECT * from patient
```

In order for the example above to work properly, both tables must contain the same number of fields with correlating data types. The fields themselves do not have to be named the same, but the order in which they occur in the table and their data type must correspond. For the sake of simplicity, suppose for a minute that the Patient table includes only the LastName, FirstName, and MiddleInitial fields, all of which are character data types. The Temp_patient table needs to have corresponding fields in the same order with those data types. So, the Temp_patient table structure needs to look like LName, FName, and MI, all of which should be character data types. If the fields in theTemp_patient table are ordered by Fname, Lname, and MI, then the result of the above SQL statement is that the LastName values from the Patient table gets inserted into the Fname field in the Temp_patient table. This does not raise a database error, but it does cause a data integrity error.

Another way to accomplish the task of getting all of the data from the Patient table into Temp_patient is to specify each field explicitly, as shown below:

```
INSERT INTO temp_patient (LName, FName, MI, Addr, City, State,
   Zip, Age, Gender, BirthDate)
SELECT LastName, FirstName, MiddleInitial, Address, City,
   State, Zip, Age, Gender, DOB
FROM Patient
```

The field names are not exactly alike, but they are in corresponding order. For example, Lname in the Temp_patient table is being populated from LastName in the Patient table; Fname in the Temp_patient table is being populated from FirstName in the Patient table; and so on. The field names do not have to match each other at all, but they must at least be of the same general data type in order for that data to insert correctly into the table without generating an error. Again, the order they appear in the `Insert` statement does not have to match with the order they occur in the table.

The prior example inserted the entire contents of the Patient table into the Temp_patient table. If only certain records from the Patient table are to be inserted into the Temp_patient table, `WHERE` criteria can be specified to limit the records selected, as shown in the example below:

```
INSERT INTO temp_patient (LName, FName, MI, Addr, City, State,
   Zip, Age, Gender, BirthDate)
SELECT LastName, FirstName, MiddleInitial, Address, City,
   State, Zip, Age, Gender, DOB
FROM Patient
WHERE LastName = 'Doe'
```

The result of this statement is that all patient records with a last name of Doe will be inserted into the Temp_patient table. However, the user is not limited to just selecting the results from one table, as in the example above. A complicated SQL statement can insert those results into an existing table.

```
INSERT INTO temp_patient (LName, FName, MI, Addr, City, State,
   Zip, Age, Gender, BirthDate, HomePhone, WorkPhone, Email,
   RelativeContact, RelativePhone)
SELECT p.LastName, p.FirstName, p.MiddleInitial, p.Address,
   p.City, p.State, p.Zip, p.Age, p.Gender, p.DOB, c.Hphone,
   c.Wphone, c.Email, c.RelativeName, c.RelativePhone
FROM Patient p JOIN Contacts c on p.patient_id = c.patient_id
WHERE p.LastName IN ('Doe', 'Jones', 'Smith') and (c.Email is
   not null or c.Hphone is not null or c.Wphone is not null)
ORDER BY p.LastName, p.FirstName, p.MiddleInitial
```

The result of this statement is that any patient in the Patient table with a last name of Doe, Jones, or Smith who had a specified e-mail, home phone, or work phone in the Contacts table will be inserted into the Temp_patient table. For this statement to work, the Temp_patient table would have to contain these additional fields (HomePhone, WorkPhone, and so on) in the table structure.

Making SQL Statements Easy to Read

To make SQL statements easy to understand, three steps should be followed:

1. Capitalize the keywords in the statement (`SELECT`, `FROM`, `INSERT`, `WHERE`, `GROUP BY`, `JOIN`, `IN`, and so on).
2. Start each major keyword on a new line.
3. Indent sections that wrap onto the next line with a tab. For simpler SQL statements like the ones shown earlier in this chapter, this may not seem necessary, but is still worth the effort. Complicated SQL statements that are not structured like this can become extremely difficult to understand.

The SQL statement below does not follow these guidelines and is noticeably harder to read than the example above:

```
insert into temp_patient (LName, FName, MI, Addr, City, State,
Zip, Age, Gender, BirthDate, HomePhone, WorkPhone, Email,
RelativeContact, RelativePhone) select p.LastName, p.FirstName,
p.MiddleInitial, p.Address, p.City, p.State, p.Zip, p.Age,
p.Gender, p.DOB, c.Hphone, c.Wphone, c.Email, c.RelativeName,
c.RelativePhone from Patient p join Contacts c on p.patient_id =
c.patient_id where p.LastName in ('Doe', 'Jones', 'Smith') and
(c.Email is not null or c.Hphone is not null or c.Wphone is not
null) order by p.LastName, p.FirstName, p.MiddleInitial
```

Inserting the results of an Execute into a table

Yet another way to insert data into a table is to insert the results of a stored procedure execution into a table. Assume the user has the following stored procedure already established in his MSDE database:

```
CREATE PROCEDURE get_patient_data AS
   SELECT LastName, FirstName, MiddleInitial, Address, City,
        State, Zip, Age, Gender, DOB
   FROM Patient
```

The syntax for executing that stored procedure and inserting the results into the Temp_patient looks like this:

```
INSERT INTO temp_patient
EXECUTE get_patient_data
```

The above statement can be used only when all of the fields in the Temp_patient table are being populated from the stored procedure. If only certain fields are being populated, then the field names in the `Insert` statement must be explicitly specified, as shown below:

```
INSERT INTO temp_patient(LName, FName, MI, Addr, City, State,
   Zip, Age, Gender, BirthDate)
EXECUTE get_patient_data
```

The `get_patient_data` stored procedure could be slightly more complicated and accept a parameter to limit the results by the LastName:

```
CREATE PROCEDURE get_patient_data @LastN char(40) AS
   SELECT LastName, FirstName, MiddleInitial, Address, City,
        State, Zip, Age, Gender, DOB
   FROM Patient
   WHERE LastName = @LastN
```

If the user wants to insert into the Temp_patient table all patient records with a LastName of Doe, the `Doe` value should be passed as a parameter when the stored procedure is called. The syntax to do this is as follows:

```
INSERT INTO temp_patient(LName, FName, MI, Addr, City, State,
   Zip, Age, Gender, BirthDate)
EXECUTE get_patient_data 'Doe'
```

For more details about creating stored procedures, please refer to Chapter 15.

The Execute statement shown above can also be used to execute a statement stored in a string, such as a batched SQL statement read from a file like the example below with a local string variable `@sqlstatement` that was declared and populated with the following statements:

```
BEGIN
    DECLARE @sqlstatement char(200)
    SET @sqlstatement = 'SELECT LastName, FirstName,
      MiddleInitial, Address, City, State, Zip, Age, Gender,
      DOB FROM Patient WHERE LastName = ''Doe'''
END
```

In this statement, there are two consecutive single quotes surrounding `Doe`, followed by another single quote at the end. Two consecutive delimiters such as these let the server know that they are intended to be part of the string itself versus a delimiter that ends the string. The final single quote in the statement is the ending delimiter for the entire string.

To execute the contents of that string variable and insert the results into the Temp_patient table, use this syntax:

```
INSERT INTO temp_patient(LName, FName, MI, Addr, City, State,
   Zip, Age, Gender, BirthDate)
EXECUTE (@sqlstatement)
```

The parentheses surround the variable name in the statement above. This tells the server that a string is being executed versus a stored procedure. If the surrounding parentheses are left out, then the server will look for a stored procedure with that name and generate an error if one does not exist.

See *Writing Flexible Code with Variables* and *Sending Batches of Commands to the Server* in Chapter 13 for more details about declaring variables and about executing statements that are stored in strings.

Creating and populating a new table with the results of a Select

Oftentimes, a user may want to create a brand-new table from the results of a `Select` statement. This can be accomplished in one step, saving the user the trouble of creating a table structure first and then inserting the records into that table as a separate step. This also efficiently allows the user to select data from multiple tables in one SQL statement and automatically put the combined results into a new table.

If the Temp_patient table used in prior examples had not been created yet, a user might wish to copy all of the records in the Patient table to another table for further analysis. Copying all of the data into another table allows for manipulation of the data without harming the live Patient table. The syntax to select all records from the Patient table into a new table called Temp_patient looks like this:

```
SELECT *
INTO temp_patient
FROM patient
```

After running this SQL statement, the Temp_patient table will be created with an identical table structure as the Patient table. This means that the field names, data types, order of appearance in the table, and records themselves will exactly match the Patient table.

In the example above, every record in the Patient table got inserted into the Temp_patient table. If a user wanted to select only records in the Patient table that had a LastName of Doe and insert those into a new table called Temp_patient for a case study on the Doe family, the statement would look like this:

```
SELECT *
INTO temp_patient
```

```
FROM patient
WHERE LastName = 'Doe'
```

In the two prior examples, all the fields in the Patient table were created in the Temp_patient table. There will be times when not every field in the existing table needs to be a field in the new table. The fields desired for creation in the new table can be specifically selected, as shown below:

```
SELECT LastName, FirstName, DOB
INTO temp_patient
FROM patient
WHERE LastName = 'Doe'
```

The LastName, FirstName, and DOB fields are specified instead of *. After executing that statement, the Temp_patient table will be created with those three fields and with those values from the Patient table where the LastName is `Doe`.

Users are not limited to duplicating the contents of a single table. They can also insert the results of a `Select` statement that joins multiple tables together and limits the records by specific criteria into a new table. The Contacts table has HPhone, WPhone, Email, RelativeName, RelativePhone fields and relates to the Patient table on `patient_id`. If a user wants to insert information about all patients of the Smith family that have e-mail addresses into a new table to analyze in further detail, the statement to do so would look something like this:

```
SELECT p.LastName, p.FirstName, p.MiddleInitial, p.Address,
   p.City, p.State, p.Zip, p.Age, p.Gender, p.DOB, c.Email
INTO temp_patient
FROM patient p JOIN contacts c ON p.patient_id = c.patient_id
WHERE p.LastName = 'Smith' and c.Email is not null
```

The structure of the new table is determined by the fields that were used to create it. The field names and data types will be inherited from those used to create it. So, after executing the statement above, the Temp_patient table will have the following fields: LastName, FirstName, MiddleInitial, Address, City, State, Zip, Age, Gender, DOB, and Email. The data types of these fields will match with those from the original tables.

Selecting into a permanent table, as shown in the previous examples, requires the `Select into/bulkcopy` option to be set for the database. This option can be set for an MSDE database using SQL Server Enterprise Manager. Another way to turn on the `Select into/bulkcopy` option is to execute the following command in Query Analyzer or from an application:

```
sp_dboption databasename, 'select into/bulkcopy', 'true'
```

A Select...Into is a nonlogged operation. This means that the user will not be able to use the transaction logs to re-create it in the event of a problem. For this reason, a backup should be performed after executing Select...Into statements, especially when they deal with critical or large volumes of data.

An alternative that does not require that the `Select into/bulk copy` option be enabled is to select the results into a local temporary table or a global temporary table. A local temporary table is visible only to the user's session, while a global temporary table is visible to any active session. The syntax for selecting into a local temporary table is as follows:

```
#tablename
```

The syntax for selecting into a global temporary table is as follows:

```
##tablename
```

Once they are no longer being used, local and global temporary tables are automatically deleted from the MSDE database. A local temporary table gets deleted when the current session ends, except for those temporary tables that are created in stored procedures. Local temporary tables created in a stored procedure get deleted when the stored procedure ends. A global temporary table, on the other hand, gets deleted when the session that created it ends and when all other sessions that have a reference to it stop referencing it.

If a user wanted to put all of the Doe family records into a temporary table for further analysis during his current session, the statement would look like this:

```
SELECT *
INTO #temp_patient
FROM patient
WHERE LastName = 'Doe'
```

The temporary table (#temp_patient) created here will be available until the user exits the session it was created in. Upon exit, the temporary table gets deleted from the database. If the data in that table needs to be retained beyond the life of the user's session, it should be put into a permanent table (by dropping the # sign) instead of a temporary one.

The Update Statement

Users will frequently need to update data in one or more tables in the MSDE database. As with adding new records, a user can always update records through a graphical tool such as Access. However, it is probably more likely that a SQL statement will be used to run the updates programmatically. This can be accomplished using the `Update` statement.

Changing an existing row

The Update statement can be used to update fields for a single record in a table. The syntax for an Update statement is shown below.

```
UPDATE
        {
         table_name WITH ( <table_hint_limited> [...n])
          | view_name
          | rowset_function_limited
        }
        SET
        {column_name = {expression | DEFAULT | NULL}
        | @variable = expression
        | @variable = column = expression } [,...n]
```

If a user needs to update the Mary Smith patient record because she has moved to a new home in her current city, the Update statement to do that looks like this:

```
UPDATE patient
SET address = '123 New Place'
WHERE LastName = 'Smith' and FirstName = 'Mary'
```

If Mary moves to another city and her Address, City, State, and Zip fields must be updated, then a statement like this could be used:

```
UPDATE patient
SET address = '123 New Home Place', city = 'Somewhere New',
   state = 'IN', zip = '46060'
WHERE LastName = 'Smith' and FirstName = 'Mary'
```

Each of the fields to be updated is separated by commas in the Update statement. As many fields as desired can be listed to update in the table, all separated by commas. In the Where clause above, Mary's patient_id could have been used to update her patient record instead of using LastName and FirstName. For example, if Mary's patient_id = 3, then executing this statement would accomplish the same thing as the statement above:

```
UPDATE patient
SET address = '123 New Home Place', city = 'Somewhere New',
   state = 'IN', zip = '46060'
WHERE patient_id = 3
```

A user is not limited to updating a single row using the Update statement. All records with a certain value could be updated, such as all patients with a last name of Smith. If all the Smiths in America were moving to Smithville, the addresses of each Smith could be updated in the Patient table all at once. To accomplish this, the user would execute the following Update statement:

```
UPDATE patient
SET address = '123 Somewhere In Smithville', city =
```

```
   'Smithville', state = 'IN', zip = '46060'
WHERE LastName = 'Smith'
```

To update all records in a table with a certain value, the Where clause must be eliminated, as shown in the example below:

```
UPDATE patient
SET address = '123 Somewhere In Smithville', city =
'Smithville', state = 'IN', zip = '46060'
```

This statement will update every record in the Patient table with that address information. Without the Where clause, the effect of the above statement is very dangerous. However, there may actually be situations where an update of every single record in a table is intended. Here's a good example: If a doctor is doubling all of his service fees to account for the increased cost of medical malpractice insurance, the shortage of qualified physicians, and increasing inflation, a single Update statement can be issued to update all of the fees in the Fee table at once. Here's what that statement will look like:

```
UPDATE fees
SET fee_amt = fee_amt * 2
```

The Update statement works well in this situation; however, the user should always exercise caution when leaving off a Where clause or when the Where clause contains only the table joins themselves, because the user may be updating more records than intended.

Changing one or more rows based on information in another table

Sometimes, the user needs to update a table based on information in another table. For example, all patient address changes get written to an interim table called Temp_patient_addresses until a nightly process runs that executes an Update statement. If the Temp_patient_addresses table has an identical table structure to the Patient table, a single Update statement can be issued to select all of the records in the Temp_patient_addresses table and update the Patient table with those changes. The Update statement will look something like this:

```
UPDATE patient
SET address = t.address, city = t.city, state = t.state, zip =
   t.zip
FROM patient p, temp_patient_addresses t
WHERE p.patient_id = t.patient_id
```

The above example uses the older and more common join syntax (ANSI-89). Using the newer join syntax (ANSI-92), which is now the method recommended by Microsoft, the statement looks like this:

```
UPDATE patient
```

```
SET address = t.address, city = t.city, state = t.state, zip =
   t.zip
FROM patient p JOIN temp_patient_addresses t
ON p.patient_id = t.patient_id
```

The From clause in the two previous examples contains the Patient and Temp_patient_addresses tables. However, a table name does not always need to be specified in the From clause. An alternative to specifying a table name in the From clause is to use a Select statement. The MSDE Data Engine will treat the Select the same as if it were a table. It is helpful to think of it as being a virtual table. For example, the Update statement shown above could also be written as shown below to accomplish the exact same task—to update the Patient table with address information contained in the Temp_patient_addresses table:

```
UPDATE patient
SET address = t.address, city = t.city, state = t.state, zip =
   t.zip
FROM (select * from temp_patient_addresses) as t
WHERE patient.patient_id = t.patient_id
```

The From clause contains a Select statement that selects all records from the Temp_patient_addresses table. Then, the Where clause specifies how the Patient table and the Select statement (the "virtual table") relate to each other.

In both of these examples, all records that are in the Temp_patient_addresses table are updating information in the Patient table. If only certain records with values that are in the Temp_patient_addresses table should be updated, the Where clause must be further limited to select only those records. For example, if only the addresses of the Jones and Smith families will be updated, then the following Update statement would be run:

```
UPDATE patient
SET address = t.address, city = t.city, state = t.state, zip =
   t.zip
FROM patient p, temp_patient_addresses t
WHERE p.patient_id = t.patient_id AND (t.LastName = 'Smith' OR
   t.LastName = 'Jones')
```

In the Where clause of the above statement, after the AND, there are parentheses surrounding the OR criteria. The placement of these parentheses is important because it lets the database know exactly how the criteria should be executed. Any time ANDs and ORs are mixed in a Where clause, parentheses should be used to explicitly designate the intended execution priority. The parentheses in the statement above tell MSDE that the records must relate by patient_id and that the last name must be either 'Smith' or 'Jones'. If the parentheses are left out in situations like this, unexpected results may occur. This is because without them, the database has to try to determine what is intended. For example, there is a big difference in the meaning of 'X and Y or Z' versus 'X or Y or Z'.

In the previous examples, one table was updated with data from another. However, users are not limited to just updating a table based on the data in one other table. They can update a table with values that come from multiple tables, as in the following example:

```
UPDATE patient
SET address = t.address, city = t.city, state = t.state, zip =
   t.zip, age = m.age, gender = m.gender, dob = m.dob
FROM patient p, temp_patient_addresses t, temp_patient_misc m
WHERE p.patient_id = t.patient_id AND p.patient_id =
   m.patient_id
```

This example conveys well the concept of updating one table with information in more than one table. However, it updates patient records only for those patients that exist in all three tables, so this exact statement may not be the most useful in practice.

The Delete Statement

Just as with inserts and updates, a user can delete records one by one with Access or another graphical tool. Alternatively, the `Delete` statement can delete records programmatically.

Removing a row from a table

If a user wants to remove one or more rows that meet certain predetermined criteria from an existing table, a `Delete` statement such as the one below can be issued:

```
DELETE
FROM patient
WHERE patient_id = 4
```

This statement will delete any records in the Patient table that have a patient_id of 4. In this case, there will only be one patient record with that id, since the patient_id is the unique key.

If all of the patients in the Jones family who lived at 123 Somewhere Street in Anytown, Indiana, are moving out of state, the following `Delete` statement can be issued to remove their information from the Patient table:

```
DELETE
FROM patient
WHERE LastName = 'Jones' AND Address = '123 Somewhere Street'
   AND city = 'Anytown' AND state = 'IN'
```

Removing one or more rows based on information in another table

Records can be deleted based on information in another table just as they can be updated based on information in another table. For example, the patient_ids of all patient records to be deleted get written to an interim table called Temp_patient_delete until a nightly process runs that executes a Delete statement to delete all of them at once. This procedure can be accomplished with the following Delete statement:

```
DELETE
FROM patient
FROM patient p JOIN temp_patient_delete t ON p.patient_id =
   t.patient_id
```

When this statement is executed, every record in the Patient table that has a matching patient_id in the Temp_patient_delete table will be deleted.

The above statement contains two From clauses. The first From clause specifies the table name that the records are to be deleted from. The second specifies the table source(s) followed by the criteria. The first From clause is optional, but the second is required when deleting based upon criteria from one or more tables. If the optional From clause is omitted, a user still has to specify which table the records are to be deleted from, followed by the required From statement that joins the other tables together. If omitting the optional first From clause, the statement looks like this:

```
DELETE patient
FROM patient p JOIN temp_patient_delete t ON p.patient_id =
   t.patient_id
```

Instead of listing the table names in the From clause as was done in the previous examples, a user could also use a Select statement as a virtual table to accomplish the same thing. The statement below will delete the same records as the one above:

```
DELETE
FROM patient
FROM (select * from temp_patient_delete) as t
WHERE patient.patient_id = t.patient_id
```

A user may need to delete records based on information contained in more than one table. The user might want to delete all of the patients in the Temp_patient_delete table, but only if they do not have any historical records in the patient_history. If patient records are deleted but they still have related history in the History table, then the data will become fragmented. One way around this is to issue a Delete statement that removes those patients only if they do not have historical information in the Patient_history table. The Delete statement to accomplish this will look like this:

```
DELETE
FROM patient
WHERE patient_id IN (SELECT patient_id FROM temp_patient_delete
WHERE
   NOT EXISTS (SELECT patient_id FROM patient_history WHERE
   patient_id = temp_patient_delete.patient_id))
```

There are nested `Selects` in the `Where` clause, and the `NOT EXISTS` is being used. The second `Select` looks to see if the patient to be deleted exists in the Patient_history table. Then, if that patient does NOT exist in the Patient_history table, it becomes part of the IN clause that deletes those records from the Patient table.

Removing all rows with the Truncate Table command or Delete statement

There are two ways to remove all rows in a table with a single statement. The first way is to use the `Delete From` statement followed by the table name with no criteria. For example, to delete all rows in the Patient table, this statement can be issued:

```
DELETE FROM patient
```

Without the `Where` clause to limit the records, all records will be affected by the statement. Another way to eliminate all the records in the patient table is to use the `Truncate Table` command. This is the more commonly used way of eliminating all records in a table. Here's how all records in the Patient table can be removed with the `Truncate Table` command:

```
TRUNCATE TABLE patient
```

With both of these examples, all records in the table are being removed, but the table structure itself remains. However, with the `Truncate Table` command, the removal of each row is not a logged operation. This means that the `Truncate Table` command deletes the rows faster than the `Delete` command does. Both of these commands are different from the `Drop Table` command that not only removes all records from the table, but also deletes the table structure itself from the database.

Advanced SQL Examples

This section will use a hypothetical scenario to demonstrate some advanced uses of the SQL statements discussed in this chapter, such as selecting results into new and existing tables, as well as the grouping/aggregate functions discussed in Chapter 11.

Background information

A programmer is hired by a doctor's office to do some database/programming work. The doctor's assistant provides the following business specifications:

The doctor is doing a complicated study funded by a federal grant to analyze the impact that heredity has on diseases that led to deaths versus the natural occurrence of such events. He has been a doctor for 35 years and has an extensive database of patient history for the hundreds of patients he has treated. He has practiced medicine in the same small city his entire practice. Of his patient base, the majority of patients who share the same last name are somehow related.

He needs to have complicated SQL statements run against the MSDE patient database to generate the following summary information:

1. The top five fatal diseases that occurred and the quantity of each
2. The number of patients with fatal diseases with the same last name (if single or a male) as another patient with a fatal disease
3. A summary of the age groups those persons with the top five fatal diseases were in
4. The average duration of treatment before the patient died of the disease

The doctor is aware that these results will not be 100 percent accurate based on the above rules, but knows that they will still provide valuable results for his study.

Assume that the following MSDE database tables are those that contain the information needed for the study:

Table 12-1
Patient Table

Field	***Data Type***
PatientId	Int (primary key)
LastName	Char(40)
FirstName	Char(40)
MiddleInitial	Char(1)
Address	Char(100)
City	Char(50)
State	Char(2)
Zip	Numeric
Gender	Char(1)

Field	Data Type
MaritalStatus	Char(1)
DateOfBirth	DateTime
DateOfDeath	DateTime

Table 12-2 **Fatal_Diseases Table**	
Field	***Data Type***
PatientId	Int (part of primary key)
TreatmentDate	DateTime (part of primary key)
DiseaseId	Int
Comments	Char(200)

Table 12-3 **Treatment_Codes Table**	
Field	***Data Type***
DiseaseId	Int (primary key)
DiseaseDescription	Char(100)

Solution to requirement one

The first business requirement is determining "the top five fatal diseases that occurred and the quantity of each." This information can be gathered from the Fatal_Diseases and Treatment_Codes tables. The Fatal_Diseases table contains a record for each patient visitation where a fatal disease that ultimately led to death was involved. The Treatment_Codes table contains a description of what those diseases were. The programmer can run the following SQL statements to get the results the doctor is looking for:

```
SELECT DISTINCT PatientId, DiseaseId
INTO Distinct_Fatal_Diseases
FROM Fatal_Diseases
```

Since the Fatal_Diseases table contains multiple records for each visit that patient had, the statement above must be run to limit the records to a single record per patient for each disease. Now that there is a table containing the distinct disease each patient had, it can be used for further analysis in this solution and the others.

To determine the top five diseases that occurred in the doctor's patient base, execute the following SQL statement:

```
SELECT TOP 5 t.DiseaseDescription, COUNT(d.DiseaseId) as Total
INTO solution_one
FROM Distinct_Fatal_Diseases d JOIN Treatment_Codes t ON
   d.DiseaseId = t.DiseaseId
GROUP BY t.DiseaseDescription
ORDER BY Total Desc
```

The statement orders the records in descending order. Descending order will make the highest totals come first, and then the top five of those will be selected. If the descending `order by` clause is left out, then the query will use the default, which is ascending, and the five lowest totals will be returned. Thus, it is important to include the descending `order by` statement.

Solution to requirement two

The second requirement, "The number of patients with fatal diseases with the same last name (if single or a male) as another patient with a fatal disease," is not as easy to calculate as the first. It will be addressed in two steps.

First, the SQL to select those patients with fatal diseases who are Male or Single into an interim table called Temp_Diseases_Lname should be written. Since the programmer does not want to include married females who have that last name by marriage, he eliminates records based on the patient being male or single. He can use the Distinct_Fatal_Diseases table created in solution one as one of his information sources. His first SQL statement appears as follows:

```
SELECT p.PatientId, p.LastName, d.DiseaseId
INTO Temp_Diseases_Lname
FROM Distinct_Fatal_Diseases d JOIN Patient p ON d.PatientId =
   p.PatientId
WHERE p.Gender = 'M' OR p.MaritalStatus = 'S'
```

Those that get inserted into this table are males or single people. To find out how many of them have the same last name, a self join is used:

```
SELECT Temp_Diseases_Lname1.LastName,
   COUNT(Temp_Diseases_Lname1.LastName) as Total
INTO solution_two
FROM Temp_Diseases_Lname Temp_Diseases_Lname1 JOIN
   Temp_Diseases_Lname Temp_Diseases_Lname2 ON
   Temp_Diseases_Lname1.LastName =
   Temp_Diseases_Lname2.LastName
WHERE Temp_Diseases_Lname1.PatientId <>
   Temp_Diseases_Lname2.PatientId
GROUP BY Temp_Diseases_Lname1.LastName
ORDER BY Temp_Diseases_Lname1.LastName Asc
```

The Temp_Diseases_Lname table is joined to itself to determine which of the patients have the same last name. Self joins are helpful to accomplish such tasks. They allow a user to treat the same table as though it is really two separate tables by listing the first table with a unique alias, followed by the same table again with another unique alias.

The `order by` clause specified above sorts the query results in alphabetical order by patient LastName.

Solution to requirement three

The third business requirement, which is "a summary of the age groups those persons with the top five fatal diseases were in," is not as complicated to determine as the previous requirement. The Patient table contains the DateofBirth and the DateofDeath, and the Distinct_Fatal_Diseases table contains the disease each patient had. Using the date difference and count aggregate functions, the desired results can be gathered from those two tables using the following SQL statements:

```
SELECT p.PatientId, DATEDIFF(year, p.DateOfBirth,
   p.DateOfDeath) as PatientAge
INTO patient_age
FROM Distinct_Fatal_Diseases d JOIN Patient p ON d.PatientId =
   p.PatientId
```

The statement above calculates the age of each patient who died of a fatal disease. The `DATEDIFF` function determines the age of the patient by calculating the number of years from the point they were born to the point they died. Once the age of each patient who died of a fatal disease is known, the breakdown of age groups those patients were in can be calculated. Here's what that SQL statement looks like:

```
SELECT a.PatientAge, COUNT(d.DiseaseId) as Total
INTO solution_three
FROM Distinct_Fatal_Diseases d JOIN patient_age a ON
   d.PatientId = a.PatientId
GROUP BY PatientAge
ORDER BY PatientAge Asc
```

The `order by` clause in this statement sorts the results in order from youngest to oldest. The `COUNT` function totals up how many patients in that age group had fatal diseases.

Solution to requirement four

The fourth requirement, which is "the average duration of treatment before the patient died of the disease," can be met by summarizing data found in the Patient and Fatal_Diseases tables.

To determine the average length of treatment before each patient died, the programmer must first look up the date the patient first had treatment, as well as the date they died. The SQL statement to do that follows:

```
SELECT p.PatientId, MIN(f.TreatmentDate) as FirstTreatment,
   p.DateOfDeath
INTO Treatment_Duration
FROM Fatal_Diseases f JOIN Patient p ON f.PatientId =
   p.PatientId
GROUP BY p.PatientId, p.DateOfDeath
ORDER BY p.PatientId Asc
```

Using the information in the Treatment_Duration table that was just created, the programmer can use date functions with aggregate functions to determine the average duration of treatment across all patients who died of a fatal disease:

```
SELECT AVG(DATEDIFF(month, FirstTreatment, DateOfDeath)) as
   AverageTreatmentDuration
INTO solution_four
FROM Treatment_Duration
```

The statement above will return a single record result that will contain the average number of months the patients were treated before death occurred. The interval in the `DATEDIFF` function could have been changed to year or days, if the doctor wanted to see those increments instead.

Sharing the results with the doctor

Now that the results have been successfully compiled into four tables in the database (`solution_one` – `solution_four`), the programmer can share his results with the doctor. There are a number of ways the information can be presented. One approach is to print off the results from a tool like Query Analyzer after a `Select * SQL` statement is run against each of those four tables. However, it is likely that the doctor will want these results in an electronic format so he can further analyze them.

Probably the best approach is to give the doctor both a printout of the results AND the results in an electronic file format, such as tab-delimited files, so he can easily import those records into Excel or another tool if he so desires.

There are many ways to export the results of each business requirement into a file. A couple examples follow:

✦ From Query Analyzer (that comes with SQL Server), the query can be run and the results that are shown in the results window can be exported. To export the results shown in the query window, the cursor must be in the query results window and then the Save Query/Result button on the toolbar should be clicked. Ctrl+S is a keyboard shortcut for this function. A prompt will request a specific path and filename to save the file. The file will be saved in a fixed-width format.

✦ From Microsoft Access, the query can be run and the results previewed in Print Preview mode. From Print Preview mode, there is an option to export the results to another format. The Analyze With Excel option should be chosen to export the query results into an Excel format.

Cleaning up the database after the study is completed

After the study is completed and the SQL scripts and data are backed up, the tables created to complete the project should be deleted. To do so, the following `Drop Table` commands should be issued:

```
DROP TABLE solution_one
DROP TABLE solution_two
DROP TABLE solution_three
DROP TABLE solution_four
DROP TABLE Distinct_Fatal_Diseases
DROP TABLE Temp_Diseases_Lname
DROP TABLE Treatment_Duration
DROP TABLE patient_age
```

These tables must be manually deleted because they were created as permanent tables in the database, as opposed to temporary tables that would automatically get deleted when the session ends.

Summary

The Structured Query Language provides a powerful and flexible way to add, update, and delete data from databases. New records can be added into existing tables or into new tables altogether. A single record can be added to an existing table with the `Insert` statement, or a group of records that meet certain criteria can be added. Records in existing tables can be modified with the `Update` statement. The `Update` statement can be simple or can be based on a complex set of requirements, such as the results of another query or the result of joining multiple tables together. Records can also be deleted from a table based upon simple or complex criteria. The `Delete` and `Truncate Table` commands allow records to be deleted. Mastering the `Insert`, `Update`, and `Delete` statements is necessary in order to effectively modify data in an MSDE database.

✦ ✦ ✦

CHAPTER 13

Programming with SQL

In This Chapter

Executing SQL statements in batches

Local and global variables

Using the Begin...End statement

Using the If...Else statement

Using the Case statement

Using the While loop

Using the Goto statement

The Structured Query Language is very much a programming language itself, although people do not always think of it as one. As with any programming language, there are statements that allow users to control how the code gets executed. SQL can be used with MSDE databases and other databases such as SQL Server and provides a great deal of flexibility in controlling how the commands get executed by the database.

For example, statements can be batched together for processing at the same time. Variables can be declared and used to store values. Blocks of statements can be grouped together in a kind of routine using the Begin...End statements. Statements can be executed under certain conditions with the If...Else statement. Similarly, records can be processed conditionally using the Case statement. Other statements can be executed multiple times until a certain condition is met by using the While loop. The order a routine is executed in can be interrupted and modified using the Goto statement.

Sending Batches of Commands to the Server

Multiple SQL statements can be sent together to the server to execute one after another, instead of each of them being sent individually. The advantage to sending statements in batches is that they will execute faster together because the time it takes to transmit individual statements across the network is eliminated. Batching commands is appropriate in scenarios where the statements do not have to be executed immediately but can be batched together.

A batch is compiled into a single execution plan. The downside to this is that a single syntax error will abort the whole batch. A runtime error, on the other hand, does not abort the whole batch, just the current transaction.

The benefit of the batch having a single execution plan is that MSDE will cache and reuse execution plans if the batch is the same or very similar to a prior batch. This means that repetitive code can be sent in similar batches, improving performance.

A simple way to send batches of commands to the server is to separate the statements by a semicolon and then pass them to the server for execution all at once. The syntax looks like this:

```
Statement1; Statement2; ... . StatementN
```

If a user has a Visual Basic program that stores several statements that need to be executed in a string variable called `strSQL`, each time another statement needs to be batched for execution, it just gets concatenated to the end of the `strSQL` string variable preceded by a semicolon. After three statements have been batched, `strSQL` has the following value:

```
UPDATE patient SET Address = '123 Somewhere New' where
patient_id = 3; INSERT INTO patient (LastName, FirstName,
Address, City, State, Zip) values ('Doe', 'John', '321
Somewhere Else', 'Anytown', 'IN', 46060); DELETE FROM patient
WHERE patient_id = 8
```

When the Visual Basic program is ready to pass the statements to the MSDE database for execution, it just sends the above string as the SQL statement to be executed. The Visual Basic code to send this batch to the server for execution might look something like the following (Note: Lines that continue on but unintentionally wrap to the next line have been indicated with an underscore at the end of the first line.):

```
Sub Execute_Batch(strSQL as string, strDSN as string, strUID _
as string, strPwd as string)

'Establish a connection to the MSDE database
Dim oConn as New adodb.connection
oConn.ConnectionString = "Data Source=" & strDSN & _
        ";UserID=" & strUID & ";Password=" & strPwd & ";"
oConn.Open

'Execute the batch of SQL statements that are stored in the
'strSQL variable
oConn.execute strSQL

'Close the connection and deallocate the memory
oConn.close
```

```
set oConn = nothing
End Sub
```

The example above assumes that the strSQL variable that is passed into the Execute_Batch procedure contains the string value mentioned earlier. It also assumes that a valid Data Source Name (DSN), User ID, and Password are passed into the procedure as well. This example uses the ADO connection object to connect to the database. It then calls the Execute method of the connection object to have it execute the statements stored in the `strSQL` variable. This example will work if the `strSQL` variable contains one SQL statement or if it contains a batch of statements separated by semicolons, as in the above example.

As previously mentioned, a syntax error anywhere in the batch will abort the entire batch. The statement below will cause a syntax error:

```
UPDATE patient SET Address = '123 Somewhere New' where
patient_id = 3; INSERT INTO patient (LastName,
FirstName, Address, City, State, Zip) values (Doe,
'John', '321 Somewhere Else', 'Anytown', 'IN', 46060);
DELETE FROM patient WHERE patient_id = 8
```

In the middle Insert statement, `Doe` is missing the single quotes (`Doe` instead of `'Doe'`), a syntactic error that will prevent any of the statements from running when this statement attempts to run against an MSDE database. It doesn't matter where in the batch the syntax error occurs; none of the statements will be executed. This is because MSDE checks the syntax of the entire batch before executing the first statement.

The second way that a batch of statements can be executed together by MSDE is to write statements to a text file from the application and have the database read and execute the statements in the file at one time. In a Visual Basic program that writes several SQL statements to a file called c:\updates.txt, the program appends a carriage return at the end of each statement written to the file. For the sake of simplicity, assume that the contents of the c:\updates.txt file look something like this:

```
UPDATE patient SET Address = 'Somewhere' where patient_id = 3
INSERT INTO patient (LastName ) values ('Doe')
DELETE FROM patient WHERE patient_id = 8
```

Assume also for the purpose of this example that after each statement in the text file above there is a carriage return. This will become important later. Then, in the Visual Basic code, an execution statement can be sent to the database to have it read from the file and execute all of the statements together.

The example below creates a table called Statements to hold the string values (which are really SQL statements) that are in the c:\updates.txt text file. Then, the BULK INSERT statement reads from that file and imports those string values into the newly created Statements table. At that point, it creates a cursor to store all of those statements and then loops through the cursor, executing each statement one by one.

```
--Create a new table to hold the sql statements
CREATE TABLE statements
(sql_statement char(200))

--Read the statements from the file into the statements table
--Each statement is separated by a carriage return (\n)
BULK INSERT statements
    FROM 'c:\updates.txt'
    WITH
        ( ROWTERMINATOR = '\n' )

--Loop through a cursor containing each statement
--and execute them
BEGIN
    declare @nextstatement char(200)

DECLARE batch_statements CURSOR FOR
SELECT sql_statement from statements

    OPEN batch_statements

--get the first record in the cursor
--and store it in the @nextstatement variable
    FETCH NEXT FROM batch_statements
    INTO @nextstatement

    --while there are more records in the cursor
    WHILE @@FETCH_STATUS = 0
        BEGIN
            --execute the current sql statement
            execute (@nextstatement)

            --get the next record in the cursor
        FETCH NEXT FROM batch_statements
            INTO @nextstatement
        END
    CLOSE batch_statements
   DEALLOCATE batch_statements
END
```

The code above assumes that the Statements table does not exist prior to execution. The Statements table is created first, and then the Bulk Insert statement inserts the entire contents of the c:\updates.txt file into the Statements table. The `ROWTERMINATOR` option of the Bulk Insert specifies that each record is delimited with a carriage return (\n). Then, the batch_statements cursor is created by selecting each statement in the Statements table. The first string value, which is actually a valid SQL statement, is read into a local variable called `@nextstatement`. A While loop begins next and executes each statement in the cursor that was read into the `@nextstatement` variable. The Execute statement is followed by parentheses encapsulating the variable `@nextstatement`. This tells MSDE that code stored in a string is being executed as opposed to executing a stored procedure in the database.

The While loop in the above example is executed until the `@@FETCH_STATUS` variable returns a value not equal to 0. This variable is a global variable that contains the status of the cursor. As long as its value is 0, there are more records in the cursor. When there are no more records in the cursor, the While loop terminates and the Close and Deallocate statements are executed. The Close and Deallocate statements are important to execute upon completion because they close the cursor and free up the memory it is allocating.

There are a variety of methods that can be used to execute the above code. For example, it can be passed to the MSDE database for execution from a Visual Basic program, it can be run interactively in Query Analyzer, or it can be placed into a stored procedure in the MSDE database and executed with the Execute statement.

Writing Flexible Code with Variables

The ability to use variables with the SQL language provides a great deal of flexibility. Variables can be used for many purposes, such as for a counter to keep track of the number of times a loop is executed. There are two types of variables: local and global. They will be described in the following two sections.

Local variables

A local variable allows the user to store a value of a specific data type. Declaring a local variable uses the following syntax:

```
DECLARE @variablename datatype
```

If a user wants to declare a variable that will be used as an integer for a counter, the following statement could be used to declare it:

```
DECLARE @intCount INT
```

The @ sign appears before the name `intCount` and is followed by the integer data type, which is the desired counter variable. The @ sign must be included prior to the variable name. This lets MSDE know that it is a local variable. After it is declared, the @ sign must always be included as part of the variable name when later referencing the variable.

Tip

The variable `@intCount` in the example above starts with `int`. This was done to indicate that the `@intCount` variable can hold integer values. It is a good idea to start a variable with a letter or letters that indicate what data type it is. The advantage to doing so is that the code does not have to be examined where the variable was declared just to see what type of value it can store.

Multiple variables, like an integer variable and a data variable, can be declared together to be used in a procedure with the following syntax:

```
DECLARE @intCount INT, @dStartDate DATETIME
```

The above statement separates each variable declaration with a comma. This statement declares two local variables: `@intCount` and `@dStartDate`. More than two variables can be declared together as long as they are separated with a comma.

After a variable is declared, it can be assigned a value in two ways. The first of these ways is by using the SET statement with syntax that looks like this:

```
SET variablename = value
```

An example follows:

```
DECLARE @intCount INT
SET @intCount = 0
WHILE (select count(*) from test_numbers) < 100
BEGIN
    Insert into test_numbers (quantity) values (@intCount * 2)
    SET @intCount = @intCount + 1
END
```

This example uses a local variable to count the number of times the While loop gets executed. After the `@intCount` variable is declared, it gets initialized to 0 using the SET statement. Then, as long as the Test_numbers table contains fewer than 100 records, new records get inserted into it. The While loop causes that code block to execute until Test_numbers contains 100 records. If it already contains 100 records to start with, then the code inside the loop will never be executed. If it contains fewer than 100 records, the Insert statement and incrementing of the `@intCount` counter will happen multiple times until it reaches that requirement. The `@intCount` variable is used in the Insert statement to help determine the value to insert (`@intCount * 2`). The SET statement on the line that follows was used to increment `@intCount` by one.

With the SET statement, users are not limited to just assigning their variable to an explicit value. They can also set the variable equal to the result from a select list. Here's an example:

```
SET @intCount = SELECT count(*) from test_numbers
```

In this case, the SET statement is setting the `@intCount` variable equal to the total number of records in the Test_numbers table, whose value is not known until the Select statement is executed. Caution should be exercised when using the SET statement to set variables to the results of Select statements, because if more than one row can be returned from the Select statement, an error will occur. An example of a statement that will generate an error is shown below:

```
SET @intCount = SELECT quantity from test_numbers
```

If the Test_numbers table has five records, after statement execution, an error message similar to the following will result:

```
"Subquery returned more than 1 value. This is not permitted
when the subquery follows =, !=, <, <= , >, >= or when the
subquery is used as an expression."
```

Whenever the SET statement is used to assign a value to the results of a Select, a user should make sure that only one record can be returned.

Another way to assign a value to a variable without using the SET statement is to assign the value in a Select statement. This concept is different than what was just discussed above with respect to using the SET statement in conjunction with a Select. This is a way to assign a value to a variable without using the SET statement at all. Here's an example:

```
SELECT @intCount = count(quantity)
FROM test_numbers
```

This example is assigning the `@intCount` value based on the count of the number of records in the Test_numbers table as part of the Select statement. A similar example appeared earlier in this section where the SET statement was used to assign the value to the number of records in the Test_numbers table. This statement above accomplishes the same result, but with `the @intCount` variable being assigned a value within the Select statement itself.

When using the SET statement to assign the value to a Select statement, problems can occur when a value is assigned such that more than one record can be returned, although an error is not raised. Instead of receiving an error, the variable will be assigned to the last value in the resultset. This still may not yield the desired results. An example of what can happen follows:

```
SELECT @intCount = quantity
FROM test_numbers
```

Assuming that the Test_numbers table has four records (with the quantity field for those four records equaling 1, 2, 3, and 4, consecutively), executing the statement above will not raise an error. However, the `@intCount` variable will be assigned a value of 4, which is the last record in the resultset. Again, this problem can be avoided by assigning a variable in a Select statement that will return only one record from the Select statement. A good way to make sure of this is to always use the COUNT function, or other aggregate functions, that can return only one record.

In the Select statement above there was a FROM clause. The FROM clause was used to assign the variables to the quantity value in the Test_numbers table. However, to assign a variable using the Select syntax, a FROM clause is not required to reference another table. Here's an example:

```
SELECT @intCount = 0
```

There is no FROM clause in the above example. The Select statement is simply being used to assign a value to a variable. This is a common way of assigning values to variables. It accomplishes the same result as the following:

```
SET @intCount = 0
```

To display the value contained in the variable, use this syntax:

```
Select @intCount
```

In this example, the Select statement was used, followed by the variable name, to have it display the value contained in @intCount. Another way to display the value contained in the variable is to use the Print statement:

```
PRINT @intCount
```

The Print statement is also followed by the variable name. Displaying the variable value using the Select or Print statements described above is especially helpful when running SQL code interactively in a tool like Query Analyzer to visually see the values change to verify that the code is working properly.

A discussion about local variables is not complete without mentioning scope. The variable itself is only available until the stored procedure or batch it was declared in completes. So once another batch or procedure begins, that variable is no longer available for use. The example below shows a variable that has gone out of scope. Running this code will generate an error:

```
DECLARE @intCount INT
SET @intCount = 25
GO
SELECT @intCount
```

Running the above statement generates an error message similar to the following:

```
"Server: Msg 137, Level 15, State 2, Line 1
Must declare the variable '@intCount'."
```

In the example above, the @intCount variable goes out of scope as soon as the Go statement is encountered. This is because the Go statement terminates the batch. The Select statement following the Go statement is in a new batch, and since the @intCount variable is not declared in that batch, an error is generated. A large stored procedure or a code block can utilize local variables, but as soon as that stored procedure or code block ends, those local variables go out of scope.

Although a variable may go out of scope, the value it contains, in some situations, can be returned and assigned to a variable in the calling procedure, such as assigning the return result of a stored procedure to a local variable. In this respect, the variable itself may be out of scope, but the value it contained can be carried on through another variable. The following is an example of that concept, assuming there is a stored procedure defined as follows:

```
CREATE PROCEDURE get_patient_records
AS

DECLARE @intNumber INT

IF (SELECT count(*) FROM patient) > 0
    set @intNumber = 2
ELSE
    set @intNumber = 1

RETURN @intNumber
```

The stored procedure get_patient_records selects the total number of records in the Patient table and returns a 2 to the calling procedure if records exist in the table or a value of 1 if no records exist. The Return statement exits the user immediately from a stored procedure and gives the calling procedure the return value assigned if it is expecting one.

The following code declares a local variable, assigns that variable to the return result of the get_patient_records stored procedure, and displays the returned value:

```
DECLARE @intResult INT
EXECUTE @intResult = get_patient_records
SELECT @intResult
```

After the @intResult variable is declared, the Execute statement runs the get_patient_records stored procedure and assigns the return value to the @intResult variable. This is slightly different than the typical syntax for calling a stored procedure, since a variable assignment is involved. Immediately following the Execute statement is the variable name, followed by an equal sign and then the stored procedure name. This syntax must be followed in order for the @intResult variable to be assigned the value returned by the stored procedure and for the stored procedure to even be executed.

Although the @intNumber local variable went out of scope when the get_patient_records stored procedure ended, the value it contained was passed on to the @intResult variable. It is worth noting that variables can also be used to declare cursors. Cursors can be local or global in scope.

Please see Chapter 17 for more information about cursors.

Global variables

Global variables are available to any batch or stored procedure in the current connection. A number of global variables automatically get assigned values in an MSDE database, such as when statements are executed. These global variables are not declared or assigned. However, a user can make use of the helpful information they contain.

An example of a global variable was seen earlier in this chapter in the section *Sending Batches of Commands to the Server*. The @@FETCH_STATUS global variable was used to determine when the cursor no longer contained more records. The @@FETCH_STATUS global variable contains the result of the last cursor fetch and can contain a value of 0, -1, or –2. A value of 0 means that the Fetch statement was successful and that a record was retrieved. A value of –1 means the Fetch statement failed to retrieve a record. A value of –2 means the fetched row is missing (for example, has been deleted).

The @@FETCH_STATUS variable is global to all cursors within a single connection. To determine the result of a fetch, a user should check the variable immediately after the Fetch statement. Otherwise, another fetch within the connection could overwrite the value it contains.

Another helpful global variable is the @@ROWCOUNT variable. This variable returns the number of rows impacted by the last executed statement. The Update statement below will further the explanation:

```
UPDATE patient
SET Address = 'Somewhere New'
WHERE LastName = 'Doe'
```

After executing this statement, the @@ROWCOUNT value can be accessed to determine how many records were affected. A user wants to change the addresses of all patients with a last name of 'Doe' to 'Somewhere New', but if no patients have a last name of 'Doe', she wants to instead change the 'Smith' family's address to 'Somewhere New'. She can use the @@ROWCOUNT variable to determine if any 'Doe' records were affected and then take the appropriate action. Here's an example of that scenario:

```
BEGIN
UPDATE patient
```

```
SET Address = 'Somewhere New'
WHERE LastName = 'Doe'

IF @@ROWCOUNT = 0
UPDATE patient
SET Address = 'Somewhere New'
WHERE LastName = 'Smith'
END
```

The Update statement gets executed to change the `'Doe'` family addresses to `'Somewhere New'`. If the `@@ROWCOUNT` variable contains a 0, which indicates that no rows were updated by the prior statement, then another Update statement is executed to change the Smith family addresses.

Another helpful global variable is the `@@ERROR` variable, which stores the error number for the last statement executed. The `@@ERROR` variable receives a value of 0 if the statement runs successfully, or it receives the error number if an error occurs. This is similar in concept to the Visual Basic Err object (Err.Number). As with a Visual Basic program, a user can write a SQL code in such a way that it handles certain known errors, displays the error, or doesn't commit the entire transaction unless everything succeeds. The `@@ERROR` variable might be used as follows:

```
BEGIN TRAN

DECLARE @intPatient INT, @intTempPatient INT

BEGIN

INSERT INTO patient (LastName, FirstName)
VALUES ('Doe', 'John')

SET @intPatient = @@ERROR

    INSERT INTO temp_patient (LastName, FirstName)
    VALUES ('Doe', 'John')

    SET @intTempPatient = @@ERROR

    IF @intPatient = 0 and @intTempPatient = 0
        COMMIT TRAN
    ELSE
        ROLLBACK TRAN

END
```

The example above declares two local variables that will store the results of each attempted insert. Only if both inserts succeed is the transaction committed. This is because the insert should not take place in only one of those two tables if something goes wrong. If something goes wrong, neither should be committed. The two local variables get set to the @@ERROR global variable at different points. The reason for this is to preserve the status of both inserts separately. As discussed earlier, since the @@ERROR is global, its value gets reassigned the next time another statement is executed. Therefore, the result of the first insert should be stored in the Patient table before executing the next insert statement.

These are just three of many global variables available in MSDE. Table 13-1 shows most of the available global variables, as well as a brief description of what value they store.

Table 13-1
MSDE Global Variables

Global Variable	*Description*
@@CONNECTIONS	Number of connections since MSDE was last started
@@CPU_BUSY	Time in milliseconds that the processor spent working since MSDE was last started
@@CURSOR_ROWS	Number of qualifying rows currently in the last cursor that was opened on the connection
↓TEFIRST	Returns the value that the SET DATEFIRST parameter is currently set to, which specifies which day is being used as the first day of the week
@@DBTS	Value of the current timestamp data type for the current database, which is guaranteed to be unique in the database
@@ERROR	Error number for the last SQL statement executed
@@FETCH_STATUS	Value indicating status of last cursor fetch
@@IDENTITY	Value of the last inserted identity
@@IDLE	Time in milliseconds that MSDE has been idle since last started
@@IO_BUSY	Time in milliseconds that MSDE has spent performing I/O operations since last started
←NGID	Local language identifier of the language in use
←NGUAGE	Language currently in use by MSDE
@@LOCK_TIMEOUT	Lock time-out, in milliseconds, for the current session
@@MAX_CONNECTIONS	Maximum number of simultaneous connections allowed on MSDE
@@MAX_PRECISION	Shows the precision the decimal and numeric data types on the server are set to

Global Variable	*Description*
@@NESTLEVEL	Nesting level of the current stored procedure being executed
@@OPTIONS	Information about current SET options
@@PACK_RECEIVED	Number of input packets read from the network since MSDE last started
@@PACK_SENT	Number of output packets written to the network since MSDE last started
@@PACKET_ERRORS	Number of network packet errors that have occurred since MSDE last started
@@PROCID	Stored procedure identifier of the current procedure
@@REMSERVER	Name of the remote MSDE database server as shown in the login record
@@ROWCOUNT	Number of rows impacted by the last executed statement
@@SERVERNAME	Name of local server running MSDE
@@SERVICENAME	Name of registry key where MSDE is running
'ID	Server process identifier of the current user process
@@TEXTSIZE	Current value of TEXTSIZE option, which shows the maximum length, in bytes, of text or images that a Select statement returns
@@TIMETICKS	Number of microseconds per tick
@@TOTAL_ERRORS	Number of errors occurred in MSDE reading/writing to disk since it last started
@@TOTAL_READ	Number of disk reads since MSDE last started
@@TOTAL_WRITE	Number of disk writes since MSDE last started
@@TRANCOUNT	Number of active transactions for the current connection
@@VERSION	Processor type, version, and date of the current installation of MSDE

As seen from the list above, there is a wealth of information available in these global variables. However, since they are indeed global in scope, the value of these should be checked at the correct time before they get reset with a value from another operation.

Controlling the Flow of Operation

SQL possesses a variety of commands used to control the order and manner in which statements get executed.

- ✦ **The Begin...End statement** — segments code into statement blocks.
- ✦ **The If...Else statement** — can conditionally execute certain statements.
- ✦ **The Case statement** — can process data conditionally.
- ✦ **The While loop** — repeats certain statements or operations multiple times until a certain event occurs.
- ✦ **The Waitfor statement** — can set a statement to occur at a specific time.
- ✦ **The Goto statement** — can change the flow of operation of code.

Creating code blocks with Begin...End

Code blocks are an important part of the SQL programming language. They not only provide users with a way to organize their code in a readable fashion, but they are also required in order for that code to execute as expected.

The syntax for a code block is as follows:

```
BEGIN
[statements go here]
END
```

The following simple example demonstrates how code blocks are used. Suppose the user wants to execute three statements together. They can be separated with a Begin...End statement, as shown below:

```
BEGIN
    SELECT * FROM PATIENT
    SELECT * FROM TEMP_PATIENT
    SELECT * FROM CONTACTS
END
```

A more complicated example supposes there is a patient with a last name of Smith whose patient id is thought to be 3. If patient 3 is indeed a Smith, his last name will be changed to Test. The example further supposes that the statement is running in Query Analyzer so results can be viewed interactively. Therefore, a `SELECT * FROM patient` statement before and after the Update statement confirms the before and after results. Here's what the code to accomplish all of this looks like:

```
BEGIN
    DECLARE @lastname char(40)
```

```
    SELECT @lastname = LastName
FROM patient where patient_id = 3

    IF @lastname = 'Smith'
        BEGIN
            --display the contents of the patient table before
            --the update statement
            SELECT * FROM patient

            --update the patient table for patient 3
            UPDATE patient
  SET LastName = 'Test'
  WHERE patient_id = 3

            --display the contents of the patient table after
            --the update statement
            SELECT * FROM patient
        END
END
```

This example uses two sets of Begin...End statements. The first Begin...End statement is used to surround the entire code segment. There is also an inner Begin...End statement after the If statement. Any time another control statement (If, Else, While, and so on) is used within the code block, another Begin...End statement should be used. If a Begin...End is not used after a control statement and the user is planning to execute multiple statements after it, then it is possible that only the first statement after the control statement will be executed.

Executing code conditionally with If...Else

An If statement can be used to execute a SQL statement if the condition is satisfied. Or, in the alternative, a user can employ the Else part of the statement to execute another SQL statement if the requirement is not satisfied. The syntax for an If...Else is as follows:

```
IF condition
    sql statement
[ELSE
    sql statement]
```

The Else part of the If statement is optional, as indicated with the brackets above. If a user wants to update the patient address record for patient_id 3, but only after he has first verified that a patient with that id exists, the If statement to accomplish that looks like this:

```
IF (SELECT count(patient_id)
FROM patient
WHERE patient_id = 3)  > 0
```

```
UPDATE patient
SET address = 'testing if statement'
WHERE patient_id = 3
```

The above If statement checks to see if patient_id 3 exists, and if so, the Update statement to change the address gets executed. In this example, a Select statement was used as part of the If condition. However, a variety of other types of statements can also be used as part of the If statement. For example, a user can check the value of a variable in the If statement. Here's an example of how that looks:

```
IF @intPatientExists = 1
UPDATE patient
SET address = 'testing if statement'
WHERE patient_id = 3
```

This example assumes that the `@intPatientExists` variable has already been declared and assigned a value. The user can also employ the optional Else portion of the If statement to specify what should happen if the condition is not satisfied. Patient 3's record will be updated if it exists. If not, the highest patient id with that same value will be updated. This is accomplished by the following:

```
IF @intPatientExists = 1
UPDATE patient
SET address = 'testing if statement'
WHERE patient_id = 3
ELSE
UPDATE patient
SET address = 'testing if statement'
WHERE patient_id = (select max(patient_id) from patient)
```

The desired alternative condition was placed after the Else statement. This section will be executed when the condition after the If statement is not met. If executing multiple statements after the If or Else statement, Begin...End statements should be included to separate the code. Otherwise, only the first statement after the If or Else may be executed.

```
IF @intPatientExists = 1
    BEGIN
UPDATE patient
SET address = 'testing if statement'
WHERE patient_id = 3

SELECT * FROM patient
    END

ELSE
    BEGIN
UPDATE patient
SET address = 'testing if statement'
```

```
WHERE patient_id = (select max(patient_id) from patient)

SELECT * FROM patient
    END
```

The Begin...End statements immediately followed the If and Else statements. This explicitly tells the MSDE database exactly how to execute the statements and avoids the possibility that only one statement after the condition will be executed.

Nested If statements are also an option, as in the example below:

```
IF @intPatientExists = 1
    BEGIN
        SELECT count(*) FROM temp_patient
        IF @@ROWCOUNT > 0
            SELECT * FROM temp_patient
    END
```

There is an If statement nested inside the outer If statement. If the `@intPatientExists` condition is met (for example, it is 1), then the inner statement block is executed and the second If statement is encountered. The second If statement does not have a Begin...End immediately following it. That is because if a user is just executing one statement after a condition such as an If statement, following it with the Begin...End statement is not necessary.

Processing records conditionally using Case

Although the Case statement was already described in Chapter 11, it is appropriate to review it in this chapter. The Case statement is another SQL statement that allows a user to control how code gets processed.

For example, if the user wants to rename values in the select query so that patients with a LastName of `'Doe'` have one value and patients with a LastName of `'Hoffenheimer'` have another value, the following statement could be used:

```
SELECT
    CASE LastName
        WHEN 'Doe' THEN 'Common'
        WHEN 'Hoffenheimer' THEN 'Uncommon'
    END as Occurrence_Frequency
FROM patient
```

The Case statement was followed by the field to be evaluated and then by the When statements of what values are to be modified. The Case statement is ended with the End statement, followed by the name to call this newly calculated field. The Case statement provides a powerful way to conditionally process data in a Select statement.

Looping using While

A While loop can be used to execute certain statements multiple times until a certain condition is met. Code similar to the following could be employed by a user who wants to keep inserting more records into the Temp_patient table until the record count is three:

```
BEGIN
    DECLARE @patient_id as int
    SELECT @patient_id = 1
WHILE (select count(patient_id) from temp_patient) < 3
        BEGIN
            INSERT INTO temp_patient (patient_id, age) values
(@patient_id, @patient_id+1)
            SELECT @patient_id = @patient_id + 1
        END
END
```

Running the above code will cause the While loop to execute multiple times until the Temp_patient table has three records in it. If the Temp_patient table already contains three records, then the Insert and Select statements in the While loop will never be executed.

It is important to make sure caution is taken when using a While loop. If a user is not careful, the loop could execute forever. A While loop should be created in such a way that it will always have a certain point of completion or that it will exit the loop.

The above example shows a While loop that gets executed until the specified Select criteria is met. However, a user could also employ a variety of other conditions to evaluate the While loop other than a Select statement. If a user wants to insert a new record into the Temp_patient table but then wants to keep trying because for some reason the statement does not get executed, they could use the following code:

```
BEGIN
    INSERT INTO temp_patient (patient_id, age) values (1, 25)

WHILE @@ERROR <> 0
        INSERT INTO temp_patient (patient_id, age)
VALUES (1, 25)
END
```

If the @@ERROR global variable returns a 0, which means that there were no errors, then the While loop will not execute. If, however, an error gets returned, then MSDE will keep trying to execute the Insert statement until an error is not returned. This is a good example of the type of scenario where the user should exercise caution and use such a condition only if confident it will be able to finish at some reasonable point.

In scenarios similar to the one above where the user has chosen to keep trying to insert the statement but does not know for sure that it will ever succeed, the user can keep track of a counter and have it break out of the loop when that statement has been executed some predetermined number of times. Here's an example:

```
DECLARE @intCounter INT

BEGIN
    INSERT INTO temp_patient (patient_id, age) values (1, 25)

WHILE @@ERROR <> 0
    BEGIN
INSERT INTO temp_patient (patient_id, age)
VALUES (1, 25)

SET @intCounter = @intCounter + 1

IF @intCounter = 100
    BREAK
ELSE
    CONTINUE
END
END
```

The `@intcounter` keeps track of how many times the Insert has been attempted and then either issues a Break or Continue, depending on whether it has hit the predetermined number of times that statement can be attempted. The Break statement causes an exit from the innermost While loop. The Continue statement causes the While loop to restart. If the Insert statement has not succeeded after 100 attempts, then the Break is executed and the While loop ends. Otherwise, the loop continues until the record gets inserted successfully (`@@ERROR = 0`) or until it has tried 100 times.

A Begin...End statement should be used anytime more than one statement is used together, as was discussed in the section about Begin...End statements. Otherwise, it is possible that only the first statement will be executed.

Changing program flow using Goto

A user can employ the Goto statement to cause the flow of execution to change to a different section of a code block or procedure. There is a two-part syntax for using a Goto statement.

First, the label must be defined by using a label name followed by a colon, as shown below:

```
LabelName:
```

Then, to alter the execution of the code segment and have it jump to the area where the label is located, the Goto statement is issued, as shown below:

```
GOTO LabelName
```

This concept will become clear after looking at the following SQL code block:

```
DECLARE @intUserSelection INT

EXECUTE @intUserSelection = get_user_selection

IF @intUserSelection = 1
    GOTO Display_Patient_Records

IF @intUserSelection = 2
    GOTO Display_Contact_Records
ELSE
    BEGIN
SELECT * FROM patient
SELECT * FROM contacts
    END
    RETURN

Display_Patient_Records:
    SELECT * FROM patient
    RETURN

Display_Contact_Records:
    SELECT * FROM contacts
    RETURN
```

In addition, the user has a stored procedure called `get_user_selection` and a Patient and Contacts table in the database. The user selection is retrieved from the `get_user_selection` stored procedure and assigned to the `@intUserSelection` variable. Then, if the user wants to see the patient records (for example, the value was one), the Goto statement jumps the code execution to the `Display_Patient_Records` section in the code. If the user wants to see the contact records (for example, the value was two), then the Goto statement jumps the code execution to the `Display_Contact_Records` label. There is a Return statement at the end of the main code block and after each label. The Return statement terminates the procedure. Without the Return statement or some other method of terminating the procedure, the code that comes after the Return statement will also be executed, and the user will not get the desired results.

The label can appear at the beginning or the end of the code block. Whether it comes prior to or after the Goto statement in terms of physical location is not important. It matters only that the label exist somewhere in the same code block or procedure where the Goto statement gets issued.

As the above example portrays, the Goto statement provides a great deal of flexibility in altering the order and manner in which SQL statements are executed. Caution should be exercised when using Goto statements, however, to ensure that the code will execute in the order and manner expected.

Summary

The Structured Query Language provides ultimate power and flexibility by allowing the user to control how and when statements are executed, just as with any other programming language. SQL statements can be batched together and executed at a single time and gain performance advantages by sending repetitive code in similar batches. Local variables can be declared to store values for use during the procedure.

However, the user is not limited to just using variables or batches. A variety of other statements can control how code is executed. For example, the user can create blocks of code routines using the Begin...End statement. The user can conditionally execute certain statements using the If...Else statement or manipulate the flow of operation using the Goto statement. Using the Case statement allows the user to conditionally process records in a Select or similar statement. Statements can be continuously executed until a certain condition is met using the While loop. Mastering these statements will equip the user with the tools needed to effectively control how code gets executed against the MSDE database.

✦ ✦ ✦

P A R T

IV

Advanced Database Structures

This part explores how views provide users with the ability to simplify and reorganize data, the different types of stored procedures and how they are managed, how triggers provide the user with the ability to have logic execute at any time and automatically enforce data integrity, and the benefits of accessing data with cursors.

In This Part

Enhancing Data Access with Views

In This Chapter

Using views to simplify data

Using views for security reasons

View limitations

Using SQL to manage views

Using Access to manage views

Using Enterprise Manager to manage views

Using DMO to manage views

Views provide users with the ability to create a virtual table to organize the data in a database in a different manner than it exists in the underlying tables. A view is really just a query that is being stored in the MSDE database. It can be treated as if it is a table; for example, users can select information from a view, as well as update data in it. Views are helpful for a variety of reasons: to simplify data that is otherwise complex, or to prevent access to columns or rows in a table that contain sensitive information but allow access to other data that is not sensitive. Views can be managed through SQL statements, from a graphical tool such as Access or Enterprise Manager, or with the DMO object model in programming languages such as Visual Basic.

Simplifying Database Structure with Views

Views are particularly beneficial when it comes to simplifying data in the MSDE database, especially if the database is complex and contains numerous tables. Suppose, for example, that the MSDE database contains approximately 50 tables that have to be joined together on one or more keys to retrieve the complete set of information. Non-technical users, who shouldn't be expected to learn the intricacies of the SQL language to look up basic information, may find this situation frustrating. Views, however, can be created to summarize the data in one (or a few) formats. Then, all the user has to know is how to retrieve information from that simplified source.

The SQL code to create a view looks like this:

```
CREATE VIEW PatientView
AS
SELECT LastName, FirstName, MiddleInitial
FROM patient
```

A view should be given a name that somehow indicates that it is a view. Being able to identify a view immediately—instead of looking through all the tables in the database for it—saves a great deal of time.

The `Create View` statement comes first in the above example, followed by the `Select` statement. After the view has been declared, it can be referenced in the same way as a table. For example:

```
SELECT *
FROM PatientView
```

`PatientView` is listed after the From clause. Upon execution, this statement returns all records from the PatientView virtual table (for example, the view), resulting in the selection of the LastName, FirstName, and MiddleInitial fields from the Patient table. Even developers familiar with the database and educated in advanced SQL syntax can benefit from the simplicity that views provide. The developer can put common SQL queries into a view so that the SQL syntax only has to be written one time. The information can be accessed in that common view as though it were in a physical table. The developer is able to keep the underlying table structure intact, yet access the information in a simplified way.

Developers and end-users of data can benefit from the simplicity that views provide. The next example involves an MSDE database that contains many tables, called Patient, Contacts, Patient_Stats, Patient_Insurance, and Insurance.

The Patient table contains the following fields:

PatientId

LastName

FirstName

MiddleInitial

Address

City

State

Zip

DOB

Gender

The Contacts table contains the following fields:

PatientId

HomePhone

WorkPhone

Email

RelativeLName

RelativeFName

RelativePhone

The Patient_Stats table contains the following fields:

PatientId

Weight

Height

Race

The Patient_Insurance table contains the following fields:

PatientId

InsuranceCoId

DateEffective

NameOnPlan

The Insurance table contains the following fields:

InsuranceCoId

InsuranceCompanyName

ContactName

Address

City

State

Zip

Phone

Fax

These tables are broken into small, logical chunks, and most relate to each other on PatientId. Any time a user needs to get a combination of data from these tables, a query must be written to join them together. A better approach would be to write the common SQL query one time, and store it in a view to be taken advantage of in the future.

A user might frequently need to access the following fields that come from the above tables: LastName, FirstName, MiddleInitial, HomePhone, WorkPhone, Weight, Race, InsuranceCompanyName, InsurancePhoneNumber, and InsuranceFaxNumber. The syntax for creating a view called PatientCommonView with these fields follows:

```
CREATE VIEW PatientCommonView
AS
SELECT p.LastName, p.FirstName, p.MiddleInitial, c.HomePhone,
    c.WorkPhone, s.Weight, s.Race, i.InsuranceCompanyName,
    i.Phone as InsurancePhone, i.Fax as InsuranceFax
FROM Patient p, Contacts c, Patient_Stats s, Patient_Insurance
    pi, Insurance i
WHERE p.PatientId = c.PatientId AND p.PatientId = s.PatientId
    AND p.PatientId = pi.PatientId AND pi.InsuranceCoId =
    i.InsuranceCoId
```

The `Create View` statement is followed by the SQL Select query that retrieves the necessary information. Unless the fields are renamed using an alias, they will maintain the same name in the view as in their source tables. In the example above, the Phone was renamed to InsurancePhone and the Fax to InsuranceFax so they would not be mistaken for patient phone or contact phone.

After creating the PatientCommonView, the user can access its information as if it was a table. For example, to look up the last name, first name, and insurance company information for patient John Doe without having to write a query to join the normalized tables together, just select that information from the view already created:

```
SELECT LastName, FirstName, InsuranceCompanyName,
    InsurancePhone, InsuranceFax
FROM PatientCommonView
WHERE LastName = 'Doe' AND FirstName = 'John'
```

This is much simpler than writing the query against the tables themselves, which would look like this:

```
SELECT p.LastName, p.FirstName, i.InsuranceCompanyName,
    i.Phone, i.Fax
FROM patient p, patient_insurance pi, insurance i
WHERE p.PatientId = pi.PatientId AND pi.InsuranceCoId =
    i.InsuranceCoId AND p.LastName = 'Doe' AND p.FirstName =
    'John'
```

Providing Security with Views

Views can act as security mechanisms, to restrict employees from having access to confidential information, but to allow them access to information that is not confidential. For example, employee salary information should be protected, but other non-sensitive information should be accessible to all employees. If the underlying employee table contains the fields LastName, FirstName, MiddleInitial, Address, City, State, Zip, DateOfHire, and Salary, then only the Human Resources department should see an employee's salary. The rest of the company should be able to look up the home address and hire date information of any other employee. A view can be created to be accessed by employees instead of the employee table itself.

```
CREATE VIEW EmployeeInfoView
AS
SELECT LastName, FirstName, MiddleInitial, Address, City,
    State, Zip, DateOfHire
FROM employee
```

The Salary field is not included in the above `Select` statement, but every other field in the Employee table is included. This is an example of "column level security," which restricts the columns the user can have access to in the database.

"Row level security" can also be achieved with views. Row level security means that the `Select` statement in the view limits which rows can be accessed by specifying a Where clause, as shown below.

```
CREATE VIEW EmployeeInfoView
AS
SELECT *
FROM employee
WHERE LastName = 'Doe'
```

This view limits which rows can be accessed to those patients with a last name of Doe. The user is kept from accessing rows where the last name is not Doe.

A combination of row and column level security can be used together.

```
CREATE VIEW EmployeeInfoView
AS
SELECT LastName, FirstName, MiddleInitial, Address, City,
    State, Zip, DateOfHire
FROM employee
WHERE LastName = 'Doe'
```

The above view provides column level security by not allowing the Salary field to be accessed and row level security by not allowing patient records other than last names of Doe to be accessed.

Views can also restrict data accessible to summary information only, as in the following scenario. A table containing detailed data about books sold to each store in a chain must be accessed by an employee who needs summary information about sales, but who should not have access to the underlying detail records for each store. The following view is created, summarizing the sales information and granting the employee access to the view.

```
CREATE VIEW SalesSummaryView
AS
SELECT SalesDate, sum(TotalSold) as TotalSold
FROM Sales
GROUP BY SalesDate
```

The view summarizes the sales for each date, but hides the details about which stores those books were sold to. If the employee needs to see the sales that occurred for a given date range, such as for March 2000, she can run the following SQL statement:

```
SELECT *
FROM SalesSummaryView
WHERE SalesDate BETWEEN '03/01/2000' AND '03/31/2000'
```

Limitations of Modifying Data Through Views

There are a number of limitations on how data can be modified through views. Since a view is a virtual table that can be made up of information from one or more tables with simple or complex criteria, issuing an `Update` statement against a view can be complicated. It is possible, however, to update data through a view as long as certain conditions are met.

The MSDE database engine is really the SQL Server database engine with a few limitations. With SQL Server 2000, a number of improvements have been made to allow views to be updateable in more situations. Those improvements are also available in MSDE.

Two enhancements have been made to view updates. Instead Of triggers can now be created on a view to make that view updateable. In addition, if the view is a Partitioned View, it can be updated as long as certain restrictions are met. Both of these new features will be discussed later in this section.

The general requirements for a view to be updateable are:

✦ The `Select` statement cannot contain any aggregate functions such as `Sum` or `Count`, or any `Top`, `Union`, `Group By`, or `Distinct` clauses (except the Partitioned View, which uses a `Union` and can be updateable in certain scenarios).

✦ The `From` clause must reference at least one table.

✦ The `Update` or `Insert` statement must only reference one of the tables in the view.

✦ The `Delete` statement must only reference a view that selects from a single table.

If the requirements above are not met, then the view cannot be updated, unless it is based on the new Instead Of trigger or Partitioned View features. The following view is updateable:

```
CREATE VIEW PatientView
AS
SELECT PatientId, LastName, FirstName, MiddleInitial, Address,
       City, State, Zip
FROM patient
```

Since this view does not contain any aggregate functions and does contain a table in the From clause, it can be updated using the following `Update` statement against the view:

```
UPDATE PatientView
SET LastName = 'Doe'
WHERE FirstName = 'Jane' AND LastName = 'Single'
```

The statement executes an update against the PatientView to change Jane Single's name to her new married name, Jane Doe. The end result is that the patient record for Jane will also be updated in the Patient table.

Identity columns and timestamp columns cannot be updated through a view. The example above would not work if the user had also tried to update the PatientId identity column.

For the next example, the PatientView has been declared as shown below:

```
CREATE VIEW PatientView
AS
SELECT p.PatientId, p.LastName, p.FirstName, p.MiddleInitial,
       c.Email
FROM patient p JOIN contacts c ON p.PatientId = c.PatientId
```

A user attempts to issue the following `Update` statement against the PatientView:

```
UPDATE PatientView
SET LastName = 'Doe', Email = 'JaneDoe@yahoo.com'
WHERE FirstName = 'Jane' AND LastName = 'Single'
```

The Update statement will not work because it is trying to make updates to more than one table in the database (Patient and Contacts). An error similar to the following will result:

```
Server: Msg 4405, Level 16, State 2, Line 1
View 'PatientView' is not updatable because the FROM clause
names multiple tables.
```

The new feature allows a user to create an Instead Of trigger to update a view, permitting updates to views that would otherwise not be updateable. When an Instead Of trigger is created for a view, it gets executed instead of any Insert, Update, or Delete statements made on that view.

Earlier in this chapter, the PatientView was defined to select information from both the Patient and Contacts table, as shown below:

```
CREATE VIEW PatientView
AS
SELECT p.PatientId, p.LastName, p.FirstName, p.MiddleInitial,
       c.Email
FROM patient p JOIN contacts c ON p.PatientId = c.PatientId
```

Running the statement to update both the LastName and Email for Jane Single causes an error because it tries to update two underlying tables. If an Instead Of trigger is created for the PatientView, then the desired update will work.

```
CREATE TRIGGER IO_Trig_UPD_PatientView ON PatientView
INSTEAD OF UPDATE
AS
BEGIN
     UPDATE patient
          SET LastName = i.LastName, FirstName = i.FirstName,
               MiddleInitial = i.MiddleInitial
          FROM patient p, inserted i
          WHERE p.PatientId = i.PatientId
     UPDATE contacts
          SET Email = i.Email
          FROM contacts c, inserted i
          WHERE c.PatientId = i.PatientId
END
```

The trigger created above uses the INSTEAD OF UPDATE syntax. It will be executed instead of the Update statement against the PatientView. This trigger has an Update statement for each underlying table in the view. It joins each Update statement to an "inserted" table. The inserted table is a logical table that all inserts and updates are placed into. The inserted table contains the same fields as the view itself. The underlying Patient and Contacts tables are updated by joining to the inserted table on the key field, which is PatientId.

Now, when the Update statement is issued, it will work.

```
UPDATE PatientView
SET LastName = 'Doe', Email = 'JaneDoe@yahoo.com'
WHERE FirstName = 'Jane' AND LastName = 'Single'
```

When the Update statement above is executed, the Instead Of trigger runs in its place. The values to be updated will be changed in both the Patient and Contacts tables.

The key to utilizing the Instead Of trigger is to break the trigger down so that each of the underlying tables in the view is updated. Please consult Chapter 16 for more details on how to create and use triggers.

The other new feature available with view updates, Partitioned View, is used to join multiple tables together into one virtual table using the Union All statement. For example, patient history records may be archived by year into separate tables, but each of those history tables contains the same table structure. A partitioned view can join them together and treat them as one table. These tables can exist on the same server or on different servers. An example of such a partitioned view follows:

```
CREATE VIEW PatientHistoryView
AS
SELECT *
FROM PatientHistory1997
UNION ALL
SELECT *
FROM PatientHistory1998
UNION ALL
SELECT *
FROM PatientHistory1999
```

The partitioned view can be updated if the following requirements are met:

- ✦ Values must be specified for all required fields (for example, all fields that cannot be null).
- ✦ Primary keys, identity and timestamp columns cannot be updated.

The new Instead Of triggers and Partitioned View updates greatly improve the ability to make previously impossible updates against views.

Creating, Deleting, and Modifying Views

Views can be managed through such tools as Enterprise Manager and Access, through SQL code, or through DMO.

Creating views with SQL

The syntax for creating views follows:

```
CREATE [ < owner > ] VIEW view_name [ ( column [ ,...n ] ) ]
[ WITH < view_attribute > [ ,...n ] ]
AS
select_statement
[ WITH CHECK OPTION ]

< view_attribute > ::=
    { ENCRYPTION | SCHEMABINDING | VIEW_METADATA }
```

There are some options and attributes included above: `With Check Option`, `Encryption`, `Schemabinding`, and `View_Metadata`.

Specifying the `With Check Option` in a view will not allow any insert or update to be made to the view unless that record still meets the Select criteria for the view. Any modification that will cause the row to disappear from the view will be cancelled and will generate an error as follows:

```
CREATE VIEW PatientView
AS
SELECT PatientId, LastName, FirstName, MiddleInitial, Address,
       City, State, Zip
FROM patient
WHERE LastName = 'Doe'
WITH CHECK OPTION
```

The above view is defined in a user's database and the `Update` statement below is executed against it:

```
UPDATE PatientView
SET LastName = 'Single'
WHERE LastName = 'Doe' AND FirstName = 'Jane'
```

The `With Check Option` is defined on the view, so the statement will generate an error similar to this:

```
Server: Msg 550, Level 16, State 1, Line 1
The attempted insert or update failed because the target view
either specifies WITH CHECK OPTION or spans a view that
specifies WITH CHECK OPTION and one or more rows resulting from
```

```
the operation did not qualify under the CHECK OPTION
constraint. The statement has been terminated.
```

The error occurs because if the `Update` statement is executed, Jane Doe will be Jane Single and her record will no longer appear in the view (last name = Doe). The `Encryption` attribute causes MSDE to encrypt the system table columns containing the text of the `Create View` statement. The view cannot be published as part of replication because it is encrypted.

The `Schemabinding` attribute binds the view to the database schema. It forces the user to specify table ownership in the `Select` statements in the view. The owner must be specified before each object name (for example, dbo.tablename). The `Schemabinding` attribute locks the structure of all the underlying tables or views and keeps their structures from being modified. Attempting to modify the structure of one of the underlying tables or views will generate an error. Before one can be modified, the view with the `Schemabinding` attribute must be dropped or altered to turn off the `Schemabinding` attribute.

A view can reference a maximum of 1,024 columns. A view can also reference another view, as shown in this example:

```
CREATE VIEW PatientViewLimited
AS
SELECT LastName, FirstName
FROM PatientView
```

The new view, PatientViewLimited, references an existing view, PatientView. Referencing a view within a view can be helpful if a slight variation of an existing view is needed and complex SQL joins that have already been specified in an existing view are not desired in the new view.

Creating indexes on views with SQL

Indexes can be created on views and can greatly improve the performance of views, especially when the views are extremely complex.

In past versions of SQL Server, views could not be indexed. SQL Server 2000 and MSDE views now support indexes.

If a view is not indexed, then its resultset is not stored in the database anywhere. Any time a non-indexed view is referenced in a SQL statement, MSDE builds the resultset at that moment from the data in the underlying tables. A complicated non-indexed view can run very slowly because MSDE has to build the resultset at execution time. The moment a view is created with a unique clustered index, that view is executed and its results stored in the database the same way as results for tables with clustered indexes. As changes are made in any underlying table that the view references, the index gets updated as it does with a normal table. A view with an index can execute much faster, especially where large amounts of data or complex joins are involved. The first index created on a view must be a unique clustered index. By being unique, MSDE can find the rows in the index faster. Additional non-clustered indexes can then be added. The code for creating a unique clustered index on a view follows:

```
CREATE UNIQUE CLUSTERED INDEX iPatientView
ON PatientView(PatientId)
```

Once an index has been created on a view, that index can be used even when the view is not being accessed. Suppose, for example, that you have already created the index shown above and that the PatientView still exists from the last example we used it in (for example, that it selects the PatientId, LastName, FirstName, MiddleInitial, Address, City, State, and Zip columns from the Patient table). If you run a SQL statement against the Patient table without using the view, the MSDE optimizer can use the index you created to retrieve results from the Patient table faster. Thus, when you execute the SQL statement below against the Patient table, the index on the PatientView will be utilized:

```
SELECT count(LastName)
FROM patient
WHERE LastName = 'Doe'
```

Existing SQL statements that reference underlying tables can benefit from indexes created on views that reference the same tables.

Altering views with SQL

Once created, a view can be altered. The SQL syntax for altering a view is:

```
ALTER VIEW view_name [ ( column [ ,...n ] ) ]
[ WITH < view_attribute > [ ,...n ] ]
AS
    select_statement
[ WITH CHECK OPTION ]

< view_attribute > ::=
    { ENCRYPTION | SCHEMABINDING | VIEW_METADATA }
```

The `Alter View` syntax is nearly identical to the `Create View` syntax. Everything the view is to include must be specified. The only difference is that this view happens to exist already, and will replace old statements with the new ones specified. Altering a view leaves the permissions already granted intact. A dropped view loses all permissions. For an `Alter View` statement to preserve the existing permissions, column names must remain the same. An example of an altered view follows:

```
ALTER VIEW PatientView
AS
SELECT PatientId, LastName, FirstName, MiddleInitial
FROM patient
```

The old definition of PatientView gets replaced with the one above. Any permissions that were granted on the columns being selected in the `Select` statement remain intact.

Deleting views with SQL

The SQL syntax for deleting a view is:

```
DROP VIEW { view } [ ,...n ]
```

Following the `Drop` statement, the view name is specified. When dropping multiple views in one statement, view names should be separated with commas, as shown as follows:

```
DROP VIEW PatientView, PatientCommonView
```

After executing the above `Drop View` statement, the PatientView and the PatientCommonView will be deleted from the MSDE database.

Managing views with Enterprise Manager and Access

To add a new view using Enterprise Manager, a user should:

1. Go to the database to which the new view will be added.
2. Expand the tree to see the objects that exist in that database, including Views.
3. Click on the Views node in the tree to see all current views on the right half of the screen.
4. To create a new view, right-click where it says Views and a pop-up menu will appear with the New View option. Select the New View option from the list and the View Designer screen will appear. The drop-down menus can be utilized instead by choosing Action, New View. Once New View is chosen with either of these methods, the screen shown in Figure 14-1 will appear.

To add tables to the view, a user can click the Add Table button and select the desired table(s) from the list. Once the desired tables are added to the list, individual fields from those tables can be selected to include in the view and any criteria desired to limit the results can be specified. Properties of the view can be modified by clicking on the Properties button.

To modify an existing view using Enterprise Manager, the user can go to the Views node in the tree and double-click on the view to be modified, which displays the screen shown in Figure 14-2.

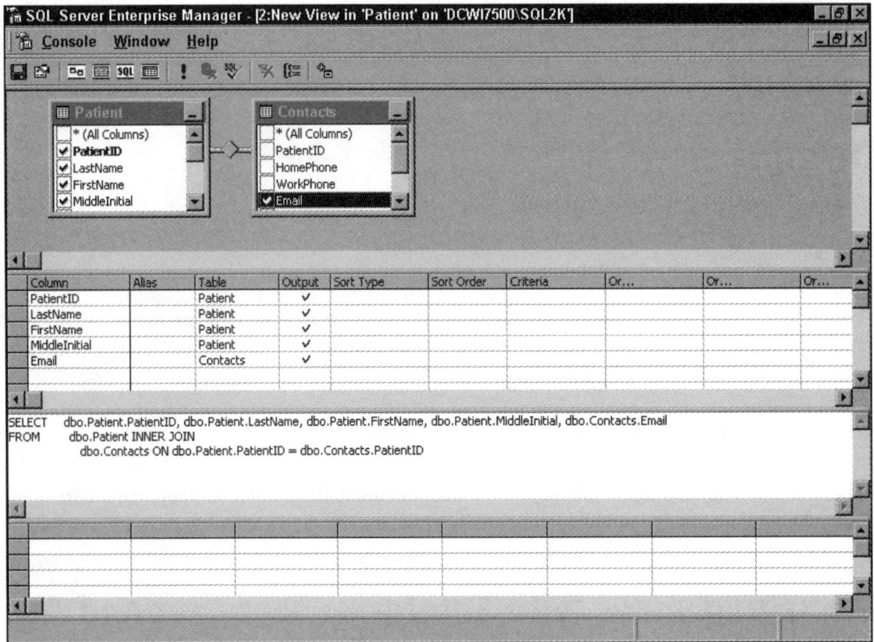

Figure 14-1: Creating a view with Enterprise Manager

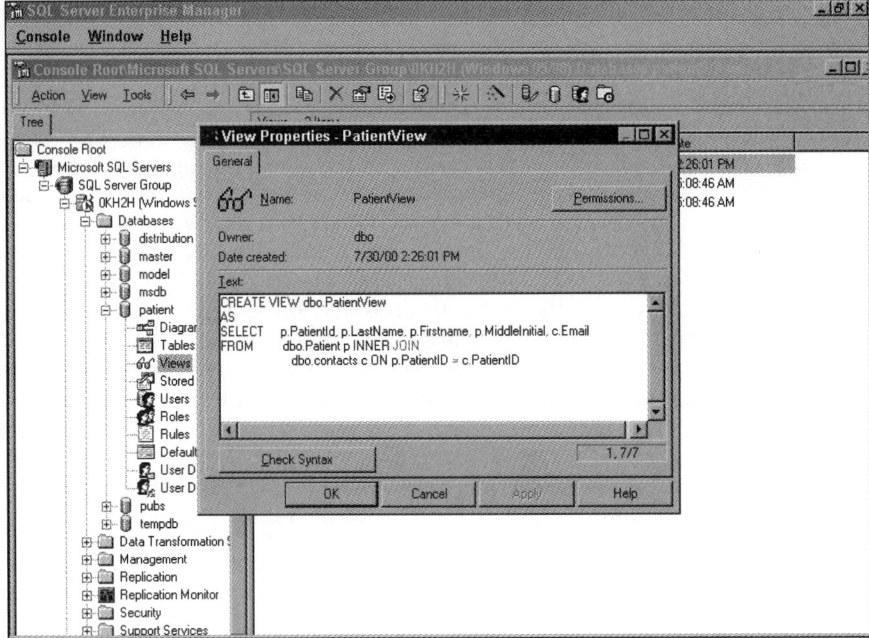

Figure 14-2: Modifying an existing view with Enterprise Manager

Changes can be made to the view by altering the SQL syntax in the text box.

To manage MSDE views using Access 2000, a user must create a new Project. A Project is an Access file that connects to an MSDE or SQL Server database through OLE DB and allows the user to manage the Tables, Stored Procedures, and Views of that database. To create a new Project in Access, the user should select File, New, and then choose Project (Existing Database). A wizard will then guide the user through the steps of establishing a connection to that database. If an MSDE database has not been created yet, choosing Project (New Database) will begin the process of creating a Project for a new database.

When the new Project has been created, the Tables, Stored Procedures, Views, and Triggers list will appear on the left side of the screen. When Views is selected, the Open, Design, New, and Delete buttons become enabled. The user can click the Open button to execute the selected view and see the data it returns. The user can click the Design button to view the SQL code for the selected view and/or to make changes to it. The New button will create a new view, and the Delete button will delete the selected view.

Managing views with DMO

As mentioned in Chapter 5, the DMO object model can modify the MSDE database from any programming environment that can work with COM objects.

DMO objects can be used to create views. To create the PatientView using DMO, the following Visual Basic code, as shown in Listing 14-1, can be run to access the DMO view object and add the new view to the MSDE database:

Listing 14-1: Visual Basic Code Using DMO to Create a New View

```
'This example creates a new view called PatientView in your
'MSDE database called MSDESample.  You can change MSDESample to
'any valid MSDE database name.

'declare the server object
Dim oMSDEServer As sqldmo.SQLServer
Set oMSDEServer = New sqldmo.SQLServer
oMSDEServer.LoginTimeout = 15
oMSDEServer.ODBCPrefix = False

'declare the database object
Dim oDatabase As sqldmo.Database

'declare the view object
Dim oView As New sqldmo.View
```

Continued

Listing 14-1 *(continued)*

```
'Declare and populate the server, userid, and
'password variables here...(Typically, you would
'pass them in to a routine such as this or declare
'them in a module versus declaring them here.  This
'is done for simplicity here.)
Dim strServerName As String
Dim strUserId As String
Dim strPassword As String

'In our example the server is (local).  This would
'be different if the database is on an NT server
'separate from the machine where you're running this
'code
strServerName = "(local)"
strUserId = "sa"
strPassword = ""

'log in and connect to the MSDESample database
oMSDEServer.Connect strServerName, strUserId, strPassword
Set oDatabase = oMSDEServer.Databases("MSDESample")

'Set the text value (the create view statement) for this view
'object
oView.Text = "CREATE VIEW PatientView AS SELECT * from patient"

'Give the view a name.  This name should match with the create
'statement
oView.Name = "PatientView"

'Add the new view to the database
oDatabase.Views.Add oView

Set oView = Nothing
Set oDatabase = Nothing
```

The code declares a database and view DMO object and connects to the MSDESample database. Then the Text and Name properties of the View object are assigned values. The Text property is assigned the `Create View` syntax and the Name property is assigned the name of the view. Once they have values that define how the view will be structured, the view object gets added to the database object. The act of adding the view object to the database object creates the view on the database.

In order for the above code to work, the project must include a reference to DMO. A reference can be added by selecting Project, References, and choosing Microsoft SQLDMO Object Library from the list.

To alter the view on the database, the following code in Listing 14-2 can be inserted beneath the oMSDEServer.connect line shown in Listing 14-1 above to replace the code that followed the Connect statement above.

Listing 14-2: Visual Basic Code Using DMO to Alter an Existing View

```
Set oView =
oMSDEServer.Databases("MSDESample").Views("PatientView")

'string to hold the new view syntax
Dim strViewSyntax As String

strViewSyntax = "CREATE VIEW PatientView AS SELECT * from
     patient WHERE LastName = 'Doe'"

'alter the view in the database to the new value
oView.Alter (strViewSyntax)

Set oView = Nothing
Set oDatabase = Nothing
```

A connection is made directly to the view PatientView on the MSDESample database. The Alter method of the view object is executed to update the view on the database. Please consult Chapters 5, 15, and 16 for more examples of using DMO in your programs.

Summary

Views provide a powerful and flexible means for simplifying and securing underlying data in the MSDE database. Views are stored SQL statements that are treated like virtual tables. Selects, updates, and deletes can be issued against views just as with tables (with certain restrictions). Indexes created on views can make them execute faster. Views can be created and modified with SQL statements, from a graphical tool such as Access or Enterprise Manager, or with the DMO object model in programming languages such as Visual Basic. Mastering the concept of views is essential to effectively utilize the MSDE database.

✦ ✦ ✦

CHAPTER 15

Packaging SQL in Stored Procedures

✦ ✦ ✦ ✦

In This Chapter

System stored procedures defined

Extended stored procedures defined

User-defined stored procedures defined

How MSDE processes stored procedures

Using SQL to manage stored procedures

Using Access to manage stored procedures

Using Enterprise Manager to manage stored procedures

Using DMO to manage stored procedures

✦ ✦ ✦ ✦

Stored procedures provide the user with the ability to create reusable code modules in the MSDE database for common tasks. The user-defined stored procedure can then be executed any time that task needs to be performed. Executing a stored procedure is similar to writing reusable Visual Basic or C++ procedures that can be called any time that task needs to be performed. The main difference is that stored procedures are actually stored in the MSDE database and typically deal with database-related tasks. Business logic for company programs can be put in stored procedures and can thus minimize the need for developers or end-users to have an in-depth knowledge of the database structure.

Users can also take advantage of system stored procedures that get installed automatically with MSDE. These system stored procedures automate common database functions that are not specific to any particular database. In addition to system stored procedures and user-defined stored procedures, there are extended stored procedures, which are stored in external DLL's or files. Stored procedures can be managed in a variety of ways: through SQL statements, from a graphical tool such as Access or Enterprise Manager, or with the DMO object model in programming languages such as Visual Basic.

Understanding the Types of Stored Procedures

There are three types of stored procedures: system stored procedures, extended stored procedures, and user-defined stored procedures. As I previously mention, system stored procedures and user-defined stored procedures reside in the MSDE database. Extended stored procedures, on the other hand, reside in an external DLL. All three of these types of stored procedures are discussed in detail in this section.

System stored procedures

System stored procedures are installed automatically when MSDE is installed. They were created by Microsoft to automate many administrative tasks or to provide users with common database information. A stored procedure can be identified as a system stored procedure because it starts with a `sp_` prefix. So, for example, if Enterprise Manager is opened and the tree under the master database is expanded, Stored Procedures are included in the list. If Stored Procedures is then selected from the list, all of the stored procedures for the master database are displayed on the right side of the screen. Those that start with `sp_`, such as `sp_addlogin`, are system stored procedures.

One very helpful system stored procedure is `sp_help`. A user can run `sp_help` to get information about a database object, such as a table or view. If, for example, the following `sp_help` stored procedure for the Patient table is executed:

```
EXEC sp_help Patient
```

results similar to those shown in Listing 15-1 are returned (although a few columns have been removed for clarity).

Listing 15-1: Results of sp_help for the Patient Table

```
Name          Owner      Type      Created_datetime
--------------------------------------------------------
patient       dbo     user table  2000-05-14 22:50:36.597

Column_name     Type     Comp  Len Prec Scale Null  TrimTrail
                         uted                 able  ingBlanks
-----------------------------------------------------------------
PatientId       int       no   4   10     0    no   (n/a)
LastName        char      no   40              yes  no
```

```
FirstName      char     no  40              yes  no
MiddleInitial  char     no  1               yes  no
Address        char     no  100             yes  no
City           char     no  50              yes  no
State          char     no  2               yes  no
Zip            numeric  no  9    18    0    yes  (n/a)
Sex            char     no  1               yes  no
MaritalStatus  char     no  1               yes  no
DateOfBirth    datetime no  8               yes  (n/a)
DateOfDeath    datetime no  8               yes  (n/a)

Identity        Seed      Increment     Not For Replication
-----------------------------------------------------------
PatientId       1         1             0

RowGuidCol
-------------------------------
No rowguidcol column defined.

Data_located_on_filegroup
-------------------------------
PRIMARY

index_name              index_description           index_keys
-----------------------------------------------------------------
_WA_Sys_PatientId       nonclustered, statistics,   PatientId
_0AD2A005               auto create located on
                        PRIMARY
_WA_Sys_Sex_            nonclustered, statistics,   Sex
0AD2A005                auto create located on
                        PRIMARY
_WA_Sys_MaritalStatus   nonclustered, statistics,   MaritalStatus
_0AD2A005               auto create located on
                        PRIMARY
_WA_Sys_DateOfDeath     nonclustered, statistics,   DateOfDeath
_0AD2A005               auto create located on
                        PRIMARY

No constraints have been defined for this object.

No foreign keys reference this table.
```

The information above describes the table structure for the Patient table, when it was created, the type of indexes that have been created for it, and the primary key. Users can run the `sp_help` stored procedure to retrieve similar information for tables, views, etc. The code that implements `sp_help` can be viewed by double-clicking `sp_help` in the Stored Procedures node of the tree under the master database.

The stored procedure sp_who returns a list of the current users and processes. This is helpful when monitoring the database to see who is currently logged in to the database. Here's an example of the results of running sp_who:

```
spid status      loginame hostname blk dbname      cmd
-----------------------------------------------------------------
1    sleeping    sa                0   master      SIGNAL
                                                   HANDLER
2    background  sa                0   MSDESample  LOCK MONITOR
3    background  sa                0   MSDESample  LAZY WRITER
4    sleeping    sa                0   MSDESample  LOG WRITER
5    sleeping    sa                0   MSDESample  CHECKPOINT
                                                   SLEEP
6    background  sa                0   MSDESample  AWAITING
                                                   COMMAND
7    runnable    sa       DEFAULT  0   MSDESample  SELECT
```

Some system activities are displayed, as well as those awaiting a command or running a command. The database name, the login name, and the command that is running can also be seen. Sp_who can also be used to kill a process that a user started but now needs to terminate. By finding out the process id (spid) of that process using sp_who, the user can execute the KILL command, followed by the spid, to terminate that process.

There is a whole series of system stored procedures for performing administrative tasks, such as adding users, roles, etc. A good example of an administrative system stored procedure is the sp_adduser procedure. Suppose the following command is executed:

```
EXEC sp_adduser 'JDoe', 'JDoe', 'key_user'
```

This example adds the user JDoe to the key_user role using the existing login of JDoe. The sp_adduser procedure accepts three parameters and then uses those parameters in running the commands to add that new user to the database.

The Books Online should be consulted for a detailed list of all available system stored procedures.

Extended stored procedures

Extended stored procedures are procedures that reside in exported DLLs and are thus created the same way as any other exported DLL—with C/C++ or the Windows API, for example. Before MSDE can take advantage of an extended procedure that is in a DLL, the user must let MSDE know about that procedure by registering it. (This does not mean registering it in the Windows registry but simply giving MSDE some information to make it aware of that procedure).

Follow these steps to register an extended procedure:

1. Go to the master database in a graphical tool such as Enterprise Manager.
2. Double-click to expand the tree to see the objects in the master database, including extended stored procedures.
3. Click the Extended Stored Procedures node. The list on the right side of the screen displays any extended procedures that MSDE is already aware of, such as those that are automatically included when a user installs MSDE.
4. To add a reference to another extended stored procedure, select Extended Stored Procedure in the node and right-click.
5. Choose New Extended Stored Procedure from the pop-up list that appears.
6. A dialog box appears with a prompt requesting the procedure name and the path to the DLL in which the procedure resides. The exact name of the procedure must be entered as it appears in the DLL.

Extended stored procedures can only be added to the master database. Thus, extended stored procedures in Enterprise Manager are only seen under the master database tree structure.

When creating an extended procedure in a DLL from C/C++ or similar tools, it is recommended that a standard naming convention, such as `xp_userdefined_procedurename`, be used. This identifies it as a custom-created extended procedure rather than one of the extended procedures that comes with MSDE.

Extended stored procedures are executed the same way as system or user-defined stored procedures:

```
EXEC procedurename
```

Alternately, the following command could be used:

```
EXECUTE procedurename
```

If a single command is running in the Query Analyzer window, the user can omit the execute syntax and just specify the name of the stored procedure, like this:

```
procedurename
```

Any parameters required by the stored procedure should follow the name of the procedure.

User-defined stored procedures

User-defined stored procedures are those created by developers or DBAs to perform a specific task. This type of procedure can contain several SQL statements and control of flow statements (such as `IF..Then`, `Begin...End`), or it can be very simple and contain a single statement. Whenever developers talk about creating stored procedures, they are referring to user-defined stored procedures. Once created, these procedures are physically stored in the MSDE database. Unlike extended stored procedures, which can only be created in the master database, a user-defined stored procedure can be created in any MSDE database. The remainder of this chapter demonstrates how to create user-defined stored procedures.

How Stored Procedures are Processed by MSDE

No matter how many statements are included in a stored procedure, they are all compiled into a single execution plan for that procedure. The stored procedure gets compiled when it is executed, just like any other SQL statement. MSDE retains execution plans for all stored procedures and SQL statements. When a stored procedure is executed again, MSDE reuses the execution plan that is in the procedure cache for that stored procedure. The speed of executing the same stored procedure multiple times versus executing the same code without a stored procedure multiple times is equal because, in both cases, the execution plan is being reused.

Creating, Deleting, and Modifying Stored Procedures

There are a variety of ways stored procedures can be created, deleted, and altered. For example, stored procedures can be managed through such tools as Enterprise Manager and Access, through SQL code, or through DMO.

Managing stored procedures with SQL

SQL statements can be used to efficiently manage stored procedures (by creating, altering, and deleting them).

Creating stored procedures

The syntax for creating a stored procedure is:

```
CREATE PROC [ EDURE ] procedure_name [ ; number ]
    [ { @parameter data_type }
```

```
        [ VARYING ] [ = default ] [ OUTPUT ]
    ] [ ,...n ]

[ WITH
    { RECOMPILE | ENCRYPTION | RECOMPILE , ENCRYPTION } ]

[ FOR REPLICATION ]

AS sql_statement [ ...n ]
```

The preceding code employs the following parameters:

✦ `Procedure_name` is the specified name of the stored procedure.

✦ `Number` is an optional integer that specifies more than one set of procedures with that same name.

✦ `@Parameter` is a parameter (variable) being used in the procedure.

✦ `Data_type` is the data type of the parameter.

✦ `Varying` means that the output parameter can have varying output (e.g., that it is a cursor that can return multiple rows).

✦ `Default` is a default value for the input parameters.

✦ `Output` defines the specific parameter as an output parameter instead of an input parameter.

The additional options available are `Recompile`, `Encryption`, and `For replication`. `With recompile` forces the stored procedure to be recompiled each time instead of having MSDE reuse the existing execution plan for it. Using the `With encryption` option causes MSDE to encrypt the text of the `Create Procedure` statement as it is stored in the syscomments table. This keeps the stored procedure from being published as part of replication. The `For replication` option defines the stored procedure so that it can only be executed during replication.

The last part of the Create Procedure syntax is the `sql_statement`. It is in this part of the declaration that the core code resides for what the stored procedure is supposed to do. The user can use the Control of Flow language discussed in Chapter 13. This part of the stored procedure contains the SQL code that gets executed when the stored procedure runs. It can be long and complex or as simple as a single statement. Following the `CREATE PROCEDURE` statement, the user specifies the name of the procedure and an optional number (as shown in the preceding syntax). The optional number allows the user to define multiple stored procedures with the same procedure name but with different numbers. For example:

```
CREATE PROCEDURE get_patient_records; 1
AS
SELECT *
FROM patient
```

The next example identifies the same procedure name but uses a different number.

```
CREATE PROCEDURE get_patient_records; 2
AS
SELECT LastName, FirstName
FROM patient
```

The first procedure, `get_patient_records`, is followed by the number one, and the second procedure is followed by the number two. This allows them both to share the procedure name but to be distinguished from each other by the number. The number option is helpful when a user wants to be able to delete a series of related stored procedures with one simple command. To execute a stored procedure that is declared with the number option, the number must be explicitly specified after the procedure name, like this:

```
EXECUTE get_patient_records; 2
```

If a user does not want to use the number option, the stored procedure can be declared without it, like this:

```
CREATE PROCEDURE get_patient_records
AS
SELECT *
FROM patient
```

Input and output parameters are often used with stored procedures. If a user wishes to create a procedure that returns a record for a patient by passing the patient's LastName and FirstName to the stored procedure and then having the stored procedure return the patient's record, input parameters can be used to allow the stored procedure to accept last name and first name as parameters. Here's an example:

```
CREATE PROCEDURE get_patient_records
@LastName varchar(40),@FirstName varchar(40)
AS
SELECT *
FROM patient
WHERE LastName = @LastName AND
FirstName = @FirstName
```

The input variables are declared after the procedure name. After the variable name, the data type is specified. The variable's data type must be specified so MSDE knows what type of value to expect. Then, the Select statement uses the variables to determine which record to select. The following command runs this stored procedure:

```
EXECUTE get_patient_records 'Doe', 'John'
```

The variable name can be explicitly stated if the user prefers:

```
EXECUTE get_patient_records @LastName = 'Doe', @FirstName =
      'John'
```

Alternately, the following command could be used:

```
EXECUTE get_patient_records @FirstName = 'John', @LastName =
        'Doe'
```

By specifying the variable name explicitly as shown, the variable values do not have to appear in the exact order as they are declared in the stored procedure.

Instead of using the EXECUTE statement to run this procedure, EXEC can be specified instead. EXECUTE and EXEC have the same effect. It is simply a matter of user preference.

After executing the get_patient_records stored procedure and passing the John Doe variables, the record for John Doe is returned. If the results are to be available to a batch, external procedure, or multiple SQL statements, an OUTPUT variable must be used:

```
CREATE PROCEDURE get_patient_id
@LastName varchar(40), @FirstName varchar(40),
@PatientId int OUTPUT
AS
SELECT @PatientId = PatientId
FROM patient
WHERE LastName = @LastName AND
FirstName = @FirstName
```

In the stored procedure above, the patient id gets returned to the calling procedure, as follows:

```
DECLARE @PatientIdentifier int
EXECUTE get_patient_id 'Doe', 'Jane', @PatientIdentifier OUTPUT
```

The EXECUTE statement passes in the last name and first name variables for input, and then puts the output variable into the @PatientIdentifier variable that is declared prior to executing the statement. The stored procedure get_patient_id only returns the patient id. There may be times when a user needs to return multiple results to the calling procedure. There are two ways to pass multiple pieces of information back to the calling procedure. One way is to have more than one output variable, as in the following example:

```
CREATE PROCEDURE get_patient_address_info
@LastName varchar(40), @FirstName varchar(40),
@PatientId int OUTPUT, @Address varchar(40) OUTPUT,
@City varchar(40) OUTPUT, @State varchar(2) OUTPUT,
@Zip int OUTPUT
AS
SELECT @PatientId = PatientId, @Address = Address, @City = City,
@State = State, @Zip = Zip
FROM patient
WHERE LastName = @LastName AND
FirstName = @FirstName
```

The preceding stored procedure includes five output variables that contain the patient's address information. To call this stored procedure and return the values for use in the calling procedure, a user can execute a statement similar to the one shown below:

```
DECLARE @PatientIdentifier int, @Address varchar(40),
        @City varchar(40), @State varchar(2), @Zip int
EXEC get_patient_address_info 'Doe', 'John',
     @PatientIdentifier OUTPUT, @Address OUTPUT, @City OUTPUT,
     @State OUTPUT, @Zip OUTPUT
SELECT @PatientIdentifier, @Address, @City, @State, @Zip
```

This example declares five local variables to store the return values from the stored procedure. Then, it calls the stored procedure and passes the empty variables to the stored procedure for population. Last, it displays the values interactively to show what is returned.

The second way to pass multiple pieces of information back to the calling procedure is to return the information in an output cursor, which is similar to a recordset. An output cursor can be declared the same way as any other output variable, but the result is that it can contain multiple records. Here's an example:

```
CREATE PROCEDURE get_patient_records
@patient_cursor CURSOR VARYING OUTPUT
AS
BEGIN
    SET @patient_cursor = CURSOR
        FORWARD_ONLY STATIC FOR
        SELECT *
        FROM patient

    OPEN @patient_cursor
END
```

The `@patient_cursor` is declared as an output variable, and its data type varies. The syntax `CURSOR VARYING OUTPUT` is the correct way to declare any cursor that is to be output from the stored procedure. Then, the cursor variable gets set up as forward only and gets populated with the results of the `SELECT` statement. Here's how the calling routine can call this stored procedure:

```
DECLARE @PatientRecords CURSOR
EXECUTE get_patient_records @patient_cursor =
      @PatientRecords OUTPUT
WHILE (@@FETCH_STATUS = 0)
BEGIN
    FETCH NEXT FROM @PatientRecords
END
CLOSE @PatientRecords
DEALLOCATE @PatientRecords
```

In the preceding example, a local cursor variable is assigned, and then the `get_patient_records` stored procedure is called. The local cursor gets assigned to the output variable from the stored procedure, and the `WHILE` loop executes for each record that is returned. Then, the cursor is closed and deallocated. For more information about cursors, please consult Chapter 17.

There may be times when it is necessary to specify a default value for an input variable. By specifying a default value, the stored procedure can be executed even when the calling routine doesn't include the parameters. This makes the input parameters "optional." Here's an example of a default value for a parameter:

```
CREATE PROCEDURE get_patient_records
@LastName varchar(40) = '%', @FirstName varchar(40) = '%'
AS
SELECT *
FROM patient
WHERE LastName like @Lastname AND FirstName like @Firstname
```

The input variables are declared, and then they are set to a default value (%). The default value in the preceding example causes the stored procedure to return all records in the Patient table if the input parameters are not specified. The Like statement selects everything like '%', which returns everything. With such default values assigned, the following statement can be executed to call the stored procedure:

```
EXECUTE get_patient_records
```

Because the input variables have default values, the above statement executes without error, and the default values are used in the procedure. However, if the variables in the stored procedure declaration do not have default values specified, an error similar to the following is returned from MSDE after executing the above statement:

```
Server: Msg 201, Level 16, State 1, Procedure
get_patient_records, Line 0
Procedure 'get_patient_records' expects parameter
'@patient_cursor', which was not supplied.
```

So far, the examples presented in this section have been relatively simple. However, one of the common uses of stored procedures is to create complex code routines to perform common tasks and to keep end users and/or developers from needing to know the underlying table structure in detail. If a user wants to create a routine that updates the Patient table with any value that has changed for a patient but any or all of the fields in the Patient table have changed, a single stored procedure that uses default values for all of the input parameters so that they are treated as "optional" may be created. Those input variables that have values other than the defaults are updated in the database. Here's the syntax for creating such a stored procedure:

```
CREATE PROCEDURE update_patient_record
@PatientId int, @LastName varchar(40) = '%', @FirstName
```

```
varchar(40) = '%', @MiddleInitial varchar(1) = '%', @Address
varchar(60) = '%', @City varchar(60) = '%', @State varchar(2) =
'%', @Zip int = 1
AS
BEGIN
    IF @LastName <> '%'
       UPDATE patient
       SET LastName = @LastName
       WHERE PatientId = @PatientId

    IF @FirstName <> '%'
       UPDATE patient
       SET FirstName = @FirstName
       WHERE PatientId = @PatientId

    IF @MiddleInitial <> '%'
       UPDATE patient
       SET MiddleInitial = @MiddleInitial
       WHERE PatientId = @PatientId

    IF @Address <> '%'
       UPDATE patient
       SET Address = @Address
       WHERE PatientId = @PatientId

    IF @City <> '%'
       UPDATE patient
       SET City = @City
       WHERE PatientId = @PatientId

    IF @State <> '%'
       UPDATE patient
       SET State = @State
       WHERE PatientId = @PatientId

    IF @Zip <> 1
       UPDATE patient
       SET Zip = @Zip
       WHERE PatientId = @PatientId

END
```

All of the input variables are defined as optional except the patient id. This is because the patient id is required and used to update the appropriate record depending on the patient values that have changed. If patient Jane Single has married John Doe and has moved into his home, her last name and address have to be updated. Assuming that Jane has a patient id of four, the following statement executes the stored procedure and updates her information:

```
EXECUTE update_patient_record @PatientId = 4, @LastName =
'Doe', @Address = 'The home of John', @City = 'Somewhere
Special', @State = 'IN', @Zip = 46060
```

Jane Single's patient id is specified, as well as the values that need to be updated for her patient record. This example demonstrates how default parameters can be used to determine which statements in the stored procedure need to be executed.

A chapter on stored procedures is not complete without mentioning a few other important details. Stored procedures can be nested within stored procedures. In the declaration of one stored procedure, another stored procedure can be called. This is the same concept as calling one routine from within another as you can in development tools such as Visual Basic. Another useful stored procedure tool is an option that allows a stored procedure to be executed every time the database starts. The user can set this option by running the `sp_procoption` system stored procedure with the stored procedure name as the parameter.

Altering stored procedures

Once a stored procedure is created, it can be altered. The SQL syntax for altering a stored procedure is:

```
ALTER PROC [ EDURE ] procedure_name [ ; number ]
    [ { @parameter data_type }
        [ VARYING ] [ = default ] [ OUTPUT ]
    ] [ ,...n ]
[ WITH
    { RECOMPILE | ENCRYPTION
        | RECOMPILE , ENCRYPTION
    }
]
[ FOR REPLICATION ]
AS
    sql_statement [ ...n ]
```

The `ALTER PROCEDURE` syntax is nearly identical to the `CREATE PROCEDURE` syntax. When a stored procedure is altered, it is basically defined in the same way as if it is being created. The user specifies everything the stored procedure is to include. The only difference is that this stored procedure happens to exist already, and it replaces the old statements with the new statements that are specified. The primary advantage of using an `ALTER PROCEDURE` syntax instead of just dropping the stored procedure and re-creating it is that when a user alters a stored procedure, the permissions that have already been granted remain intact. When a stored procedure is dropped, all permissions are lost and must be re-created. A stored procedure can be altered as follows:

```
ALTER PROCEDURE get_patient_records @PatientId int
AS
SELECT *
FROM patient
WHERE PatientId = @PatientId
```

The old definition of `get_patient_records` with the two input parameters gets replaced with the preceding one that now has `PatientId` as the parameter. Any execute permissions that are granted on the stored procedure remain intact after this statement is issued.

Deleting stored procedures

In addition to creating and altering stored procedures, a user can delete them. The SQL syntax for deleting a stored procedure is as follows:

```
DROP PROCEDURE { procedure } [ ,...n ]
```

Following the Drop statement, the stored procedure name is specified. Issuing the following command drops the `get_patient_records` stored procedure from the database:

```
DROP PROCEDURE get_patient_records
```

Multiple stored procedures can be dropped in one statement by separating them with commas after the `DROP PROCEDURE` statement, as follows:

```
DROP PROCEDURE get_patient_records, update_patient_records
```

After executing the `DROP PROCEDURE` statement, the `get_patient_records` and `update_patient_records` stored procedures are deleted from the MSDE database.

Suppose a user has declared some stored procedures with the same name by declaring them with the `Number` option described earlier. If the Drop statement is issued against the stored procedure series name, it drops all stored procedures with that name, regardless of their number. Being able to drop them in one simple statement is really the advantage of using the `Number` option. The stored procedures in a user's MSDE database—`get_patient_records; 1`, `get_patient_records; 2`, and `get_patient_records; 3`—can be dropped at once with the following syntax:

```
DROP PROCEDURE get_patient_records
```

The name of the stored procedure series is specified above. This tells MSDE to drop all stored procedures in that series.

Managing stored procedures with Enterprise Manager and Access

In addition to using the SQL syntax to manage stored procedures, there is the option of using the Enterprise Manager or Access 2000 graphical tools to create, alter, and delete stored procedures.

To add a new stored procedure using Enterprise Manager:

1. Go to the database to which the new stored procedure is added and expand the tree to show the objects that exist in that database, including Stored Procedures.
2. Click the Stored Procedures node in the tree for a listing of all the stored procedures on the right half of the screen.
3. To create a new stored procedure, right-click Stored Procedures, and select the New Stored Procedure option from the pop-up menu that appears. The stored procedure designer screen appears next. The drop-down menus can also be used to create a stored procedure by selecting Action, then New Stored Procedure. Once New Stored Procedure is chosen with either of these methods, the screen in Figure 15-1 appears:

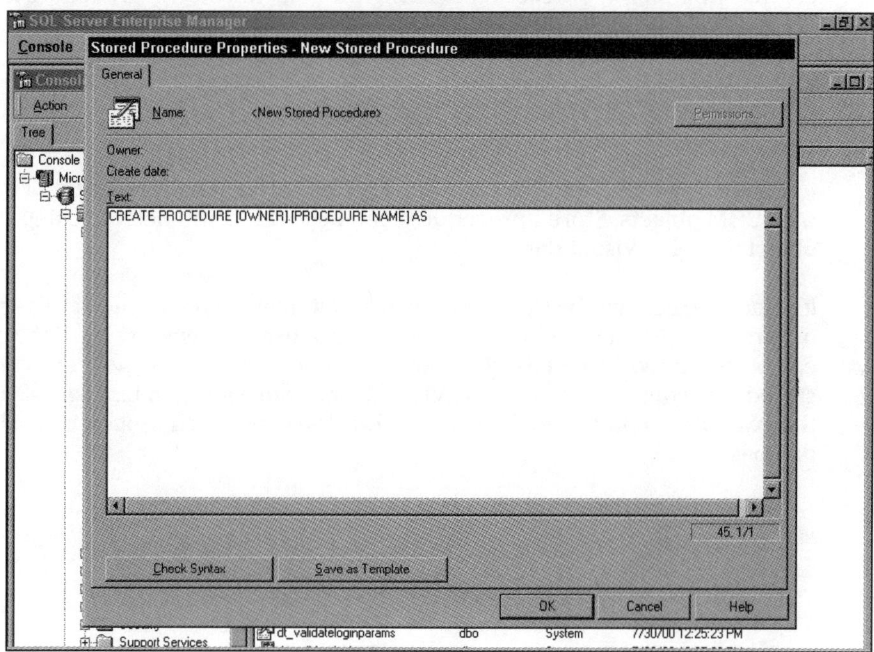

Figure 15-1: Creating a stored procedure using Enterprise Manager

The `CREATE PROCEDURE` syntax has been started automatically. The user must then specify the procedure name and the SQL code that the stored procedure is to be composed of and click the Check Syntax button to make sure there are no syntax errors in the statements. For more information about the proper syntax for creating stored procedures, consult the *Managing Stored Procedures With SQL* section of this chapter.

To manage MSDE stored procedures using Access 2000, a new project must be created. A Project is an Access file that connects to an MSDE or SQL Server database through OLE DB and then allows the user to manage the Tables, Stored Procedures, Views, and Triggers of that database. To create a new Project in Access, select File, New, and then choose Project (Existing Database). A wizard guides the user through the steps of establishing a connection to that database. If an MSDE database has not been created, a user can choose Project (New Database), and the wizard then guides the user through the process of creating a project for a new database.

Once a project has been created with Access, the Tables, Stored Procedures, and Views objects are listed on the left side of the screen. Stored procedures can be selected to see which stored procedures already exist in the database. This also enables the Run, Design, New, and Delete buttons. A user can click the Run button to run the selected stored procedure, the Design button to view the SQL code for the selected stored procedure and/or to make changes to it, or the New button to create a new stored procedure. Deleting the selected stored procedure is a matter of choosing the Delete button.

Managing stored procedures with DMO

As mentioned in Chapter 5 and Chapter 14, the DMO object model allows the user to modify the MSDE database from any programming environment that can work with COM objects. Stored procedures can be created and deleted using the DMO object model in Visual Basic.

Instead of executing the Create Procedure statement in a tool such as Query Analyzer or through a Visual Basic program with ADO, a user can employ the DMO objects to create the stored procedure. If a user wants to create the `get_patient_records` stored procedure using DMO, the Visual Basic code shown in Listing 15-2 accesses the DMO stored procedure object and adds the new stored procedure to the MSDE database:

Listing 15-2: Visual Basic Code Using DMO to Create a New Stored Procedure

```
'This example creates a new stored procedure using DMO

'declare the server object
Dim oMSDEServer As sqldmo.SQLServer
Set oMSDEServer = New sqldmo.SQLServer
oMSDEServer.LoginTimeout = 15
oMSDEServer.ODBCPrefix = False

'declare the database object
Dim oDatabase As sqldmo.Database
```

```
'declare the stored procedure object
Dim oSP As New sqldmo.StoredProcedure

'Declare and populate the server, userid, and
'password variables here...(Typically, you would
'pass them in to a routine such as this or declare
'them in a module versus declaring them here.  This
'is done for simplicity here.)
Dim strServerName As String
Dim strUserId As String
Dim strPassword As String

'In our example the server is (local).  This would
'be different if the database is on an NT server
'separate from the machine where you're running this
'code
strServerName = "(local)"
strUserId = "sa"
strPassword = ""

'log in and connect to the MSDESample database
oMSDEServer.Connect strServerName, strUserId, strPassword
Set oDatabase = oMSDEServer.Databases("MSDESample")

oSP.Text = "CREATE PROCEDURE get_patient_records " & _
           "@LastName varchar(40),@FirstName varchar(40) " & _
           "AS " & _
           "SELECT * " & _
           "FROM patient " & _
           "WHERE LastName = @LastName AND " & _
           "FirstName = @FirstName"
oSP.Name = "get_patient_records"

'Add the new stored procedure to the database
oDatabase.StoredProcedures.Add oSP

Set oSP = Nothing
Set oDatabase = Nothing
```

The code in Listing 15-2 declares a database and stored procedure DMO object and then connects to the MSDESample database. After connecting to the database, the `Text` and `Name` properties of the stored procedure object are assigned values. The `Text` property gets assigned to the Create Procedure syntax and the `Name` property gets assigned the name of the stored procedure. Once they have values that define how the stored procedure is structured, the stored procedure object gets added to the database object. The act of adding the stored procedure object to the database object creates the stored procedure on the MSDE database.

For the above code to work, the user must first add a reference to DMO to the project. To add a reference, select Project, References, and then choose Microsoft SQLDMO Object Library from the list.

If the user decides to delete this stored procedure after creating it on the database, the following code in Listing 15-3 can be inserted beneath the oMSDEServer.connect line, shown in Listing 15-2, to replace the code that originally follows the Connect statement. (Note: The first Set statement in this listing is too long to fit across the page, so the line is continued below and indented even though it is representative of a single line.)

Listing 15-3: Visual Basic Code Using DMO to Delete an Existing Stored Procedure

```
'This example removes the stored procedure from the database
Set oSP = oMSDEServer.Databases("MSDESample").StoredProcedures
     ("get_patient_records")

oSP.Remove

Set oSP = Nothing
Set oDatabase = Nothing
```

By directly connecting to the stored procedure `get_patient_records` on the MSDESample database, the user is able to execute the Remove method of the stored procedure object to remove the stored procedure from the database. These are just a few examples of how the DMO object model can be used to modify stored procedures on the MSDE database. Please consult Chapters 5, 14, and 16 for more examples of using DMO in programs.

Summary

Stored procedures are an important part of the MSDE database. They provide the power to create code modules that organize common database tasks into reusable formats. MSDE comes with a number of system stored procedures that can be used to perform common database tasks not specific to any particular database. Routines in extended stored procedures can be accessed from MSDE after the DLL is registered with MSDE. Extended stored procedures can be created in development tools that allow the user to create exported DLL's, such as C/C++. User-defined stored procedures can be created to store the business logic for the database and then accessed from multiple applications, such as Visual Basic or C++, that connect to the MSDE database. Stored procedures can be created and modified in a number of ways: through SQL, in the Access or Enterprise Manager graphical tools, or programmatically from environments such as Visual Basic. Understanding how to create stored procedures and how to take advantage of the system stored procedures is an important step in effectively utilizing the MSDE database.

✦ ✦ ✦

Using Triggers to Enforce Data Integrity

In This Chapter

Triggers compared to constraints, rules, and defaults

When to use Insert, Update, or Delete triggers

How and when to use the Inserted virtual table

How and when to use the Deleted virtual table

Using SQL to manage triggers

Using Enterprise Manager to manage triggers

Using Access to manage triggers

Using DMO to manage triggers

Triggers provide the user with the ability to have logic execute any time an `Insert`, `Update`, or `Delete` statement is issued against a table. A defined trigger specifies which action or actions (Insert, Update, or Delete) should cause the code to execute. The main benefit of using triggers is that they enforce data integrity and certain business rules in the MSDE database automatically. Triggers can be created to execute `AFTER` the table insert, update, or delete occurs — for example, to notify someone in the company that a certain event has occurred or to modify the data inserted if it doesn't meet certain requirements. A trigger can also be created to execute `INSTEAD OF` the table insert, update, or delete. A powerful benefit of the `Instead Of` trigger is that it allows the user to update views that would otherwise not be updateable. The specific details about the differences between `Instead Of` triggers versus `After` triggers will be described in this chapter. Triggers can be managed in a variety of ways: through SQL statements, from a graphical tool such as Access or Enterprise Manager, or with the DMO object model in programming languages such as Visual Basic.

Comparing Triggers to Constraints, Rules, and Defaults

Triggers can provide similar functionality to constraints, rules, and defaults. Constraints are part of the `Create Table` statement and specify criteria that get applied to every record.

Those records that do not meet the constraint criteria are not added to that table. Here's an example of a constraint:

```
CREATE TABLE Indiana_Patients
(
PatientId int,
LastName varchar(40),
FirstName varchar(40),
MiddleInitial varchar(1),
Address varchar(60),
City varchar(60),
State varchar(2),
Zip int,
CONSTRAINT chk_state CHECK (State = 'IN')
)
```

The `Create Table` statement above has a check constraint declared on the state field. This check constraint ensures that only records with a value of `'IN'` get added to the Indiana_Patients table. This is just one example of a constraint. Other examples include primary keys, foreign keys, not nullable columns, and unique constraints. All of these types of constraints are defined in the `Create Table` syntax. Rules allow the user to specify acceptable values that can be inserted into a particular column. A rule performs the same function as the check constraint in the above example, where only Indiana patients are allowed to be added to the Indiana_Patients table. Check constraints are the recommended method, but rules are included in SQL Server 2000 and MSDE because prior versions of SQL Server used them. A rule gets created with the `Create Rule` statement. The following command will create that same restriction using a rule:

```
CREATE RULE rule_Indiana_patients
AS
@State = 'IN'
```

After creating this rule, a user must associate it with the state column in the Indiana_Patients table. To do so, the `sp_bindrule` system stored procedure should be executed.

Defaults, the values that get inserted into a column when no other value has been specified, can be created in two ways. One way is to specify the default as part of the `Create Table` syntax, as shown as follows:

```
CREATE TABLE default_example
(
RecId int,
Description varchar(25) DEFAULT 'Hello'
)
```

The example above creates a Default_example table and sets the default description to `'Hello'`. If a record gets inserted into the Default_example table and a description is not specified, then `Hello` will be inserted into that column.

Another way to create a default table is to use the Create Default statement. After the default has been created this way, it has to be associated with the column and table using the sp_bindefault system stored procedure. This latter method is not recommended any more but is included in SQL Server 2000 and MSDE because prior versions of SQL Server used them.

Triggers contain statements that get executed any time data on the specified table is modified. A trigger can be created to do the same thing that a constraint, rule, or default can. However, using constraints, rules, and defaults is recommended whenever possible.

The following syntax will create a trigger to make sure the record inserted into the Indiana_Patients table has a state equal to 'IN' if constraints, rules, or defaults were not an option.

```
CREATE TRIGGER indiana_state_trigger
ON Indiana_Patients
FOR INSERT, UPDATE
AS
BEGIN
    DECLARE @intCount int

    SELECT @intCount = count(*)
    FROM Indiana_Patients
    WHERE state <> 'IN'

    IF @intCount > 0
        BEGIN
            RAISERROR ('You attempted to insert a state other
            than Indiana into the Indiana_patient table.
            The non-Indiana rows have been deleted.',1,1)
            DELETE FROM Indiana_Patients
            WHERE state <> 'IN'
        END
END
```

This trigger accomplishes the same result as the Check Constraint example we saw earlier. Triggers normally work in conjunction with constraints, rules, and defaults to provide ultimate data integrity over the MSDE database.

Choosing a Trigger Type: Insert, Update, or Delete

A trigger can be automatically fired whenever an Insert, Update, or Delete statement is executed against the specified table. A single trigger can execute when any of these events happen, or a trigger can be created to execute when only one of these events happens. Oftentimes, it may be desirable to have one trigger that runs when inserts or updates take place, and another one that runs when deletes take place. All of these combinations are possible.

```
CREATE TRIGGER trig_ins_patient
ON patient
AFTER INSERT
AS
BEGIN
    DECLARE @MaxPatientId int

    SELECT @MaxPatientId = max(PatientId)
    FROM inserted

    IF @MaxPatientId > 10000
            RAISERROR ('Time for Doctor to retire!  Over
                       10,000 patients served.',1,1)
END
```

The purpose of this trigger is to raise an error telling the doctor to retire after he sees patient #10,000. Any time a record gets inserted into the Patient table, this trigger will be automatically executed. The key part of the `Create Trigger` syntax that imparts this information is `ON patient AFTER INSERT`. This specifies that the Patient table is the table this trigger is to be associated with and that this trigger should execute `AFTER` any insert.

Tip The trigger in the above example is named by beginning with the prefix `trig` to indicate that it is a trigger; followed by `ins` to symbolize that it happens on insert, and `patient` to symbolize the table it is associated with. This, or a similar naming convention, is recommended so that what the trigger is impacting is easily identifiable.

The type of trigger chosen depends entirely on when that event is to occur. In the example above, only `insert` was appropriate because the purpose was to notify the doctor once the Patient table had more than 10,000 records. A delete or an update was not necessary in that situation. However, there may be times when a check is needed to verify that any changes made to data still meet a certain business rule. In such a situation, the insert and update would be used together, like this:

```
CREATE TRIGGER trig_ins_upd_patient
ON patient
AFTER INSERT, UPDATE
AS
    INSERT INTO patient_history
    SELECT * from inserted
```

This example inserts a record into the Patient_history table any time a new patient record is added or if an existing record is updated. The `INSERT` and `UPDATE` are specified together, separated by commas following the `After` statement. Triggers such as this example are very common for maintaining historical or audit information about all changes made to a table.

More examples of when triggers might be used will be discussed throughout the remainder of this chapter.

Understanding the Inserted and Deleted Virtual Tables

When creating triggers, a programmer or administrator should make use of the Inserted and Deleted tables. These are virtual tables in the MSDE database that store the rows affected by the insert, update, or delete operation. For a trigger to know which records have changed (for example, the records that were inserted, updated, or deleted and that caused the trigger to run), it must reference one of these virtual tables.

The Inserted table contains the values that were inserted as a result of an `Insert` statement. It also contains the new values that were changed as a result of an `Update` statement. The Deleted table also serves two purposes. It stores any records that were deleted as a result of a `Delete` statement, and it stores the prior value for a record that was updated as the result of an `Execute` statement. An update will end up having a record in the Deleted table as well as the Inserted table.

The Inserted and Deleted tables have the identical column structure as the table they refer to. The same fields can be referenced in them that are in the original table, as in the following example:

```
CREATE TRIGGER trig_ins_patient
ON patient
AFTER INSERT
AS
BEGIN
    DECLARE @MaxPatientId int

    SELECT @MaxPatientId = max(PatientId)
    FROM inserted

    IF @MaxPatientId > 10000
            RAISERROR('Time for Doctor to retire!  Over 10,000
                        patients served.',1,1)
END
```

The highest patient id is being selected from the Inserted table. The PatientId field exists in the Inserted table because it also exists in the Patient table. At the moment this trigger executes, the Inserted virtual table will contain the rows that just got inserted into the Patient table. To see if any of these newly inserted rows meet the criteria (in this case, whether the doctor has seen his 10,000th patient yet), a user can simply select from the Inserted table. The Deleted virtual table works in a similar way. If a user wants to delete the contact record for a patient whose patient record has also been deleted, the following trigger could be used:

```
CREATE TRIGGER trig_del_patient
ON patient
AFTER DELETE
AS
DELETE
FROM contacts
FROM contacts c JOIN deleted d ON c.PatientId = d.PatientId
```

This example executes any time a patient record is deleted. The `Delete` statement joins to the Deleted table to determine which records in the Contacts table need to be deleted. Any records that are in the Deleted table were just deleted, and by joining to that table on PatientId, the corresponding files from the Contacts table are identified for deletion.

Tip: Because the Inserted and Deleted tables are virtual tables and exist only in the server's memory, accessing them is nearly always faster than accessing a real table, which might require reading the disk. To improve trigger performance, evaluate their code to see if they are accessing a real table when they could access a virtual table (the first trigger example in this chapter is a prime offender), and change the code to access the virtual table instead.

Creating, Deleting and Modifying Triggers

Triggers are created, altered, and deleted in a variety of ways, with tools like Access and Enterprise Manager, through SQL code, or through DMO.

Creating triggers with SQL

Although examples of what a trigger looks like have already been introduced, the syntax for creating them should be explored for its included options.

```
CREATE TRIGGER trigger_name
ON { table | view }
[ WITH ENCRYPTION ]
{
    { { FOR | AFTER | INSTEAD OF }
        { [ DELETE ] [ , ] [ INSERT ] [ , ] [ UPDATE ] }
        [ WITH APPEND ]
        [ NOT FOR REPLICATION ]
        AS
```

```
            sql_statement [ ...n ]
        }
        |
        { ( FOR | AFTER | INSTEAD OF ) { [ INSERT ] [ , ]
        [ UPDATE ] }
            [ WITH APPEND ]
            [ NOT FOR REPLICATION ]
            AS
            { IF UPDATE ( column )
                [ { AND | OR } UPDATE ( column ) ]
                    [ ...n ]
            | IF ( COLUMNS_UPDATED ( ) { bitwise_operator }
            updated_bitmask )
                    { comparison_operator } column_bitmask [ ...n ]
            }
            sql_statement [ ...n ]
        }
}
```

The `WITH ENCRYPTION` attribute is used to enhance security and causes MSDE to encrypt the System table columns that contain the text of the `Create Trigger` statement. A byproduct of using this option is that the trigger cannot be published as part of replication because it is encrypted.

The `NOT FOR REPLICATION` option prevents the trigger from being executed when a replication process makes the table change. This option is normally used when it is known that an equivalent trigger was implemented on the server that the replicated data originated from. In that case, there is no need to run an identical trigger on the same data a second time.

`INSTEAD OF` is a unique type of trigger that executes instead of the `Insert`, `Update`, or `Delete` statement.

As mentioned in Chapter 14, the `Instead Of` trigger is new to SQL Server 2000 and is included in MSDE.

A major benefit to the `Instead Of` trigger is that a user can update views that previously could not be updated. As discussed in Chapter 14, there are several limitations on when views can be updated. One example is trying to update columns in a view that comes from multiple tables. The `Instead Of` trigger provides a way to overcome this limitation, because it executes instead of the insert or update on the view. Here is an example:

Create a View in the database as follows:

```
CREATE VIEW PatientView
AS
SELECT p.PatientId, p.LastName, p.FirstName, p.MiddleInitial,
       c.Email
FROM patient p JOIN contacts c ON p.PatientId = c.PatientId
```

The following `Update` statement will fail because it tries to update columns that impact more than one underlying table in the view:

```
UPDATE PatientView
SET LastName = 'Doe', Email = 'JaneDoe@yahoo.com'
WHERE FirstName = 'Jane' AND LastName = 'Single'
```

If an `Instead Of` trigger is created on the PatientView table, then it will execute instead of the `Update` statement.

```
CREATE TRIGGER IO_Trig_UPD_PatientView ON PatientView
INSTEAD OF UPDATE
AS
BEGIN
     UPDATE patient
          SET LastName = i.LastName, FirstName = i.FirstName,
               MiddleInitial = i.MiddleInitial
          FROM patient p, inserted i
          WHERE p.PatientId = i.PatientId
     UPDATE contacts
          SET Email = i.Email
          FROM contacts c, inserted i
          WHERE c.PatientId = i.PatientId
END
```

This trigger will execute any time an update is attempted on the PatientView table. It checks the Inserted table to see what is supposed to be inserted, and does two separate inserts: one into the Patient table and the other into the Contacts table. The insert into the view works this time because the trigger handles the inserts and breaks them down into their base tables. An `Instead Of` trigger can run against tables as well as views. Unlike `After` triggers, which allow multiple `Insert`, `Update`, or `Delete` triggers to be defined per table or view, only one `Instead Of` trigger can be defined for each `Insert`, `Update`, or `Delete` statement per table or view.

Another important trigger feature is the `IF UPDATE (column)` clause. This clause can be specified in the SQL statement section of the trigger and can be used to test for whether a particular column has been updated, as in this example:

```
CREATE TRIGGER trig_ins_upd_patient
ON patient
FOR INSERT, UPDATE
AS
BEGIN
    IF UPDATE (Address)
        INSERT INTO patient_history
        SELECT Address from inserted
END
```

This trigger contains the `IF UPDATE (Address)` statement. If the address field was updated or inserted, then a record gets inserted into the Patient_history table. The If `Update` statement can be used on any column in the table.

Triggers can be created to have an automatic e-mail sent when a specific event occurs. The following trigger, without an e-mail option, returns an error:

```
CREATE TRIGGER trig_ins_patient
ON patient
AFTER INSERT
AS
BEGIN
    DECLARE @MaxPatientId int

    SELECT @MaxPatientId = max(PatientId)
    FROM inserted

    IF @MaxPatientId > 10000
            RAISERROR('Time for Doctor to retire!  Over 10,000
                        patients served.',1,1)
END
```

If, instead of raising an error, a trigger sent the doctor an e-mail message telling him it's time to retire, the system would be more efficient. Here's an example:

```
CREATE TRIGGER trig_ins_patient
ON patient
AFTER INSERT
AS
BEGIN
    DECLARE @MaxPatientId int

    SELECT @MaxPatientId = max(PatientId)
    FROM inserted

    IF @MaxPatientId > 10000
            EXECUTE master..xp_sendmail 'DoctorKhan@yahoo.com',
                  'You have served patient # 10,000.  It is
                  time to retire!!!'
END
```

The `Raiserror` statement is replaced with a statement that executes the extended stored procedure `sendmail` to send the doctor a message letting him know it's time for him to retire.

Another valuable trigger allows the user to issue a rollback transaction to undo any insert, update, or delete that occurred that doesn't meet the specified business rules. In the previously shown Indiana_Patients table, instead of issuing a `Delete` statement to remove any records that were added with states other than Indiana, the transaction can be rolled back, as in the following example:

```
CREATE TRIGGER indiana_state_trigger
ON Indiana_Patients
FOR INSERT, UPDATE
AS
BEGIN
    DECLARE @intCount int

    SELECT @intCount = count(*)
    FROM Inserted
    WHERE state <> 'IN'

    IF @intCount > 0
        BEGIN
_              RAISERROR ('You attempted to insert a state other
_              than Indiana into the Indiana_patient table',1,1)
_           ROLLBACK TRANSACTION
        END
END
```

If the number of invalid records exceeds 0, then the transaction is rolled back and an error is raised.

Altering triggers in SQL

Once a trigger has been created, it can be altered. The SQL syntax for altering a trigger is as follows:

```
ALTER TRIGGER trigger_name
ON ( table | view )
[ WITH ENCRYPTION ]
{
    { ( FOR | AFTER | INSTEAD OF ) { [ DELETE ] [ , ]
    [ INSERT ] [ , ] [ UPDATE ] }
        [ NOT FOR REPLICATION ]
        AS
        sql_statement [ ...n ]
    }
    |
    { ( FOR | AFTER | INSTEAD OF ) { [ INSERT ] [ , ]
    [ UPDATE ] }
        [ NOT FOR REPLICATION ]
        AS
        { IF UPDATE ( column )
        [ { AND | OR } UPDATE ( column ) ]
        [ ...n ]
        | IF ( COLUMNS_UPDATED ( ) { bitwise_operator }
```

```
            updated_bitmask )
            { comparison_operator } column_bitmask [ ...n ]
            }
            sql_statement [ ...n ]
        }
    }
```

The Alter Trigger syntax is nearly identical to the Create Trigger syntax. The user must specify everything the trigger is to include. The only difference is that the trigger happens to exist already, and it will replace the old statements with the new ones that were specified.

An earlier example showed how to inform a doctor when he had consulted with his 10,000th patient. If the doctor now decides to retire after 15,000 patients, the original trigger can be altered:

```
ALTER TRIGGER trig_ins_patient
ON patient
AFTER INSERT
AS
BEGIN
    DECLARE @MaxPatientId int

    SELECT @MaxPatientId = max(PatientId)
    FROM inserted

    IF @MaxPatientId > 15000
            RAISERROR('Time for Doctor to retire!  Over 15,000
                        patients served.',1,1)
END
```

The old definition of trig_ins_patient gets replaced with the one above. The trigger declaration replaces the 10000 with 15000 in both the If statement and the Raiserror notice.

Deleting triggers in SQL

In addition to being created and altered, triggers can also be deleted. The SQL syntax for deleting a trigger is as follows:

```
DROP TRIGGER { trigger } [ ,...n ]
```

The Drop statement is followed by the specified trigger name. To drop the Trig_ins_patient trigger from the database, the following command would be issued:

```
DROP TRIGGER trig_ins_patient
```

Multiple triggers can be dropped in one statement by separating them with commas after the `Drop Trigger` statement, as shown as follows:

```
DROP TRIGGER trig_ins_patient, trig_ins_upd_patient
```

After executing the `Drop Trigger` statement above, both of the triggers will be deleted at once from the MSDE database.

Managing triggers with Enterprise Manager and Access

Triggers can be created, altered, or deleted using the Enterprise Manager or Access 2000 graphical tools.

In Enterprise Manager a trigger is bound to a table, so before a trigger can be added or modified, a table must be selected. To add a new trigger using Enterprise Manager, a user should do the following:

1. Go to the database to which the new trigger will be added. Then, expand the tree to see the objects that exist in that database, including Tables.
2. Click on the Tables node in the tree to see all of the existing tables on the right half of the screen.
3. To create a new trigger, select the table for which triggers will be viewed/ added. Then, right-click and select All Tasks, then Manage Triggers. An example of that screen is shown in Figure 16-1.

The drop-down menus may be used instead of the pop-up windows to create a trigger. Assuming the desired table has been selected, a user can choose Action, All Tasks, and then Manage Triggers from the toolbar. Once Manage Triggers is chosen with either of these methods, the screen shown in Figure 16-2 will appear.

On the Trigger Properties screen, the SQL syntax must be used to specify what the trigger should do. Once the trigger syntax has been specified, the user can click the Check Syntax button to make sure there are no syntax errors. Clicking the OK button will save the trigger with that table.

To modify an existing trigger, the same steps described above should be followed to open the Trigger Properties window (see Figure 16-2). Where it says Name and defaults to New, the user can select the drop-down list and see any other triggers that have been defined for that table and select the trigger from the list that is to be updated.

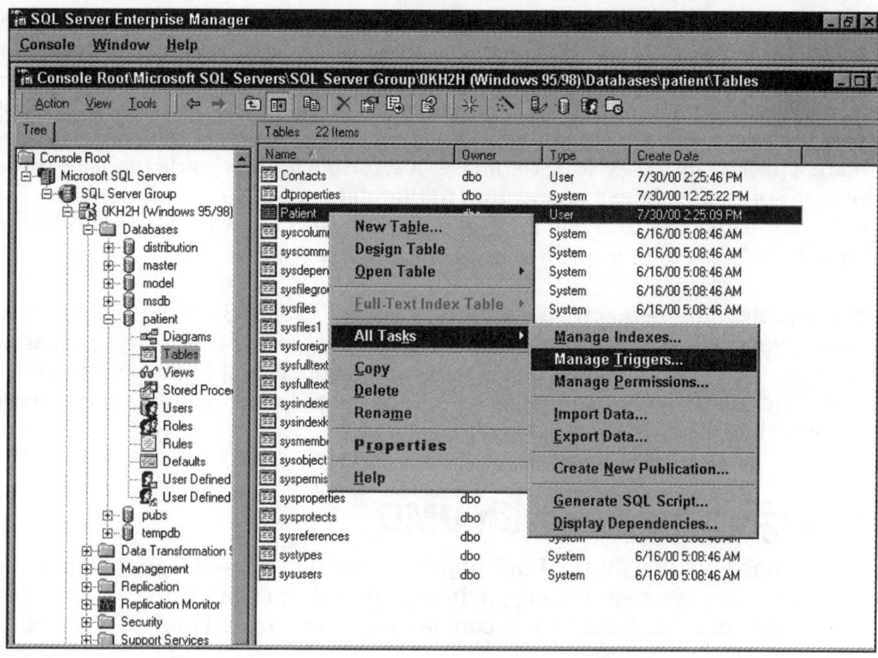

Figure 16-1: Selecting Manage Triggers from Enterprise Manager

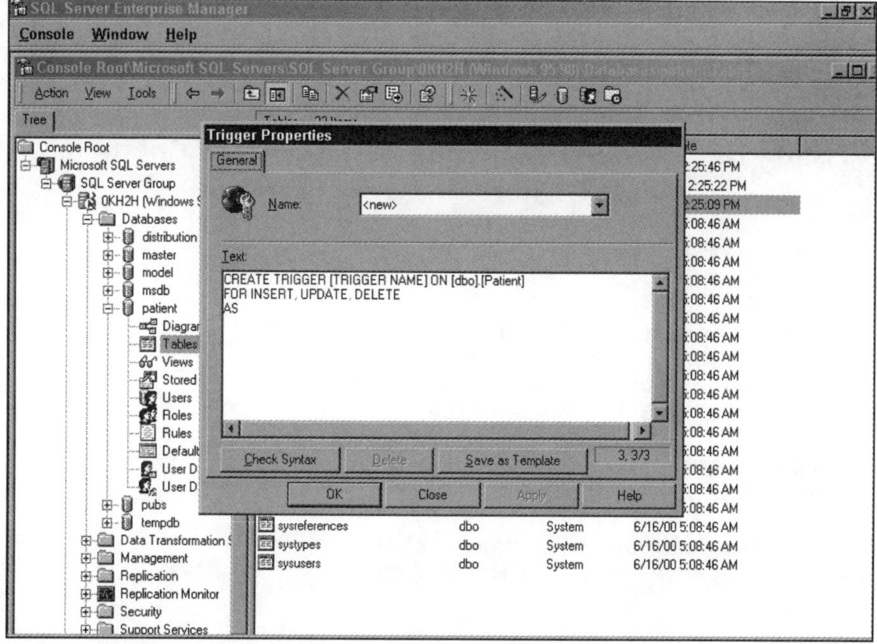

Figure 16-2: Creating a new trigger using Enterprise Manager

To manage MSDE triggers using Access 2000, a new project must first be created. A Project is an Access file that connects to an MSDE or SQL Server database through OLE DB and then allows the user to manage the Tables, Stored Procedures, Views, and Triggers of that database. A user can create a new Project in Access by selecting File, New, and then choosing Project (Existing Database). This will allow the user to create a project for an existing database. A wizard will then guide the user through the steps of establishing a connection to that database. If an MSDE database has not yet been created, the user can instead choose Project (New Database) and be guided through the process of creating a project for a new database.

Once a project has been created with Access, the Tables, Stored Procedures, and Views objects will be listed on the left side of the screen. Since a trigger is associated with tables, a table must be selected and right-clicked to display the pop-up menu. The user can choose Triggers from that pop-up menu and then the screen to create the trigger will be displayed.

Managing triggers with DMO

As mentioned previously, the DMO object model allows modification of the MSDE database from any programming environment that can work with COM objects. The DMO object model in Visual Basic can be used to create and update triggers.

Instead of executing the `Create Trigger` statement in a tool such as Query Analyzer or through a Visual Basic program with ADO, the DMO objects can also be used to create the trigger. To create a Trig_ins_patient trigger using DMO, The Visual Basic code in Listing 16-1 accesses the DMO trigger object and adds the new trigger to the MSDE database:

Listing 16-1: Visual Basic Code Using DMO to Create a New Trigger

```
'This example creates a new trigger using DMO

'declare the server object
Dim oMSDEServer As sqldmo.SQLServer
Set oMSDEServer = New sqldmo.SQLServer
oMSDEServer.LoginTimeout = 15
oMSDEServer.ODBCPrefix = False

'declare the database object
Dim oTable As sqldmo.Table

'declare the stored procedure object
Dim oTrigger As New sqldmo.Trigger
```

```
'Declare and populate the server, userid, and
'password variables here...(Typically, you would
'pass them in to a routine such as this or declare
'them in a module versus declaring them here.  This
'is done for simplicity here.)
Dim strServerName As String
Dim strUserId As String
Dim strPassword As String

'In our example the server is (local).  This would
'be different if the database is on an NT server
'separate from the machine where you're running this
'code
strServerName = "(local)"
strUserId = "sa"
strPassword = ""

'log in and connect to the MSDESample database
oMSDEServer.Connect strServerName, strUserId, strPassword
Set oTable =
oMSDEServer.Databases("MSDESample").Tables("patient")

oTrigger.Text = "CREATE TRIGGER trig_ins_patient " & _
                "ON patient " & _
                "AFTER Insert " & _
                "AS " & _
                "BEGIN " & _
                    "DECLARE @MaxPatientId int " & _
                    "SELECT @MaxPatientId = max(PatientId)" & _
                    " FROM inserted " & _
                    "IF @MaxPatientId > 10000 " & _
                        "RAISERROR ('Time for Doctor " & _
                        "retire!  Over 10,000 patients " & _
                        "served.',1,1) " & _
                "End"

oTrigger.Name = "trig_ins_patient"

'Add the new trigger to the table
oTable.Triggers.Add oTrigger

Set oTrigger = Nothing
Set oTable = Nothing
```

The code in this listing can be found on the CD-ROM in the file named `Ch 16\CreateTrigger.txt`.

The above code declares a table and trigger DMO object and then connects to the MSDESample database. After connection to the Patient table in the database, the Text and Name properties of the Trigger object are assigned values. Once they have values that define how the trigger will be structured, the Trigger object gets added to the Table object. The act of adding the Trigger object to the Table object adds the trigger to the MSDE database.

In order for the above code to work, a reference to DMO must first be added to the project. To add a reference, select Project, References, and then choose Microsoft SQLDMO Object Library from the list.

If after creating this trigger on the database, a user decides to delete it, the code shown in Listing 16-2 would accomplish the task:

Listing 16-2: Visual Basic Code Using DMO to Delete an Existing Trigger

```
'This example deletes a trigger from the database

'declare the server object
Dim oMSDEServer As sqldmo.SQLServer
Set oMSDEServer = New sqldmo.SQLServer
oMSDEServer.LoginTimeout = 15
oMSDEServer.ODBCPrefix = False

'declare the database object
Dim oTable As sqldmo.Table

'Declare and populate the server, userid, and
'password variables here...(Typically, you would
'pass them in to a routine such as this or declare
'them in a module versus declaring them here.  This
'is done for simplicity here.)
Dim strServerName As String
Dim strUserId As String
Dim strPassword As String

'In our example the server is (local).  This would
'be different if the database is on an NT server
'separate from the machine where you're running this
'code
strServerName = "(local)"
strUserId = "sa"
strPassword = ""

'log in and connect to the MSDESample database
oMSDEServer.Connect strServerName, strUserId, strPassword
```

```
Set oTable = _
oMSDEServer.Databases("MSDESample").Tables("patient")
'Remove the trigger from the database
oTable.Triggers.Remove "trig_ins_patient"

Set oTable = Nothing
```

The code in this listing can be found on the CD-ROM in the file named `Ch 16\DeleteTrigger.txt`.

In this example, a trigger object was not declared. Only the Table object was required because the `trigger.remove` method of the Table object can be executed to remove the Trig_ins_patient table. These are just two examples of how the DMO object model can be used to modify triggers on the MSDE database. Chapters 5, 14, and 15 contain more examples of using DMO in programs.

Summary

Triggers provide a powerful and flexible way for programmers and administrators to automatically enforce business rules and maintain data integrity in their MSDE database. Triggers are really just stored procedures that are programmed to fire automatically when an `Insert`, `Update`, or `Delete` occurs on the table they were defined on. A trigger can be set to execute `INSTEAD OF` or `AFTER` the database modification event. Triggers can be created and modified with SQL statements, from a graphical tool such as Access or Enterprise Manager, or with the DMO object model in programming languages such as Visual Basic. In order to fully harness the power of the MSDE database and maintain the integrity of the data, a firm understanding of triggers is essential.

✦ ✦ ✦

CHAPTER 17

Accessing Data with Cursors

In This Chapter

Scrolling through records with cursors

Types of cursors

Server-side cursors versus client-side cursors

Declaring a cursor

Opening a cursor

Retrieving records from a cursor

Updating records in a cursor

Deleting records in a cursor

Closing a cursor

Deallocating memory used by a cursor

Cursors provide users with the ability to retrieve a set of results from the MSDE database and to utilize those results in their procedures. Cursors are powerful tools that allow stored procedures and other SQL statements to make use of recordsets (for example, to scroll through the cursor one record at a time and to perform some action). Chapter 13 discusses how SQL is a programming language, though not always thought of as one. Cursors are another feature of the SQL language that can be used with MSDE to fully take advantage of its programming capabilities.

There are several types of cursors: static cursors, keyset cursors, dynamic cursors, and fast-forward cursors. There are two possible locations for a cursor: client or server. To make use of cursors in the MSDE database, the cursor must first be declared by assigning it a `Select` statement for the records to be retrieved. Then the cursor can be opened, and rows can be fetched from it. Once the cursor is open, data in it can be updated, deleted, or used to determine another course of action, such as in a `Control of Flow` statement. When finished with the cursor, a user can close and deallocate the memory for it.

Using Cursors to Scroll through Records

The primary purpose of a cursor is to provide users with a way to retrieve a set of records from the MSDE database for further use in its stored procedures or batch statements. For example, a user may be writing a stored procedure that needs to loop through a specific set of records and to perform certain actions depending on the values contained in those records. A cursor provides more flexibility than an `Update` statement because the user can utilize the cursor to perform different actions for each record in the set, whereas an `Update` statement issues a single update to a group of records that meets a certain criteria. Cursors should only be used when their particular flexibility is called for. For example, consider a stored procedure that needs to do the following:

1. Select all patients with a last name of Doe.
2. If the Doe patient lives in Nowhere, Indiana, delete the record.
3. If the Doe patient lives in Somewhere, Indiana, change the address to Somewhere New, Indiana.
4. If the Doe patient has a first name of John, change the address to Somewhere Special.

In this case, the stored procedure can use a `Delete` statement followed by two `Update` statements instead of a cursor. For any reasonably large table, the performance using set operations is much better than the performance using a cursor. However, if a stored procedure is intended to select patients for clinical trials the following steps should be performed:

1. Select patients matching a standardized profile.
2. Perform complex analysis on each patient to ensure that the trials are safe for the patient.
3. Perform more analysis to make sure the patient fits into a desired category for the trials.
4. Determine if more patients for that category are necessary to meet the statistical requirements of the trials.
5. If the patient meets all of the criteria, encrypt the patient's ID and add it with category information to the table that is used for the trials.

In this case, a cursor may be necessary because there is probably no way to write an SQL statement that satisfies these needs. In addition, a cursor can loop through a resultset and take actions that have nothing to do with database updates. For example, if a user wants to send a reminder notice through e-mail to all patients who have an appointment in the upcoming two weeks, the user can create a cursor to select all patients with upcoming appointments, loop through the cursor and — for each patient with an e-mail address — send an e-mail reminder. The SQL code for implementing this example is listed at the end of this chapter in the section, *Putting It All Together.*

Choosing a Cursor Type

Different types of cursors — static, dynamic, keyset, and fast_forward — are used and different options are set depending on what needs to be accomplished. Table 17-1 shows the different types of cursors and a description of what each can be used for.

Table 17-1
MSDE Cursor Types

Cursor Type	*Description*
Static	Creates a cursor that makes a temporary copy of the data in the Tempdb table. Changes made in the underlying tables are not reflected in the cursor.
Keyset	Creates a cursor that makes a temporary copy of the unique identifiers for each record in the Tempdb table. As records are fetched, the keys are read from the Tempdb table and their corresponding data is looked up in the original tables. Any changes made to existing records on non-key fields are visible through this cursor. Any inserts are not visible because those identifiers for the new records are not in the Tempdb table. When a record is fetched in the cursor that has been deleted, the `@@FETCH_STATUS` returns a `-2`. If the key fields are updated outside of the cursor, then an insert and delete in effect take place. The insert of the new data is not visible to the cursor and the deleted row returns `@@FETCH_STATUS` of `-2` when it is retrieved. To make updates to the key values visible to the cursor, the updates should be done through the cursor itself using the `Where Current Of` clause in the `Where` clause of the `Update` statement.
Dynamic	Creates a cursor that reflects the current data with each fetch. This is the most resource-intensive of the four cursor types because it always shows the most current data.
Fast_Forward	Creates a cursor that can only move forward and is read-only (for example, cannot be updated).

In addition to declaring a specific cursor type, options exist that further supplement the cursor type, as shown in Table 17-2.

Table 17-2
Additional Cursor Options

Cursor Option	*Description*
Read_Only	Specifies that the cursor is read-only and cannot be updated.
Update [of column]	A cursor is updateable by default, but a user can explicitly specify that it can be updated by using the `update` option. In addition, a user can specifically limit which columns can be updated by following the `update` option with the column name(s) that can be updated.
Scroll	Specifies that the cursor can be navigated around using Next, Prior, First, Last, Absolute, and Relative. If the `scroll` option is not specified, then only the Next operation can be performed to move through the recordset. If the fast_forward type of cursor is being used, then scroll cannot be specified.
Forward_Only	Specifies that the cursor can only move forward through the results. This cannot be used with a fast_forward type of cursor because `forward_only` is inherently in the fast_forward cursor.
Scroll_Locks	Also referred to as pessimistic locking, this guarantees that positioned updates and deletes made on the cursor succeed because the rows are locked as they are read into the cursor. This option cannot be used with fast_forward because a fast_forward cursor is read-only.
Optimistic	Often called optimistic locking, it guarantees that positioned updates and deletes made on the cursor do *not* succeed if the record has been updated after being modified in the cursor read. This option increases performance as long as other processes do not update the records. It is called optimistic because the programmer hopes that no other processes update the records while the cursor is in use.

MSDE provides flexibility in cursor operation, and the user must determine which cursor is best suited for a given scenario. For example, a user encounters the following situation: A cursor must be created to retrieve a list of patients who have not been sent an invoice for their visit. The cursor is scrolled through record by record, and an invoice is generated. In addition, each night a process runs to batch update the patient database with any changes of name, address, details about the visit, charges, and so on. In this situation, the cursor does not need to be dynamic since the user is not concerned that the data is outdated while it's being used (the nightly process makes the changes for the day). The keyset cursor can be used, but, once again, the user is not concerned about data being outdated.

A static cursor is the best choice for this hypothetical situation because the temporary copy created in the Tempdb table contains everything the user needs to know to retrieve the specified list.

The user should also specify the `forward_only` and `read_only` options because the task does not require moving any direction other than forward, and no data needs to be updated.

Specific examples of the syntax used for declaring these cursor types are described in a later section, *Defining a Cursor.*

Choosing the Location for a Cursor: Client or Server

A cursor can be implemented in two locations: on the client or on the server. Client-side cursors are returned to the requesting client and stored in local memory. Server-side cursors remain on the server and return chunks of records to the client as requested.

Transact-SQL cursors are located on the server. Transact-SQL cursors are used in MSDE stored procedures, triggers, and other SQL code blocks. From programming languages such as Visual Basic and Visual C++ and other similar programs that support ODBC, OLE DB, or ADO, both client- and server-based cursors can be utilized. Using ADO in Visual Basic, for example, a user can specify whether to create a recordset (the ADO equivalent to a cursor) implemented on the client or on the MSDE server.

It is appropriate to use server-side cursors when accessing a small portion of data because they are faster than client-side cursors. Only fetched records are transmitted over the network. With client-side cursors, all of the records are returned to the client, regardless of how many records the client ends up using. Client-side cursors support updates and deletes, but they are really just create SQL statements that later get sent to the server for updating.

For more information about choosing the appropriate cursor location to use from external programs, data access references, such as the ADO references, should be consulted.

Defining a Cursor

Several steps are involved in using a cursor.

1. The cursor must be declared and opened.
2. The records can be fetched from the cursor, and the information (including any updates or deletes) can be used in a procedure or SQL statement.
3. The cursor should be closed, and the memory it uses should be deallocated.

Declare

The first step in working with a cursor is to declare it. The syntax for declaring a cursor is the following:

```
DECLARE cursor_name CURSOR
[ LOCAL | GLOBAL ]
[ FORWARD_ONLY | SCROLL ]
[ STATIC | KEYSET | DYNAMIC | FAST_FORWARD ]
[ READ_ONLY | SCROLL_LOCKS | OPTIMISTIC ]
[ TYPE_WARNING ]
FOR select_statement
[ FOR UPDATE [ OF column_name [ ,...n ] ] ]
```

The Declare statement is followed by the name of the cursor. Additional parameters can be specified following the declaration.

The `local` and `global` options specify whether the cursor is local to the current batch or procedure or global to all operations using the current connection. Local cursors can only be referenced in the current batch or stored procedure and cannot be used anywhere outside that scope. Global cursors can be referenced by any other stored procedure or batch running on the current connection.

The cursor type and options are the next part of the declaration. Types and options are described in Tables 17-1 and 17-2.

The `type_warning` option specifies that the client should be sent a message to notify it any time a cursor is converted from the original type to another type.

The `FOR select_statement` portion of the `Declare` statement lists the SQL `Select` statement that the cursor is to be based on.

The `For Update [Of column_name]` option can be explicitly specified to allow records in the cursor to be updated. By default, you can update data in the cursor, but this option lets you specify that you definitely want the columns to be updated.

If the `For Update` option is used without the additional `Of column_name` portion, then all of the columns in the cursor can be updated. However, if you do use the `column_name` option, then only those columns can be updated in the cursor.

The following is a `Declare` statement with no options specified:

```
DECLARE patient_cursor CURSOR
FOR select * from patient
```

The above declares a `patient_cursor` as every record in the Patient table.

```
DECLARE patient_cursor CURSOR
GLOBAL
SCROLL
DYNAMIC
FOR SELECT LastName, FirstName, Address, City, State, Zip
    FROM patient
FOR UPDATE
```

In this example, the `patient_cursor` is defined with the additional options: `global`, `scroll`, `dynamic`, and `for update`. The global specification allows this cursor to be available to any batch or procedure on the same database connection. The `scroll` option allows the cursor to be scrolled in all directions. The dynamic cursor type specified allows all changes in the data to be reflected as the records are fetched. The `for update` option explicitly specifies that all columns in the cursor can be updated.

The `Select` statement in the preceding declaration can be very complex as opposed to very simple. Any valid SQL statement that runs against the MSDE database can be used in a cursor, but `Compute`, `Compute By`, and `Insert Into` statements cannot be used in a cursor declaration.

Once a cursor has been declared, a local variable of the data type "cursor" can be assigned to it as follows:

```
DECLARE patient_cursor CURSOR
GLOBAL
SCROLL
DYNAMIC
FOR SELECT LastName, FirstName, Address, City, State, Zip
    FROM patient
FOR UPDATE

DECLARE @patient_cursor CURSOR

SET @patient_cursor = patient_cursor
```

The global patient_cursor is declared first, and then a local @patient_cursor variable is declared of cursor data type. Following the declaration of the local cursor variable, it gets assigned to the global cursor. A cursor variable, in addition to the cursor itself, can be used in situations where a local variable is assigned to the values already stored in a cursor.

Open

The act of opening the cursor executes the SQL statement and populates the cursor. The syntax for opening a cursor that is defined is the following:

```
OPEN { { [ GLOBAL ] cursor_name } | cursor_variable_name }
```

The Open statement is followed by the global keyword if the cursor is global and then by the name of the cursor. The statement to open an already declared patient_cursor looks like this:

```
OPEN GLOBAL patient_cursor
```

The reason for specifying "global" is to open the global cursor previously declared as global. If the user is working with a local cursor, the Open statement looks like this:

```
OPEN patient_cursor
```

Fetch

After the cursor has been opened, the Fetch statement can be used to retrieve records from the cursor. The syntax for the Fetch statement is as follows:

```
FETCH
        [ [ NEXT | PRIOR | FIRST | LAST
                | ABSOLUTE { n | @nvar }
                | RELATIVE { n | @nvar }
            ]
            FROM
        ]
{ { [ GLOBAL ] cursor_name } | @cursor_variable_name }
[ INTO @variable_name [ ,...n ] ]
```

The Fetch statement is followed by options for records intended to be fetched. If the cursor with the scroll option is not declared, then only NEXT records can be fetched in the resultset. If the scroll option is specified, then the Next, Prior, First, Last, Absolute, and Relative directions are available.

Next fetches the next record in the cursor. Prior fetches the prior record in the cursor. First fetches the first record in the cursor. Last fetches the last record in the cursor. Absolute is followed by a negative or positive number. If Absolute is followed by a positive number, then that row number from the beginning of the cursor is retrieved. If Absolute is followed by a negative number, then that row number from the end of the cursor is retrieved (for example, absolute 15 retrieves the 15th record in the cursor). Relative is very similar to absolute, but it starts from the current position. Specifying a positive number after Relative fetches the row that is the number of rows before the current record. Specifying a negative number after Relative fetches the row that is the number of rows after the current record.

The `From` statement comes next in the declaration statement and is followed by the cursor name. If users wants to put the fetched value or values into local variables, they can specify the `INTO @variablename` as the last part of the declare.

If the cursor has already been declared and opened with the following statements, use the following.

```
DECLARE patient_cursor CURSOR
GLOBAL
SCROLL
KEYSET
FOR SELECT LastName, FirstName, Address, City, State, Zip
    FROM patient
FOR UPDATE

OPEN GLOBAL patient_cursor
```

To fetch the next record from the cursor, the user should execute the following statement:

```
FETCH NEXT
FROM GLOBAL patient_cursor
```

After the user executes this statement, the next record is retrieved, and the current position of the cursor is moved to that record. To fetch the 15th record from the cursor, use this statement:

```
FETCH ABSOLUTE 15
FROM GLOBAL patient_cursor
```

The 15th record is returned, and the current position of the cursor is moved to record 15. To retrieve the 15th to last record in the cursor, the user can employ this statement:

```
FETCH ABSOLUTE -15
FROM GLOBAL patient_cursor
```

The preceding Fetch returns the record that is 15 rows from the end of the cursor. It also moves the current position of the cursor to that record.

If a user has local variables to put the cursor values into, a statement such as the one that follows accomplishes this:

```
DECLARE @LastName varchar(40)
DECLARE @FirstName varchar(40)
DECLARE @Address varchar(40)
DECLARE @City varchar(25)
DECLARE @State varchar(2)
DECLARE @Zip int

FETCH NEXT
FROM GLOBAL patient_cursor
INTO @LastName, @FirstName, @Address, @City, @State, @Zip
```

All of the fields in the cursor must be included in the local variables of the Into clause. They should also be listed in the same order as they appear in the cursor. Otherwise, the data may get inserted into the wrong variable.

Caution should be exercised when scrolling around recordsets. If users scroll too far, they can generate errors.

A patient cursor is declared and opened as follows:

```
DECLARE patient_cursor CURSOR
SCROLL
DYNAMIC
FOR SELECT LastName, FirstName, City, State, Zip
    FROM patient

OPEN patient_cursor
```

For purposes of understanding this example, there are four records in the cursor. The user starts by fetching the first record:

```
FETCH NEXT
FROM patient_cursor
```

Because the cursor has just been opened, the result of the FETCH NEXT is that the first record is returned. Executing three more FETCH NEXT statements puts the current position pointer at the fourth (last) record in the cursor, as is shown in the Figure 17-1:

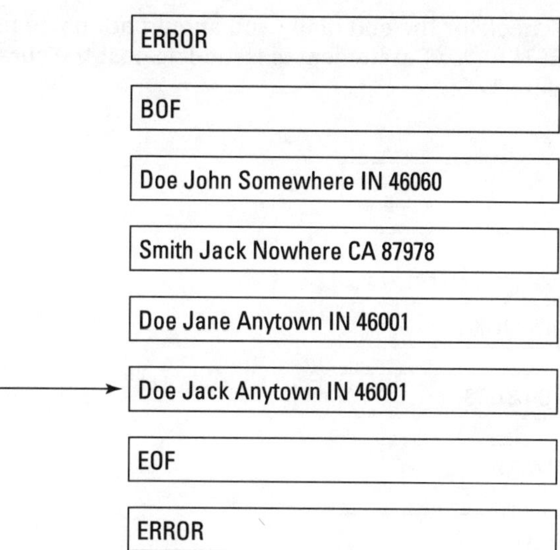

Figure 17-1: Current cursor position is on last record

The current cursor position is located on Jack Doe's record. Jack Doe is the last record in the cursor. Issuing another `FETCH NEXT` statement moves the cursor position beyond the last record to the End of File (EOF), as shown in Figure 17-2.

ERROR

BOF

Doe John Somewhere IN 46060

Smith Jack Nowhere CA 87978

Doe Jane Anytown IN 46001

Doe Jack Anytown IN 46001

EOF

ERROR

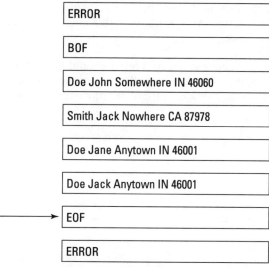

Figure 17-2: Current cursor position is at end of file

At this stage, the code should check for the end of file and should not try to move forward. However, if another `FETCH NEXT` statement is issued against the cursor, an error is raised, as shown in Figure 17-3:

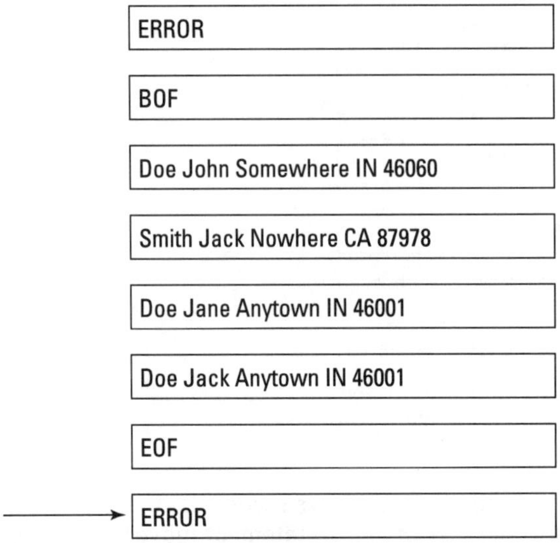

ERROR
BOF
Doe John Somewhere IN 46060
Smith Jack Nowhere CA 87978
Doe Jane Anytown IN 46001
Doe Jack Anytown IN 46001
EOF
→ ERROR

Figure 17-3: Current cursor position raises an error

Figure 17-3 shows what can happen if you do not appropriately check for the beginning or end of file when scrolling through your cursors with a client program written in a language such as Visual Basic.

Whenever a user loops through a recordset, the first fetch should be performed before entering the loop, if the loop performs a condition assuming there is a valid record. The loop should be written to check that there are more records before continuing.

```
--Loop through a cursor containing each statement
--and execute them
BEGIN
    declare @nextstatement char(200)

    DECLARE batch_statements CURSOR FOR
    SELECT statement from statements

    OPEN batch_statements

   --get the first record in the cursor
   --and store it in the @nextstatement variable
```

```
        FETCH NEXT FROM batch_statements
        INTO @nextstatement

        --while there are more records in the cursor
        WHILE @@FETCH_STATUS = 0
            BEGIN
                --execute the current sql statement
                execute (@nextstatement)

                --get the next record in the cursor
            FETCH NEXT FROM batch_statements
                INTO @nextstatement
            END
        CLOSE batch_statements
      DEALLOCATE batch_statements
END
```

The first record in the batch_statements cursor is retrieved first. If a valid record is returned (for example, @@FETCH_STATUS was 0), the loop is entered, the Sql statement gets executed, and the next record in the cursor is fetched. The loop is exited when the end of the cursor is reached.

If a users have not closed the cursor and need to use it later in the procedure, they must remember that they are at the end of the file. They can always issue a Fetch First command to move back to the beginning before trying to use the cursor again. Here's an example:

```
FETCH FIRST
FROM batch_statements
```

After moving back to the beginning of the recordset, it is safe to move forward when looking at the records. However, a FETCH PRIOR should not be issued too many times; an error similar to the one shown in Figure 17-3 results.

Update

Once the cursor has been opened and records have been fetched from it, the data in the cursor can be updated if necessary, assuming the user is not working with a read-only cursor that cannot be updated. By updating data through a cursor, the data is updated in the underlying table, and changes are shown in the cursor as well.

To update the current record in a cursor, the user utilizes the standard Update statement but with the Where Current Of clause:

```
UPDATE patient
SET LastName = 'Doe'
WHERE CURRENT OF GLOBAL patient_cursor
```

This `Update` statement updates the LastName value of the patient table record that is the same record as the current record in the cursor. The underlying table name is specified after the `Update` statement, but the `Where Current Of` clause specifies the current cursor record as the criteria for the update.

Delete

Assuming a user is working with an updateable cursor, deleting a row through a cursor deletes the row in the underlying table and from the cursor itself.

To delete the current record in a cursor, a user should implement the standard `Delete` statement but with the `Where Current Of` clause:

```
DELETE FROM patient
WHERE CURRENT OF GLOBAL patient_cursor
```

The `Delete` statement deletes the underlying record in the Patient table that matches the current record in the cursor. As with the updates, the underlying table name is specified after the `Delete` statement, but the `Where Current Of` clause specifies the current cursor record as the criteria for the delete.

Close

When a user is finished working with the cursor, it must be closed. The syntax for the `Close` statement is:

```
CLOSE { { [ GLOBAL ] cursor_name } | cursor_variable_name }
```

The `Close` statement is followed by the `global` option and the name of the cursor or cursor variable. To close the global `patient_cursor` previously created, the following statement should be issued:

```
CLOSE GLOBAL patient_cursor
```

If the user is only working with a local cursor, then the following `Close` statement would be used instead:

```
CLOSE patient_cursor
```

If a local cursor variable is defined to store the results of the cursor, the `Close` statement for the local cursor variable looks like this:

```
CLOSE @patient_cursor
```

Deallocate

The last step in utilizing a cursor is to deallocate the memory that is being used by that cursor. Memory used by a cursor is not freed by just closing the cursor. In addition, a cursor name cannot be reused until the original has been deallocated. The syntax for the `Deallocate` statement is:

```
DEALLOCATE { { [ GLOBAL ] cursor_name } | @cursor_variable_name
}
```

It follows the same general syntax as the `Open` and `Close` statements: the `Deallocate` statement is followed by the `global` option and then by the name of the cursor or cursor variable.

To deallocate the memory that the global `patient_cursor` is using, the following statement should be run:

```
DEALLOCATE GLOBAL patient_cursor
```

If instead a local `patient_cursor` has been used, the statement is:

```
DEALLOCATE patient_cursor
```

If a local cursor variable is defined to store the results of the cursor, the `Deallocate` statement to free the memory of the local cursor variable looks like this:

```
DEALLOCATE @patient_cursor
```

Putting It All Together

Define the following stored procedure in an MSDE database:

```
CREATE PROCEDURE get_patient_records
@patient_cursor CURSOR VARYING OUTPUT
AS
BEGIN
    SET @patient_cursor = CURSOR
        FORWARD_ONLY STATIC FOR
        SELECT LastName, FirstName
        FROM patient

    OPEN @patient_cursor
END
```

This stored procedure returns a cursor as output. The cursor is populated from the Patient table. Next, execute the following statements to call the stored procedure:

```
DECLARE @PatientRecords CURSOR

DECLARE @LastName varchar(40), @FirstName varchar(40),
        @DisplayName varchar(80)

EXECUTE get_patient_records @patient_cursor =
      @PatientRecords OUTPUT
WHILE (@@FETCH_STATUS = 0)

BEGIN
    FETCH NEXT
    FROM @PatientRecords
    INTO @LastName, @FirstName

    SELECT @DisplayName = @LastName + ',' + @FirstName
    PRINT @DisplayName
END

CLOSE @PatientRecords
DEALLOCATE @PatientRecords
```

The example declares a local cursor variable (`@PatientRecords`) to hold the results of the varying output cursor returned by the stored procedure. The stored procedure is called, and its results are put into the local cursor variable. Each record in the local cursor variable is fetched, and the patient name, formatted in "Last Name, First Name" format, is displayed interactively. After all of the records in the cursor have been accessed, the cursor is closed and deallocated.

If patient appointments are contained in the Appointments table and the e-mail address is contained in the Contacts table, the following code creates a cursor of all patients with upcoming appointments and then loops through the cursor, sending each patient an e-mail:

```
DECLARE @ApptDateTime DATETIME, @LastName varchar(40),
        @FirstName varchar(40), @Email varchar(100),
        @Message varchar(200)

DECLARE patient_appointments_cursor CURSOR
SCROLL
STATIC
FOR SELECT a.ApptDateTime, p.LastName, p.FirstName,
           c.Email
    FROM appointments a, contacts c, patient p
    WHERE a.patientid = c.patientid AND
          c.patientid = p.patientid AND
          a.ApptDateTime BETWEEN '10/01/00' AND '10/15/00'
          c.Email IS NOT NULL
```

```
OPEN patient_cursor

FETCH NEXT
FROM patient_appointments_cursor
INTO @ApptDateTime, @LastName, @FirstName, @Email

    --while there are more records in the cursor
    WHILE @@FETCH_STATUS = 0
        BEGIN

            @message = select 'Dear ' + @FirstName + ' ' +
                       @LastName + ', This is to remind you of
                       your appointment scheduled for ' +
                       @ApptDateTime + '   Sincerely, Your
                       Doctor'
            EXECUTE master..xp_sendmail @Email, @Message

            FETCH NEXT
            FROM patient_appointments_cursor
            INTO @ApptDateTime, @LastName, @FirstName, @Email
       END

CLOSE patient_appointments_cursor
DEALLOCATE patient_appointments_cursor
```

The cursor is declared and opened to retrieve the patient records for those that have appointments from October 1, 2000 to October 15, 2000. The first patient record is fetched, and the While loop executes to send each patient an e-mail reminder.

These are just two of the many ways that cursors can be used in stored procedures or SQL batches.

Summary

Cursors provide a great deal of power in retrieving results and in taking action based on those results. Cursors are really just SQL queries that get returned into a recordset variable that can be used in procedures. Cursors are based on a SQL `Select` statement. Cursors can be used in stored procedures and other SQL statements in the same manner as recordsets in a Visual Basic or C++ program. Different types of cursors can be declared based on how information is to be used. Static cursors can return a quick set of results but are inefficient for reflecting immediate changes and updating the data in the cursor. Keyset cursors can be used to reflect immediate changes made to existing records but do not accommodate new records that are added. When a user is unconcerned about speed but needs to have all data changes reflected in the active resultset, a dynamic cursor can be used. Read-only and other similar options are often used in conjunction with keyset, static, or dynamic cursors.

A cursor can be client-side or server-side. Client-side cursors return the recordset to the client machine, but server-side cursors remain on the server, with records returned as requested. The Transact-SQL cursors described in this section are server-side cursors. A series of SQL statements must be issued each time a cursor is used: `Declare`, `Open`, `Fetch`, `Update` (if applicable), `Delete` (if applicable), `Close`, and `Deallocate`. Understanding how to utilize cursors is critical to taking full advantage of the SQL programming capabilities available to the MSDE database.

✦ ✦ ✦

P A R T

V

Working with External Data

This part explores the tools used to transfer blocks of data focusing on using Data Transformation Services (DTS) to migrate data between different databases and using replication mechanisms for copying and distributing data from one database to another. This part further explains how to use transactions to distribute data and guard against data fragmentation.

✦ ✦ ✦ ✦

In This Part

✦ ✦ ✦ ✦

CHAPTER 18

Importing and Exporting Data

In This Chapter

Choosing import and export tools

Using bcp

Using Bulk Insert

Optimizing Bulk Copy operations

Using the DTS Import/Export Wizard

Moving data into and out of databases is a common maintenance task. In this chapter, the tools used to transfer blocks of data will be explored. Several common tools, such as `Bulk Insert`, `bcp`, and the DTS Import/Export Wizard, will be explained in detail.

Choosing Import and Export Tools

There are a variety of tools designed for importing and exporting data. The tool a user chooses depends on the features required for the given task. Some of these tools include the following:

- **Bulk Insert** — This is a T-SQL command that rapidly imports data from a text file into a SQL Server database. It performs imports only from text files. It can be included in a T-SQL script or stored procedure. It offers very high performance.
- **Bcp** — This is a command-line utility that can rapidly import or export data from or to a text file. Data can be stored in character format or SQL Server's native format. It can import or export data from text files or ODBC sources. It can be executed from a command line or batch files. It has a programmatic interface and offers very high performance.
- **DTS Import/Export Wizard** — Found in the SQL Tools (not shipped with the SQL Server Desktop Engine), this wizard can import data from or export data to any OLE DB or ODBC data source. It can also import text file data. The wizard allows transformation of data during export. It features a graphical user interface and a programmatic interface. The wizard produces packages that can be scheduled to run automatically through the SQL Server Agent.

- **Replication** — Replication can create snapshots of data on a linked server. The SQL Server Desktop Engine can act as a subscriber to this replication, but cannot publish data. Replication can import from text files, OLE DB sources, and ODBC sources. It can export to OLE DB and ODBC sources. Replication can be accessed through the command line and batch files. It can also be accessed through T-SQL scripts and provides a programmatic interface. Replication jobs can be scheduled through the SQL Server Agent.
- **Select Into/Insert Into** — These are T-SQL commands that move data. `Select Into` creates a new data structure and populates it. `Insert Into` appends data to an existing data structure. They can be included in T-SQL scripts. They can access data through linked servers, including OLE DB and ODBC source data structures.

Bulk inserting data from a text file using `Bulk Insert` or `bcp` must be in a row, field format. Delimiters that can be described to these processes must separate fields. Delimiters must also separate rows. The columns in the source need not be in the same order as columns in the destination. The data must be in character or SQL Server's native format.

The destination table must already exist but does not need to have the same number of columns as the source text file. If columns in the destination table are not mapped to the source text file, they must either allow nulls or have a default value specified. Bulk copy operations can perform parallel scans on the source data. This means there is no guarantee that the order in the source file will be the order in which the data is inserted into the destination. The exception is sorted data inserted into tables with clustered indexes. If the destination table has a clustered index and the source data is sorted into the same order as the clustered index, the speed of the insertion can be improved.

Both `Bulk Insert` and `bcp` allow a specified number of rows in the source to be inserted into the destination. Long inserts can be broken into smaller chunks.

Data can be imported and exported through linked servers. This provides simple T-SQL access to source and destination data. While the source and destination data source must exist, internal data structures, such as tables, can be created on the fly through the scripts. Select Into creates a table based on the rows in the select before populating the table. The DTS Import/Export Wizard can define its own connections within the context of the package and create destination data structures as well.

Bcp

The bulk copy program (`bcp`) is a command-line executable built on the ODBC bulk copy Application Programming Interface (API). It allows rapid insertion of data and extraction of data into a data file. `Bcp`'s speed comes from reducing the amount of logging performed.

`Bcp`-inserted rows do not, by default, fire triggers. If the user optionally chooses to fire triggers, the inserted table will have all the rows in the `bcp` batch (typically, the inserted table has only one row). This will affect how triggers are implemented. Firing triggers will also cause the `bcp` operation to be fully logged, and thus slow performance down.

Bcp file types

`Bcp` supports four types of data file formats:

- **Native** files store data in the same internal format as the SQL Server database. The file can be read only by SQL Server bulk copy software. These files take less room and load faster than other types of data file formats. These files are meant primarily for transferring data between identical tables on different databases. They are used by replication when creating snapshots of data to send to subscribing SQL Server databases.
- **Character** files store data as ANSI characters. Any software that can read ANSI text can open and read these files. By default, individual fields are delimited with [Tab] characters, and rows are delimited with a line feed character. This style of file is the most universal.

Bulk copy operations convert characters to OEM format when exporting and into ANSI format when importing. However, this may cause a loss of extended characters or misinterpretation of data. If the source uses a different codepage than the destination, the source codepage can be specified as a command switch. Storing the data in a Unicode format will also assure that characters are properly maintained.

- **Unicode Native** files store noncharacter data in native format. Character data types (char, nchar, nvarchar, ntext, and text) data is stored using Unicode characters. Data stored in this format can be read only by SQL Server bulk copy software. Files stored in this format are larger than native format because each Unicode character requires 2 bytes of storage rather than 1. Storing character data in Unicode format assures the preservation of data transferred between servers with different default codepages. Noncharacter data is stored in native format, saving time to convert that data.
- **Unicode Character** stores all data as Unicode data. Any software that can read Unicode ANSI text can read these files. Since Unicode characters consume 2 bytes for each character rather than 1, these files consume more space. They preserve extended characters and can facilitate transferring data between servers that have different default codepages.

Formatting data

`Bcp` needs to know the format of data when importing and exporting data. If an import or export is run without a format file or the appropriate command switches, `bcp` will query the user for the following information for each column in the table.

File Storage Type defines the data type of each column. This determines how the data is formatted. Use Table 18-1 to specify the appropriate data type. These codes are case sensitive.

Table 18-1
Data Type Coding

Data Type	*Code As:*
char	c[har]
varchar	c[har]
nchar	w
nvarchar	w
text	T[ext]
ntext	W
binary	x
varbinary	x
image	I[mage]
datetime	d[ate]
smalldatetime	D
decimal	n
numeric	n
float	f[loat]
real	r
int	i[nt]
bigint	B[igint]
smallint	s[mallint]
tinyint	t[inyint]
money	m[oney]
smallmoney	M
bit	b[it]
uniqueidentifier	u
sql_variant	V[ariant]
timestamp	x

Prefix allows bcp to compact the size of the data file by specifying the size of the field in a prefix that precedes the field. The size of this prefix varies depending on the data type and file type. Columns that can contain nulls will store –1 in the prefix if the value is null. A positive value indicates there is data. Table 18-2 shows the prefix sizes in characters.

Table 18-2
Comparison of Bcp Native and Character Formats

SQL Server	*Native Format*		*Character Format*	
Data Type	***Not Null***	***Null***	***Not Null***	***Null***
Char	2	2	2	2
Varchar	2	2	2	2
Nchar	2	2	2	2
Nvarchar	2	2	2	2
Text	4	4	4	4
Ntext	4	4	1	1
Binary	1	1	2	2
Varbinary	1	1	2	2
Image	4	4	4	4
Datetime	0	1	1	1
Smalldatetime	0	1	1	1
Decimal	1	1	1	1
Numeric	1	1	1	1
Float	0	1	1	1
Real	0	1	1	1
Int	0	1	1	1
Bigint	0	1	1	1
Smallint	0	1	1	1
Tinyint	0	1	1	1
Money	0	1	1	1
Smallmoney	0	1	1	1
Bit	0	1	0	1
Uniqueidentifier	1	1	1	1
Timestamp	1	1	2	2

Field Length indicates the maximum number of characters a field can consume. This is particularly important when converting to character type data files. If storing in native mode, noncharacter data does not require this parameter. Table 18-3 indicates the various data sizes.

Table 18-3
Bcp Data Type Sizes

Data Type	*Length*	*Default Length For Native Mode*
Char	Length defined for the column	-
Varchar	Length defined for the column	-
Nchar	Twice the length defined for the column	-
Nvarchar	Twice the length defined for the column	-
Text	0	-
Ntext	0	-
Bit	1	1
Binary	Twice the length defined for the column + 1	Length defined for the column
Varbinary	Twice the length defined for the column + 1	Length defined for the column
Image	0	0
Datetime	24	8
Smalldatetime	24	4
Float	30	8
Real	30	4
Int	12	4
Bigint	19	8
Smallint	7	2
Tinyint	5	1
Money	30	8
Smallmoney	30	4
Decimal	41	Varies with precision
Numeric	41	Varies with precision
Uniqueidentifier	37	16
Timestamp	17	8

Field Terminators are optional characters used to separate fields. They are not required when prefixes and field lengths are used. The characters must be used uniquely to separate fields and cannot appear in the data. This can be difficult to assure when native mode files are used, because noncharacter data may randomly contain the designated character codes. A distinct character is also used to indicate the end of a row. Table 18-4 is a list of typical terminators. The backslash is used to indicate escape characters to produce control characters.

Table 18-4
Bcp Control Characters

Field Terminator	*Indicated By:*
Tab	\t
Newline character	\n
Carriage return	\r
Backslash	\\
Null terminator	\0
Any printable character	* , . : ~ | ` and so on
Any string up to 10 characters	******, |-|-|, !!!!!, @@@@, and so on

Format files

Format files are ASCII character files that provide the formatting data used by `bcp`. The file can be built by executing `bcp` interactively, as shown in Figure 18-1. `Bcp` will query the user for all the required format information for the source column. Once collected, `bcp` will ask for a file name for the format file.

The format file can be reused when the same operation is repeated. Figure 18-2 shows a sample format file. The first row contains the `bcp` version number. The second row contains the number of columns. There is one row for each column with the following fields:

- **Host file field order** indicates the order of the column within the data file (this does not necessarily correspond to the order in the source table or view).
- **Host file data type** indicates the data type used in the host file. In a character type file, this will always be SQLCHAR.
- **Prefix length** is a number between zero and four.
- **Host file data length** indicates the maximum number of characters consumed by the field.
- **Terminator** indicates the delimiter character.

✦ **Server column order** indicates the order of the column as it exists in the source table or view.

✦ **Server column name** indicates the name of the column as it exists in the source table or view.

✦ **Collation** indicates the collation used to store character data within the data file.

```
BCP
C:\WINDOWS\Desktop>bcp northwind..products out c:\projects\msdebible\products.tx
t -Smarkropolis -Usa -P

Enter the file storage type of field ProductID [int]:
Enter prefix-length of field ProductID [0]:
Enter field terminator [none]:

Enter the file storage type of field ProductName [nvarchar]:
Enter prefix-length of field ProductName [2]:
Enter field terminator [none]:

Enter the file storage type of field SupplierID [int-null]:
Enter prefix-length of field SupplierID [1]:
Enter field terminator [none]:

Enter the file storage type of field CategoryID [int-null]:
Enter prefix-length of field CategoryID [1]:
Enter field terminator [none]:

Enter the file storage type of field QuantityPerUnit [nvarchar]:
Enter prefix-length of field QuantityPerUnit [2]:
Enter field terminator [none]:

Enter the file storage type of field UnitPrice [money-null]:
```

Figure 18-1: Using `bcp` interactively to define a format file

```
products.fmt - Notepad
8.0
10
1       SQLINT        0   4    ""    1    ProductID         ""
2       SQLNCHAR      2   80   ""    2    ProductName       SQL_Latin1_General_CP1_CI_AS
3       SQLINT        1   4    ""    3    SupplierID        ""
4       SQLINT        1   4    ""    4    CategoryID        ""
5       SQLNCHAR      2   40   ""    5    QuantityPerUnit   SQL_Latin1_General_CP1_CI_AS
6       SQLMONEY      1   8    ""    6    UnitPrice         ""
7       SQLSMALLINT   1   4    ""    7    UnitsInStock      ""
8       SQLSMALLINT   1   4    ""    8    UnitsOnOrder      ""
9       SQLSMALLINT   1   4    ""    9    ReorderLevel      ""
10      SQLBIT        0   1    ""    10   Discontinued      ""
```

Figure 18-2: Format file created when exporting the Products table from the Northwind database

If the data file has fewer columns than the destination table, rows must be added for these missing columns in the file. Adding a field with a prefix length of 0, hosts data field length of 0, and terminator of "" indicates that the columns do not exist in the host data file.

If the format file has more columns that the destination table, setting the server column order to 0 indicates that the column should not be inserted. Changing the server column order also allows the user to map fields in the host data file to different columns in the destination table.

Using Bcp

In the following section, `bcp` will be used to import and export data. To export the Products table from the Northwind database using `bcp` interactively:

1. Confirm that SQL Server is running on the host computer.
2. Open a command window.
3. Enter the following command:

   ```
   Bcp northwind..products out c:\products.txt -Sservername
    -Usa -Ppassword
   ```

   where *servername* is the name of the database server and *password* is the password for the sa account.
4. For each column in the table, a prompt will appear for a field data type, prefix-length, and terminator character. Press Enter at each prompt to accept the default setting.
5. At the prompt, save the format information as a file by entering **Y**. Enter **C:\Products.fmt** as the name of the file.
6. The export should run, creating a products.fmt format file and products.txt export file on c:\.

The file will save the data in native format. To repeat the export using the format file created, add the `-f` switch to the command line and specify the fully qualified name of the format file.

```
Bcp northwind..products out c:\products.txt -Sservername
     -Usa -Ppassword -fc:\products.fmt
```

Next, to import data into a copy of the Products table:

1. Create a table in Northwind called Products2 that has the same schema as the Products table. (Hint: Use Generate SQL Scripts to create a SQL statement that will re-create the table. Using only the `Create Table` statement, change the name, remove the identity constraint on ProductID, and run the command in the SQL Query Analyzer.)
2. Import the data from products.txt using `bcp`. Enter the following command in a command window:

   ```
   Bcp northwind..products in c:\products.txt -Sservername
        -Usa -Ppassword -fc:\products.fmt
   ```

3. Use SQL Query Analyzer to confirm that the rows have been inserted into the Products2 table.

The `format` option allows the user to create a format file without executing the copy. The following line can help interactively create a format file for the Suppliers table:

```
Bcp northwind..suppliers format c:\suppliers.txt
-Sservername -Usa -Ppassword -fc:\suppliers.fmt
```

The source of a `bcp` export can also be a SQL query. You will export a list of products with their product categories and suppliers using the following command:

```
Bcp "select productname, categoryname, companyname from
products p join categories c on p.categoryid = c.categoryid
join suppliers s on p.supplierid=s.supplierid" queryout
c:\prodlist -Sservername -Usa -Ppassword -C
```

Bcp command line

`Bcp` can import data from a text file into an existing SQL table. It can also export data from a table, view, or query, and can be used to create format files without performing the copy. `Bcp` also has a large number of command switches that allow the user to control the manner in which it operates. The syntax is as follows:

```
bcp {[[databasename].[owner].]{tablename | viewname} | "query"}
{ in | out | queryout | format} datafilename ( command line
switches)
```

The case-sensitive command line switches are listed in Table 18-5:

Table 18-5
Bcp Command Line Switches

Command Switch	*Function*
-m max_errors	Sets the number of errors that can occur during the copy process before the process terminates. The default is 10. Each row that cannot be copied counts as one error.
-f format_file	Specifies the fully-qualified name of a format file. If the file exists, it will be used to format the copy, and the user will not be prompted for format information. If used with the `FORMAT` parameter, it indicates where to create the resulting format file.
-e err_file	Specifies the fully qualified name of the error file. Places copies of rows that cannot be copied into the database in this file.

Command Switch	*Function*
-F first_row	Specifies the first row in the data source on which to begin importing or exporting data. The default is 1.
-L last_row	Specifies the last row in the data source on which to end importing or exporting data. The default is 0, indicating all the rows in the source should be copied.
-b batch_size	Specifies the number of rows to include in a single batch. Each batch is handled as a single transaction. If unspecified, all rows are considered a single batch. Do *not* use this parameter in conjunction with `-h "ROWS_PER_BATCH = bb"`.
-n	Specifies that native data types are being used. This mode does not prompt for format information; it simply uses the native data formatting.
-c	Specifies character data types are used. This mode does not prompt for format information. All data is stored as a char type. By default, all fields are separated by tab characters (\t) and rows by the newline character (\n).
-w	Specifies using the Unicode character data type. This mode does not prompt for format information. All data is stored as a nchar type. By default, all fields are separated by tab characters (\t) and rows by the newline character (\n). This switch is applicable only for SQL Server 7.0 or higher.
-N	Specifies that native data types are being used. This mode does not prompt for format information. Character data is stored in nchar format, and all other data is stored in native format. This switch is applicable only for SQL Server 7.0 or higher.
-V (60 | 65 | 70)	Specifies using an earlier version of SQL Server to define the data format. Even when using this switch, all data will be saved in ODBC formats. Also, null bit data types will be written as 0, because versions previous to 7.0 did not support nullable bit columns. This option should be used with the character (`-c`) or native (`-n`) format.
-6	Specifies using version 6/6.5 data types. Included for backward compatibility. The preferred option is `-V`.
-q	Specifies setting quoted identifiers in the connection between `bcp` and the database server. Required when any part of the fully qualified name of the database includes spaces or quotation marks.
-C *code_page*	Specifies the codepage of the source data. It is provided for backward compatibility and should be replaced with a collation for each column. Legal values include the following: ACP – ANSI/Microsoft Windows (ISO 1252) OEM – default code page of the client RAW – no code page conversion; provides highest performance *nnn* – specific code page used (for example, 850)

Continued

Table 18-5 *(continued)*

Command Switch	*Function*
-t term_character	Specifies the field termination character. By default, it is the tab character (\t).
-r term_character	Specifies the row termination character. By default, it is the newline character (\n).
-i input_file	Specifies a file that contains the responses to the format prompts when using `bcp` interactively. This option is not necessary when `-6`, `-c`, `-n`, `-N`, or `-w` are used.
-o output_file	Specifies the name of a file to which the output of `bcp` can be redirected.
-a packet_size	Specifies the size of network packets `bcp` constructs. This overrides the default packet size used by the SQL Server engine. Default packet size is 4096 bytes. On some networks, increasing packet size can improve performance. The maximum value is 65535.
-S server_name	Specifies the name of the SQL Server server. If connecting to a named instance, it is servername\instancename. If connecting through TCP/IP, an IP address can be used.
-U login_id	Specifies the user name that `bcp` should use to connect to the SQL Server when using SQL authentication.
-P password	Specifies the password of the login ID. If omitted, `bcp` prompts for a password. `-P` is specified. However, no password parameter is supplied, and the password is set to null.
-T	Specifies that `bcp` should connect using a trusted connection. `Bcp` will use the security context of the process that executes `bcp`. If used, `-U` and `-P` are not required nor prompted for.
-v	Specifies that `bcp` should return the version number.
-R	Specifies that currency and datetime values should be expressed using the regional locale settings of the client computer. If unspecified, regional settings are ignored.
-k	Specifies that null columns should retain their null setting rather than be replaced with default values.
-E	Specifies that values for an identity column exist in the source file and should be imported. If not specified, the values will be ignored and SQL Server will create new identity values as the rows are imported.

Command Switch	Function
-h hint	Specifies a hint to be used during the operation. This option is available for version 7.0 or higher. Hints include the following: ORDER(column (ASC | DESC), ...)—If data being imported is in the same order as a clustered index, bcp can improve performance. If the destination table is not clustered, the hint is ignored. ROWS_PER_BATCH= bb—This specifies the number of rows that should be considered a single batch when committing into the database if -b is not specified. KILOBYTES_PER_BATCH = cc—This specifies the number of kilobytes of data that can be copied before the batch is committed. TABLOCK—This specifies that the table should be locked during copy operations. This should be used carefully if the table is in use while copies are being performed. CHECK_CONSTRAINTS—This specifies that constraints should be checked as the data is loaded. By default, constraints are ignored during bcp operations. This also slows performance. FIRE_TRIGGERS—This specifies that triggers should be fired as data is inserted during bcp operations. By default, triggers are not fired.

Bulk Insert

Bulk Insert allows the user to import data from text files in a manner very similar to bcp. Bulk Insert is a Transact-SQL command and can be included in SQL scripts and stored procedures. DTS even has a special task for Bulk Insert operations. Unlike bcp, Bulk Insert cannot be used to export data.

Using Bulk Insert

To perform the next series of steps, the user must first create a table in the Northwind database called Products2. The table should have the same schema as the Products table. The user must also use bcp to export a copy of the Products table to a text file. Instructions on using bcp in this fashion are found earlier in the chapter.

MakeProducts2.sql is a SQL script. It can be opened with the SQL Query Analyzer to build the Products2 table. Products.txt contains the export of the Products table.

The following steps demonstrate a basic use of the Bulk Insert command.:

1. Copy products.txt to c:\ or create it using bcp.
2. Open Query Analyzer and connect to the SQL Server database.
3. Choose the Northwind database.

4. Check for the Products2 table. If it does not exist, create it. (Note: MakeProducts2.sql from the CD can be used to create this table.)
5. Execute the following command:

```
BULK INSERT Products2 FROM 'C:\Products.txt WITH (DataFileType=
'Native')
```

6. From Query Analyzer, execute the following command to confirm that the records were imported:

```
Select * from Products2
```

Bulk Insert command syntax

The syntax for `Bulk Insert` is as follows:

```
BULK INSERT tablename FROM datafile WITH (options)
```

The *`tablename`* is a table within the SQL Server database. It can be a fully qualified object name, allowing the user to perform inserts on linked servers.

`Datafile` is a fully qualified path to the datafile. The *`datafile`* must comply to the same parameters as files imported with `bcp`.

The options are expressed as parameters. Many map to the command arguments used with `bcp`. The list is as shown in Table 18-6:

Table 18-6
Bulk Insert Command Options

Option	*Description*	*Bcp Argument*
BATCHSIZE = *n*	Specifies the number of rows per batch. Each batch is processed as a single transaction. By default, the entire import is considered one batch.	`-b`
CHECK_CONSTRAINTS	Specifies that constraints should be checked as rows are inserted. By default, constraints are not checked.	`-h CHECK_CONSTRAINTS`

<table>
<tr><th>Option</th><th>Description</th><th>Bcp Argument</th></tr>
<tr><td>CODEPAGE = <<em>ACP | OEM | RAW | nnn</em> ></td><td>Specifies the codepage of the data. Can be replaced with column collation specifications in a format file.</td><td><code>-C</code></td></tr>
<tr><td>DATAFILETYPE = <<em>char | native | widechar | widenative</em>></td><td>Specifies the type of data file being imported:
char=Character data files
native=Native data files
widechar=Unicode character data files
widenative=Unicode native data files</td><td><code>-c, -n, -N, -w</code></td></tr>
<tr><td>FIELDTERMINATOR=a</td><td>Specifies the field termination character. The default is the tab character (\t).</td><td><code>-t</code></td></tr>
<tr><td>FIRSTROW=n</td><td>Specifies the first row in the data file on which to begin the import.</td><td><code>-F</code></td></tr>
<tr><td>FIRETRIGGERS=n</td><td>Specifies whether triggers should be fired as rows are inserted. By default, triggers are ignored.</td><td><code>-h FIRE_TRIGGERS</code></td></tr>
<tr><td>FORMATFILE=path</td><td>Specifies a fully qualified path to a format file. <code>BULK INSERT</code> uses the same format files as <code>bcp</code>.</td><td><code>-f</code></td></tr>
<tr><td>KEEPIDENTITY</td><td>Specifies that values for Identity columns should be imported from the file (similar to using an Identity Insert).</td><td><code>-E</code></td></tr>
<tr><td>KEEPNULLS</td><td>Specifies that null values in the data file should be inserted as nulls in the destination table and not replaced with default values.</td><td><code>-k</code></td></tr>
<tr><td>KILOBYTES_PER_BATCH= n
<code>KILOBYTES_</code></td><td>Specifies the number of bytes that should be imported to comprise a single batch. Each batch is individually committed to the database. By default, the entire import is considered a single batch.</td><td><code>-h</code>
<code>PER_BATCH</code></td></tr>
</table>

Continued

Table 18-6 *(continued)*

Option	*Description*	*Bcp Argument*
LASTROW=*n*	Specifies the last row to be imported from the data file. The default is 0, indicating all rows should be imported.	`-L`
MAXERRORS=*n*	Specifies the maximum number of errors that can occur in a batch before it is rolled back. By default, the number is 10.	`-m`
ORDER (column ASC|DESC, ..)	Specifies the order of rows in the data file. If the order in the data file matches the order of a clustered index on the destination table, it will improve performance. If the destination table does not have a clustered index, the option is ignored.	`-h ORDER`
ROWS_PER_BATCH=*n*	Specifies the number of rows that comprise a batch. Each batch is a single transaction.	`-h ROWS_PER_BATCH`
ROWTERMINATOR=*a*	Specifies the row terminator character. By default, the value is the newline character (\n).	`-r`
TABLOCK	Specifies that the destination table should be locked while the data is being inserted.	`-h TABLOCK`

Optimizing Bulk Copy Performance

Both `bcp` and `Bulk Insert` use the same API. There are a variety of things that will optimize performance of these operations.

✦ **Using nonlogged operations**. Bulk copy operations can insert data into the database with minimal logging. This increases speed and reduces log file consumption. For nonlogged inserts to occur, the `Select Into/Bulk Copy` option on the database must be enabled. The destination table must have no indexes, or the indexes must be empty before the import begins. The table must be locked during the import, and the table must not be published through replication while being filled.

✦ **Parallel loading.** Multiple clients can simultaneously bulk copy data into a table. This can speed the process of large loads. The rows must be partitioned by the clients (firstrow and lastrow are quite useful for this). The table must be locked and must not contain indexes.

✦ **Dropping indexes**. Indexes slow the process of inserting data into a new table. In many instances, it may be worthwhile to drop the indexes, insert the data, and then rebuild the indexes. The general rule of thumb is if a table has a clustered index and 25 percent or more new rows of data are being inserted, it is quicker to drop the index, insert the data, and then rebuild the index. With more than two nonclustered indexes, drop and rebuild if inserting more than 50 percent new rows.

There are exceptions. If all the data inserts at the end of a clustered index (say, in the case of a clustered primary key that is defined as an identity field) or if the data file has the same order as the clustered index, the user need not remove the existing index. As with most optimizations, the more often a user performs the same action, the more effort it merits to optimize.

✦ **Using native mode loads**. When moving data between two instances of SQL Server, it is best to use native mode data files. The files require less conversion and import and export faster.

✦ **Avoid triggers and constraint checks**. If each row has to be checked for constraints before it is inserted, operations are slowed. Also, firing triggers places the entire batch in a single transaction. That means the inserted table has a row for each imported row. If the validity of the data can be confirmed before it is imported, a great deal of time can be saved.

DTS Import/Export Wizard

The DTS Import/Export Wizard is designed to leverage the power and convenience of Data Transformation Services to move data between any two OLE DB sources. It can include transformation of the data while copying, making it very powerful.

The wizard is available as part of the tools that ship with all editions of SQL Server 2000 except the Desktop Engine and CE versions of the product. The wizard can be used to create a package that can be executed by the Desktop Engine, even though the wizard is not distributed with the Engine.

The wizard builds a basic DTS package. It helps the user build connections to the source and destination databases. The user must be able to create OLE DB or ODBC connections to both the source and destination. Neither must be a SQL Server database.

The wizard can help build tables on the destination source. The user can perform many of the transformation functions that are performed by other DTS packages (see Chapter 19 for more information on Data Transformation Services). The user can copy data, transform data, and even use ActiveX scripts to change the data as it is copied from the source to the destination.

The wizard provides a graphical, step-by-step interface for creating the package. The package can be run once or saved and run over and over again. The saved package can be scheduled to run by SQL Server Agent if the import or export occurs on a regular basis. The user can also run the package from the command line using `DTSRUN.EXE`.

A user can create a new database and transfer objects to it from the Northwind database using the DTS Import/Export wizard, as in the following example:

1. Create a new database named Southwind. Accept the default settings for the database.
2. Choose Import and Export Data from the Microsoft SQL Server program group.
3. Connect to the source database (if working on the source SQL Server computer, choose (local)), as shown in Figure 18-3.
   - **a.** Set security. If working in a Windows NT/2000 domain, Integrated security may work. If not, SQL authentication can be used.
   - **b.** Click Refresh to connect and build a list of databases on the destination server. Choose Northwind as the database.

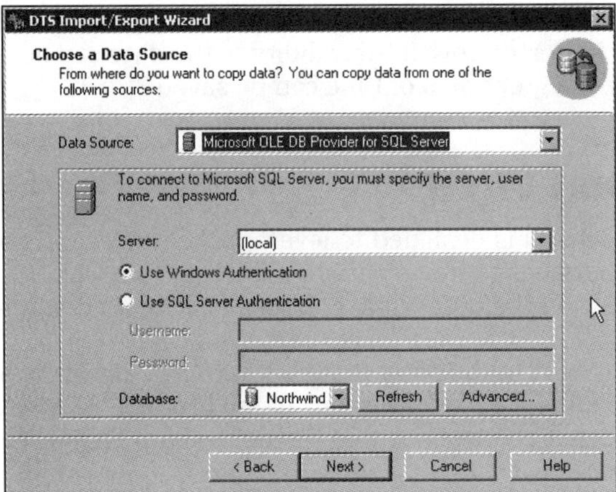

Figure 18-3: Connecting to a source database with the DTS Import/Export Wizard

4. Connect to the destination database (if working on the source SQL Server computer, choose (local)), as shown in Figure 18-4.
   - **a.** Set security. If working in a Windows NT/2000 domain, Integrated security may work. If not, SQL authentication can be used.
   - **b.** Click Refresh to connect and build a list of databases on the destination server. Choose Southwind as the database.

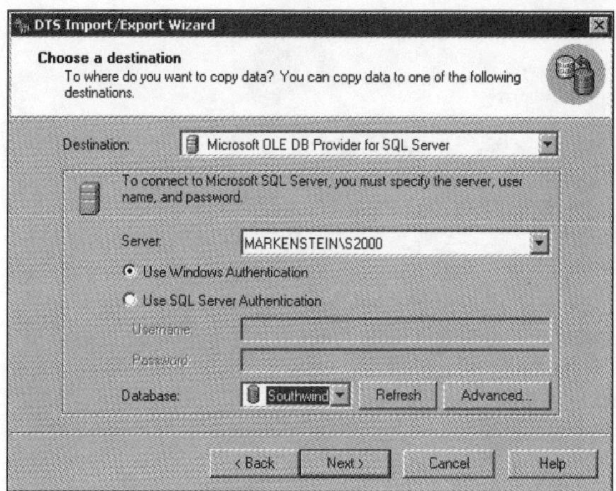

Figure 18-4: Connecting to a destination database with the DTS Import/Export Wizard

5. Choose the table to copy or query, as shown in Figure 18-5. The source can be an existing table or a SQL query. Choose to transfer objects between SQL Server databases. This allows the user to copy the tables and associated objects, such as triggers, indexes, stored procedures, security settings, and so on.

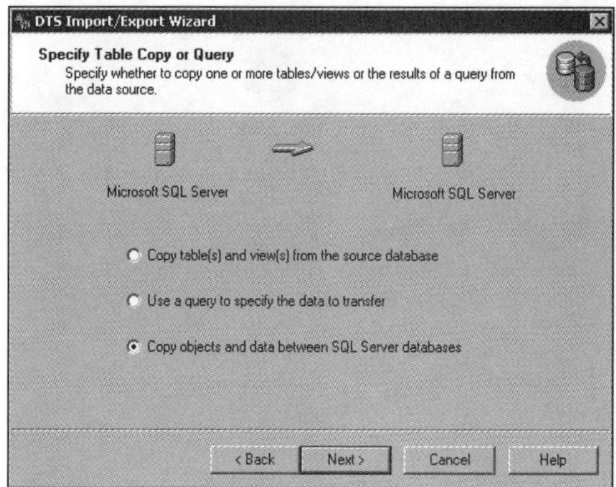

Figure 18-5: Selecting a table copy or query with the DTS Import/Export Wizard

6. Determine which objects to copy, as shown in Figure 18-6. The user can choose to create or re-create the table schemas on the destination database. The user can choose whether to include dependent objects or can just copy the data into existing table structures on the destination database. For this example, leave the default settings.

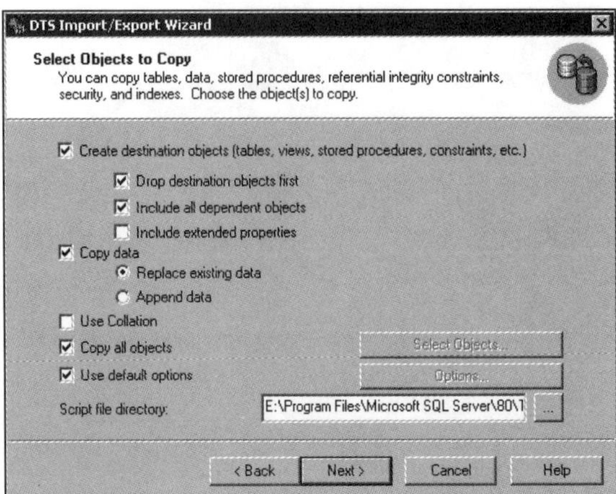

Figure 18-6: Choosing the objects to transfer using the DTS Import/Export Wizard

7. Choose how the job should be scheduled to run, as shown in Figure 18-7. The user can run immediately or choose to save the package. The saved package can be run on demand or scheduled as a SQL Server Agent job. Choosing "Use replication to publish destination data" will launch the Replication Publication Wizard to help configure replication. For this example, choose Run immediately.

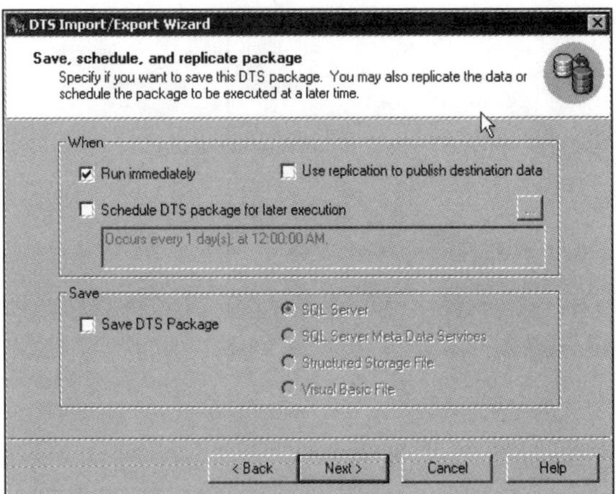

Figure 18-7: Saving and running DTS Import/Export Wizard packages

The following steps demonstrate how to export the Products table from Northwind to a Microsoft Access database.

1. Create an empty Microsoft Access database named export.mdb. (Note: EXPORT.MDB can be copied from the CD-ROM to the hard drive or created with Microsoft Access 2000.)
2. Start the DTS Import/Export Wizard by choosing Import and Export Data from the Microsoft SQL Server program group.
3. As in the previous example, set the source database to Northwind on the SQL Server computer.
4. Set the destination to the export.mdb database, as shown in Figure 18-8. First, set the destination to Microsoft Access. Then specify the path to the export.mdb file. (Note: The Builder button can be clicked to access the File dialog box and to point to the file graphically.)

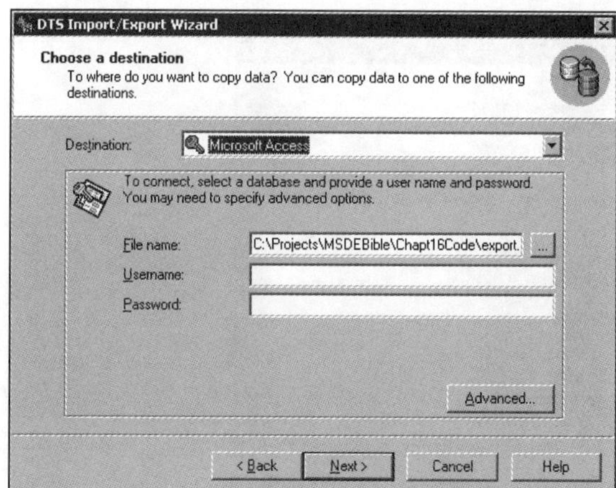

Figure 18-8: Connecting to a Microsoft Access database using the DTS Import/Export Wizard

5. Choose to use a query as the source of the data to transfer.
6. Use the query builder to build a query that joins the Products, Categories, and Suppliers tables to produce a list of product ids, product names, product categories, and supplier names.
   a. Click the Query Builder button, shown in Figure 18-9, to access the query builder.
   b. Choose the columns that should appear in the destination table, as shown in Figure 18-10. From the Products table, choose ProductID and ProductName. From the Categories table, choose CategoryName. From the Suppliers table, choose Company Name.

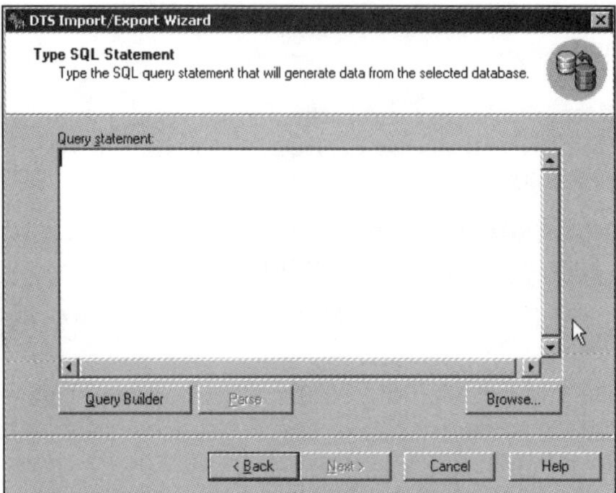

Figure 18-9: Accessing the query builder

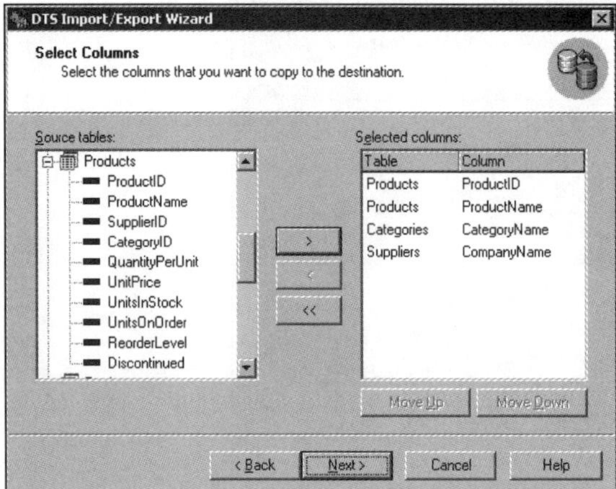

Figure 18-10: Choosing columns using the DTS Import/Export Wizard query builder

c. Choose a sort order for the data, as shown in Figure 18-11. Choose CategoryName, then ProductName, and then CompanyName. Do not include ProductID.

d. Specify row selection criteria, as shown in Figure 18-12. This will build a `WHERE` clause in the SQL statement. In this example, the `WHERE` clause will specify how to join the tables. Products.CategoryID must equal Categories.CategoryID and Products.SupplierID must equal Suppliers. SupplierID. Products that are discontinued should be excluded. Choose rows where the Products.Discontinued column does not equal 1 (1 indicates the product has been discontinued).

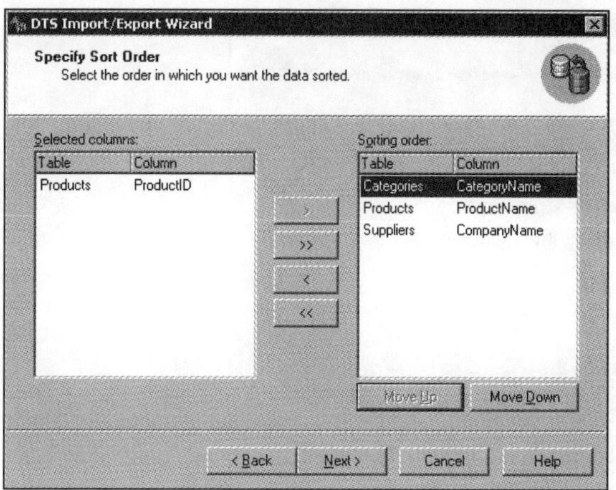

Figure 18-11: Setting a sort order in the query builder

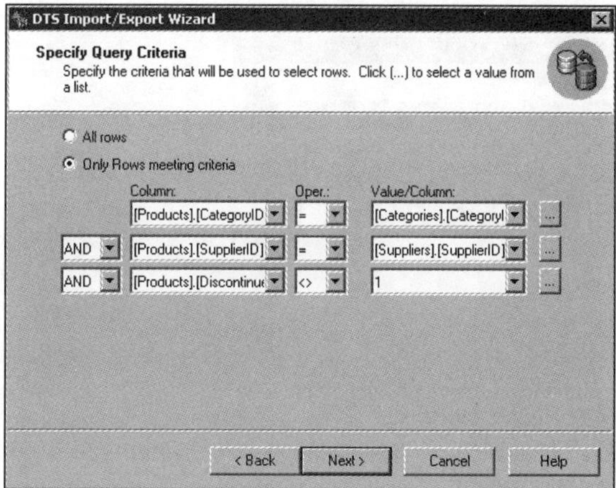

Figure 18-12: Specifying query criteria in the query builder

  e. The final step is to examine the SQL statement produced by the builder, as shown in Figure 18-13. This statement can be manually modified before it is used.

7. Prepare a transformation for the new table, as shown in Figure 18-14. Change the name of the destination table from Result to ProductsCategories and click the Transform button.

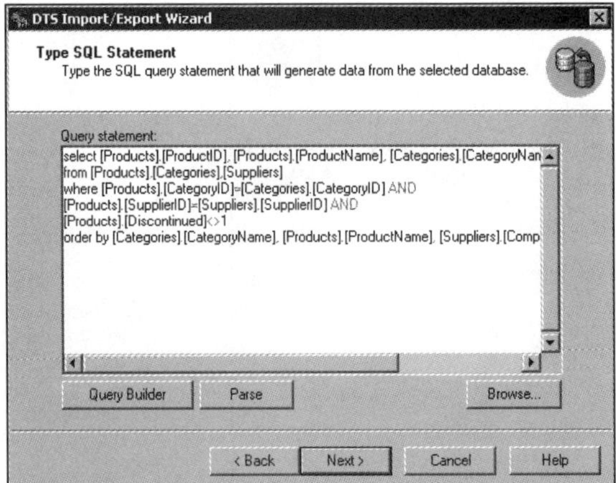

Figure 18-13: Examining the SQL statement built by the query builder

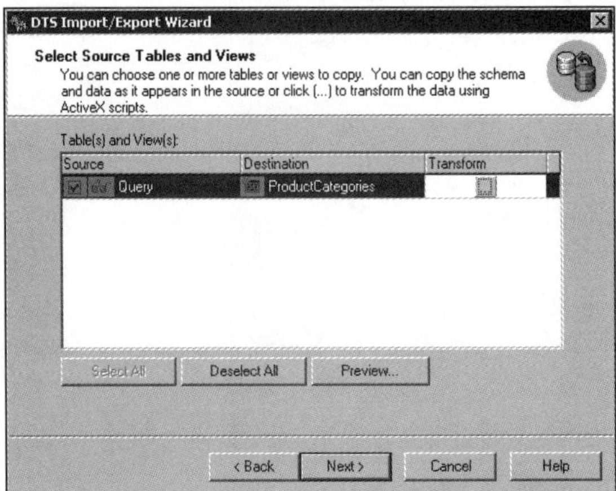

Figure 18-14: Selecting a source and destination table

8. On the transformation dialog, shown in Figure 18-15, the user can choose to create a new table as part of the process or drop any existing table and re-create it. (This will not enable the user to violate referential integrity on the destination database.) The user can also choose to create or modify the ActiveX transformation script to perform more advanced conversions and transformations. In this example, accept the default responses.

9. The next dialog allows the user to save the package. It can be run immediately, saved to run on demand, or scheduled as a SQL Server Agent job. This is similar to the dialog in the previous example.

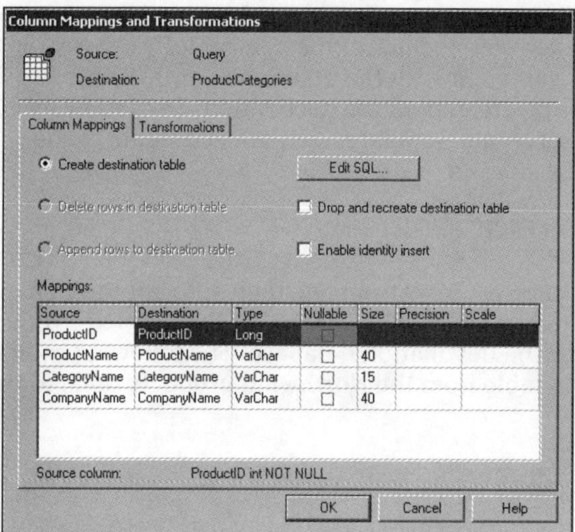

Figure 18-15: Creating column mappings and transformations

The DTS Import/Export Wizard can provide a simple, effective method of creating Data Transformation Service packages that move data from one OLE DB source to another.

Other methods of importing and exporting data

There are a variety of other tools and techniques for moving data into and out of SQL Server databases. Each one presents its own advantages and disadvantages. The following sections summarize these methods.

Replication

SQL Server's replication can be used to create snapshots of the contents of tables within the database. The destination can be any OLE DB source that is set as a linked server. This can be useful for exporting data.

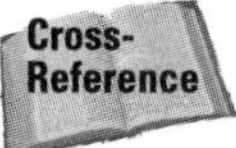

More information on replication can be found in Chapter 20 and more on linked servers can be found in Chapter 21.

Transact-SQL

There are two key SQL statements that are very useful in importing and exporting data: `SELECT INTO` and `INSERT INTO`.

`SELECT INTO` creates a new table on the destination database and then inserts the rowset produced by the select statement into the new table. It follows the same syntax as an ordinary `SELECT` statement with the addition of an `INTO` clause. The `INTO` clause names the table to be created on the destination. The following SQL batch will create a temporary table and populate it with the contents of the Products table in Northwind:

```
SELECT * INTO #Products FROM Products
```

`INSERT INTO` allows the user to insert rows from one table into another. The values clause can be replaced with a query. Unlike `SELECT INTO`, `INSERT INTO` requires the destination table to exist on the destination database. The following example copies the rows in the Products table from the Northwind products table to the Southwind products table:

```
INSERT INTO Southwind..Products
SELECT * FROM Northwind..Products
```

Summary

Maintaining databases frequently requires sharing data with other systems. In this chapter, the tools for importing and exporting data were explored. Bulk copy (`bcp`) provides the fastest means for importing and exporting data between text files and the database. The Transact-SQL equivalent command, `Bulk Insert`, can be used to import text file data into a SQL Server database. The DTS Import/Export Wizard uses Data Transformation Service and can transform data on a row-by-row basis while importing or exporting, adding flexibility to the process. A variety of other techniques, including replication and Transact-SQL statements, can also be used to import and export data.

✦ ✦ ✦

CHAPTER 19

Transforming Data With DTS

In This Chapter

Understanding DTS architecture and object model

Building packages

Executing packages

Saving and retrieving packages

Managing packages

Optimizing DTS

This chapter provides an overview of Data Transformation Services (DTS) and how it is used to migrate data between different databases. It will describe the DTS object model, which is used to build packages that connect databases and to move and transform data. Readers will learn how to execute these packages from the command line and as scheduled jobs with the SQL Server Agent. You will also discover techniques for managing changes to DTS packages and optimizing DTS operations.

When working with data, developers and administrators alike deal with a common difficulty. Data is stored throughout the organization in a wide variety of formats. From file-server databases such as Microsoft Access and Visual FoxPro to client-server databases such as Oracle, Sysbase, and Informix to legacy and mainframe databases, the data critical to management information systems must be collected, collated, and placed in order for simple access and retrieval.

Microsoft developed Data Transformation Services (DTS) to serve this purpose. It uses the OLE DB Application Programming Interface (API) to connect to a wide variety of data sources. Once connected, this data can be moved from one source to another. If the data needs to be transformed, DTS can take the data one row at a time and programmatically transform the information during the move. DTS can be programmed to move data in steps, allowing one step to complete before another. It can also inform operators of success or failure in operations and can be used to transfer objects between databases.

Uses for Data Transformation Services

There are a variety of business uses for DTS. One common use is collecting and collating data. An MSDE-based application can be developed and placed on the laptop of each person in a sales force, who can then use the database application to create and modify orders while disconnected from the home office. At the end of the day, each sales force member can connect to the home office, uploading the data he or she modified to the corporate database and loading changes in the data at the central office into his or her local database.

Another use for DTS is converting data. Personnel use spreadsheets to work with salary increases. A DTS package can convert the data in the personnel database into a spreadsheet format to provide personnel with the current data for analysis.

DTS can also import data received from the mainframe and place it into a database. It can even move data from an Access database into an Oracle database. Neither the source nor the destination need to be MSDE or SQL Server databases.

Administrating Data Transformation Services

DTS is bundled in a package. The package consists of database connections, individual tasks, and workflow constraints. It can be stored in the database itself or as a COM file.

The package can be run as a job in the database. For regularly scheduled tasks, such as weekly imports or exports, daily updates, and so on, the package can be executed as a scheduled task by SQL Server Agent. The package can also be executed from the command line. `DTSRUN` is used to invoke the package.

Package security depends on the storage method. If the package is stored in the database, standard database security can be used to control access to DTS. If the package is stored as a COM file, it can be given password security. The file can support two distinct passwords: one password to allow a user to execute the package, and another to allow a user to edit the contents of the package.

Data Transformation Services Architecture

The heart of DTS is dtspump.dll. When a DTS package runs, the information stored in the package directs the actions of dtspump. The package consists of connections, tasks, transforms, and workflows.

Connections provide the necessary information to make an OLE DB connection to the data source. DTS uses ActiveX Data Objects (ADO) to achieve this. An OLE DB or ODBC provider is also necessary to connect to the data.

The OLE DB provider for ODBC will work with any ODBC driver that is version 3.0 or higher.

Tasks define the operations the package should perform. These include executing SQL statements, running ActiveX scripts, sending mail, executing shell commands, and a variety of other activities.

Data transforms allow data to be modified as it flows from a source to a destination database. The rows are accessed one at a time. Transforms can be as simple as mapping a column in the source to the destination or can include using COM objects or ActiveX scripts to change field values.

Workflows determine the order in which operations are executed. They allow tasks to be sequenced. Workflows also provide for conditional branching when a task succeeds or fails.

The dtspump.dll runs within the dtsrun executable. This can be run from the command line or executed by the SQL Server Agent. DTS also relies on the Microsoft Distributed Transaction Coordinator to enact transactions across databases.

DTS has an internal object structure (see Figure 19-1). Using this object structure, programming languages such as Visual Basic and Visual C++ can be used to create packages or used as interfaces to help users create their own packages.

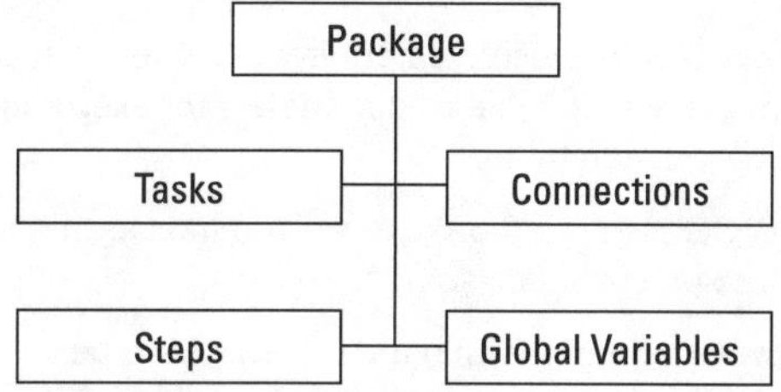

Figure 19-1: DTS package object collections

DTS in MSDE has extended the object model. Many objects have a second version with additional properties, methods, and events (for example, DataPumpTask2, Package2, and so on). Having two versions of the objects allows packages to remain backward compatible with SQL Server 7.0. If a package must run on both platforms, only the original version objects should be used.

The root object is the package. It has several collections that allow the user to program the actions of the data pump object. By adding objects to these collections and defining their properties and methods, the user can build a DTS package programmatically.

Understanding the object structure can help those with programming experience understand how DTS works and how to create custom interfaces to help users build packages when they need them.

The most common objects are task objects, listed in Table 19-1. They allow DTS to perform a variety of operations.

Table 19-1
Available Task Objects

Task	*Description*
ActiveScriptTask	This task allows an ActiveX script to be executed by a DTS package. Since this task is not directly involved in using the data pump itself, it does not have access to the connections, source, or destination tables. This object does, however, have full access to the GlobalVariables collection, allowing a method of data sharing.
BulkInsertTask	Based on the SQL Bulk Insert, this task provides the ability to import data into a SQL Server table. This provides high speed copying of data from a flat file, such as a mainframe dump.
CreateProcessTask/ CreateProcessTask2	This task allows the user to run a Win32 executable or batch file from within a DTS package.
DataDrivenQueryTask/ DataDrivenQueryTask2	This task allows DTS to execute parameterized queries. It can use data from the source table as parameters for executing tasks on the destination table.
DataPumpTask/ DataPumpTask2	This task uses OLE DB to import, export, and transform data between heterogeneous data sources.
DynamicPropertiesTask	This task allows properties within a DTS package to be modified when the package is executed. This allows DTS packages to become parameterized.
ExecutePackageTask	This task allows one DTS package to call another. Global variables from the calling package can be passed to the called package.
ExecuteSQLTask/ ExecuteSQLTask2	This task allows one or more SQL commands to be executed on a connection within the package.
DTSFTPTask	This task transfers file(s) from one directory to another using TCP/IP File Transfer Protocol (FTP).
DTSMessageQueueTask	This task allows messages to be sent to or received from a message queue. This task can participate in transactions if Microsoft Distributed Transaction Coordinator is running.

Task	*Description*
ParallelDataPumpTask	This is similar to DataPumpTask2 and DataDrivenQueryTask2, except this task can handle hierarchical rowsets. This task is only available programmatically. The DTS Designer does not expose it.
SendMailTask	This task uses SQL Mail to send e-mail. Typically it is used to notify operators of successful, failed, or completed DTS operations.
TransferObjectTask/ TransferObjectTask2	This task is used to transfer objects between SQL Server databases. Objects can include dependent objects, such as indexes, constraints, triggers, and logins.

Connection objects allow DTS to locate and connect to data sources. The connection object must store the necessary information to allow ActiveX Data Objects (ADO) to connect to the data source. In the case of a file-server database, such as Microsoft Access or Visual FoxPro, Inprise dBase, Paradox, and so on, it would include a path to the file. In the case of a client-server database, such as Microsoft SQL Server, Oracle, Sybase, IBM DB2, and so on, it would include a network path (for example, a NetBIOS name or TCP/IP address). In the case of a text file, all that is required is the location of the file. The connection will also need to include the appropriate provider software and security information. Since each data source has different requirements, the provider may have specific properties unique to the data source that may also be required.

Step objects control the flow of execution of tasks within a package. A step is associated with each defined task. Precedence constraints are used to determine when a step executes. A task will not execute until the conditions of all Precedence constraints are met (for example, this step will not execute until the step containing ClearDataTables has completed successfully).

The Global Variables collection allows variant data types to be created and shared across steps. This allows data to be passed from one step to the next. Programmers can explicitly add global variables to a package with ActiveX scripts.

The configuration of these objects will follow later in the chapter.

Building DTS Packages

There are two basic means of constructing DTS packages. The DTS Designer is a graphical tool that ships with SQL Server 2000 Personal and higher. Users can also build packages programmatically using Microsoft Visual Studio or any other COM-compliant programming language.

Building DTS packages with the DTS Designer

The DTS Designer is part of the Enterprise Manager. This tool ships with all versions of SQL Server 2000, except the Desktop Engine and Window CE versions. The Enterprise Manager has a Data Transformation Services folder for managing the packages. The following example will serve as an introduction to building simple packages with DTS. In the first set of steps, you copy the data from the pubs database to an empty Microsoft Access database.

1. Connect to the local server by expanding Microsoft SQL Servers, SQL Server Groups, *<local server name>*.
2. Expand Data Transformation Services by clicking the plus in front of the folder.
3. Right-click Local Packages and click New Package from the pop-up menu.
4. The DTS Designer opens a new window within the Enterprise Manager, as shown in Figure 19-2.

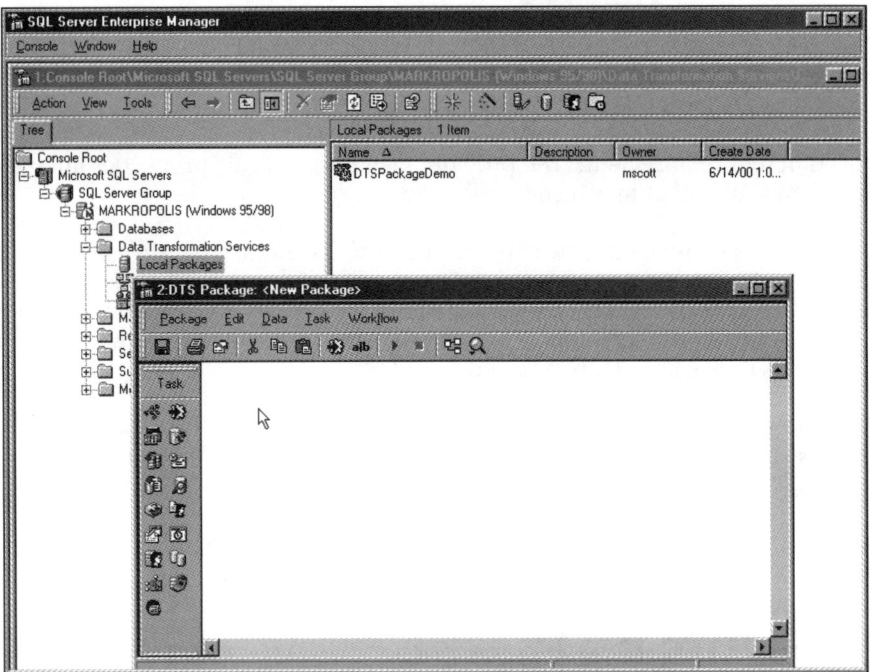

Figure 19-2: Creating a new DTS package with the DTS Designer

The next series of steps establishes a connection from the package to the SQL Server database instance. This connection is used to identify and access data. It contains security information and specific instructions that help the package connect to the server.

1. Locate the Microsoft OLE DB Provider for SQL Server icon in the toolbox on the left side of the Designer.
2. Drag and drop a copy of the icon onto the Designer surface.
3. Set the properties of the dialog box, as shown in Figure 19-3.
   a. Set the name to Pubs.
   b. Set the server to (local).
   c. Set security to Use SQL Server Authentication.
   d. Fill in the appropriate user name and password (for example, sa and the sa account password).
   e. Click Refresh to get a list of the databases to which this account has access.
   f. Choose the pubs database and click OK.

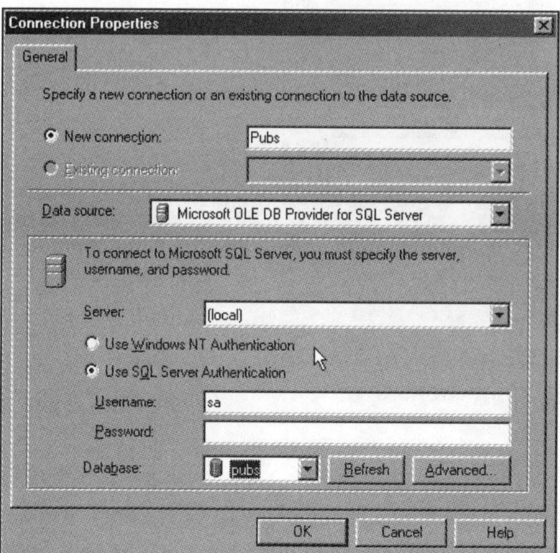

Figure 19-3: Configuring a SQL Server connection

The next series of steps will connect to a Microsoft Access database. This is typical of connecting to database files like Access, FoxPro, dBase, and others. Like the connection to SQL Server, it contains security information and information used by DTS to connect to the data. The Access MDB must exist before you can create a connection to it. You can create a blank database using Microsoft Access or copy the database provided on the CD to the hard drive. The assumption is that the database is located at C:\MSDE\pubs.mdb. The path should be corrected accordingly if it is not.

1. Drag and drop a Microsoft Access connection icon from the toolbox onto the design surface.
2. In the dialog box that opens, set the following, as shown in Figure 19-4:
   a. Set the name to AccessPubs.
   b. Set the path to the location of the Access database file. Click the Builder button to get a dialog box and visually navigate to the file.
   c. If the database is password-protected, a valid user name and password must be supplied.

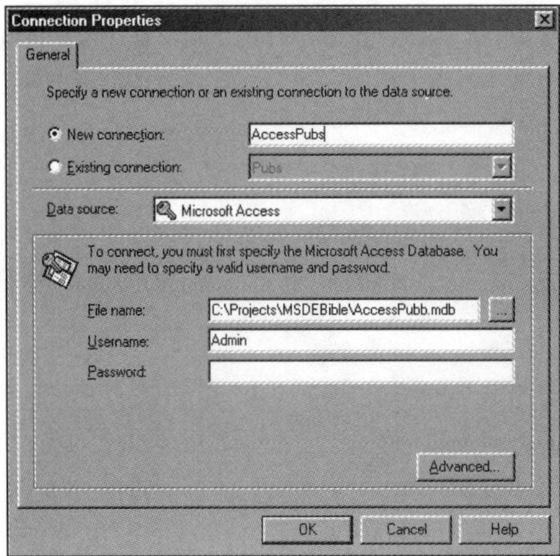

Figure 19-4: Configuring connections to an Access database

The next series of steps create a data transformation task that will move data from the SQL Server pubs database into the Access database. Data transformation allows you to define what happens as data is moved from the source to the destination.

1. Click to select the Pubs connection. Hold the Ctrl key and click the AccessPubs connection.

The order in which the connection icons are selected determines the source and destination within the data transformation. Click the source first, then the destination.

2. Right-click on the AccessPubs connection to access the pop-up menu. Choose Transform Data Task from the menu. A line will appear between the icons with an arrowhead pointing to the AccessPubs connection.
3. Right-click the line between the connections to access the pop-up menu. Choose Properties to access the Transform Data Tasks Properties dialog box.
4. On the Source tab of the dialog box, as shown in Figure 19-5, set the Description to Copy Authors' Table. Note that the source can be a table, view, or SQL Query. Leave the Table/View set to [pubs].[dbo].[authors].

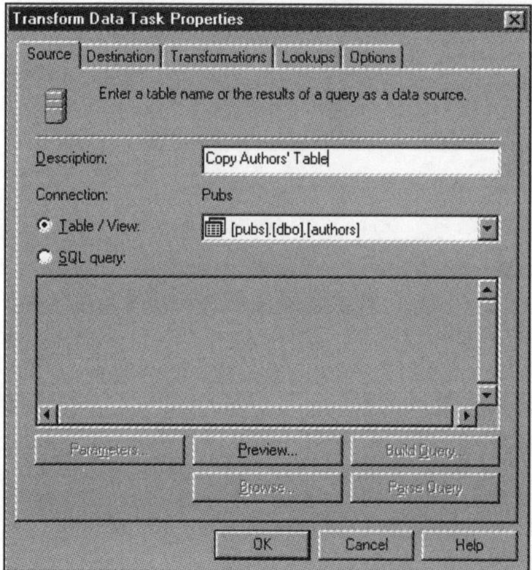

Figure 19-5: Configuring the transform source

5. Click the Destination tab. If the Access database currently has no tables defined, DTS will create a table modeled after the table selected in the source, as shown in Figure 19-6. You can select an existing table or can create a new table using the Create button.
6. Click the Transformations tab, as shown in Figure 19-7. The source table is represented on the left, and the destination table is represented on the right. The lines stretching between the fields indicate that the data will be moved from the source field to the target field. Click OK to close the dialog box.

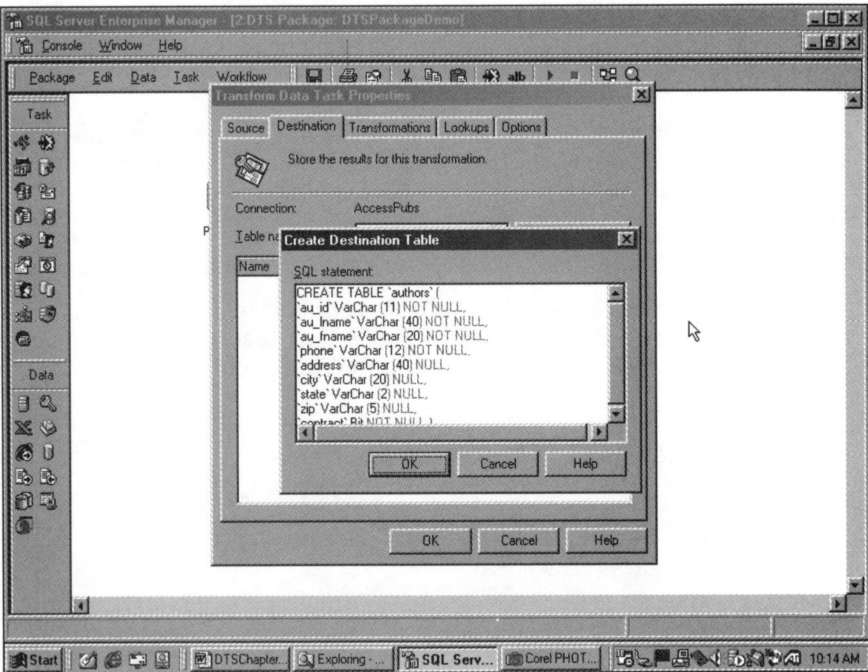

Figure 19-6: DTS can create a new table as the destination for the data.

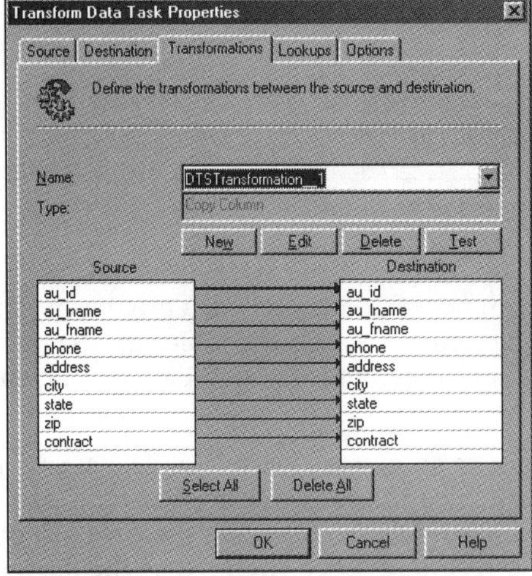

Figure 19-7: Transforming data from the source to the destination

7. To execute the transformation, as shown in Figure 19-8, right-click on the design surface and choose Execute from the pop-up menu.

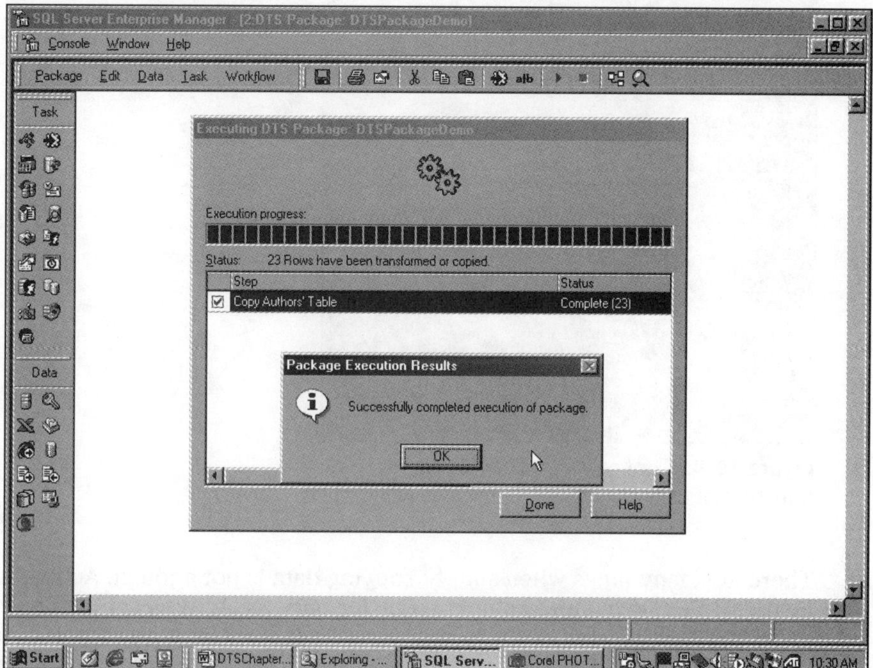

Figure 19-8: Executing a DTS package from the DTS Designer

You can do more than copy single columns. By copying a group of columns, the DTS package becomes more efficient. In the following series of steps, a custom transformation is created.

1. Click Transformations in the Transform Data Task Properties dialog box. Click and delete each existing line between the source and destination tables. This will clear the existing transforms.
2. While holding the Ctrl key, click to select the following fields, first in the Source box, then in the Destination box: au_id, phone, address, city, state, zip, and contact.
3. Click the New button. Choose Copy Column in the dialog box, as shown in Figure 19-9.
4. Name this the MoveAddress transform. Click OK to save the configuration.
5. Use the Test button to check the results.

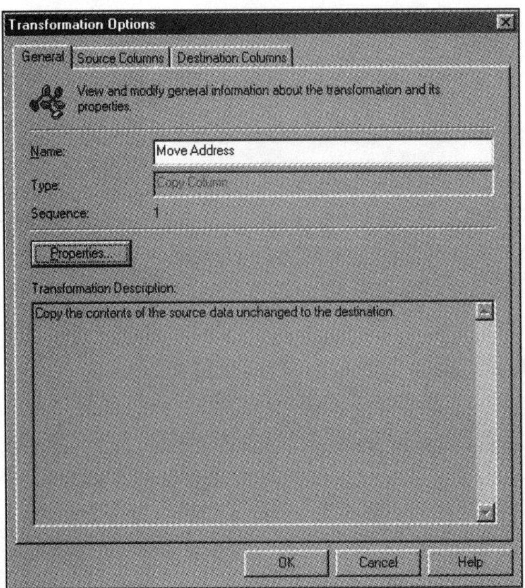

Figure 19-9: Configuring a Copy Column transformation

There are many times when simply copying data is not enough. ActiveX scripts can be used to perform more complex transformations. ActiveX scripts can be written in VBScript, JScript, and other languages to allow these more complex data conversions and transformations. The following series of steps serve as an example of how to add an ActiveX Script transform:

1. Choose the Transformation tab from the Transform Data Task Properties dialog box.
2. Holding the Ctrl key, click the `au_fname` and `au_lname` in the Source box. Repeat the selections in the Destination box.
3. Click New. Click ActiveX script in the dialog box.
4. Name this task UpperCaseNames. Click the Properties button.
5. In the dialog box, shown in Figure 19-10, you create an ActiveX script by typing the following VBScript to make the name all uppercase as it is moved from the source to the destination:

```
'*************************************************************
**
'  Visual Basic Transformation Script
'*************************************************************
**
```

```
'  Copy each source column to the destination column
'  Convert the data to all uppercase
Function Main()
    DTSDestination("au_fname") =UCase(DTSSource("au_fname"))
    DTSDestination("au_lname") = UCase(DTSSource("au_lname"))
    Main = DTSTransformStat_OK
End Function
```

6. Click Parse to test the code. Correct any errors.
7. Click Test to assure the code runs properly.
8. Click OK to save the changes and again to close the dialog box.

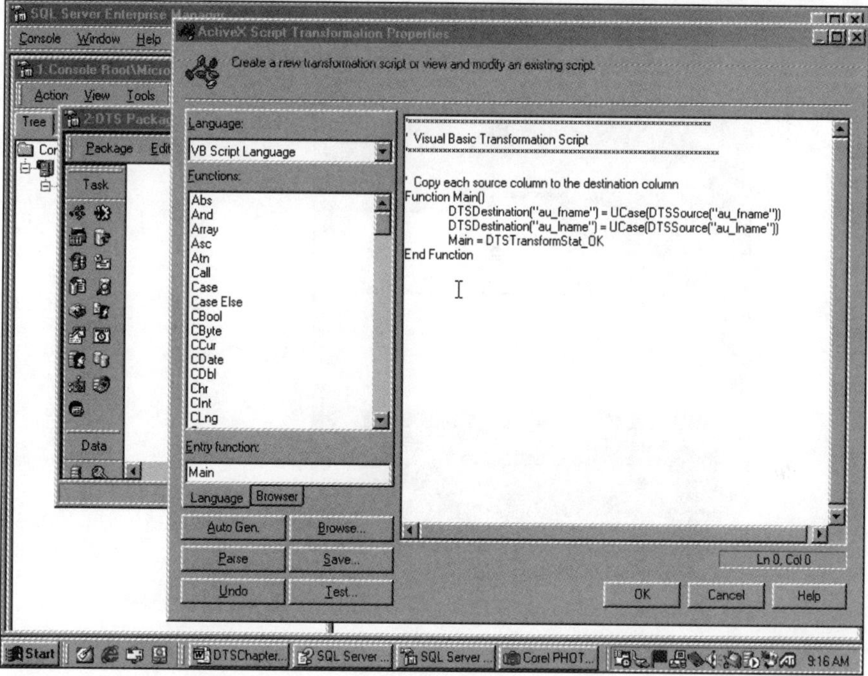

Figure 19-10: Configuring an ActiveX script transform

DTS can also perform standard SQL tasks written in ANSI-92 SQL. The next series of steps demonstrate how to use a SQL task to clear the table in the Access database before data is copied from the SQL Server database source.

1. Drag and drop an Execute SQL Task onto the design surface.
2. In the dialog box, configure the following parameters, as shown in Figure 19-11:
   a. Name the task Clear Authors Table.
   b. Set the connection to AccessPubs.
   c. Set the SQL Statement to delete all the rows in the Authors table in the Access database.
   ```
   Delete from Authors
   ```
   d. Click Parse Query to check the code.
3. Click OK to save the modifications and again to close the dialog box.

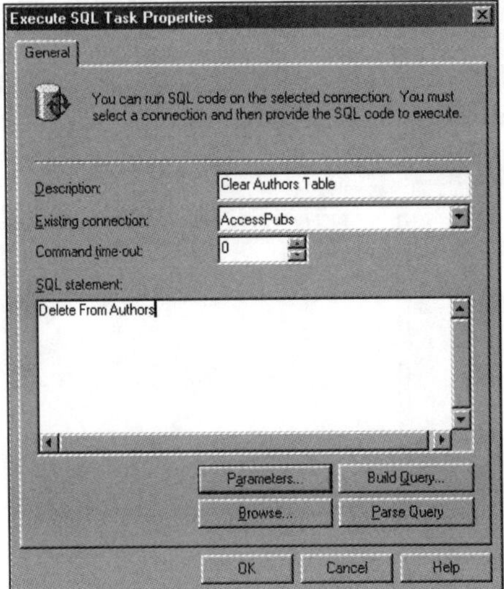

Figure 19-11: Configuring an Execute SQL Task

You should create a Precedence constraint so the table is cleared before data is moved.

1. Click to select the Clear Authors Table icon. Holding the Ctrl key, click to select the Pubs icon.
2. Right-click on the Pubs icon to access the pop-up menu. Click Workflow from the pop-up. Click On Success. A green line will appear between the Execute SQL Task and the Pubs connection, as shown in Figure 19-12.

This brief example has been a rudimentary introduction to using the DTS Designer to build DTS packages. The next section will explain how to build packages programmatically using Visual Basic.

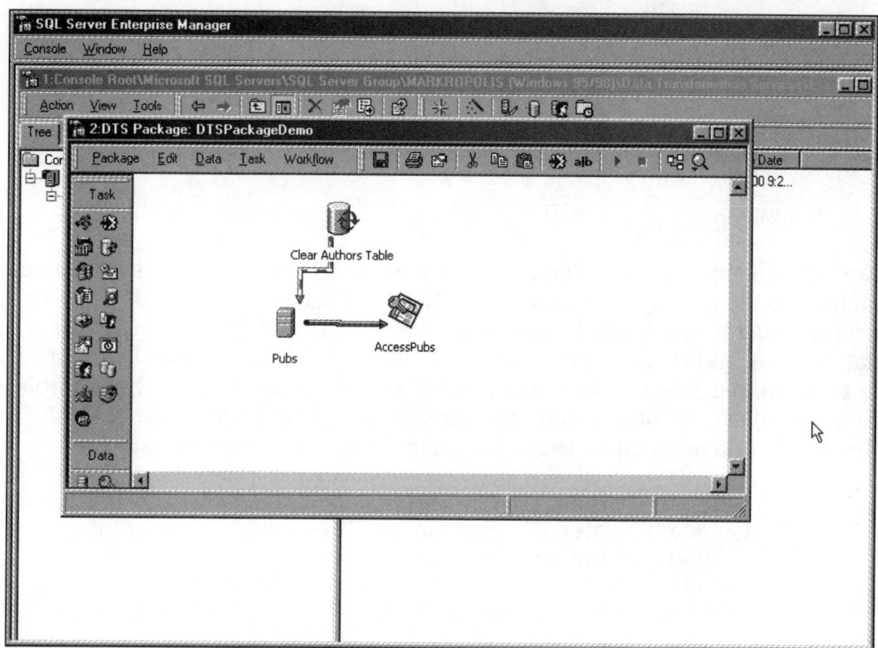

Figure 19-12: Configuring Precedence constraints

Building DTS packages with Visual Basic

The object structure of DTS allows packages to be constructed with COM-compliant languages. Programmers can create custom DTS interfaces to include with their applications. The following section will demonstrate how to build a simple DTS package using Visual Basic.

The Visual Basic project DTSPackageBuilder is a sample application that builds a package that copies data from one SQL Server table to another. It can be used as an example of how to programmatically build COM applications that allow users to configure DTS packages.

The first step in building a DTS package in Visual Basic is to reference the DTSPackage Object Library. This will provide access to the DTS object structure. The following sections of code from the sample application build a simple DTS package for copying data from one SQL Server table to another. It serves as a basic tutorial for examining the process of programming DTS packages.

The first step is to instantiate the package. Then you can create connections to the source and the destination. First, the package must be declared:

```
Private pkgNew As DTS.Package2
```

Next, it must be initialized. The code destroys any existing package in memory and creates a fresh one:

```
'Initialize package object
    If Not pkgNew Is Nothing Then
        Set pkgNew = Nothing
    End If
    Set pkgNew = New DTS.Package2
```

Now, connections must be built. Connection objects are created using the `New` method of the package object's Connections collection. Once created, the connection must be configured. Connections require the OLE DB provider name, the data source, and security information. In the case of database servers that can host multiple databases, an initial catalog will also be needed. In the example, the user provides most of this data through text boxes on the form. Once configured, the connection must be added to the package Connections collection.

```
'Build connections to the source and destination servers
 If Len(cboSourceCat) = 0 Or Len(cboDestCat) = 0 Or _
 Len(cboSourceTables) = 0 Or Len(cboDestTable) = 0 Then
     MsgBox "You must select source and destination " _
     & "tablesbefore you can build a package", _
     vbInformation, "Cannot Build Package"
 Else
     Set objSourceConn = _
     pkgNew.Connections.New("SQLOLEDB.1")
     With objSourceConn
         .ID = 1
         .DataSource = txtSourceDB
         .UserID = txtSourceUser
         .Password = txtSourcePassword
         .Catalog = cboSourceCat
     End With
     Set objDestConn = pkgNew.Connections.New("SQLOLEDB.1")
     With objDestConn
         .ID = 2
         .DataSource = txtDestDB
         .UserID = txtDestUser
         .Password = txtDestPassword
         .Catalog = cboDestCat
     End With
     pkgNew.Connections.Add objSourceConn
     pkgNew.Connections.Add objDestConn
```

Once the connections are built, the user can build a task. For this example, the data pump task can be used. This object allows row-by-row access and manipulation of data. To instantiate the task, first instantiate a custom task within the DTS Tasks collection. ObjDataPump becomes the interface for the custom task. It allows the user to set the connection source and object name, and the destination source and object name.

```
Set objTask = pkgNew.Tasks.New("DTSDataPumpTask")
   Set objDataPump = objTask.CustomTask
   With objDataPump
       .Name = "MoveColumnData"
        .SourceConnectionID = 1
        .SourceObjectName = cboSourceCat & ".." & _
        cboSourceTables
        .DestinationConnectionID = 2
        .DestinationObjectName = cboDestCat & _
        ".." & cboDestTable
```

Next, the user must add a transformation. This is done with the New method of the Transformations collection of the data pump task. The transformation is a copy task. Once created and configured, it must be added to the Transformations collection of the data pump task. Once complete, the object task can be added to the Tasks collection of the package.

```
        Set objTransform = _
        .Transformations.New("DTS.DataPumpTransformCopy")
        objTransform.Name = "CopyData"
        .Transformations.Add objTransform
   End With
   pkgNew.Tasks.Add objTask
```

The final step in this simple package is to place the task in a step so that it can execute. Like previous objects, the step object is created by using the New method of the Steps collection. The step object must be configured with a name and a data pump task. Once configured, the task can be added to the Steps collection of the package.

Note When creating tasks in Visual Basic, the ExecuteInMainThread property must be set to true because Visual Basic does not allow free threading. Other languages, such as C++ or Java, may allow tasks to run on separate threads.

```
Set objStep = pkgNew.Steps.New
With objStep
   .Name = "CopyingData"
   .TaskName = objDataPump.Name
   .ExecuteInMainThread = True
End With
pkgNew.Steps.Add objStep
```

Once built, the package can be executed from Visual Basic. The package has an execute method. If the package will be executed more than once, the UnInitialize method should be run before the package is executed again.

```
If pkgNew Is Nothing Then
   MsgBox "You must build the package before you " & _
     "can execute it", vbInformation, "Cannot Execute Package"
End If
```

```
pkgNew.Execute
pkgNew.UnInitialize
MsgBox "Package completed without errors", vbInformation, _
"Package Ran Without Errors"
```

By default, DTS package errors are not returned to Visual Basic. If the user wants to use VB to detect and enumerate the errors, the `FailOnError` property must be set to `true` and then enumerated through the Error collection of the package.

Performing tasks with DTS

The following is a description of the task objects available in the DTS programming interface. Each task is described and key properties are mentioned. These tasks are also available through the DTS Designer.

ActiveScriptTask

`ActiveScriptTask` allows an ActiveScript to execute within the DTS package. It can be used to perform tasks that do not utilize the database connections defined within the data pump object. ActiveScripts can be written in VBScript, JScript, PERL, or XML. ActiveScriptTask's key properties are as follows:

- `ActiveXScript`—string that contains the script to be executed.
- `AddGlobalVariables`—Boolean that determines if the task can add global variables to the package. Setting this to `false` can improve performance if global variables are not required.
- `Description`—string that contains a description string to the task.
- `FunctionName`—string that contains the name of a specific function within the script to be called during a step.
- `Name`—string that contains the name of the script.
- `ScriptingLanguage`—string that identifies the language of the script.

The `CheckSyntax` command will check the syntax of the script before execution, and the `Execute` command will complete the task.

CreateProcessTask

`CreateProcessTask` allows the user to run a Win32 executable file or batch command. This can be used to execute tasks that would normally be executed from the command line, such as executing batch processes to export data or generate reports. Its key properties are as follows:

- `Description`—string to describe the process.

- `FailPackageOnTimeout`—Boolean that determines if the package should fail when the timeout expires for the executed task.
- `Name`—string that names the task.
- `ProcessComandLine`—string that contains the Universal Naming Convention (UNC) path to the file to execute and any required command-line parameters.
- `SuccessReturnCode`—long value that the process should return if it succeeds. If the return code does not match this value, the task is noted as failed.
- `TerminateProcessAfterTimeout`—Boolean that determines if the process should be terminated by the package once the timeout has been exceeded.
- `Timeout`—long value that specifies, in seconds, the timeout period.

ExecuteSQLTask

`ExecuteSQLTask` allows the user to execute one or more SQL statements using the connections established within the package. This task's key properties are as follows:

- `CommandProperties`—pointer to the OLEDBCommand Properties collection of the connection.
- `CommandTimeout`—long value that sets the command timeout period in seconds. Default value of 0 allows an infinite timeout period.
- `ConnectionID`—long value that indicates which connection within the package to use when performing the SQL tasks.
- `Description`—string that allows the user to add a description to the task.
- `Name`—string that allows the user to name the task.
- `SQLStatement`—string that contains the SQL statement(s) to be executed.

TransferObjects

`TransferObjects` allows the user to transfer objects between SQL Server databases. Objects include tables, views, stored procedures, indexes, referential integrity constraints, defaults, rules, and user-defined data types. Key properties of this command are as follows:

- `CopyAllObjects`—Boolean that determines if all the objects in one database should be transferred to another.
- `CopyData`—DTSTransfer_CopyDataOption enumerated value, shown in Table 19-2, that determines whether data replaces existing data, appends to existing data, or is not copied.

Table 19-2
Enumerated Values

Enumeration	*Value*	*Description*
DTSTransfer_DontCopyData	0	No data is copied.
DTSTransfer_ReplaceData	1	Data is copied and replaces existing data.
DTSTransfer_AppendData	2	Data is copied and added to existing data.

- `CopySchema`—Boolean that determines if the schema of the objects should be copied. If set to `false`, only data is copied (if `CopyData` is set to `true`).
- `Description`—string that contains a description of the task.
- `DestinationDatabase`—string that contains the name of the database (or catalog) to which the object is transferring.
- `DestinationLogin`—string that contains a user name on the destination database. Required when trusted connections are not in use. Must be used in coordination with the `DestinationPassword` property.
- `DestinationPassword`—string that contains the password for the `DestinationLogin` user on the destination database. Required when trusted connections are not in use.
- `DestinationServer`—string that contains the address of the database server to which the object(s) are transferring.
- `DestinationUseTrustedConnection`—Boolean that determines if Integrated or standard SQL security is to be used in the transfer. If the value is set to `false`, `DestinationLogin` and `DestinationPassword` must be set.
- `DropDestinationObjectsFirst`—Boolean that determines if existing objects on the destination database with the same name as objects from the source database should be dropped before the objects are transferred.
- `IncludeLogins`—Boolean that determines if logins on the source database should be added to the destination database.
- `IncludeUsers`—Boolean that determines if users in the source database should be added to the destination database.
- `Name`—string that contains the name of the transfer task.
- `ScriptFileDirectory`—string that contains the path to where the script files and log files are written.
- `ScriptOptionEx`—`DTSTransfer_ScriptOptionsEx` enumerated type used to set extended scripting options (see Microsoft SQL Server Books Online for a complete listing of values).

- SourceDatabase — string that contains the address of the source database (or catalog).
- SourceLogin — string that contains a user name on the source database. Required when trusted connections are not in use. Must be used in coordination with the SourcePassword property.
- SourcePassword — string that contains the password for the SourceLogin user on the destination database. Required when trusted connections are not in use.
- SourceServer — string that contains the address of the database server from which the object(s) are transferring.
- SourceUseTrustedConnection — Boolean that determines if Integrated or standard SQL security is to be used in the transfer. If the value is set to false, SourceLogin and SourcePassword must be set.

TransferObjects employs the following methods for smooth execution:

- AddObjectsForTransfer — adds objects on the source database to the collection of objects to be transferred to the destination database using the parameters ObjectName, OwnerName, and Type (as a DTSSQLObjectType constant). See Table 19-3 for a list of DTS database object types.

Table 19-3
DTS Database Objects Types

Enumeration	*Value*	*Description*
DTSSQLObj_AllDatabaseObjects	4607	System and database objects are transferred
DTSSQLObj_Default	64	User-created database objects
DTSSQLObj_Rule	128	Database rule object
DTSSQLObj_StoredProcedure	16	Stored procedure
DTSSQLObj_SystemTable	2	System table
DTSSQObj_Trigger	256	Trigger
DTSSQLObj_UserDefinedDatatype	1	User-defined data type
DTSSQLObj_UserDefinedFunction	4096	User-defined function
DTSSQLObj_UserTable	8	User table
DTSSQLObj_View	4	View

- `CancelExecution`—cancels asynchronous execution of transfer. Must be called on a thread other than the thread executing the transfer.
- `Execute`—executes the object transfer.
- `GetObjectForTransfer`—provides a list of the individual objects to be transferred using the parameters `Index`, `ObjectName`, `OwnerName`, and `Type` (as a `DTSSQLObjectType` constant).
- `ResetObjectsList`—clears the current list of objects to be transferred.

SendMailTask

`SendMailTask` allows the DTS package to send an e-mail to a designated recipient. This can be used to report the status of DTS package executions to operators, to send reports or other files as mail attachments, and to perform a variety of other tasks. `SendMailTask`'s key properties are as follows:

- `CCLine`—string that contains e-mail addresses that receive copies of the message. Semicolons separate multiple addressees.
- `Description`—string that contains a description of the task.
- `FileAttachments`—string that contains UNC paths to attached files. Semicolons separate multiple files.
- `IsNTService`—Boolean set to `true` only when process executing the package is configured as a Windows NT or Windows 2000 service. The default is `false`.
- `Message`—string containing the body of the e-mail message.
- `Password`—string that contains the password to the MAPI mail client to allow a MAPI session to be instantiated.
- `Profile`—string that contains the name of the mail profile to be used when instantiating the MAPI mail client.
- `SaveMailInSentItemsFolder`—Boolean that determines if a copy of the message should be stored in the Sent Items folder. The default is `false`.
- `Subject`—string that contains the subject of the message.
- `ToLine`—string that contains the e-mail addresses of the recipients of the message. Semicolons separate multiple recipients.

`SendMailTask` employs the following methods to execute its properties:

- `Execute`—sends the e-mail message.
- `GetDefaultProfileName`—returns the name of the default mail profile.

✦ `InitializeMAPI`—initializes the MAPI session.

✦ `Logoff`—ends the MAPI session.

✦ `Logon`—creates the MAPI session.

✦ `ResolveName`—returns a string that contains a qualified e-mail address from a partial string supplied as a parameter.

✦ `UninitializeMAPI`—uninitializes the MAPI provider.

BulkInsertTask

`BulkInsertTask` allows fast insertion of data from delimited text files. Based on the SQL `Bulk Insert` command, it uses bcp-style format files to parse text files and rapidly insert data into a table. Its key properties are as follows:

✦ `BatchSize`—Long value that includes the number of rows to include as a single transaction. The default, `0`, inserts all rows as a single transaction.

✦ `CheckConstraints`—Boolean that determines whether constraints are checked as data is inserted. The default, `false`, provides better performance, but requires foreknowledge that the data will violate no integrity constraints.

✦ `Codepage`—string that indicates the codepage to use while inserting the data. The default is `"OEM"`.

✦ `ConnectionID`—Long value that identifies the connection to the SQL Server database.

✦ `DataFile`—UNC path that contains the path to the input file.

✦ `DataFileType`—`BulkInsert_DataFileType` enumeration value that indicates the type of source file, as shown in Table 19-4.

Table 19-4
Bulk Insert Task File Storage Types

Enumeration	*Value*	*Description*
DTSBulkInsert_DataFileType_Char	0	Character data
DTSBulkInsert_DataFileType_Native	1	SQL Server native mode data
DTSBulkInsert_DataFileType_WideChar	2	Unicode character data
DTSBulkInsert_DataFileType_WideNative	3	Unicode SQL Server native mode data

✦ `Description`—string containing a description of the task.

✦ `DestinationTableName`—string containing the name of the destination table.

✦ `FieldTerminator`—string type that contains the character used to separate fields. Default value is `[Tab]`.

✦ `FirstRow`—variant data type that indicates the first row in the source table to import. The default is `1` (the first row in the file).

✦ `FormatFile`—string that contains the UNC path to a bcp-style format file.

✦ `KeepIdentity`—Boolean that determines whether the inserts are done as IdentityInserts. The default is `false`, which means identity fields are automatically incremented by the database, rather than receiving values from the source table.

✦ `KeepNulls`—Boolean that determines whether null field values should be retained or replaced with the default value for the column. The default is `false`, replacing the nulls with the default value.

✦ `LastRow`—variant data type that stores the number of the last row to be imported. The default is `0`, which indicates all rows in the source will be imported.

✦ `MaximumErrors`—Long value that stores the number of errors that can occur during the load before the task is considered a failure. The default value is `10`. If batches are used, each failed batch counts as a single error. If the task is performed in fast mode and the batch size is left at the default, `0`, a single error will roll back the entire task.

✦ `RowTerminator`—string that contains the character used to terminate rows within the source file. The default is the line feed character.

✦ `SortedData`—string that contains an `Order` clause used by the T-SQL `Bulk Insert`. The string indicates the order in which the data is sorted in the source file. If that sort order is the same as the clustered index of the table, it will improve efficiency. If the table has no clustered index, the property is ignored.

✦ `TableLock`—Boolean that determines if the entire table should be locked during the loading operation. The default value is `false`.

DataDrivenQueryTask

`DataDrivenQueryTask` allows parameterized queries to be executed. This facilitates the use of stored procedures of data stored in tables to modify the behavior of a query at run time. DataDriven queries are good for updating and deleting data. `DataDrivenQueryTask`'s key properties are as follows:

✦ DeleteQuery—string that contains a parameterized SQL Delete statement. Although named DeleteQuery, this query can perform any SQL function.

✦ DeleteQueryColumns—returns a pointer to the DeleteQuery Columns collection.

✦ Description—string that contains a description of the task.

✦ DestinationColumnDefinitions—returns a pointer to a collection of column definitions.

✦ DestinationCommandProperties—returns a pointer to the OLE DB Command Properties collection for the destination connection.

✦ DestinationConnectionID—Long value that contains the ID of the destination.

✦ DestinationObjectName—string that contains the name of the destination table or view.

✦ DestinationSQLStatement—string that contains the SQL statement to be performed on the destination rowset.

✦ ExceptionFileColumnDelimiter—string that contains the character used to separate columns in the exception file. The default character is |.

✦ ExceptionFileName—string that contains the UNC path to the exception file.

✦ ExceptionFileRowDelimiter—string that contains the characters used to delimit rows within the exception file. The default is carriage return/line feed.

✦ FetchBufferSize—Long value that contains the number of rows to fetch with each OLE DB operations. The default is 100. The value is ignored if Binary Large Objects, such as Image fields, are being addressed.

✦ FirstRow—variant that indicates the first row in the source to be used. The default value is 1, indicating that the operation will begin with the first row.

✦ InsertQuery—string that contains a parameterized SQL Insert statement. Although named InsertQuery, this query can perform any SQL function.

✦ InsertQueryColumns—returns a pointer to the InsertQuery Columns collection.

✦ LastRow—variant that indicates the last row to be used from the source. The default value is 0, indicating all rows will be used.

✦ MaximumErrorCount—Long value that indicates the number of errors that can occur before the task is aborted. The default is 0, allowing an infinite number of errors.

✦ Name—string that contains the name of the task.

- ProgressRowCount—Long value that determines the number of rows processed before the task fires an alert to the connection point. The default value is 1000.
- SourceCommandProperties—returns a pointer to the OLE DB Command Properties collection for the source connection.
- SourceConnectionID—Long value that contains the ID of the source connection.
- SourceObjectName—string that contains the name of the source table or view.
- SourceSQLStatement—string that contains the SQL statement to be performed on the source rowset.
- UpdateQuery—string that contains a parameterized SQL Update statement. Although named UpdateQuery, this query can perform any SQL function.
- UpdateQueryColumns—returns a pointer to the UpdateQuery Columns collection.
- UserQuery—string that contains a parameterized SQL statement.
- UserQueryColumns—returns a pointer to the UserQuery Columns collection.

The DataDrivenQueryTask object also has two key collections. The Lookups collection is a grouping of lookup object definitions that define named, parameterized query strings that allow a transformation to retrieve data from a location other than the row being transformed. The Transformation collection is a grouping of objects that define transformation processes and operations.

ExecutePackageTask

ExecutePackageTask allows one DTS package to call and execute another. This allows complex packages to be broken down into smaller, simpler, reusable packages. ExecutePackageTask's key properties are as follows:

- Description—string that contains a description of the task.
- FileName—string that contains a UNC to the DTS package file.
- InputGlobalVariableNames—string that contains a list of global variables to be passed between packages. Variable names are separated by semicolons.
- Name—string that contains the name of the task.
- PackageID—string that contains the Globally Unique Identifier (GUID) for the package. Packages stored in the repository are automatically assigned GUIDs to distinguish between packages.
- PackageName—string that contains the name of the package.

- PackagePassword—string that contains the password for a package.
- RepositoryDatabaseName—string that contains the name of the repository database where the meta-data for the DTS package is stored.
- ServerName—string that contains the name of the server where the DTS package is to be run.
- ServerPassword—string that contains the password of the user account in whose context the DTS package runs. Used in conjunction with the ServerUserName property. Not required if trusted connections are used.
- ServerUserName—string that contains the name of a user on the server in which the DTS package runs. Used in conjunction with the ServerPassword property. Not required if trusted connections are used.
- UseRepository—Boolean that determines if the DTS package should be retrieved from the repository database.
- UseTrustedConnections—Boolean value that determines whether Integrated or standard SQL Server security should be used to create a context within which the DTS package will run.
- VersionID—string that contains the GUID for the specific version of this package. When storing modifications to a DTS package in the repository, each version is saved and given a unique version GUID. This can be used for maintaining data lineage.

ExecutePackageTask's key collection is GlobalVariables, which is a collection of variables that allows data to pass between packages and between steps within a package.

DynamicPropertiesTask

DynamicPropertiesTask allows properties within the package to be set at run time. This has the effect of parameterizing a DTS package. A DynamicPropertyTaskAssignment is placed where the property would go, and a value for that property is programmatically placed in the Dynamic Properties collection. The key properties of this function are as follows:

- Assignments—returns a pointer to the DynamicPropertiesTaskAssignments collection.
- Description—string that contains a description of the task.
- Name—string that contains the name of the task.

DynamicPropertiesTaskAssignments is the key collection used with DynamicPropertiesTask. This collection of DynamicPropertyTaskAssignment objects allows property values to be assigned at run time.

DTSFTPTask

`DTSFTPTask` allows DTS to move files through TCP/IP network connections using FTP. It can be used to move import and/or export files. `DTSFTPTask`'s key properties are as follows:

- `Description`—string that contains a description of the task.
- `DestSite`—string that contains the destination path of the file.
- `Name`—string that contains the name of the task.
- `NonOverwritable`—Boolean that determines whether the destination file can be overwritten with a new version if the destination file already exists.
- `NumRetriesOnSource`—Long value that determines the number of times the connection to the source will be tried before it is considered a failure.
- `SourceFilename`—string containing the path, name, and size of the file(s) to be transferred. String should be formatted as 'path';'filename';'size';'path'; "filename';"size'. Size is used by the DTS Designer and is not required when building the property programmatically. If the `SourceSite` property is set, it will be appended to the filename to produce a fully qualified path.
- `SourceLocation`—Long value that indicates the source of the file(s). This can be an Internet site (0) or network directory (1).
- `SourcePassword`—string that contains the password of the `SourceUserName` account on the source FTP server.
- `SourceSite`—string that contains the location of the source file(s). If the `SourceLocation` is set to `0`, `SourceSite` must be set to an Internet address.
- `SourceUserName`—string that contains the name of a user that has access to the source location and files to transfer on the source. Used in conjunction with the `SourcePassword` property.

DTSMessageQueueTask

`DTSMessageQueueTask` allows the user to use the Microsoft Message Queue server to send information to other processes in a store-and-forward manner. This allows the receiving system to collect the message when it has the time and resources and not hold the DTS package while it awaits the results.

DTS lookups

DTS lookups allow data in another source to be included in the transformation. The most common use is lookup tables. A foreign key may be stored in the source table. A user may wish to include the name or description of the entity rather than the key in the destination. DTS lookups can retrieve that data from the parent table.

To use a DTS lookup, a distinct connection for the query must first be created, followed by a parameterized query. In the following example, a parameter is used to look up a company name based on the CompanyID field value. Note that a question mark is used to indicate the parameter:

```
Select CompanyName from Companies Where CompanyID = ?
```

To use the query, the user should create an ActiveX Script using data from the source table to serve as the parameter, as in this example:

```
DTSDestination("CompanyName") = _
DTSLookup("CompanyName").Execute(DTSSource("CompanyID"))
```

The DTSSource CompanyID field acts as the parameter when the query is executed.

If a DTS lookup returns multiple rows based on the query, only the first row is used. If the query returns no row, the lookup returns an empty variant. A user can test for this, using a function such as `ISEmpty`. The following code skips a line if the lookup cannot return a value:

```
If IsEmpty(LookupResults) Then
    Main = DTSTransformStat_SkipRow
Else
    Main = DTSTransformStat_OK
End If
```

This could also be used to insert a default value:

```
If IsEmpty(LookupResults) Then
    DTSDestination("CompanyName") = "Unknown"
End If
```

Lookup queries can be used to perform updates and deletes. In the following example, a parameterized delete query is formulated:

```
Delete From Inventory Where LotID = ?
```

The following script would delete the lots identified by the DTSSource rowset.

```
DTSLookups("DeleteLots").Execute(DTSSource("LotID"))
```

Multiple lookups can be used in the same transformation. Each lookup is created and named, and can be individually accessed. Lookups can also be used to supply parameters for data-driven queries.

Executing DTS Packages

There are several methods for executing DTS packages. They can be executed from within Enterprise Manager from the DTS Designer. They can be scheduled and run with SQL Server Agent, which will store a history of the package operations enabling the package to run repeatedly. COM applications can execute packages, and packages can also be run from the command line using `dtsrun`.

`Dtsrun.exe` is a command-line executable that can open and execute a DTS package. `Dtsrun` has the following command line switches:

- `/?` — lists the command prompt options.
- `~` — placed in front of a parameter that is encoded as hexadecimal text. Encoding parameters can provide added security for exposed parameters such as server, user name, password, package name, package GUID, package version GUID, package password, filename and repository database name.
- `/S server_name[\instance_name]` — indicates which server to specify. If the instance of the database is other than the default instance, add the instance name to the server name, separated by a backslash.
- `/U user_name` — specifies a user name on the server to which you wish to connect.
- `/P password` — specifies password for the aforementioned user name.
- `/E` — indicates the use of trusted connections. When set, user name and password are not required.
- `/N package_name` — specifies the name of the DTS package.
- `/G package_guid_string` — specifies the GUID of the original version of the package.
- `/V package_version_guid_string` — specifies the version number of the iteration of the package you wish to use.
- `/M package_password` — specifies the password required to execute the package. This parameter is required only if a password was added to the package.
- `/F filename` — specifies the UNC path to a COM structured DTS file. The contents of this file can be overwritten by the contents of a package stored on the server if the `/S` switch is also set.
- `/R repository_database_name` — specifies the name of the repository database in which the DTS package is stored.
- `/A global_variable_name:typeid=value` — is added for each global variable that needs to be set for the package. The typeid is an integer that indicates the data type for the variable, as shown in Table 19-5.

Table 19-5
DTS Global Variable Data Type Enumeration

TypeID	*DataType*
2	Integer (small)
3	Integer
4	Real (4-byte)
5	Real (8-byte)
6	Currency
7	Date
8	String
11	Boolean
14	Decimal
16	Integer (1-byte)
17	Unsigned integer (1-byte)
18	Unsigned Integer (2-byte)
19	Unsigned integer (4-byte)
20	Integer (8-byte)
21	Unsigned integer (8-byte)
22	Int
23	Unsigned int
25	HRESULT
26	Pointer
30	LPSTR
31	LPWSTR

✦ `/L log_file_name`—specifies the name of the package log file.

✦ `/W NT_event_log_completion_status`—specifies True to write completion to the NT Application log. False and completion status will not be written to the log.

✦ `/!X`—allows the contents of a DTS package to be retrieved from the server and to overwrite an existing file without executing the package itself.

- ✦ `/!D`—deletes a package stored in SQL Server (COM structured file can be deleted by merely deleting the file). The package does not execute.
- ✦ `/!Y`—displays the encrypted command used to execute the DTS package without executing it.
- ✦ `/!C`—copies the command used to execute the DTS package to the Microsoft Windows Clipboard. This option can also be used in conjunction with `/!X` and `/!Y`.

The DTS Run utility for Windows provides a graphical interface for running or scheduling DTS packages without using the Enterprise Manager. To access the utility, execute `dtsrunui.exe` from the command line. The interface facilitates running packages immediately or scheduling them to run under SQL Server Agent, as shown in Figure 19-13.

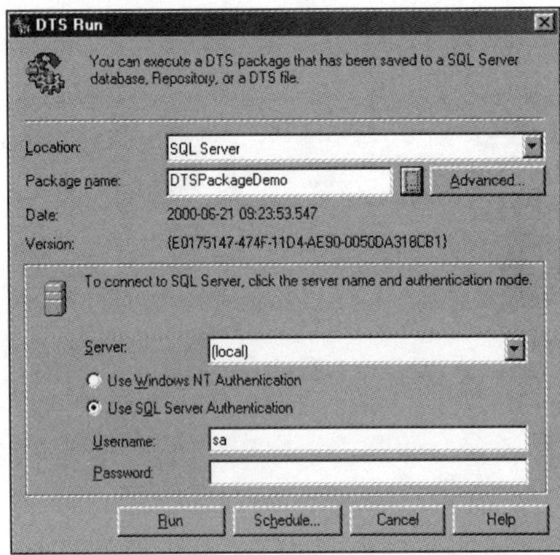

Figure 19-13: The DTS Run utility for Windows

Saving DTS Packages

There are four places in which DTS packages can be saved. Each has its own advantages and disadvantages.

Local SQL Server packages are stored in msdb. They provide a convenient means of storing and organizing the files for a given database server. Multiple versions can be stored and deleted as required. The DTS package is stored as a binary large object (BLOB) in msdb. Packages stored in msdb can be password-protected.

Packages can be stored in SQL Server 2000 Meta Data Services (also known as the repository). Meta Data Services tracks the Package GUIDs and Version GUIDs. It keeps a history of changes made to the packages. By adding the Package and Version GUIDs to the base tables, a user can track which version of each package transformed and copied data into a table. This can provide data lineage. Packages stored in Meta Data Services cannot be password protected, but Meta Data Services provides its own security mechanisms for restricting access.

Packages can be stored as COM structured files. The files can easily be moved between computers. A single file can store several versions of the package. COM structured files also offer optional password protection.

Packages can be saved as Visual Basic script files. This saves the file as a Visual Basic script that can be executed from the Windows Scripting Host or opened and added to a Visual Basic project. This option can speed development by creating packages in the DTS Designer, then scripting them to add to an application. Visual Basic script files do not support password protection.

Managing DTS Packages

There are a variety of package properties that can be viewed and configured to help maintain DTS packages. Most are properties within the package. They can be accessed programmatically or viewed on the Package Properties property pages in the DTS Designer, as shown in Figure 19-14. These properties include the following:

- `Package Identification`—lists the package GUID, version GUID, package name, creator name, creation date, computer name, and package description.
- `Error information`—the user can configure the location of the error log file and can also set whether errors are noted as step failures or abort the entire package.
- `Microsoft Windows events`—the user determines whether the status of the package is written to the Windows NT event log. The user can step the process priority of threads and the maximum number of threads a package can spawn.
- `Global Variables`—the user can view, add, edit and delete global variables for the package. These variables are available to any ActiveX Script within the package and can be passed to other packages.
- `Data Lineage`—using Meta Data Services, the user can track which version of which package added or modified each row within the database.

✦ `Meta Data Services scanning`—the user can relate objects referenced by the DTS package to catalog meta data in Meta Data Services.

✦ `Transactions`—the user can group steps together into transactions. Steps can be committed or rolled back as part of a transactional unit, with the support of the Microsoft Distributed Transaction Coordinator.

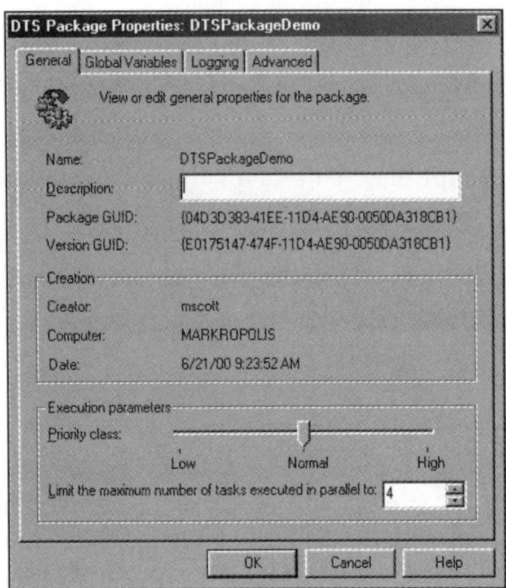

Figure 19-14: Managing DTS package properties

DTS packages built with the Designer require connection to source and destination data sources. This helps assure that properties are set correctly and errors avoided. There may be times, however, when the source and/or destination are not available. When this occurs, the user can build packages using disconnected editing by right-clicking on the Designer and choosing Disconnected Edit from the pop-up menu. The Edit All Package Properties window will display all editable properties, as shown in Figure 19-15. The user can use this tool to adjust any of the properties.

This feature will allow properties to be set to values that will cause the package to fail. It should be used only when no other options are available for editing the package.

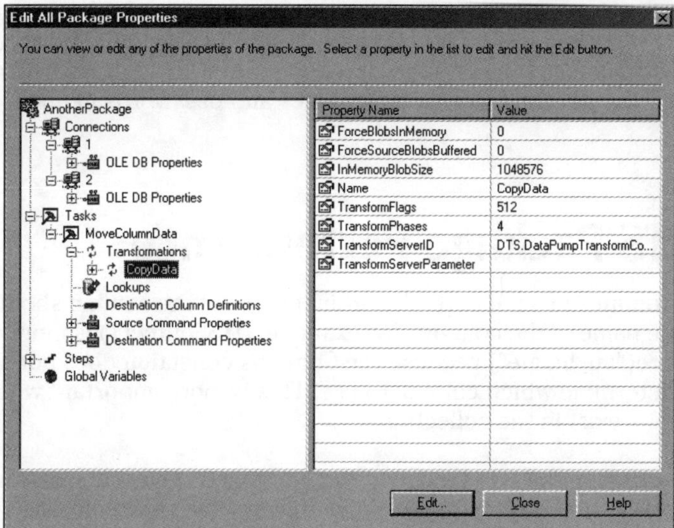

Figure 19-15: Editing packages while disconnected

DTS Package Security

Security for packages depends on the means by which the package was saved. Local SQL Server packages and COM structured files support password protection. Two passwords can be supplied. The user password allows a user to execute the package without modifying it. The owner password allows the user to open and modify the package contents.

Packages stored in the Meta Data Services database or as Visual Basic scripts cannot be password protected. Meta Data Services can use SQL Server security mechanisms to restrict access to the packages on a user-by-user basis. Visual Basic script files require an external form of security, such as Microsoft Visual SourceSafe or Windows 2000 file encryption.

When packages are run interactively, such as those run from the command line or launched from the Enterprise Manager manually, they run in the context of the user who launches them. This affects the operating system resources the package can access. When scheduled to run under the SQL Server Agent, the package runs in the security context of the SQL Server Agent account. If a user in the sysadmin role owns the job, the job will also utilize the security context of the SQL Server Agent when run. If a user not in the sysadmin role owns the package, it will execute in the security context of the SqlAgentCmdExec account. This is a local account and may have difficulty accessing network databases and resources on other servers.

DTS packages can store connection information in Microsoft User Data Link files (.udl). These are unencrypted files that store text strings. UDLs should be used with trusted connections. Trusted connections will rely on the credentials of the user who executes the file, rather than storing user names and passwords in unencrypted text files.

Enhancing DTS Package Performance

When referring to columns in a package, the ordinal value of the column should be used rather than the name of the column. For example, DTSSource(1) is more efficient than DTSSource("au_lname") because the Columns collection does not need to be searched to determine which column to use. This is more important when more than 20 columns exist in the collection.

When building a package in the DTS Designer, each column is given an individual mapping and transformation. This is relatively inefficient. If several columns can be moved in the same manner, a single many-to-many mapping can be created by selecting all the source columns and all the destination columns at once, as shown in Figure 19-16.

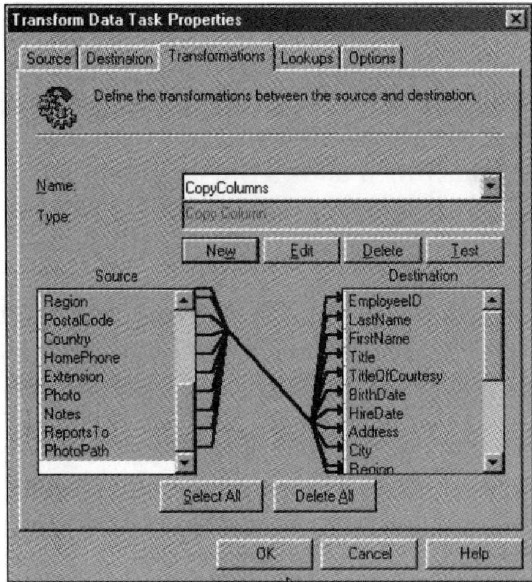

Figure 19-16: Create many-to-many column mappings when possible

By default, data transforms use fast load when inserting data into an MSDE database. This is faster than the process used by the data-driven query. A user should avoid using data-driven query tasks when inserting data into a MSDE table.

Bulk Insert is the fastest means for inserting data into a MSDE table from a text file. Bcp and data transform that copy columns are roughly the same speed. Bcp is the fastest way to export data to a text file or MSDE's native format.

A user should avoid using ExecuteOnMainThread whenever possible. By using multiple threads, DTS packages can run operations concurrently. While C++ and Java allow creation of additional thread, Visual Basic does not. Custom tasks written in Visual Basic 6 or earlier must be executed on the main thread. Also, operations that run concurrently should have distinct connections. For safety reasons, DTS will allow only one task to use a connection at a time.

Many tasks can be performed more efficiently as T-SQL batches. This leverages the batch processing strength of MSDE. When transformations are not required, copying data using `SELECT INTO` or `INSERT INTO` provides the best performance.

Summary

Data Transformation Services provides MSDE with the means to move and transfer data to and from OLE DB data sources. In the chapter, the creation of DTS packages using the DTS Designer and Visual Basic was explored. The individual objects within the DTS model were explained. The process of storing and executing DTS packages was discussed. The chapter also relayed techniques for improving DTS package performance.

✦ ✦ ✦

CHAPTER 20

Using Replication to Distribute Data

✦ ✦ ✦ ✦

In This Chapter

Choosing replication types

Assigning servers to roles

Creating publications

Subscribing to publications

✦ ✦ ✦ ✦

SQL Server provides replication mechanisms that can automatically copy and distribute data from a database to other databases. Users can choose from several types of replication to best suit the needs and limitations of their environment. Users can also choose to use different servers in different roles, although there are restrictions on which roles MSDE can play. The replication type and server role determine where data can be modified and where it can only be read, and applications must be written to accommodate the replication model.

Replication allows data to be moved closer to the users who need it. By having a local copy of data, users don't have to be as dependent on the operations of a network and server in a distant city. Having local data can also provide performance and cost benefits because less network bandwidth is needed.

Replicating data requires careful planning. There should not be more than one copy of a single piece of data in a relational database. Having more than one copy opens the door to a number of potential errors. For example, more than one user can update the data at the same time, causing a conflict that must be resolved. For this reason, the type of replication must be chosen carefully, and any applications written should accommodate conflict resolution.

Understanding the Roles Servers Play in Replication

The tasks performed by replication are divided into roles in order to define how each server will participate in the replication. The terms for these roles are taken from the publishing industry; they are publisher, distributor, and subscriber. A single server can play more than one role in replication, and more than one server can perform the publishing and subscribing roles.

Publisher

The server that plays the publisher role has control over any modifications to the data being published. In most cases, the data originates at the publishing server and is subsequently copied out to subscribers. It is possible to allow subscribers to modify data, in which case a distributed transaction extends the modification back to the publisher so that the publisher still controls the data modification. When using merge replication, the publisher does not control the modification of the data; however, it does control the synchronization and conflict resolution processes and is responsible for the ultimate outcome of the data.

MSDE cannot participate as a publisher when you use transactional replication.

Distributor

The distributor is used as a storage location for data waiting to be moved to subscribers. It also serves as a platform from which to run the services that pull data from the publisher. By using the distributor for both of these functions, the publisher is saved from a possible significant hit to its performance and disk space. The distributor stores information about the state of all subscribers.

Data is stored in a distribution database on the distributor and in the file system. The database stores transactions, if transactional replication is in use, and status information about subscribers for all types of replication. The file system is used to store entire copies, or snapshots, of the data being replicated. These snapshots can be used for all types of replication.

Subscriber

The subscriber is the ultimate consumer of the replicated data. When replication is initiated, a snapshot of the replicated data is moved to each of the subscribers. Subsequent updates can take place as transactions, merge synchronizations, or additional snapshots.

MSDE can participate as a subscriber in any type of replication.

Selecting the Type of Replication

There are three primary types of replication — snapshot, transactional, and merge — and an option for immediate updating of subscribers that can be used along with two of them. The type of replication determines the mechanism used to decide which data is to be moved from the publisher to the subscriber and how that data is to be moved.

Snapshot

Snapshot replication involves making a period copy of the data to be published and sending it to the subscribers via the distributor. Taking a snapshot is the first step in initiating any kind of replication because there must be an initial copy of the data on the subscriber before any changes can be applied.

There are several ways to get a snapshot from the publisher to a subscriber. The replication service can automatically create a snapshot and store it on the distributor. From there, the snapshot can be moved to a subscriber immediately, on a scheduled basis, or manually. Once publication has been moved to one subscriber, the subscribed database can be detached and copied as a file to other subscribers. When it is attached to the new server, the new server automatically be subscribes to the publication.

Transactional

Transactional replication uses a log-reader agent to gather information about every transaction that takes place on the publisher and records the changes caused by the transactions. The original batches that create the transactions are not saved, but the changes to the database are. The batch that executed on the publisher might have a different effect if it is executed on the subscriber. For example, if a subscriber receives replicated data from several publishers into a single table and if one publisher executes a batch that modifies all rows with a date that falls into a particular range, there might be more rows on the subscriber that fall into this range; clearly, only those rows that come from the first publisher should be modified. Any rows that are modified on the publisher are uniquely identified, and these uniquely identified changes are stored in the distribution database to be moved to the subscriber at a later time.

Merge

Merge replication is similar to snapshot replication in that an original copy of all of the published data is copied to the subscriber. Merge replication can modify rows on the publisher or on any subscriber. The subscribers are periodically synchronized with the publisher, at which time the publisher resolves any conflicts according to the conflict resolution rules that are set up by the administrator. There are many predefined conflict resolution rules, such as allowing the publisher to always win, assigning a weight to various servers and using the value from the server with the highest weight, or allowing the earliest change to win.

Whatever method is used to resolve conflict, both the application that uses the database and users of the application must be prepared to accept the undoing of committed transactions. Merge replication works best in environments where conflict is avoided rather than resolved. An example of avoiding conflict is allowing traveling sales representatives to enter orders in their laptop computers. When the orders are entered, they are inserted into a table and identified by the representative's name, region employee ID, and so on. During synchronization, there are no conflicts because the only action is insertion and all rows are identified by representatives.

Updating subscriber

Both transactional and snapshot replication allow the user to configure updating subscribers. Data is replicated from the publisher to one or more subscribers. These subscribers can modify the replicated data, and a distributed transaction is created that performs the update on the publishing server as well as on the subscriber.

Controlling Replication

Because replication is so complex, the following examples use Enterprise Manager to describe how to control replication. It is also possible to control replication with DMO or stored procedures; books online can be consulted for documentation on how to use these APIs.

Configuring the servers

Before a publication can be created, replication must be enabled and configured on the publisher and distributor. Before a user can subscribe to a publication, replication must be enabled and configured on the subscriber.

Configuring the distributor

The first server that must be configured is the distributor. In Enterprise Manager, a user should right-click the Replication container and choose Configure Publishing, Subscribers, and Distribution. The first screen welcomes the user to the wizard. The second screen allows a choice of using a local or remote distributor. The third screen, shown in Figure 20-1, gives the user the opportunity to specify the configuration for the distribution database or to accept the default settings.

The defaults are summarized at the bottom of the screen. The local server is configured as publisher and distributor. Other editions of SQL Server allow a remote computer to be used as the distributor. All registered servers are configured as possible subscribers. The distribution database and logs are stored in the default location for databases on the local server.

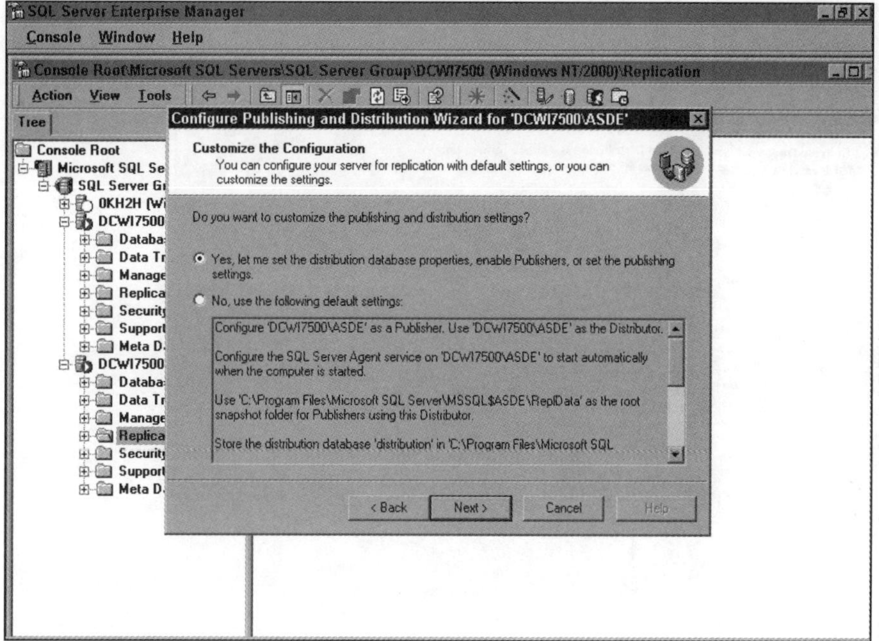

Figure 20-1: Setting up the distributor

Tip

The wizard only appears the first time a user chooses Configure Publishing, Subscribers, and Distribution. Subsequently, the Properties dialog box appears, allowing the user to change individual aspects of replication. If replication is completely removed from the server, the wizard reappears the next time this menu item is chosen.

If the default configuration is chosen for the distributor, clicking Next displays the last screen in the wizard; when Finish is selected, the distribution database is created, and the publisher and potential subscribers are configured.

The first screen displayed for custom distribution database properties is shown in Figure 20-2. The user should enter the name for the database. It defaults to "distribution," the recommended name, but it can be changed if desired. The user can also specify the location for the files that contain the data and log portions of the distribution database. The replication process is completely asynchronous relative to the production database, so locating the distribution database on a different physical drive or RAID array may be a good idea if much contention is expected.

Enabling the publisher

The third screen allows the user to specify additional properties for any publishers, which, at this point, is only the local server. Clicking the Ellipsis button at the right of the screen shown in the background of Figure 20-3 displays the screen shown in the foreground.

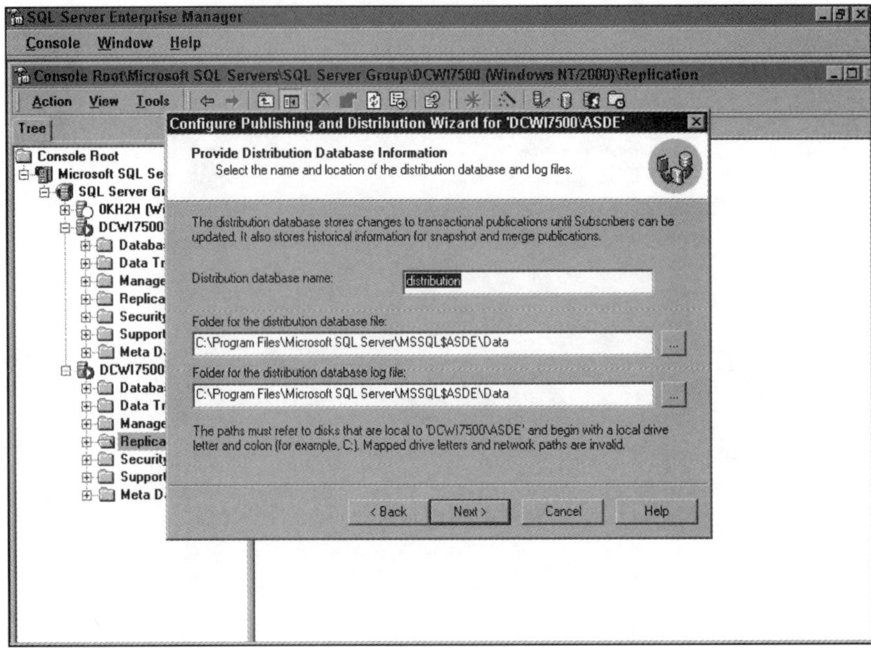

Figure 20-2: Distribution database name and files

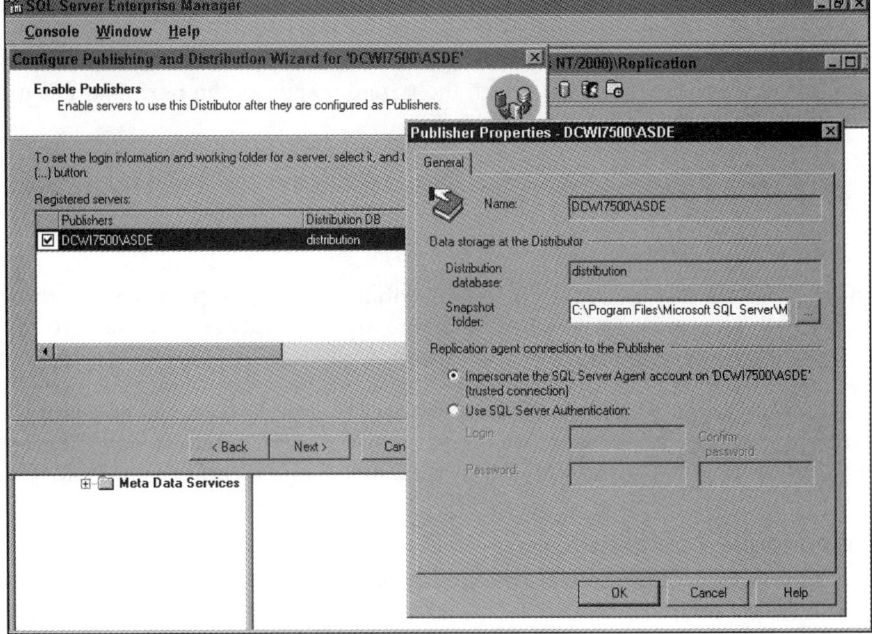

Figure 20-3: Publisher properties

The distribution database is specified in the first text box; this should agree with the name given to the distribution database in the previous screen. The snapshot folder is specified in the second text box. It defaults to a local path but should be set to a network path if pull subscriptions are to be performed (an appropriate network share must be set up prior to entering this information).

The bottom half of the dialog box shown in Figure 20-3 allows the user to configure the security context for the replication agent when it connects to the publisher. The user can choose to use the credentials of the SQL Agent service account (assuming it is not running in the local system account) or can specify a login that uses SQL Server authentication. The sa login should probably not be used for this, even though it's the default. A new login should be created specifically for this purpose and granted administrative privilege in the databases to be replicated.

The next screen allows the user to enable databases for transactional or merge publication. Databases must be enabled for replication before a publication can be created in them.

Figure 20-4 shows the Enable Publication Databases dialog box. If a user who is a database owner but not a member of the sysadmin group is to be allowed to create a publication, the database to be published must be enabled for publishing by a sysadmin. Merge or transactional replication (or both) can be selected in this dialog. MSDE does not support transactional publication, but selecting the transactional replication check box in this dialog enables the database for snapshot publication.

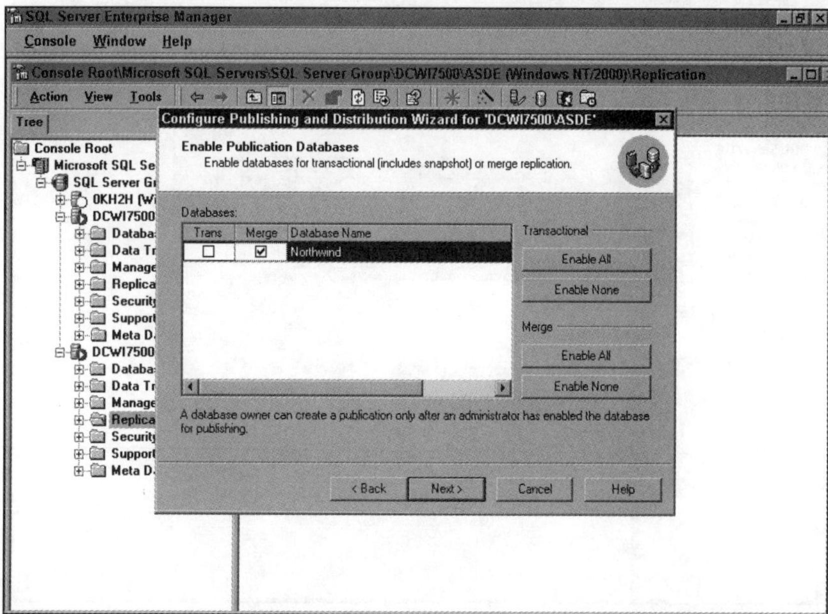

Figure 20-4: Enable publication databases

Enabling subscribers

After enabling and configuring the properties for the publisher, the next screen in the wizard allows the user to enable and set properties for subscribers. This screen is shown in Figure 20-5. Enabling a subscriber in this screen makes another server a potential subscriber to a publication on the local server. A user can enable all, none, or some of the servers in this list by using the buttons on the right or the individual check boxes on the left. The Ellipsis button can also be clicked to set properties, as shown in Figure 20-5.

The General tab in the Subscriber Security dialog box, shown in Figure 20-6, allows the user to enter an individualized description for each subscribing server. At the bottom of this dialog, the user can enter the security context that is used by replication agents when communicating with subscribing servers. Again, the SQL Server Agent account or a SQL Server authenticated login can be chosen. If all of the servers are administered by the same person or group of people, the SQL Agent service account probably suffices. In some environments in which the administration of the servers is distributed among different people, departments, or companies, it may be a security risk to do so because the SQL Agent service account must have administrative privilege. The subscription replication agent does not need administrative privilege; it needs only write permission in the database being replicated. Creating specific accounts to be used only for replication and giving those accounts the minimum level of permission necessary can help segment and compartmentalize security.

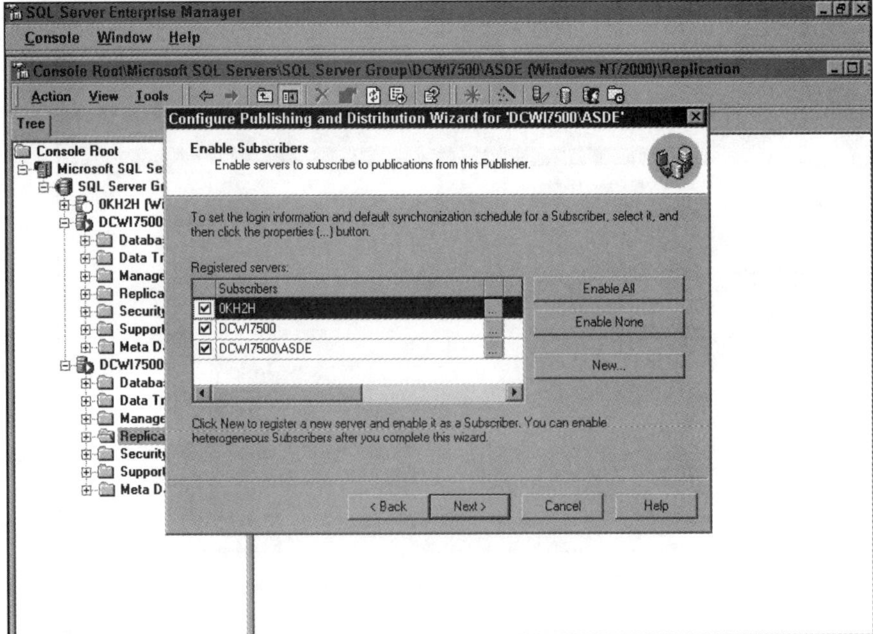

Figure 20-5: Enabling subscribers

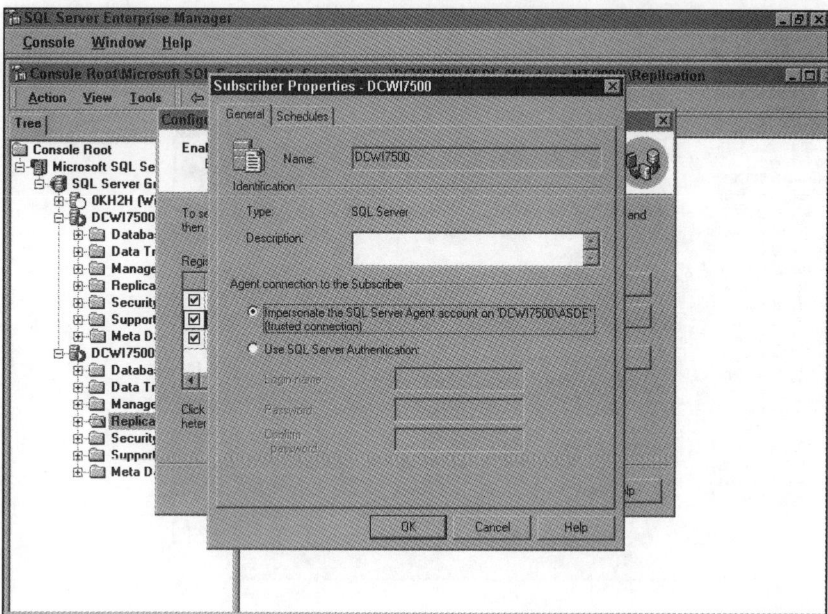

Figure 20-6: Subscriber security

The Schedules tab, shown in Figure 20-7, allows a user to create a custom schedule for each subscriber for the distribution agent and the merge agent. Creating custom schedules can spread out the replication activity to prevent the distribution server and network from becoming overwhelmed.

Once the subscriber properties are configured, the custom settings are complete. The next screen in the wizard is the final screen, and clicking Finish creates the distribution database and enables and configures the publisher and subscribers.

A dialog box informs the user of the status and of any error messages. If the path for the snapshot directory is specified as a local path (the default), a warning dialog informs the user that only pull subscriptions can be used. Another dialog box informs the user that the replication monitor has been added to the Enterprise Manager hierarchy, allowing the user to see detailed status of replication and thus to diagnose problems.

Creating a publication

A publication can be created when all servers are enabled and configured.

To create a publication, a user should expand the Replication container, select the Publication container, right-click anywhere in the right pane, and choose Create New Publication. The Create New Publication wizard begins and displays the dialog shown in Figure 20-8.

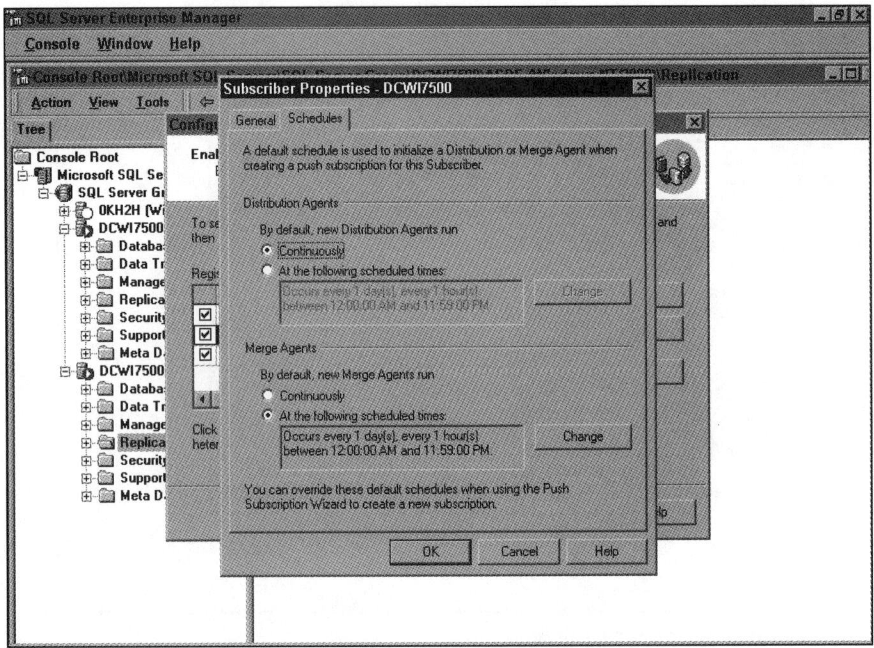

Figure 20-7: Subscriber schedules

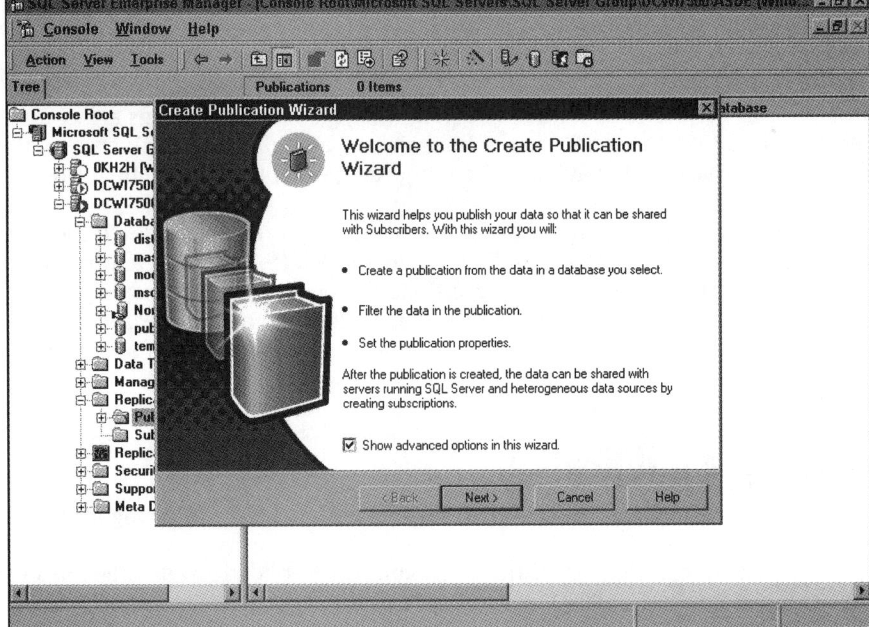

Figure 20-8: Enabling advanced options

Selecting the "Show advanced options in this wizard" check box at the bottom of the dialog allows the user to choose immediate or queue updating subscribers or to specify whether data is transformed as it is replicated using DTS. These features (except immediate updating subscribers) are not supported on previous versions of SQL Server. Updating subscribers and replication data transforms are not supported with merge replication. Merge replication has its own mechanisms for allowing subscribers to update data, and transforms are not permitted.

Figure 20-9 shows the second dialog in the Create New Publication wizard. This dialog allows the user to select the database for which the publication is created. Only a single database can be selected in this dialog, and only a single publication can be created at one time. To publish multiple databases or to create multiple publications for a single database, the wizard must be run multiple times.

Figure 20-10 shows the Select Publication Type dialog box. In this dialog, a user can select either snapshot or merge replication. The option for transactional replication is disabled because the Desktop Engine does not support this type of replication.

Snapshot replication takes an image of the published data and periodically copies it to the subscribers. By default, data can only be modified on the publisher when using snapshot replication. Modifications can be permitted on subscriber by using immediate or queue updating subscribers, in which case severe restrictions are placed on the modifications, and the modifications are transmitted more or less directly to the publisher.

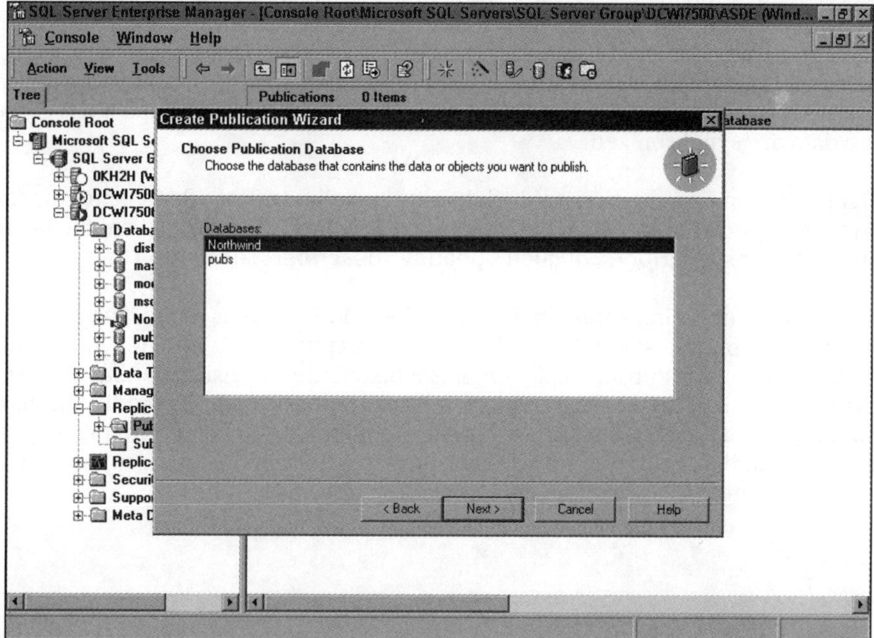

Figure 20-9: Selecting a database to publish

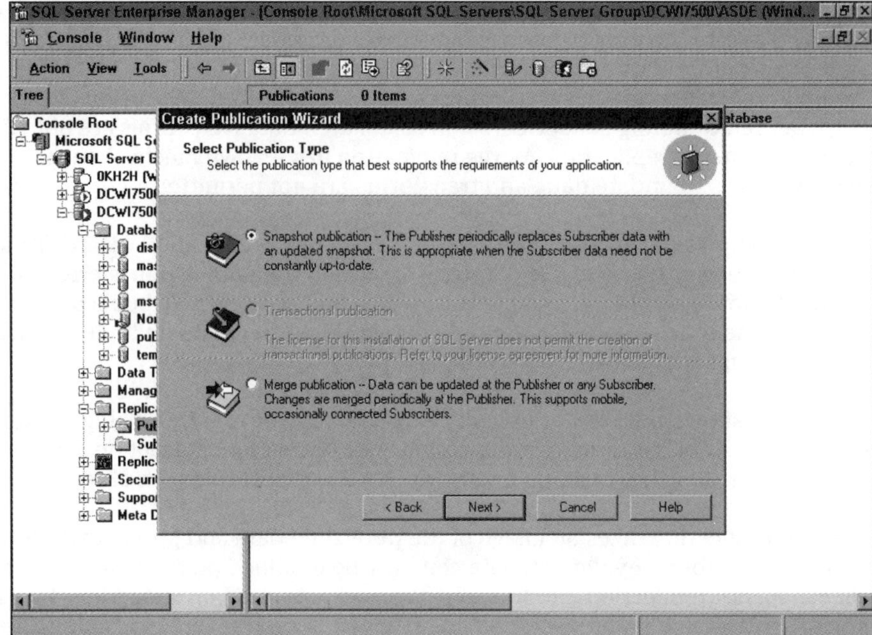

Figure 20-10: Selecting the publication type

Merge replication makes an initial copy of the replicated data but allows modifications to be made at the publisher or at any subscriber. Periodically, a connection is made between the publisher and subscribers. Any changes are synchronized between the computers. Conflict resolution mechanisms resolve any conflicts that occur if data is changed at more than one computer before the replicated copies of the data are synchronized.

Figure 20-11 shows the Updatable Subscriptions dialog box, which is not displayed if merge replication is selected. Using this dialog box, the user can enable immediate updating subscribers, queued updating subscribers, or both.

If immediate updating subscribers is enabled, modifications can be made to replicated data from the subscriber. When a data modification is initiated at the subscriber, the server automatically creates a distributed transaction that performs the same modification on the publisher. Prior to performing the modification, the data on the subscriber is verified against the publisher to ensure that it is synchronized. Immediate updating subscribers rely on a full-time network connection to the publishing server to support the distributed transactions.

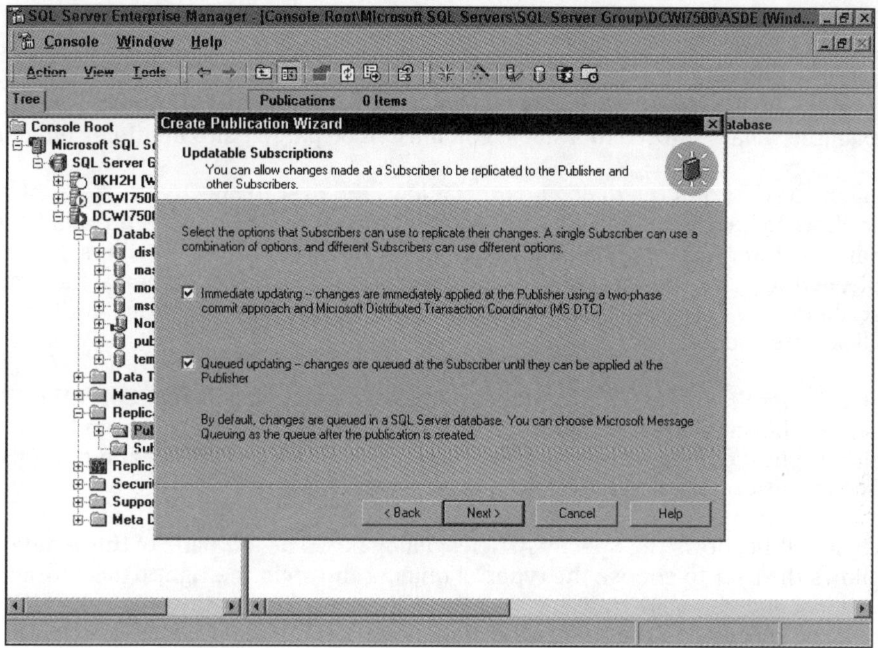

Figure 20-11: Enabling immediate updating subscribers or queued updating subscribers

Updates on snapshot replication subscribers without a full-time network connection can be performed using queued updates. A queued update allows the update at the subscribing server, but stores the update in a queue. The queued portion of the update is executed on the publishing server when a connection is made. The updates are queued in a system table by default. A user can enable the use of the Microsoft Message Queue (MSMQ) after the publication is created.

If immediate and queued updates are enabled, the modifications at the subscribers use immediate updating by default and queue the update only if communication with the publisher fails. Using this configuration provides more resiliency than using only immediate updates but requires applications to be designed to accommodate the possible reversal of a queued update. Using immediate updates only simplifies the design of the applications because a transaction either succeeds or commits immediately and is durable once it is committed.

The updating subscriber setting is immutable once a publication is created. The entire publication must be deleted and re-created to disable this setting.

Figure 20-12 shows the Transform Published Data dialog box, in which the user can select whether or not to add a transformation of any data that occurs during replication. This dialog box is not displayed in selected merge replication. A data transformation processes data as it is being copied in the replication process. For example, a name stored in a single column can be parsed into multiple columns.

Figure 20-13 shows the dialog box that allows the user to specify the types of subscribers to be used. If only SQL Server 2000 is selected, all options are available. Some features are unavailable for SQL Server 7.0 and ODBC subscribers; for example, neither views nor stored procedures can be replicated to either of these subscribers. The dialogs that follow in the wizard show only the options available for all selected subscriber types.

SQL Server CE can only subscribe to publications that use merge replication. The screen shown in Figure 20-13 is displayed if merge replication is selected. If snapshot replication is selected, only SQL Server 2000, SQL Server 7.0, and heterogeneous subscribers are shown as choices in this dialog.

Figure 20-14 shows the Specify Articles dialog box. The left pane of this dialog allows the user to choose the types of objects shown in the right pane. Stored procedures and views are only shown if the SQL Server 2000 is the only subscriber type, as specified in the previous dialog.

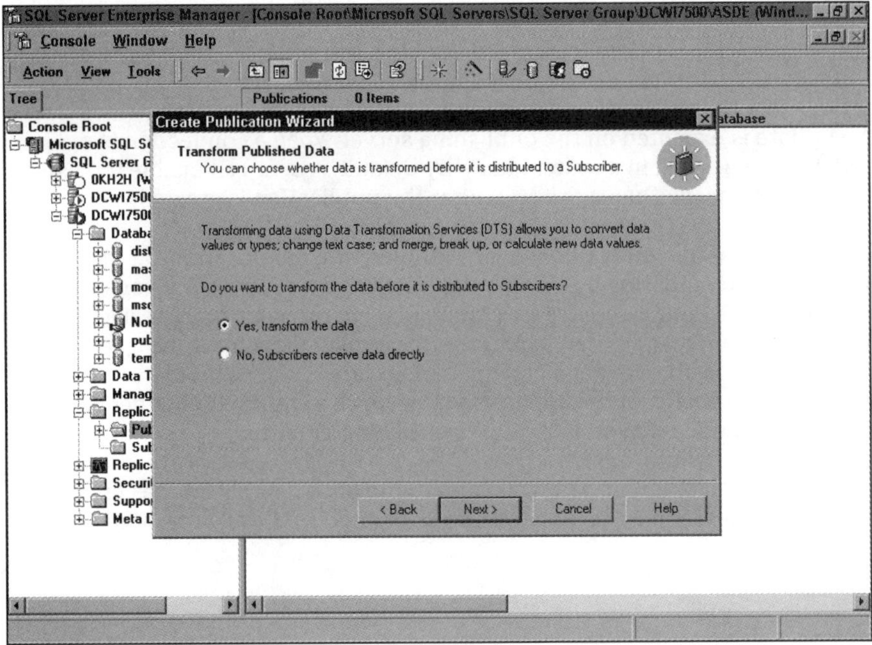

Figure 20-12: Enabling data transformation

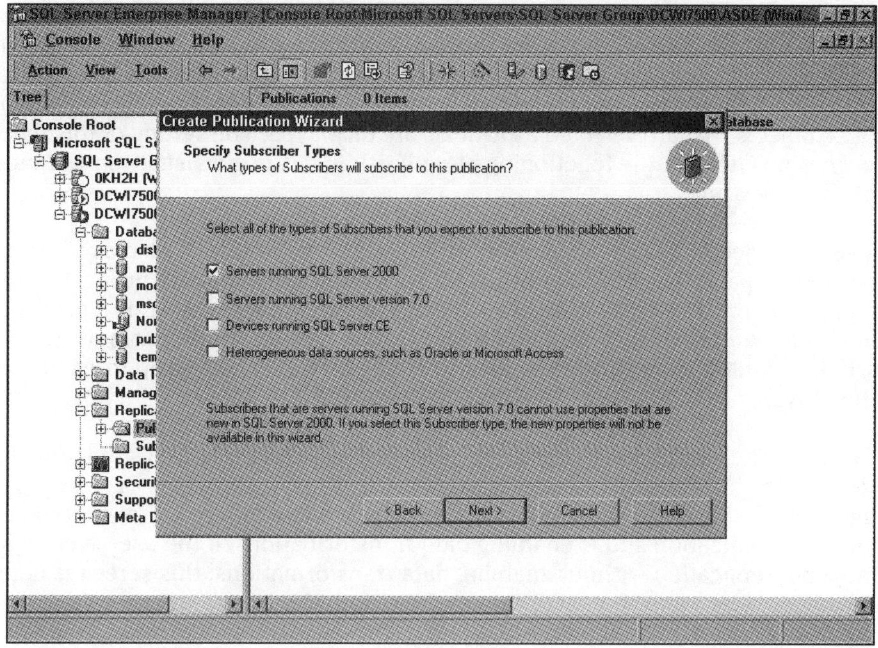

Figure 20-13: Selecting subscriber types

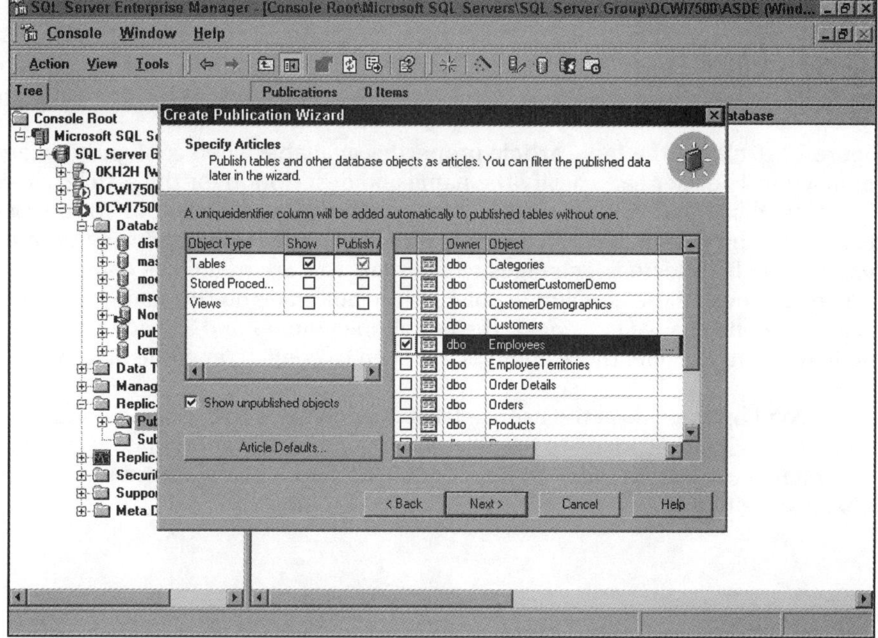

Figure 20-14: Specifying articles

Clearing the "Show unpublished objects" check box allows the user to more easily see the objects selected and to set properties for those objects. When the check box is selected, all objects in the database are displayed, both those that are selected as articles for publication and those that are not. When the check box is cleared, only those objects that are selected as articles are displayed. The setting of the check box has no effect on the functioning of replication; it is just a visual convenience for the dialog box.

When an object is selected for publication, an Ellipsis button is displayed next to it in the right pane. The Ellipsis button allows the user to configure properties for the object. The properties that are available are different for views, stored procedures, and tables, and they vary depending on the type of replication that is used. The Article Default button allows the user to configure the default properties for each object type.

The properties for objects vary slightly depending on other settings that are chosen.

Figure 20-15 shows the table article properties available when a user is configuring snapshot replication and is enabling data transformations. If the user is configuring snapshot replication without enabling data transformations, this screen is nearly the same, except that the check box at the bottom for horizontal partitioning is not displayed.

In this dialog box, the user can specify a name and description for the article, as well as the owner name and table name that is used for the table on the subscriber.

Enabling horizontal partitioning by DTS allows a unique, customizable partitioning mechanism for each subscriber. A replication DTS package has to be attached to each subscriber. This package determines which rows are sent to each subscriber.

Figure 20-16 shows the table article properties available when configuring merge replication. The user can specify the name and description for the article, as well as the owner name that is used for the object on the subscriber. At the bottom of this dialog box, the criteria used to determine the scope of a conflict during synchronization can be selected. If changes to the same row are treated as conflicts, there is a conflict even if the conflicting changes are not made on the same column. For example, if one change is made to the telephone number and a second change is made to the first name, these changes are seen to conflict, and one of them is lost.

The second option allows the user to treat only changes to the same column as a conflict. If a change is made to the telephone number and another change made to the first name, these changes do not conflict, and both changes survive and merge into all subscribers.

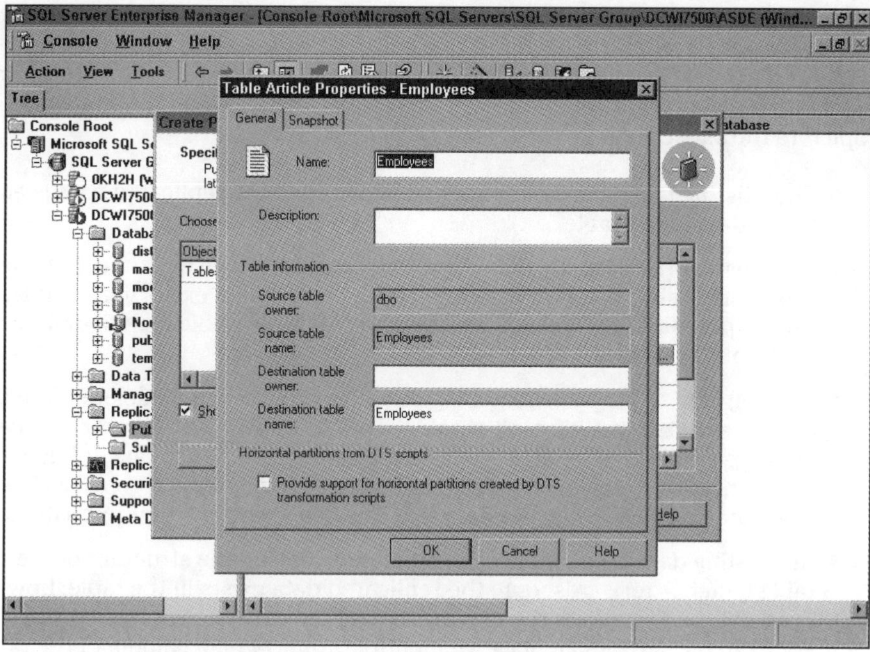

Figure 20-15: Table article properties for snapshot replication

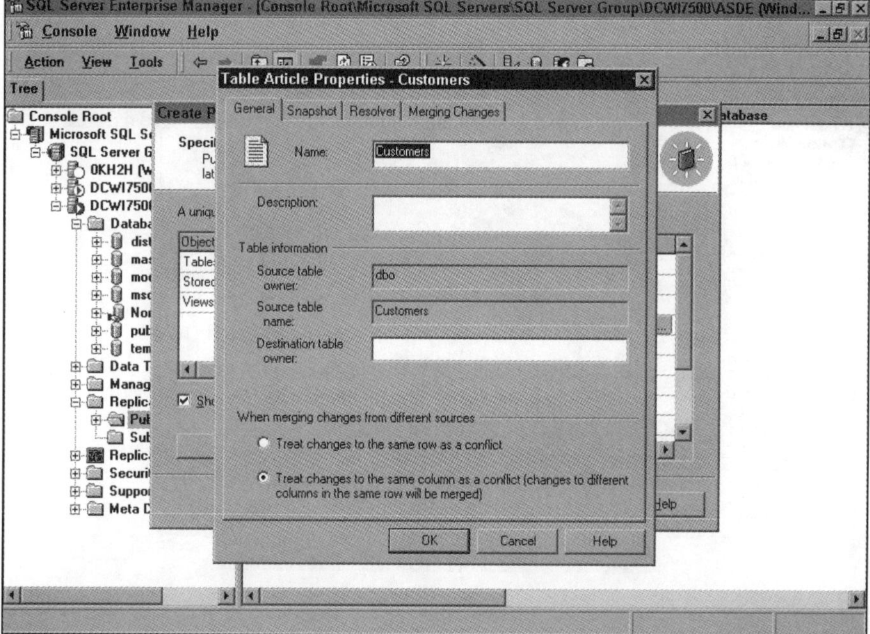

Figure 20-16: Table article properties for merge replication

Figure 20-17 shows the Table Article Snapshot Properties dialog box, which allows the user to configure the behavior of the snapshot used in both snapshot and merge replication. The top half of the dialog allows the user to specify the actions that takes place if a table of the same name already exists when the snapshot is copied to the subscriber.

- The existing table can be left as-is, in which case the replicated data is added to the data in the table.
- The existing table can be deleted and re-created, losing any data that may exist in the table. Afterwards, only the replicated data exists in the table. This setting precludes the possibility of having multiple publishers of data to the same table.
- Existing data in the table matching the filter criteria can be deleted, leaving any other data remaining in the table. This setting allows the user to have multiple publishers replicate data to the same table. When one publisher sends its data, it deletes the data that it sent previously and replaces it with new data, not disturbing the data that has been sent by other publishers.
- All existing data in the table can be deleted, leaving the structure of the table intact. Afterwards, only the replicated data exists in the table; however, this setting allows the user to control the existence of table properties. For example, a user can place an identity property on a column of the table that is not otherwise created by the replication process.

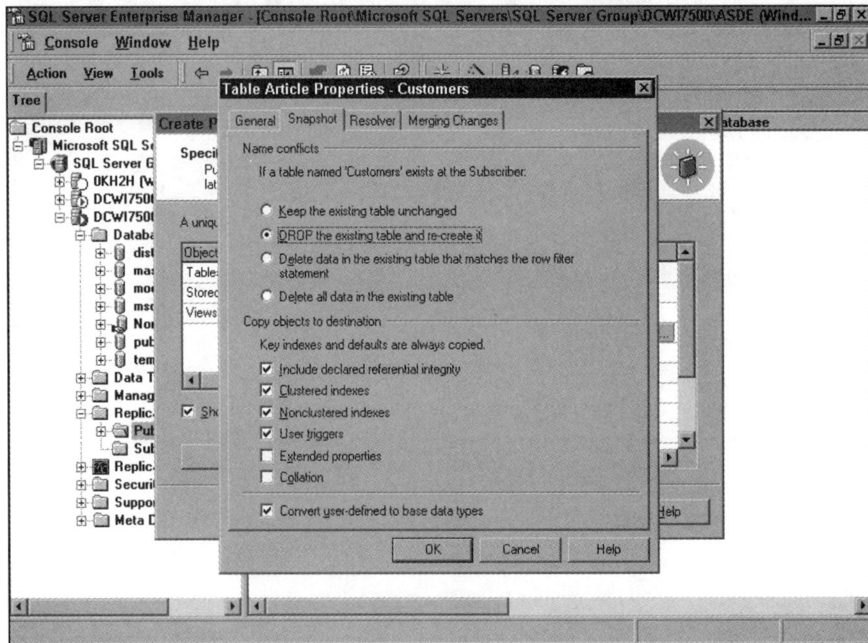

Figure 20-17: Table article snapshot properties

The lower half of the dialog box allows the user to configure which objects associated with the table are replicated to the subscribers.

✦ The user can replicate declarative referential integrity objects, which re-creates primary key, unique, and foreign key constraints on the subscriber.

✦ The user can choose to replicate indexes, both clustered and non-clustered.

✦ The user can replicate user-defined triggers, extended properties, and collation. Extended properties are primarily user-defined properties.

The user can also choose to convert user-defined data types to the underlying base data type. If not, these data types have to be manually created on the subscriber before replication is initiated.

Figure 20-18 shows the Resolver dialog box, in which the user can specify the resolver to be used when a conflict is detected during merge replication synchronization. The user can select the default resolver or a custom resolver. The default resolver allows the administrator to configure priority levels for each server involved with replication, and the highest priority wins in the case of a conflict. Users can write their own custom resolver or can select one from those included with SQL Server:

✦ **Additive** — sums the conflicting values and stores the result.

✦ **Averaging** — averages the conflicting values and stores the result.

✦ **DateTime Earlier** — the first changed conflicting value is saved; values changed later are discarded.

✦ **DateTime Later** — the last changed conflicting value is saved; values changed at an earlier time are discarded.

✦ **Maximum** — stores the largest of the conflicting values.

✦ **Minimum** — stores the smallest of the conflicting values.

✦ **Subscriber** — the value from the subscriber always takes precedence over the value from the publisher.

✦ **Stored Procedure** — runs a stored procedure and stores the results.

Depending on the needs of the chosen custom resolver, additional information may be needed. For example, the DateTime resolver requires the name of a column that contains the DateTime value used to determine the winner of the conflict.

Interactive conflict resolution can be enabled for use during on-demand synchronization. This type of conflict resolution allows the user that initiates the synchronization to manually choose the winning value in the event of a conflict.

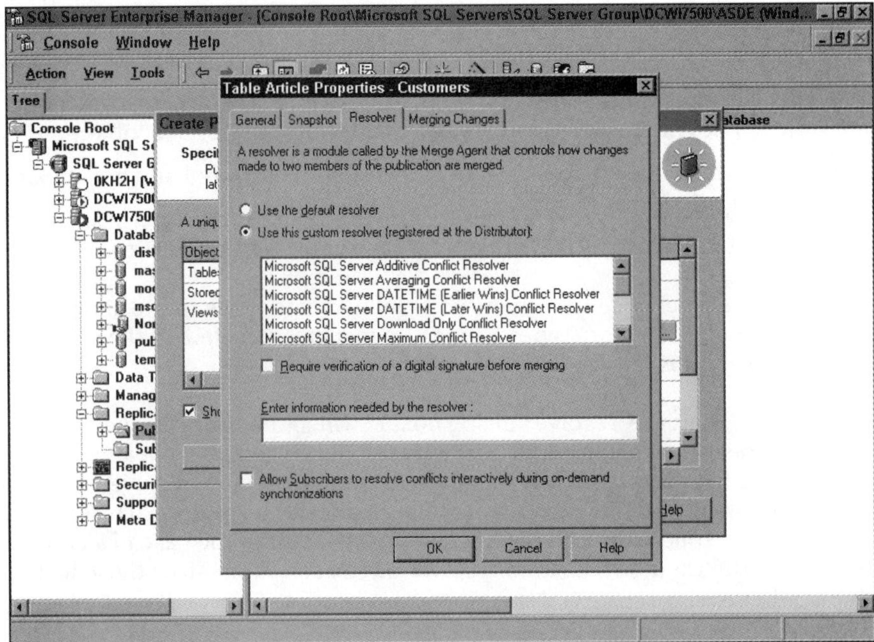

Figure 20-18: Configuring merge conflict resolution behavior

Figure 20-19 shows the Merging Changes dialog box in which the user can specify that the subscriber merge agent operates in a security context that has insert, update, and/or delete permissions to upload the data modifications to the publisher. The check box at the bottom of this screen allows the user to configure the merge agent to use a single update for an entire row, rather than individual updates for each modified column during synchronization.

After the articles to be included in the publication are selected and configured, the screen shown in Figure 20-20 is displayed. A summary of all settings is shown at the bottom of this screen. The current settings can be accepted and the publication created, or additional properties can be customized. The additional properties allow the user to create article filters, to allow anonymous subscriptions, and to preserve snapshots for future subscribers.

If a user chooses to set additional properties, a dialog is displayed, allowing the user to enable either horizontal or vertical filters (partitioning).

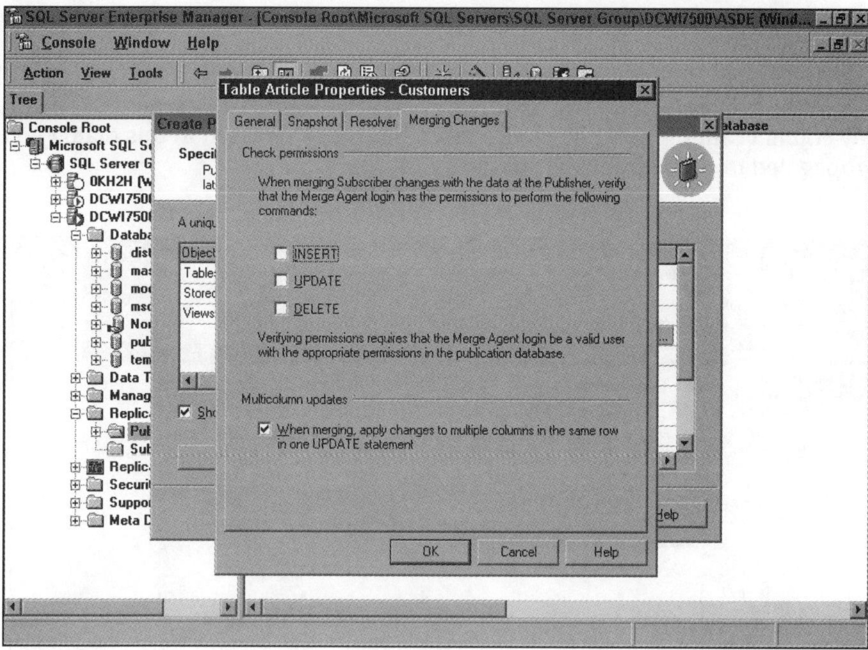

Figure 20-19: Merging changes properties

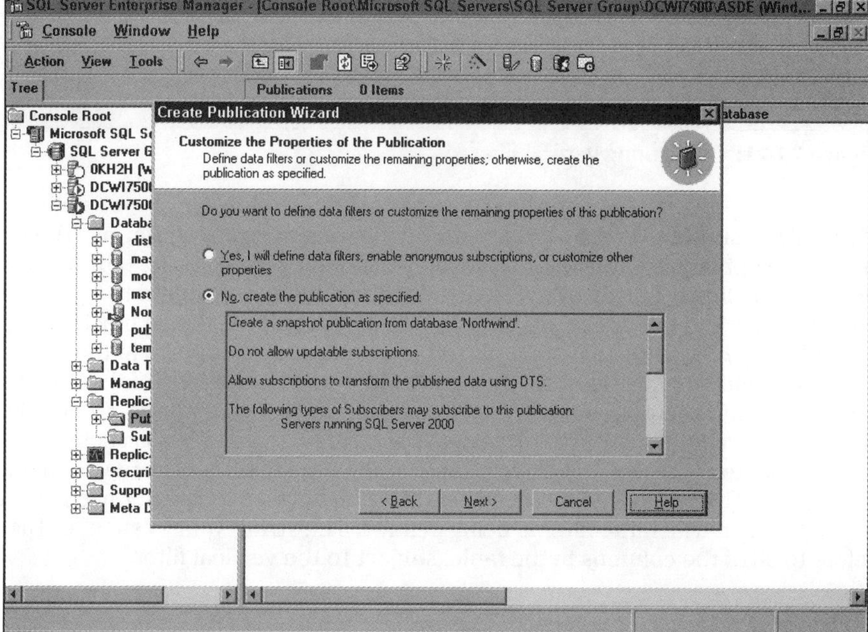

Figure 20-20: Customizing publication properties

Figure 20-21 shows the dialog displayed when a user chooses to include a vertical filter in a publication. All of the published tables are displayed in the left pane. The selected table's columns are displayed in the right pane. Any columns with a check box in the first column of the right pane can be selected or deselected. The primary key column cannot be deselected. Any columns not selected in this dialog box are propagated from the publisher to the subscribers.

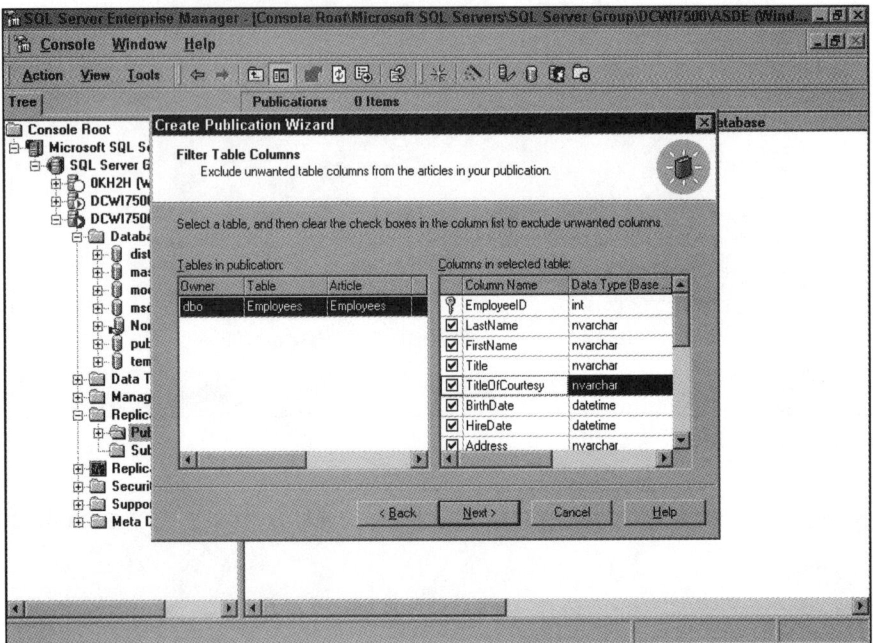

Figure 20-21: Configuring vertical filters

Figure 20-22 shows that dialog boxes for configuring horizontal filtering. The dialog box at the upper left of the figure is displayed first. It lists all of the tables in the publication. An Ellipsis button at the right side of this dialog, obscured in Figure 20-22, should be clicked to choose the table to be filtered, and the dialog box in the lower left of Figure 20-22 is displayed. A partial Select statement appears in the window. The user should define the filter by completing the Where clause of the Select statement. All of the components of the Select must remain as they appear when the window opens except for the Where clause. The string `<<Table>>` is essentially a variable set to represent the current table at the time the filter is processed during replication. This string can be reused in the Where clause if the user needs to refer to the table on which the filter is being defined. The string `<published_columns>` refers to all of the columns in the table, subject to the vertical filter.

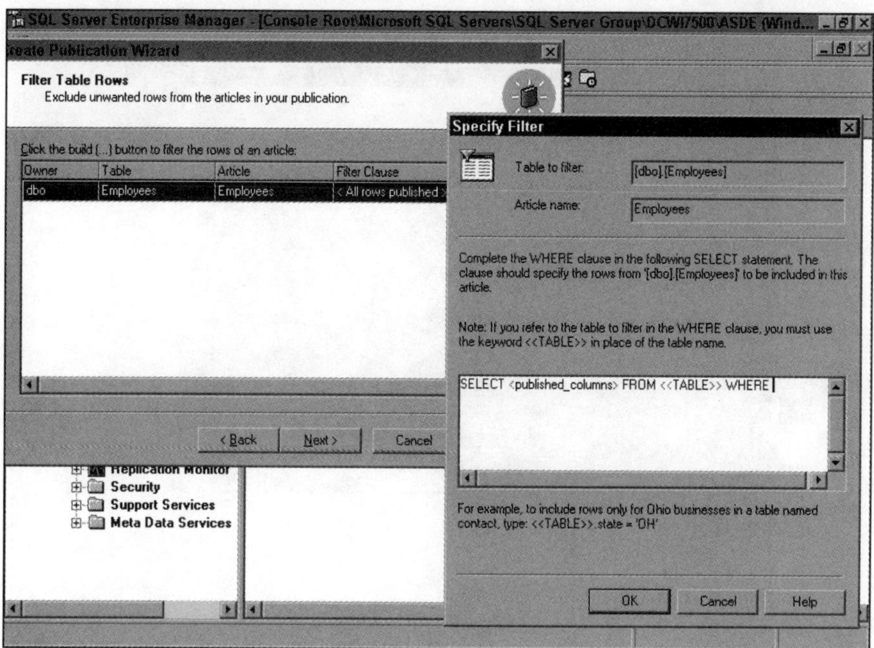

Figure 20-22: Configuring horizontal filters

The next dialog box displayed after configuring any horizontal or vertical figures is shown in Figure 20-23. This dialog allows the user to enable anonymous subscriptions. Anonymous subscriptions are subscriptions configured without previously specifying the subscribing server during publication configuration on the publishing server. Several factors should be considered when deciding whether or not to allow anonymous subscriptions.

- ✦ Anonymous subscriptions do not reduce the level of security for the replication environment. The replication agents must still have all appropriate permissions for connecting to and accessing data on the publisher/distributor.
- ✦ Information is not stored about all subscribers. This can significantly ease administration if there are a large number of subscribers.
- ✦ Only anonymous subscribers can be used when replicating via the Internet (FTP). This type of replication may be necessary if the subscriber and the distributor are on opposite sides of a firewall. Firewalls are often configured so that normal connections made by the replication agents are not allowed. Internet replication stores data in an FTP directory, and the agents retrieve the data using the FTP protocol. Only the FTP protocol must pass through the firewall in this configuration.

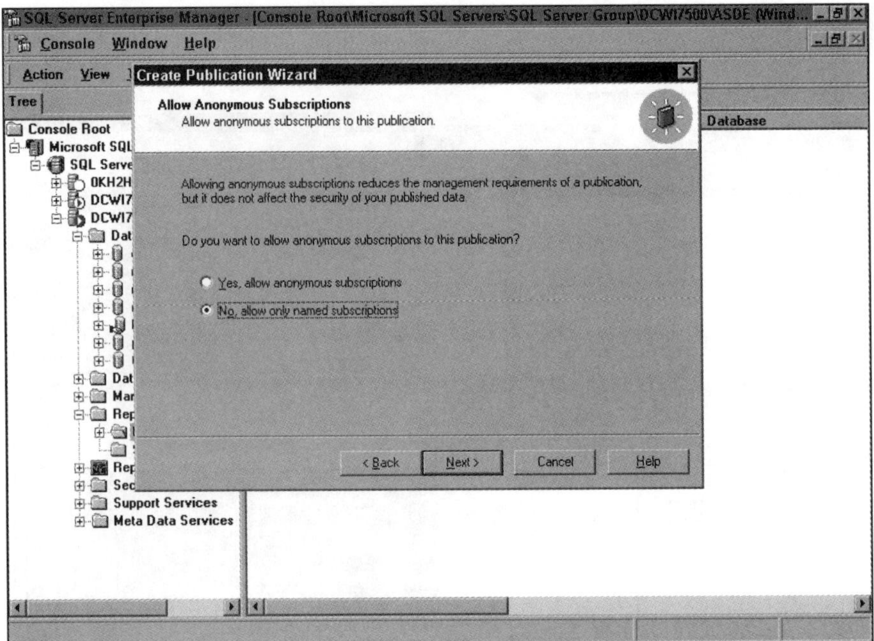

Figure 20-23: Allowing anonymous subscriptions

Figure 20-24 shows the last dialog box in the Create New Publication wizard. Using this dialog box, the snapshot agent can be scheduled to periodically re-create a new snapshot image of the published data in a database. The user can also configure the agent to create a snapshot immediately after the wizard is complete. Scheduling periodic snapshots ensures that fresh images are available for new subscribers for either snapshot or merge replication.

Whenever the Create New Publication is run after the first publication is created, an additional dialog is presented as the second screen of the wizard. This screen, the Use Publication Template, is shown in Figure 20-25. Using a template presets all of the configuration settings in the wizard to be the same as the selected publication. Templates can simplify and speed the process of creating a new publication.

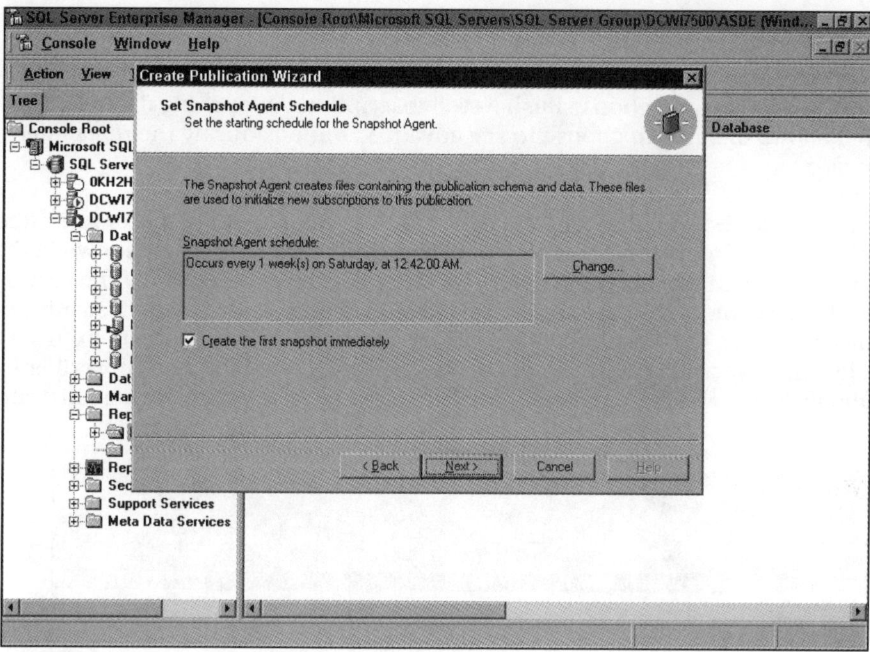

Figure 20-24: Scheduling the snapshot agent

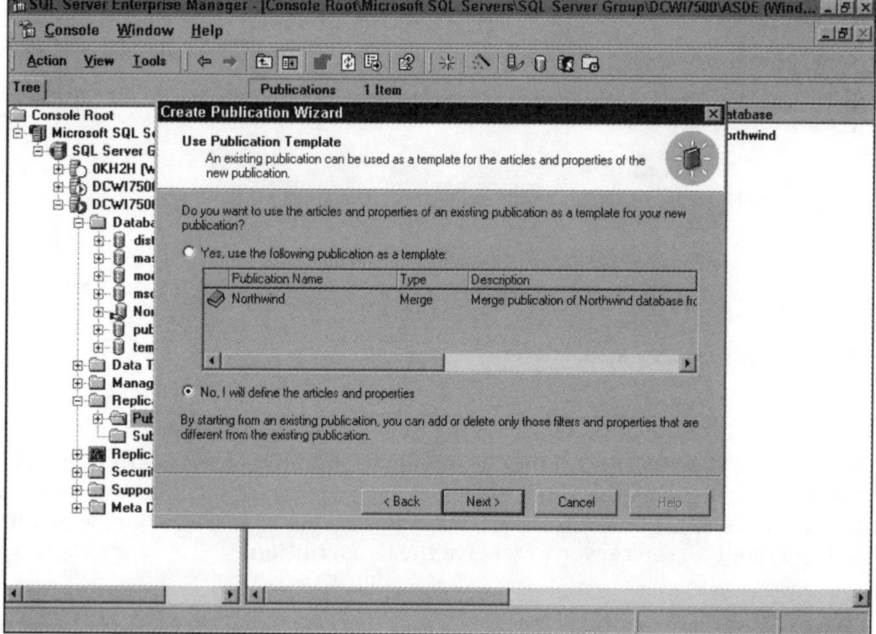

Figure 20-25: Using a publication template

Creating a push subscription

To create a push subscription, a user can open the Publication container, right-click the publication, and choose Push New Subscription. An opening dialog is displayed that allows the user to choose to see advanced options during the remainder of the wizard.

Figure 20-26 shows the second dialog in the Push Subscription. All servers either registered in Enterprise Manager or configured as a subscriber are shown in this dialog. A user with administrative privilege can select any server, and if the server has not been enabled as a subscriber, it is enabled. A user without administrative permission (e.g., a database owner who is not a member of the sysadmin fixed server role) can only push a subscription to a server that is enabled as a subscriber by an administrator. Heterogeneous subscribers must be enabled by the administrator.

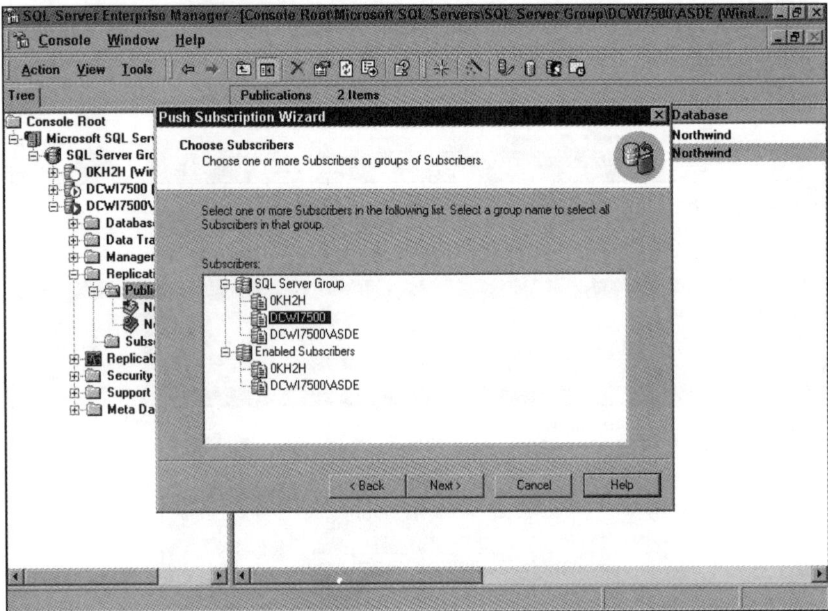

Figure 20-26: Selecting a subscriber

One or more servers should be selected to which the subscription can be pushed (using the Ctrl key to select multiple servers). If multiple servers are selected, the database that receives the subscription at each server must already exist and must have the same name on each server. If a single server is selected, a new database can be created on the server to receive the subscription.

After a server is selected to receive the subscription, the screen shown in the upper left of Figure 20-27 is displayed. The user can type the name of the database to receive the subscription or click the Browse or Create button to display the dialog box shown in the lower right of Figure 20-27. This dialog displays all of the candidate databases on the destination server. System databases are not displayed because they cannot be used in replication. The user can select the correct database or create a new one.

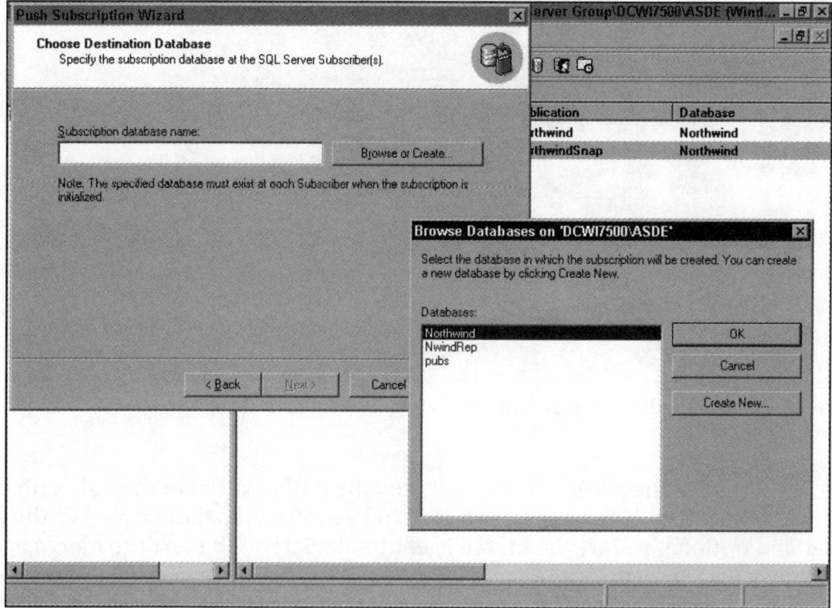

Figure 20-27: Selecting a database.

Figure 20-28 shows the Set Merge Agent Schedule dialog box, which allows the user to run the Merge Agent continuously or on a schedule basis. Whenever the merge agent runs, it performs synchronization of data modifications between the subscriber and publisher.

If a snapshot publication is being pushed, the corresponding scheduling screen offers the same options; however, it is used to configure the distribution agent, which recopies the snapshot to the subscribers any time it is updated. Normally, the distribution agent is not run continuously for snapshot replication. The option is offered primarily for push subscriptions of a transactional publication on versions of SQL Server other than MSDE. Transactional publications and snapshot replication use many of the same dialog boxes for configuration.

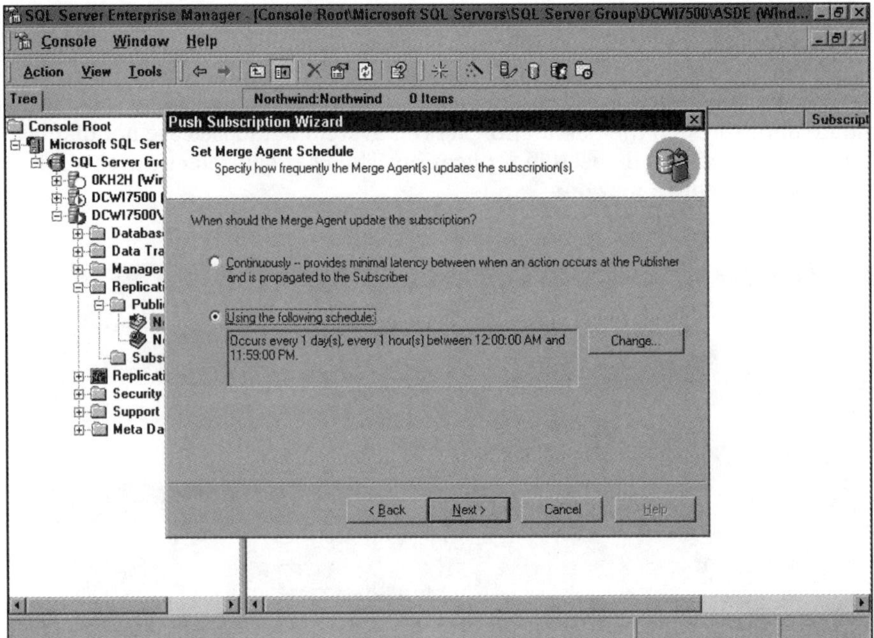

Figure 20-28: Configuring the schedule

Figure 20-29 shows the screen that configures the initialization of the subscriber for merge replication. The user can choose to have the snapshot copied to the subscriber and optionally start the merge agent immediately. To start the merge agent successfully and immediately, a snapshot must have been created for the publishing database. If a snapshot does not exist, the check box should go unchecked, and the merge agent should be started manually. The appropriate schema and data must be created on the subscriber. The most automatic way to accomplish this is to apply the snapshot to the subscriber, but the task can be performed manually by restoring a backup tape or running scripts and bulk copies, etc.

The corresponding screen for snapshot replication is the same as that shown in Figure 20-29, except that the check box allows the user immediately to start the distribution agent.

If you are using the default conflict resolution resolver, conflicts are resolved based on the priority assigned to each change. The priority scheme is configured in the screen shown in Figure 20-30. The first option, "Use the Publisher as a proxy for the Subscriber when resolving conflicts," does not assign a specific priority to the subscribers. Subscribers configured in this way are called local subscribers. When you are using this option, the publisher accepts whichever change is merged first. The accepted change takes on the priority assigned to the publisher. Any future conflicts are resolved according to priority. If another local subscriber conflicts, the publisher wins. If another global subscriber (one that has an assigned priority) conflicts, the server with the higher priority wins.

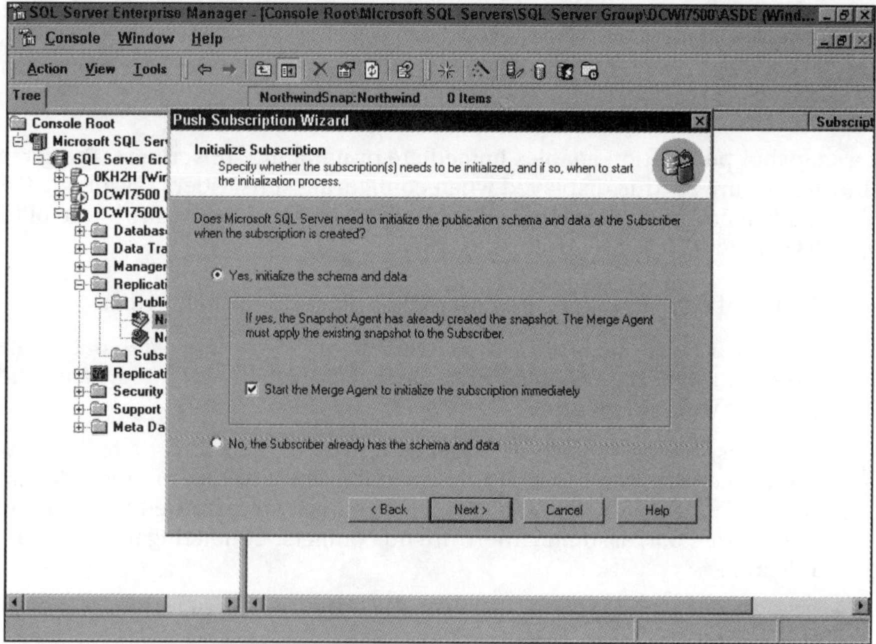

Figure 20-29: Initializing the subscription

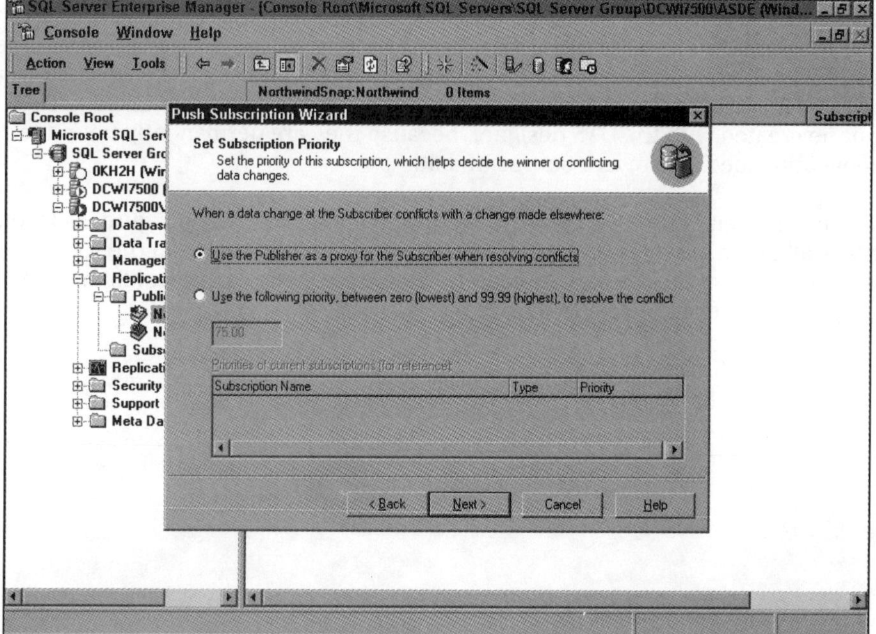

Figure 20-30: Setting subscription priority for merge subscribers

The second option allows the user to configure a specific priority value for each server that participates in replication. Each time data is synchronized between two servers, any conflict is resolved by accepting the value from the higher priority server. Any subscriber that republishes data must be a global subscriber.

If a snapshot publication enables immediate or updating subscribers, the screen shown in Figure 20-31 is displayed when configuring subscribers (assuming the display of advanced options is enabled in the first screen of the wizard). One of four options can be selected for each subscriber:

- No updating of the replicated data takes place on the subscriber.
- The subscriber can perform an immediate update of replicated data. Whenever replicated data is updated at the subscriber, a distributed transaction is initiated with the publisher.
- The subscriber can perform a queued update of replicated data. Whenever replicated data is updated at the subscriber, the changes are recorded in a queue. The queued changes are asynchronously transmitted to the publisher and carried out, assuming there are no conflicts. Conflicting updates are rejected.
- The subscriber can perform immediate updates if the publisher is available. If the publisher is not available, the update is queued.

If a snapshot publication is configured to allow data transformations, the screen shown in Figure 20-32 is displayed in the Push New Subscription wizard. This screen allows the user to select a replication DTS package stored on the distributor or on the subscriber to transform the data as it is replicated. Replication DTS packages can be created by right-clicking the publication and choosing Define Transformation of Published Data. These packages can also be created programmatically. They cannot be created with the DTS designer, because they are permanently bound to the replication mechanism as a source of data.

The last screen in the Push New Subscription wizard, shown in Figure 20-33, displays all of the services that must be started to run replication in the way it is configured. If any of these services need to be started, they can be configured to start automatically from this screen.

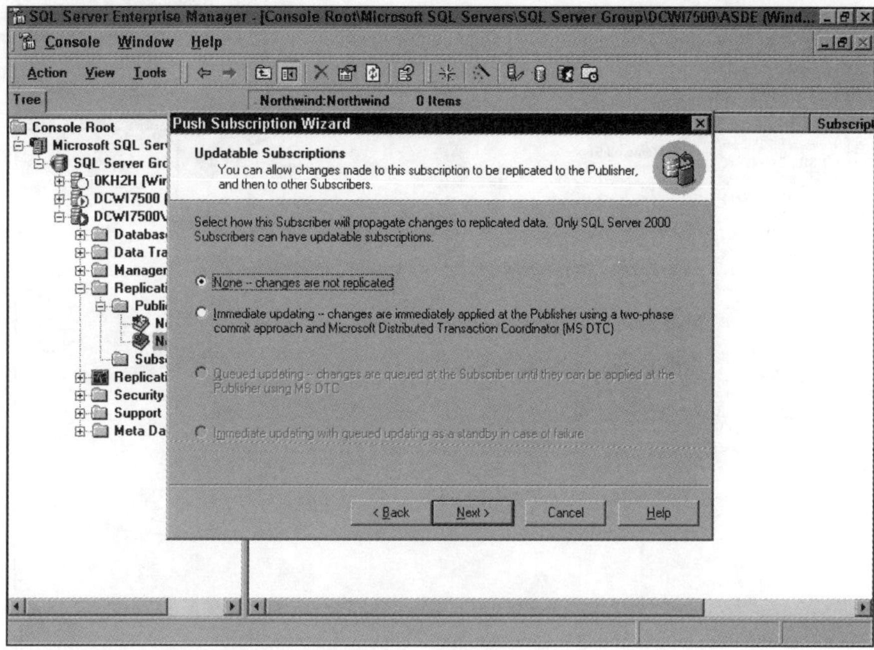

Figure 20-31: Configuring an updating subscriber

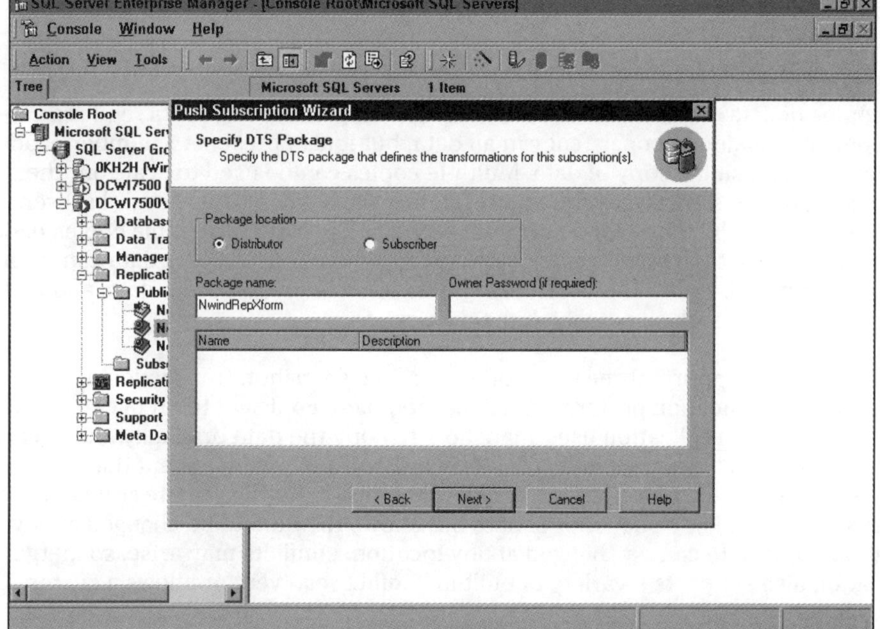

Figure 20-32: Specifying a replication DTS package

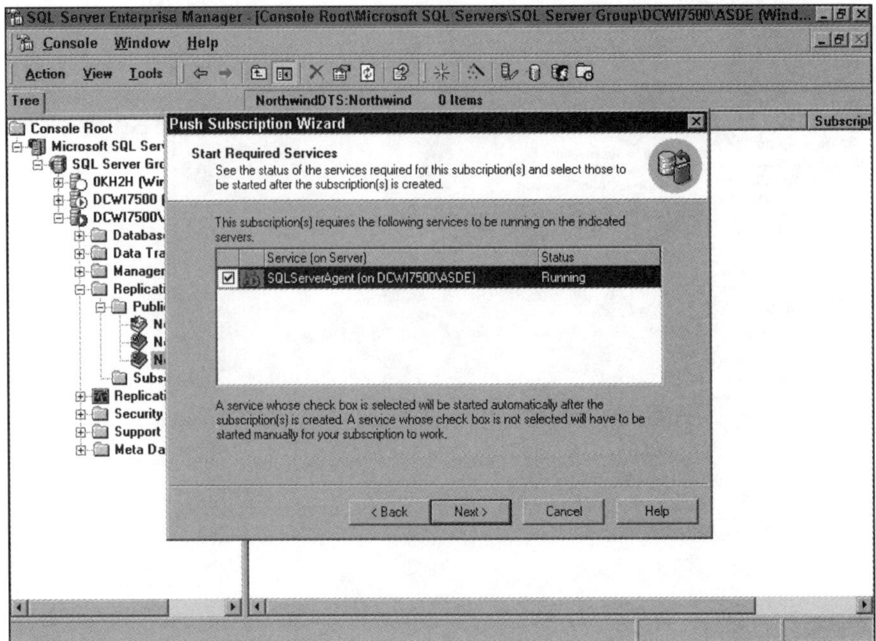

Figure 20-33: Starting the SQL Server Agents

Summary

Replication is a technology that provides a number of mechanisms for maintaining copies of data on multiple servers. Having multiple copies of data requires careful control to maintain consistency in all data, but it also presents a number of advantages over a single copy of data. Multiple copies can be used to scale out the database and take advantage of the performance gains when using several servers, each of which may be tuned for a particular application. Having multiple copies of data also allows data to be moved closer to users who need it. Closer data can mean lower network traffic and costs, lower network latency to access data, and more autonomy for each site at which the data exists.

SQL Server supports three types of replication: snapshot, transactional, and merge. Snapshot replication performs periodic, complete copies of the replicated data. Transactional replication uses snapshots to copy the data originally and occasionally to refresh the data, but it relies primarily on a log reader agent that copies the results of each transaction and transfers the results to the remote server. Merge replication makes a snapshot of data but allows the data to be changed at any location. When data can be changed at any location, conflicts may arise, so merge replication also supports a variety of built-in conflict resolvers or allows a custom resolver to be created. Transactional and snapshot replication both support two mechanisms for modifying data at any location but place more stringent controls on those data modifications. The modifications that occur on the copied data are brought back to the original copy either through a distributed transaction or through a message queue.

✦ ✦ ✦

CHAPTER 21

Using Transactions to Distribute Data

✦ ✦ ✦ ✦

In This Chapter

Accessing external data using OpenRowset in an ad hoc query

Accessing external data using OpenDatasource in an ad hoc query

Linking to an external server

Accessing external data using linked servers

Understanding transactions

Understanding distributed transactions and the two-phase commit

Understanding Microsoft Transaction Server (MTS) and Component Services

✦ ✦ ✦ ✦

Distributing data across multiple locations and data formats is the norm in many companies. Users can connect to external data sources such as Access from their MSDE database on an ad hoc basis using the `OpenRowset` function in MSDE. Or they can use the `OpenDatasource` function to connect to external data sources, such as remote MSDE databases, that adhere to the three-part naming convention (database.owner.tablename). When users need to regularly connect to those external sources, they can link to the remote server using the `sp_addlinkedserver` stored procedure. After linking to a server, they can then use a shorter syntax for referencing it in their SQL statements.

Transactions provide users with a mechanism for ensuring that all parts of the transaction either succeed or fail, so that data does not become fragmented. In MSDE, the BEGIN TRANSACTION statement followed by the COMMIT TRANSACTION or ROLLBACK TRANSACTION can be used to create a transaction. If the data is on multiple servers, then users can execute distributed transactions. The Distributed Transaction Coordinator manages distributed transactions from the server that initiates the transaction. Users can also take advantage of distributed transactions, database connection pooling, and server resource power by utilizing Microsoft Transaction Server to manage their business layer objects.

Referencing Multiple Servers in Ad Hoc Queries

One way to access data that is on a different server than the MSDE database is through a distributed ad hoc query. If the user does not need to access the information frequently, then accessing the data through a distributed ad hoc query is a good choice. Information can be retrieved from multiple sources on an ad hoc basis. If the user will need to access that data frequently, then linking that server should be considered (as is described in the next section).

The MSDE `OpenRowset` and `OpenDatasource` functions enable the user to retrieve information from OLE DB data sources. The `OpenRowset` function can be used to retrieve data from any OLE DB data source that can return a rowset. The `OpenDatasource` function can be used only with providers that support the multipart object name: database.owner.tablename (for example, msdesample.dbo.patient). The `OpenRowset` and `OpenDatasource` functions cannot be used interchangeably. However, there are some data sources that are supported by both, such as MSDE and SQL Server.

The OpenRowset function

If a user's MSDE database contains patient medical history, billing address, and other such information, and the user's Access database contains the patient contact information, then the user could look up each patient's e-mail and home and work phone number by using the `OpenRowset` function to retrieve the information from Access by running the following statement against the MSDE database:

```
SELECT PatientId, Email, HPhone, WPhone
FROM OPENROWSET('Microsoft.Jet.OLEDB.4.0', 'c:\my
     documents\patientdb.mdb';'admin';'',Contacts)
```

The first part of the SELECT statement resembles a normal SELECT statement. Then, the `FROM` clause makes use of the `OpenRowset` function to specify the OLE DB provider information that is needed to connect to the patientdb.mdb Access database. After the database path, the user ID and password are specified, followed last by the name of the table. The above example retrieves the patient ID, patient e-mail, home phone, and work phone from the Access database.

If after running this query, the user realizes that the patient's last and first names need to be included to identify with whom the contact information goes, the user must get that information from the patient table in the MSDE database because patient names are not contained in the Contacts table in the Access database. The user can join the Patient table on the MSDE database to the Contacts table in the Access database together in a single query to get the patient name, e-mail, and phone numbers.

```
SELECT p.PatientId, p.FirstName, p.LastName, c.Email, c.HPhone,
       c.WPhone
FROM OPENROWSET('Microsoft.Jet.OLEDB.4.0', 'c:\my
     documents\patientdb.mdb';'admin';'',Contacts) as c
JOIN patient p ON c.PatientId = p.PatientId
```

The OpenRowset function is specified in the first part of the FROM clause to obtain data from the Access Contacts table, followed by the JOIN to the Patient table. The OpenRowset function can be used in any part of the SQL statement that would usually use the explicit table name, such as in the FROM clause or after an UPDATE or DELETE statement. So if the user decides to update some data in the Access Contacts table from MSDE, it can be done. To update Patient #1's home phone number to (317) 888-9999, the following statement could be run against MSDE:

```
UPDATE OPENROWSET('Microsoft.Jet.OLEDB.4.0', 'c:\my
       documents\patientdb.mdb';'admin';'',Contacts)
SET HPhone = '(317) 888-9999'
WHERE PatientId = 1
```

In this example, the OpenRowset function is used following the update statement instead of the FROM clause. That is because with an UPDATE statement, the table to be updated must be specified immediately following the UPDATE statement itself.

With the OpenRowset function, users are not limited to joining to databases that are stored in a single external file as they are with Access. They can also link to databases such as MSDE and SQL Server. For example, if the Contacts table resides on a remote MSDE database instead of in the Access database, a user could execute a query against the local MSDE database to join to the remote database to retrieve the patient phone list as shown below:

```
SELECT p.PatientId, p.FirstName, p.LastName, c.Email, c.HPhone,
       c.WPhone
FROM OPENROWSET('SQLOLEDB', 'MSDEDb2';'sa';'','select
     PatientId, Email, HPhone, WPhone from
     msdesample.dbo.contacts') as c
JOIN patient p ON c.PatientId = p.PatientId
```

This example uses the OpenRowset function to connect to the Contacts table on the remote MSDEDb2 database and joins it to the local Patient table. By using the OLE DB provider for ODBC, the same result can be accomplished:

```
SELECT p.PatientId, p.FirstName, p.LastName, c.Email, c.HPhone,
       c.WPhone
FROM OPENROWSET('MSDASQL', 'DRIVER={SQL SERVER};SERVER=MSDEDb2;
     UID=sa;PWD=', msdesample2.dbo.contacts) as c
JOIN patient p ON c.PatientId = p.PatientId
```

In the example above, the MSDASQL provider is specified. It will use the ODBC driver for SQL Server (that is, MSDE) to connect to the remote MSDEDb2 database. Notice how the three-part name is used: msdesample2.dbo.contacts. The above example assumes that the user has a remote MSDE server called MSDEDb2 and a database on that server called msdesample2. Either of the above examples (OLE DB or OLE DB using ODBC) will work well to connect to remote MSDE databases. It is really a matter of preference.

The OpenDatasource function

In addition to using the `OpenRowset` function to connect to remote servers in ad hoc queries, users can also use the `OpenDatasource` function. However, the `OpenDatasource` function cannot be used to retrieve information from Access because the `OpenDatasource` function supports only multipart object references. The `OpenDatasource` function can be used to retrieve data from the remote MSDE database, as in the examples shown before:

```
SELECT PatientId, Email, HPhone, WPhone
FROM OPENDATASOURCE ('SQLOLEDB', 'Data Source=MSDEDb2;User
Id=sa;Password=') .MSDESample2.dbo.Contacts
```

The `FROM` clause contains the `OpenDatasource` function, followed by the OLE DB provider information and the three-part object name. The `OpenDatasource` function can be used only with databases that can be accessed using the three-part object name, such as MSDE, SQL Server, and Oracle.

If a user wants to retrieve that patient phone list again and some data exists in the local MSDE database while the contact information exists in the remote MSDE database, then the user can employ the `OpenDatasource` function to accomplish that result. Here's how:

```
SELECT p.PatientId, p.FirstName, p.LastName, c.Email, c.HPhone,
       c.WPhone
FROM OPENDATASOURCE ('SQLOLEDB', 'Data Source=MSDEDb2;User
Id=sa;Password=') .MSDESample2.dbo.Contacts as C
JOIN patient p ON c.patientid = p.patientid
```

The example above is similar to the prior one, except that the table join to the local Patient table was added. Just as with the `OpenRowset` function, the `OpenDatasource` function can be used in any part of a SQL statement where a table name would normally be used. Instead of being used in the `FROM` clause, the `OpenDatasource` function can also be used as part of an UPDATE or DELETE statement, directly following the statement itself, as shown below:

```
UPDATE OPENDATASOURCE ('SQLOLEDB', 'Data Source=MSDEDb2;User
Id=sa;Password=') .MSDESample2.dbo.Contacts
SET Email = 'somewherenew@yahoo.com' WHERE patientid = 2
```

In this example, the OpenDatasource function follows the UPDATE statement. This example will update the e-mail address in the remote Contacts table for patient 2. Being able to connect to remote and external databases on an ad hoc basis is an easy and powerful tool, but again, should be used only when the user does not need to connect to them on a regular basis.

Using Linked Servers for Frequent Access

The first step in working with a linked server is to *register* the server so that the MSDE database knows that it exists. After a remote server has been linked, users can then retrieve data from it.

Linking and configuring linked servers

To link to a remote server that will be used frequently, the sp_addlinkedserver stored procedure in MSDE should be used. Here is the syntax:

```
sp_addlinkedserver [@server =] 'server'
    [, [@srvproduct =] 'product_name']
    [, [@provider =] 'provider_name']
    [, [@datasrc =] 'data_source']
    [, [@location =] 'location']
    [, [@provstr =] 'provider_string']
    [, [@catalog =] 'catalog']
```

Each of the above-mentioned parameters can be passed into the sp_addlinked server stored procedure. Not all of these parameters are required in order to link to a server, but each has a specific use.

- **@server**— This is the name chosen to call the linked server. Because this name will be used in future queries that reference the remote server, it should be distinct and easy to remember.
- **@srvproduct**— This parameter is the OLE DB name for the product the user wants to link to. Some examples are SQL Server, Oracle, and OLE DB Provider for Jet.
- **@provider**— This parameter is the unique program ID of the OLE DB provider that is stored in the registry. Some examples of valid values for the provider parameter are SQLOLEDB, MSDASQL, and Microsoft.Jet.OLEDB.4.0.
- **@datasrc**— This parameter is the name of the data source as OLE DB interprets it. In the case of an Access database, it is the complete path to the file. In the case of SQL Server, it can be the servername or instancename. Two examples are c:\my documents\patientdb.mdb and MSDEDb2.

✦ **@location** — This parameter is the location of the database as OLE DB interprets it.

✦ **@provstr** — This parameter is the unique data source connection string specific to OLE DB. Some examples are DRIVER={SQL Server}; SERVER=MSDEDb2; UID=sa; and PWD=.

✦ **@catalog** — This parameter specifies the catalog that should be used when connecting to the OLE DB provider.

If a user is frequently using ad hoc queries to connect to the patient Contacts table in the Access database, the user could create a link to that server for efficiency's sake with the following code:

```
EXECUTE sp_addlinkedserver @server = 'PatientContacts',
        @provider = 'Microsoft.Jet.OLEDB.4.0',
        @srvproduct = 'OLE DB Provider for Jet',
        @datasrc = 'c:\my documents\patientdb.mdb'
```

The above statement defines a new linked server called PatientContacts using the OLE DB provider for Jet. The location of the Access database that is being linked is c:\my documernts\patientdb.mdb. Only a few of the parameters that can be passed to the `sp_addlinkedserver` stored procedure are used in this case. After executing the above statement, the user will receive a message indicating that the server has been added (if that database is on the user's computer in that location).

Now that the Access database is successfully linked, MSDE must be granted permission to connect to it. To do so, the user must execute the `sp_addlinkedsrvlogin` stored procedure. The following example demonstrates how the user can grant permission to connect to the PatientContacts linked database from MSDE:

```
EXECUTE Sp_addlinkedsrvlogin PatientContacts, False, sa, null,
        null
```

The `sp_addlinkedsrvlogin` stored procedure is called and passed to the linked server name PatientContacts: `False` for the UseSelf parameter, `sa` for the LocalLogin parameter, and null for the Remote User and Remote Password logins. The UseSelf parameter determines which login id will be used to log in to the remote server. If `True` is specified, then the logged in user's credentials will be used to log in to the remote server, and the Remote User and Remote Password arguments will be ignored. In the above example, `False` has been specified for the UseSelf parameter, which will ignore the logged in user's credentials and will instead log in to the remote server with the values specified for Remote User and Remote Password. The effect of the above statement is that MSDE will be capable of connecting to the Access database on behalf of the user. For more details about how the linked server login options can be set, consult the SQL Server books online.

If a user wants to create a link to the remote MSDE database used in prior examples, it can be done as follows:

```
EXECUTE sp_addlinkedserver @server = 'PatientContacts',
        @provider = 'SQLOLEDB',
        @srvproduct = '',
        @datasrc = 'MSDESample2'
```

This time, the OLE DB provider for SQL Server (that is, MSDE) is being used. The data source parameter is set to the name of the server and/or instance, which, in this example, is MSDESample2.

The `sp_addlinkedsrvlogin` stored procedure must be run to assign login permissions to the remote database as in the previous example.

At some point after creating a linked server, the user will need to know how to drop the link to that server. To drop a link to a server, the `sp_dropserver` stored procedure must be used in the following way:

```
EXECUTE sp_dropserver ServerName[, DropLogins]
```

The `sp_dropserver` call is followed by the `ServerName` parameter and an optional `DropLogins` parameter. The server name is the given name of the linked server. The `DropLogins` parameter will drop all logins associated with that server. If the user has existing logins assigned to the linked server and tries to drop the server, it will generate an error. Thus, the `DropLogins` option will drop the logins at the same time it drops the server. Here's an example of how the user can drop the PatientContacts linked server and any associated logins:

```
EXECUTE sp_dropserver PatientContacts, DropLogins
```

Dropping means that the link is removed from the database. It does not mean that any data will be harmed in any way. The example above will eliminate the PatientContacts as a linked server in the MSDE database.

Using data on linked servers

After a user has linked to a remote server, a shortened syntax can be used to reference it in SQL statements. For example, to select from the Contacts table in the Access patientcontacts linked database, the user can use the following syntax:

```
SELECT *
FROM patientcontacts...contacts
```

A four-part syntax is used, but only two parts of the syntax are specified. The server name is followed by three periods and the table name on the remote server. If instead of running a SELECT statement against the linked server, a user wanted to issue an UPDATE statement, the user could use the same type of syntax following the UPDATE statement. Here's an example:

```
UPDATE patientcontacts...contacts
SET Email = 'somewhere@yahoo.com'
WHERE patientid = 2
```

Understanding the Distributed Transaction Coordinator and Microsoft Transaction Server

Whenever a transaction is used, the Distributed Transaction Coordinator (DTC) on the machine where the transaction is originating will coordinate the transaction with the other servers. Microsoft Transaction Server (MTS) is an extension of DTC. A user can register a COM object with MTS on an NT Server and let MTS handle the creation and destruction of the object in a more efficient way. Windows 2000 Server has integrated the features of MTS into the operating system and calls them Component Services.

Understanding transactions

With a database transaction, there may be several database changes that need to be made in the underlying tables, but if any one of those changes fails, the whole transaction is rolled back. The database can become inconsistent if a user is updating various tables with related data and one of the updates fails. Without using a transaction, some of those tables will be updated with the new information, but some of them will not. By using database transactions, these data inconsistency problems can be eliminated.

A transaction uses a two-phase process. The first phase is called the preparation phase, during which all of the SQL statements are executed against the database to see if they are successful. This is often referred to as the BEGIN TRANSACTION phase. After the server determines that all of the SQL statements are successful, the second phase begins. The second phase commits all of the changes to the database if they are successful or rolls all of them back if one of the SQL statements is unsuccessful. This is often called the COMMIT or ROLLBACK phase of the transaction.

In MSDE, the user can use the BEGIN TRANSACTION statement to start the first phase, the COMMIT TRANSACTION statement to commit the successful transaction, or the ROLLBACK TRANSACTION statement to roll back the unsuccessful transaction.

```
BEGIN TRANSACTION

DELETE FROM patient
```

```
WHERE patientid = 2

DELETE FROM contacts
WHERE patientid = 2

DELETE FROM charges
WHERE patientid = 2

IF @@ERROR = 0
    COMMIT TRANSACTION
ELSE
    ROLLBACK TRANSACTION
```

The BEGIN TRANSACTION statement appears first, followed by the SQL statements. If any statement fails, then the transaction is rolled back, and none of the deletes will take place. If all of the deletes are successful, they will all be committed to the database. The example above deals with a single local MSDE server. There is also a BEGIN DISTRIBUTED TRANSACTION statement in MSDE that can be implemented when a user is dealing with multiple (distributed) servers, such as those discussed earlier in this chapter.

If a user attempts to make changes to the Patient table on the local MSDE database and to the Contacts table on the linked remote MSDE database and if either of those changes fails, then the user will want to make sure the transaction gets rolled back so that the data will not become inconsistent. Here's the SQL syntax to accomplish this:

```
BEGIN DISTRIBUTED TRANSACTION

DELETE FROM patient
WHERE patientid = 2

DELETE FROM PatientContacts...Contacts
WHERE patientid = 2

IF @@ERROR = 0
    COMMIT TRANSACTION
ELSE
    ROLLBACK TRANSACTION
```

The BEGIN DISTRIBUTED TRANSACTION statement appears first in order to let MSDE know to prepare for the transaction. The first DELETE statement is deleting the patient record for patient #2 on the local MSDE database. The second DELETE statement is deleting the contact record for that patient on the linked server PatientContacts. After both of these DELETE statements are attempted, if either fails, then they are both rolled back. Otherwise, they are both committed to the database.

Distributed Transaction Coordinator

Whenever a distributed transaction is used, as in the previous example, the Microsoft Distributed Transaction Coordinator (DTC) coordinates the transaction from the machine where the transaction was started. The DTC will send the appropriate SQL statements to each remote and local server and will wait for a response. If any server returns a failure, then all of the statements are rolled back. If all of the statements succeed, then the DTC instructs each server to commit the transaction.

DTC is a service that once was just part of SQL Server; now, however, it is a core component of Microsoft Transaction Server and Component Services. DTC is also installed with MSDE. If the machine starting the transaction does not have DTC installed or running, then the distributed transaction will fail. To start DTC, if it is not already running, a user must open the Service Manager program, choose MSDTC as the service, and click Start. The Service Manager program is typically added to the startup group as part of the MSDE install. It should appear in the taskbar as an image of a server with a green or red arrow.

The MS DTC Administrative Console is a graphical tool that enables the user to see information about the distributed transactions managed by DTC as well as to specify some of the DTC settings. A user does not automatically have the Administrative Console with MSDE. The Administrative Console is one of the graphical tools that are part of the SQL Server installation program, just as the Enterprise Manager and Query Analyzer programs. The Administrative Console can be used to specify the log file for the distributed transactions, see any current transactions, and see the number of distributed transactions that have executed since the DTC service was last started. The Statistics tab, shown in Figure 21-1, displays the number of active transactions, the number of transactions committed, and the number of transactions aborted when the DTC service was started, as well as other helpful information.

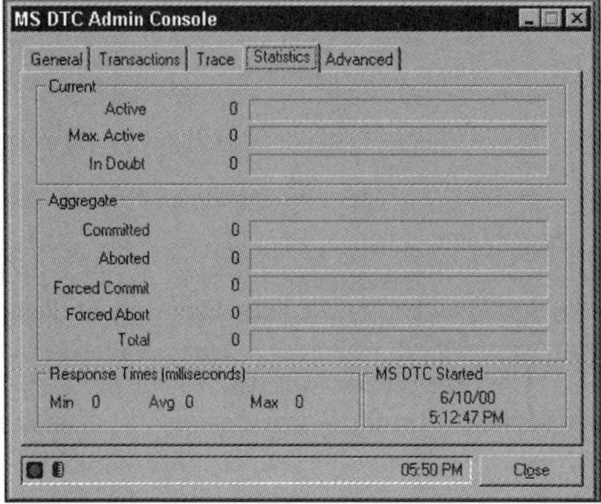

Figure 21-1: MS DTC Administrative Console Statistics tab

A user can work with distributed transactions from MSDE using the syntax shown earlier (BEGIN DISTRIBUTED TRANSACTION, and so on) and can even use transactions from software applications such as Visual Basic (such as with ADO's `begintrans` and `committrans` methods of the connection object).

MTS provides another powerful way to manage transactions as well as other benefits.

Microsoft Transaction Server

On Windows NT Server 4.0, MTS can be installed from the NT 4.0 Option Pack or the Visual Studio 6 Enterprise Edition installation programs. On Windows 2000 Server, the features of MTS are built into the operating system and called Component Services. Since Component Services is a superset of MTS, we will refer to MTS, but the following sections are equally for the Windows 2000 platform.

MTS is used by a number of developers to implement a three-tiered architecture. A typical three-tier architecture scenario consists of the front-end user interface running on the client, some or all of the business rules running on a server (such as NT), and the database actions running on the database server. By having the servers process the business rules and the database activities, the client machine is relieved of much of the processing. MTS fits into this three-tiered scenario because it can manage COM objects (often called DLLs) in the business rules tier, keep COM objects loaded in memory, and keep database connections open for a certain amount of time behind the scenes so that when the next client requests that COM object or connection, it will already be open. This can be a huge performance benefit, especially in large-scale applications. MTS cannot keep the COM object or connection open indefinitely, or the server will become bogged down, so time out limits can be specified. MTS also manages the transactions behind the scenes, so if any of them fail, the whole transaction is rolled back.

Users can create their own MTS component and take advantage of its benefits by using any programming tool, such as Visual Basic or Visual C++, that enables them to create a COM object as an ActiveX DLL. After the COM object is created, it has to be registered with MTS. The client and development machines have to be made aware of how to communicate with the MTS server before the COM object can be used. After creating and running a setup program to make the development machine aware of the MTS COM object, a user can then create or change the front-end or other COM objects to call the MTS COM object.

Step 1: Create the MTS component

The first step is to use Visual Basic to create the COM object that will run under MTS. To do so, the user should open Visual Basic and create a new ActiveX DLL project. Then the user needs to add a reference to MTS and ADO to the project by selecting Project ➪ References ➪ ActiveX Data Objects 2.0 Library (or the highest version available) ➪ Microsoft Transaction Server Type Library. After adding these references, the user should change the name of the class module from class1 to something more meaningful. At this point, the user can start adding the code to the class module as shown in Listing 21-1.

Listing 21-1: Sample Visual Basic Code to Create ActiveX DLL to Run in MTS

```
Option Explicit

Public Function GetRecords(strConnection As String, strSQL As
String) As ADODB.Recordset

'The purpose of this function is to execute the SQL statement
'passed in from the client and return the recordset to the
'client.  This function should be used for selects.

On Error GoTo GetRecords_Error

Dim oContext As ObjectContext

Dim oConnection As ADODB.Connection
Dim rsResults As ADODB.Recordset

Set oContext = GetObjectContext()

Set oConnection = GetConnection(strConnection)
Set rsResults = New ADODB.Recordset

rsResults.CursorLocation = adUseClient
rsResults.Open strSQL, oConnection, adOpenStatic,
adLockOptimistic
rsResults.ActiveConnection = Nothing

Set GetRecords = rsResults

rsResults.Close
Set rsResults = Nothing

oConnection.Close
Set oConnection = Nothing

oContext.SetComplete

Exit Function

GetRecords_Error:
    Set rsResults = Nothing
    Set oConnection = Nothing
```

```
    oContext.SetAbort
    Err.Raise "MTSDb - GetRecords", Err.Number, Err.Description
    Exit Function

End Function

Public Function RunSQL(strConnection As String, strSQL As
String) As Boolean

'The purpose of this function is to execute the SQL statement
'and let the client know that the statement was successful.
'This function should be used for deletes and updates.

On Error GoTo RunSQL_Error

Dim oContext As ObjectContext

Dim oConnection As ADODB.Connection

Set oContext = GetObjectContext()

Set oConnection = GetConnection(strConnection)

   oConnection.BeginTrans
oConnection.Execute strSQL


oConnection.Close
Set oConnection = Nothing

oConnection.CommitTrans

RunSQL = True

oContext.SetComplete

Exit Function

RunSQL_Error:
    Set oConnection = Nothing
    oConnection.RollbackTrans
    oContext.SetAbort
    RunSQL = False
    Err.Raise "MTSDb - RunSQL", Err.Number, Err.Description
    Exit Function

End Function

Private Function GetConnection(strConnection As String) As
ADODB.Connection
```

Continued

Listing 21-1 *(continued)*

```
'This is an internal function that uses the connection string
'passed in from the client to establish a connection to the
database.
On Error GoTo getconnection_error

Dim oConnect As New ADODB.Connection

oConnect.Open strConnection

Set GetConnection = oConnect

oConnect.Close
Set oConnect = Nothing

Exit Function

getconnection_error:

    Err.Raise "MTSDb - GetConnection", Err.Number,
Err.Description
    Exit Function

End Function
```

The code in Listing 21-1 has three functions: `GetRecords`, `RunSQL`, and `GetConnection`. The `GetRecords` function will return a recordset to the client based on the connection string and SQL statement passed to it. The `RunSQL` function will execute the SQL statement that is passed to it and let the client know whether that statement succeeded. The `GetConnection` function is an internal function used by the other two to connect to the database.

Now, the user needs to set the threading model of the project to apartment threading. This can be done in the Project Properties on the General tab. The project name should also be set here. It will become the default name of the DLL and will be referenced in MTS by that name. A project description may be optionally added in the Project Description field on the General tab.

Next, the user must set the transaction mode of the class module to UsesTransaction by selecting the class module and changing the `MTSTransactionMode` property to 3—Uses Transaction. This will enable the component to support transactions if the calling program wants there to be a transaction.

When the user is finished coding the DLL, the project should be saved. Then the user can compile the project into a DLL by selecting File ➪ Make dllname.dll. An ActiveX DLL, or, more appropriately, a COM object, that can be used by MTS has successfully been created.

Step 2: Add the DLL to MTS

MTS must be informed that it should handle the COM object, meaning that the COM object will run in the process space on the server and MTS will manage it. To add the COM object to MTS, Microsoft Transaction Server must be opened. The user should select and double-click the server that the COM object is going to run on (which is likely to be the same computer running MTS) and go into the Packages for that server. Then, select File ➪ New. The Package Wizard shown in Figure 21-2 will appear.

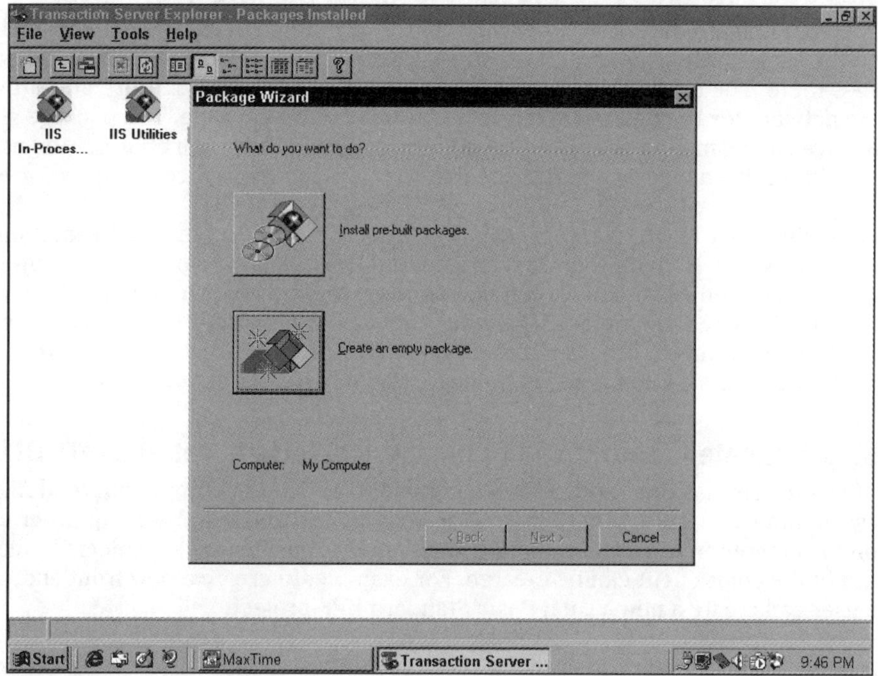

Figure 21-2: Microsoft Transaction Server Package Wizard

The user should click the button to Create an empty package, name the package an appropriate name, and click Finish. The new package should appear among the other packages listed on that machine. From there, the user should do the following:

1. Double-click on the package that was just created and then double-click on the components of the package.
2. Select File ➪ New and then click the Install New Components button.
3. Click the Add Files button and browse the network to locate the appropriate DLL file. Then click the Finish button.

The COM object has been successfully added to MTS. While still in MTS, the setup program (as described in step 3 below) can be created to register the MTS component on the development and client machines.

In Windows 2000, Component Services is accessed through the Administrative Tools in Control Panel. MTS packages are the equivalent of Component Services applications, and rather than using the File menu item, use the Action menu item to create new objects.

Step 3: Create the setup program to install the MTS component

In MTS, to create the setup program, the user should go back to the list of packages on the server. The user should see the MTSDbSample package among all the packages there. The user should right-click on that package, select Export, and browse the network for the desired location to save the setup package. The package should be given a meaningful name and saved. After clicking the Export button, the user should receive a message indicating that the package was successfully exported.

In the directory in which the package is saved, a .pak file is created. In addition, a client directory is created underneath containing a setup program. The setup program can be run on the development computer and on any client computers to register the MTS COM object. The setup program will install a mini copy of the COM object in the c:\program files\remote applications directory, which will contain the information it needs to locate the MTS server.

Step 4: Create the front end or business objects to call the MTS DLL

After the user has created the MTS component, added the component to MTS, created the setup program to install the component, and run the setup program on the computer, the front-end application and/or business rules objects to make use of the component can be created. For example, to create a new front end, a user can create a new Visual Basic Standard EXE project.

A reference should be added to the recently created and installed server version of the MTS COM object. To do so, the user should select Project ➪ References and choose the MTS component from the list. It may be listed by the description given to it in the VB project and not readily apparent, in which case it may be necessary to browse the network to the c:\program files\remote applications location.

References to any other libraries, such as ADO, that the program will use must also be added. After the user is finished coding the front-end program, it can be distributed by creating a setup package. The client program and the setup program for the MTS component must both be distributed. If the MTS component setup program is not run on the client machine, then the client will not be able to find or use the MTS component, and the front end will generate an error.

Listing 22-2 is an example of Visual Basic code that calls an MTS DLL to retrieve records from the MSDE database:

Listing 22-2: Sample Visual Basic Code to Use the MTS Component

```
Dim oMTSDb As MTSDb.clsMTSDb
Dim rsResults as ADODB.recordset
Dim strConn as string

StrConn = "Data Source=MSDESample;User ID=sa;Password=;"

'create a new instance of the MTS object
Set oMTSDb = New MTSDb.clsMTSDb

'call the GetRecords method in the MTS object to retrieve
'the query results
Set rsResults = oMTSDb.GetRecords(strConn, "select * from
                patient")

Set oMTSDb = nothing
```

The code in Listing 22-2 calls an MTS object called MTSDb with a class module called clsMTSDb. After declaring the MTS object, the `GetRecords` method is called to retrieve the results from the SQL statement. The `GetRecords` method in the MTS object handles the connection to the MSDE database, retrieves the results, and then passes them back to this routine. The code for the MTS object referenced in this example can be found in the Step 1 section of this chapter.

Step 5: Turn on connection pooling

To turn on connection pooling for the MSDE database:

1. In the Control Panel on the server on which MTS is running, open ODBC Data Sources (32 Bit).
2. Select the Connection Pooling tab.
3. Choose the SQL Server driver from the list (which is what MSDE uses) and double-click. Connection pooling is turned on to the selected driver, and the connection time out can be set.

If the user uses MTS to handle all database transactions for programs and turns on connection pooling, then similar connection strings will be kept open and reused. What this means to the user is that for the duration specified in the time out, MTS will keep an active connection to the database open. When the next client requests a similar connection, MTS will just reuse the one that is already open. This can result in a significant performance boost in applications, especially across the network when the time to connect to the database is often longer than the time it takes to run the SQL statement itself.

A user should consider creating an application user ID and password on the database server so that the program uses the same connection string every time. Connection pooling only works with similar connections. If the connection string changes to include each user ID and password, then the user may not gain any advantage from pooled connections.

The connection pooling feature of ODBC and MTS is one of the biggest advantages to using an MTS component to handle all database connections and retrieval of data.

Summary

If a user has multiple servers or data sources involved, connecting to those different sources can be tedious. MSDE has functions that help alleviate this problem. On an ad hoc basis, the user can connect to external data sources such as Access, for example, from the MSDE database by using the `OpenRowset` function. Or the user can implement the `OpenDatasource` function to connect to external data sources that adhere to the three-part naming convention (database.owner.tablename). If the user needs to regularly connect to those external sources, the server can be linked using the `sp_addlinkedserver` stored procedure. After linking to a server, the user can employ a shorter syntax for referencing it in SQL statements.

Using distributed transactions with rollbacks and commits is another important capability. The Distributed Transaction Coordinator manages distributed transactions from the server that initiates the transaction. Microsoft Transaction Server is an extremely powerful software package that can be used to take advantage of distributed transactions, as well as database connection pooling, and to have DLLs run in the server's process space instead of on the client machine.

✦ ✦ ✦

PART

VI

Database Administration

This part explores the methods for starting and stopping required services and explains the existing back ups and their uses in safeguarding and recovering data. It clarifies the function and use of the different programming tools for accessing data from the MSDE database and explains how to administer the complex security in MSDE. It goes on to explore MSDE's flexible capabilities for automating administrative tasks on a database and database server, and explains the methods of creating Web pages.

✦ ✦ ✦ ✦

In This Part

✦ ✦ ✦ ✦

CHAPTER 22

Controlling MSDE

✦ ✦ ✦ ✦

In This Chapter

Starting and stopping the SQL Server service

Starting and stopping the SQL Server Agent service

Starting and stopping the Distributed Transaction Coordinator

✦ ✦ ✦ ✦

An important part of planning for and administering MSDE is to make sure that the services are running when they are needed and to be able to stop and restart the services as required. Special considerations for starting services may come into play when recovering from disasters and when performing certain maintenance functions.

There are three basic categories of service controllers: programs with a graphical interface, programs with a command-line interface, and APIs for use with other programs.

MSDE Control Mechanisms

There are three programs with a graphical interface that can be used to control the MSDE services:

- ✦ The Service Manager is installed by default with MSDE. Its only purpose is to control the MSDE services. It also adds an icon to the system tray, which not only allows controlled services but also provides a real-time display of the status of the service.
- ✦ Enterprise Manager is the general-purpose management tool for MSDE and SQL Server. It does not ship with MSDE, but is available in the Developer Edition of SQL Server.
- ✦ The services applet is available in the Control Panel on computers with Windows NT and Windows 2000. It provides control for all services, including those associated with MSDE.

There are three kinds of command-line interfaces for controlling services:

✦ The Service Control Manager command-line interface provides complete control for services on Windows NT and Windows 2000 and can also be used to control the MSDE services on Windows 98.

✦ The `net` command, available on Windows NT and Windows 2000, provides the means for viewing running services and starting, pausing, and stopping services, including those associated with MSDE.

✦ The SQL Server service and the SQL Server Agent service each have a command-line executable command that can be used to start the service for maintenance and troubleshooting.

There are two programmatic interfaces for controlling services in MSDE:

✦ SQL-NS, the SQL Namespace, provides all of the same functionality as Enterprise Manager and is an object-oriented interface.

✦ SQL-DMO, the SQL Distributed Management Objects, is an object-oriented interface for performing any kind of management function in MSDE. This includes all of the functionality available with Enterprise Manager or the Data Definition Language (DDL) components of SQL.

One additional mechanism for controlling the SQL Server service is with SQL commands. A `shutdown` command within SQL allows the database engine to be stopped. SQL does not include commands for starting the database engine or for starting or stopping the SQL Server Agent service.

The Service Manager

The Service Manager is a program that is installed with MSDE. By default, it is available in the Start menu in the Microsoft SQL Server group. It also places an icon in the system tray in the lower right corner of the screen.

The Service Manager can be invoked from the Start menu or by double-clicking the icon in the system tray. The GUI for the Service Manager is shown in Figure 22-1.

Figure 22-1: The SQL Server Service Manager

The drop-down list at the top of the Service Manager dialog box displays the name of the server that is currently being monitored. This drop-down list is disabled on Windows 98, displaying only the name of the current server. On Windows NT and Windows 2000, the drop-down list allows the user to select the server they would like to monitor and control.

The second drop-down list in Service Manager displays the name of the service that is currently being monitored and controlled. The status of this service is shown with an icon in the white circle on the left of the dialog box.

- ✦ A green triangle indicates that the service is running.
- ✦ Two vertical black bars indicate that the service has been paused.
- ✦ A red square indicates that the service has been stopped.

To change the service that is being monitored and controlled, select the desired service from the drop-down list. To start, pause, or stop any service, select the desired service from the drop-down list and then use the buttons on the right side of the dialog box.

When you start and stop services, it may take from a few seconds to several minutes for the process to complete. The SQL Server service must run the recovery process on all databases when it starts, and it attempts to end all transactions before it shuts down. The SQL Server Agent service may be configured to initiate jobs automatically when it starts, and it has a configurable waiting period for jobs to end if any are in progress when the Stop command is given.

The check box at the bottom of the dialog box allows you to configure each service to start automatically when the operating system starts. On Windows 98, only the SQL Server service and the Distributed Transaction Coordinator (DTC) service can be auto-started.

On Windows NT and Windows 2000, all three services can be auto-started. The SQL Server Agent service is dependent on the SQL Server service, so whenever the Agent starts, the SQL Server service also starts. Conversely, when the SQL Server service is stopped, the SQL Server Agent service also stops if it is running.

When the service displayed in the Service Manager is changed, the icon and status of the icon in the system tray change to reflect the new service. Even when the Service Manager has been closed, the icon in the system tray continues to reflect the last service that was displayed in Service Manager.

The service displayed in the system tray can also be changed by right-clicking the icon in the system tray, choosing Current service on \\servername, and selecting the service to be displayed. The services can also be started, paused, and stopped by right-clicking the icon in the system tray and choosing the appropriate menu item.

Pausing the SQL Server service does not stop the functions of the service, but it does prevent new connections from being established. Pausing can be a convenient prelude to stopping the server and can also be used for performing maintenance or testing with a specific set of users.

The component of the Service Manager that runs the icon in the system tray polls the displayed service periodically to determine its state. The default period that it uses between polls is five seconds. To change the polling interval, right-click the icon in the system tray, choose Options, and then enter a length of time in seconds. The polling of the service is visible as a small red dot at the lower left corner of the icon that appears during the poll.

The options for the Service Manager icon can also be used to turn off the verification of service control actions. When verification is turned on, the user is prompted for confirmation before starting, pausing, or stopping any services.

The Enterprise Manager

Once an instance of MSDE is registered in Enterprise Manager, that instance can be fully controlled from within Enterprise Manager.

Server registrations in Enterprise Manager are organized into groups. The groups exist solely for the purpose of administrative convenience in locating a particular server or instance. The default group is called SQL Server Group, but other groups can be created by right-clicking the Microsoft SQL Servers container and choosing New SQL Server Group. A new group is created and immediately displayed in the left pane hierarchy.

To register a server in Enterprise Manager, right-click any existing group and choose New SQL Server Registration. Depending on previous configuration, you will be presented with either a wizard or a dialog box.

The registration wizard walks the user through the steps of registering a server. The first screen is the wizard welcome screen. It contains a check box that allows the user to choose not to use the wizard in the future. The second screen allows the user to choose a server to register. It displays a list of known, available, unregistered servers on the left. Even if a server is not displayed in the list, the user can type its name and click Add. When a server is added, its name appears in the list on the right. The user can register multiple servers by adding multiple names to the list on the right. When all the desired servers have been added to the register, the user proceeds to the next screen, which allows the user to choose the authentication mode. The authentication mode can be either Windows NT authentication, or SQL Server authentication. If SQL Server authentication is chosen, a screen will be presented to allow entering of the login name and password or to give the option of always being prompted for the account information at the time of connection. The next screen allows the user to choose the group to which the servers will be added or to create a new group. The next screen shows a list of all the servers that will be registered when Finish is clicked, after which the dialog box will display the status as Enterprise Manager attempts to connect to end register each of the servers chosen.

If the user chooses to register servers without the wizard, a single dialog box will be presented that allows the user to choose or type a server name, to choose the authentication mode and optionally enter a login name and password (if SQL Server was chosen for the authentication mode), and to choose a server group. The Ellipsis button at the top of this dialog box allows the user to perform an Active Directory search for servers. The following options are also available:

✦ **Display SQL Server state in the Enterprise Manager console.** If this is selected, Enterprise Manager will poll MSDE every few seconds to determine if it is running and display an icon to show if the service is running, paused, or stopped.

✦ **Show system databases and objects.** If this option is selected, Enterprise Manager will display system databases (master, model, msdb, and tempdb), as well as system tables, views, and stored procedures. If the option is not selected, all of these objects will be hidden.

✦ **Automatically start the SQL Server service during connection.** If this option is selected, Enterprise Manager will start MSDE if it is not already started whenever a user accesses the server.

By default, Enterprise Manager shows the system state of the SQL Server service whenever a server is displayed. This display uses the same icons as the Service Manager icon in the system tray. The SQL Server service can be started, paused, stopped, and polled for status by right-clicking the server and choosing the appropriate menu item. Figure 22-2 shows these features in Enterprise Manager. The first server in the SQL Server Group, 0KH2H, is currently stopped. The second server in the SQL Server Group, DCWI7500, is started and connected (the squiggle line on the right side of the icon indicates that Enterprise Manager has an open connection to the server). In this figure, the second server has been right-clicked, and the context-sensitive menu is displayed, with options available to poll the service state or to stop or pause the SQL Server service. The option to start the service is not available because it is already running.

The SQL Server service can also be automatically started by connecting to the server in Enterprise Manager. This behavior is configurable; it can be turned off by right-clicking a server, choosing Edit SQL Server Registration properties, and deselecting the last option displayed in the dialog box.

The SQL Server Agent service can be controlled in Enterprise Manager by expanding the Management container and right-clicking the SQL Server Agent icon. This icon displays the state of the service; however, it does not periodically poll the service. The service can be manually polled by right-clicking the icon and choosing Poll Service State. Figure 22-3 shows the context-sensitive menu for controlling the SQL Server Agent service in Enterprise Manager. The service cannot be paused—only started and stopped.

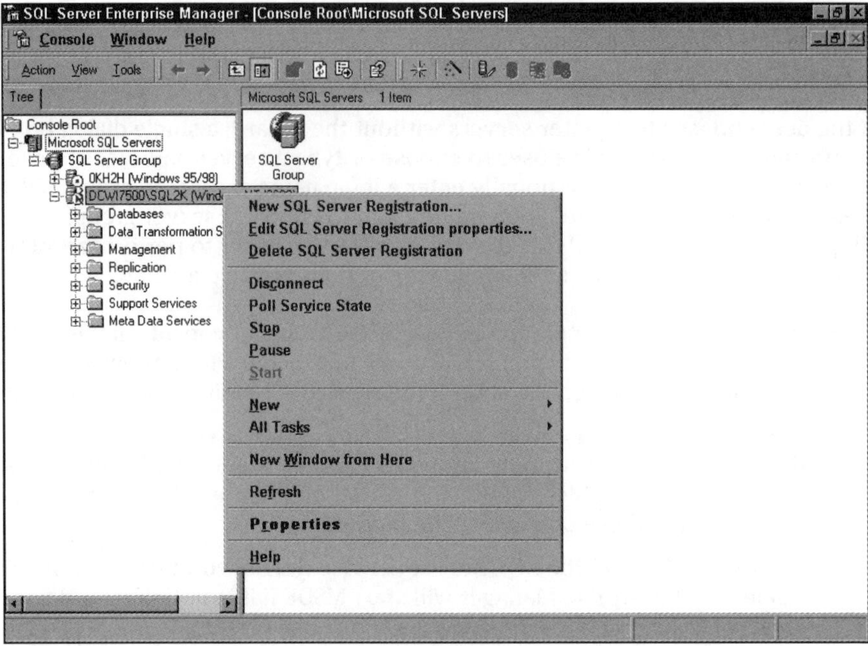

Figure 22-2: Controlling SQL Server service with Enterprise Manager

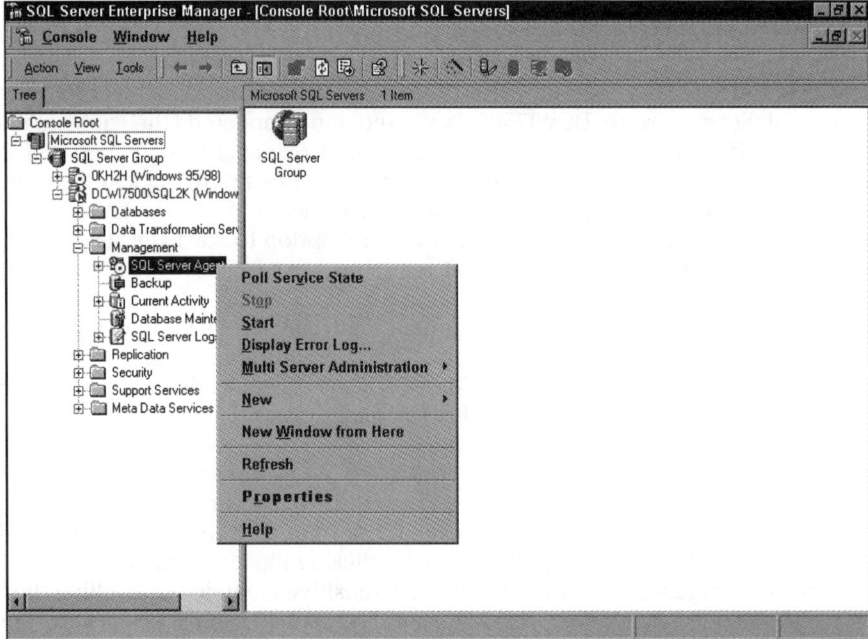

Figure 22-3: Controlling the SQL Server Agent service with Enterprise Manager

The DTC service can be controlled by expanding the Support Services item in the left pane of Enterprise Manager, as shown in Figure 22-4. Right-click the Distributed Transaction Coordinator and choose Start or Stop from the context-sensitive menu. There is also an option in the menu to poll the service state. As with the SQL Server Agent, Enterprise Manager does not periodically poll the state of the DTC; it must be done manually.

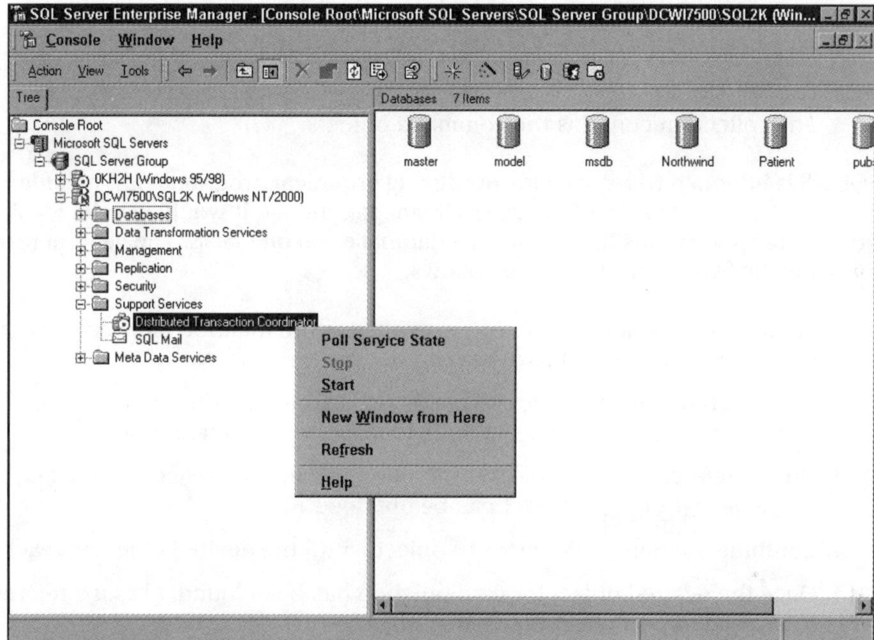

Figure 22-4: Controlling DTC with Enterprise Manager

The Programmatic Control Mechanisms

The services in MSDE can be manipulated programmatically through two mechanisms: the SQL-NS (Namespace), which is an object model and can be accessed by any programming language that is COM compliant; and SQL-DMO, which is also a COM-compliant object model.

Chapter 5 contains sample code in Visual Basic that illustrates the use of SQL-NS.

SQL-NS

SQL-NS is an object model containing only three objects and one collection:

- ✦ One object represents the entire namespace equivalent to the entire left pane of Enterprise Manager.
- ✦ Another object refers to any of the individual items within the namespace, such as a server, database, or table.
- ✦ The final object refers to any of the commands that can be executed: an object in the namespace.
- ✦ The collection contains the command objects.

SQL-NS is intended to be used for producing graphical programs that include some of the functionality of Enterprise Manager, though it would also be ideal for producing applications in support of a database run on MSDE. The general process for using the SQL Namespace is as follows:

1. Initialize the namespace object, providing authentication information that can be used to connect to a server.
2. Obtain a reference to a root object, which can be the root of the entire namespace, a server group, an individual server, or a database.
3. Once a reference to an object is obtained, further references to objects contained within that object can be obtained.
4. Continue obtaining references to objects until the desired object is reached.
5. Once the desired object for manipulation has been found, obtain a reference to the command collection for that object.
6. Execute an appropriate command from the command collection.

A sample Visual Basic program called the SQL Namespace Object Browser is available with SQL Server. To access the sample, when installing SQL Server, choose the development tools. The SQL Namespace Object Browser will be available in the directory C:\Program Files\Microsoft SQL Server\80\Tools\DevTools\Samples\sqlns\vb\browse.

This program allows the user to interactively obtain a reference to one of the four types of root objects and then browse through the object using a tree control. This program is shown in Figure 22-5 having obtained a reference to the root of the namespace and browsed down into an SQL Server. The server is highlighted, and the right pane shows the commands collection for that object. In this case, the first three commands for a server object allow the user to start, stop, or pause the SQL Server service.

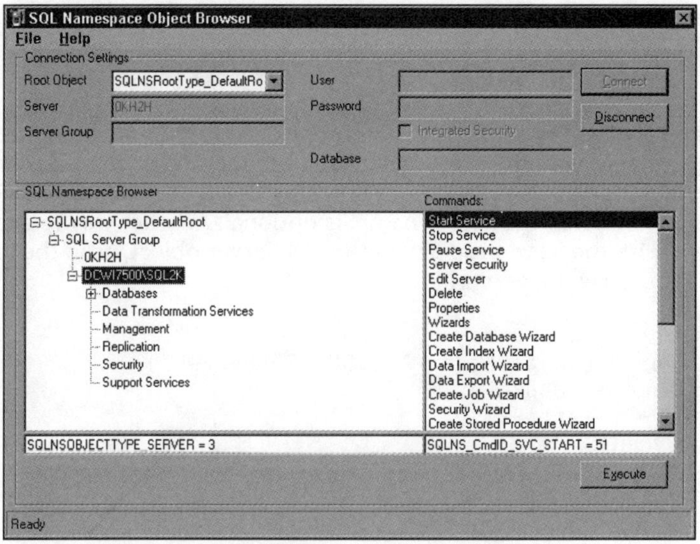

Figure 22-5: The SQL Namespace Object Browser

Users can also browse down into the Management container and find the SQL Server Agent service with its commands collection. Text boxes at the bottom of the program window show the string and integer representation of each object and each command.

Working with the SQL Namespace Object Browser will give the user a feel for how the SQL-NS object model is used in practice. The source code is available in the directory mentioned above and is extremely useful for users who want to apply SQL-NS when they create their own programs. Source code for this program is also available in Visual C++.

DMO

DMO can be used to start, pause, or stop the SQL Server service and start or stop the SQL Server Agent service.

The code that starts SQL Server service with DMO is one of the very few places where it is not necessary to make a connection to a server:

```
Dim oMSDEServer
set oMSDEserver = CreateObject("SQLDMO.SQLServer")
call oMSDEserver.Start(False, "0kh2h")
```

This code can be found on the CD-ROM in the file named `Ch 22\StartServer.vbs`.

The first parameter for the `Start` method determines whether or not a connection should be made to the server after starting it. Although there is no reason to make this type of determination in a script, a more fully functional program might wish to do so. The second parameter, the server name, is optional. Another way to specify the server name is with the `Name` property of the SQLServer object, as in the following code, which also starts the server:

```
Dim oMSDEServer
set oMSDEserver = CreateObject("SQLDMO.SQLServer")
oMSDEServer.Name = "Okh2h"
call oMSDEserver.Start(False)
```

This code can be found on the CD-ROM in the file named `Ch 22\StartServer2.vbs`.

The SQL Server service can be stopped using DMO with two different methods in the SQLServer object. To shut the server down gracefully, use the `Shutdown` method. To bring the server to a crashing halt, use the `Stop` method.

The following code stops the SQL Server service using the optional `Wait` parameter for the `Shutdown` method. If the `Wait` parameter is True, checkpoints are issued for all databases, and all currently running commands are allowed to finish. If the `Wait` parameter is set to False, all user connections are immediately terminated, checkpoints are not issued, and any transaction that is active at the time of the shutdown will be rolled back. The default for the `Wait` parameter is True.

```
Dim oMSDEServer
set oMSDEserver = CreateObject("SQLDMO.SQLServer")

oMSDEserver.connect "Okh2h","sa",""
call oMSDEserver.Shutdown(True)
oMSDEserver.disconnect
```

This code can be found on the CD-ROM in the file named `Ch 22\StopServer.vbs`.

Only two objects are needed to control the SQL Server Agent service with DMO: the SQLServer object, which must be created, and the JobServer object, which is automatically created as a property of the SQLServer object. The JobServer object has `Start` and `Stop` methods that can be called without parameters.

The following code starts the SQL Server Agent service. The SQL Server service must be started for this script to function, since a connection must be created to the server before the `Start` method can be called.

```
Dim oMSDEServer
set oMSDEserver = CreateObject("SQLDMO.SQLServer")

oMSDEserver.connect "Okh2h","sa",""
call oMSDEserver.JobServer.Start()
oMSDEserver.disconnect
```

This code can be found on the CD-ROM in the file named `Ch 22\StartAgent.vbs`.

The only modification needed so that the previous code stops the SQL Server Agent is to change the name of the `Start` method to `Stop`.

SQL

Naturally, the SQL Server service itself cannot be started with a SQL command, since it would have to be running first in order to process the command. SQL Server can, however, be shut down with the `SHUTDOWN` command.

The `SHUTDOWN` command can be issued only by someone with the appropriate permission. The fixed server roles that have the permission to shut the server down are sysadmin and serveradmin.

When the `SHUTDOWN` command is issued, the server disables new logins, waits for currently executing commands and stored procedures to complete, and issues a checkpoint on all databases. The server can be shut down more quickly by a member of the sysadmin role. A member of sysadmin can issue the `SHUTDOWN` command with the `With NoWait` parameter, in which case all user connections are immediately terminated, checkpoints are not issued, and any transaction that is active at the time of the shutdown will be rolled back.

The Command Prompt

There are several methods of starting services from the command prompt, and the number of methods varies depending on the operating system being run. The methods that apply only to Windows NT and Windows 2000 will be addressed in the following section. This section will cover the commands that can be used to start the services without regard to the operating system.

The Service Control Manager is available from a command-line interface in the form of the `scmexe` command, which can control any of the MSDE services. The individual services can also be started using their executables.

The SCM command line

The `scm` command requires two parameters: `-Action` and `-Service`. The `-Action` parameter accepts an integer value between one and seven to determine what the `scm` command will do to the service specified by the `-Service` parameter. The possible values (and a short description of each) for `-Action` are as follows:

- `1`—Start
- `2`—Restart
- `3`—Return Status
- `4`—Delete
- `5`—Install
- `6`—Stop
- `7`—Modify

The `-Service` parameter accepts the name of the service (for example, MSSQL for the SQL Server service or SQLSERVERAGENT). If there is a named instance of MSDE, then the name of that instance must be used with the service name, for example, MSSSQL$SQL2K (where SQL2K is the instance name).

So, to start the default instance of the SQL Server service, use the following command:

```
Scm -action 1 -service MSSQL
```

The Restart action (`2`) is convenient when configuration changes have been made to the server that require the SQL Server service to be shut down and started again.

The command line for the Service Control Manager has other functionalities in addition to being able to start and stop the MSDE services. It can control many services, and with Windows NT or Windows 2000, it can install, modify, uninstall, or delete services. Other parameters for the Service Control Manager command line are as follows:

- `Server`—allows you to specify the server name for controlling services across a network.
- `Pwd`—allows you to specify a password for operations that require specific authentication.
- `StartupOptions`—allows you to specify options to be used by the service when it starts. This option is used only when installing or modifying a service. An example of a startup option would be specifying the path of the master database data and log files.

✦ `ExePath`—allows you to specify the path to the service executable. This option is used only when installing or modifying a service.

✦ `SvcStartType`—allows you to specify whether a server should start automatically or manually. Automatic startup is specified with the number 1; manual startup is specified with the number 2. This option is used only when installing or modifying a service.

✦ `SvcAccount`—specifies the user account to be used by the service for security context when it starts. This option is used only when installing or modifying a service.

✦ `SvcPwd`—specifies the password that will be used for the service account when the service starts. This option is used only when installing or modifying a service.

✦ `Dependencies`—creates dependencies among services so that one may start only if another is already running. This option is used only when installing or modifying a service.

The SQL Server service command line

The SQL Server service can be started with the `sqlservr` command. When this is done, the SQL Server service is run as part of the user process. The screen will show a list of the processes taking place while the server initializes. When the screen stops scrolling, the service has started; there is no prompt or specific message indicating the start. Other processes can now connect to databases and work normally.

The `sqlservr` command will return an error message if the SQL Server service is already running. On a Windows 98 computer, executing `sqlservr` when the service is already running will also cause Service Manager and Enterprise Manager to incorrectly believe that the service has stopped.

When the SQL Server service has been started from the `sqlservr` command, it can be stopped with Service Manager, Enterprise Manager, or with the `SHUTDOWN` command. The SQL Server service can also be terminated by pressing Ctrl+C; however, this is equivalent to issuing `SHUTDOWN With NoWait` or using the `Stop` method in DMO. No checkpoints are executed and all transactions are terminated immediately.

The `sqlservr` command should not be used to run MSDE for production purposes. It makes the server much more vulnerable to being peremptorily shut down by accidental user activity.

The `sqlservr` command line can be used for several useful administrative and maintenance purposes. `Sqlservr` has a parameter that supports like safemode:

```
Sqlservr -f
```

The previous command starts the service in minimally configured mode, which temporarily resets all configurations to values just large enough to start the server. Using the -f parameter can resuscitate a server that was killed by accidental misconfiguration. The sp_configure stored procedure can be used to reconfigure the server to start again normally.

The -m parameter starts the SQL Server service in maintenance mode:

```
Sqlsrvr -m
```

Maintenance mode is a single-user mode that does not initiate the checkpoint process. This mode should be used only for specific maintenance tasks, usually repairing system databases.

It is occasionally desirable to start the SQL Server service with a master database that is not in the default or configured location. The -d parameter allows this:

```
Sqlservr -dc:\lowpath\Scotland\master.mdf
```

When using the -d parameter, it is usually necessary to also specify the -l parameter with the path to the master database log file.

The -y parameter is used to specify an error message. When the specified error is encountered, the server writes extended information about the error to the error log.

The SQL Server Agent service command line

The command line for the SQL Server Agent service, sqlagent.exe, is used only for diagnosing errors and has just two parameters.

The -c parameter isolates the service so that it cannot be terminated by the Service Control Manager.

The -v parameter logs extended information about errors.

The SQL Server Agent service should never be run from the command line for production use.

Windows NT and Windows 2000 Methods

MSDE services run as true services on Windows NT and Windows 2000, and all of the mechanisms for services control used in those operating systems will control the three MSDE services. Specifically, there is an applet in Control Panel that is used for configuring and controlling services and a command-line command that can also be used to control services.

Control Panel

On Windows NT 4.0, the services applet is located directly in Control Panel. In Windows 2000, services is within Administrative Tools in Control Panel. In Windows 2000, the services applet is also available by right-clicking My Computer on the desktop, choosing Manage then expanding Services and Applications, and clicking Services.

The services applet presents a list of all installed services. A computer with MSDE installed should show two services for each instance of MSDE, the SQL Server service and the SQL Server Agent service. Only one instance of the Distributed Transaction Coordinator is required for any number of MSDE instances.

The SQL Server service is called MSSQL for the default instance. If any named instances are installed, they are called MSSQL$InstanceName.

The SQL Server Agent service is called SQLSERVERAGENT for the default instance and SQLAgent$InstanceName for named instances.

Service can be started and stopped with the buttons at the top of the dialog box, by right-clicking the service name, or by double-clicking the service name and using the buttons that appear in the resulting Service Properties dialog box.

The Service Properties dialog box can also be used for configuring the startup conditions for each service. Each service can be configured to start automatically or manually or to be disabled. For services that are not disabled, the security context in which the service runs can be specified. The service can also be configured to run in the context of the local system account or to run in the context of a specific user account. The local system account has administrative privilege on the local computer, but no privilege on the network, while a user has whatever privilege assigned to it.

Startup parameters can also be assigned in the Service Properties dialog box. The SQL Server service account can be configured to look in a nondefault directory for the master database and log file, for example.

Net commands

Windows NT and Windows 2000 have a command-line interface to control services: the `net` command. The three forms of the command relevant to controlling the MSDE services are as follows:

```
NET START servicename
NET PAUSE servicename
NET STOP servicename
```

These commands use the same service name that appears in the Services Applet dialog box. For a list of running services, type `NET START` with no parameters.

Summary

This chapter has shown many ways of controlling the three services associated with MSDE: the SQL Server service, the SQL Server Agent service, and the Distributed Transaction Coordinator. The services can be controlled with the graphical tools, Enterprise Manager, Service Manager, and Control Panel. They can be controlled programmatically through three different interfaces: the SQL Service Control Manager API, the SQL Namespace object model, and the SQL Distributed Management Objects object model (although there is no representation of the DTC in DMO). The services can also be controlled with several different commands from the command prompt.

✦ ✦ ✦

Chapter 23

Backing Up and Restoring Data

In This Chapter

Understanding types of backups

Creating a full backup

Creating a differential backup

Creating a transaction log backup

Understanding checkpoint and recovery

Restoring backups

Creating a standby server

A critical aspect of designing and administering a database is creating and implementing an effective disaster recovery plan. Creating a disaster recovery plan involves a complete analysis of all business practices and the amount of sustainable risk. Although such analysis goes far beyond the scope of this book, key components of any disaster recovery plan are the backup and restore strategies.

Many questions must be answered to develop a comprehensive backup and restore strategy. A thorough understanding is needed of what data exists in a database, the consequences of losing that data, and whether or not there are any mechanisms for re-creating data in the event of loss. Additionally, procedures must be put in place to ensure that regular backups of data occur and that these backups are tested on a regular basis. Backups must be implemented so they do not interfere with the normal operation of the database. Interfering with normal operations can usually be avoided by performing backups after business hours on a daily basis. However, many businesses are moving toward 24-hour operations.

MSDE's built-in utilities for backing up and restoring databases allow the implementation of a number of different strategies. Several different types of backups have varying degrees of impact on other operations in the database. Backups can be performed in single-user mode, so that the backup completes as quickly as possible while preventing users from working while backup occurs. Backups can also be performed while numerous operations are occurring on the database. Performing backups while people are working in the database will naturally slow both the backup and the performance of the database with respect to all other users.

Another important aspect of designing a backup strategy is to consider the effect of restoring the data. The length of time required for a restore can be an important factor in the impact of a disaster on a company's operations. Restoring data to a computer can often take as long as acquiring and configuring replacement hardware in the event of equipment failure.

Backup Types

MSDE provides three types of backups: full backup, differential backup, and transaction log backup. Each of these types of backups has its own characteristics with regard to the amount of data it backs up, the length of time it takes to back up, and methods used to restore the data.

Full backups

A full backup copies the contents of all data pages that have been allocated to any objects from the database to the backup device. A full backup first forces a checkpoint of the database that is being backed up. The checkpoint ensures that all committed transactions are written to the data files on disk. The backup process then records the Log Serial Number (LSN), which indicates the current location in the transaction log. All data pages in the database are then copied to the backup media. The backup process places locks only on the data it is actively reading, so other users can be connected to the database and operational during the backup. When all of the pages in the database have been copied to the backup media, they do not reflect a single point in time, as some may have been modified during the time backup process took to complete. Therefore, at the end of the backup process, the transaction log is also stored on the backup media. The transaction log contains a record of all modifications to the database. When a full backup is restored, all of the data pages are written back to disk, and the transaction log is restored and replayed to bring the system back to the state it was in at the very end of the backup process. Full backups can be restored only to the single point in time at which they finished, unlike transaction log backups.

Differential backups

A differential backup copies only those pages to the backup medium that have been modified since the last full backup. The highest LSN from the transaction log is recorded during a full backup and retained for use in determining which pages have changed between the time of the full backup and the time the differential backup is run. Whenever a data page is modified, the LSN is recorded in the page. So, a differential backup scans the LSNs on each data page, and a page that has a higher LSN than the one recorded at the last full backup will be copied to the backup medium. A differential backup, like a full backup, is a point-in-time snapshot of the database and can be restored only to that specific point in time. The advantage of a differential backup over a transaction log backup is that the differential backup relies only on the last full backup and itself in order to restore the database. Transaction log backups rely on the last full backup and every transaction log backup after that full backup.

Transaction log backups

Transaction log backups are similar to incremental backups for operating systems. They record all changes that have taken place since the last backup of any kind. Transaction log backups do not write data pages to the backup medium—they write the transaction logs, as their name implies. Because the transaction log records all normal modifications to data, transaction log backups can be restored to any point in time by restoring the log and replaying only those transactions that were committed prior to the point in time desired.

To perform a transaction log backup, both of the database options Truncate Log on Checkpoint and Select Into/Bulk Copy must be turned off. In addition, the database must not have its recovery models set to simple.

Recovery Models

Recovery models are configurations that can be set on a database to facilitate the type of backup and recovery strategy being used. The three recovery models are full, bulk-logged, and simple.

The full recovery model provides the greatest flexibility in terms of backing up and restoring data to any point in time. It enables the use of full, differential, and transaction log backups. When a database is in full recovery mode, it cannot perform nonlogged operations, such as fast bulk copies or selecting into a permanent table.

The bulk-logged recovery model allows nonlogged operations and turns on the Select Into/Bulk Copy database option. All three types of backups can be performed; however, transaction log backups are modified slightly so that they record all pages touched by any nonlogged operation. Recording these pages makes the backup itself larger and prevents point-in-time restoration. Transaction log backups taken in this mode can be restored only to the point in time at which they were taken, just like full backups and differential backups.

The simple recovery model allows nonlogged operations and turns on the Truncate Log on Checkpoint database option. With this option turned on, it is impossible to perform transaction log backups. Full backups and differential backups are permitted. Turning on this mode does not actually change the recovery process; it changes the way transaction logs are maintained and thus the way backups can be taken.

Each time the checkpoint process runs, in addition to verifying that committed transactions are written to data pages on disk, it marks committed transactions for truncation. A transaction that is marked for truncation will be deleted from the transaction log by a background process. These committed transactions are not necessary for the recovery process, because the recovery process only reads the transaction log starting at the last checkpoint. Recovery always ignores checkpointed transactions. So, setting the simple recovery mode in no way interferes with the stability of your database; if your backup strategy relies primarily on full and differential backups, this may be the most appropriate recovery model to choose.

Backup Methods

Once the types of backups possible in MSDE are understood, a plan can be formulated to integrate those backups into the business environment. Three primary questions must be answered for this plan: Who will backup the data, where will the data be backed up, and, most importantly, when will the data be backed up?

Who can back up data

To execute a backup in MSDE, a person must be appropriately prepared. By default, three roles have permission to perform backups: the sysadmin fixed server role, the db_owner fixed database role, and the db_backupoperator fixed database role. Permissions can be directly granted to any role or user to be able to perform backups.

In addition to the permissions required to perform a backup, three types of activities are prohibited during a database backup. The prohibited activities are creating or modifying the database, creating indexes in the database, and performing any nonlogged operation in the database, such as Select Into or Bulk Copy.

Where data can be saved

The backup utility in MSDE enables data to be stored on one of three types of physical devices: a file system file, which could reside on a hard drive local to the database or a hard drive on a network server; a tape drive; or a named pipe. Named pipes are a network communication mechanism supported by Microsoft as well as many other companies. Using them enables the backup and restore mechanisms built into MSDE to be used with third-party software that provides additional capability such as tape library management, distributed backup and restore across a network, and centralized management of backup operations.

Several factors can be considered when deciding where to save the backups and what kind of media to use. Hard drives are becoming faster than tape drives. So, for companies that are sensitive to the length of time the backup takes, several options can be explored to make backup faster. The backups can be saved to hard disk first and subsequently to a tape for off-site storage. In addition, several tape drives can be employed simultaneously to speed up the backup. MSDE can multi-thread the backup process and devote a thread to each tape drive so that the backup to two tape drives becomes almost twice as fast as the backup to one tape drive. The backup to three tape drives is almost three times as fast. Backups made to multiple tape drives do not need to be restored by using the same number of tape drives on which they were made.

Standby servers

A standby server contains a copy of the data on a production server and can be quickly brought online in case of failure of the production server. To implement a standby server, backups are made on the production server on a regular basis, and each backup is immediately restored to the standby server. In such a scenario, performing backups initially to a hard drive, restoring to the standby server from the hard drive, and using another backup program to copy the files from hard drive to tape can facilitate the process. The standby server may simply be an unused server that can be made ready for production very quickly, or it can actually be put to use as a read-only database. The read-only database could be used for extensive reporting, decision support, or analytical processing. One drawback to a standby server being put to use is that no one can use the databases that are being restored during the process.

To set up a standby server, follow these steps:

1. Install MSDE on a second computer with sufficient hard disk space to host the production database, as well as an undo file. The undo file is used to store information that can undo the recovery process performed after each tape is restored. The size of this file will vary depending on the size in number of uncommitted transactions in the transaction line at the time of each backup.
2. Perform a full database backup on the production database.
3. Restore the full database backup on the standby server using the `STANDBY` parameter.
4. Periodically perform transaction log backups on the production server.
5. Restore the periodic transaction backups on the standby server using the `STANDBY` parameter.

In the event of failure of the production server, use the following steps to bring the standby server online:

1. If the transaction log is available on the production server, perform a backup of the transaction log. It may be necessary to use the `NO_TRUNCATE` option if the data portion of the database is unavailable.
2. Restore any transaction log backups to the standby server that have not yet been restored, including the one created in the previous step.
3. When restoring the last transaction log to the standby server, use the `RECOVERY` parameter. If there are no remaining backups to restore, the recovery process can be initiated by using the `restore` command with the `RECOVERY` parameter, and omitting any backup device.
4. Optionally change the name of the standby server to that of the former production server. This will require a reboot of the standby server. When it restarts, change the name of the server in the sysservers system table by running `sp_dropserver <old_standby_servername>` and `sp_addserver <production_servername>, 'Local'`. These commands will reestablish MSDE's knowledge of its name and enable processes such as replication to continue. It is not absolutely required to change the server's name; if the name is not changed, however, there must be some mechanism through which the client computers are informed to use a new name when connecting to the server.
5. Client computers can reconnect to the standby server and continue with normal operations.

Two servers with the same name cannot reside on the network at the same time. If you want to bring the standby server online as the new production server, you can temporarily disconnect the network from one of the servers and change the name of both servers. If the production server is being taken offline for maintenance or some other temporary reason and it will be returned to production use at some later time, then it is not necessary to run the stored procedures that change the name of the server in the sysservers table.

Alternatives to the standby server

If the database requires a high degree of fault tolerance, beyond what can be provided by fault-tolerant server hardware and a backup strategy, there are some alternatives that require the Enterprise version of SQL Server 2000. The log-shipping alternative in the Enterprise version is similar to the standby server. It utilizes a service to copy the transaction log entries from the production server to the backup server. This method also requires manually changing over the servers if the production server fails.

A more elaborate and expensive alternative in the Enterprise version of SQL Server 2000 is the Microsoft Cluster Service. Running a database cluster removes much of the administrative overhead required for a standby server and automates the process of failover. A cluster requires two similar servers that share a disk subsystem. Both servers can operate at the same time, improving performance and providing hot failover fault tolerance.

Databases hosted on MSDE are not generally large enough or used heavily enough to consider a server cluster. However, databases grow, and the upgrade to other editions of SQL Server is very easy. Some third-party clustering alternatives may not require the Enterprise edition of SQL Server.

Storage media

The physical storage of backup media is a crucial question for database administrators. Backing up to a hard drive is fast, but buys nothing if the hard drive fails. The most common backup medium is tape of one kind or another. Backup tapes are cheap, convenient, and easy to move and store. Other media, such as optical disks, are also available.

Whichever media is chosen for backups, off-site storage and media rotation must also be planned. If all media are not stored off-site, then the backups are only as secure as an organization's building, and no building is absolutely secure, particularly in the case of fire. Even storing tapes in fireproof safes is not absolute security, as was demonstrated in the case of a high-rise fire in which temperatures grew so high that tapes inside fireproof safes were melted. The security of the off-site storage location should be verified. A business owner once walked into the third-party tape storage location without identifying himself or being stopped. He was further able to walk into the tape storage rooms and remove his tapes. Needless to say, he never returned his tapes to that location.

No medium lasts forever, particularly not metal oxide-coated film. Tapes need to be thrown away after they've been used or aged sufficiently. An adequate system for tracking tape aging and usage and reliably destroying tapes should be developed. Data-sensitive tapes should be erased and made physically unusable, rather than simply discarded.

Choosing a backup schedule

Of the three backup types, the full backup takes the longest, usually followed by the differential backup, with the transaction log backup coming in as the quickest possible backup. Occasionally, differential backups are faster than transaction log backups if there are many transactions and the transactions modify data located within a relatively small number of pages because differential backups copy only the changed pages whereas the transaction log backups record every change. Backups should be timed when a backup strategy is initially set up and should continue to be monitored as the database grows larger and more heavily used.

Full backups

A typical scenario is to perform a full backup periodically when there is little usage of the database system or when the system can be scheduled down with no user connections. This full backup may occur once a week on weekends, once a month on a scheduled day of the month, or perhaps even nightly if it doesn't interfere too much with normal operations.

Differential and transaction log backups

In between the full backups, it may be prudent to schedule additional backups. The additional backups could be differential, transaction log, or a combination of both. Again, the determination can be made only by examining the size and frequency of data modification. An important determining factor in how often a backup should be scheduled is the size of the transaction logs. Transaction logs grow larger as more and bigger transactions are performed, and they grow smaller as backups are performed that truncate the logs. In a highly transactional environment, it may be necessary to run transaction log backups every hour, or even every 15 minutes, to keep the transaction logs at a reasonable size.

When deciding on the combination of differential and transaction log backups, the length of time required to restore the backup should be considered. If the full backup is made once a week, and transaction log backups are made four times every day, then it is possible that a system failure shortly before the full backup could cause 25 different backups to have to be restored to make the system operational. A scenario like this increases the exposure to risk, because if any tape fails, then the backup can be restored only to the final point before the failed tape. On the other hand, if differential backups are performed periodically throughout the week, then the number of tapes that need to be restored is significantly reduced, and there is less risk that a single failed tape will invalidate a large amount of data.

System databases

In addition to backing up user data, the system databases should be backed up periodically. The master database, in particular, should be backed up anytime another database is created or deleted. The msdb database contains information about all jobs and schedules configured for the SQL Server Agent and should be backed up as often as major changes are made in MSDE automation, or at least frequently enough so that lots of administrative work is not lost. If possible, all the system databases (master, model, and msdb) should be backed up simultaneously. If the master database ever needs to be re-created or restored, all three of these databases will be re-created.

If the master database is ever damaged beyond usability, the SQL Server service will be unable to start. The first step toward recovering such a system is to create a new master database by running the rebuildm.exe program located in the subdirectory with the other MSDE executables. This process will create a new master database, as if MSDE had just been installed. The new master database will enable the SQL Server service to start, at which point the master database can be restored from backup if a good backup exists. If no valid backup of the master database exists, but the user databases still exist in good condition, the user databases can be added to MSDE by running the stored procedures `sp_attach_db` or `sp_attach_single_file_db`, which create new entries in the system tables of the master database.

Transaction Logs

Transaction logs serve two purposes in MSDE: They provide a mechanism for the recovery process, guaranteeing the consistency of the database in case of failure, and they provide a mechanism for performing incremental backups of the database that record only changes in the data.

Whenever data is to be written to the database, it is first written to the transaction log. When a transaction finishes writing data to the database, it commits those changes. By committing changes, an indication is written in the transaction log, which allows the data to be written to the underlying database file. Once the changes for transaction have been committed, they become durable and remain in the database without regard to any errors or failures of the server. Prior to being committed, changes in a transaction are susceptible to being rolled back by errors in code or failures of the database or database server.

Checkpoint

Periodically, the server runs the checkpoint process that examines the transaction logs to find any committed transactions that have not previously been checkpointed and determines whether or not the changes corresponding to the transactions have been written to the data pages on disk. If the changes have not been written to disk, the checkpoint process writes the changes. The checkpoint process also writes a transaction into the transaction log showing that the checkpoint has occurred and recording which transactions have been checkpointed. The checkpoint process acts as a guarantee that the transactions have been written to the disk.

MSDE must know which transactions have been written to the data pages on disk in order to fulfill the guarantee of durability for committed transactions. Once a transaction is checkpointed, and therefore guaranteed to have been written to the data pages on disk, the server need not be concerned with that transaction. Until a transaction has been checkpointed, that is while the transaction is still in progress or when it has been committed but is waiting to be checkpointed, the server must carefully track the status of the transaction. Should the server fail during this period, it takes one of several actions, depending upon the status of the transaction.

Recovery

The recovery process runs automatically whenever the SQL Server service starts. Recovery can also be manually initiated. In some ways, the recovery process is like an elaboration of the checkpoint process. It examines the transaction logs starting with the last checkpoint in the log because all transactions prior to the last checkpoint are guaranteed to have been both completed and written to disk. Those transactions that have not yet been checkpointed must be analyzed to determine their state. The primary determinant of state is whether the transaction has committed. If a transaction has committed, the recovery process will roll a transaction forward. Rolling forward verifies that the changes associated with the transaction are written to the data pages on disk and writes them there if they have not yet been written. If a transaction is not committed, then the recovery process will roll that transaction back. Rolling back verifies that the changes have not yet been written to the data pages on disk, and if they have, undoes those changes from the disk. Any transaction that was committed before the server failed is made durable. Any transaction not committed before the server failed is undone, and the database is considered consistent because no transactions are left in a state of partial completeness.

Understanding the recovery process is crucial to understanding the backup and restore processes. Recovery is an integral part of restoring a backup. All backups, whether they are full, differential, or transaction log backups, store the transaction logs at the time of the backup. When a backup is restored, the recovery process must be run to make the database operational. The state of the database at the time of a backup restoration is analogous to the state of the database at the time it is restarted after a system failure. The transaction logs must be scanned by the recovery process to roll back uncommitted transactions before any new transactions can be started. If new transactions were permitted to begin before the recovery process ran, there would be no way to distinguish between transactions that had begun prior to the system failure or backup and those that had begun after the system was restarted or restored but had not yet completed. Any transaction that had begun before the system failed or was backed up would have no way of ever completing because any connection with the client that started the transaction would long since have been destroyed.

Performing Backups and Restores

Database backups and restores can be initiated from within Enterprise Manager by using SQL statements or initiated programmatically by using DMO.

Using Enterprise Manager

Enterprise Manager contains a series of dialog boxes associated with backup and a series of dialog boxes associated with restore.

Backup

To initiate a backup using Enterprise Manager, right-click the database and choose All Tasks ➪ Backup Database. The dialog box shown in Figure 23-1 is displayed.

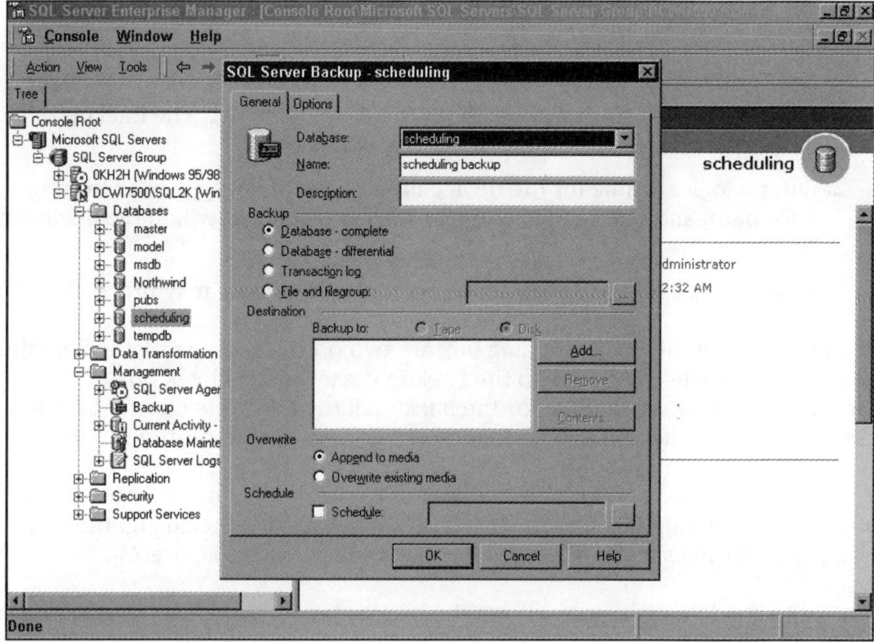

Figure 23-1: The Backup dialog box in Enterprise Manager

The top of the dialog box shown in Figure 23-1 enables the user to choose the database to back up. A description for the backup may also be included.

A descriptive and memorable name and description should be entered for every backup. Too many abbreviations can lead to memory lapses, especially under the strain of trying to recover from a disaster.

The section just below the name and description offers a choice of four types of backup: complete (or full), differential, transaction log, or file and file group.

Just below the backup type selection is the section used to select a destination for the backup. The possible destinations for a backup are a temporary file or a backup device. A backup device can consist of a file system file or a tape drive.

A backup device may be chosen for the current database by clicking the Add button. The Select Backup Destination is displayed. The user can choose a temporary file by selecting the first option button, called File name, and typing in or browsing to a file path and name. The user can choose a backup device by selecting the second option button, called Backup device. If the option for backup device is chosen, a backup device can be selected from the drop-down list.

A new backup device may also be created.

1. Choose <New Backup Device> from the drop-down list. The Backup Device Properties dialog box for a new device will display.
2. Enter a logical name for the device in the name field, type in or browse to a file path, and enter a name for the file system file in which the device will be stored.
3. When OK is clicked, the device is created and backup may proceed.

At the bottom of the Backup dialog box are two option buttons that enable the user to either overwrite or append to the backup device and a check box that enables the user to choose a schedule for the backup. If the schedule check box is not checked, the backup will initiate immediately when the OK button is clicked.

If the schedule check box is selected, the default schedule of every week is enabled on Sunday at midnight. The schedule can be changed by clicking on the ellipsis button, which displays the Edit Schedule dialog box shown in Figure 23-2.

The Edit Schedule dialog box allows the user to type a name for the schedule and select whether it is enabled or not. It also allows four choices for the schedule type. The first schedule type is to start automatically when the SQL Server Agent starts. The SQL Server Agent starts when a server boots, so choosing the first option would start a backup every time the server starts.

The second option offers the choice to start the backup whenever the CPU becomes idle. The default conditions for CPU idle are when the processor activity falls below 10 percent for a period of 10 minutes. The CPU idle condition can be configured in the properties of the SQL Server Agent.

The third option allows the user to schedule a single backup for a future date and time. Configuring a one-time backup is convenient if you need to come in at night or on a weekend to perform system maintenance, and you would like the backup to begin automatically before you arrive.

The fourth option (the default) allows the user to configure a recurring backup on a regular schedule. The default schedule begins every week on Sunday at midnight. To change the schedule, click the Change button, and the Edit Recurring Job Schedule dialog box is displayed. This dialog box is shown in Figure 23-3.

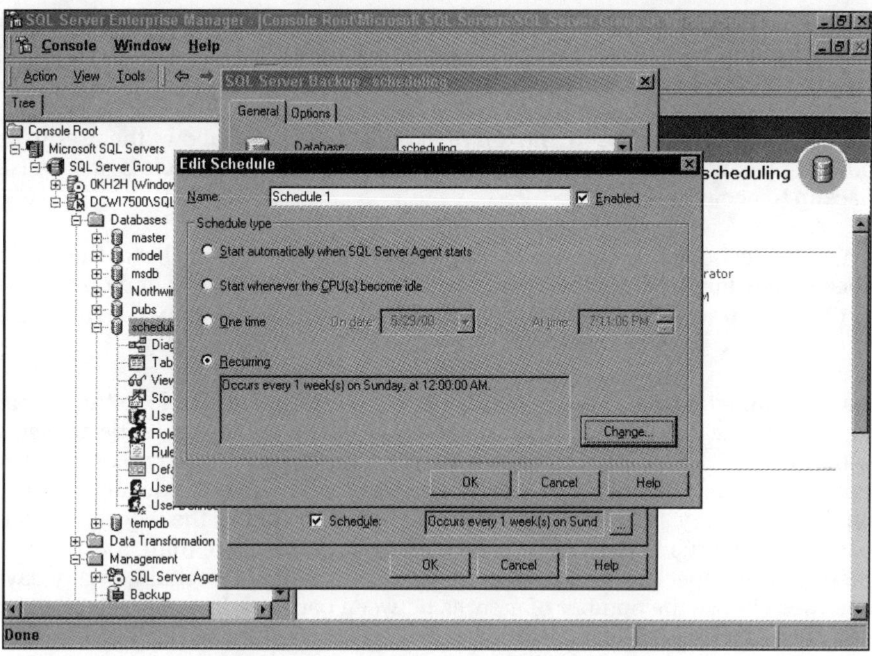

Figure 23-2: The Edit Schedule dialog box in Enterprise Manager

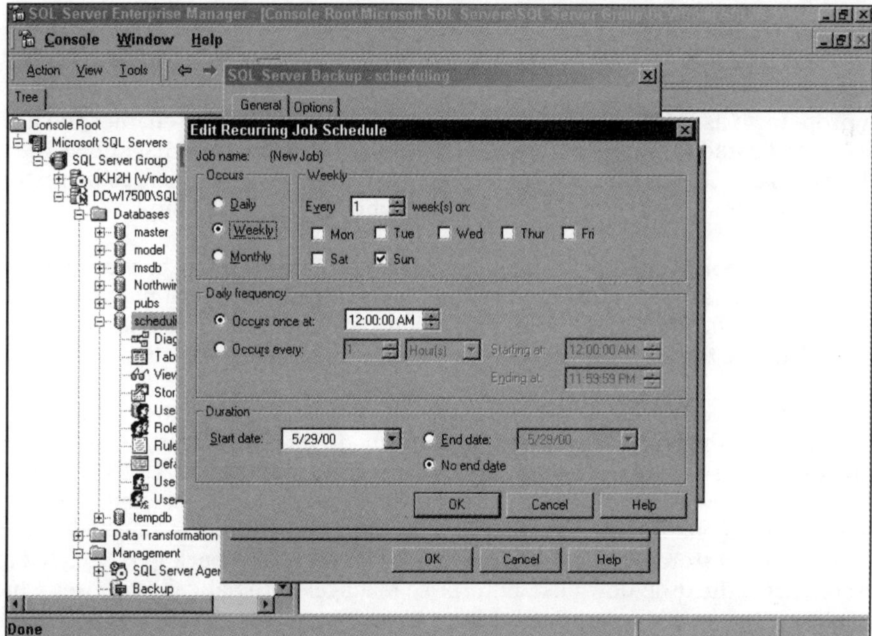

Figure 23-3: Edit Recurring Job Schedule dialog box

The top left of the scheduling dialog box allows the user to choose the type of schedule that will be used. The top right of the dialog box varies slightly, depending upon which type of schedule is chosen.

If a daily schedule is chosen, the top right of the dialog box allows the user to specify how many days the system will wait between backups. The default is one, causing the backup to occur every day.

If a weekly schedule is chosen, the top right of the dialog box allows the user to specify how many weeks the system will wait between backups and on which days of the backup week the backup will run. The default for weeks between backups is one, running a backup every week. The default for days is Sunday.

If a monthly schedule is chosen, a number of choices are available to the user at the top right of the dialog box. The cardinal day of the month must first be chosen, along with the period of months between which backups are run. This choice could, for example, set the backup for the 15th of every second month; the default is to back up on the 1st of every month. Alternatively, the user can choose the day on which the backup should run in the following way: choose first, second, third, fourth, or last; then choose a specific day of the week—a weekend day, a weekday, or any day—and then choose the number of months between backups. By using this last choice, you could back up on the last Friday of every sixth month and the first Monday of every month, or any other combination of intervals.

Restore

To initiate a restore of a database, right-click on the database and choose All Tasks ➪ Restore Database. The Restore database dialog box shown in Figure 23-4 is displayed.

A drop-down list at the top of the Restore database dialog box enables the user to select the database to be restored. To be clear, this drop-down list shows the name the database will have after it is restored. MSDE allows a database to be restored under a different name than the one it had when it was backed up.

The capability to restore to a different database name is useful in two common situations. Use the capability to perform periodic restores to test the backup media without interfering with the production database, and use it to create a test database that is populated with data very similar to the production database.

After users have selected the database to which the backup will be restored, they should select the type of restore to be performed. Selecting a restore option changes the way the rest of the dialog box allows the user to find the source for the restore. Figure 23-4 shows the dialog box when the database option is selected. The rest of the dialog box enables the user to view the history of backups for a chosen database. This history is stored in the msdb database. When the first backup is selected to restore from the drop-down list, Enterprise Manager automatically chooses what it thinks are the most appropriate backups to restore.

For example, Figure 23-4 was created after the Scheduling database had been backed up three times. The history of these backups can be seen at the bottom of the dialog box. The first backup was a full backup, the second was a transaction log, and the third was differential. The backup set name column shows the name that was typed in at the time of the backup; in this example, the names were set to describe the type of backups performed.

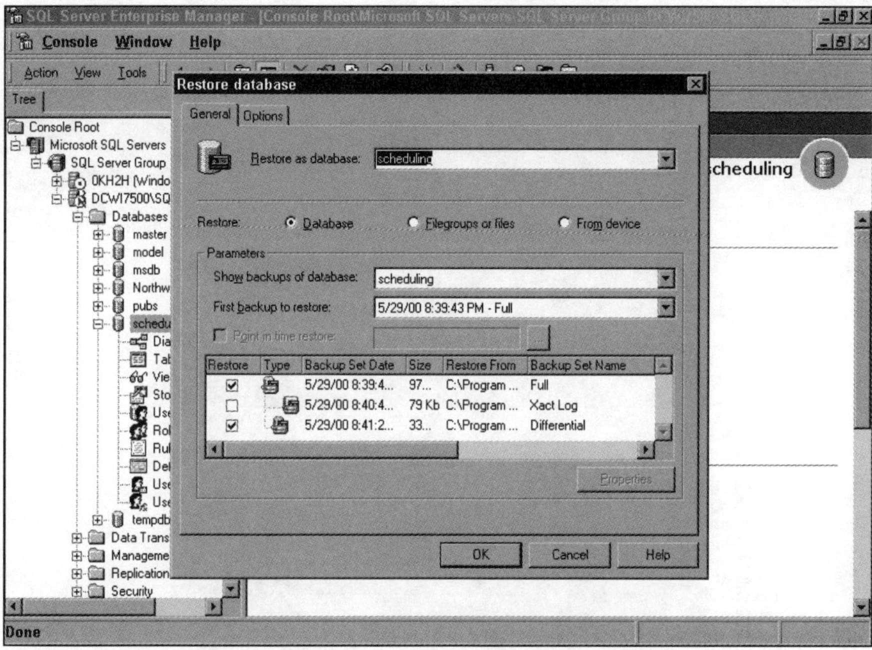

Figure 23-4: The Restore database dialog box in Enterprise Manager

Notice that the full and differential backups are both selected but the transaction log backup is not. That selection is chosen by default because Enterprise Manager attempts to restore the database to the most current possible state based on the backup chosen in the First backup to restore drop-down list. The differential backup contains all the changes since the last full backup; therefore, there is no need to restore the transaction log backup. Although the dialog box shows only three history items, if there had been another transaction monitor backup after the differential backup, Enterprise Manager would have selected that transaction log backup in addition to the full and differential backups. Additional information is available about each backup by clicking the backup and then clicking the Properties button.

Figure 23-5 shows the Restore database dialog box with the Filegroups or files option selected. With the dialog box in this configuration, a user can select any individual file or filegroup, as well as the transaction logs, to restore. When the Filegroups or files option is selected, Enterprise Manager automatically selects the appropriate transaction lines to restore. Selecting the check box and a subset of backup sets enables the user to filter the list of backups that are shown. The filtering can be done by the hard drive on which the files exist by the time after which the backups were taken or by the names of the files and filegroups.

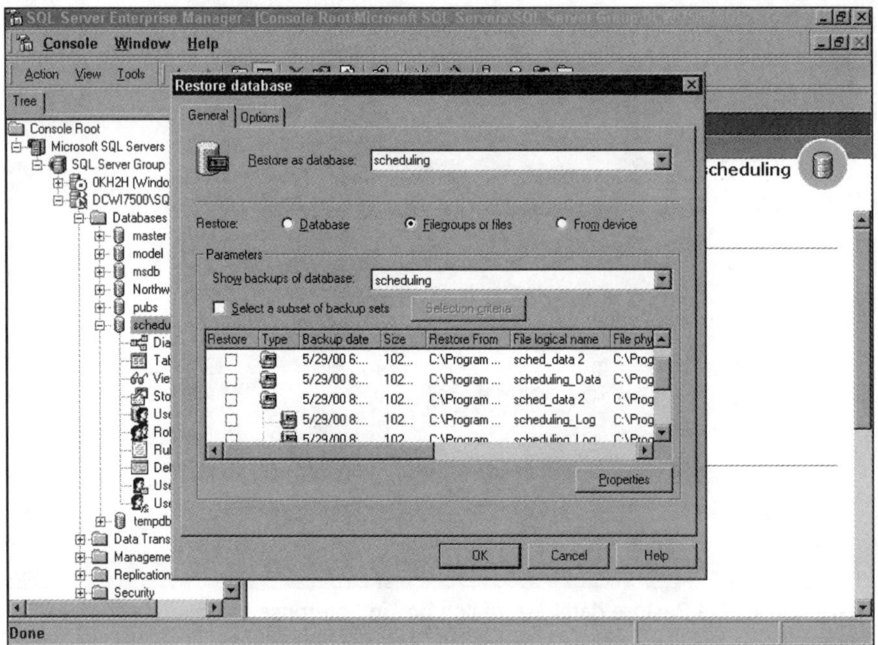

Figure 23-5: Restoring files or filegroups in Enterprise Manager

Figure 23-6 shows the Restore database dialog box with the From device option selected. With the dialog box in this configuration, any backup device can be selected. This configuration is useful if the backup device is a temporary file or if the backup is no longer stored in the history in the msdb database. The Select Devices button invokes a dialog box from which the user can browse to a file or choose a backup device from a list. After a backup device has been selected, details about the backups stored in that device can be displayed by clicking the View Contents button. The option buttons at the bottom of the dialog box allow the user to restore the backup set, choose the appropriate type of backup, or read the information about the backup device and record it in the history kept in the msdb database. After the information is read into the msdb database, it will appear in the Restore database dialog box when the database option is selected.

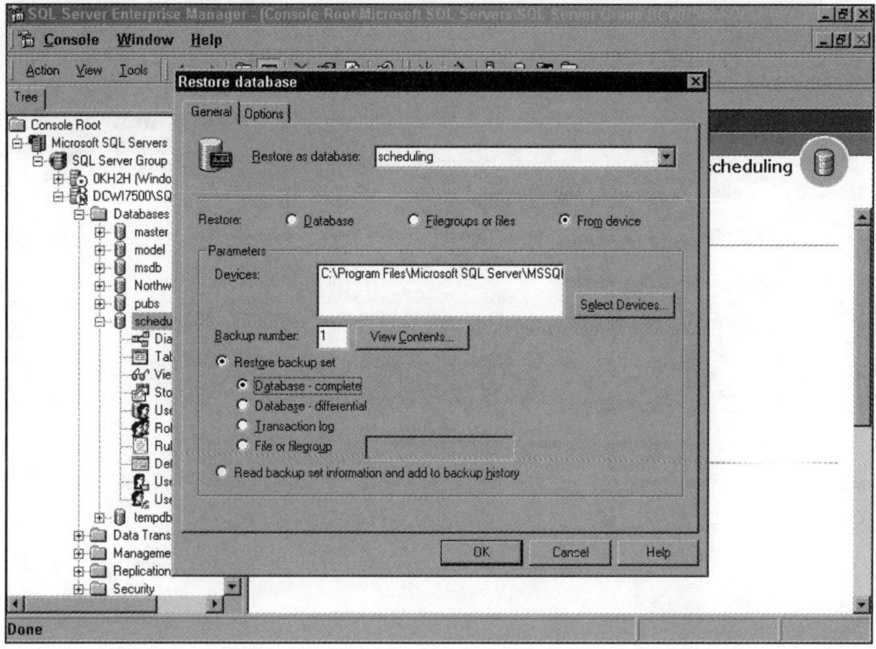

Figure 23-6: Restoring from temporary files in Enterprise Manager

The dialog box shown in Figure 23-7 contains the option settings for restoring a database backup.

- ✦ The top check box is self-explanatory: tapes are automatically ejected after backup if a tape drive is being used.
- ✦ The second check box prompts the operator between each backup. For example, if the backup set being restored contains a full backup, a differential backup, and two transaction logs, then the operator will be prompted four times to proceed with the backup.
- ✦ The third check box is used to restore the database over an existing database if the existing database is not exactly the same as the database that is contained on the backup media.

The center section of the Restore Options dialog box allows the respecification of each filename associated with the original database. Figure 23-7 shows a backup set of a database that consists of three files. The details are not available in the figure, but one of the files must be a log file, one must be a data file, and the third must be a second data file. Each of these files could individually be restored to a different location or filename.

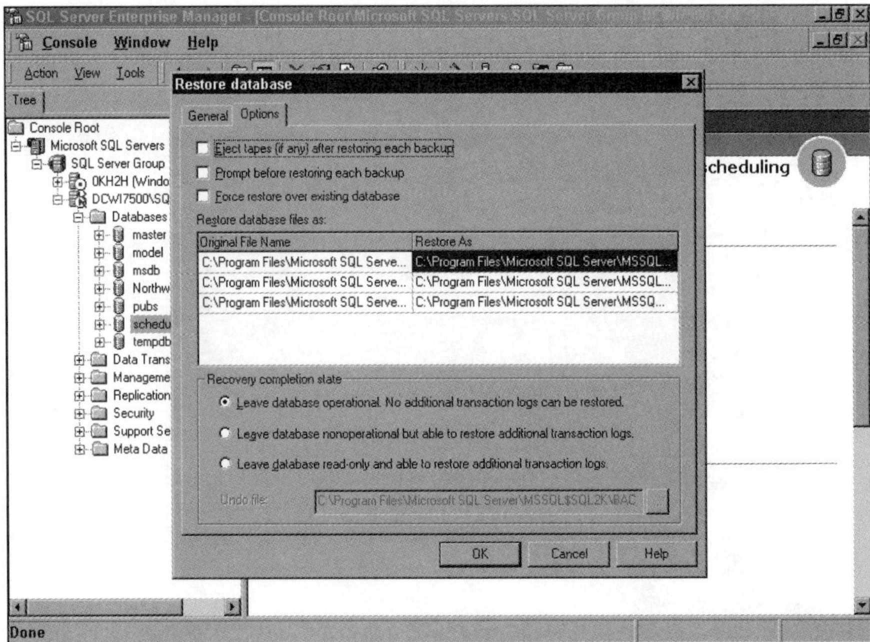

Figure 23-7: Restore Options dialog box in Enterprise Manager

The bottom section of the Restore Options dialog box has three option buttons that control the recovery completion state.

✦ The first option button leaves the database operational after the restore in such a way that no additional transaction logs can be restored. This option causes MSDE to run the recovery process after the backup has been restored. The recovery process reads the restored transaction months, rolls all committed transactions forward, and rolls all uncommitted transactions back. No additional transaction logs can be restored because rolling back transactions causes a gap in the activity of the database.

✦ The second option leaves the database nonoperational but able to restore more transaction logs because it does not run the recovery process. This means that any transaction logs that are restored are left on disk in an unrecovered state with potentially both committed and uncommitted transactions. Because no transactions are rolled back, there is no gap in the activity of the database if additional transaction logs are restored.

✦ The third option, which is sometimes called standby, leaves the database in read-only mode but still able to restore additional transaction lines. When the third option is chosen, a text box at the bottom of the dialog box becomes active for specification of an undo file. When the database is restored into a standby mode, the recovery process is run; however, an undo file is created that stores any activity that would otherwise be lost due to rolling back transactions that were uncommitted at the time of the backup. If additional transaction lines are restored, the undo file is accessed, the rolled back transactions are restored, and any additional transactions are appended to the transaction log. While the server is in standby mode, it must be read-only because any modifications to the data would cause transactions to be written to the transaction log, which would interfere with the application of the undo file and additional transaction logs.

The first recovery option is the most common. When restoring a database to an operational state, the operator normally specifies all of the necessary components of the backup set — for example, a full backup, perhaps a differential backup, and as many transaction logs as are necessary to make the database current. If all of the necessary components of the backup set are specified, then recovery can be specified to run at the completion of the restore. MSDE will automatically defer recovery until the last component of the recovery set is restored.

The standby option is also common in environments in which having a hot spare server (a spare server that is running and ready to take over for the production server) double as a read-only server is desirable. For example, in a heavily transactional environment, one server can be set up to perform the online transaction processing, while a standby server can be set up for decision support. Periodically throughout the day, backups can be taken of the OLTP server and can be restored onto the standby server. Reporting and analytical processing can be performed on the standby server. If the OLTP server ever goes down, recovery can be run on the standby server, and it can quickly be brought into service handling transaction processing.

The second recovery option, leaving the database nonoperational, will usually be employed only in an environment in which a hot spare server is needed, but on which no additional processing needs to be run. Clustering technologies have become available, making such a scenario with labor-intensive techniques obsolete.

Using SQL

The basic syntax to perform a full backup is as follows:

```
BACKUP DATABASE <database>
TO <backup device>
[WITH <with clause options>]
```

The backup device can be either the logical name of a backup device that has already been created or the physical path to a file system file or a tape drive (in which case, the programmer must additionally supply the keywords DISK= or TAPE=). For example, the following command backs up the scheduling database:

```
BACKUP DATABASE Scheduling
TO DISK = 'C:\backup\sched\Tuesday.bak'
```

This code will create the file Tuesday.bak if it does not already exist. To specify whether the backup process should overwrite existing data in the file, the WITH INIT or WITH NOINIT parameters can be used. For example, the following code modifies the previous example to always overwrite the file:

```
BACKUP DATABASE Scheduling
TO DISK = 'C:\backup\sched\Tuesday.bak'
WITH INIT
```

To pre-create a backup device, use the sp_addumpdevice (note the double, not triple, 'd') stored procedure:

```
sp_addumpdevice
'disk','SchedDev','C:\backup\sched\weeklydev.bak'
```

To perform a differential backup, add the keyword DIFFERENTIAL to the WITH clause, as in this example:

```
BACKUP DATABASE Scheduling
TO SchedDev
WITH NOINIT, DIFFERENTIAL
```

This code will add a differential backup to the SchedDev device created in the previous example.

To back up the transactions log for a database, the following generalized syntax should be used:

```
BACKUP LOG <database>
TO <backup device>
[WITH <with clause options>]
```

For example, the following code adds a transaction log backup to the file created above:

```
BACKUP LOG Scheduling
TO DISK = 'C:\backup\sched\Tuesday.bak'
WITH NOINIT
```

All of these examples presuppose that the directory C:\backup\sched exists. Backup will create a file for the backup, but will not create the directories.

The database can be placed in either restore mode or standby mode with the `BACKUP LOG` command using `WITH NORECOVERY` or `WITH STANDBY = <undo filename>`. The following command backs up the active portion of the transaction log and leaves the database in restore mode, which is a state in which the database is nonoperational but transaction log backups can be restored.

```
BACKUP LOG Scheduling
TO DISK = 'C:\backup\sched\LogTail.bak'
WITH NORECOVERY
```

Once the database is in this state, recovery must be run before normal operations can be resumed.

The general syntax to restore a database is as follows:

```
RESTORE DATABASE <database>
[FROM <backup device>]
[WITH <with clause options>]
```

For example, to restore the backup created in the first example in this section, use the following code:

```
RESTORE DATABASE Scheduling
FROM DISK = 'C:\backup\sched\tuesday.bak'
```

The general syntax to restore the transaction log for a database is as follows:

```
RESTORE LOG <database>
[FROM <backup device>]
[WITH <with clause options>]
```

When either a database or the transaction log for a database is restored, the user can specify whether the database should go into normal operation, restore mode, or standby mode. The corresponding `WITH` clause parameters used to accomplish this are `RECOVERY`, `NORECOVERY`, or `STANDBY`. For example, the following code restores a transaction log and causes the recovery process to be executed, leaving the database operational:

```
RESTORE LOG Scheduling
FROM SchedDev
WITH RECOVERY
```

If the recovery process needs to be executed on the database, it can be done manually with the `restore` command. For example, if you have restored to transaction logs and specified no recovery and later need to execute recovery, execute `RESTORE DATABASE <database> WITH RECOVERY`.

The restore command can be used to restore an individual filegroup by specifying a file or filegroup immediately before the FROM clause in the restore command. If any changes have been made to the filegroup after the backup has been taken, the user will be notified in the messages returned from the restore and will be required to restore transaction logs in order to bring the filegroup up-to-date.

Filegroups can also be restored to a new location by themselves without restoring the rest of the database by using the PARTIAL parameter in the WITH clause of the restore. Performing a partial restoring this way can facilitate retrieving data that was accidentally deleted or damaged.

Using DMO

The DMO hierarchy for backup and restore is as follows:

```
Backup
Restore
SQLServer
    BackupDevices
        BackupDevice
```

The Backup and Restore objects are created independently of a SQLServer object; however, a SQLServer object must be created and connected to an MSDE Server in order to execute the SQLBackup or SQLRestore methods. A connected SQLServer object must be passed to these methods at the time of execution.

The following code performs a full backup of the scheduling database:

```
dim oBackup
dim oMSDEServer

set oMSDEServer = CreateObject("SQLDMO.SQLServer")
set oBackup = CreateObject("SQLDMO.Backup")

oBackup.Database = "Scheduling"
oBackup.Files = "C:\Backup\Sched\DMOFull.bak"
oBackup.Initialize = True
oBackup.MediaName = "DMOFullBack"

oMSDEserver.connect "Okh2h","sa",""
oBackup.SQLBackup(oMSDEServer)
oMSDEserver.disconnect
```

You can find this code on the CD-ROM in the file named Ch 23\FullBack.vbs.

The file property of the Backup object is used to specify a temporary file; it serves the same purpose as the WITH DISK = parameter in the SQL backup command. Alternatively, the DEVICE, PIPE, or TAPE parameters can be used to specify a predefined backup device, a named pipe, or a tape device, respectively. Only one of the four properties may be given a value. The Initialize property can be set to true or false and is used to determine whether the backup will overwrite the existing contents of the backup media. The MediaName property is used to specify a descriptive name for the backup; there is also a MediaDescription property that was not used in this sample.

To perform a differential backup, the Action property of the Backup object should be set to 1. The following example performs a differential backup and appends it to the predefined backup device called SchedDev:

```
dim oBackup
dim oMSDEServer

set oMSDEServer = CreateObject("SQLDMO.SQLServer")
set oBackup = CreateObject("SQLDMO.Backup")
oBackup.Database = "Scheduling"
oBackup.Devices = "SchedDev"
oBackup.Initialize = False
oBackup.Action = 1
oBackup.MediaName = "DMODiffBack"

oMSDEserver.connect "Okh2h","sa",""
oBackup.SQLBackup(oMSDEServer)
oMSDEserver.disconnect
```

You can find this code on the CD-ROM in the file named Ch 23\DiffBack.vbs.

To perform a transaction log backup, the Action property of the Backup object should be set to 3. All other properties are the same as the backup for full or differential. The following code performs a transaction log backup:

```
dim oBackup
dim oMSDEServer

set oMSDEServer = CreateObject("SQLDMO.SQLServer")
set oBackup = CreateObject("SQLDMO.Backup")
oBackup.Database = "Scheduling"
oBackup.Files = "C:\Backup\Sched\DMOLog.bak"
oBackup.Initialize = True
oBackup.MediaName = "DMOTLBack"
oBackup.Action = 3
```

```
oMSDEserver.connect "0kh2h","sa",""
oBackup.SQLBackup(oMSDEServer)
oMSDEserver.disconnect
```

You can find this code on the CD-ROM in the file named `Ch 23\TLBack.vbs`.

To perform a restore using DMO:

1. Instantiate a Restore object and set the `database` property.
2. Create a SQLServer object and connect it to an instance of MSDE.
3. Call the `SQLRestore` method of the Restore object, passing the name of the SQLServer object.

The following code restores the full backup that was created in a previous example:

```
dim oRestore
dim oMSDEServer

set oMSDEServer = CreateObject("SQLDMO.SQLServer")
set oRestore = CreateObject("SQLDMO.Restore")
oRestore.Database = "Scheduling"
oRestore.Files = "C:\Backup\Sched\DMOFull.bak"

oMSDEserver.connect "0kh2h","sa",""
oRestore.SQLRestore(oMSDEServer)
oMSDEserver.disconnect
```

You can find this code on the CD-ROM in the file named `Ch 23\RestData.vbs`.

To restore a differential backup, the same techniques used for the full restore can be employed. A differential restore must follow a full restore, and the full restore must leave the database in either restore mode or standby mode. Setting the `LastRestore` property of the Restore object to `false` will leave the database in restore mode. To leave the database in standby mode, the `LastRestore` property should be set to `false` and the `StandByFiles` property should be set to a valid filename. The file will be created if one does not exist, but the directory in which it will be created must be preexistent. The following code restores a database and leaves it in standby mode:

```
dim oRestore
dim oMSDEServer
```

```
set oMSDEServer = CreateObject("SQLDMO.SQLServer")
set oRestore = CreateObject("SQLDMO.Restore")
oRestore.Database = "Scheduling"
oRestore.Files = "C:\Backup\Sched\DMOFull.bak"
oRestore.LastRestore = False
oRestore.StandByFiles = "C:\Undo.und"

oMSDEserver.connect "Okh2h","sa",""
oRestore.SQLRestore(oMSDEServer)
oMSDEserver.disconnect
```

You can find this code on the CD-ROM in the file named `Ch 23\RestSB.vbs`.

To restore a transaction log, the same techniques used for the full and differential restores apply, but the `Action` property must be set to `2`. The following code restores a transaction log backup and leaves the database in restore mode so that additional transaction logs can be restored:

```
dim oRestore
dim oMSDEServer

set oMSDEServer = CreateObject("SQLDMO.SQLServer")
set oRestore = CreateObject("SQLDMO.Restore")
oRestore.Database = "Scheduling"
oRestore.Files = "C:\Backup\Sched\DMOLog.bak"
oRestore.LastRestore = False

oMSDEserver.connect "Okh2h","sa",""
oRestore.SQLRestore(oMSDEServer)
oMSDEserver.disconnect
```

You can find this code on the CD-ROM in the file named `Ch 23\RestLog.vbs`.

Recovery should be specified on the last transaction log restored when using DMO. There is no way to specify that a database should be recovered without actually restoring something.

Summary

A strategy for backing up and restoring databases is a key component of the disaster recovery scheme. MSDE has integrated backup and restore facilities with a high degree of flexibility to meet any disaster recovery requirements. The backup utility supports full, differential, and transaction log backups depending on the recovery model that is used. The restore utility supports restoring databases to different servers or locations, performing partial restores, and resuming interrupted restores. Backup and restore are both supported by a fully functional job scheduling mechanism. Backup center stores can be performed via file system files, streaming tape, or named pipes. All of the relevant features of the backup and restore utilities should be molded together into a comprehensive plan for the protection of data, and that plan should be regularly tested.

✦ ✦ ✦

CHAPTER 24

Accessing Data from Programs, Scripts, and Web Pages Using ADO and XML

✦ ✦ ✦ ✦

In This Chapter

Using the ADO connection object

Using the ADO command object

Using the ADO recordset object

Using Access and VBA to connect to MSDE

Using Visual Basic to connect to MSDE

Using Active Server Pages to connect to MSDE

Using XML to connect to MSDE

Using Windows Scripting Host and VBScript to connect to MSDE

✦ ✦ ✦ ✦

Microsoft ActiveX Data Objects (ADO) is a powerful object model that allows users to connect to MSDE and other databases from external programs. Once a connection is made using the ADO connection object, the command and recordset ADO objects can be used to execute SQL statements against the database. Although the variety of programming tools that can be used to access data from the MSDE database may seem overwhelming, this chapter will clarify the function and use of these tools. It will also cover some helpful tips on how to choose one tool over the other.

Understanding ActiveX Data Objects

Chapter 5 discusses how ActiveX Data Objects (ADO) is a high-level data access model that can be used to communicate with ODBC or OLE DB from any programming language that can access COM objects. For example, when you write a Visual Basic, C++, or Access program to communicate with your MSDE database, ADO is the recommended method to access the data. It might be helpful to take a look at the ADO object model as it is presented in Chapter 5.

- Connection
  - Error
  - Property
- Command
  - Parameter
  - Property
- Recordset
  - Field
  - Property

There are three primary object collections in the ADO object model: Connection, Command, and Recordset. The collection objects listed below each collection contain additional information about their parent object. Because each object collection has numerous properties and methods (for example, the connection object has a method called `Open`), it is not possible to list them all here. However, I will briefly recap what each of these object collections is used for.

The connection object maintains information about the database connection, such as the connection string, default database, and so on. A SQL statement can also be executed against the connection object.

The command object maintains information about a command, such as the SQL string to be executed, parameters being passed, and so on. Under certain circumstances, SQL statements can be executed without using the command object, such as with the connection and recordset objects. The command object is best suited for executing a SQL statement or stored procedure that doesn't return any records, but it can also be used with statements that return records. If records are being returned, however, a recordset will have to be assigned to the results of the command.

Whenever records need to be retrieved from the database, the recordset object should be used to execute the SQL statement and retrieve the records.

The error object contains information about any errors that occur when using the connection object. The property object can be used with the connection, command, or recordset object to retrieve additional information about them. ADO has several built-in properties that can be used with any data source, but also allows for data providers to provide their own dynamic properties. These dynamic properties allow each data provider (such as SQL Server/MSDE engine) to provide its own special features.

Controlling connections to MSDE using the connection object

The ADO connection object allows a user to specify the connection parameters, such as the ODBC or OLE DB provider information, and connect to that data source. To declare a new connection object, use the following syntax:

```
Dim oConn as New ADODB.connection
```

Before the ADO functionality can be used, a reference to the project must be added to the Microsoft ActiveX Data Objects 2.0 Library (or the highest available version).

After a new connection object is declared, connection properties can be set that tell the program how ADO can communicate with the desired database. When using an ODBC data source, this syntax opens the connection:

```
oConn.Open "MSDESample", "sa", ""
```

This code uses the `Open` method of the connection object to connect to a database using an ODBC data source name (DSN) named MSDESample. MSDESample contains the server name and the database name and may contain other specifications about how the connection is to be made. The parameters following the DSN are the user id and password. The connection object also allows all the connection information to be specified in one string, instead of being separated by commas, as shown in the previous code example. The following syntax specifies a single string to connect to the ODBC data source with ADO:

```
OConn.Open "DSN=MSDESample;User Id=sa;Password=;"
```

To connect to the database through OLE DB instead of ODBC, the following ADO syntax can be used:

```
Dim strConnect as string
StrConnect = "Provider=SQLOLEDB;Server=MSDEServer;" & _
             "Database=MSDESample;User Id=sa;Password=;"
oConn.Open strConnect
```

In this example, the SQLOLEDB provider is specified, and a server called MSDEServer is used. Next, the database name, user id, and password are specified. For this example to work, access to a server called MSDEServer and an MSDE database called MSDESample that resides on that server is necessary.

Once an open connection has been established, a SQL statement can be executed against the connection object, the command object, or the recordset object. Executing a SQL statement against the connection object itself without using the command or recordset objects can be done with an `Insert`, `Update`, or `Delete` (that is, an action that does not return any rows). An example of the ADO syntax for executing a SQL statement with the connection object follows:

```
Dim strSQL as string
strSQL = "UPDATE patient SET Address = 'Somewhere New' WHERE
        patientid = 2"
oconn.Execute strSQL
```

In this example, a SQL string is defined, and the `Execute` method of the connection object is called to execute that SQL statement. No specific variable is needed to hold the SQL string before executing it. The following code also accomplishes the same result:

```
OConn.Execute "UPDATE patient SET Address = 'Somewhere New'
             WHERE patientid = 2"
```

In this example, the SQL string is placed immediately following the `Execute` method of the connection object.

Sending SQL commands to MSDE with the command object

Assuming there is now an open connection to the MSDE database, commands can be sent to it by using the command object. The following statement declares the new command object:

```
Dim oCommand as New ADODB.Command
```

Once declared, the command object's properties and methods can be accessed. For example, you can set the `CommandText` property to a string containing a SQL statement:

```
oCommand.CommandText = "UPDATE patient SET Address = 'Somewhere
                        New' WHERE patientid = 2"
```

This example assigns the `CommandText` property of the command object, which contains the SQL statement to be executed. After the command object has been told what SQL statement to execute, an active connection must be assigned to specify which database connection to use, as shown in the following code:

```
oCommand.ActiveConnection = oconn
```

Finally, the statement can be executed against the MSDE database and can call the command's `Execute` method to do so:

```
oCommand.Execute
```

As the CommandText and ActiveConnection properties have already been set, the statement will be executed against the database when the Execute method is called. Had the SQL statement and connections to be used not been specified before trying to run the Execute method, an error would have occurred.

A common way developers use the command object is to execute stored procedures and assign the parameter values to be passed into the stored procedure. For example, a stored procedure called get_patient_records on the MSDE database that accepts LastName and FirstName as parameters and then returns the patient information for that patient can use the code shown in Listing 24-1 to have the command object run that stored procedure:

Listing 24-1: Command Object Executing a Stored Procedure with Parameters

```
Dim oCommand As New ADODB.Command
Dim rsExecute As New ADODB.Recordset

Dim pLastName As ADODB.Parameter
Dim pFirstName As ADODB.Parameter

rsExecute.CursorLocation = adUseClient
oconn.CursorLocation = adUseClient

oCommand.CommandText = "get_patient_records"
oCommand.CommandType = adCmdStoredProc

Set pLastName = oCommand.CreateParameter("LastName", adChar,
                adParamInput, 40)
Set pFirstName = oCommand.CreateParameter("FirstName", adChar,
                 adParamInput, 40)

oCommand.Parameters.Append pLastName
oCommand.Parameters.Append pFirstName

pLastName.Value = "Doe"
pFirstName.Value = "John"

Set oCommand.ActiveConnection = oconn
Set rsExecute = oCommand.Execute

Set dgResults.DataSource = rsExecute
```

The code in Listing 24-1 first declares a command, parameter, and recordset object. It assumes that the oConn connection object is still open from before. Then, it sets the recordset and connection cursor locations to the client. The rest of the code sets up the command object to call the stored procedure and pass in the parameters.

The CommandText property of the command object gets set to the stored procedure name to be executed (get_patient_records, in this case). The CommandType property of the command object gets set to a stored procedure. The next step is to use the parameter variables that were declared to set up the LastName and FirstName parameters that have to be passed into the stored procedure. The LastName and FirstName parameters are created using the CreateParameter method of the command object. Once created, these parameters are added to the command object and assigned their values to be passed into the stored procedure. The active connection for the command is set to the currently open connection. Then, the command is executed, and the results are put into the recordset. These recordset results are displayed in a data grid that is on the form.

Accessing rows returned from MSDE with the recordset object

A recordset object can be used whenever data needs to be returned from MSDE or another database. Again, the first step in using a recordset is to declare the recordset object:

```
Dim rsResults as New ADODB.Recordset
```

Once declared, the recordset can be used with or without a command object. Previous examples have shown a recordset used with a command object to retrieve the results from a stored procedure. A recordset can also be opened independently with its own SQL statement, as shown in the following:

```
Dim rsResults As New ADODB.Recordset
rsResults.CursorLocation = adUseClient
rsResults.Open "select * from patient", oconn, adOpenKeyset,
                  adLockBatchOptimistic
Set rsResults.ActiveConnection = Nothing

Do While Not rsResults.EOF
    'do nothing
    rsResults.MoveNext
Loop
```

The preceding example declares a new recordset object and executes the Open method of the recordset object to retrieve all of the patient records from the database. The CursorLocation and ActiveConnection properties of the recordset work together to "disconnect" the recordset from the data source. A disconnected recordset is in the memory of the client and has no further connection to the original source. This example also shows how to loop through the recordset to take some action.

Choosing a Programming Environment

Every application programming project involves choosing a programming environment. Applications can be developed in Access, Visual Basic, or a Web environment using Active Server Pages (ASP). Within each of these environments, there may be additional choices regarding the languages that are available and the ways in which data may be represented. This section describes these environments and how they interact with MSDE, as well as the Visual Basic for Applications (VBA), Visual Basic, and VBScript languages. The Extensible Markup Language (XML) is also covered as a generic mechanism for data representation.

Access and Visual Basic for Applications

Microsoft Access is a very powerful and commonly used programming language/database program that uses the Visual Basic for Applications (VBA) language. Access is often used to create databases with forms, queries, macros, and reports and to link to external data sources in order to manipulate them in a user-friendly environment.

Many people use Access to develop applications because Access is part of the Microsoft Office product suite. In addition, Access stores everything in a single file and can be run on client computers that have Access (which most have nowadays) without having to create a complicated setup program. Access can easily link to external data sources like MSDE and manipulate that data using VBA code or graphical tools such as the Query Builder.

Access can be used to create a form and to place controls — such as text boxes, labels, data grids, and command buttons — on that form. New modules can then be created that contain procedures and functions to perform database operations. From the form, these modules can be called and executed. Since Access uses Visual Basic for Applications as its programming language, it is possible to cut and paste Visual Basic code into Access, and vice versa. Occasionally, a few changes may have to be made, but for the most part, the code stays the same.

To create a function that will accept a string as a parameter and then connect to the MSDESample database and return the results of the SQL statement to the calling routine, open Access so that a new blank database can be created. Then, click on Modules to create a new module. The code to create the routine can be placed in the module, as shown in Figure 24-1.

Figure 24-1 shows the Access environment, as well as the module where the `GetRecords` function is pasted. The `GetRecords` function uses ADO to open a connection, retrieve the recordset, and return the recordset to the calling function. The same syntax will work in Visual Basic. Once the function is created, a form can be designed to call that function and pass the SQL statement to that function.

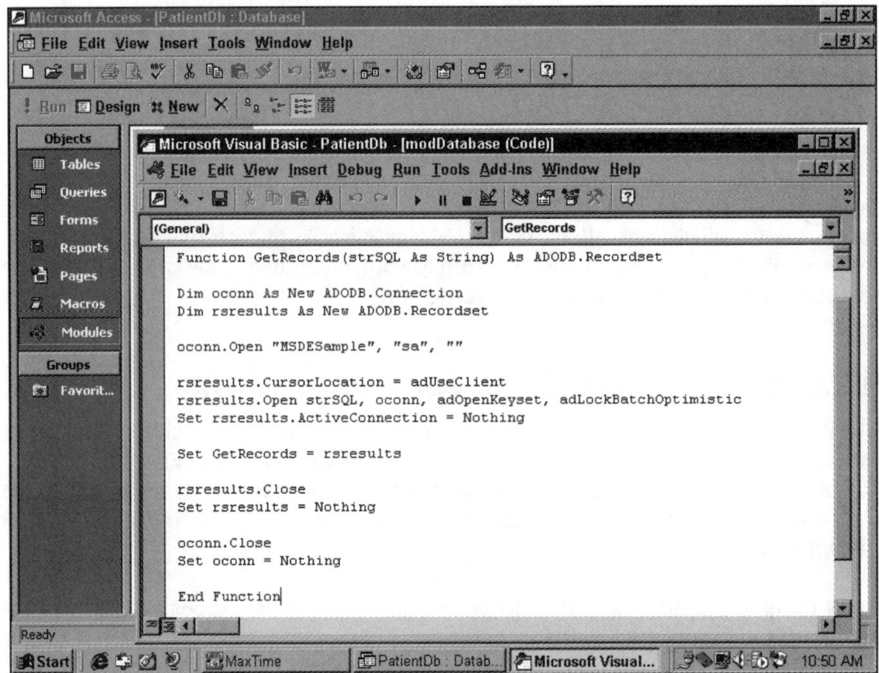

Figure 24-1: Using Access and VBA to create the `GetRecords` function to retrieve data

Access is an ideal tool for organizations that already have it on their computers and do not wish to purchase any additional programming tools. Access is also well suited for smaller applications with a small number of users that do not require huge amounts of code to be stored in the Access database.

Visual Basic

Visual Basic is another powerful programming tool that allows a programmer to create ActiveX DLLs for common code routines and executables for front-end applications.

Visual Basic can store several different types of files: forms, modules, class modules, user controls, and so on. Unlike Access, which stores everything in the .mdb file, Visual Basic stores each of these in a separate file. These files can be compiled into an executable, ActiveX DLL, or ActiveX control (OCX), depending on whether the program has any user interface elements, such as forms, or whether it just contains code modules.

Code to call the MSDE database can be put under forms, in modules, or in class modules. However, it is recommended that the designer of a Visual Basic application create functions and procedures for all of the data access methods and other business rules that will be compiled into separate DLLs. The forms can then handle the user interface elements and call these DLLs to retrieve the data from the database. Using this structure will make it easier to migrate programs to Microsoft Transaction Server/COM+ in the future and will make your code much more reusable.

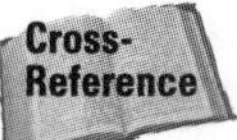

For more information about Microsoft Transaction Server, refer to Chapter 21.

Earlier in this chapter, several examples (in Visual Basic code) were used to show how the ADO command, connection, and recordset objects can be used to connect to the MSDE database Listing 24-2 gives one more example of Visual Basic code that can retrieve data from the MSDE database.

Listing 24-2: **Visual Basic Code to Execute SQL Statements and Display Results in Grid**

```
Screen.MousePointer = vbHourglass
Dim oconn As New ADODB.Connection

'Use the MSDESample ODBC driver
oconn.ConnectionString = "Data Source=MSDESample;User
    ID=sa;Password=;"
oconn.Open

'if it is a select, then display the results in the grid...
'otherwise, just execute the statement
If Left(UCase(txtSQL.Text), 6) = "SELECT" Then
    Dim rsExecute As New ADODB.Recordset
    rsExecute.CursorLocation = adUseClient
    rsExecute.Open txtSQL.Text, oconn, adOpenKeyset,
        adLockBatchOptimistic

    Set rsExecute.ActiveConnection = Nothing
    Set dgResults.DataSource = rsExecute
Else
    oconn.Execute txtSQL.Text
End If

'close the database connection
oconn.Close
Set oconn = Nothing

Screen.MousePointer = vbNormal
```

This example will read the SQL statement that is in the txtSQL text box on the form, and it will then run that SQL statement against MSDE. If that SQL statement starts with `SELECT` (that is, if the `LEFT` six characters are `SELECT`), then this code will run the SQL statement and put the results into a recordset. That recordset will then be displayed in a data grid called dgResults that is on the form. However, if the SQL code begins with something other than `SELECT`, such as `Update`, `Insert`, or `Delete`, then the code just runs the `Execute` method of the connection object to execute that statement.

An illustration of the Visual Basic programming environment is provided in Figure 24-2. First, note the form with the data grid and the text box that is used to call the routine that retrieves the records from the database or execute the statement against the database. Also note that the left portion of the screen provides controls in a toolbox and that the right portion of the screen shows the project contents (frmMSDESample) as well as the form properties.

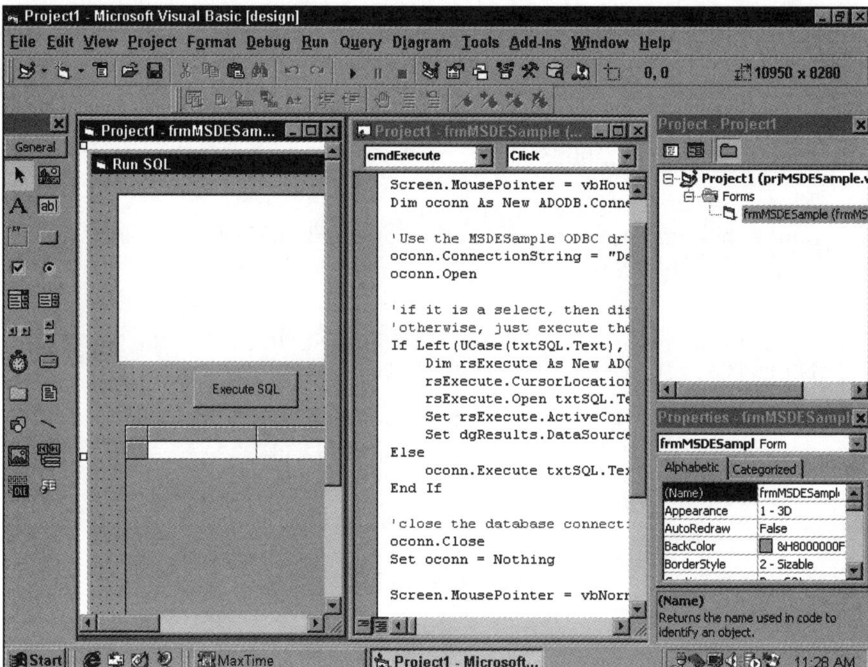

Figure 24-2: The Visual Basic environment

Visual Basic is an excellent choice for creating DLLs that contain business logic, even if the application will be run on the Web. Web-based applications can call COM objects (DLLs) that were created in Visual Basic. If the application is not going to be

Web-based, then a user interface (the EXE) can also be created in Visual Basic. DLLs can be called from a Visual Basic front end for applications that are not Web-based and can also be called from Web-based applications. Thus, for a Web-based application, those same DLLs can be reused. Only the user interface elements will have to be re-created. That is a huge advantage!

Active Server Pages

Active Server Pages (ASP) is a hot topic among developers nowadays. ASP allows developers to connect to their databases from a Web browser. It can also be intermixed with HTML code and can use ADO to connect to MSDE and other data sources. Listing 24-3 provides a complete code listing of an ASP document called QueryWiz.asp:

Listing 24-3: ASP Code to Execute SQL Statement Gathered from User and Display Results in Web Browser

```
<html>

<head>
<title>MSDE Bible Query Wizard</title>
</head>

<body>

<%
  if request.querystring("action") = "" then
     'wait while information is being gathered from the user
%>

<form action="QueryWiz.asp?action=validate" method=post>
  <p align="center"><b>Welcome To The MSDE Bible Query
     Wizard</b></p>
  <p>Please Type Your SQL Select Statement Here And Then Click
     Submit:</p>
  <p><textarea rows="3" name="txtSQL" cols="81"></textarea></p>
<p align="center"><input type="submit" value="Submit"
   name="cmdSubmit"></p>
</form>

<%
   else
      'user took action

%>
```

Continued

Listing 24-3 *(continued)*

```
<h1>Here Are The Results Of Your Select Statement:</h1>

<%
      call get_data
   end if
%>

<%

sub get_data()
   dim oConn   'as an ADODB connection
   dim rsResults 'as an ADODB recordset
   dim strOutput 'string to hold output
   dim i   'integer

   set oconn = server.createobject("ADODB.connection")
   oconn.open "MSDESample", "sa", ""

   set rsResults = oconn.execute (request("txtSQL"))

   Do While Not rsResults.EOF
       for i = 0 to rsresults.fields.count - 1
        strOutput = strOutput & rsresults.fields(i).value & " "
       next

       response.write "<li>" & strOutput
       strOutput = ""

       rsResults.MoveNext
   Loop

   oconn.close
end sub

%>

</body>

</html>
```

Listing 24-3 is a mixture of HTML and ASP code. The HTML code is what creates the display, and the ASP code uses VBScript to process the user's selection. The first part, which consists of HTML, creates an input text box that allows the user to type a SQL Select statement. It also displays a Submit button so the user can see the results when the SQL Select statement has been added. Figure 24-3 shows what the user interface looks like when this .asp file is executed.

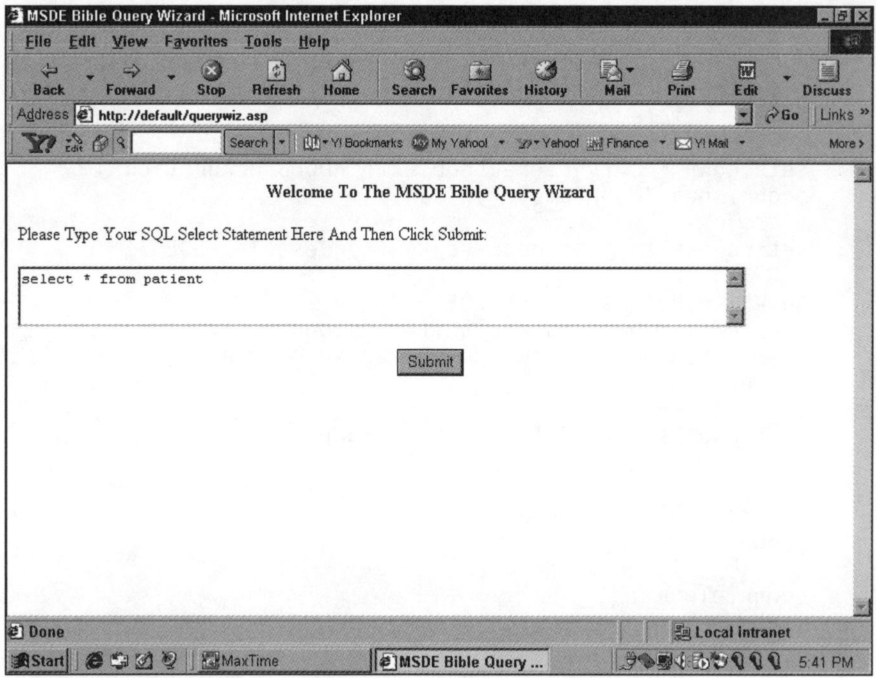

Figure 24-3: Using ASP to run a user-specified SQL statement

In Figure 24-3, the user has typed a SQL statement to select all of the patient records from the database. Once the Submit button is clicked, this portion of the code from Listing 24-3 gets called:

```
<%
   else
      'user took action

%>

<h1>Here Are The Results Of Your Select Statement:</h1>

<%
      call get_data
```

```
   end if
%>

<%

sub get_data()
   dim oConn  'as an ADODB connection
   dim rsResults 'as an ADODB recordset
   dim strOutput 'string to hold output
   dim i   'integer

   set oconn = server.createobject("ADODB.connection")
   oconn.open "MSDESample", "sa", ""

   set rsResults = oconn.execute (request("txtSQL"))

   Do While Not rsResults.EOF
       for i = 0 to rsresults.fields.count - 1
        strOutput = strOutput & rsresults.fields(i).value & " "
       next

       response.write "<li>" & strOutput
       strOutput = ""

       rsResults.MoveNext
   Loop

   oconn.close
end sub

%>

</body>

</html>
```

The `get_data` routine is called once the user takes action. The `get_data` routine contains the ADO code to connect to the MSDE database through an ODBC DSN called MSDESample. The SQL statement specified by the user is passed as the SQL string `(request("txtSQL"))`. Then, for each record in the recordset, the response is written to the Web browser, along with a line feed. In order to capture every field that may possibly be in a Select statement, the Fields collection of the ADO recordset object is used to loop through each field that was returned and add it to the output screen. This allows the code to work no matter how many fields are in the Select statement.

Figure 24-4 shows an example of what the output from the Select statement might look like. Each record that was retrieved from the patient table is displayed. Each field is separated by a space, which is what the code concatenated at the end of each field in the loop.

For more information about ASP, refer to Chapter 27.

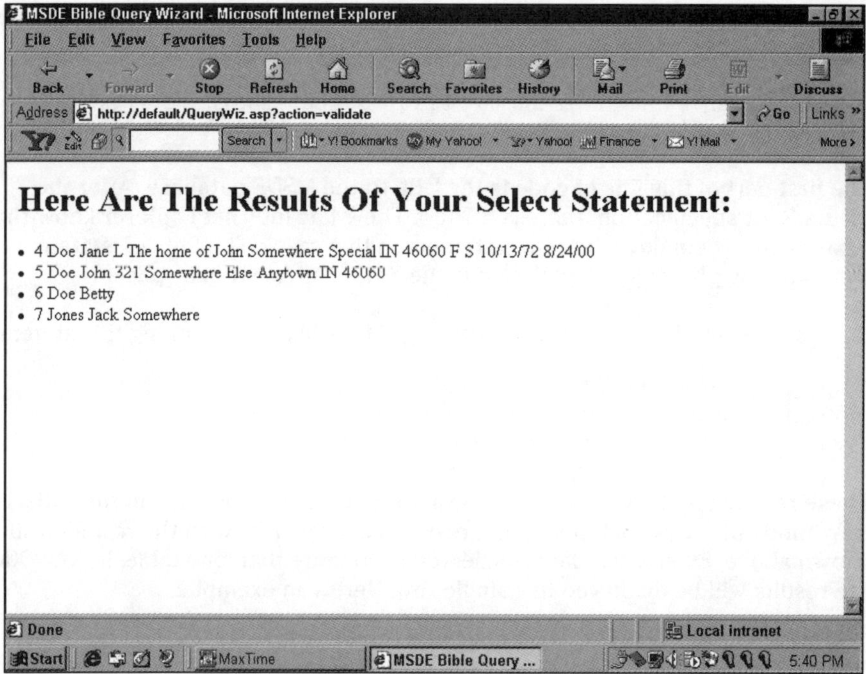

Figure 24-4: Results from a SQL statement

XML

A powerful new feature available as part of SQL Server 2000 and MSDE is XML support. The XML syntax can be used in a Web browser to run SQL statements against the MSDE database. Stored procedures can be executed against the MSDE database from a Web browser using the XML syntax. Queries and stored procedures can be created in the database to return the results in an XML format instead of the standard format.

With SQL Server 2000 and MSDE, support for XML is available.

To make use of these features, a virtual root on IIS (Internet Information Server) must first be defined so that a URL will be associated with the MSDE database.

As part of the graphical interface tools install that comes with SQL Server 2000, there is a utility called IIS Virtual Directory Management for SQL Server.

After a virtual directory pointing to the MSDE database has been assigned, SQL statements can be executed in a Web browser using the XML syntax. To select all patient records from the patient table while in Internet Explorer — and to display the results in XML format — type the following command in the URL line of Internet Explorer:

```
http://ServerName/VirtualRoot?sql=SELECT+LastName,+FirstName+
FROM+Patient+FOR+XML+RAW
```

The first part of this line of code is the URL to the MSDE database. After the VirtualRoot specification, there is a `?sql`. The ? lets Internet Explorer know that a parameter is coming (the SQL statement in this case). The `SELECT` statement is separated by plus signs. A plus sign is the XML equivalent of a space.

Here is an example of what the results might look like after running this statement:

```
<row LastName="Doe" FirstName="John" />
<row LastName="Doe" FirstName="Jane" />
<row LastName="Smith" FirstName="Jack" />
```

These results are displayed in RAW XML format, as was specified in the URL. The RAW mode displays each row in the result in a single row with the row identifier shown above. Even when data is selected from more than one table, in RAW XML the results will be displayed in a single row. Here's an example:

```
http://ServerName/VirtualRoot?sql=SELECT+p.LastName,+p.
FirstName,+c.HPhone+FROM+Patient+p+JOIN+Contacts+c+ON
+p.patientid+=+c.patientid+FOR+XML+RAW
```

After executing this statement in the Web browser, results such as the following will be displayed:

```
<row LastName="Doe" FirstName="John" HPhone="317-111-2222" />
<row LastName="Doe" FirstName="Jane" HPhone="317-111-2222" />
<row LastName="Smith" FirstName="Jack" HPhone="999-222-3333" />
```

The `LastName`, `FirstName`, and `HPhone` fields are displayed together on the row for each record, even though they came from two different tables. There is an AUTO mode that will separate each table into a subcategory.

```
http://ServerName/VirtualRoot?sql=SELECT+p.LastName,+p.
FirstName,+c.HPhone+FROM+Patient+p+JOIN+Contacts+c+ON
+p.patientid+=+c.patientid+FOR+XML+AUTO
```

This is the same statement as the previous one except that it sets the display mode to AUTO instead of RAW. Here are some sample results:

```
<Patient LastName="Doe" FirstName="John">
    <Contacts HPhone="317-111-2222">
</Patient>
<Patient LastName="Doe" FirstName="Jane">
    <Contacts HPhone="317-111-2222">
</Patient>
<Patient LastName="Smith" FirstName="Jack">
    <Contacts HPhone="999-222-3333">
</Patient>
```

This time, the contact information for each record is displayed on a separate line from the last name and first name.

XML in the Web browser can also be used to run an MSDE stored procedure with or without parameters. The `get_patient_records` stored procedure might be defined in the MSDE database as follows:

```
CREATE PROCEDURE get_patient_records
AS
    SELECT *
    FROM patient
    FOR XML AUTO
```

This stored procedure can then be executed with the following URL:

```
http://ServerName/VirtualRoot?sql=EXECUTE+get_patient_records&root=ROOT
```

Since the stored procedure doesn't take any parameters, all that has to be done is to assign the SQL to be executed to the `get_patient_records` stored procedure name, as is shown in the preceding example. If the `get_patient_records` stored procedure had instead been defined to accept parameters, it might look like this:

```
CREATE PROCEDURE get_patient_records
@LastName varchar(40), @FirstName varchar(40)
AS
    SELECT *
    FROM patient LastName
    WHERE = @LastName AND FirstName = @FirstName
    FOR XML AUTO
```

To execute the stored procedure, the following URL can be used:

```
http://ServerName/VirtualRoot?sql=EXECUTE+get_patient_records+
@LastName='Doe'+@FirstName='John'
```

For more information about using XML with the MSDE database, the XML help files that come with SQL Server 2000 can be referenced.

Windows Scripting Host and VBScript

Windows Scripting Host (WSH) is a scripting tool that allows the running of Visual Basic Script or Java Script natively within the base operating system of the client, such as Windows 95, Windows 98, or Windows NT. A similar concept to WSH is a DOS batch file, which runs the script against the local machine. WSH provides a similar feature. If a WSH script file is sent to a user, he or she can double-click and run the file directly from the desktop, Windows Explorer, and so on. It does not have to be run from within an HTML Web document.

Figure 24-5 shows a sample VBScript document in Windows Explorer. The Windows operating system already recognizes the file as a VBScript Script file. Once the file is double-clicked from Windows Explorer, the script will run. If any compiler errors exist in the script, it will bring up a dialog box identifying the line in which the error occurs.

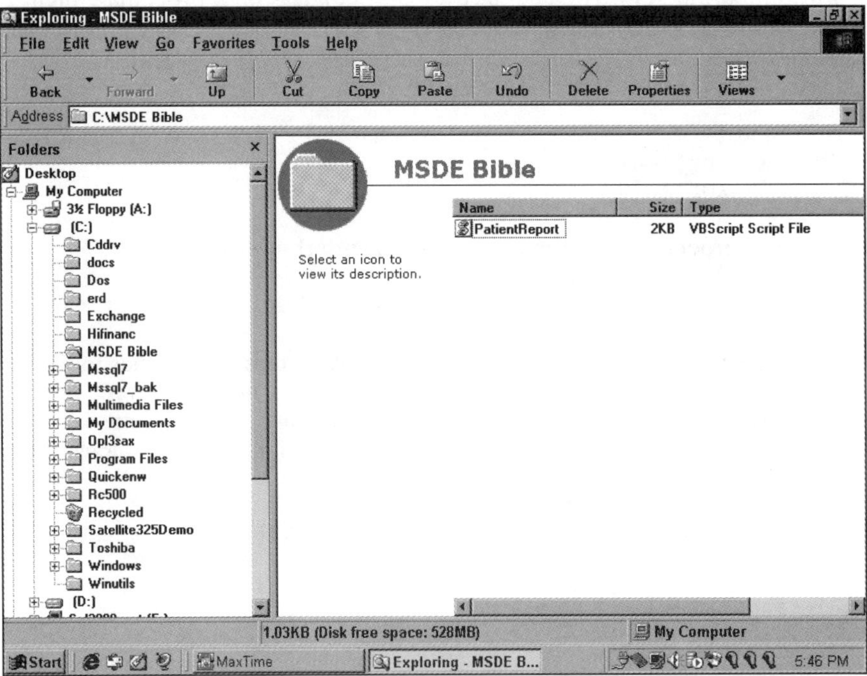

Figure 24-5: VBScript (VBS) file from Windows Explorer

WSH is much more powerful than DOS batch files because it exposes many more features. WSH allows users to use the languages they already know (such as VB) and create automated scripts for common tasks, such as login scripts.

If a programmer wanted to execute a SQL statement every morning to see what patients would be coming into the office that day, he could open Access or Query

Analyzer and run a SQL statement against the MSDE database to get those results. However, the following WSH VBScript code, shown in Listing 24-4, makes it possible to create a script to execute the SQL statement and automatically send the results to the printer on a daily basis.

Listing 24-4: WSH (VBScript) Code to Print a Report

```
Dim oConn 'to become ADO connection
Dim rsResults 'to become ADO recordset
Dim strMessage 'to store the data to output

Dim oPrinter 'printer object
Dim oFileSystem 'file system object
Dim oNetwork 'network object

'connect to the MSDE database using the MSDESample ODBC DSN
Set oConn = CreateObject("ADODB.Connection")
oConn.open "MSDESample", "sa", ""

Set rsResults = CreateObject("ADODB.Recordset")

'retrieve the results from the MSDE database
rsResults.open "SELECT p.LastName, p.FirstName FROM Patient p
    JOIN Visits v ON p.patientid = v.patientid WHERE
    v.VisitDate='06/11/2000'", oConn

'loop through the recordset and put the records into the string
Do While not rsResults.EOF
  strMessage = strMessage & rsResults("LastName") & ", " &
rsResults("FirstName") & chr(13)
  rsResults.MoveNext
Loop

'get ready to print the document
Set oFileSystem = CreateObject("Scripting.FileSystemObject")
Set oNetwork = CreateObject("WScript.Network")
oNetwork.AddPrinterConnection "LPT1", "networkprinterpath",
     false, "UserId", "Password"
Set oPrinter = oFileSystem.CreateTextFile("LPT1:", True)

'output the string to the printer
oPrinter.write(strMessage)

oPrinter.close

Set oFileSystem = nothing
Set oPrinter = nothing
set oNetwork = nothing
Set rsResults = nothing
Set oConn = nothing
```

This example uses ADO to connect to an ODBC data source. Those records for patients that are coming into the office on a certain date are retrieved into a recordset. The script can be modified to use the MSDE function for today so that when run daily, no changes have to be made to the script. Once the records are returned from the database, the results get placed into a string variable. After the string variable is fully populated with the values that need to be sent to the printer, the printer, file system, and network objects are used to communicate with the printer, and the report gets printed.

This process saves the trouble of having to create a Visual Basic program, to compile it into an executable, to distribute the necessary files to the system on which they will run, and so on. Once a script is created, that script can run by itself, without any separate file having to be created. This is just one of the ways VBScript and WSH can be used to automate common tasks. More information on Windows Scripting Host can be found on the Microsoft Web site at: `http://msdn.Microsoft.com/scripting/`

Summary

Programmers can access data in an MSDE database from application programs using the ADO object model. The connection object provides a link from the application to the database, and the command and recordset objects provide a way to run SQL statements against that database and to retrieve records. Applications can be developed in Access, Visual Basic, or a Web environment. The Visual Basic language is available in several forms, Visual Basic for Applications, VBScript, and the full Visual Studio version. Web applications can be created with server-side code using Active Server Pages. Data can be handled within a program in the native format provided by ADO or in the more generic format provided by XML.

✦ ✦ ✦

CHAPTER 25

Administering Security

In This Chapter

Setting the security mode

Configuring logins

Configuring users

Assigning roles to logins and users

Setting permissions for statements

Setting permissions on objects

Understanding the ownership chain

The security in MSDE is complex and must be understood and used correctly. For most organizations in the modern world, data is one of the most, if not the most, important assets they own. If security is not set up correctly that asset can easily be damaged accidentally, damaged maliciously, or even stolen. It is incumbent upon database designers to consider this during design, deployment, and ongoing support.

There are several steps to setting up security for MSDE. It must be configured to use NT authentication only or to use both NT authentication and its own authentication. Logins must be created to provide access to the MSDE server. Then users must be created within each database and associated with logins. Roles, which allow permissions to be granted to more than one user at a time, can be assigned at the server level to logins and at the database level to users. Finally, at the most granular level, individual permissions can be assigned for each object within a database.

Understanding Authentication

Whenever an application attempts to connect to MSDE, whether it is on the same computer or across the network, it must be authenticated before being granted even the most rudimentary access to the server. MSDE supports two different kinds of authentication: Windows NT authentication and SQL Server authentication. The authentication used for a particular connection depends upon the security mode setting configured in MSDE; the operating system platform on which MSDE is running; the Net-Library in use by the connection; and the settings configured in the connection itself.

There may be additional requirements for a user to connect to the MSDE server, depending on the network configuration. If the user attempts to connect using the named pipes Net-Library, the user must have permission to connect to the IPC$-named pipe on the server before the user can make the connection to the MSDE-named pipe. If a user attempts to make a connection through a firewall, the firewall must be configured to allow the type of network traffic associated with the Net-Library; for example, the TCP/IP Net-Library uses port 1433 by default, and this port must be opened through the firewall.

Security Modes

The two available security modes for MSDE are Windows NT Integrated and Mixed. Windows NT Integrated mode accepts only those connections that can be authenticated by Windows NT or Windows 2000. Mixed mode accepts connections that have been authenticated by Windows NT or that can have MSDE perform the authentication itself.

The security mode can be set in Enterprise Manager by right-clicking on the server, selecting properties, selecting the security tab, and then choosing the appropriate option button. This dialog box also supports setting the audit level, which determines whether or not connections to the server are logged.

The login mode setting is stored in the Registry under the following key:

```
HKEY_LOCAL_MACHINE\
SOFTWARE\
Microsoft\
MSSQLServer\
MSSQLServer\
LoginMode
```

Windows NT Integrated security mode

Windows NT Integrated security mode is supported only when MSDE is running on Windows NT or 2000. A connection using Windows NT Integrated security is called a trusted connection because MSDE trusts that the operating system has properly authenticated it. When the connection is being initiated, MSDE performs pass-through authentication. This process accepts the security credentials associated with the connection and passes them to a domain controller for authentication. If this process succeeds, the connection is accepted and associated with a login in the syslogins table in the master database by the security identifier (SID). If the process fails, the connection is denied.

Mixed security mode

When MSDE is configured for Mixed mode security, it can accept trusted or non-trusted connections. Trusted connections are described above. Nontrusted connections must supply login credentials directly to MSDE. These credentials (login name and password) are verified against values stored in the syslogins table.

The client connection may request to be authenticated either as a trusted connection or as a nontrusted connection. However, the process varies slightly depending upon which Net-Library is being used. The named pipes and multiprotocol Net-Libraries perform pass-through authentication before the connection is checked for its requested authentication type. That means that even if the client requests a non-trusted connection, it must still have some kind of domain credentials. The TCP/IP Net-Library, on the other hand, checks for the requested connection type first and then either performs the SQL Server authentication or calls the operating system's security support provide interface (SSPI) to request the pass-through authentication.

NT Integrated mode is the default mode when MSDE is installed on Windows NT or 2000. Mixed mode is the only available mode when MSDE is installed on Windows 95 or 98.

Using MSDE Logins to Grant Server Access

When a connection is made to the MSDE server, one of the authentication mechanisms described above verifies the security credentials and makes an association with a row in the syslogins table. There is only one syslogins table in an installation of MSDE and it is stored in the master database. Logins can be created and deleted with Enterprise Manager or by running a stored procedure from osql, Query Analyzer, or any other utility that will send a SQL command to the server. A login associated with a user that owns objects cannot be deleted. To delete such a login, the owned objects must first be deleted or have their ownership changed. Then the login and any users associated with it can be deleted. Membership in the Security Administrators or System Administrators role is required to create or delete a login.

A Windows NT–authenticated login can reference a user or group account in the NT domain. If it references a user, then the user must be logged into the NT domain as that user in order to gain access to MSDE. This type of login otherwise functions as if it were authenticated by MSDE. If a login references a Windows NT group, then anyone who is logged onto NT as a member of that group can create a connection to MSDE in the security context of the login. Managing logins can be complicated because grouping can be done at two different levels simultaneously: the NT group level, which equates to a single MSDE login, and the MSDE role level, which can be used to group MSDE users or logins (which can themselves be NT groups).

To simplify management, make a decision during the early stages of planning and implementation for the database about where and how grouping is to be done and by whom (the network administrators at the NT level or the database administrators (DBAs) at the MSDE level).

Another sometimes-confusing aspect of creating MSDE logins that refer to Windows NT groups is object ownership. An MSDE login referring to NT groups can be created, and a User can then be created in a database for that login. Having an MSDE login point to an NT group means that the group appears as a single user within a database, which is fine until one of its members creates an object. MSDE will not permit an object to be owned by such a group, so it will automatically create a new user in the database to become the owner of the object. The new user will be given the same name as the NT user that created the object. A clear indication of the user's origin as a group login will appear in the properties of that user. There are no other security implications regarding this DBMS-created user.

Managing logins with Enterprise Manager

Logins can be created in Enterprise Manager by right-clicking in the Logins container within the Security container and selecting New. The process varies at this point depending upon whether the login is being created for NT authentication or for authentication by MSDE.

For an NT-authenticated login, the login name may be typed in the Name field or selected from a list by clicking the ellipsis button to the right of the Name field. When the Windows NT authentication option button is selected, the domain drop-down list will be enabled, and when the appropriate domain is selected, it will automatically be inserted in the field. There is also an option button allowing access to be granted or denied.

If most, but not all of the people in an NT group are to be able to access the MSDE server, create a login that grants access to the group and then create logins that deny access to the people who shouldn't have access. If the group is large and there are more than one or two people who shouldn't have access, another NT group can be added that contains those who shouldn't have access with a denying login.

For an MSDE-authenticated user, any name can be typed in so long as it is unique to the server. When the SQL Server authentication option button is selected, the password field is made available. When the New Login dialog box is dismissed, a prompt is displayed to confirm the password.

Whichever kind of login is created, it should have its default database set to the database that will be used most often by the user's application. The default value of master is rarely a good choice. Setting a database to be default for a login does not give that login any permission in the database; such permission must be defined separately either on the Database Access tab or in the properties of the database itself. The default language can also be set in this dialog box if it is different than the system default.

Deleting logins in Enterprise Manger is as simple as selecting the login and using the delete key, or right-clicking on the login and choosing delete from the menu. If the login is associated with any users, the users are automatically deleted as long as they do not own any objects.

Managing logins with Access

To manage MSDE logins using Access:

1. Open a project that references the MSDE server.
2. Select Tools, then Security, and finally Database Security from the menu.
3. The dialog box shown in Figure 25-1 is displayed. It provides a button to add, edit, and delete logins. The Add and Edit buttons display the same dialog box used by Enterprise Manager to access the properties of a login.

Deleting logins with this dialog is subject to the same rules that apply to other means of delete. Again, if the login is associated with a user in a database that owns objects, the login cannot be deleted. It can be slightly more difficult to resolve this in Access because a project focuses on only a single database. If the problematic objects exist in a different database, a correspondingly different project must be loaded into Access (or the objects could be dealt with using a script or by another method).

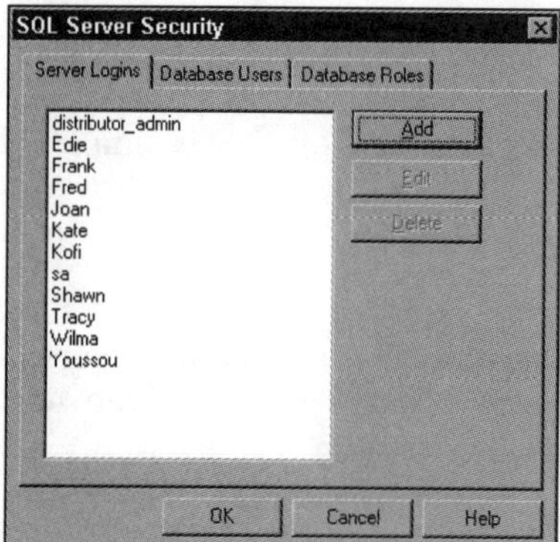

Figure 25-1: Access 2000 Database Security dialog box

Managing logins with SQL

Logins can also be created and deleted using stored procedures. There are two different sets of stored procedures depending upon whether the logins are to be authenticated by Windows NT or MSDE.

`Sp_addlogin` is used to create logins that will be authenticated by MSDE. The syntax is as follows:

```
sp_addlogin [@loginame =] 'login'
    [,[@passwd =] 'password']
    [,[@defdb =] 'database']
    [,[@deflanguage =] 'language']
    [,[@sid =] 'sid']
    [,[@encryptopt =] 'encryption_option']
```

The first four parameters are the same as the parameters from the dialog in Enterprise Manager: login name, password, default database, and default language. It also accepts a security identifier (SID). A SID is not normally used for MSDE-authenticated logins; however, it can be used when scripting logins to be re-created on a different server. The last parameter is the encryption option, which is also used primarily for scripting the re-creation of logins. The password is normally encrypted, but if the encrypted value is to be read from one server and copied to another server, the copied value should not be re-encrypted. Here is an example of adding a user with a stored procedure:

```
sp_addlogin 'Frank', 'frankspw', 'pubs'
```

The `sp_droplogin` procedure deletes a login that has been created for authentication by MSDE. Any users associated with a login must be deleted before this procedure is run. The syntax requires only the name of the login:

```
sp_droplogin [@loginame =] 'login'
```

Creating a login that will be authenticated by Windows NT or 2000 is simple. The syntax is as follows:

```
sp_grantlogin [@loginame =] 'login'
```

The 'login' must take the form of 'domain\username.' This procedure creates a login that grants access. To deny login permission to an NT user, the following stored procedure must be used:

```
sp_denylogin [@loginame =] 'login'
```

This command creates a row in syslogins that specifically prevents an NT user of that name from accessing MSDE. A denying login would be used if a login had been created (using `sp_grantlogin`) for a Windows NT group, and a member of that group should not be allowed access to MSDE.

Deleting a login created with `sp_grantlogin` or `sp_denylogin` is accomplished with `sp_revokelogin`.

```
sp_revokelogin [@loginame =] 'login'
```

This command removes the row from syslogins. Paradoxically, if someone was a member of an NT group that had been granted access and this person had been denied access to the server with `sp_denylogin`, using `sp_revokelogin` with their name would actually allow them access to the server. Access appears to be granted by the revoke because there is no longer a row in syslogins that specifically denies that person access; there is, however, a row that grants them access by virtue of their group membership.

Managing logins with DMO

The DMO hierarchy for logins is as follows:

```
Server
    Logins
        Login
```

The following VBScript creates a login called Fred:

```
dim oMSDEserver
set oMSDEserver=CreateObject("SQLDMO.SQLServer")

dim oLogin
set oLogin=CreateObject("SQLDMO.Login")
oLogin.name="Fred"
oLogin.type=2

oMSDEserver.connect "Okh2h","sa",""
oMSDEserver.logins.add(oLogin)
oMSDEserver.logins("Fred").SetPassword "","password"
oMSDEserver.disconnect
```

You can find this code on the CD-ROM in the file named `Ch 25\addlogin.vbs`.

The first section creates a server object. The second section creates a login object, sets the name property to Fred, and sets the `type` property to 2. The `type` property determines whether the login will be an NT-authenticated or MSDE-authenticated login. The possible values are as follows:

✦ 0 is a Windows NT user. The `name` property must match an NT username exactly.

✦ 1 is a Windows NT group. The `name` property must match an NT group name exactly.

✦ 2 is an MSDE-authenticated login. For this type of login, the initial password is always null.

The third section of code creates a connection to the MSDE server named 0kh2h using the sa login with a null password. It then adds the login object created earlier to the Logins collections. No password has yet been entered, so the next line calls the `SetPassword` method and sets it to password. Finally, the script disconnects from the server.

Only members of the System Administrators role can execute the `SetPassword` method. Security Administrators do not have this privilege.

To delete a login with DMO, connect to the server and execute the `Remove` method of the Logins collection with the name of the login as a parameter.

```
dim oMSDEserver
set oMSDEserver=CreateObject("SQLDMO.SQLServer")

oMSDEserver.connect "0kh2h","sa",""
oMSDEserver.logins.remove("Fred")
oMSDEserver.disconnect
```

You can find this code on the CD-ROM in the file named `Ch 25\remlogin.vbs`.

For this code to work properly, the login Fred must not be associated with any users. In practice, additional code would be added to check for this condition, delete the users, and then delete the login.

Creating Users to Link Logins with Databases

Just as logins give access to the MSDE server, users give access to individual databases located on the server. A user can be associated with one login. The name of the user and login are often the same, but do not have to be. There is a user named dbo (database owner) in every database that corresponds to the login that created the database, and which has all permissions in the database. The dbo can be changed with `sp_changedbowner`.

Users can be added to roles within the database to receive permissions, or they can be granted specific permissions to any object. Developers take different approaches to the use of database users. Some applications are written with their own internal security systems, in which case there may be a need for only a single user in the database other than dbo. Any users running the application would connect as this user, and all security and auditing would be handled in the application. Occasionally applications are written to use dbo in this way, but it is considered better practice to create a user and grant that user all necessary permissions instead.

Another special user sometimes created for databases is guest. Guest is the only user not associated with a particular login. When such a user is created, it enables anyone who has a valid login on the MSDE server, but not a valid user in the database, to access the database. In other words, whenever a connection attempts to access a database, MSDE checks the login associated with the connection and looks to see if there is a user associated with it. If there is, that user will provide the security context for the connection. If there is not, MSDE will use the guest user as a security context if it exists or, otherwise, will deny any access to the database. Guest is not usually created in user databases unless every person who has access to the server should also have access to the database. Having a guest user in the database does not give unrestricted access to the database, but it does guarantee access for all logins on the server. Permissions may be granted or denied to the guest user just like permissions may be granted or denied any other user.

Again, users cannot be deleted if they own an object in the database without first deleting the object or changing the object's ownership. An object is deleted or its ownership changed with the following:

```
sp_changeobjectowner [@objname =] 'object', [@newowner =]
'owner'
```

Managing users with Enterprise Manager

Users can be managed in two places in Enterprise Manager: from the properties of a login or from the Users container within a database.

A Database Access tab appears in the properties dialog box for each login, as shown in Figure 25-2. This dialog box lists all databases that exist in MSDB. When the Permit column is selected next to a database, a user is created within that database and associated with the currently selected login. The default username will be the same as the login name; a different name, however, can be typed in the User column. Using this dialog box, a User can be deleted by deselecting the Permit column.

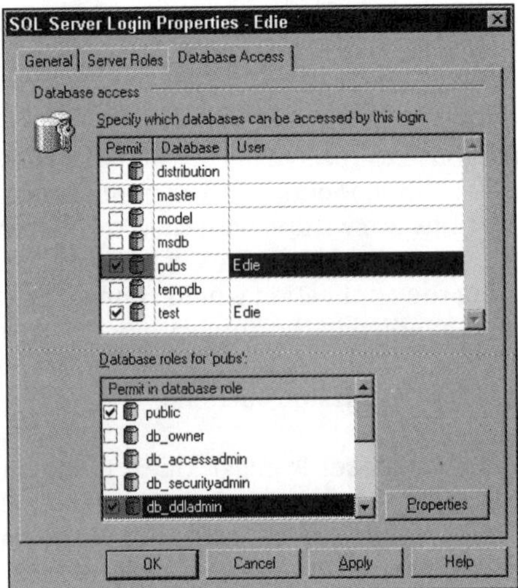

Figure 25-2: Managing users from the Login Properties dialog box

Each database has a Users container. New users can be created by right-clicking in this container and choosing New Database User. A dialog box will display with a drop-down list from which the appropriate login can be selected. Again, the default username will match the login name, but can be changed. Existing users can be modified by right-clicking and choosing Properties and can be deleted by right-clicking and choosing Delete.

Managing users with Access

In Access, users can be managed from the same dialog box used for logins by opening a project that references the appropriate database on the MSDE server; selecting Tools, Security, and then Database Security from the menu; and clicking on the Database Users tab. A dialog box will display showing all of the users currently defined in database, as well as buttons that enable users to be added, edited, or deleted. These buttons bring up the same dialog boxes found in Enterprise Manager for managing users.

Managing users with SQL

The stored procedures used to manage users are `sp_grantdbaccess` and `sp_revokedbaccess`. There are other stored procedures (`sp_adduser` and `sp_dropuser`) that perform the same function, but that are intended for backward compatibility with SQL Server versions prior to 7.0. The syntax for these procedures is as follows:

```
sp_grantdbaccess [@loginame =] 'login'
    [,[@name_in_db =] 'name_in_db' [OUTPUT]]
```

The login name is required. If the name in db is not supplied, it will be set to the same as the login name. If the name in db is supplied as a null with the `OUTPUT` parameter, the user name will be set to the same as the login name and will be returned through this parameter.

```
sp_revokedbaccess [@name_in_db =] 'name'
```

If the user owns any objects, an error will be returned along with a list of owned objects.

Managing users with DMO

The DMO hierarchy for users is as follows:

```
Server
    Databases
        Database
            Users
                User
```

To create a user, a connection must be established to a server and a reference to the database in which the user is to be created must be acquired. Then the `Add` method of the Users collection can be called, passing a User object that has been declared, instantiated, and had its properties set. In the following code, a user is created in Pubs and associated with the login Fred.

```
dim oMSDEserver
set oMSDEserver = CreateObject("SQLDMO.SQLServer")

dim oUser
set oUser = CreateObject("SQLDMO.User")
oUser.Login = "Fred"

oMSDEserver.connect "Okh2h","sa",""
oMSDEserver.databases("pubs").users.add(oUser)
oMSDEserver.disconnect
```

You can find this code on the CD-ROM in the file named `Ch 25\addUser.vbs`.

In deleting a user, there is no need to instantiate a User object, and the `Remove` method is called instead of the `Add` method. The `ListOwnedObjects` is a method that can be used to determine which, if any, objects are owned by a particular user. This method can be used in combination with the `Owner` property of objects to change ownership of all owned objects before attempting deletion.

Grouping Users and Permissions with Roles

MSDE supports the ANSI SQL concept of roles. These are similar to operating system groups in that they allow permissions to be granted to, or denied from, groups of users. They can ease the burden of administration enormously, particularly on systems that support many users. There are four types of roles available on MSDE:

- **Fixed server roles** are used to delegate server-wide administration.
- **Fixed database roles** are used primarily to delegate administrative functions within a database.
- **User-defined database roles** are used to grant permissions within a database to groups of users.
- **Application roles** are used to grant special permissions to users when they are running particular applications (for example, a user might have read-only permission while running Excel, but have modify and delete permission while running a custom accounting application).

Server

MSDE is installed with seven built-in, fixed server roles. These roles cannot be changed in any way, they cannot be deleted, and new server roles cannot be added. They are used to assign privileges to logins so that they can perform server-wide administrative functions. Fixed server roles are the only way a login receives privileges directly. Privileges can otherwise be assigned only to users within a database.

Every server role has at least one right; any member of the role can add any other login to the same role. For example, any Security Administrator can make any other login a Security Administrator.

The privileges of the fixed server roles can be examined in Enterprise Manager by right-clicking on the role, choosing properties, and then clicking on the Permissions tab. The functions of each role are summarized below:

- **System Administrators**—This role can perform any function on the server.
- **Setup Administrators**—This role can configure linked servers and specify that a stored procedure should automatically run whenever MSDE is started.

✦ **Server Administrators**—This role can configure server options and shutdown MSDE.

✦ **Security Administrators**—This role can manage logins, read the error log, and manage the Create Database statement permission (which can be assigned to users in the master database).

✦ **Process Administrators**—This role can kill processes on the MSDE server.

✦ **Disk Administrators**—This role can run a series of commands that are used to manage disk devices that were used in versions of SQL Server prior to 7.0.

✦ **Database Creators**—This role can create, modify, and delete databases.

Managing server roles with Enterprise Manager and Access

Logins can be added to fixed server roles with Enterprise Manager or Access by opening the properties of the login, clicking the Server Roles tab, and selecting the roles to which the login should be added. This dialog box is shown in Figure 25-3. In Enterprise Manager, logins can also be added to server roles through the Server Roles container within the Security container by right-clicking a role and choosing Properties. A list of logins that are currently members of the role will be displayed, and logins can be added or removed from this screen.

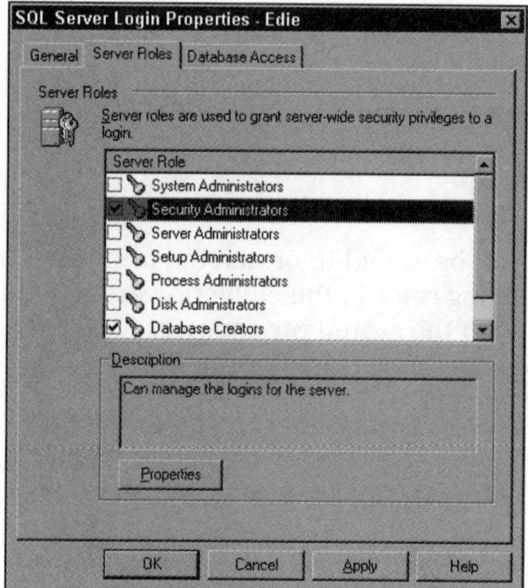

Figure 25-3: Managing server roles from the Login Properties dialog box

Managing server roles with SQL

Logins can be added to and removed from fixed server roles by using the following stored procedures:

```
sp_addsrvrolemember [@loginame =] 'login', [@rolename =] 'role'
sp_dropsrvrolemember [@loginame =] 'login', [@rolename =]
'role'
```

These stored procedures use abbreviated role names that must be entered exactly as shown in the list below:

- **sysadmin** — System Administrators
- **securityadmin** — Security Administrators
- **serveradmin** — Server Administrators
- **setupadmin** — Setup Administrators
- **processadmin** — Process Administrators
- **diskadmin** — Disk Administrators
- **dbcreator** — Database Creators

Managing Server Roles with DMO

The DMO hierarchy for server roles is as follows:

```
Server
    ServerRoles
        ServerRole
```

Because server roles are fixed, nothing can be added to or deleted from the ServerRoles collection. However, the existing roles in the collection are identified with the same abbreviated names used with the stored procedures. They each have an `AddMember` method and a `DropMember` method. The VBScript below adds the login Fred to the database creator's server role:

```
dim oMSDEserver
set oMSDEserver=CreateObject("SQLDMO.SQLServer")

oMSDEserver.connect "Okh2h","sa",""
oMSDEserver.serverroles("dbcreator").addmember("Fred")
oMSDEserver.disconnect
```

You can find this code on the CD-ROM in the file named `Ch 25\modSrvrole.vbs`.

Removing a member would use exactly the same code except for substituting dropmember for addmember.

Database

Every database is automatically configured with ten fixed roles that can be used for configuring users to perform database administration, or to assign or block read and write permissions across all objects in the database. The first nine roles (along with their abbreviated role name for use with stored procedures and DMO) are as follows:

- **Database owners** (db_owner)—This role includes a superset of the permissions granted to all other roles. Members of this role can create objects and specify that they are owned by dbo or any other user.
- **Database access administrators** (db_accessadmin)—This role can add users to and delete users from the database.
- **Database security administrators** (db_securityadmin)—This role can grant, revoke, or deny permissions and can manage database roles.
- **Database DDL administrators** (db_ddladmin)—This role can create, modify, or delete any object in the database. Members of this role can create objects and specify that they are owned by dbo or any other user.
- **Database backup operators** (db_backupoperator)—This role can back up the database, issue a checkpoint, and run various dbcc maintenance commands.
- **Database data readers** (db_datareader)—This role has Select permission for all objects in the database.
- **Database data writers** (db_datawriter)—This role has Insert, Update, and Delete permissions for all objects in the database.
- **Database deny data readers** (db_denydatareader)—This role is explicitly denied the Select permission for all objects in the database.
- **Database deny data writers** (db_denydatawriter)—This role is explicitly denied the Insert, Update, and Delete permissions for all objects in the database.

The fixed roles within a database are managed in exactly the same way as user-defined roles, except that the fixed roles can neither be created nor deleted.

Every database has a role called Public. By default, Public has only Select permissions on the schema views in a database; any other permissions must be granted by an administrator. Every user in the database is automatically a member of Public and cannot be removed from that role. Therefore, any permissions assigned to

Public are inherited by every user including dbo and guest, if they exist. Permissions granted to Public can be denied elsewhere. For example, Select permission can be granted to Public for a series of tables, but it may not be desirable to have guest able to access these tables. In this case, these permissions can be denied to guest, which will override the grant to Public. Permissions should never be denied to Public.

User-defined

User-defined roles can be added to a database. Unlike the fixed roles, user-defined roles will have no inherent permissions. They are created solely for assigning object and statement permissions to groups of users at one time. User-defined roles are particularly useful when there are groups of users who require similar access to the database or when groups of people change frequently. For example, a user-defined role might be defined for accounts receivable clerks. Permissions could then be assigned to this role for all the different tables, views, and stored procedures to which these clerks require access. Additionally, temporary workers can easily be added to and removed from the role as needed. Figure 25-4 shows the properties of a user-defined role called AR. Three users are currently members of the role, and users can be added or deleted from the role using this dialog box. Permissions can be accessed using the button in the upper-right of the dialog box.

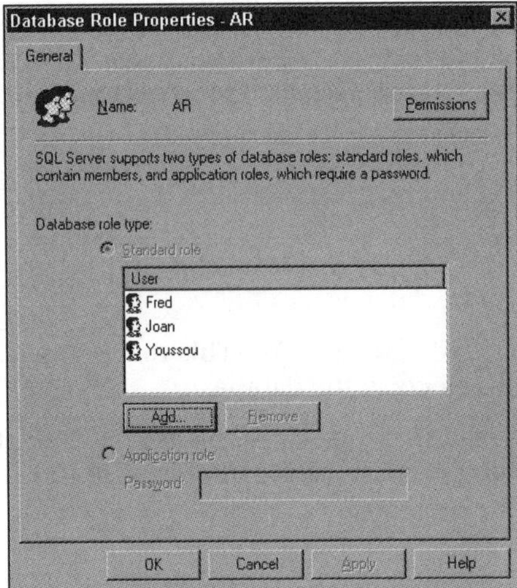

Figure 25-4: Database Role Properties

Managing database roles with Enterprise Manager and Access

User-defined roles can be managed in Enterprise Manager through the Roles container within each database. Users can be added to and removed from these roles through the properties of the roles or the properties of the users. In Access, the database Security dialog box is used; it has a Database Roles tab with Add, Edit, and Delete buttons. Access also allows the membership of user-defined roles to be controlled through the properties of either the role or the user.

Managing database roles with SQL

User-defined roles can be added and deleted with the following stored procedures:

```
sp_addrole [@rolename =] 'role' [,[@ownername =] 'owner']

sp_droprole [@rolename =] 'role'
```

The membership of roles, both fixed and user-defined, can be modified with the following stored procedures:

```
sp_addrolemember [@rolename =] 'role',
    [@membername =] 'security_account'

sp_droprolemember [@rolename =] 'role',
    [@membername =] 'security_account'
```

Managing database roles with DMO

The DMO hierarchy for database roles is as follows:

```
Server
    Databases
        Database
            DataBaseRoles
                DataBaseRole
```

The following code creates a new, user-defined database role called AR:

```
dim oMSDEserver
set oMSDEserver=CreateObject("SQLDMO.SQLServer")

dim oDBrole
set oDBrole = CreateObject("SQLDMO.DatabaseRole")
oDBrole.Name = "AR"

oMSDEserver.connect "Okh2h","sa",""
oMSDEserver.databases("pubs").databaseroles.add(oDBrole)
oMSDEserver.disconnect
```

You can find this code on the CD-ROM in the file named `Ch 25\addDBrole.vbs`.

Once the role has been created, users can be added to it by name with the AddMember method:

```
dim oMSDEserver
set oMSDEserver=CreateObject("SQLDMO.SQLServer")

oMSDEserver.connect "Okh2h","sa",""
oMSDEserver.databases("pubs").databaseroles("AR").addmember("Fr
ed")
oMSDEserver.disconnect
```

You can find this code on the CD-ROM in the file named `Ch 25\modDBrole.vbs`.

Application

Application roles act differently than any other roles. Permissions are assigned to application roles, but they have no membership. The user receives the permissions that are assigned to an application role when that application role is specifically activated in the user's connection. The activation requires a password to which the user is not normally privy. The activation code and password are normally imbedded in a custom application, hence the name.

Application roles fill a security need because there are so many easily accessible and powerful tools with which a user can access a database. With these tools, such as Excel or Access, a user who has read and write access in a database might be tempted to download data from the database to their local PC, manipulate data, and upload it back to the database. While creating a local copy of data may appear to be convenient for the user, it can destroy the consistency of the database. In the past, steps were taken to combat this situation by denying users direct access to the database and programming the application they used to create a connection including sending a login name and password. The drawback to that solution was that all connections used the same security context, which effectively prevented auditing. With application roles, users retain their identity, but use different sets of permissions depending on what they use to access the database.

In a typical scenario, user Fred connects to the database and receives any permissions that have been specifically assigned to his user, as well as any permissions by way of membership in a role. The permissions that Fred now has are probably primarily Select permissions. The application Fred starts to enter data into the database was written to activate an application role. As soon as the role activates, Fred loses all of his previous permissions and gains the permissions that were assigned to the application role. The only permissions that survive the activation of an application role are those assigned to Public because every user is always a member of Public, whether or not they are running an application role.

The code an application uses to activate an application role is as follows:

```
sp_setapprole [@rolename =] 'role' ,
    [@password =] {Encrypt N 'password'} | 'password'
    [,[@encrypt =] 'encrypt_style']
```

This procedure can be used with an unencrypted password or an encrypted password. In either case, the role name must be supplied, followed by the password. To send a plain text (unencrypted) password, the role name must simply be followed with the password. It is not necessary to send the encryption style parameter if the password is unencrypted. The unencrypted password will be sent across the network in a form that can be read by anyone with a packet sniffer (a device that can read all of the information that passes through a network). Here is an example of activating an application role called AcctRole with a password of l0pht:

```
sp_setapprole 'AcctRole','l0pht'
```

The alternative is to have ODBC encrypt the password before it is sent across the network and inform MSDE of the encryption so that it can be decrypted. In this case, `Encrypt` is an ODBC function, `N` indicates the use of Unicode, which is required for the encryption, and `odbc` lets MSDE know that the password has been encrypted.

```
sp_setapprole 'AcctRole', {Encrypt N 'l0pht'}, 'odbc'
```

Both of these samples will work without any changes taking place on the server. It is up to the application programmer to turn on the encryption.

After an application role is invoked, its permissions are in effect until the connection is ended. There is no way to deactivate the application role or to change to another role.

Managing application roles with Enterprise Manager or Access

Application roles can be created in Enterprise Manager by right-clicking in the Roles container of a database and choosing New Database Role. The Database Role Properties dialog box is displayed. This dialog box is available in Access by using the Tools, Security, Database Security menu, and then choosing the Database Roles tab. In either case, the only information required to create an application role is the name of the role and the option button that indicates that the role is an application role.

Application roles can be deleted from the same screens. Editing the properties of an application role allows permissions to be set.

Managing application roles with SQL

Application roles can be created with the following stored procedure:

```
sp_addapprole [@rolename =] 'role', [@password =] 'password'
```

They can be deleted with the following:

```
sp_dropapprole [@rolename =] 'role'
```

Managing application roles with DMO

DMO treats application roles the same as other database roles, with the exception that the AppRole property is set to true. The following code creates an application role called AcctRole with a password of l0pht.

```
dim oMSDEserver
set oMSDEserver=CreateObject("SQLDMO.SQLServer")

dim oDBrole
set oDBrole = CreateObject("SQLDMO.DatabaseRole")
oDBrole.Name = "AcctRole"
oDBrole.AppRole = "True"
oDBrole.Password = "l0pht"

oMSDEserver.connect "0kh2h","sa",""
oMSDEserver.databases("pubs").databaseroles.add(oDBrole)
oMSDEserver.disconnect
```

You can find this code on the CD-ROM in the file named `Ch 25\AddAppRole.vbs`.

Securing Data with Permissions

Setting permissions appropriately is one of the most important parts of administering MSDE. It takes time and attention to detail to be able to make the data as secure as possible while enabling all users to perform their jobs. If the data is made too secure, users may be unable to execute a necessary task. Some administrators try to alleviate problems of this nature by granting too much permission, which can endanger their system and perhaps their entire organization. Good security administration is knowing how to walk the thin line between giving too much and taking too much.

Permissions are primarily granted to groups of users on tables and views. Rarely does each user need their own specific set of permissions, which is why roles are so helpful in a database environment.

In addition to the permissions associated with objects, permissions can be associated with statements that create something (because the object does not exist before the statement has been run the permission to create it cannot be associated with that object).

Because permissions can be granted (or denied) to roles and users and a user can be a member of multiple roles, a user can inherit multiple, possibly conflicting sets of permissions. When a user has multiple sets of permissions, all grants are additive, but any deny overrides the corresponding grant. For example, if a user is a member of two roles, role A and role B, and role A is granted only Select permission on a table, while role B is granted only Insert permission on the same table, the user's effective permissions are Select and Insert. However, if role A has been granted Select permission on a table and role B has been denied Select permission on that table, then user who is a member of both roles A and B is also denied Select. Even if a permission is specifically given to a user, if that same permission is denied to a role in which the user is a member, the user will be denied that permission.

Statement permissions

Table 25-1 shows the statement permissions. The table includes the names of the permissions used by the SQL Grant statement, the abbreviated name used by Enterprise Manager, and the numeric representation used by DMO.

Table 25-1
Statement Permissions

SQL Grant	*Enterprise Manager*	*DMO Value*
Create Database	Create DB	256
Create Table	Create Table	128
Create View	Create View	512
Create Procedure	Create SP	1024
Create Default	Create Default	4096
Create Rule	Create Rule	16384
Backup Database	Backup DB	2048
Backup Log	Backup Log	8192

Except for the Create DB permission, all of these permissions apply only to the database in which they have been granted.

All of these permissions are included in one or more fixed roles, so it is not strictly necessary to use these permissions. They are advantageous when database administration needs to be delegated in a very granular or specific way.

Managing statement permissions with Enterprise Manager

In Enterprise Manager, statement permissions can be set in the Properties dialog box of a database. This dialog is shown in Figure 25-5. The Create DB statement permission can be granted only in the master database, so a person must have a user defined in the master to receive this permission. The Create DB column is not shown in Figure 25-5 because it displays the properties of a database other than master (it is the first column in this dialog box for the master database). The alternative is to make the person's login a member of the `db_creator` fixed server role.

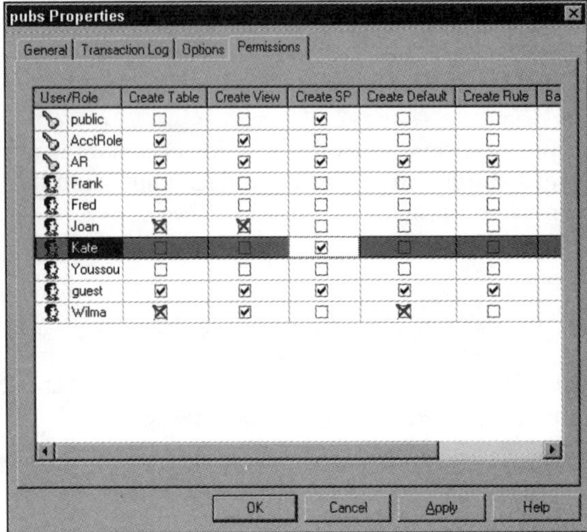

Figure 25-5: The statement permissions dialog box

The checkboxes used for assigning permissions in Enterprise Manager and Access can be set to three different states.

- ✦ A blank box means that the permission has neither been granted nor denied. A user may have been granted or denied this permission elsewhere (for example, in other roles of which the user is a member).
- ✦ A black check mark means that the permission has been granted. If the user has not been denied elsewhere, then he or she can exercise the permission.
- ✦ A red X means that the permission has been denied. If this is set for a role, then no member of the role can exercise the permission without regard to any permissions granted at the role or user level. If a specific user is denied, that user will be unable to exercise the permission even if it is granted to roles of which the user is a member.

Managing statement permissions with SQL

The same command is used to grant statement and object permissions, and the full syntax of that command is shown below. When granting statement permissions, the middle section of the command, in which objects are specified, is not used.

```
GRANT
    {ALL [PRIVILEGES] | permission[,...n]}
    {
        [(column[,...n])] ON {table | view}
        | ON {table | view}[(column[,...n])]
        | ON {stored_procedure | extended_procedure}
    }
TO security_account[,...n]
[WITH GRANT OPTION]
[AS {group | role}]
```

To simplify this diagram, the command is as follows:

```
Grant permission To User/role
```

For example, the following SQL statement grants the user Fred Create Database statement permission. The `Use` command sets master as the default database.

```
Use master
Grant Create Database to Fred
```

The `WITH GRANT OPTION` is used if the user to whom the permission is given should be able to give the permission to other users. For example, when a person gives his car keys to his teenaged nephew, he *never* uses the `WITH GRANT OPTION` because his nephew may have unreliable friends. On the other hand, when the man lends his old sweatshirt with the really thin elbows and paint spots to his daughter, he is happy to use the `WITH GRANT OPTION`, because he can't quite work up the courage to throw it away and is hoping his daughter will lend it to someone who won't return it.

When the `WITH GRANT OPTION` has been used and the permissions have been granted to a role, the `AS` role parameter comes into play. For example, Wendy grants Create Table with grant option to a role called UnderGrad. Amy is a member of UnderGrad, and she would like to grant Create Table to Pete, who is not a member of UnderGrad. Because Amy has not been granted the `WITH GRANT OPTION` directly, but through a role, she must use the `AS` parameter to specify the role through which she receives the permission. The statement she uses would look like this:

```
Grant Create Table to Pete AS UnderGrad
```

The `Deny` command can be used to specifically deny permissions for a user or role. The syntax is:

```
Deny permission to User/role [cascade]
```

The cascade option denies the user the permission, but also revokes anyone to whom that user has given permission by virtue of `WITH GRANT OPTION`. For example, the following statement denies Fred the ability to create databases, even if he is a member of a role that has been granted that permission. If Fred has granted Wilma Create Database, her permission to create a database is also revoked (she might still be able to create a database by virtue of some role membership, which is an important distinction between being denied and being revoked).

```
Use master
Deny Create Database to Fred cascade
```

Both `Grant` and `Deny` add a row to the sysprotects table, which is searched whenever a user attempts to run a command. The `Revoke` command reverses either of these by removing the row from sysprotects. The syntax for `Revoke` is as follows:

```
Revoke permission from User/role
```

The following command revokes whatever permission Fred had previously been given. If he had been granted permission, he is no longer granted. If he had been denied, he is no longer denied. After running this command, Fred is at the mercy of any roles of which he is a member for permissions to run Create Database.

```
Use master
Revoke Create Database from Fred
```

Multiple permissions and multiple users can be specified in the same command for `Grant`, `Deny`, and `Revoke`.

Managing statement permissions with DMO

The database object has a `Grant` method whose syntax is as follows:

```
Databaseobject.Grant permissionValue, grantee
```

The permissionIDs for statement permissions are listed in Table 25-1. The code below grants the user Fred the statement permission for Create Database in the master database, which is number 256. Fred must exist in master before running this script.

```
dim oMSDEserver
set oMSDEserver=CreateObject("SQLDMO.SQLServer")

oMSDEserver.connect "Okh2h","sa",""
oMSDEserver.databases("master").grant 256,"Fred"
oMSDEserver.disconnect
```

You can find this code on the CD-ROM in the file named `Ch 25\GrantStmt.vbs`.

Multiple permissions can be granted in the same command by adding the numeric representations. For example, Fred could have been granted Create Database (256) and Create Table (128) by using 384 as the permissionID in the grant.

There are similar `Deny` and `Revoke` methods of the database object. The code shown above can be used by replacing `grant` with `deny` or `revoke`.

Object permissions

Object permissions are set on tables, views, and stored procedures. Individual columns can also have permissions, although this can needlessly increase the administrative workload. When it is necessary to grant permissions on a subset of columns within a table, a view can be created and permission can be granted on the view but not the underlying table. This method is every bit as secure as setting permissions on columns but easier to administer.

The permissions that are available for tables are as follows:

- **Select**—This permission enables a user to view the contents of rows in the table.
- **Insert**—This permission enables a user to add new rows to the table.
- **Update**—This permission enables a user to make modifications to existing rows in the table.
- **Delete**—This permission enables a user to remove rows from the table.
- **DRI** (also known as References)—This permission enables foreign key constraints to be checked. For example, a table, PublicStuff, has a foreign key that refers to a column in the table, SecretStuff, so that new rows can be added to PublicStuff only if the new row has a value that matches some value in SecretStuff. If a user has no permissions in SecretStuff, the values cannot be checked, and an insert will fail. If a user has Select permission on SecretStuff, the insert will succeed, but the data in SecretStuff will not be very secret. The DRI permission walks the middle ground between these scenarios. Given the DRI permission on SecretStuff, the user will be able to read SecretStuff, but only to check a foreign key constraint, and not for any other reason.

A stored procedure can be assigned only one permission—Execute. As long as the ownership chain is unbroken, a user who has Execute permission on a stored procedure can do anything that the stored procedure will permit. It is certainly possible to include security checks in a stored procedure's code, so the possibilities for security configuration are limitless.

Managing object permissions with Enterprise Manager and Access

Enterprise Manager and Access provide a dialog box, shown in Figure 25-6, for managing object permissions from the properties of database users or roles. It is displayed by clicking the Permissions button. This dialog box lists all of the objects in the database along with the appropriate checkboxes (Execute for stored procedures; Select, Insert, Update, and Delete for tables and views; DRI is also available for tables). Each object type is identified by its own icon. Stored procedures are boxes with wavy lines, tables are boxes with columns and rows of dashes, and views are eyeglasses. The checkboxes have three states: empty means that there are no permissions (they have been revoked), a black check mark means that permissions have been granted, and a red X means that permissions have been denied. An option button controls which objects are displayed in the list. The choices are to see all objects in the database, which is the default, or to see only those objects to which the user has been granted or denied permission. The second option is useful for determining what permissions exist when there are a large number of objects in the database.

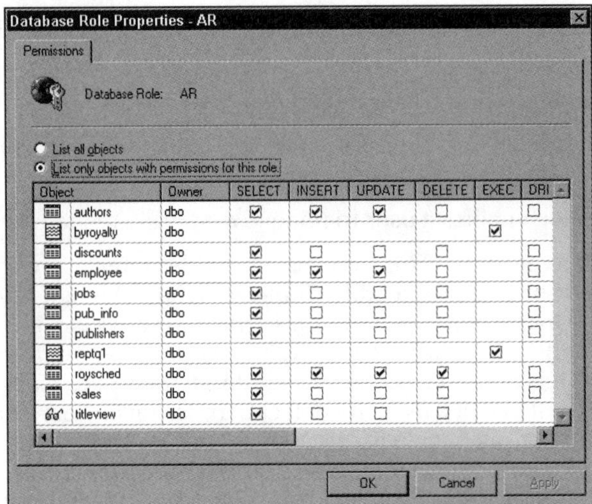

Figure 25-6: Object permissions viewed from a role

Enterprise Manager also has a dialog box for assigning permissions that is accessible from the properties of any object by clicking the Permissions button. This dialog box is shown in Figure 25-7 and has two options: displaying all users or only those assigned permissions to the currently selected object.

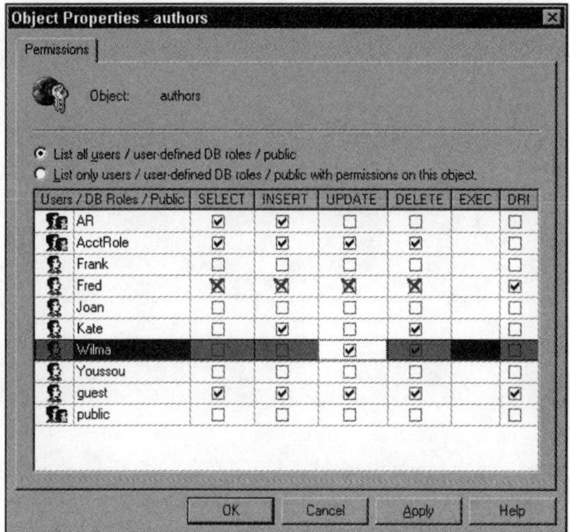

Figure 25-7: Object permissions viewed from a table

There is no way to see or manage the `WITH GRANT OPTION` from Enterprise Manager or Access.

Managing object permissions with SQL

The `Grant`, `Deny`, and `Revoke` commands work for object permissions very much like they do for statement permissions. In addition to the syntax used for statement permissions, they must have the object listed for which permissions are to be modified. The following example grants select permission to Fred on the authors table in the pubs database.

```
Use pubs
Grant select on authors to Fred
```

This code revokes both Select and Insert permissions:

```
Use pubs
Revoke select, insert on authors from Fred
```

Here is the statement to deny Fred Execute permission on the stored procedure `byroyalty`:

```
Use pubs
Deny execute on byroyalty to Fred
```

Managing object permissions with DMO

DMO table and view objects have methods for Grant, Deny, and Revoke. They use numeric values for each permission as shown in Table 25-2. These values can be added to handle multiple permissions with a single method call.

Table 25-2
DMO Values for Object Permissions

Permission	*DMO Value*
Select	1
Insert	2
Update	4
Delete	8
References (DRI)	32

The syntax for the Grant method is as follows:

```
Object.grant permission value, User/role, [columns],
[grantgrant], [AS role]
```

Columns are optional and should rarely be used, but two commas are required as a placeholder if using the grantgrant or AS role parameters. The grantgrant parameter must be either True or False, and functions in the same way as WITH GRANT OPTION in the SQL Grant command. The AS role parameter also follows the SQL functionality. The code below grants Fred the Select permission on the authors table WITH GRANT OPTION.

```
dim oMSDEserver
set oMSDEserver=CreateObject("SQLDMO.SQLServer")

oMSDEserver.connect "Okh2h","sa",""
oMSDEserver.databases("pubs").tables("authors").grant
1,"Fred",,True
oMSDEserver.disconnect
```

You can find this code on the CD-ROM in the file named Ch 25\GrantSelect.vbs.

The syntax for the deny method is as follows:

```
Object.deny permission value, User/role, [columns], [cascade]
```

The cascade option must be either `True` or `False`. When `True`, any other users or roles that have been granted permission by the user or role currently being denied will have that permission revoked. This is functionally identical to the SQL `Deny` command. The following sample denies Fred the Select permission on the authors table and cascades the deny so that if Fred had granted anyone Select on authors, they would now be revoked.

```
dim oMSDEserver
set oMSDEserver=CreateObject("SQLDMO.SQLServer")

oMSDEserver.connect "Okh2h","sa",""
oMSDEserver.databases("pubs").tables("authors").deny
1,"Fred",,True
oMSDEserver.disconnect
```

You can find this code on the CD-ROM in the file named `Ch 25\DenySelect.vbs`.

The syntax for the `Revoke` method is as follows:

```
Object.revoke permission value, User/role, [columns],
[cascade], [RevokeGrantOption], [As role]
```

As with the `Deny` method, cascade must be `True` or `False`. The `RevokeGrantOption` enables the `Revoke` method to revoke only the `WITH GRANT OPTION` part of a grant. If Fred was granted Select `WITH GRANT OPTION` and is subsequently revoked with `RevokeGrantOption`, he will still have Select permission, but will no longer be able to grant the Select permission to others. The sample code below revokes only the grant option. When `RevokeGrantOption` is `True`, cascade must also be `True`.

```
dim oMSDEserver
set oMSDEserver=CreateObject("SQLDMO.SQLServer")

oMSDEserver.connect "Okh2h","sa",""
oMSDEserver.databases("pubs").tables("authors").revoke
1,"Fred",,True,True
oMSDEserver.disconnect
```

You can find this code on the CD-ROM in the file named `Ch 25\RevokeGrant.vbs`.

Simplifying Security by Maintaining Unbroken Ownership Chains

In MSDE, views and stored procedures are dependent on the objects they reference. Stored procedures can perform operations on tables or views, and views can refer to other views or to underlying tables. When objects are dependent on each other in this way, a chain is formed. Of particular interest is the ownership of objects along this chain. If all of the objects that depend on each other have the same owner, there is an unbroken ownership chain. Conversely, if any of the objects has a different owner, the ownership chain is broken. The ownership chain is important when understanding how MSDE evaluates permissions.

MSDE always checks the permissions on the object that a user references. If a user attempts to run a stored procedure, the user must have the execute permission on that stored procedure. When a user attempts to select a row from a view, the user must have Select permission on the view.

MSDE will check only the permissions on objects to which the original object refers where the ownership chain is broken. So, a user must have permission on a stored procedure to run it, but if the stored procedure inserts rows into a table, the user needs only Insert permission on the table if the table has a different owner than the stored procedure. The same is true of views, which explains why views are so useful for implementing security. If there are particular columns or rows in a table to which some users should not have access, a view can be created on the table that excludes those columns or rows. The user is given permission on the view but not on the underlying table. As far as the user is concerned, the excluded columns or rows do not even exist (unless they happen to examine the table schema, but they still don't have access to the contents).

It is often a goal of database designers to make dbo the owner of all (or most) objects within a database. Having a single owner allows the use of views and stored procedures as security devices. If many different users own objects, administration and troubleshooting can be very complex. It is quite simple to create objects that are owned by dbo. Any user who is a member of the `db_ddladmins` or `db_owner` can create an object and specify the owner as dbo. For example, the following code creates a table called payroll that is owned by dbo:

```
Create table dbo.payroll (col1 int)
```

Summary

Security is an important part of all database designs and administration. Analysis must be performed to decide on the appropriate authentication mechanism based on operating systems, Net-Libraries, physical location (are users connecting through firewalls), and so on. The logistics for administering logins, from Windows NT, MSDE, or both, must be defined. An ongoing part of administering a database will include creating users in the database, making a user a member of appropriate roles, assigning permissions to roles, and sometimes assigning permissions directly to users. If security has not played a sufficient part in the design of a database and the applications that use the database, then day-to-day operations of the database may be severely affected. The time to troubleshoot inadequate permissions can be greatly extended if ownership chains are broken. Planning and executing security always requires forethought and intelligent choices to balance ease of user access with security of the data.

✦ ✦ ✦

CHAPTER 26

Automating Tasks with SQL Agent

✦ ✦ ✦ ✦

In This Chapter

Creating jobs

Scheduling jobs

Creating alerts

Configuring alerts

Sending feedback to operators

✦ ✦ ✦ ✦

MSDE provides a set of very flexible capabilities for automating administrative tasks on a database and database server. The tasks can predefine repetitive work and reduce errors. They can schedule work so that operator intervention is not required, and they can automatically respond to predefined situations on the server.

Given sufficient planning and setup, MSDE should be able to detect, respond to, and often correct errors automatically. MSDE can also notify operators and administrators through e-mail, pagers, and pop-up windows whenever errors occur and when the errors have automatically been corrected.

Configuring the SQL Server Agent

All of this automation is handled through the SQL Server Agent, a service separate from the SQL Server service. The Agent itself must be configured appropriately for the environment, and then jobs, alerts, and operators can be configured.

- ✦ **Jobs** — predefine tasks to be executed on a schedule or as the result of an error condition.
- ✦ **Alerts** — define possible error conditions and specify what actions should be taken because of those conditions.
- ✦ **Operators** — define the e-mail address, pager addresses, and the address of people to whom the SQL Server Agent should send notifications when jobs or alerts are activated.

If MSDE is running on a Windows 98 computer, then the SQL Server Agent runs in the security context of the logged on user, making the automation system somewhat less robust than that which runs on Windows NT or Windows 2000. Some automation is still possible with Windows 98; however, the notifications system should be considered unreliable because e-mail connectivity cannot be consistently guaranteed. Windows 98 installations of MSDE are outstanding candidates for creating jobs that will simplify complex tasks for users.

When configuring the SQL Server Agent on a Windows NT or Windows 2000 computer, the first tasks are to set up a user account with which the SQL Server Agent can log on and to provide e-mail connectivity to that account. Although the Agent can be run as a system account, this prevents the Agent from communicating with other computers across the network and prohibits it from sending e-mail, replicating, and participating in distributed transactions.

Providing e-mail connectivity for the SQL Server Agent service account is not unlike providing e-mail for any other user. A mailbox must be created on the e-mail server, and permission must be granted so that the SQL Server Agent service account has permission to access the mailbox. Then an e-mail profile must be created on the database server. The easiest way to create an e-mail profile is to log on as the service account and start an e-mail client such as Outlook. When Outlook is first started, it automatically starts a wizard to create an e-mail profile. The information required to create the profile is the server name and the mailbox name.

Using Jobs to Organize Work

Having configured the SQL Server Agent, the user can proceed to create jobs. A job consists of a series of steps containing a series of instructions. The instructions can be of various types; they can be SQL commands, operating system commands, ActiveX scripts, or any of several other specialized command types that are used primarily for replication.

After the steps to be taken during execution of the job are defined, the user must define when the job will run. A job can be configured to run once at a specific point in time, repetitively on a schedule, or because of an activated alert. The user can also specify the kind of notification to be performed upon completion of the job. Notification consists of sending an e-mail to a mailbox or a pager address or popping up a window on the computer screen. Each kind of notification can be sent conditionally based on whether the job completes successfully, fails, or ends without regard to its success or failure.

Defining job steps

A job consists of any number of steps, and each step can be any of the following types:

- ✦ **Transact SQL Script** (TSQL) — A transact SQL script step enables the user to specify the database to be used, and one or more valid SQL commands. These commands, for example, can be any commands that could be entered into Query Analyzer. They can include stored procedures and conditional logic, allowing for a great deal of flexibility and complexity within a single step.
- ✦ **Operating System Command** (CmdExec) — An operating system command step enables the user to specify the exit code for a successful command and one or more commands that could be executed at the operating system command line for the computer on which the job will run. This step could include an executable file, a batch file, an operating system internal command, or a series of such commands. One of the difficulties of using this kind of step is determining when the operating system command has failed. For example, when a copy command is initiated, it succeeds if the command itself executes, whether or not the file is actually copied. If an attempt is made to copy a file and that file does not exist, the copy command nonetheless reports success. Operating system batch files allow some conditional logic and can specify return values, or exit codes, which can help to identify failure conditions.
- ✦ **ActiveX Script** — An ActiveX script step enables the user to specify the ActiveX script language and one or more commands in that language. Scripting capability is based on the Windows Scripting Host (WSH). The two default languages are Visual Basic Script and JScript. Other scripting languages, such as Rexx or Perl, can be installed into the WSH and can be used for an ActiveX script step. Scripting provides the maximum flexibility of any type of job step. Fully featured conditional logic, string handling, and other advanced functions are all available. Visual Basic script tends to be the fastest performing script; in environments with programmers who are more familiar with other scripting languages, however, convenience and ease of maintenance may override VB's slight performance edge. ActiveX scripts can also instantiate COM objects, giving them nearly unlimited power and flexibility.

The step types can be mixed within the same job, and a job can consist of an SQL command, followed by an operating system command, followed by an ActiveX script. The user can also specify flow control for the job by indicating which step within the job will be the first to run and by specifying the step that will follow each step if the current step is successful, if it fails, or when it completes, regardless of whether it has succeeded or failed. This control of flow capability enables the user to create sophisticated error handling, and adaptable jobs with many branches of execution can be selected based upon current conditions on the database server.

Running jobs on a schedule

When a job is created, it can be scheduled or unscheduled. If the job is unscheduled, it can be initiated manually at any time or by an alert. A scheduled job can be set up in any of the following ways:

- ✦ A job can start automatically whenever the SQL Server Agent starts. The SQL Server Agent may be scheduled to start when the computer starts, or it can be started manually. The choice for when to start the Agent will depend upon the type of environment in which MSDE is running. For example, if MSDE is running on a laptop computer that is only infrequently connected to a network and to other database servers, the user may choose not to start the Agent automatically. In this case, a job may be created that performs backups or maintenance functions and starts automatically when the Agent starts. In this way, the user can simply start the Agent periodically to perform all of the necessary maintenance on the system.
- ✦ A job can start when the CPU becomes idle. The definition of CPU idle is specified as a property of the SQL Server Agent. The default idle condition is defined as a period of 600 seconds (10 minutes) or longer during which the CPU runs at less than 10 percent capacity. Using this setting allows the user to create a job that interferes with user performance as little as possible. An example of a job with this kind of start condition is manually updating index statistics if you choose not to have them updated automatically. Having the most up-to-date possible index statistics gives users' queries the best possible performance, even though allowing them to be updated automatically can occasionally have a detrimental effect on performance because they are updated at the time a query runs.
- ✦ A job can be configured to run once. This configuration setting enables the user to define sometime in the future by date and time at which the job will run. This is a convenient setting for administrators who would like to perform off-hour maintenance. A maintenance job can be scheduled to run in the middle of the night, and the administrator can show up just as the job is finishing.
- ✦ A job can be set up to run on a recurring schedule. Recurring schedules can be daily, weekly, or monthly. They can occur on specific days of the week or month. They can run at a specific time or multiple times during the day when they are scheduled to run.

An individual job can be set up with multiple schedules. This allows flexibility to do things such as run a job on the last day of every week and the last day of every month, which would be impossible without multiple schedules.

If a job doesn't run when it's expected to, the schedules should be checked to verify that they, and the job itself, are enabled. Because each schedule can individually be disabled, as well as the entire job, there are many places to look (or fail to look) when troubleshooting a problem with a job.

For a job to send notifications on its completion, success, or failure, one or more operators must be configured. An operator is an e-mail address, an e-mail address that is set up to call a pager, or a net send address, which is the logon name on the network to which the job will send a pop-up dialog box.

Using Alerts to Automate Responses

Creating alerts enables the user to have the SQL Server Agent monitor the system for possible danger signs, instead of having an administrator do so or waiting until a user complains about a problem. There are two types of alerts: event alerts and performance condition alerts. Event alerts look for error messages, and performance condition alerts look for the value of performance counters to fall outside the normal range.

When an alert is activated based on an error or a performance counter value, a user can define the actions it will take. The actions can include notification through e-mail, pager, or pop-up window. They can also include running a job. It is also possible to have event forwarding, so that one computer, perhaps a SQL server, can have alerts that respond to events that occur on many other computers, perhaps running MSDE at users' workstations.

As with jobs, alerts require operators in order to send notification about their activation.

Event alerts

An event alert can be configured to activate upon one of two basic types of conditions. The first condition is the occurrence of an error with a specific error number being written to the error log. The second general condition is the appearance in the error log of some error of a specific severity. In either condition, users can filter the errors that cause a specific alert to be activated by indicating which database they are interested in or indicating a particular text string that must occur in the error message.

Every error message written to the error log has a specific number that uniquely identifies that error. The error numbers and messages that MSDE uses are predefined in the system table sysmessages, which is located in the master database. Programmers and administrators can add additional error messages to the sysmessages table and can cause those errors to be raised within a program, SQL script, or stored procedure.

Every error that can be raised also has a severity level. A higher severity level indicates a more critical problem. Errors with a severity of ten and below are informational only. Errors with a severity of 19 or higher are fatal.

Care should be taken when creating alerts using severity levels. There are 3700 rows in the sysmessages table out of the box and only 25 severity levels, of which 10 are either reserved or not used initially. That means on average there are almost 250 error messages for a particular severity level. Creating an alert on a severity level is painting in broad strokes. If a severity alert is created, filters should be included on the database and text string to help make your alert more specific.

Performance condition alerts

Performance condition alerts can be created on any of the SQL Server performance counters available in Performance Monitor. Having a performance condition alert defined does not mean that the user needs to be running Performance Monitor, because the SQL Server Agent handles that function.

To define a performance alert, the user must specify the performance object, which is a functional grouping for the individual counters. The counters are the specific metrics that can be collected. For certain counters, the user may also have to specify the instance, if there is more than one object of the same type. For example, the database object has an instance for each database that exists on the computer.

The objects available for performance condition alerts are as follows:

✦ **Access Methods**—Provides counters to measure the number and kind of accesses to database structures, for example, the number of pages that are allocated, deallocated, or split each second; the number of indexing searches each second; and the number of full scans through tables for indexes each second.

✦ **Buffer Manager**—Provides counters to measure how efficiently MSDE is using memory with regard to input in output. This object includes counters for such things as the number of pages written by checkpoint each second; the number of pages written by the LazyWriter each second; the number of pages read from disk each second; and so on.

✦ **Buffer Partition**—Provides counters to examine the state of the freelist, which controls pages in memory that are available for allocation.

✦ **Cache Manager**—Provides counters to measure the efficiency of memory usage with regard to the cache, such as how often objects are found in cache rather than in going to disk. The cache manager has multiple instances to examine overall performance or to examine specific types of execution plans, such as those generated by stored procedures, some ad hoc queries, or triggers.

✦ **Databases**—Provides many counters for measuring utilization and size of databases. There is one instance for each database.

✦ **General Statistics** — Provides counters for the number of logins and logouts per second as well as the total number of user connections to the MSDE server.

✦ **Latches** — Provides counters to measure the utilization of latches, which are lightweight locks used internally by MSDE.

✦ **Locks** — Provides counters to measure the utilization of locks, including how many locks are being placed, how many are waiting, and how many are being deadlocked.

✦ **Memory Manager** — Provides counters to measure the utilization of memory, particularly with regard to how much memory is allocated to which kinds of objects.

✦ **SQL Statistics** — Provides counters that reflect heat compilation of queries into execution plans.

✦ **User Settable** — Provides up to ten administrator-customizable counters. To perform the customization, a stored procedure, with a name such as sp_user_counter_1, must be created that returns an integer value. The customized stored procedure is run at the Performance Monitor sampling rate, and return values are recorded.

Creating, Deleting, and Modifying Jobs and Alerts

The job and alert system in MSDE is quite complex, and the graphical user interface in the Enterprise Manager is well suited for the task. If users have access to it, they will find that using Enterprise Manager is the easiest way to create and manage jobs and alerts. Nonetheless, jobs and alerts can also be managed using SQL or DMO.

Managing jobs and alerts with Enterprise Manager

Before configuring jobs and alerts, it is important that MSDE, and the SQL Server Agent in particular, are set up correctly.

Configuring the SQL Server Agent

Most of the configuration for the overall automation systems in MSDE is done by right-clicking the SQL Server Agent container in the left pane of Enterprise Manager. The General properties dialog box is displayed in Figure 26-1.

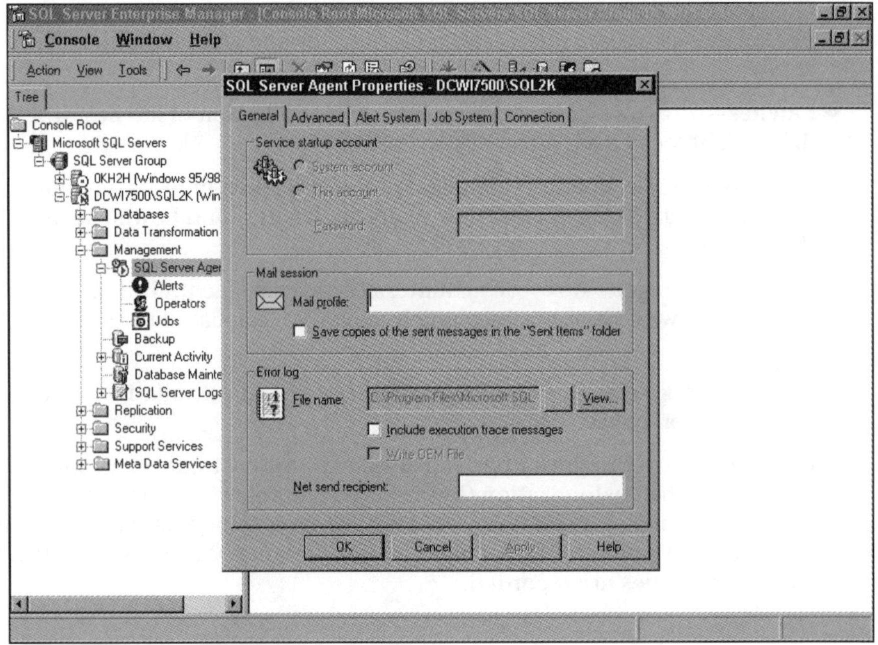

Figure 26-1: SQL Server Agent properties

The option buttons at the top of the dialog box allow the user to choose whether to run the SQL Server Agent in the security context of the system account or in the security context of a user account. If the user is going to take advantage of any of the capabilities of the SQL Server Agent that involve communications with other servers, the Agent should be configured to run in the context of a domain user account.

The middle of the General properties dialog box contains the configuration for the SQL Server Agent mail session. If any e-mail profiles have been set up for the SQL Server Agent service account, those profiles will appear in a drop-down list.

Tip

The e-mail profiles shown in the SQL Server Agent Properties dialog box are not those associated with the account to which the user is logged on, but with the service account for the Agent. If no profiles show up in the list, the user should log out and log back in as the SQL Server Agent service account. Then an e-mail profile should be created and tested by sending the e-mail.

The bottom of the SQL Server Agent General properties dialog box enables the user to configure an error line into which the Agent can write diagnostic information.

Figure 26-2 shows the Advanced properties for the SQL Server Agent. The top two check boxes are used for restarting the MSDE services in case of error. The middle of this dialog box enables the user to configure event forwarding. When event forwarding is turned on, any error message written to the error log with a source of MSDE and a severity equal to or greater than what is specified in the drop-down list will be sent to the specified server. That server can then be configured to generate alerts based on these events. Option buttons enable the filtering of the events that are sent. If the user chooses to send only unhandled events (which is usually the best choice), then any event with a configured alert on the local server will not be forwarded.

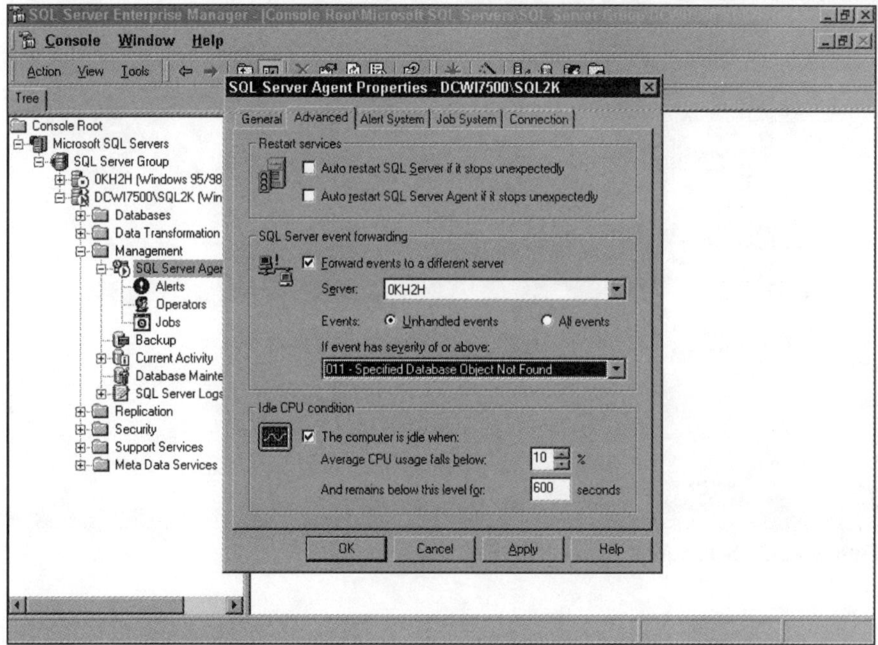

Figure 26-2: SQL Server Agent Advanced properties

The bottom of the Advanced properties dialog box enables the user to configure the idle CPU condition. If the check box in this section is cleared, then there will be no idle CPU condition, and jobs that are configured to start on the idle CPU condition will never start. If the box is checked, then the maximum CPU utilization and length of time can be specified. Only when these conditions are met will jobs configured to start on idle CPU be executed.

Figure 26-3 shows the Alert System configuration. The top of this dialog box enables the user to add prefixes and suffixes to the e-mail addresses and subjects used in notification for jobs and alerts. In the center of the dialog is a check box that allows the user to include the body of the e-mail, which includes error message and description, in notifications sent to pagers. For this to be effective, alphanumeric pagers prepared to accept messages must have been configured.

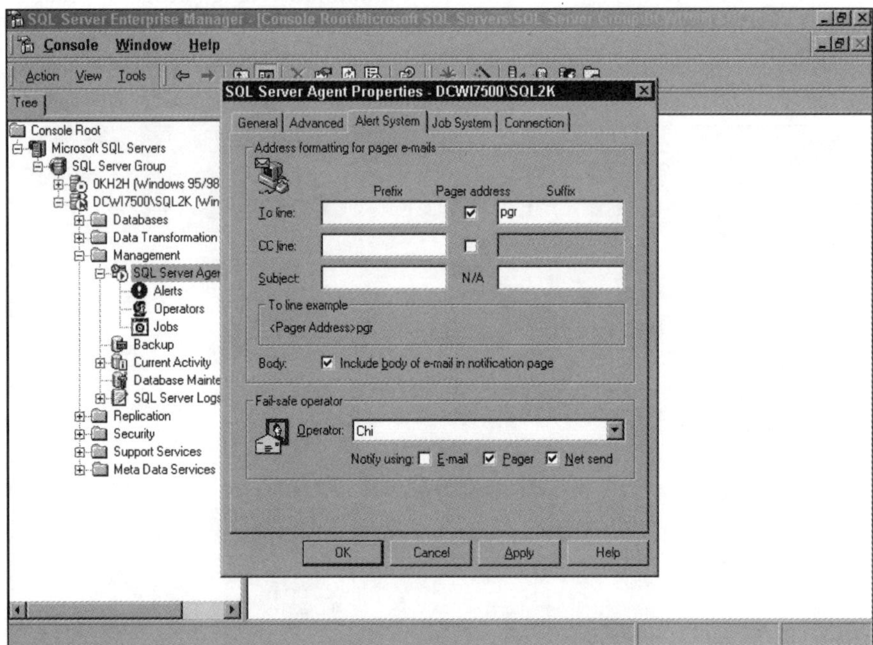

Figure 26-3: SQL Server Agent Alert System properties

The bottom of the Alert System dialog box enables the user to specify a fail-safe operator. If a job or alert tries to send a notification to a pager but no pagers were scheduled to receive the message, then the fail-safe operator will receive notification.

Figure 26-4 shows the Job System properties for the SQL Server Agent. The top of this dialog box enables the user to determine whether or not there should be a limitation on the number of rows that are stored to record the history of executed jobs. These rows are stored in the msdb database. If the limitation box is checked, then two numbers can be entered. The first number specifies the total number of job history rows to be stored. When this number is reached, MSDE will start overwriting the earliest rows. Because some jobs run more frequently than others, there is a second number that can be provided to limit the maximum number of rows that are stored for any one job. For example, if one job is configured to run backup four times a day and another job is configured to run a process every six months, then there will only ever be a single row of history for the biannual job because it will constantly be overwritten by the job that runs four times a day. By limiting the maximum number of rows per job, a reasonable amount of history can be kept for every job.

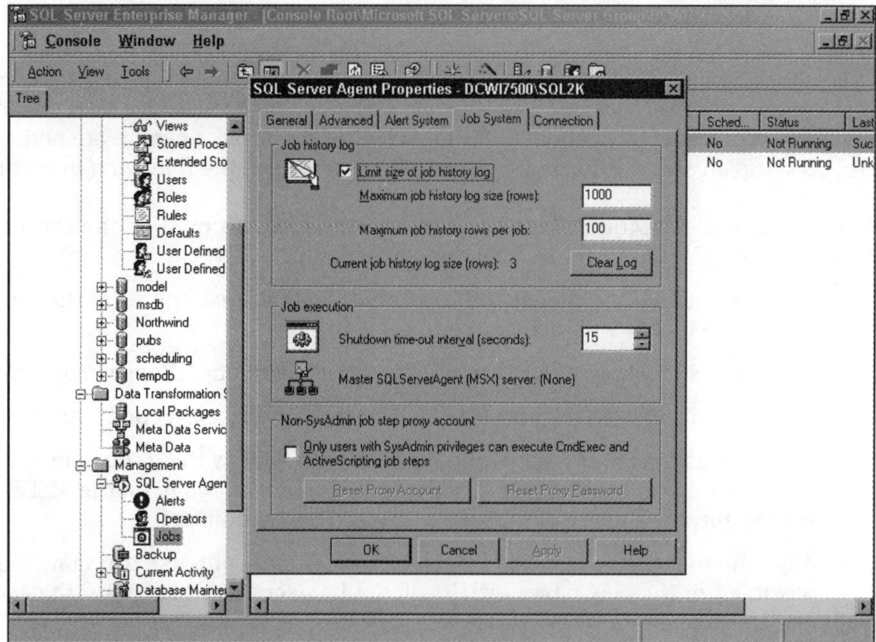

Figure 26-4: SQL Server Agent Job System properties

The middle section of this dialog box includes a setting for how long the SQL Server Agent will wait for jobs to shut down when it has been given the instruction to shut down. Just below this is an informational item that reports the name of the master server if one exists.

At the bottom of the Job System properties dialog box are the controls for configuring the behavior of jobs with respect to users who are not members of the sysadmin role. If the user is not a member of the sysadmin role, but needs to be able to launch a job, the user can be made the owner of the job. In this case, operating system command steps and ActiveX script steps act slightly differently than they would if the owner were a member of sysadmin. This behavior varies because job steps normally run within the security context of the SQL Server Agent service account, which has administrative privilege. If the user is the owner of a job, they can both modify and run the job. Because the job runs in the security context of the administrator of the computer, the user is effectively given administrative control of the computer. To control this, there are two settings at the bottom of the Job System properties dialog box.

If the check box is selected, then only users who are members of sysadmin can execute preexisting commands and ActiveX script job steps. In this case, if the user who is not a member of sysadmin runs a job that has an operating system command or ActiveX script steps, the step will fail.

If the check box is left clear, non-sysadmin users can execute operating system commands or ActiveX script steps, but the steps will be executed within the security context of a special account that the MSDE administrator can create and configure. To setup an account for non-sysadmin job steps, use the following procedure:

1. Create a user account. This account can be a local account on the server that is running MSDE, or it can be a domain account.
2. Assign rights and privileges to the account so that it can perform the job steps for which it will be responsible.
3. In Enterprise Manager, right-click SQL Server Agent and choose Properties.
4. Click the Job System tab and then click the Reset Proxy Account button.
5. Enter the user account name and password, as well as the domain in which the account was created. If the account was created locally on the MSDE server, enter the name of the server instead of the domain.
6. Any time that the password is changed for this account, use the same dialog box to enter the new password. It will not be necessary to reenter the account name or domain.

The Reset Proxy Password button is used only when Enterprise Manager is used to administer MSDE 1.0 or SQL Server 7.0. These versions automatically generate an account called SQLAgentCmdExec, the password to which can be reset only with this button.

Configuring jobs

All existing jobs are displayed in the Jobs container, which is in the SQL Server Agent container under the Management container. New jobs can be created by right-clicking anywhere in the right pane while the Jobs container is displayed or by right-clicking the Jobs container itself in the left pane and selecting New Job from the menu.

Figure 26-5 shows the General properties page for a job. This dialog box is displayed when a new job is created or when a user right-clicks a job and chooses Properties. At the top of the dialog box is the job name; every job must have a unique name, but the name can be changed at any time. MSDE tracks the time and date of job creation and displays them just below the job name. To the right of the creation date is a check box that can be used to enable or disable the job. If a job is disabled, it cannot be run manually, on a schedule, or by an alert.

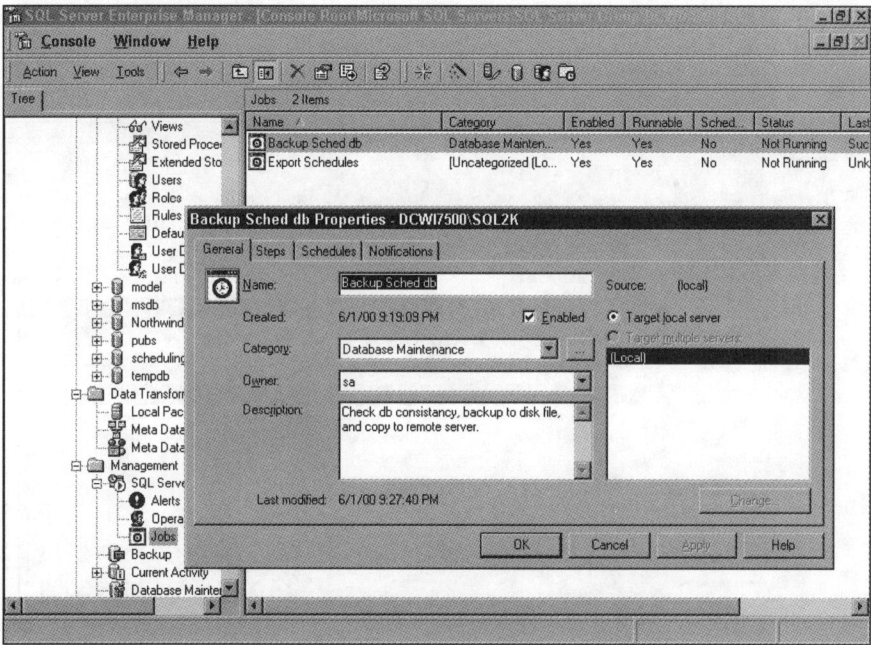

Figure 26-5: Job General properties

In the center of the dialog box is a drop-down list for category. Categories can be used to organize jobs, although they have no functional effect on how a job runs. Categories can be created and organized with a utility that is available by right-clicking the Jobs container and choosing All Tasks ➪ Manage Job Categories. All system-created jobs are automatically categorized.

The owner of a job can be selected from the drop-down list. By default, the owner is the creator of the job. The primary reason to change the owner is to enable someone who is not a member of the sysadmin role to run or modify the job. Below the owner is a text box that can be used to include a description for the job. At the bottom of the dialog box is the date and time of the last modification to the job. The right side of the dialog box is used for controlling multiserver jobs.

Figure 26-6 shows the Steps page of the job properties dialog box. This page shows all steps currently configured for the job and allows the steps to be created, deleted, modified, and reordered. The small green flag marks the first step that will be executed when the job is started. The start step can be configured with the drop-down lists located in the bottom center of the dialog box. The steps can be reordered with the up and down arrows in the lower left of the dialog box. Also shown in this dialog box are the behaviors that will be executed on the success or failure of each step. This behavior can be modified by using the Advanced properties of the step, which are accessible by selecting the step, clicking the edit button, and then choosing the Advanced step properties. The resulting Advanced properties dialog box for a job step is shown in Figure 26-7.

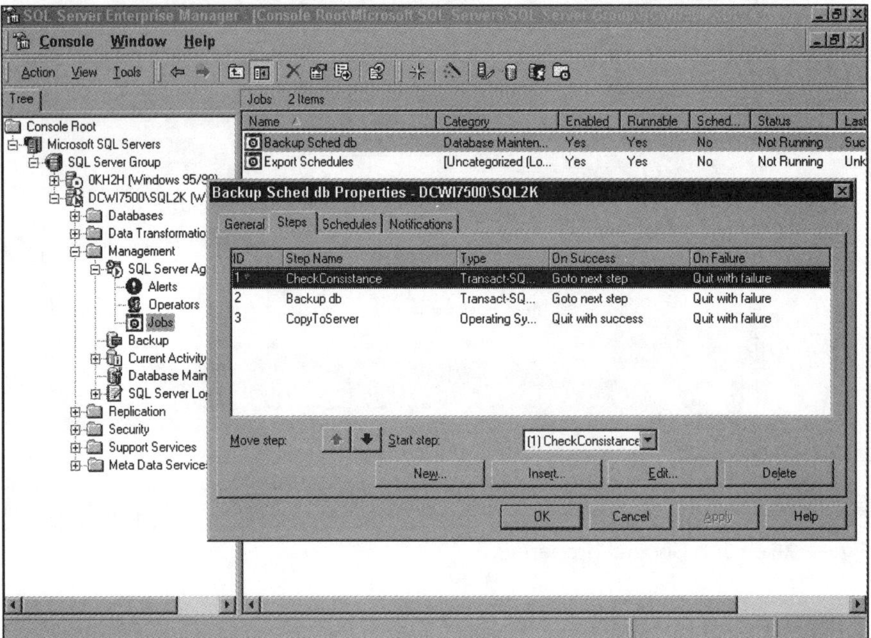

Figure 26-6: Job Steps

The top of the Advanced step properties dialog box enables the user to control what will happen when the step has completed. There is a separate drop-down list for success action and a failure action. Each of these drop-down lists contains options to quit the job successfully, quit the job with failure, go to the next step in order, or go to some other step.

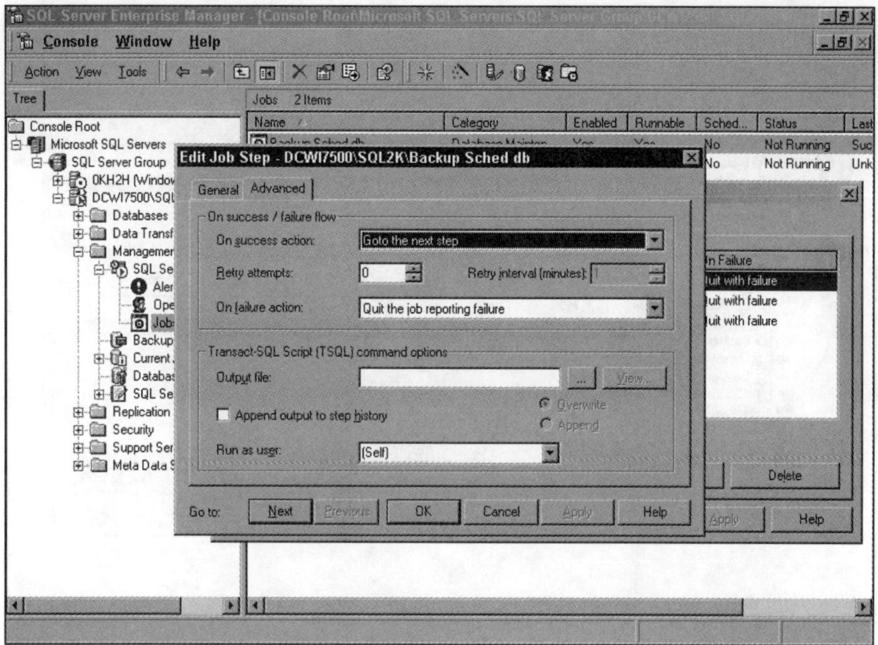

Figure 26-7: Advanced step properties

This dialog box also enables the user to specify whether the step will be retried on failure, and if so, how many times it will be retried and how long the system will wait between each retry. The bottom of this dialog box varies slightly depending upon the type of step. For operating system command steps and SQL steps, an output file can be specified to contain any output generated by the commands contained within the step. In SQL, there is also an option to specify which user within the database will run the step. The selected user must have all required permissions for executing the step or it will fail.

Figure 26-8 displays the Schedules page in the job properties dialog box. This page shows a summary of all of the configured schedules for the job. It enables schedules to be created, deleted, and modified. It also has a button that takes the user directly to the dialog box for creating a new alert. Each schedule can be individually enabled or disabled. To change this state of the schedule, the Edit button must be clicked, and the check box next to Enabled selected or deselected.

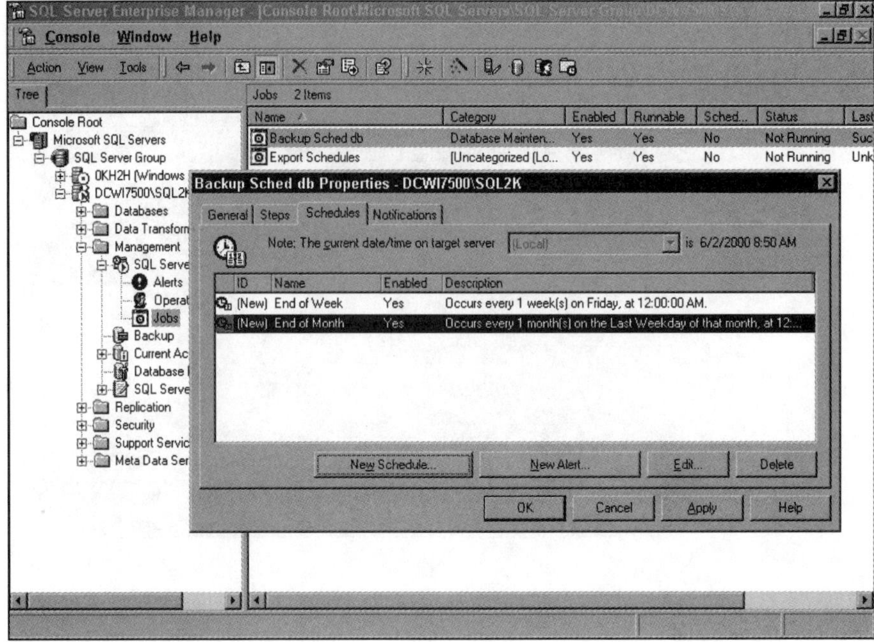

Figure 26-8: Job Schedules

Configuring operators and notification

Before configuring notification for jobs or alerts, the user must configure operators to receive those notifications. Operators can be created from within the Operators container, or they can be created from the Notifications dialog box in the properties of either a job or an alert by choosing New Operator from any operator drop-down list.

Figure 26-9 shows the Notifications page from the properties dialog box of a job. This page enables notifications to be configured in four different ways. It also enables jobs to be automatically deleted after they are run. The four different kinds of notification are as follows:

✦ **E-mail operator**—An e-mail operator can be configured to receive an e-mail containing a job status when the job completes and achieves the status selected from the drop-down list on the right. The drop-down list allows the e-mail to be sent only if a job succeeds, only if a job fails, or when it completes without regard to whether it succeeds or fails.

✦ **Page operator**—A page operator can be configured similarly to the e-mail operator. MSDE has no built-in paging capability and assumes that an organization's e-mail service is configured to be able to place a call to a pager whenever it receives an e-mail to a specific address. For example, if an operator's e-mail address is Chi, then another e-mail address, ChiPgr, might be set up that would cause Chi's pager to beep or vibrate. Page operators have one additional functionality that e-mail operators do not have: Page operators have an on-call schedule. MSDE will page someone only if they are on call (unless they are the fail-safe operator). The on-call schedule can be viewed in the operator properties, which is available by clicking the ellipsis button in the Notifications page and is shown in Figure 26-10.

✦ **Net send operator**—A net send operator will receive a pop-up dialog box in the event of being notified. This functionality depends on underlying NetBIOS messaging functionality in the network, which is not always present. Moreover, workstations can be set up to block net send messages.

✦ **Write to Windows NT application event log**—This log creates a permanent record of the notification that can be viewed by anyone with permission to examine the system application log. This notification, like all the others, is individually configurable for delivery on success, failure, or completion.

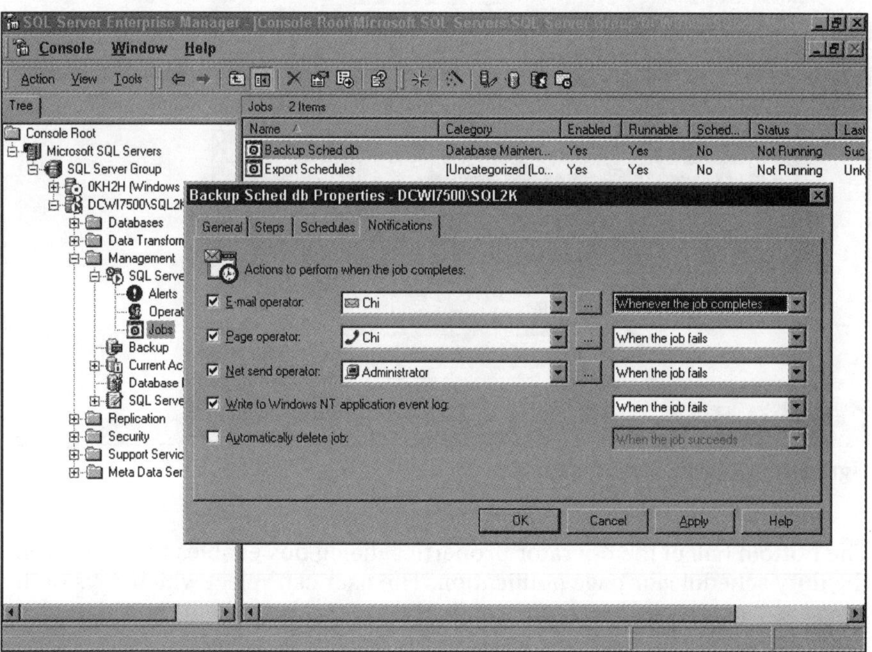

Figure 26-9: Job Notifications

Figure 26-10 shows the operator properties dialog box that is accessible from the Notifications page in the properties of alerts or jobs, or directly from the Operators container. Each operator may be given a name and can be configured individually with one or more addresses: e-mail, pager e-mail, or net send. For the e-mail and pager e-mail address, an ellipsis button will invoke the address book functionality whenever an e-mail client is installed on the computer from which Enterprise Manager is being run. Addresses can also be entered manually. Both e-mail addresses and the net send address have test buttons that will send notifications immediately that are clearly marked as tests. When a user clicks the test buttons for either e-mail address, the SQL Server Agent will send the test e-mail (rather than having it sent by the account to which the user is currently logged on) while configuring the server. For this test to succeed, the SQL Server Agent service account must have been properly configured with a MAPI profile.

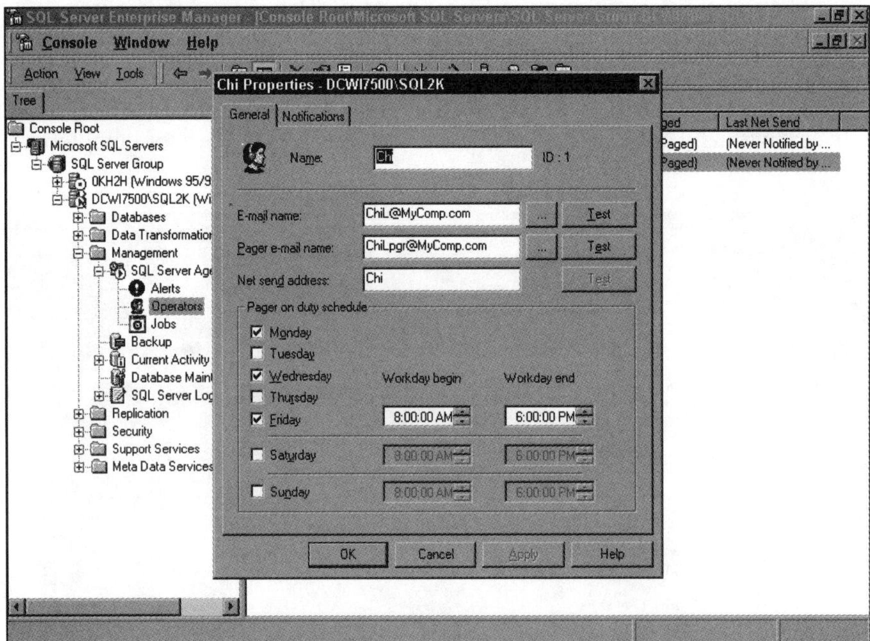

Figure 26-10: Operator properties

The bottom half of the operator properties dialog box enables the user to configure the duty schedule for page notification. The user can select which days of the week a person can be paged and can specify the times during the days, although only a single time period is available for all of the weekdays.

Examining job history

If a user needs to know whether or not a job ran and how successful it was, there are several options. First, there is the notification system built into each job. Users should take advantage of this system and have job status come to them instead of having to go to it. The job notification system should log events in the NT event log, and if an e-mail or a page is not received when expected, the event log should be checked.

Tip

When the NT event log is checked for information about jobs that were supposed to run but didn't, the system log and the security log should be examined. Sometimes, failures of other software or improperly configured security can interfere with jobs that are correctly configured.

The Job container in Enterprise Manager displays an icon to the left of a job name that will turn into a white X on a red background if the job has failed. To get more detail about why a job has failed, or just more detail about the status of a job, a user may wish to examine the job history.

The Job History dialog box is shown in Figure 26-11 and is displayed by right-clicking the job and choosing View Job History. When the Job History dialog box is first displayed, the check box in the operator is clear, and each line in the display represents a summary of the job outcome for each time it has run. The lines displayed in Figure 26-11 with a step ID of zero and a step name of (Job Outcome) are the summary lines that were displayed before the step details were included as well. The summary lines represent the overall job status. The lines just below each summary line correspond to the status of each step in the job when it was run. The top four lines of the display represent the most recent execution of the job. This execution was successful, as can be determined from step ID zero, and the entire job had a run duration of four seconds. The three steps were performed during this execution, with run durations of one second, two seconds, and one second, respectively, and with the last listed the highest in the display.

The previous execution of the job failed. You will notice that the Job Outcome result is failed, the run duration of the job was two seconds, and the small computer icon is displayed in the Notifications column. The Notifications column will display icons for any kind of notification that was performed. A small computer indicates a net send notification, and a small letter icon indicates an e-mail notification. In the case of the failed job execution, the job was configured to perform a net send notification if the job ended with failure, which it did. There are only two lines below the job outcome indicating that the second step failed and caused the entire job to terminate. The first step, CheckConsistency, ran successfully. The second step, Backup db, failed. This failed step is selected in Figure 26-11 so that the details of the step are displayed at the bottom of the dialog box. The error message indicates that the backup utility was unable to access the file in which it was supposed to save the backup. After inspecting this error message, the administrator of this system corrected the problem with the file and immediately reran the job successfully, which is confirmed by the time stamps.

Each of the lines in the Job History display represents one row that is stored in the History table in the msdb database. Understanding this will help the user to properly configure the history retention settings of the SQL Server Agent. The job history for an individual job can be removed from the History table by clicking the Clear All button in the Job History dialog box.

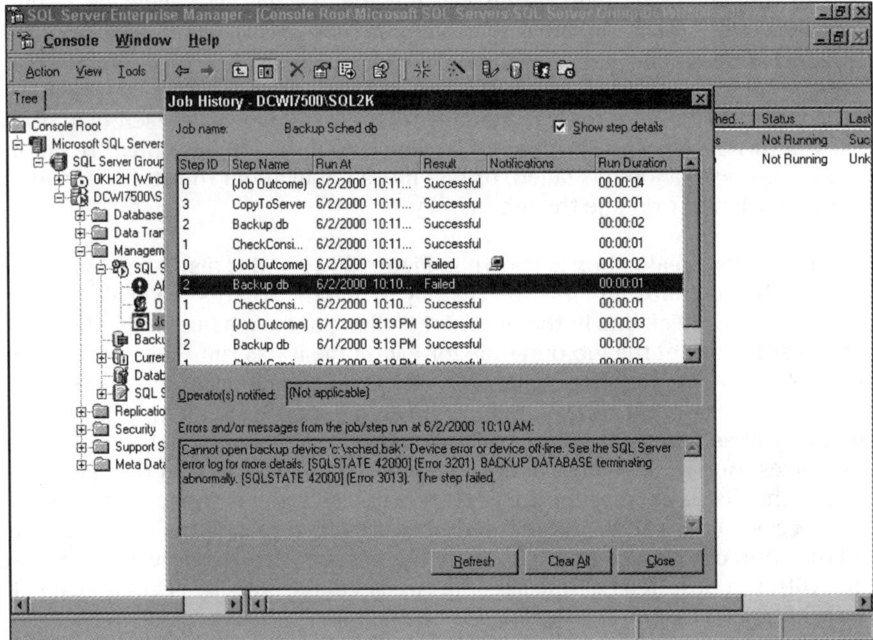

Figure 26-11: Job History dialog box

Configuring alerts

To create an alert, a user must right-click in the right pane of Enterprise Manager when the Alerts container is displayed or right-click on the Alerts container in the left pane. In the alert properties dialog box, the user must enter a name for the alert and choose whether it will be an event alert or a performance condition alert.

Event alerts

Figure 26-12 shows the properties of an event alert.

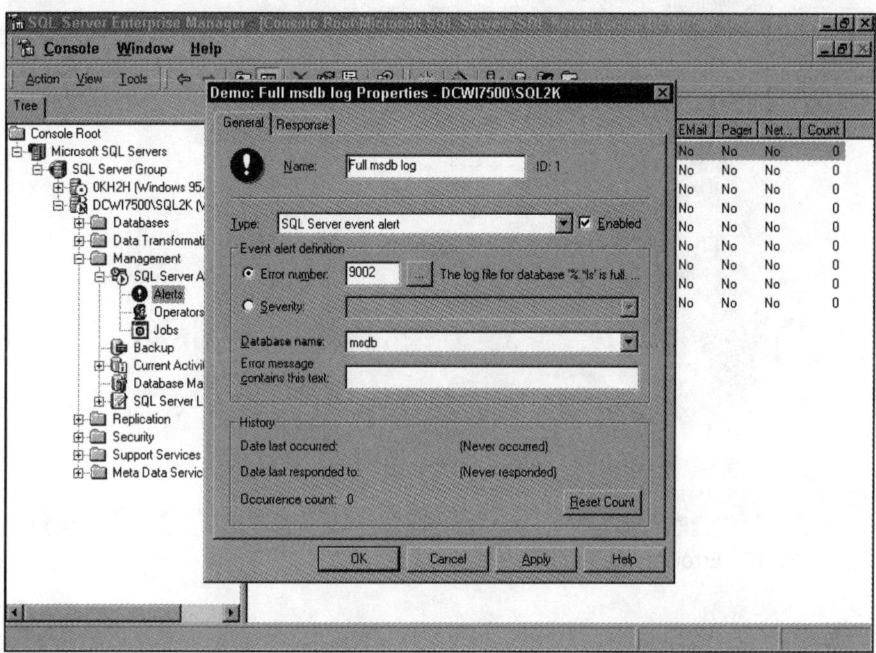

Figure 26-12: Event alert properties

In the event alert shown in Figure 26-12, a specific error number, 9002, is selected and the msdb database is specified. This alert will fire only when error number 9002 is specifically raised on the msdb database. Just below the database name, additional text can be entered. If text is entered here, then the alert will fire only if that text is also found in the actual error message.

To assist in finding a specific error number, the dialog box shown in Figure 26-13 is available for managing server messages. Clicking the option button next to Error Number and then clicking the ellipsis button to the right of the error number displays this dialog box. The search for an error message can be based on text found in the error message, the specific error number, the severity of the error, or any of the above. Once the user has entered the search criteria, the user must click the Find button. For example, if a user were looking for the log file full error, the user could type log file in the Message text that contains text box and click Find, and all of the matching messages would be displayed in the resulting Messages screen, as shown in Figure 26-14.

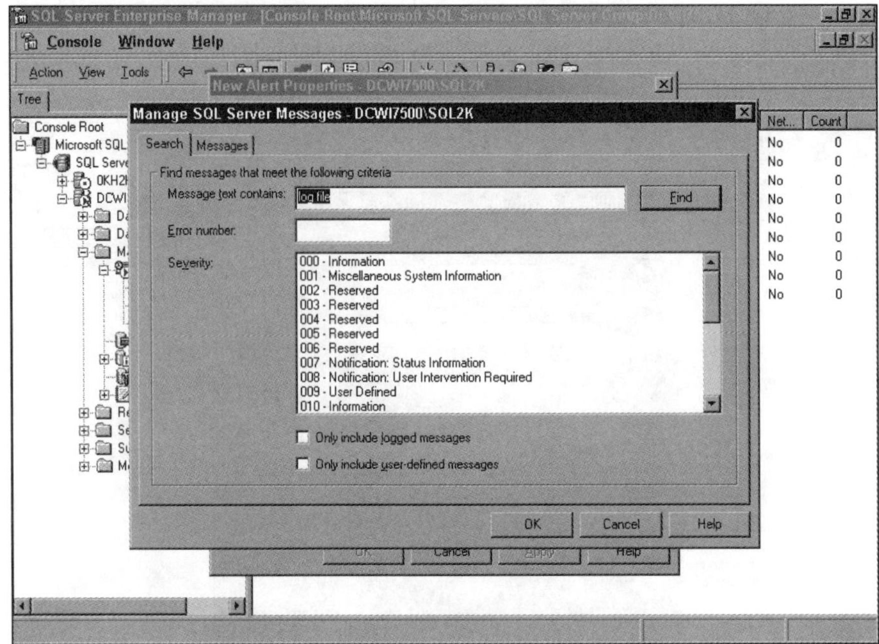

Figure 26-13: Error message Search dialog box

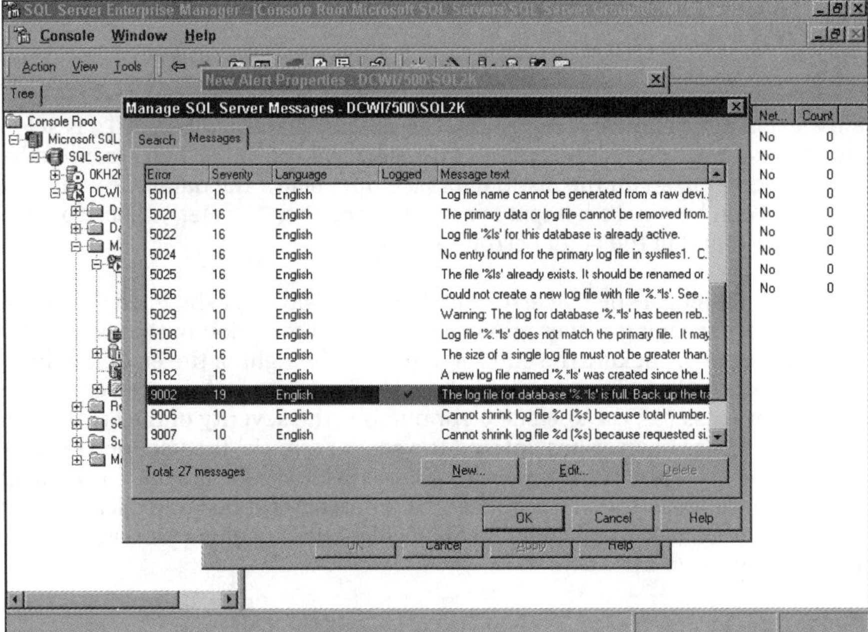

Figure 26-14: Server Messages search results

From the Manage SQL Server Messages dialog box shown in Figure 26-14, user-defined system messages can be created, modified, and deleted. When an error message is selected from this dialog box and the OK button is clicked, the selected error will be returned to the alert properties box.

To define an event alert based on the severity level, click the Severity option button and choose a severity level from the drop-down list. The user can also add a filter based on the database name and text found in the error message for severity level alerts.

Performance condition alerts

To define a performance condition alert, choose the appropriate type from the drop-down list just below the name of the alert in the dialog box. The rest of the dialog box will change as shown in Figure 26-15.

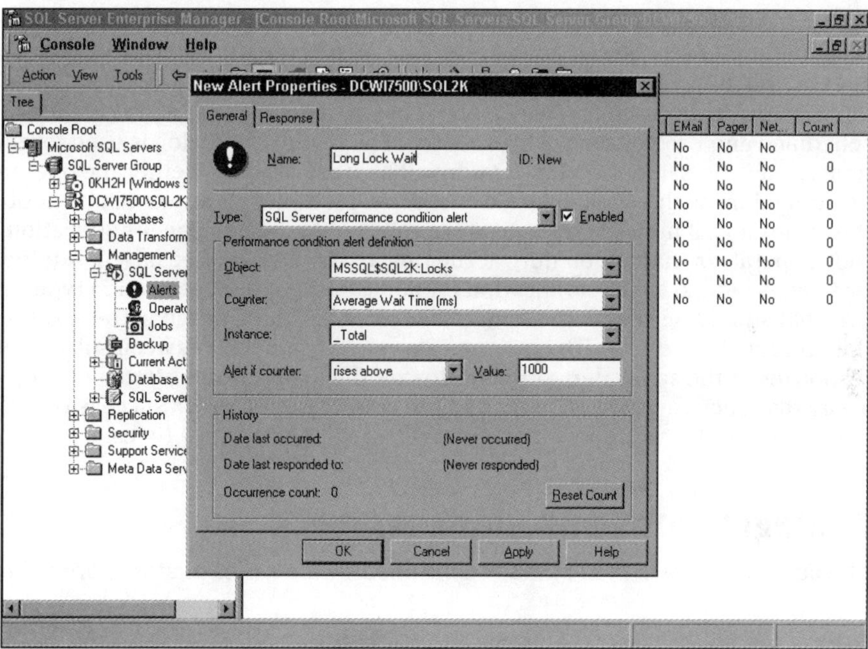

Figure 26-15: Performance condition alert properties

An object should be chosen from the performance condition alert properties dialog box. The objects are listed with the server name first followed by a colon and the object name. If a user is working with a named instance of MSDE, the name of the instance will appear next to the server name separated by a dollar sign. Having chosen the object, a counter from the drop-down list should be selected, as well as an instance of the object, if necessary. Finally, the user must specify the condition upon which the alert should be fired. The three conditions available are falls below, equals, or rises above. The user can then specify the value above which, below which, or equal to which the counter must come to fire the alert.

In the example shown in Figure 26-15, the average wait time was chosen. The instance was set to '_Total,' which provides the aggregate value across the entire server instance. The condition in this example is set to rise above 1000. So, in the example, the alert will fire if the average wait time for locks rises above 1000 milliseconds.

Alert response

Having defined the condition that will cause the alert to fire, whether it's an event alert or a performance condition alert, the user can now define the actions that the alert will take when it is fired.

Figure 26-16 shows the alert Response properties dialog box. This dialog box is the same for all types of alerts. A user can choose to automatically run a job when the alert is fired by selecting the check box at the top of the dialog box and choosing a job from the drop-down list, which will show all defined jobs (a job can be both scheduled and used as an alert response). The rest of the dialog is used for notification. A user can select which operator will be notified and whether the operator will be notified through e-mail, pager, or net send. Multiple operators can be notified for the same alert. If multiple operators are selected to receive pager notification, only those operators that are on duty at the time of the alert will be paged. Additional text can be added to the notification for some or all of the notification types. Any text that should be sent with the notification should be entered in the text box at the bottom of the dialog. The user can also specify a delay between subsequent responses to the same alert at the bottom of the dialog. Some alerts behave in such a way that once they fire, they tend to fire many times in quick succession. Specifying a delay will prevent a pager from ringing numerous times.

Managing jobs and alerts with SQL

The automation system in MSDE is controlled with a series of stored procedures.

Jobs

To create a job with SQL, the user must run a stored procedure to create the job and then run separate stored procedures to create the steps within the job and to create the schedule (if a schedule is desired). When setting the notification parameters, the user can set the notification levels, which indicate when to send notification, and the notification operator name. The notification levels are as follows:

- 0 — Perform no notification

- ✦ 1—Send notification only if job is successful
- ✦ 2—Send notification only if job fails
- ✦ 3—Send notification when job completes with success or failure

The following code creates a job similar to the example used in the figures for Enterprise Manager. The job name is Backup Sched db and will send e-mail notification to the operator, Chi, when it finishes, whether or not it succeeds. It will send pager notification to Chi and a net send notification to the administrator if it fails. An error will be written to the NT event log if the job fails.

```
USE msdb
EXEC sp_add_job @job_name = 'Backup Sched db',
   @enabled = 1,
   @description = 'Check db, backup to file, copy to server',
   @notify_level_eventlog = 2,
   @notify_level_email = 3,
   @notify_level_netsend = 2,
   @notify_level_page = 2,
   @notify_email_operator_name = 'Chi',
   @notify_netsend_operator_name = 'Administrator',
   @notify_page_operator_name = 'Chi'
```

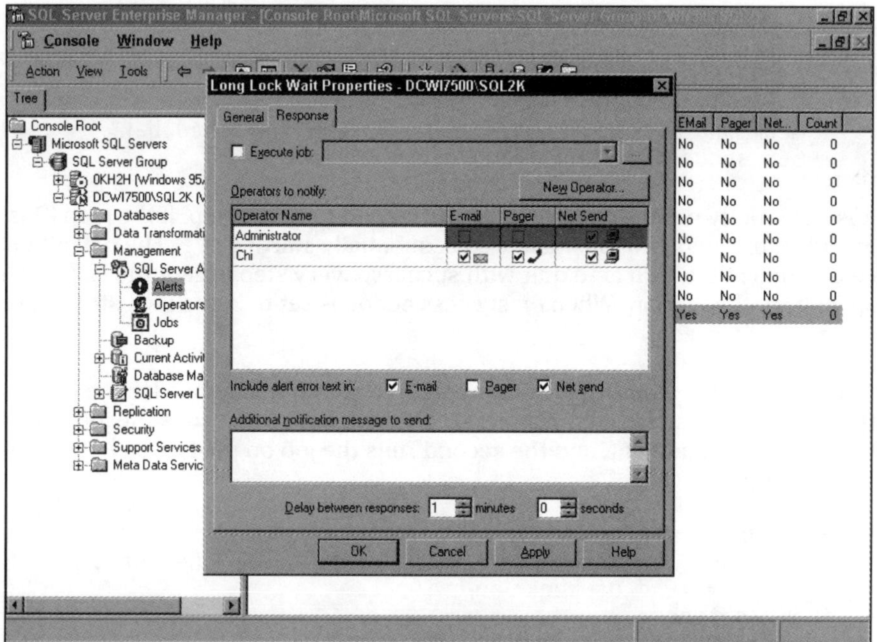

Figure 26-16: Alert Response properties

The msdb database must be used. The stored procedures used for configuring MSDE automation are only available in msdb, which is also where all automation data is stored.

After the job is created, code similar to the following will create job steps:

```
USE msdb
EXEC sp_add_jobstep @job_name = 'Backup Sched db',
   @step_name = 'Check Consistency',
   @step_id = 1,
   @subsystem = 'TSQL',
   @command = 'DBCC CheckDB',
   @database_name = 'Scheduling',
   @on_success_action = 3

EXEC sp_add_jobstep @job_name = 'Backup Sched db',
   @step_name = 'Backup Database',
   @step_id = 2,
   @subsystem = 'TSQL',
   @command = 'BACKUP DATABASE scheduling
               TO DISK = ''c:\sched.bak''
               WITH INIT',
   @database_name = 'Scheduling',
   @on_success_action = 3

EXEC sp_add_jobstep @job_name = 'Backup Sched db',
   @step_name = 'Copy To Server',
   @step_id = 3,
   @subsystem = 'CmdExec',
   @command = 'copy c:\sched.bak \\0kh2h\c\sched.bak',
   @on_success_action = 1
```

It is not strictly necessary to include the step ID for each step. If the step ID is not included, the steps will be numbered sequentially starting at 1. The default on success action is 1, which is to quit with success. Every step except the last step must specify another action. When on success action is set to 3, the next step is executed if the step succeeds.

After defining the steps, the user may wish to create a schedule for the job, as in the following example that creates two schedules. The first runs the job every Friday night at midnight, and the second runs the job on the last day of the month at midnight:

```
USE msdb
EXEC sp_add_jobschedule @job_name = 'Backup Sched db',
   @name = 'End of Week',
   @freq_type = 8,
   @freq_interval = 32,
   @freq_recurrence_factor = 1
```

```
EXEC sp_add_jobschedule @job_name = 'Backup Sched db',
   @name = 'End of Month',
   @freq_type = 32,
   @freq_interval = 8,
   @freq_relative_interval = 16,
   @freq_recurrence_factor = 1
```

There are also corresponding stored procedures for updating and deleting jobs, job steps, and job schedules.

Operators

To create an operator with SQL, the `sp_add_operator` stored procedure must be run. To determine the pager days, the numbers corresponding to the days that the operator should be on duty must be added:

- 1—Sunday
- 2—Monday
- 4—Tuesday
- 8—Wednesday
- 16—Thursday
- 32—Friday
- 64—Saturday

In the following example, the operator Al is created with a schedule of Monday, Wednesday, and Friday (2 + 8 + 32 = 42):

```
USE msdb
EXEC sp_add_operator
   @name = 'Al',
   @email_address = 'AlM@MyComp.com',
   @pager_address = 'AlMpgr@MyComp.com',
   @netsend_address = 'Al',
   @weekday_pager_start_time = 80000,
   @weekday_pager_end_time = 180000,
   @saturday_pager_start_time = 80000,
   @saturday_pager_end_time = 180000,
   @pager_days = 42
```

Alerts

To create an alert with SQL, the user should run the `sp_add_alert` stored procedure. After the alert is created, notifications must be added with `sp_add_notification`. The following example creates an alert that fires when the average wait time for locks rises above one second.

```
USE msdb
EXEC sp_add_alert @name = 'Long Lock Wait',
   @severity = 0,
   @delay_between_responses = 60,
   @performance_condition = 'MSSQL$SQL2K:Locks|Average Wait
Time (ms)|_Total|>|1000',
   @include_event_description_in = 5
```

The operator Al is added to the notification list in the next example:

```
USE msdb
EXEC sp_add_notification @alert_name = 'Long Lock Wait',
   @operator_name = 'Al',
   @notification_method = 1
```

Managing jobs and alerts with DMO

The automation system in MSDE occupies the entire JobServer subtree in the DMO object model. A somewhat abbreviated version is shown below, and more information is available in the examples:

```
SQLServer
   JobServer
      Alerts
         Alert
      Jobs
         Job
            JobSteps
               JobStep
            JobSchedules
               JobSchedule
      Operators
         Operator
```

The JobServer object is a property of the SQLServer object, so there is no need to specifically create a JobServer.

The following code creates the same backup job that was used in the two previous sections. The SQLServer and Job object are created, and then all of the properties of the Job object are set. The notification levels are the same as those presented in the previous section. After the properties of the Job object are set, a connection is made to the MSDE server, and the Job object is added to the Jobs collection of the JobServer object. The JobServer is not created in the code, but is available as soon as the SQLServer object is connected to an MSDE Server.

```
Dim oMSDEServer
Dim oJob
```

```
set oMSDEserver = CreateObject("SQLDMO.SQLServer")
set oJob = CreateObject("SQLDMO.Job")

oJob.Name = "Backup Sched db"
oJob.Description = "Check db, backup to file, copy to server"
oJob.EmailLevel = 3
oJob.OperatorToEmail = "Chi"
oJob.PageLevel = 2
oJob.OperatorToPage = "Al"
oJob.NetSendLevel = 2
oJob.OperatorToNetSend = "Chi"
oJob.EventLogLevel = 2

oMSDEserver.connect "Okh2h","sa",""
oMSDEserver.JobServer.Jobs.add(oJob)
oMSDEserver.disconnect
```

You can find this code on the CD-ROM in the file named `Ch 26\CreateJob.vbs`.

Having created the job and set the notifications, the user next needs to create the steps within the job.

To create a job step, a user must do the following:

1. Instantiate a SQLServer object and a JobStep object for each step that will be required for the job.
2. Set the properties for each job step and then create a connection to the MSDE server.
3. Obtain a reference to the job that will contain the steps and call the `Add` method of the JobSteps collection. If steps already exist in the job when new steps with the same StepID are added, the new step will be inserted, and the old StepID will be incremented to accommodate the new step.
4. The `OnSuccessAction` property uses the values 1 to 4 to indicate that the job should quit with success, quit with failure, continue with the next step, or continue with a specified step, respectively. If the job is configured to continue with a specified step, the `OnSuccessStep` property must also be set.

In the following code, three steps are added to the Backup Sched db job. The first two steps specify to continue with the next step on success; the last step specifies to quit with success on successful completion of the step.

```
Dim oMSDEServer
Dim oJob
Dim oJobStep1
```

```
Dim oJobStep2
Dim oJobStep3

set oMSDEserver = CreateObject("SQLDMO.SQLServer")
set oJobStep1 = CreateObject("SQLDMO.JobStep")
set oJobStep2 = CreateObject("SQLDMO.JobStep")
set oJobStep3 = CreateObject("SQLDMO.JobStep")

oJobStep1.Name = "CheckConsistency"
oJobStep1.StepID = 1
oJobStep1.Subsystem = "TSQL"
oJobStep1.Command = "DBCC CheckDB"
oJobStep1.DatabaseName = "Scheduling"
oJobStep1.OnSuccessAction = 3

oJobStep2.Name = "Backup Database"
oJobStep2.StepID = 2
oJobStep2.Subsystem = "TSQL"
oJobStep2.Command = "BACKUP DATABASE scheduling TO DISK =
'c:\sched.bak' WITH INIT"
oJobStep2.DatabaseName = "Scheduling"
oJobStep2.OnSuccessAction = 3

oJobStep3.Name = "Copy To Server"
oJobStep3.StepID = 3
oJobStep3.Subsystem = "CmdExec"
oJobStep3.Command = "copy c:\sched.bak \\Okh2h\c\sched.bak"
oJobStep3.OnSuccessAction = 1

oMSDEserver.connect "Okh2h","sa",""
set oJob = oMSDEserver.JobServer.Jobs("Backup Sched db")
oJob.JobSteps.add(oJobStep1)
oJob.JobSteps.add(oJobStep2)
oJob.JobSteps.add(oJobStep3)
oMSDEserver.disconnect
```

You can find this code on the CD-ROM in the file named `Ch 26\AddSteps.vbs`.

A user may wish to create schedules for the jobs after the job and job steps are configured. To do so, a JobSchedule object must be instantiated for each schedule to be created. Set the name property on the JobSchedule. The JobSchedule object has a Schedule object as one of its properties. The user must set the properties on this Schedule object, connect to the MSDE server, obtain a reference to the Job object to which the schedules should apply, and call the `Add` method of the JobSchedules collection that is a property of the Job.

The FrequencyType property of the Schedule object is set as follows:

✦ 1—One Time

✦ 4—Daily

✦ 8—Weekly

✦ 16—Monthly on a calendar day (for example, the 15th)

✦ 32—Monthly on a relative day (for example, the first Monday)

✦ 64—Start automatically when SQL Server Agent starts

✦ 128—Start when the CPU becomes idle

The FrequencyInterval property takes on slightly different meaning depending on the value of FrequencyType. Table 26-1 shows how these values can be set using samples for each FrequencyType.

Table 26-1
Settings for FrequencyInterval Property Based on FrequencyType

Interval	*Daily*	*Weekly*	*Monthly*	*Monthly Relative*
1	Every day	Sunday	1st	Sunday
2	Every 2nd day	Monday	2nd	Monday
4	Every 4th day	Tuesday	4th	Wednesday
8	Every 8th day	Wednesday	8th	Day
9	Every 9th day	Wednesday & Sunday	9th	Weekday
10	Every 10th day	Wednesday & Tuesday	10th	Weekend Day
16	Every 16th day	Thursday	16th	
32	Every 32nd day	Friday		
64	Every 64th day	Saturday		

If the monthly relative FrequencyType is chosen (the last column in Table 26-1), the user must specify both the FrequencyInterval, which specifies on what kind of day the schedule should be active (for example, Monday, Wednesday, weekday), and the FrequencyRelativeInterval, which specifies on which of what kind of day it happens (for example, the first Monday, the fourth Wednesday, the second weekday). The following are the values for FrequencyRelativeInterval. They can be added to activate the schedule multiple times per month. For example, a value of 17 for `FrequencyRelativeInterval` (FRI) and a value of 8 for `FrequencyInterval` (FI) would activate the schedule on the first (1 FRI) and last (16 FRI) day (8 FI) of the month.

- 1—1st
- 2—2nd
- 4—3rd
- 8—4th
- 16—Last

If the `FrequencyType` is set to Weekly, Monthly, or Monthly Relative, the `FrequencyRecurrenceFactor` (FRF) must also be set. The FRF indicates the interval between activation periods. For example, if the FRF is 2, the schedule becomes active every second week if the FrequencyType is Weekly, or every second month if FrequencyType is Monthly or Monthly Relative.

The following example creates two schedules for the Backup Sched db job, a weekly schedule and a monthly schedule.

```
Dim oMSDEServer
Dim oJob
Dim oJobSchedule1
Dim oJobSchedule2

set oMSDEserver = CreateObject("SQLDMO.SQLServer")
set oJobSchedule1 = CreateObject("SQLDMO.JobSchedule")
set oJobSchedule2 = CreateObject("SQLDMO.JobSchedule")

oJobSchedule1.Name = "End of Week"
oJobSchedule1.Enabled = True
oJobSchedule1.Schedule.FrequencyType = 8
oJobSchedule1.Schedule.FrequencyInterval = 32
oJobSchedule1.Schedule.FrequencyRecurrenceFactor = 1

oJobSchedule2.Name = "End of Month"
oJobSchedule2.Enabled = True
oJobSchedule2.Schedule.FrequencyType = 32
oJobSchedule2.Schedule.FrequencyInterval = 8
oJobSchedule2.Schedule.FrequencyRelativeInterval = 16
oJobSchedule2.Schedule.FrequencyRecurrenceFactor = 1

oMSDEserver.connect "dcwi7500\sql2k","sa",""
set oJob = oMSDEserver.JobServer.Jobs("Backup Sched db")
oJob.JobSchedules.add(oJobSchedule1)
oJob.JobSchedules.add(oJobSchedule2)
oMSDEserver.disconnect
```

You can find this code on the CD-ROM in the file named `Ch 26\AddSchedule.vbs.`

To create an operator, a user must instantiate an Operator object; set the name, address, and on-duty schedule properties of the Operator object; make a connection to the MSDE Server; and call the `Add` method of the Operators collection, passing the Operator object that was created.

The following example creates the operator Chi:

```
Dim oMSDEServer
Dim oOperator

set oMSDEserver = CreateObject("SQLDMO.SQLServer")
set oOperator = CreateObject("SQLDMO.Operator")

oOperator.Name = "Chi"
oOperator.EmailAddress = "ChiL@MyComp.com"
oOperator.PagerAddress = "ChiLpgr@MyComp.com"
oOperator.NetSendAddress = "Chi"
oOperator.PagerDays = 42

oMSDEserver.connect "Okh2h","sa",""
oMSDEserver.JobServer.Operators.add(oOperator)
oMSDEserver.disconnect
```

You can find this code on the CD-ROM in the file named `Ch 26\CreateOperator.vbs.`

To create an alert for MSDE using DMO, instantiate an Alert object, set the properties, connect to the server, and call the `Add` method of the Alerts collection, passing the newly created Alert object as a parameter.

Event alerts use either the `MessageID` or the `Severity` property of the Alert object to define the condition that will cause the alert to fire. Only one or the other of these two properties may be set or an error will be returned. The following example creates an alert to fire on Message 9002, log full. The `DatabaseName` property is set to msdb in order to restrict the response to errors that are raised for the msdb database. The `AddNotification` method of the Alert object must be called after the Alert has been added to the Alerts collection to configure notifications. The parameters for `AddNotification` are the operator name and the notification type, which can be one of the following values:

- ✦ 1 — Notify by e-mail
- ✦ 2 — Notify by pager
- ✦ 4 — Notify by net send

These values can be added to provide a combination of notification methods to the same operator. For example, a value of 6 will notify by pager and net send. A value of 0 will disable the operator.

```
Dim oMSDEServer
Dim oAlert

set oMSDEserver = CreateObject("SQLDMO.SQLServer")
set oAlert = CreateObject("SQLDMO.Alert")

oAlert.Name = "Full msdb Log"
oAlert.MessageID = 9002
oAlert.DatabaseName = "msdb"
oALert.DelayBetweenResponses = 60

oMSDEserver.connect "Okh2h","sa",""
oMSDEserver.JobServer.Alerts.add(oAlert)
call oAlert.AddNotification("Al", 6)
call oAlert.AddNotification("Chi", 1)
oMSDEserver.disconnect
```

You can find this code on the CD-ROM in the file named `Ch 26\EventAlert.vbs`.

To create a performance condition alert, the `PerformanceCondition` property can be used. This property is a string that is broken into components with vertical bars in the following format:

```
Server Instance:Object|Counter|Object Instance|
Comparison Operator|Value
```

The following example creates the Long Lock Wait alert used in previous examples in this chapter.

```
Dim oMSDEServer
Dim oAlert

set oMSDEserver = CreateObject("SQLDMO.SQLServer")
set oAlert = CreateObject("SQLDMO.Alert")

oAlert.Name = "Long Lock Wait"
oAlert.PerformanceCondition = "MSSQL$SQL2K:Locks|Average Wait
Time (ms)|_Total|>|1000"
oALert.DelayBetweenResponses = 60

oMSDEserver.connect "DCWI7500\sql2k","sa",""
oMSDEserver.JobServer.Alerts.add(oAlert)
call oAlert.AddNotification("Al", 6)
call oAlert.AddNotification("Chi", 1)
oMSDEserver.disconnect
```

You can find this code on the CD-ROM in the file named `Ch 26\PerfAlert.vbs.`

Summary

MSDE provides extensive capabilities for automating maintenance and administration of routine tasks through the SQL Server Agent. The SQL Server Agent runs as a separate service or background process depending upon the operating system being used. The Agent can be configured to run jobs or to monitor alert conditions. Operators can be configured to receive notification about the status of jobs or alerts.

Jobs are composed of a series of steps. Each step can consist of one or more commands that fall into three categories: transact SQL commands, which run within the context of a database; operating system commands, which can include any command that can be issued at the operating system command line prompt, including batch files and executables; and ActiveX scripts, which can be written in any language configured to run with the Windows Scripting Host. The two default languages are VBScript and JScript. The scripting languages provide full support for COM objects.

Alerts monitor the system for one of several kinds of conditions, and when the configured condition occurs, they can be programmed to respond by notifying an operator and by running a job. The two types of alerts are event alerts and performance condition alerts.

Event alerts monitor the system error log and fire based on either a particular error or an error of a particular severity. Event alerts can also be configured to fire only if the configured error is raised by a specific database or if it contains a specific substring. Performance condition alerts monitor the same counters as are available to the NT Performance Monitor. They can be configured to fire when a particular counter rises above, falls below, or becomes equal to a specific value.

If enough work is put into configuring the automation provided by the SQL Server Agent, then most of the fire fighting on which many administrators spend too much time can be eliminated, and the database administration can become proactive instead of reactive.

✦ ✦ ✦

CHAPTER 27

Creating Web Pages

In This Chapter

Using the Web Assistant Wizard to publish data to HTML documents

Using the Web Publishing Wizard to copy Web documents to the ISP

Using Active Server Pages to develop Web sites

The Web Assistant Wizard is part of Enterprise Manager and can be used to publish data in the MSDE database to HTML files. These HTML documents can then be accessed by anyone with access to the network path, or they can be posted to the Web server on the ISP or corporate site. In addition to just creating basic HTML documents using the Web Assistant Wizard, the user also has the ability to create interactive Web sites using Active Server Pages. ASPs are a powerful programming language that can take advantage of the VBScript or JavaScript languages intermixed with the HTML user interface display code.

Using the Web Assistant and Web Publishing Wizard to Create Reports on the Web

The Web Assistant Wizard allows the user to publish data to an HTML file on a one-time or scheduled basis. The user can output the results of a SQL statement to an HTML document — or choose which tables the data should come from — and the wizard will create the SQL statement. The following steps will illustrate how to do this:

1. Open Enterprise Manager.
2. Browse the tree structure and select the database for which the data will be published.
3. Select Tools, then Wizards from the drop-down menu. Another screen will appear that lists the available wizards in Enterprise Manager.

4. Expand the tree where it says Management, choose the Web Assistant Wizard, and click OK. The Welcome screen for the Web Assistant Wizard will appear.
5. Choose the database from which the data will be retrieved.
6. Specify an appropriate name for the Web Assistant Job. This screen also offers a choice between retrieving the data from specific tables and columns, from a stored procedure, or from a SQL statement.
7. If the option to retrieve the data from specific tables and columns is chosen, a screen will appear prompting a selection of which tables and columns to include in the document.
8. If the option to retrieve the data from a stored procedure is chosen, a screen will appear prompting the selection of a stored procedure.
9. If the option to retrieve the data from a SQL statement is chosen, a screen will appear prompting you for the appropriate SQL statement.
10. Once the source of the data for the HTML document has been selected, specify the frequency at which the Web Assistant Job should run on a screen called Schedule the Web Assistant Job, shown in Figure 27-1.

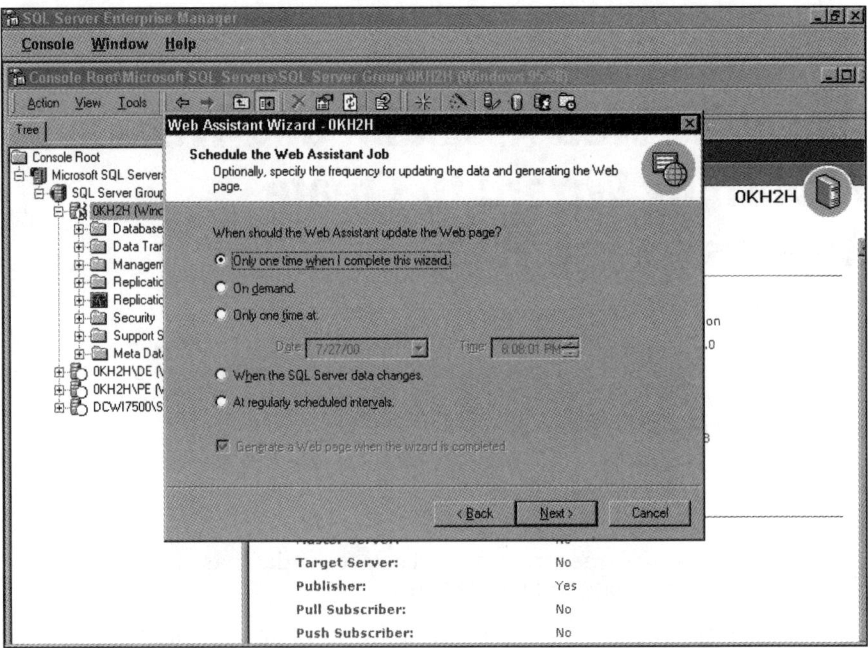

Figure 27-1: The Schedule the Web Assistant Job screen on the Web Assistant Wizard

There are several scheduling options on this screen. The job can be run only one time, if a one-time HTML report is being created, for example. It can also be run on demand, on a certain day and time in the future, whenever the underlying data changes in MSDE, or at regularly scheduled intervals. These options provide a great deal of flexibility when specifying when the HTML report should be created.

11. Once the frequency has been chosen, the last step in the wizard is to specify the location and filename for the HTML document.

12. After the export completes, the user can view the document from the Web browser by specifying the complete path to the filename.

The job is saved with an .htm extension instead of an .html extension. When specifying the filename in the Web browser, make sure to indicate .htm instead of .html.

Once the user has published the MSDE data to an HTML document, the file can be placed on the corporate network so that others in the company can access it. The user can also copy the file to the Web server or ISP host so that it will be available on the corporate Web site on the World Wide Web. Employing these options will obviously depend on the nature of the data in the report and on its intended audience. Should a user need to transfer the HTML document to the corporate Web site or ISP, a traditional FTP (File Transfer Protocol) program can be used. Another option is to use the Web Publishing Wizard that is automatically installed with a number of programs. Users can check two different locations on their system to see if the Web Publishing Wizard is available: in the Start, Programs, Microsoft Web Publishing group and in the Start, Programs, Accessories, Internet Tools group.

The Web Publishing Wizard will walk the user through a series of steps to select the files to be copied to the Web site. At the end, the wizard will begin the transfer to the Web site. It will inform the user whether it was able to connect and successfully copy the files.

Using Active Server Pages for Interactive Web Sites

Being able to publish MSDE data in an HTML document is appropriate in many situations. However, there is a way for users to create interactive Web sites that allows them to have a user interface, respond to user actions, and retrieve data from an MSDE database as appropriate: Active Server Pages, or ASPs. An ASP file can contain VBScript, JavaScript, and HTML. One of the scripting tools is used to perform the database and similar operations, while the HTML code is used to generate the user interface displayed to the user in the Web browser. ASPs can be created in a text editor, Visual Interdev, FrontPage, or any other tool that lets the user type VBScript commands. Not all of these tools (such as a text editor) give interactive feedback on whether the code entered is syntactically correct. Thus, it is advisable, when possible, to use Visual Interdev or a similar tool to test the VBScript code. A user can generate the HTML user interface portion in FrontPage pretty easily, but then has to determine which portions to paste into the ASP document and which portions to keep in a separate HTML document.

In order to run ASPs on the local development machine, Personal Web Server will need to be installed (unless IIS Server is running on the local NT machine). Personal Web Server comes on the NT 4.0 Option Pack. One place that NT 4.0 Option Pack is available is on the Visual Studio 6.0 Enterprise Edition installation CD. It can also be downloaded from Microsoft's Web site.

The rest of this chapter will focus on a hypothetical Web application created using HTML and ASPs with VBScript to connect to MSDE. This application is called "The Online Doctor's Office." It allows patients to log in with their own user id and password and then modify their contact information and view the history of their prior visits.

The first part of the Online Doctor's Office is a login screen that prompts the user to specify a user id and password before allowing them to proceed. Once the user clicks the OK button, the ASP code uses ADO to check the Users table (shown in Table 27-1) to make sure that the user and password exist.

Table 27-1
Table Structure for Users Table

Column	*Data Type*
UserId	Varchar
Password	Varchar
LastName	Varchar
FirstName	Varchar
PatientId	Integer

If that user exists, then the welcome screen (welcome.asp) is displayed. If that user does not exist or if he or she typed an invalid id or password, then the login screen gets reloaded. Listing 27-1 is the complete listing for the login functionality.

Listing 27-1: **Contents of Login.asp**

```
<%
Option Explicit

'***************************************************
' Display Login Form
'***************************************************
sub LoginForm()
%>

<html>
<head>
<title>The Online Doctor's Office</title>
</head>

<body>

<h1>Please Login To The Online Doctor's Office</h1>

<% Response.write "<form action=""" _
   & request.servervariables("script_name") _
   & "?userresponse=v"" method=POST>"

%>

<table cellpadding=2>
<tr>
  <td>User Name</td>
  <td><input type="Text" name="txtUserName" size="25"></td>
</tr>
<tr>
  <td>Password</td>
  <td><input type="password" name="txtPassword" size="25"></td>
</tr>
<tr>
  <td align=center colspan=2>
  <input type="Submit" name="cmdOK" value="Login">
  </td>
</table>

</form>
</body>
</html>
<%
end sub
```

Continued

Listing 27-1 *(continued)*

```
'*****************************************************
' Verify The UserId and Password Entered By the User
'*****************************************************
sub VerifyLogin()

    dim oConn  ' as adodb.connection
    dim rsPatient 'as adodb.recordset

    set oconn = server.createobject("ADODB.connection")
    oconn.open "MSDESample", "sa", ""

    set rspatient = oconn.execute("select * from users " & _
        whereUserId='" & request("txtUserName") & "'" & _
        " and password='" & request("txtPassword") & "'")

    if not rspatient.eof then

       'store the patientId in the session loggedin
       'parameter for later use
       session("LoggedIn") = rspatient("PatientId")

       response.redirect "welcome.asp?PatientId=" & _
                rspatient("PatientId")

    else
       loginform

    end if
end sub

'*****************************************************
' Main
'*****************************************************
sub main()

  if request("userresponse") <> "" then
    verifylogin
  else
     loginform
  end if

end sub

'*****************************************************
' Start Program
'*****************************************************

call main

%>
```

The code in Listing 27-1 is modular in structure. Modules — such as `LoginForm`, `VerifyLogin`, and `Main` — perform different functions. There is also a mixture of VBScript and HTML in this .asp document. At the very end of the script, there is a call to the `main` function, which gets the whole page going. The `Main` routine then calls the `LoginForm` to display the login screen. Once the user clicks the Submit button, the `Main` module will call the `VerifyLogin` routine.

The `LoginForm` routine uses HTML to display two text boxes: UserId and Password. It also displays an OK button. All of the code seen in that procedure is just for formatting the user interface to the user.

The first part of the `VerifyLogin` routine declares a connection and recordset object. It then creates a connection to the database using the connection object. It connects using an ODBC DSN called "MSDESample":

```
dim oConn   ' as adodb.connection
dim rsPatient 'as adodb.recordset

set oconn = server.createobject("ADODB.connection")
oconn.open "MSDESample", "sa", ""
```

Then, the SQL statement gets executed against the Users table to see if that exact user name and password exist in the database:

```
set rspatient = oconn.execute("select * from users where
    UserId='" & request("txtUserName") & "'" & " and
    password='" & request("txtPassword") & "'")
```

The recordset is set to the return value of the `execute` method of the connection object. If the recordset returns a row, then the user id and password exist in the database, and the user can continue.

```
if not rspatient.eof then

    'store the patientId in the session loggedin
    'parameter for later use
    session("LoggedIn") = rspatient("PatientId")
```

The `session("LoggedIn")` parameter is being assigned to the `PatientId`. The session object is open for the entire duration of the user session in the Web browser. This session object can be accessed from other HTML and ASP documents without having to pass in any parameters. The `LoggedIn` parameter is assigned to the `PatientId` so that in later commands requested by the user, it will already be available. It is also acting as a security mechanism to prohibit a user from jumping directly to the welcome.asp page or one of the later pages to make unauthorized changes. The way this sort of security gets implemented is that the session object will be used in the `Update` and `Select` statements as the `WHERE` criteria. If it is empty (for example, the user didn't log in), then no records will be returned, nor will any records be updated in the database.

After the session object is set to the PatientId, the validated user gets redirected to a different page: the welcome screen (welcome.asp).

```
response.redirect "welcome.asp?PatientId=" &
        rspatient("PatientId")
```

What happens if the user id and password don't exist in the database? If the recordset is at the end of file (meaning there was no match), then the Else statement gets executed:

```
else
   loginform
```

The Else statement simply calls the LoginForm procedure again to display the login screen to the user another time.

Note that everything in Listing 27-2 is HTML code. Thus, even though this file could have been saved as an HTML file, it is just as effective to save it as an ASP file.

Listing 27-2: **Contents of Welcome.asp**

```
<html>
<head>
<title>The Online Doctor's Office</title>
</head>

<body>

<h1><font color="#0000FF">Welcome </font></h1>

<form action="getselection.asp" method = POST>

<hr>
  <p><font color="#FF0000">What Would You Like To Do
      Today?</font></p>
  <p><input type="radio" name="rSelection" value="R2">Update
      Personal Information (Address and Contact
      Information)</p>
  <p><input type="radio" name="rSelection" value="R3">View
      Account Information (Office Visit History)</p>
  <p align="center"><input type="submit" value="Process My
      Request" name="cmdProcessRequest"></p>
  <p> </p>
</form>

</body>
</html>
```

The code in Listing 27-2 displays a welcome message to the user and prompts them to choose one of these options: Update Personal Information or View Account Information. Figure 27-2 displays the Welcome screen.

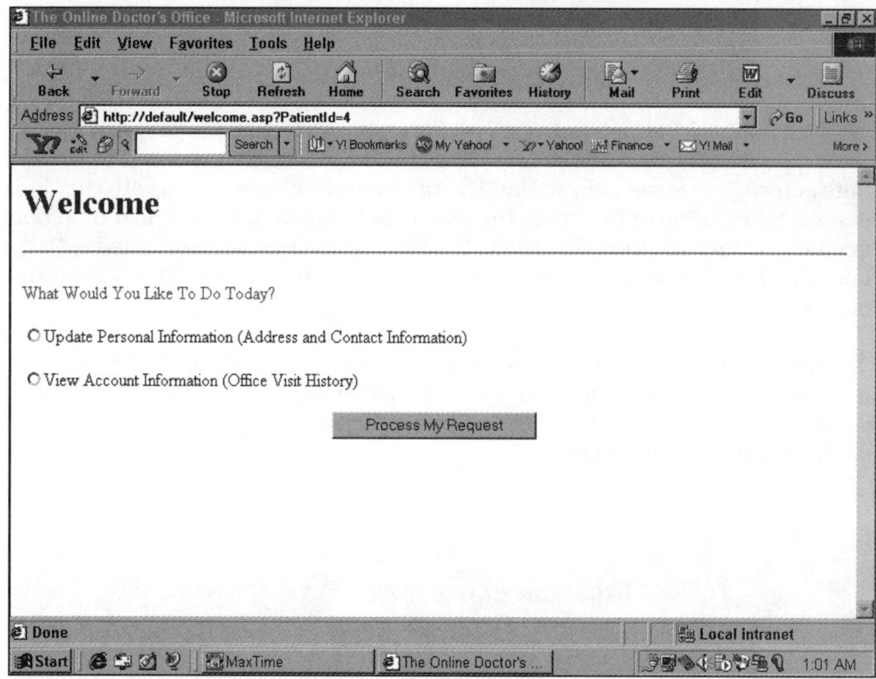

Figure 27-2: The Welcome screen (welcome.asp)

Once the user makes a selection from the option buttons and clicks the Process My Request button, the GetSelection.asp document gets called to process the user's selection. The GetSelection code is displayed in Listing 27-3:

Listing 27-3: **Contents of GetSelection.asp**

```
<%
    select case request.form("rSelection")

    case "R2"

       response.redirect "http://default/UpdatePersonal.asp"

    case "R3"

       response.redirect "http://default/ViewHistory.asp"
```

Continued

Listing 27-3 *(continued)*

```
    end select

%>
```

This file contains VBScript and no HTML formatting because the purpose of this screen is to quickly process the user's input and then redirect the user to the appropriate screen. If the user selects the "R2" option button, associated with the Update Personal Information option, then the user gets redirected to the UpdatePersonal.asp document. If, instead, the user selects the "R3" option button, associated with the View Account Information option, then the user gets redirected to the ViewHistory.asp document.

If the user selected the View Account Information option, the GetSelection.asp document would redirect the user to the ViewHistory.asp document, which would then look up the account history for the user from the Visits table (shown in Table 27-2) and display it in the browser.

Table 27-2
Table Structure for Visits Table

Column	*Data Type*
VisitId	Integer
PatientId	Integer
VisitDate	DateTime
Purpose	Varchar
Comments	Varchar

The ASP code for the View Account Information selection is shown in Listing 27-4:

Listing 27-4: Contents of ViewHistory.asp

```
<%
option explicit

'*******************************************
'  Display History
'*******************************************
```

```
sub DisplayHistory
%>

<html>

<head>
<title>View Visit History</title>
</head>

<body>
View History

</body>

</html>
<%
End Sub

'*******************************************
'  DisplayResults
'*******************************************
sub DisplayResults

    dim oConn   ' as adodb.connection
    dim rsPatient 'as adodb.recordset

    set oconn = server.createobject("ADODB.connection")
    oconn.open "MSDESample", "sa", ""

    set rspatient = oconn.execute("select VisitDate, Purpose,
        Comments from visits where patientid=" &
        session("LoggedIn"))

    if not rspatient.eof then

        do while not rspatient.eof
            response.write "<li>" & "Visit Date: " &
                    rspatient("VisitDate")
            response.write "<li>" & "Purpose: " &
                    rspatient("Purpose")
            response.write "<li>" & "Comments: " &
                    left(rspatient("Comments"),50)
            rspatient.movenext
            response.write "<li>"

        loop

    end if

end sub
```

Continued

Listing 27-4 *(continued)*

```
'******************************************
'  Main
'******************************************
sub Main

    if session("LoggedIn") <> "" then
        DisplayHistory
        DisplayResults
    end if

end sub

call Main

%>
```

This code is structured modularly, just as it was in the Login.asp file previously shown. The `DisplayHistory` routine sets the title of the window, etc. The `DisplayResults` routine gets called once the user has made a selection. It will run a SQL statement to select the patient's information from the database. The `Main` module controls how the others get executed. At the end, the call to `Main` gets everything started.

The `DisplayResults` VBScript code below uses the ADO connection object and the MSDESample ODBC DSN to connect to the MSDE database. The recordset object is also being used here.

```
dim oConn   ' as adodb.connection
dim rsPatient 'as adodb.recordset

set oconn = server.createobject("ADODB.connection")
oconn.open "MSDESample", "sa", ""
```

After the connection is opened, the SQL statement to retrieve the VisitDate, Purpose, and Comments from the Visits table is executed. The results of that select are put into the `rspatient` recordset:

```
set rspatient = oconn.execute("select VisitDate, Purpose,
    Comments from visits where patientid=" &
    session("LoggedIn"))
```

If any patient visit records are returned, then a `do while` loop is entered to display details about each visit in the Web browser to the user.

```
    if not rspatient.eof then

        do while not rspatient.eof
            response.write "<li>" & "Visit Date: " &
                    rspatient("VisitDate")
            response.write "<li>" & "Purpose: " &
                    rspatient("Purpose")
            response.write "<li>" & "Comments: " &
                    left(rspatient("Comments"),50)
            rspatient.movenext
            response.write "<li>"

        loop
```

The `response.write` method is used to write the information to the browser. The `<li>` designation causes it to place a carriage return so the data will not be garbled together.

If, instead of selecting the View Account Information option, the user chose Update Personal Information, the GetSelection.asp document would redirect the user to the UpdatePersonal.asp document, shown in Listing 27-5.

Listing 27-5: **Contents of UpdatePersonal.asp**

```
<%
Option Explicit

'******************************************************
' Display Update Form
'******************************************************
sub DisplayForm()
%>

<html>

<head>
<title>Update Personal Information</title>
</head>

<body>
<b><font color="#000080" size="5">
Update Personal Information</font></b>
<hr>

<% Response.write "<form action=""" _
   & request.servervariables("script_name") _
   & "?userresponse=v"" method=POST>"
%>
```

Continued

Listing 27-5 (continued)

```
<p>Make sure to fill out all of the fields below before you
      click Submit.  Each of the fields listed below will
      be updated in the database with the information
      below.</p>
<p>Address:        <input
      type="text" name="T1" size="20"></p>

<p>City:         &
      nbsp;     <input type="text"
      name="T2" size="20"></p>

<p>State:         
          <input type="text" name="T3"
      size="20"></p>

<p>Zip:         &n
      bsp;       <input type="text"
      name="T4" size="20"></p>

<p>Email:         
         <input type="text" name="T5"
     size="20"></p>

<p>Home Phone:  <input type="text" name="T6"
     size="20"></p>

<p>Work Phone:  <input type="text" name="T7"
     size="20"></p>

<p align="left"><input type="submit" value="Submit"
     name="B1"></p>

</form>

</body>

</html>

<%
end sub

'*****************************************************
' Update Database And Confirm To User
'*****************************************************
sub UpdateDatabase()

    dim oConn  ' as adodb.connection
    set oconn = server.createobject("ADODB.connection")
    oconn.open "MSDESample", "sa", ""
```

```
    oconn.execute("update patient set Address = '" &
          request.form("t1") & "', City = '" &
          request.form("t2") & "', State = '" &
          request.form("t3") & "', Zip = " & request.form("t4")
          & " WHERE patientid = " & session("loggedin"))

    oconn.execute("update contacts set Email = '" &
         request.form("t5") & "', HPhone = '" &
         request.form("t6") & "', WPhone = '" &
         request.form("t7") & "' WHERE patientid = " &
         session("loggedin"))

    response.write "Your personal information has been
         successfully updated!"

    oconn.close
    set oconn = nothing

end sub

'*******************************************************
' Main
'*******************************************************
sub main()

  if request("userresponse") <> "" then
    UpdateDatabase
  else
    DisplayForm
  end if

end sub

'*******************************************************
' Start Program
'*******************************************************

call main

%>
```

Again, the same modular concept has been used to structure the code. This makes it much easier to read. It is recommended that you follow this structure or a similar method when you write your own ASP code. In the UpdatePersonal code, there is a `DisplayForm` routine that will display the fields the user can update: Address, City, State, Zip, Email, Home Phone, and Work Phone. Each of these text boxes is created in the `DisplayForm` routine in HTML code. Figure 27-3 shows what the UpdatePersonal file looks like in the Web browser.

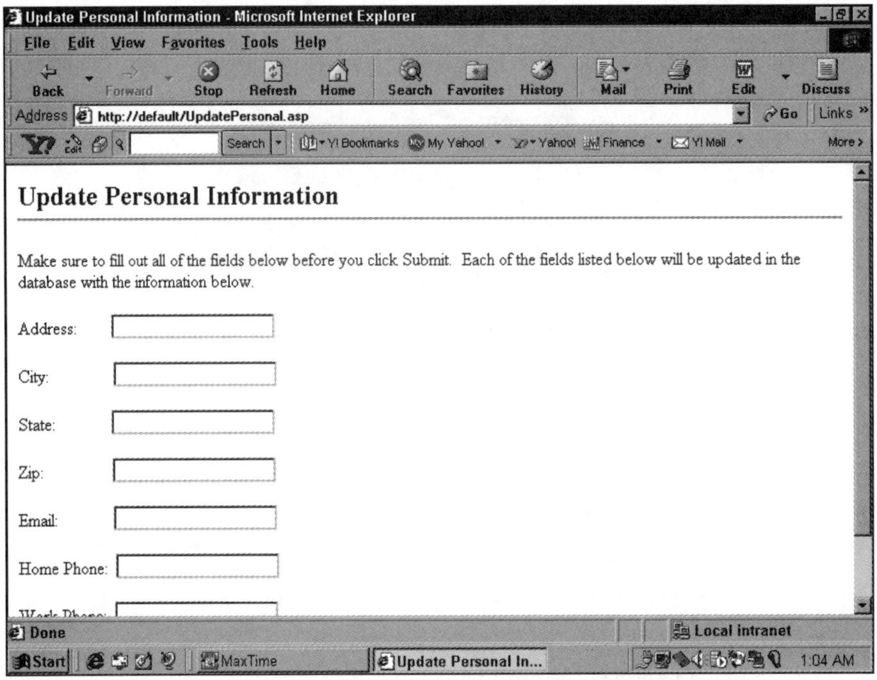

Figure 27-3: The Update Personal Information screen (UpdatePersonal.asp)

After the user clicks the Submit button, the `UpdateDatabase` routine is called and updates the Contacts and Patient tables in the MSDE database with the information the user fills out on the form. The Contacts table structure is shown in Table 27-3.

Table 27-3
Table Structure for Contacts Table

Column	*Data Type*
PatientId	Integer
HPhone	Varchar
WPhone	Varchar
Email	Varchar
RelativeName	Varchar
RelativePhone	Varchar

The Patient table structure is shown in Table 24-7.

Table 27-4
Table Structure for Patient Table

Column	*Data Type*
PatientId	Integer
LastName	Varchar
FirstName	Varchar
MiddleInitial	Varchar
Address	Varchar
City	Varchar
State	Varchar
Zip	Integer
DOB	DateTime
Sex	Varchar

The first part of the UpdateDatabase routine consists of opening the connection to the database.

```
dim oConn   ' as adodb.connection
set oconn = server.createobject("ADODB.connection")
oconn.open "MSDESample", "sa", ""
```

Next, the connection object's execute method is called to issue two update statements against the database. The first update statement updates the Patient table with the values from the t1–t4 text fields on the form.

```
oconn.execute("update patient set Address = '" &
      request.form("t1") & "', City = '" &
      request.form("t2") & "', State = '" &
      request.form("t3") & "', Zip = " & request.form("t4")
      & " WHERE patientid = " & session("loggedin"))
```

The next Execute statement updates the Contacts table with the values from the t5–t7 text fields on the form.

```
oconn.execute("update contacts set Email = '" &
     request.form("t5") & "', HPhone = '" &
     request.form("t6") & "', WPhone = '" &
     request.form("t7") & "' WHERE patientid = " &
     session("loggedin"))
```

In these two update statements, the "loggedin" value is being used in the WHERE clause to determine which records to update. If the user bypasses the login screen and tries to make changes, these updates will fail because the "loggedin" value will be empty.

After the update statements are executed against the database, the user is notified in the browser that the updates were successful.

```
response.write "Your personal information has been
     successfully updated!"
```

These last two lines perform cleanup to free up the memory that the connection object was utilizing.

```
oconn.close
set oconn = nothing
```

At this point in the application, there is nowhere else to go — unless the user clicks the Back button and returns to the Welcome screen to make another selection.

Summary

Being able to publish data in the MSDE database to an HTML report format with the Web Assistant Wizard is a valuable tool. The Web Assistant Wizard is part of Enterprise Manager and walks the user through a series of steps to specify what data will be published, how frequently, and so on. Those HTML documents can then be accessed by anyone with access to that network path, or they can be posted to the Web server on the ISP or corporate site. The Web Publishing Wizard is a tool that can help guide the user through the process of porting Web documents to an outside ISP or to the corporate Web server.

To create interactive Web sites that can access data in the MSDE database, Active Server Pages (ASPs) are a good choice. ASPs have many powerful features that allow users to take advantage of their existing knowledge of HTML user interface design, as well as VBScript and JavaScript. More and more companies are moving functionality to the Web, whether on corporate intranet sites or on public Internet sites. It is becoming increasingly important for developers to understand how to create interactive Web sites for their MSDE database.

✦ ✦ ✦

P A R T

VII

Database Monitoring, Maintenance, and Optimization

This part describes a variety of tools designed to monitor and optimize MSDE activity. It addresses Microsoft's general-purpose tool, DBCC, and SQLMaint for performing maintenance, and explores how to improve the performance of data access with indexes through proper use and maintenance.

✦ ✦ ✦ ✦

In This Part

✦ ✦ ✦ ✦

CHAPTER 28

Monitoring and Optimizing MSDE

✦ ✦ ✦ ✦

In This Chapter

Using Profiler to record database events

Analyzing commands that applications send to the database

Viewing the status of database connections

Viewing the status of locks

Examining performance counters

Setting configuration parameters on the MSDE Server

Retrieving database status from system tables

Using system stored procedures to display database status

✦ ✦ ✦ ✦

This chapter explores a variety of tools and techniques designed to impart detailed information about the inner workings of an MSDE server to decipher the most effective ways of monitoring MSDE activities and optimizing its use.

Profiler

The Profiler is a graphical tool that allows the user to capture information about events that take place on the MSDE server. The most interesting effect is usually the processing of a SQL batch. The most interesting information about that event is usually the text of the batch. In other words, the Profiler allows the user to capture all of the commands sent to, and processed by, the server.

Event information that is captured by the Profiler can be examined as it is captured. It can also be saved in a database table or an operating system file for future examination. A series of events, or trace, that is saved to a table or file can be replayed in the same order in which they originally occurred.

The Profiler can be an extremely powerful tool for debugging problems with database applications. Administrators may not have access to the source code for an application, but they can still find out exactly which commands that application is sending to the database server. Based on an examination of those commands, administrators can often resolve problems or improve performance by making modifications to the database structure.

To improve the performance of a query in an application, create a Profiler trace of the database activity associated with the query. Cut and paste the text of the query into Query Analyzer. The query can then be analyzed in detail by creating a graphical execution plan, or by running the Index Tuning wizard.

The Profiler is an independent utility run from the Start menu. When a user starts the Profiler, he can define a new trace, open a previously saved trace from a table or file, or create a new trace template, which is a collection of settings for a trace. If a new trace is started, a dialog box is displayed allowing the user to define the properties of the trace. Figure 28-1 shows the first screen (General tab) in the Trace Properties dialog box where the trace should be named and the server for the trace should be selected. A template can be chosen from the top-down list. Trace templates contain default settings for the configurations on the other screens of the Trace Properties dialog box.

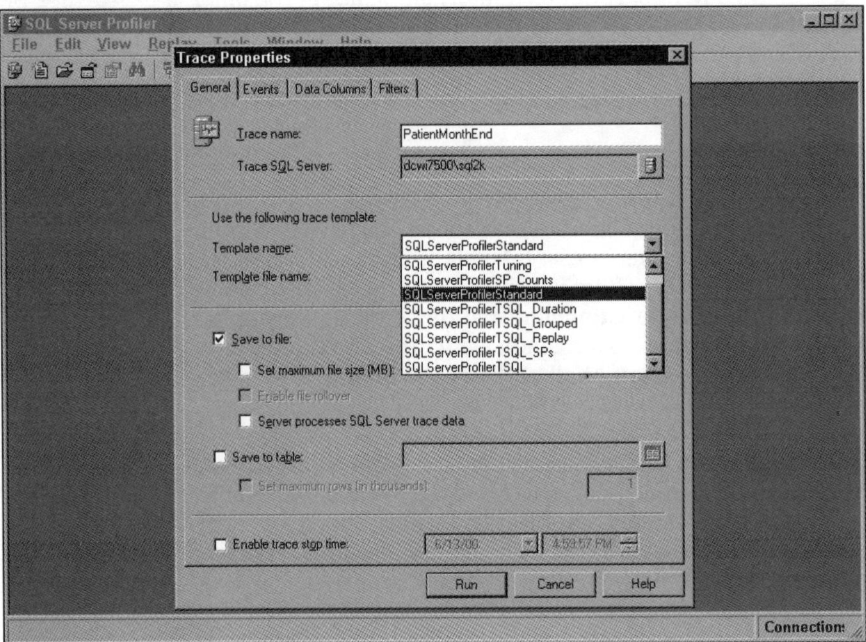

Figure 28-1: The Trace Properties dialog box

In the second half of the Trace Properties dialog box, a user can choose to save the trace to a file or table. If the trace is saved to a file, a maximum file size can be set in megabytes. If a maximum file size is set, a user can enable file rollover, which, when the file reaches its maximum size, will overwrite the earliest events in the file. If the trace is saved to a table, a maximum size can be set in thousands of rows. At the bottom of the dialog box, an automatic stop time can be set for the trace.

Figure 28-2 shows the second screen (Events tab) in the Trace Properties dialog box that allows the user to specify which events the Profiler should capture. The right side of the screen shows the events that have been preselected in the template specified on the first screen. The left side of the screen shows a list of all available events arranged in categories. Figure 28-2 shows the expanded locks category. In addition to the processing of batches, indicated as a selected event class, SQL:BatchCompleted, many other events can be captured, such as the acquisition and release of a lock, or deadlock. These events can be useful in combination with the completed batch event when trying to debug problems with locking, such as long waits or deadlock.

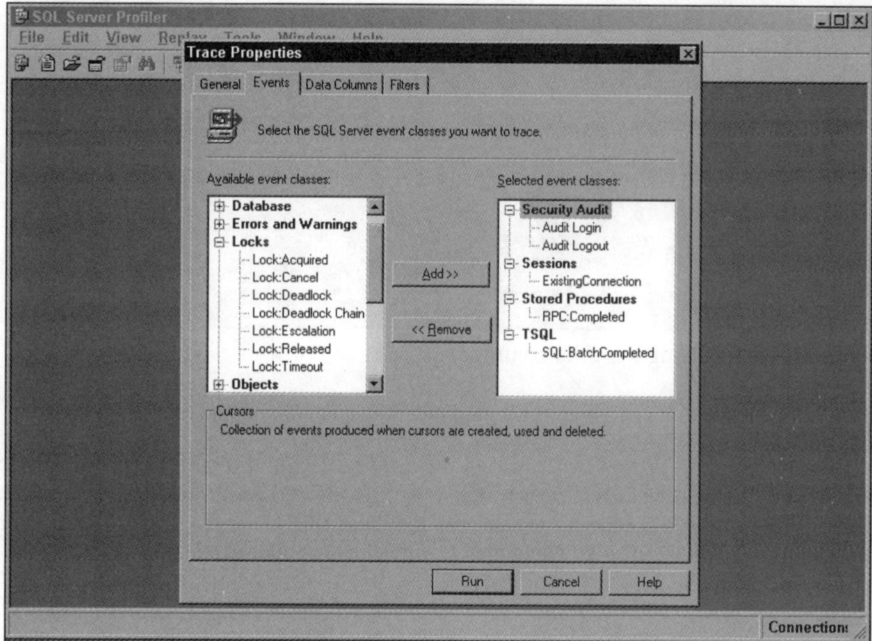

Figure 28-2: Selecting events for a trace

Other events selected by default are the audit of logins and logouts, as well as existing connections. These events are necessary to properly track the association of connections with events. The existing connections event enumerates all existing connections when the trace starts.

Figure 28-3 shows the third screen (Data Columns tab) in the Trace Properties dialog box. This screen allows the user to select the data columns that will be saved in the trace. Each of the items of data specified in this screen will be written to the trace every time one of the events defined in the previous screen occurs. Not all data columns are applicable to every event. For example, no `TextData` is associated with a login.

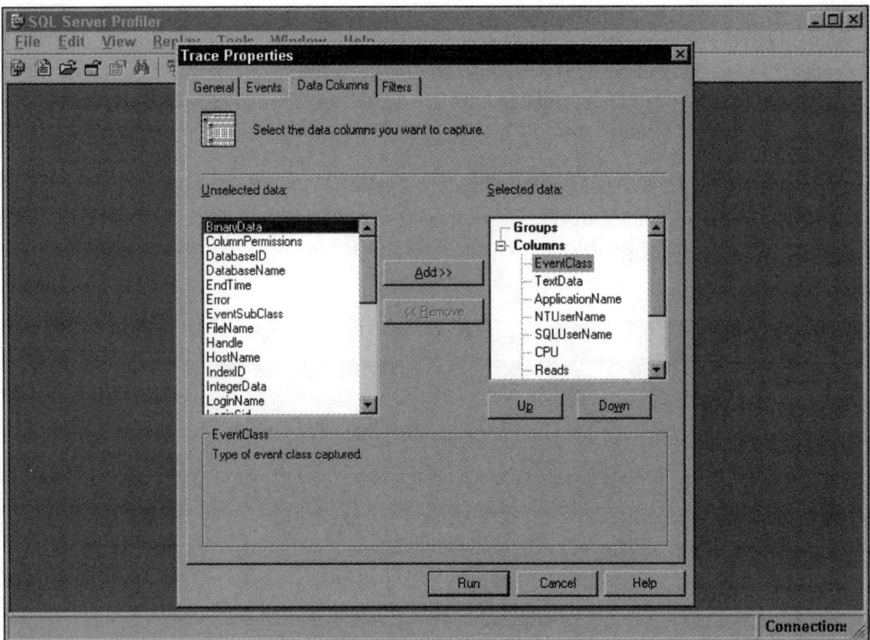

Figure 28-3: Selecting the data columns

Selected data columns can be added to one of two different areas on the right side of the dialog box: Groups or Columns. Adding data items to the Columns section will cause the data to be written to the trace. Adding data items to the Groups section will also save the data to the trace, and in addition, organize all of the events in the trace by each unique value of the grouped data items.

Figure 28-4 shows the fourth screen (Filters tab) in the Trace Properties dialog box. This screen can be used to define filters for the events saved to the trace. In each one of the categories listed in the filters, the user can choose to put a value under Like or Not Like. As shown in Figure 28-4, for example, if only saving the events associated with a single database, the user can enter the name of the database under the Like entry for DatabaseName. Profiler automatically adds a filter to prevent its own activities from being saved in the trace. This item is shown at the top of the trace event window in Figure 28-4. Filters based on numeric values allow the user to specify a value equal to, not equal to, greater than, or less than for filtering. If the check box is selected to exclude system IDs, it will set the ObjectID filter to greater than or equal to 100. Setting this filter will prevent Profiler from saving events regarding objects with IDs less than 100, which are system objects.

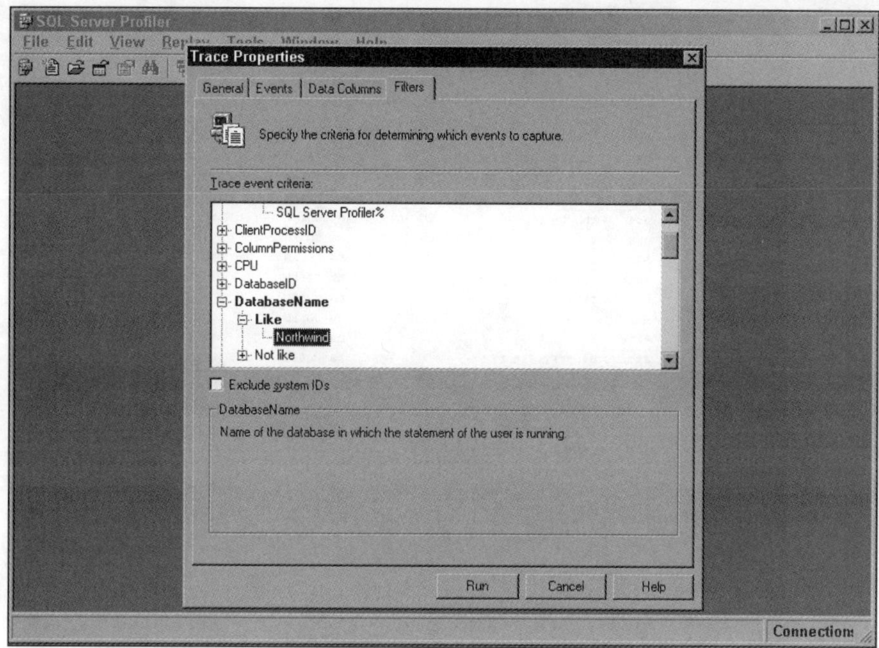

Figure 28-4: Defining a filter for a trace

When the trace has been completely configured, the Profiler will begin saving data when Run is clicked. Figure 28-5 shows a running trace collecting the default set of data items for the default events, filtered to include only those events associated with the Northwind database. The trace in this figure is not grouped, so every event is displayed on an individual line.

The text data contains the actual commands executed by each batch. The last event in the window has been selected, so its text data is shown in the gray box at the bottom of the window. The gray box contains the entire text of the batch, although some of it has scrolled past the right side of the screen. The text from this batch could be cut and pasted into Query Analyzer, for example.

The events in the trace that are not grouped are ordered according to the time at which they occurred. Seeing the sequence of commands as it happens can be useful; however, grouping events makes it easier to find particular types of events.

Figure 28-6 shows a trace of events in the Northwind database grouped by duration. To create this, the Duration data column was moved into the Group section, and the trace was rerun. The results of this trace make it easy to find the longest running batches, and to see how long they ran. In this case, the longest running batch took approximately 306,000 milliseconds, followed by a batch that took just under 54,000 milliseconds.

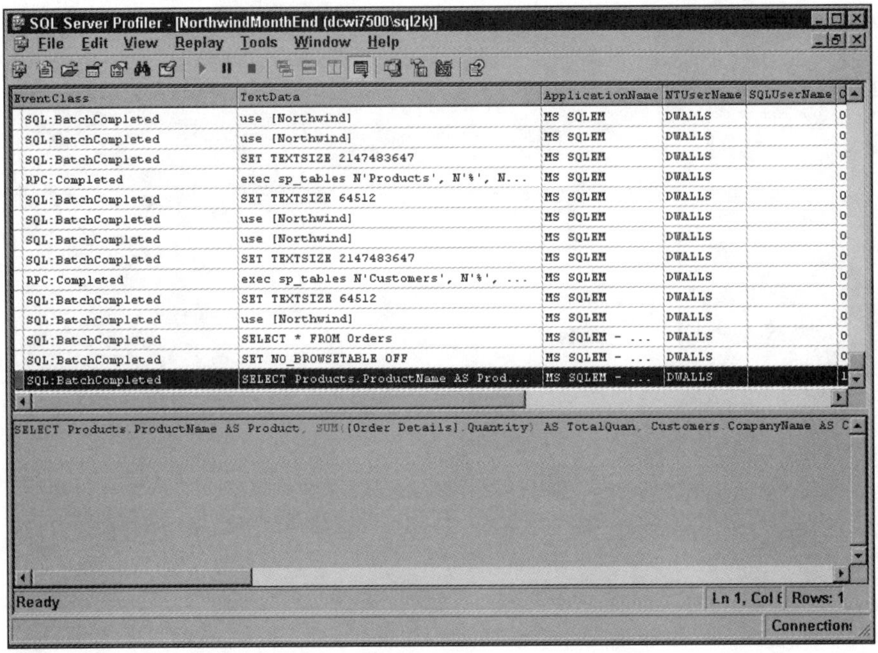

Figure 28-5: Profiler trace with no grouping

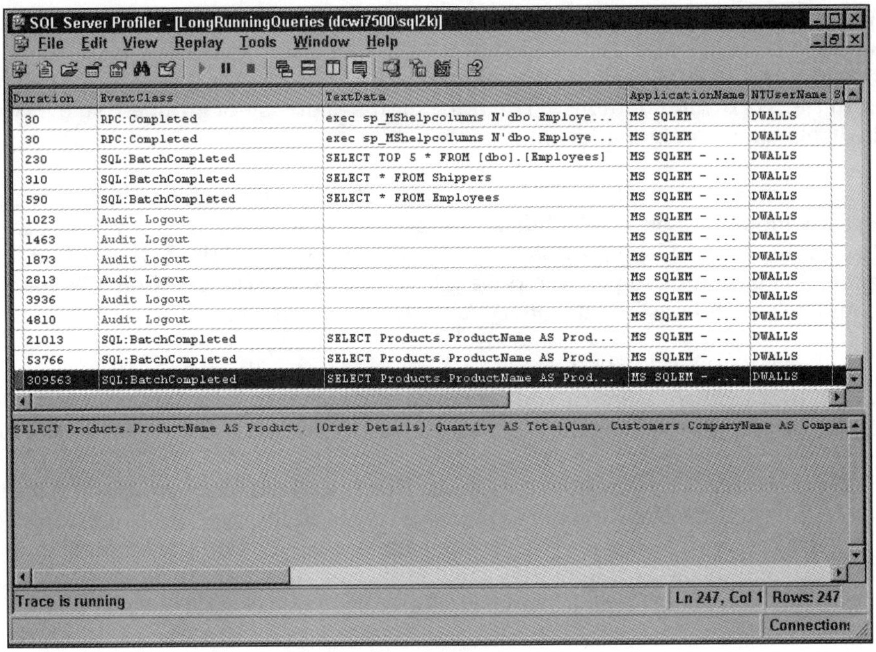

Figure 28-6: Profiler trace grouped by duration

Enterprise Manager

Enterprise Manager provides powerful, easy-to-use tools for examining most aspects of MSDE's configuration and contents, including the Current Activity and SQL Server Logs container with the Management container.

Current Activity

The Current Activity window in Enterprise Manager allows the user to examine information about all currently open connections to the database server and to examine all locks currently being held on any database objects.

Process Info

The Process Info container within the Current Activity container is shown in Figure 28-7. Each line in the window represents a connection to the database. The Process ID is shown in the first column, along with an icon representing the current status of the connection. A blank gray circle represents a background process. A gray globe indicates a sleeping process (for example, one that has executed a command, but not recently). A colored globe indicates a connection that is either currently running a command or awaiting a new command.

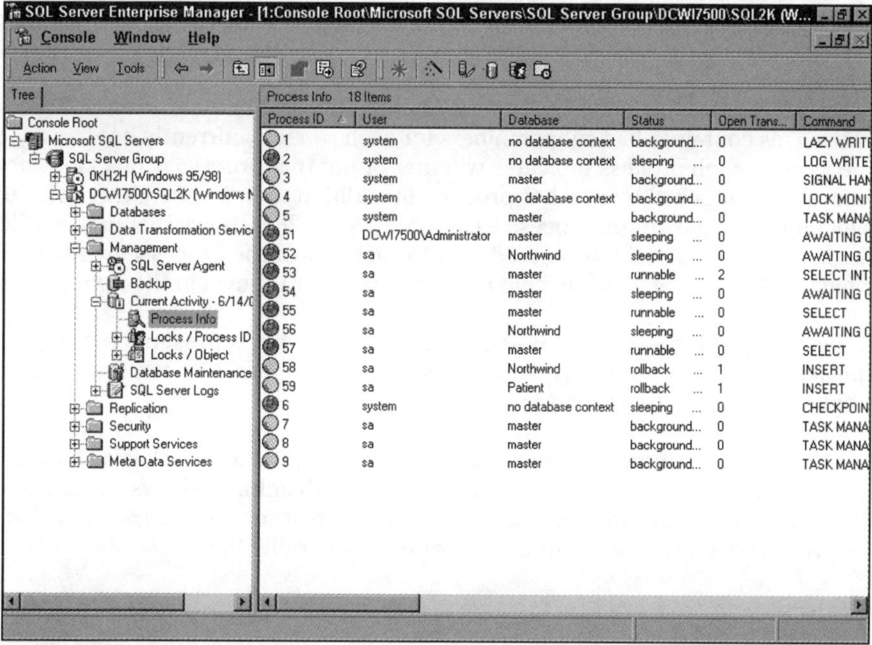

Figure 28-7: Viewing database connections

The second column displays the security context of the connection. System processes display the name system; all other processes display the name of the login used for authentication. Processes can be killed from this window by right-clicking and choosing Kill Process from the menu; however, a system process should never be killed.

The third column indicates the database context for the connection. This column either shows the default database for the connection, or if the Use command has been executed, the currently attached database.

The fourth column shows the status, which is a reiteration of the icon status in the Process ID column. The fifth column shows the number of open transactions. The sixth column shows the currently executing command, system process, or the text AWAITING COMMAND if the command is currently running. Other information is displayed which is not visible in Figure 28-7. This information includes:

- ✦ The application name if one is associated with the connection.
- ✦ The amount of time a connection has waited for a resource.
- ✦ The time at which the last batch was executed on the connection.
- ✦ The amount of system resource utilization, including CPU time, physical I/O, and memory usage.
- ✦ The blocked and blocking process numbers are shown in the last two columns of this display in the event that one process has a lock on a resource that is causing another process to wait.

Figure 28-8 shows the Locks by Process ID container within the Current Activity container. This container has subcontainers for each process currently holding a lock. The icon for each process indicates whether or not that process is blocking another process or is blocked by another process. In addition to the icons, descriptive text is included along with the Process ID number. Figure 28-8 shows that Process 52 is blocking Process 54, which is noted next to each one of the processes. Process 52 is highlighted so that all locks held by that process are shown in the right pane.

In the right pane, each object is shown with an icon that represents the object type. The second column explicitly lists the lock type. In Figure 28-8, the first lock is the database lock and the second lock is a table lock.

The third column shows the lock mode. In this case, the first lock is a shared lock, and the second lock is an exclusive lock. The fourth column shows the status of the lock, normally either grant or wait. Locks can have other statuses, such as being in the process of conversion, but these statuses are briefly held.

Locks/Process ID

The fifth column identifies the owner. Most locks are owned by the transaction. Every connection to the database, however, opens a session level shared lock on the database. MSDE uses this lock to determine whether a database is in use and by whom.

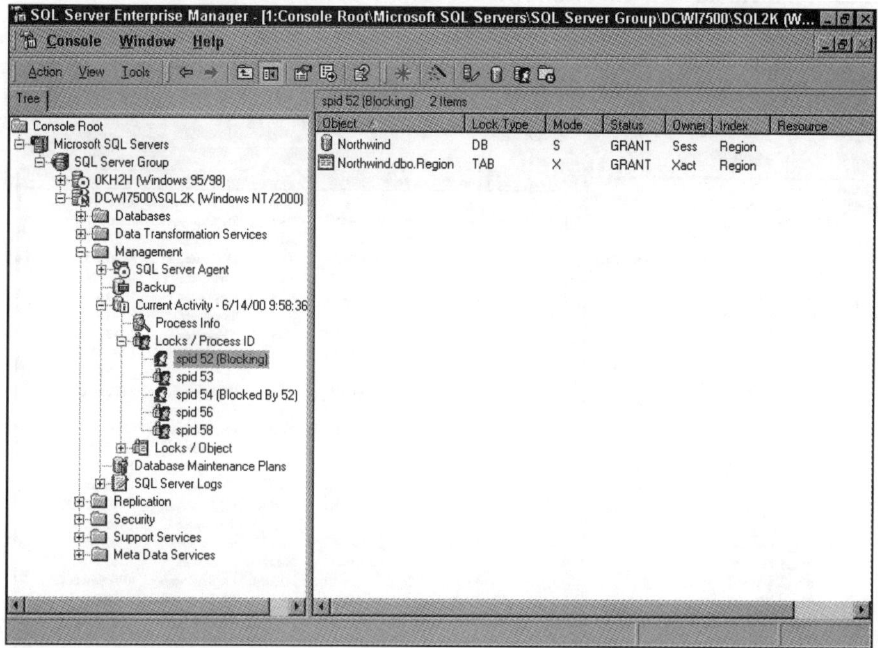

Figure 28-8: Viewing locks by process

The sixth column shows the name of the index currently in use. This column can show the name of a clustered index, a non-clustered index, or a heap. The seventh column shows the resource, if applicable. When an entire table is blocked, as indicated in Figure 28-8, no specific resource is indicated. When a page, an individual role, or a range of rows is locked, the individual resources are indicated in this column.

Right-clicking on any line in the right pane and choosing Properties from the menu will display the text of the last batch run on the connection. The dialog box that is displayed can be used to refresh the information on the screen and to kill individual processes.

Locks/Object

Figure 28-9 shows the Locks by Object container within the Current Activity container. The Locks container is expanded in the left pane, and all of the objects currently locked beneath it. The left pane shows locked objects at the database or table level. More specific information can be displayed by selecting the object in the left pane. A detailed list of each individual lock will be shown in the right pane.

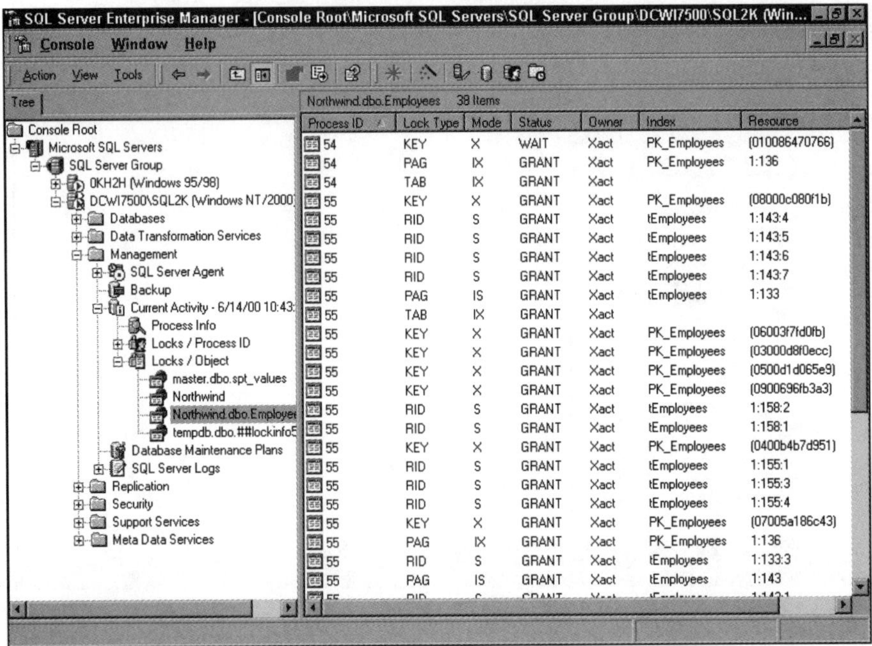

Figure 28-9: Viewing locks by object

The Employees table in the Northwind database is selected in the left pane, and all locks on the table are displayed in the right pane. Process 54 is waiting to be granted a keylock to the primary key index of the Employees table. The same functionality is available in this container for viewing the last batch of a connection, refreshing information about it, and killing processes associated with locks.

MSDE rates an enormous amount of information into its log files, and on a Windows NT or Windows 2000 computer, into the operating system application lock. The log files saved only by MSDE, without regard to the operating system, are saved as file system files in the subdirectory, Log, located by default in Program Files\Microsoft SQL Server\MSSQL.

These lines are also available from within Enterprise Manager, as shown in Figure 28-10. A new log file is created every time the SQL Server service is started. The log files are identified in Enterprise Manager according to the date and time of the latest event written to the log. There are usually several dozen lines written in the beginning of each log file representing the server startup process including database recovery.

SQL Server logs

The log file should be considered a primary source of information when attempting to diagnose a problem or gain more information on any aspect of the activity on a database server.

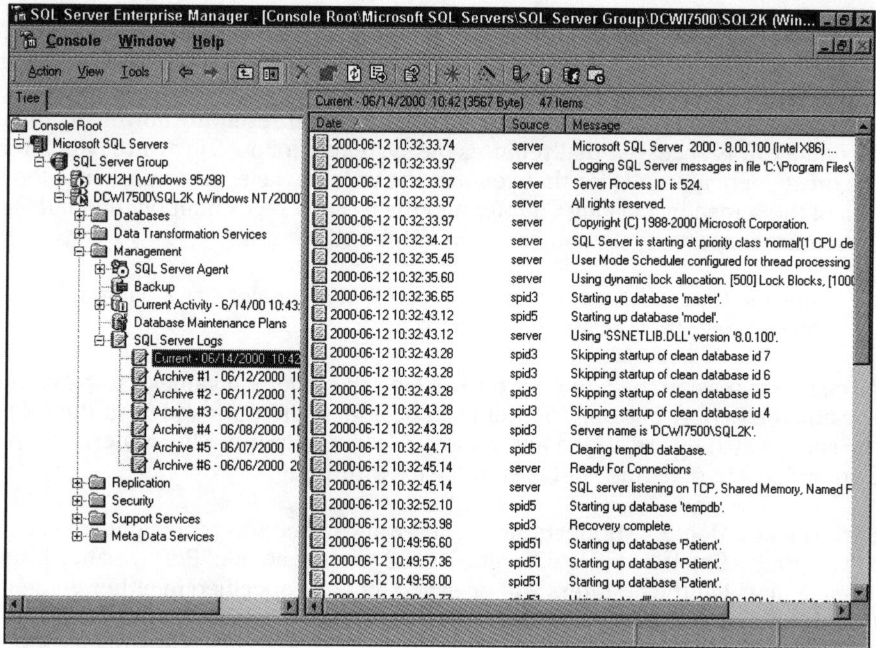

Figure 28-10: Database logs

Performance Monitor

Performance Monitor is a tool available on Windows NT and Windows 2000 computers. It allows a user to examine statistics about the operations of various services on the computer. When MSDE is installed on such a computer, a set of counters, or statistics, is installed.

See Chapter 26 for a description of the categories in which performance monitor counters are organized.

In Windows NT, Performance Monitor is available from the Start menu in the administrative tools container. In Windows 2000, it is available in the Administrative Tools container within the Control Panel. The two versions of Performance Monitor work slightly differently. However, they are both well documented in Windows books online.

Both versions of Performance Monitor have several modes of operation. When the tool is started, it displays a line graph updated in real time. Counters can be added to the graph by clicking on the button that looks like a +. When adding a counter, the user must select the server to be examined, the performance object, and the specific counter to view.

For example, if a user wants to know what performance impact forwarded records are having on the server counter, he should select the SQL Server: Access Methods performance object, and then choose the Forwarded Records per second counter. Performance Monitor will draw a line on the screen representing how many times per second a row is accessed that requires the system to follow a forwarding pointer. To see the numerical values for that counter, the user can select the counter at the bottom of the screen by clicking Counter and the last, average common minimum, and maximum values for that counter will be displayed.

Tip

The Windows 2000 version of Performance Monitor also has a bar graph, or histogram view, that updates in real time.

A report expressing the counters for tracking as numerical values can be viewed by clicking the Report button. Counters can be added and removed from the report the same way they are added and removed from the graph. The numerical report also updates in real time, and is suitable for printing.

Performance Monitor supports saving the values of counters to log files. The procedure for initiating log files is different for the two versions of Performance Monitor. The file in which the counters will be saved must be specified in either version. Counters to be recorded in the log can then be added. In the Windows NT version of Performance Monitor, entire objects must be saved to the performance log, while in Windows 2000, individual counters can be specified.

Both versions of Performance Monitor have the capability to define an alert. An alert is an action that will be performed when a specific counter rises above or falls below a defined value. In general, the SQL Server Agent provides more flexibility and better integration with MSDE than using the Performance Monitor alerts. Performance Monitor must run all the time in order for one of its alerts to take effect.

MSDE Configuration Settings

A number of configuration settings can be manipulated for an MSDE server to optimize its performance. Many of these settings are, by default, managed dynamically by the server. However, an administrator will need to make some changes. Some of these configuration settings can be controlled through a graphical interface using Enterprise Manager, but all of them can be controlled with the stored procedure, `sp_configure`.

sp_configure

`sp_configure` is a simple stored procedure. It accepts two parameters: the name of the configuration option, and the value that is to be set for that option. The configuration option names should be enclosed in single quotes.

Some options, when changed, do not immediately go into effect. To cause these parameter changes to go into effect, a user must either issue the `Reconfigure` command, or restart the SQL Server service. If one of these configuration options is changed with `sp_configure`, a message will be displayed prompting the user to run `Reconfigure`. Some commands require a restart of the SQL Server service whether or not the Reconfigure command is run.

The set of configuration options that can be changed and displayed with `sp_configure` is not the complete set of configuration options. To see the complete set, the user must set the configuration option, called Show Advanced Options, to the value 1. Show Advanced Options requires the execution of the Reconfigure command.

The following is a list of the commands that can be displayed and modified by default without turning on Show Advanced Options.

- **allow updates**—this option allows modifications to be made to system tables when it is set to the value 1.
- **default language**—set this option to the appropriate language for displaying system messages, dates, and monetary values.
- **max text repl size**—This option controls the maximum size used for replicating columns of the text or image data type.
- **nested triggers**—this option controls whether or not the trigger can cause another trigger to fire with its actions.
- **remote access**—normally turned on, this option allows stored procedures initiated from a remote server to be run on the local MSDE server (assuming the appropriate security context has been set up). When this option is turned off, stored procedures may not be initiated by remote server.
- **remote login timeout**—this option sets the timeout in seconds and will be used when the local MSDE server attempts to make a connection to a remote MSDE or SQL Server.
- **remote proc trans**—when turned on, this option will automatically initiate its committed transaction whenever a remote procedure is called.
- **remote query timeout**—this option controls the timeout that will be used when it has been initiated on a remote database server.

✦ **show advanced options** — this option allows the user to see and configure advanced options using `sp_configure`.

✦ **user options** — this option allows the default connections settings to be set for all users who connect to the MSDE server.

To display or configure advanced commands, run the following commands:

```
sp_configure 'show advanced options', 1
reconfigure
```

The following is a list of the advanced commands that should not be used with MSDE. Some of the advanced options are not included here because they either cannot work or should not be used with MSDE. These include options intended to be used with multiprocessor computers, a very large amount of memory, full text indexing, and other features that are supported in different versions of SQL Server.

✦ **c2 audit mode** — performs additional security logging to comply with the C2 security standard.

✦ **cursor threshold** — determines the size at which cursors will be built asynchronously. Cursors built asynchronously allow users to begin accessing data while the cursors are still being built.

✦ **fill factor** — controls the default fill factor used whenever an index is created without specifying the fill factor.

✦ **index create memory** — controls the amount of memory that can be used during the creation of an index for sorting values. It is dynamically configured by default.

✦ **locks** — controls the amount of memory that is allocated for tracking locks. It is dynamically configured by default.

✦ **max server memory** — controls the maximum amount of computer memory that the SQL Server service will allocate for itself. This option is normally dynamically configured. When this option is left at its default value, MSDE will attempt to use all available memory while leaving sufficient memory for all other system processes.

✦ **max worker threads** — only has an effect on Windows NT and Windows 2000 systems. It controls the number of worker threads that will be configured. Worker threads service user connections. If the number of user connections is lower than the number of worker threads, one worker thread will service each user connection. When the number of user connections rises above the number of worker threads, the worker threads will be shared. Sharing worker threads among user connections utilizes resources more efficiently, but may reduce performance.

✦ **media retention** — sets the default values for the length of time to keep backup media.

- **min memory per query**—sets the amount of memory that will be allocated for each query when it is being processed. This option is normally dynamically configured.
- **min server memory**—sets the minimum amount of memory that the SQL Server service will allocate for itself from the computer's memory. This option is normally dynamically configured. If MSDE is being starved of memory in an attempt to increase value, the system should be examined to determine if the amount of memory needs to be increased, or the number of services being run decreased.
- **network packet size**—sets the default packet size for data being transferred across the network from MSDE.
- **opened objects**—controls the amount of memory dedicated to keeping track of opened objects. This is a dynamic parameter by default, so MSDE will automatically allocate more memory to track objects as needed, and deallocate memory when it is not needed.
- **query governor cost limit**—is used to prevent the system from processing queries that would use too many system resources. When the execution planned for query is compiled, the system compares the estimated resource amount to the query governor cost limit, and if it exceeds the value, the query is never processed.
- **query wait**—controls the amount of time that a query will wait for memory to become available before it times out and returns an error.
- **recovery interval**—is used to control how often the checkpoint process will run, albeit somewhat indirectly. The system calculates how often it runs the checkpoint process by determining how long it would take to recover each database. If this length of time exceeds the recovery interval value, the checkpoint process is run. This option is normally self-configuring.
- **scan for startup procs**—stored procedures can be marked to run automatically when the SQL Server service starts with the `sp_procoption` stored procedure. That stored procedure automatically turns on this option when there are procedures to run, and turns it off when there are no procedures to run. This option can temporarily stop the processing of all stored procedures marked to run at startup.
- **set working set size**—sets a specific amount of memory that the SQL Server service will allocate for itself from the computer's memory. This option is normally dynamically configured.
- **two digit year cutoff**—is used to control how MSDE interprets a two-digit year. The default setting for this option is 2049. Any data greater than the cutoff year will be considered to be in the century prior to the cutoff year.
- **user connections**—controls the amount of memory that MSDE will allocate for managing user connections. This option is normally dynamically configured. If this amount of memory is exceeded, additional users will be denied access to the database.

System Tables

Although Microsoft does not officially support the use of system tables, there are instances when the only way to find information is by querying the system tables.

Sysobjects

A Sysobjects table exists in each database and contains a row for every object in the database. Sysobjects is commonly used to find object IDs. For example, a user can utilize Sysobjects to identify object IDs when attempting to find indexes for a particular table in the Sysindexes table, which refers to all tables by their object ID.

The following example shows a small sample of the objects from the Northwind database. All system objects have an ID less than 100. The range was chosen only to show both system objects and user objects. The xtype indicates the extended type of the object. Xtype gives slightly more detail than the type column. For example, all keys have a type of K, while primary keys have an xtype of PK and foreign keys have an xtype of F. The parent_obj column shows the object ID of the object that contains the object to which the rest of the row refers. An index object shows a parent_obj that corresponds to the table on which the index was built.

```
SELECT name, id, xtype, parent_obj
FROM sysobjects
WHERE id BETWEEN 23 and 133575514

name                id          xtype parent_obj
------------------- ----------- ----- -----------
sysprotects         23          S     0
sysfulltextnotify   24          S     0
sysfiles            95          S     0
sysfilegroups       96          S     0
PK_Suppliers        5575058     PK    2137058649
Orders              21575115    U     0
PK_Orders           37575172    PK    21575115
DF_Orders_Freight   53575229    D     21575115
FK_Orders_Customers 69575286    F     21575115
FK_Orders_Employees 85575343    F     21575115
FK_Orders_Shippers  101575400   F     21575115
Products            117575457   U     0
PK_Products         133575514   PK    117575457
```

Sysindexes

A Sysindexes table exists in each database, and contains a row for every index in the database. It also contains a row for every table that does not have a clustered index. When a clustered index is created on a table, the entry in Sysindexes for the table is removed, and the entry for the clustered index takes its place.

The following example shows the entries from sys_indexes that correspond to the Order Details table in the Northwind database. The name column shows the name of the index. The id shows the index ID; a 0 for index ID indicates a heap, a one indicates the clustered index; any other number indicates a non-clustered index or automatically generated statistics. The last two rows in this example are automatically generated statistics. Automatically generated statistics have names similar to these examples, usually starting with _WA_Sys_, followed by the column name upon which they are built, followed by a hexadecimal number. The ID column contains the object ID for the table on which the index statistics were built. The other columns not shown include information such as the number of pages allocated to the index, the original fillfactor, the group page for the index, and so on.

```
SELECT name, indid, rows, id
FROM sysindexes
WHERE id = 325576198

name                       indid  rows        id
-------------------------- ------ ----------  ----------
PK_Order_Details           1      2155        325576198
OrderID                    2      0           325576198
OrdersOrder_Details        3      0           325576198
ProductID                  4      0           325576198
ProductsOrder_Details      5      0           325576198
_WA_Sys_UnitPrice_1367E606 6      0           325576198
_WA_Sys_Quantity_1367E606  7      0           325576198
```

Indexes are covered in detail in Chapter 9.

Sysprocesses

The Sysprocesses table is a dynamically created table, existing only in the master database. It contains the same information displayed in Enterprise Manager in the Process Info container. There is a line in this table for every process running on the system, including every user connection to the server and every background process.

The following example shows a few other columns available in the Sysprocesses table. net_address, for example, shows the physical layer network address for the computer from which a connection originates, in this case an ethernet address. There are, of course, many other columns in this table. The SQL login name, as well as the NT user name, login time, memory usage, physical I/O, and many others are available.

```
SELECT spid, blocked, dbid, cpu, status, cmd, net_address
FROM sysprocesses

spid dbid cpu   status       cmd              net_address
---- ---- ----- ------------ ---------------- -----------
1    0    30    background   LAZY WRITER
```

```
2    0    6930  sleeping    LOG WRITER
3    1    10    background  SIGNAL HANDLER
4    0    0     background  LOCK MONITOR
5    1    0     background  TASK MANAGER
6    0    5969  sleeping    CHECKPOINT SLEEP
7    1    0     background  TASK MANAGER
8    1    0     background  TASK MANAGER
9    1    0     background  TASK MANAGER
51   1    26959 sleeping    AWAITING COMMAND 0050DA30832C
52   1    15763 sleeping    AWAITING COMMAND 0050049957C4
53   1    26328 runnable    SELECT           0050049957C4
54   6    26328 sleeping    AWAITING COMMAND 0050049957C4
55   6    70    sleeping    SELECT           0050049957C4
```

Syslocks

The Syslocks system table exists only in the master database, and is used by MSDE to track all locks on the server. Whenever a lock is placed, a row is automatically entered by the system into the Syslocks table.

The following example shows all of the locks that have been placed by process ID number 55. The ID column shows the object ID, page number, and so on, for the object that has been locked, with the exception of the shared lock on the database, which has the object ID of zero. The page column shows a negative one if the lock is placed on a page. The type column shows the number corresponding to the locks type. In the following output, the first lock is a shared lock, and the last two are exclusive locks.

```
SELECT *
FROM syslocks
WHERE spid = 55

id          dbid   page        type   spid
----------- ------ ----------- ------ ------
0           6      0           3      55
1977058079  6      0           8      55
136         6      -1          8      55
```

Sysperfinfo

The Sysperfinfo table is dynamically created, exists only in the master database, and contains the same information accessible through Performance Monitor. Access to this information is more easily gained through Performance Monitor. However, the occasion may arise where a user wants to write a query that can access this information, which can be done through the Sysperfinfo table.

The following example shows the Log Cache totals. The Log Cache Hit Ratio is 80 percent, which is a little on the low side, and the Log Cache Reads per second is 147, which seems to indicate the server has little activity.

```
SELECT *
FROM sysperfinfo
WHERE counter_name like 'log cache%'
and instance_name = '_Total'

object_name       counter_name                 instnc cntr_value
----------------- -------------------------- ------ -------------
MSSQL:Databases   Log Cache Reads/sec         _Total 147
MSSQL:Databases   Log Cache Hit Ratio         _Total 80
MSSQL:Databases   Log Cache Hit Ratio Base    _Total 147
```

System Stored Procedures

Since MSDE will be deployed into many environments that lack the graphical Microsoft tools such as Enterprise Manager and Profiler, developers and administrators will have to rely on other tools, primarily stored procedures, to perform administrative tasks. Stored procedures are useful for tasks that apply to the server generally, or for general-purpose tasks.

sp_help

`Sp_help` is probably the most general-purpose stored procedure in MSDE. Any object can be passed as a parameter to the stored procedure, and the results will be a general description of the object. Many objects have a dedicated stored procedure that provides more specific information about the individual type of object, but `sp_help` is always a good place to start. The following output (with a little abbreviation) was returned by running `sp_help` with a tiny test table as a parameter.

```
Name Owner Type       Created_datetime
---- ----- ---------- -----------------------
test dbo   user table 2000-06-12 10:55:11.120

Column_name Type Computed Length Prec Scale Nullable...
----------- ---- -------- ------ ---- ----- --------
col1        int  no       4      10   0     no

Identity
-----------------------------
No identity column defined.

RowGuidCol
-----------------------------
No rowguidcol column defined.

Data_located_on_filegroup
-------------------------
```

```
PRIMARY

index_name         index_description  index_keys
------------------ ------------------ -----------
PK__test__2E1BDC42 clustered, unique... col1

constraint_type         constraint_name...
----------------------- ------------------
PRIMARY KEY (clustered) PK__test__2E1BDC42

No foreign keys reference this table.
No views with schemabinding reference this table.
```

sp_helpsort

sp_helpsort returns information about the character sets and sort order in use by the MSDE server. This information can be extremely helpful when moving databases from one server to another. To install MSDE on the second server, the user must know the character sets and sort order from the first server. The following is the information returned for a server (without trying to preserve the formatting of the output):

```
Latin1-General, case-insensitive, accent-sensitive, kanatype-
insensitive, width-insensitive for Unicode Data, SQL Server
Sort Order 52 on Code Page 1252 for non-Unicode Data
```

sp_lock

sp_lock can be used to display the active locks on the server, and can be used in combination with sp_who to find out which users have what resources locked. The spid represents the process that owns the lock, and corresponds to the same number in the output of sp_who.

```
spid dbid ObjId    IndId  Type Resource         Mode     Status
---- ---- -------- ------ ---- ---------------- -------- ------
51   7    0        0      DB                    S        GRANT
52   7    0        0      DB                    S        GRANT
52   1    85575343 0      TAB                   IS       GRANT
```

See Chapter 10 for extensive coverage of locking, including the output of this stored procedure.

sp_who

sp_who shows a list of all processes active on the server. The output of this stored procedure is prodigious. It includes the process ID, the login name, the computer name from which the process originates, the current status of the process, and the currently running command.

sp_monitor

`sp_monitor` displays general statistics that reflect how busy the server is. It includes the amount of process activity, the amount of network activity, and the amount of I/O.

```
last_run                    current_run                  seconds
--------------------------- ---------------------------- -------
2000-04-18 01:53:23.693     2000-06-12 21:06:22.793      4821179

cpu_busy              io_busy               idle
--------------------- --------------------- ---------------------
83(80)-0%             22(22)-0%             36737(36671)-0%

packets_received      packets_sent        packet_errors
--------------------- ------------------- ---------------------
7655(6952)            12509(12067)        0(0)

total_read    total_write       total_errors        connections
------------- ----------------- ------------------- ------------
2032(1913)    278221(274232)    0(0)                31(20)
```

xp_loginconfig

This stored procedure displays the security mode configuration for the server—in particular, whether the login mode is mixed or NT only.

```
name                           config_value
------------------------------ ---------------------------
login mode                     Mixed
default login                  guest
default domain                 DCWI7500
audit level                    none
set hostname                   false
map _                          domain separator
map $                          NULL
map #                          -
```

sp_resetstatus

`sp_resetstatus` changes the status of a database from suspect back to normal. It requires the name of a suspect database as a parameter. When a database is marked as suspect, MSDE usually has a good reason for having done so, and the user should understand the reason before placing a suspect database back into production. This stored procedure can sometimes be useful for retrieving data from damaged databases.

sp_trace_*

There are five stored procedures that can be used to create and control traces (the same kind of traces that are created with Profiler) from within a SQL script. The following steps outline the process for creating a trace:

1. Create a new trace definition with `sp_trace_create`. Specify the file in which the trace will be saved and use the output parameter to receive a number that identifies the trace. The identification number is automatically created by MSDE.
2. Define the events that will be recorded in the trace with `sp_trace_setevent`. See books online for a complete list of values that correspond to the events and columns.
3. Define any filters to be applied to the trace with `sp_trace_setfilter`. As many filters can be applied to a trace as desired, using all of the same conditions that Profiler uses. This stored procedure uses the same numeric values to correspond to events and columns as `sp_trace_setevent`.
4. Start the trace with `sp_trace_setstatus`. This stored procedure can be used to start and stop the trace. It can also be used to delete the trace definition.

The fifth stored procedure that can be used to control traces is `sp_trace_generateevent`. This stored procedure can be used to manually cause an event to be recorded in a trace. It works with traces that are started using the stored procedures outlined above, or using the Profiler.

Working with Database Objects

Stored procedures can be used for retrieving information about databases and the objects within the databases.

✦ **sp_databases**—provides a list of the databases on the server and their size.

```
DATABASE_NAME   DATABASE_SIZE  REMARKS
--------------  -------------  ---------
master          15104          NULL
model           1152           NULL
msdb            13568          NULL
Northwind       3840           NULL
Patient         13184          NULL
pubs            2368           NULL
tempdb          9216           NULL
```

✦ **sp_helpdb**—if used without a parameter, also provides a list of the databases on the server. If given the name of the database as a parameter, it provides more detailed information about the database. The output is too long to reproduce here. However, it includes the database signs, the database owner, and a number of database settings, such as recovery mode, sort order, and compatibility level.

- **sp_helpfile**—displays the name, size, and auto growth characteristics of the files for a database.
- **sp_helpfilegroup**—displays the file groups in their IDs that are in use for a database.
- **sp_tables**—displays a list of all of the tables in use in a database.
- **sp_columns**—displays a list of all of the columns in a table (the table name must be passed as a parameter). This stored procedure also displays all of the defining characteristics of each column, including data type and links, null ability, identity property, etc.
- **sp_datatype_info**—displays the definition of all system and user data types in a database.
- **sp_helpconstraint**—displays a list of all constraints for a table whose name has been passed as a parameter. This stored procedure lists some of the properties of the constraints, but does not provide the detail of other stored procedures, such as `sp_pkeys` or `sp_fkeys`.
- **sp_pkeys**—displays the primary key columns for a table. This stored procedure requires the table name as a parameter.
- **sp_fkeys**—displays all columns in a table with a foreign key constraint, and all of their properties. A table name is required as a parameter.
- **sp_helptrigger**—displays information about any triggers that are defined on the table whose name is passed as a parameter.
- **sp_depends**—displays a list of all objects that are directly or indirectly dependent upon the object whose name is passed as parameter. These objects have to be deleted before the target object can be deleted, and they will be affected if the name of the target object is changed. In the following example, `sp_depends` has been run on the Patient table, which has only one object dependent upon it—the Patient1 view.

```
In the current database, the specified object is referenced
by the following:
name                type
----------------    ----------------
dbo.Patient1        view
```

- **sp_helprotect**—displays the permissions associated with any or all objects and statements in the database. If this stored procedure is executed with no parameters, all permissions in the database are returned. If an object or statement is passed as a parameter, then all permissions associated with the parameter are displayed.
- **sp_column_privileges**—displays all of the permissions that have been either granted or denied for a column in a table. This stored procedure accepts a table name and a column name as parameters. If only a table name is specified, permissions associated with all columns in the table are displayed. The information returned by this stored procedure is a subset of the information returned by `sp_helprotect`.

- **sp_helpindex**—displays the indexes for a table whose name is passed as a parameter. For each index displayed, the column(s) on which the index was created and the properties of the index are also displayed.
- **sp_statistics**—displays a list of all the statistics currently maintained on a table. The statistics may be associated with an index, or may have been created on a non-indexed column by the query processor if the auto-create statistics database option has been set.
- **sp_autostats**—displays each set of statistics for a table, whether each set is configured to be automatically updated, and the date and time of the last update for each set.
- **sp_spaceused**—displays the amount of space in use for a table or database (if no parameter is used). This stored procedure returns the number of rows in the table; the amount of space taken up by all pages allocated to the table; the amount of space taken up by data in the table; the amount of space taken up by indexes in the table; and the amount of space left unused in the allocated pages.

Some stored procedures retrieve information about the various objects used to grant permissions to users. These include NT users and groups, MSDE logins, users, fixed server roles, and database roles.

- **sp_helplogins**—displays all of the logins defined for the MSDE server. It also displays all of the mappings from login to database user.
- **xp_logininfo**—displays the level of privilege (admin, user, or null) possessed by an NT user or group in the MSDE server. It also shows the permission path of an NT user that has privilege on the server by virtue of membership in a group. In the following example, `xp_logininfo` is executed for an NT user who has user privilege on the server because he is a member of the DBUsers group, which is an MSDE login. The name of the domain or server on which the NT user is defined must be specified. In the example, it is 'dcwi7500.'

```
xp_logininfo 'dcwi7500\fred'

account name  type priv mapped login name permission path
------------- ---- ---- ----------------- ---------------
dcwi7500\fred user user dcwi7500\fred     DCWI7500\DBUsers
```

- **sp_helpuser**—displays all users defined for a database. The output of this stored procedure contains one line for each unique combination of user and role of which the user is a member. In other words, if a user is a member of four roles in the database, then four lines of the output will display the user.

```
UserName GroupName      LoginNa DefDBName UserID SID
-------- -------------- ------- --------- ------ -------
dbo      db_owner       sa      master    1      0x01
Patrick  db_accessadmin Patrick master    5      0x832D6...
Patrick  db_securityadm Patrick master    5      0x832D6...
Patrick  db_ddladmin    Patrick master    5      0x832D6...
```

✦ **sp_helpgroup** — lists all of the roles defined in the current database. If the name of a role is passed as a parameter, the members of the role are listed.

✦ **sp_helpsrvrole** — lists the fixed server roles.

✦ **sp_helpsrvrolemember** — lists the members of the specified fixed server role. If no role is specified, all members of all roles are listed.

✦ **sp_srvrolepermission** — displays the permissions associated with the specified fixed server role. If no role is specified, all permissions for all roles are displayed.

```
sp_srvrolepermission sysadmin

ServerRole                          Permission
----------------------------------- -----------------------------------
securityadmin                       Add member to securityadmin
securityadmin                       Grant/deny/revoke CREATE DATABASE
securityadmin                       Read the error log
securityadmin                       sp_addlinkedsrvlogin
securityadmin                       sp_addlogin
securityadmin                       sp_defaultdb
securityadmin                       sp_defaultlanguage
securityadmin                       sp_denylogin
securityadmin                       sp_droplinkedsrvlogin
securityadmin                       sp_droplogin
securityadmin                       sp_dropremotelogin
securityadmin                       sp_grantlogin
securityadmin                       sp_helplogins
securityadmin                       sp_remoteoption (update)
securityadmin                       sp_remoteoption update part
securityadmin                       sp_revokelogin
```

✦ **sp_helprole** — displays a list of all roles in the current database, the role ID, and an indicator if the role is an application role.

✦ **sp_helprolemember** — lists the members of the specified database role. If no role is specified, all members of all database roles in the current database will be listed.

✦ **sp_helpntgroup** — lists all NT groups assigned as users in the current database. This stored procedure also lists the group ID, the SID, and whether the group has access.

✦ **xp_enumgroups** — lists all of the groups in the specified or default NT domain.

Summary

This chapter has explored a variety of tools and techniques for gaining detailed information about the inner workings of an MSDE server. Database administrators, designers or programmers should have at least some familiarity with these tools and techniques.

The Profiler is an invaluable tool for performing both troubleshooting of the production system, and for testing of systems and development. It allows users to examine the conversation that takes place between a client and database server. It also allows access to some of the internal events of the database server. Additionally, it can be used for capturing information crucial for properly tuning a database, using tools such as the Indexed Tuning wizard and Query Analyzer.

Performance Monitor is a tool provided with Windows NT and Windows 2000 that allows the collection of detailed information on many processes on the operating system, including those associated with MSDE. It can be used to discover the status of the system on a moment-by-moment basis, displaying graphical charts or numerical reports. It can also collect statistics and save them into files that can be used for clear analysis, or archived for historical baselining.

The internal workings of MSDE are governed through a series of system tables. These system tables are not supported for direct user access by Microsoft. However, it can be useful in a variety of circumstances to be able to query these tables or write scripts that query these tables. They allow information to be gained about all of the processes and locks that currently exist on the system, as well as information about every object in the database.

There are many system stored procedures used for administrative purposes on an MSDE server. There are a group of stored procedures for performing general server-wide functions, a group for gathering information about the contents of a database, and a group for gathering information about the security subsystem and the ways in which users can access the server.

✦ ✦ ✦

CHAPTER 29

Maintaining Databases with DBCC

✦ ✦ ✦ ✦

In This Chapter

Using DBCC to verify database integrity

Using DBCC to correct errors

Using DBCC to examine the database

Performing maintenance from the operating system with SQLMaint

✦ ✦ ✦ ✦

DBCC, which originally stood for database consistency checker, is Microsoft's general-purpose tool for performing maintenance on MSDE databases. Many documented parameters change the nature of the function of DBCC to the point that they can be considered separate commands. There are probably nearly as many undocumented parameters, but care should be taken in using undocumented commands on a production database.

This chapter discusses some of the main areas of functionality of the DBCC command and the parameters most often used in those areas. The first section of this chapter deals with the DBCC parameters used for finding and correcting structural errors in a database and performing general maintenance tasks. The second deals with parameters used for doing analytical tasks and examining the detailed functioning of a database. The last section deals with the command-line command, `SQLMaint`, which can perform any of the same functions as a DBCC, particularly those with regard to repairing databases. You will encounter `SQLMaint` issued with every use of the Database Maintenance Plan Wizard, because the jobs it creates all use `SQLMaint`.

Repairing Databases

To determine whether there are any errors in a database, there are a series of DBCC commands that allow a user to check database structures for integrity. Based on the information retrieved from the statements, the user can make informed decisions about what steps to take to repair the database. If the user decides to automate periodic integrity checks of the database, it is often convenient to store the results of the integrity checks in tables. A number of these commands allow the use of the parameter `With No_InfoMsgs`, which will reformat the output appropriately for insertion into a table.

Verifying the structural integrity of a database

`DBCC CheckDB` performs extensive verification of the entire database structure. This command verifies the proper allocation of all pages in the database, integrity indexes, the contingent pages, and so on. If, for example, a hardware failure on a server caused an invalid pointer to be placed in the next page pointer of a page header, `DBCC CheckDB` would detect the fact that the page points forward to a page that does not point back to it. In this case, the user would want to restore the database from the good backup before too much data was written to a corrupt database. Three parameters can be used with this command that will allow it to attempt to repair any errors it finds:

- ✦ **Repair_Fast** — performs any repairs that are possible in a minimal amount of time and without possibility of data loss.
- ✦ **Repair_Rebuild** — is similar to `Repair_Fast` without the time consideration. It will not perform any repairs that would result in data loss.
- ✦ **Repair_Allow_Data_Loss** — attempts to fix any errors without regard to the length of time it will take or the possibility of losing data in the process. This parameter should be used only as an act of desperation and with great care. If used, the user must carefully analyze the data in the database to attempt to find any that may be missing. Restoring from a backup is almost always preferable to using this parameter.

Running `DBCC CheckDB` can take a long time, particularly for a large database. Three other DBCC commands perform subsets of the `CheckDB` command to allow a user to break up the verification work into smaller chunks that can be spread out over time or used individually.

- ✦ **DBCC CheckFileGroup** — performs the same tests as `DBCC CheckDB`, but within a single file group only.
- ✦ **DBCC CheckTable** — performs the same tests as `DBCC CheckDB`, but on a single table only.
- ✦ **DBCC CheckAlloc** — performs the same allocation tests performed by `DBCC CheckDB`, but does not run tests on the contents of indexes and pages to verify correct sort order, reasonable content, and so on.

The following is an example of running `DBCC CheckDB` (with partial results):

```
USE Northwind
DBCC CheckDB
```

```
DBCC results for 'Northwind'.
DBCC results for 'sysobjects'.
There are 100 rows in 2 pages for object 'sysobjects'.
DBCC results for 'sysindexes'.
There are 79 rows in 3 pages for object 'sysindexes'.
DBCC results for 'syscolumns'.
.
.
.
There are 91 rows in 3 pages for object 'Customers'.
DBCC results for 'Shippers'.
There are 3 rows in 1 pages for object 'Shippers'.
DBCC results for 'Suppliers'.
There are 29 rows in 1 pages for object 'Suppliers'.
CHECKDB found 0 allocation errors and 0 consistency errors in
database 'Northwind'.
DBCC execution completed. If DBCC printed error messages,
contact your system administrator.
```

Verifying the integrity of the contents of a database

`DBCC CheckCatalog` optionally accepts the database name as a parameter and supports the `With No_InfoMsgs` parameter. It verifies that every table and view has at least one column defined and that for every data type used in a column there is a data type definition. Results are returned only if errors are found. An example follows:

```
DBCC CheckCatalog

DBCC results for 'current database'.
```

`DBCC CheckConstraints` optionally accepts a table name or a constraint name as a parameter. It verifies that existing data in user tables complies with check and foreign key constraints. Any values that violate these constraints will be returned in the output. If the parameters are supplied, all enabled check and foreign key constraints on all tables in the database will be tested. If a table name is used, all enabled check and foreign key constraints on the table will be tested. This command also accepts the `With All_Constraints` parameter, which will test all check and foreign key constraints whether or not they are enabled.

```
DBCC CheckConstraints

(1 row(s) affected)
```

`DBCC CheckIdent` allows the user to verify and reset the identity property for a table. This command will determine if there are any values in a table that exceed the current seed value for the identity property, that is, it will tell you if the identity property will encounter a conflict at some point in the future. It can automatically reset the seed value for the identity property higher than all other values in the appropriate column and in that way avoid any future conflict. The user can also utilize this command to reset the siege value of the identity property to a specific value.

If all or a large number of rows are deleted from a table that has the identity property, a user can use the `DBCC CheckIdentity` command to avoid having a large gap in the assigned identity values.

The following example resets the seed value for the Orders table in the Northwind database.

```
USE Northwind
DBCC CheckIdent (Orders, Reseed, 24000)

Checking identity information: current identity value '17250',
current column value '24000'.
```

`DBCC UpdateUsage` is used to verify and correct, if necessary, the information stored in sysindexes pertaining to space usage in the database. Running this command immediately prior to running the `sp_spaceused` stored procedure will produce the most accurate possible results. The following example uses the parameter `0`, which is used to indicate the current database. It is shown with partial results.

```
DBCC UpdateUsage (0)

DBCC UPDATEUSAGE: sysindexes row updated for table 'sysindexes'
(index ID 255):
        USED pages: Changed from (5) to (6) pages.
        RSVD pages: Changed from (12) to (13) pages.
DBCC UPDATEUSAGE: sysindexes row updated for table 'syscolumns'
(index ID 2):
        USED pages: Changed from (2) to (5) pages.
        RSVD pages: Changed from (2) to (5) pages.
.
.
.
DBCC UPDATEUSAGE: sysindexes row updated for table 'Order
Details' (index ID 4):
        USED pages: Changed from (2) to (6) pages.
        RSVD pages: Changed from (2) to (6) pages.
DBCC UPDATEUSAGE: sysindexes row updated for table 'Order
Details' (index ID 5):
        USED pages: Changed from (2) to (6) pages.
        RSVD pages: Changed from (2) to (6) pages.
```

General maintenance

Several DBCC commands can be used to perform general maintenance on a fully functional and error-free database.

`DBCC IndexDefrag` is used to defragment indexes. Over time, as modifications are made to a database, the information in indexes becomes fragmented and is scattered out of order among many pages. Fragmentation of an index generally causes poorer performance. `DBCC IndexDefrag` is an alternative to rebuilding indexes. The defragmentation is done in place, so additional disk space is not required. This process is much faster than completely rebuilding indexes. The following example defragments the clustered index on the Order Details table in Northwind. The clustered index always has index ID 1.

```
DBCC IndexDefrag (northwind, [order details],1)

Pages Scanned Pages Moved Pages Removed
------------- ----------- -------------
2             0           0

(1 row(s) affected)
```

`DBCC DBReIndex` is used to rebuild all of the indexes in a database. For large databases, and particularly if there are many clustered indexes, this command can take quite a long time. It is preferable to use `Create Index With Drop_Existing`. The following example rebuilds all indexes on the Authors table in the Pubs database.

```
DBCC DBReIndex (authors)

DBCC execution completed. If DBCC printed error messages,
contact your system administrator.
```

`DBCC Shrinkdatabase` is used to shrink the size of the files that a database occupies. A database can never be made smaller than its original size, but this command can be used to reverse the effects of automatic growth. This command requires the database name as an argument and, optionally, a target free space percentage. When the database is shrunk, free space will be left in accordance with the target free space percentage. This command reorganizes the data within the database to consolidate the free space before it is truncated. Two other arguments can be used with this command: `TruncateOnly` or `NoTruncate`. `TruncateOnly` does not reorganize the data in the database and only removes any contiguous free space at the end. `NoTruncate` does not shrink the database, but reorganizes the data inside the database. The following example attempts to shrink the Northwind database as much as possible:

```
DBCC ShrinkDatabase (Northwind)
```

```
DbId FileId CurrentSize MinimumSize UsedPages   EstimatedPages
---- ------ ----------- ----------- ----------- --------------
6    1      320         80          312         312

(1 row(s) affected)
```

DBCC Shrinkfile reduces the size of individual files in the database. It has the same limitations as DBCC Shrinkdatabase. This command can also be used with the EmptyFile argument, which will attempt to migrate all objects out of the target file. EmptyFile should be used if a user intends to delete one of the files in a database. A file in the database can be deleted only if it is empty. The following example empties the Patient_Data2 file in the Patient database.

```
USE Patient
DBCC ShrinkFile (Patient_Data2,EMPTYFILE)

DbId FileId CurrentSize MinimumSize UsedPages   EstimatedPages
---- ------ ----------- ----------- ----------- --------------
7    3      128         128         8           8

(1 row(s) affected)
```

Examining Databases

Some of the DBCC commands do not presume a malfunction in the database, but examine specific areas of the database and retrieve information. These DBCC commands employ the following parameters:

- **ConcurrencyViolation** — allows the user to gather relevant information about the right time to upgrade from MSDE to the standard edition of SQL Server.
- **Page** — allows the user to examine the contents of any page within a database.
- **OpenTran** and **LogInfo** — allow the user to gain a better understanding of the operation of transactions in transaction logs, and most importantly, to understand the truncation behavior of transaction logs.

DBCC ConcurrencyViolation

Both MSDE and SQL Server 2000 Personal Edition are designed to be used in environments that have five or fewer concurrent processes. The limit is not a hard limit, meaning if five users are currently executing batches on an MSDE database, a sixth user can still connect to and initiate a process on the database. However, Microsoft has built in a concurrent workload governor that degrades the performance of the server when more than five processes are being executed simultaneously.

Knowing how often and by how much the limit of five concurrent batches is exceeded will allow an administrator to make an informed and cost-effective decision about when to upgrade MSDE. One should note that a limit of five concurrent batches does not equate to five concurrent users. In a typical database environment, each user has a batch executing on the server a very small percentage of time. So, an MSDE database might be able to support 10, 12, 15, or perhaps even more than 20 users without reaching the limit, or without reaching the limit very often.

Even when there are enough users on the system using the database intensely enough to reach the five concurrent batch limit on a regular basis, it may still be some time before the users notice any performance degradation. The amount of degradation to the performance of the system will be proportional to the number of concurrent batches over the limit. Even if an installation of MSDE periodically peeks at six concurrent batches, the users will still probably not notice a performance problem.

The objective for a database administrator is to be able to predict when the performance problem will become noticeable to the users. The goal is to be able to take action before performance problems reach that stage.

The database administrator could set up an alert to monitor the number of concurrent batches being processed on MSDE at any one time. There are two problems with using alerts. The first is that the SQL Server Agent service must be running at all times to properly monitor the usage of the database server. The second is that the database administrator will want to know not only when the limit has been exceeded, but by how much. Alerts are designed to fire when a counter has reached or exceeded a specific number, but they do not provide a convenient mechanism for recording by how much the counter has been exceeded.

The database administrator could also set up Windows NT Performance Monitor, and perhaps the alerts within. Doing so is subject to the same drawbacks as using a SQL Server Agent alert. Performance Monitor must be running at all times, and creating an appropriate report using Performance Monitor is difficult.

`DBCC ConcurrencyViolation` addresses both of these problems. Using it does not require any special service to be running, and the report that generates is specifically geared toward analyzing the usage of the server with regard to the limits placed on MSDE and SQL Server 2000 Personal Edition.

`DBCC ConcurrencyViolation` can be run only by members of the sysadmin fixed server role.

The four parameters for `DBCC ConcurrencyViolation` areas follows:

- **Display**—prints a report showing how many times the limit of five concurrent batches was exceeded, categorized into the number by which it was exceeded. The number of incidents is recorded since installation, the last manual reset of the counters.
- **Reset**—sets the values of all counters back to zero.

✦ **StartLog** — initiates logging to the SQL Server error log. This will record a message in the error log once per minute whenever the number of concurrently executing batches exceeds five.

✦ **StopLog** — ceases logging to the SQL Server error log.

The results of `DBCC ConcurrencyViolation (Display)` look like the following:

```
Concurrency violations since 2000-06-07 09:24:19.750
1     2     3     4     5     6     7     8     9  10-100  >100
89    13    0     0     0     0     0     0     0       0     0
Concurrency violations will be written to the SQL Server error
log.
DBCC execution completed. If DBCC printed error messages,
contact your system administrator.
```

The first line output indicates when the counters were most recently reset. The second and third lines are grouped together. The third line indicates how many times there were more than five batches executing concurrently. The second line indicates by how many batches the total number exceeded five. In the results shown above, there were 89 instances in which 6 batches where concurrently executing. These are shown in the column labeled 1 in the second line to indicate that the number of batches exceeded 5 by 1. There were 13 instances in which 7 batches were concurrently executing, as shown in the second column. During the sampling period counter, the server on which this command is run never exceeded seven concurrent batches.

The server from which the results above were gathered probably does not need to be upgraded, since it never exceeded seven concurrent batch executions. In addition to the total number of concurrent batches, the administrator should also take into account the length of time over which the statistics are collected. Even if ten concurrent batches run, if it happens only once or twice every six months, the server probably does not need to be upgraded.

DBCC Page

The `DBCC Page` command allows a user to examine the entire contents of any page in the database. There are two required parameters and two optional parameters for `DBCC Page`:

✦ **Database name** or **database ID** — a required parameter, the database ID can be found in the sysdatabases system table in the master database.

✦ **File number** — this parameter is also required and is usually 1 for databases in MSDE.

✦ **Page number** — this is a required relative number specifying which Page within the database should be examined.

✦ **Print options** (optional)—there are three possible values for `print options`. 0 prints only the header. 1 prints the header and divides the rest of the page into individual rows. 2 prints the header and the rest of the page without dividing up into rows.

✦ **Cache** (optional)—0 retrieves the page from disk. 1 retrieves a page from cache if it is available and, otherwise, retrieves it from disk.

`DBCC Page` requires that a user first run `DBCC TraceOn (3604)` to send output to the console.

To determine the page number for the page to be examined, the system tables will need to be queried. The sysindexes table contains information to find the pages associated with all tables and indexes in the database. If a table has no clustered index and is therefore a heap, it will have an entry in sysindexes underwritten name. If a table has a clustered index, then the entry in sysindexes for the data portion of the table is listed under the name of the clustered index. The three columns of interest in sysindexes are as follows:

✦ **First**—contains the first page allocated to the object.

✦ **Root**—contains the page that is the root of the B-Tree for an index.

✦ **FirstIAM**—contains the page with the first Index Allocation Map (IAM) for the object. The IAM contains a bitmap representing the pages in the database. Those pages that belong to this object have a 1, while those pages that do not belong to this object have a 0. If there is more than one IAM, then they are linked together by pointers in the header.

To find pages associated with the Authors table in the pubs database, the user must first determine if there is a clustered index. In this case, there is a clustered index for authors, called 'UPKCL_auidind'. The user can then execute the following `Select` statement:

```
SELECT name, first, root, firstIAM
FROM sysindexes
WHERE name = 'UPKCL_auidind'
```

This yields the following results:

```
Name          first          root           firstIAM
------------- -------------- -------------- --------------
UPKCL_auidind 0x580000000100 0x560000000100 0x570000000100

(1 row(s) affected)
```

The results are in a form that is easy for a computer to read, but slightly difficult for users. To translate the page numbers as presented from sysindexes, use the following steps:

1. **Break** the number apart into bytes. The first two characters, `0x`, indicate that the rest of the number is in hexadecimal. In hexadecimal, every two characters represents one byte. So the results from the first page for authors is as follows:

   ```
   58 00 00 00 01 00
   ```

2. **Reverse** the order of the bytes. The result from bytes in step 1 is as follows:

   ```
   00 01 00 00 00 58
   ```

3. **Split** the results into the file number and the page number. The first two bytes are the file number, and the last four bytes are the page number:

   ```
   file: 00 01  page: 00 00 00 58
   ```

4. **Convert** the numbers from hexadecimal to decimal. Since the file number is 1, no conversion is required:

   ```
   0x58 = 88
   ```

Using the result from the previous steps allows the following `DBCC Page` command to view the first page in the Authors table:

```
DBCC Page (Pubs, 1, 88, 1, 1)
```

This command produces a substantial amount of output. The first few lines of the output identify the page being displayed and information about the memory buffer, which will not normally be very useful.

The page header information is displayed below the buffer information. Figure 29-1 shows the page header from page 88 in the pubs database.

Some of the interesting pieces of information from the header are as follows:

✦ **m_pageId** — displays the file and page number (in decimal) of the current page.

✦ **m_objId** — is the object ID of the table or index that contains the page.

✦ **m_nextPage** — is the forward pointer to the next page if the page is linked. The example in Figure 29-1 is not linked because the table is very small and uses only a single leaf level page. If there were more leaf pages, they would have pointers to each other in this field and `m_prevPage`.

✦ **m_freeCnt** — is the count of unused bytes on this page.

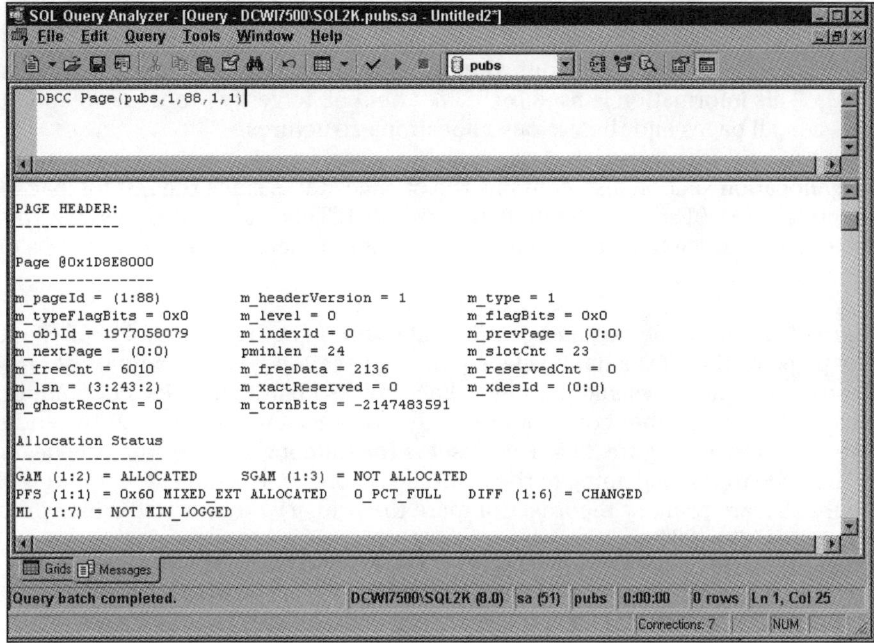

Figure 29-1: Page header shown in `DBCC Page`

✦ **m_lsn** — contains the Log Sequence Number (LSN) that identifies the most recent transaction to have updated this page.

✦ **m_ghostRecCnt** — is the count of ghost records, those records that have been marked as deleted, but not yet removed from the table.

✦ **m_indexId** — is the index ID for the object containing this page. The index ID for a heap is always 0, the index ID for the nonleaf levels of a clustered index is always 1, and the index ID for the leaf level of a clustered index (the data pages) is 0. All other indexes are assigned an index ID greater than 1 at the time of their creation.

✦ **m_freeData** — is an offset in bytes from the beginning of the page to the first available free space on the page.

✦ **m_tornBits** — is used when Torn Page Detection is turned on for the database. The bits contained in this field are used to detect a partial write of the page, in which case the database would be marked suspect.

✦ **m_prevPage** — is the reverse page pointer. See `m_nextPage`.

✦ **m_slotCnt** — is the number of slots currently on the page. A slot is the location of a row, and the rows are located within their slot by reading the row offset table at the end of the page.

Allocation status provides information about how the page has been allocated in the Global Allocation Map (GAM), Shared Global Allocation Map (SGAM), and Page Free Space (PFS) map and about whether or not the page is an Index Allocation Map (IAM). This information is used by `DBCC CheckDB` to verify proper correspondence between all pages and the various allocations structures.

The allocation section also contains the change status since the last full backup, which is `DIFF (1:6) = CHANGED` in Figure 29-1. This status indicates that this page has changed since the last full backup and should therefore be included in a differential backup.

Figure 29-2 shows the beginning of the data section in the output of `DBCC Page`. The page displayed is a data page, so the data section contains actual data rows (as opposed to index keys and pointers). Each row is identified by its slot number and offset. The slot number corresponds to the row-offset array values at the end of the page, as shown in Figure 29-4. The offset is the number of bytes from the beginning of the page to the beginning of the row. The record type is indicated; the rows in Figure 29-2 are primary records. Compare the primary records to the index records shown in Figure 29-3.

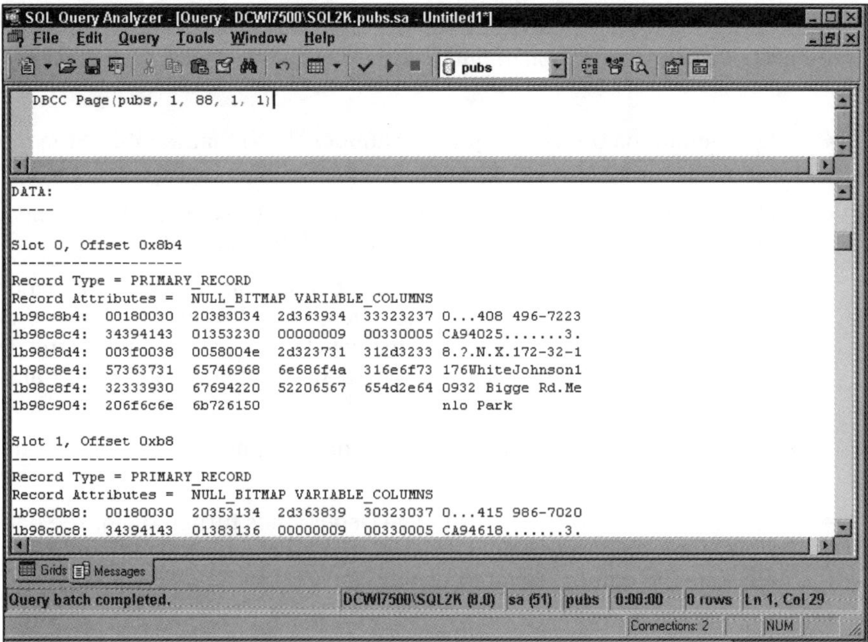

Figure 29-2: Data rows shown in DBCC Page

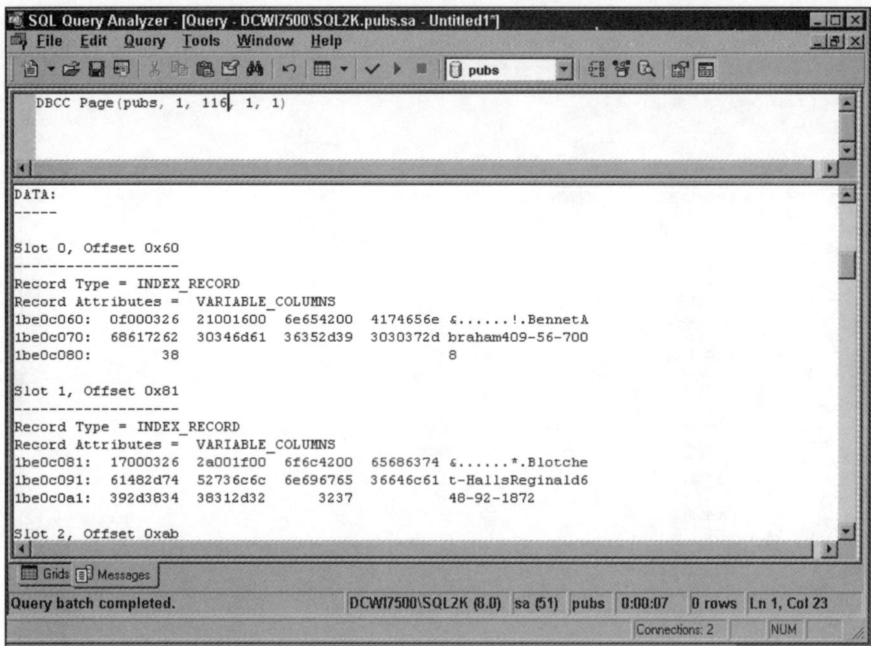

Figure 29-3: Index rows shown in DBCC Page

The index rows shown in Figure 29-3 are from the aunmind non-clustered index on the Authors table. This index was created on the columns au_lname and au_fname. The values from these columns are appended together in each row. In addition, the au_id (social security numbers in this case) acts as the pointer to the row. The au_id is present because there is a clustered index on the au_id column of the Authors table. Since there are pointers to the rows themselves in these index records, it is clear that this page is in the leaf level of the index. Otherwise, there would have been pointers to other index pages.

Figure 29-4 returns once again to page 88, the data page for the Authors table (this is the same table seen in Figures 29-1 and 29-2). In this figure, the beginning of the row-offset array is shown. The row-offset array resides at the end of each data page, starting with the first row last. Each row is assigned a number and an offset in bytes from the beginning of the page. The order of the rows in the offset array does not match the order of the rows on the page. For example, the last four rows (19, 20, 21, and 22) are in reverse order. In other words, row 22 comes closest to the beginning of the page at offset 357, while row 21 follows it at offset 448, followed by row 20 at 711 and row 19 at 1767. Row 18 breaks the pattern, falling between rows 20 and 21 at offset 619.

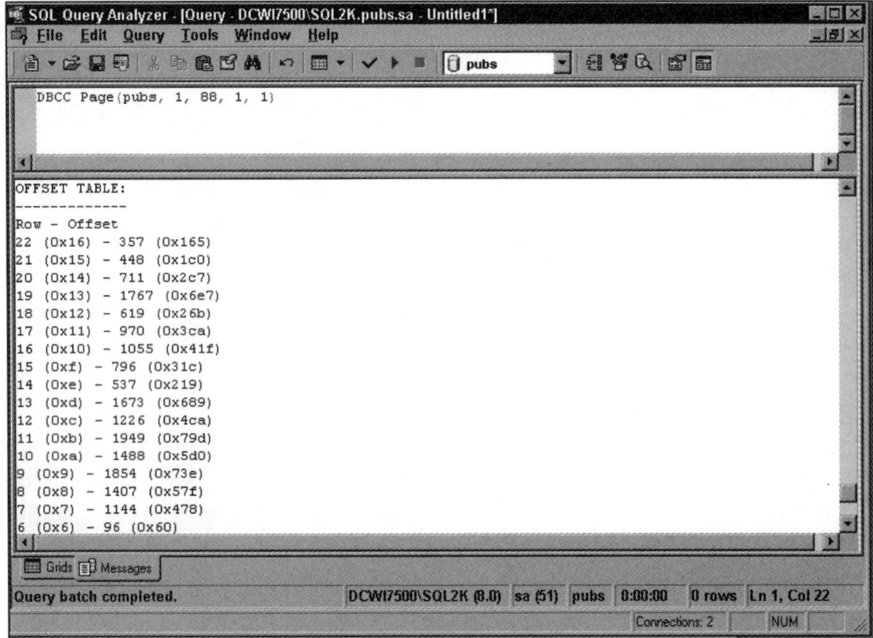

Figure 29-4: Row-offset array shown in DBCC Page

Having a row-offset array that acts like a table of contents for each page makes updates much faster. When a new row is added to a page, it is dumped in the first available slot large enough to contain it. The row-offset array is then updated, inserting the new row into the list at the ordered location. This mechanism avoids the necessity of moving large amounts of data (the rows themselves) during data updates in favor of moving just the data in the row-offset array.

Getting the status of transactions

It is sometimes useful to be able to identify the oldest active transaction, that is, the longest running transaction still running. A user may wish to do this if preparing to shut down the server or if transaction logs are not getting smaller when truncated.

`DBCC OpenTran` shows the following information about the oldest active transaction:

```
Oldest active transaction:
    SPID (server process ID) : 55
    UID (user ID) : 1
    Name          : user_transaction
    LSN           : (5:199:1)
    Start time    : Jun  7 2000  6:03:45:723PM
```

```
DBCC execution completed. If DBCC printed error messages,
contact your system administrator.
```

Once the transaction has been identified, more information about the user responsible for the transaction can be examined by running the stored procedure sp_who. Figure 29-5 shows the output of sp_who. The transaction can be matched with the output of sp_who by the server process ID (SPID). Sp_who allows one to determine the status of the connection, the login name, the host name (usually the computer name from which the user has connected to the database), the current database for the connection, and the currently running command, if any.

	spid	ecid	status	loginame	hostname	blk	dbname	cmd
1	1	0	background	sa		0	NULL	LAZY WRITER
2	2	0	sleeping	sa		0	NULL	LOG WRITER
3	3	0	background	sa		0	master	SIGNAL HANDLER
4	4	0	background	sa		0	NULL	LOCK MONITOR
5	5	0	background	sa		0	master	TASK MANAGER
6	6	0	sleeping	sa		0	NULL	CHECKPOINT SLEEP
7	7	0	background	sa		0	master	TASK MANAGER
8	8	0	background	sa		0	master	TASK MANAGER
9	9	0	background	sa		0	master	TASK MANAGER
10	51	0	sleeping	sa	OKH2H	0	pubs	AWAITING COMMAND
11	52	0	sleeping	DCWI7500\Administrator	DCWI7500	0	pubs	AWAITING COMMAND
12	53	0	sleeping	sa	OKH2H	0	pubs	AWAITING COMMAND
13	54	0	runnable	sa	OKH2H	0	pubs	SELECT
14	55	0	sleeping	sa	OKH2H	0	pubs	AWAITING COMMAND
15	56	0	sleeping	DCWI7500\Administrator	DCWI7500	0	pubs	AWAITING COMMAND

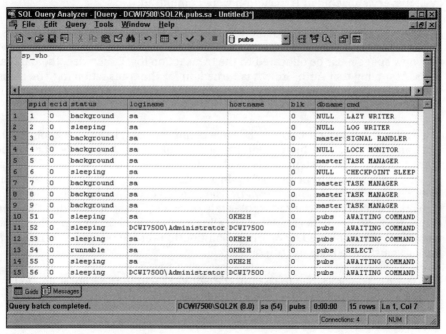

Figure 29-5: The output of sp-who

The problem of transaction logs that do not shrink when truncated can be understood by examining the internal structure of the transaction log. The transaction log is broken up into virtual log files (VLFs), similar to the data file for the database being broken up into pages. The VLFs, however, are not a fixed size. When a log file is created or expanded, MSDE breaks it up into equal sized sections, the VLFs. The size of the VLFs will vary depending on how much space was allocated. The more space that is simultaneously allocated, the larger the VLFs.

The log file is broken up into virtual log files to provide a granularity for the purpose of truncation and reuse. When a log file is truncated — that is, when old transactions, which have been committed and checkpointed, are deleted — the deletion happens to an entire VLF. In cases in which MSDE determines that it can reuse part of the transaction mind, the reuse happens on an individual basis.

Each VLF in a log file can be in one of three states: active, recoverable, or reusable. The VLF containing the oldest uncommitted, or active, transaction is active, as are any VLFs following the VLF containing the oldest active transaction. This structure makes the oldest active transaction very important. If the first transaction in a log was never committed, then all VLFs in the transaction log would always be active, even if every subsequent transaction were committed.

Active VLFs can neither be deleted nor reused. If an active transaction remains in a log, eventually all VLFs will become active. Once they are all active and the last one fills, new space must be allocated to the transaction log. Otherwise, the database halts. Assuming that Auto Growth is turned on for the transaction log, the transaction that does not commit will cause the transaction log to grow until the disk is filled.

Once all of the transactions in a VLF have committed and been checkpointed, the VLF can transition into the recoverable or reusable state. A reusable VLF can be reused any time the system needs to allocate a new VLF. A recoverable VLF is preserving transactions to be backed up in a transaction log backup. The database itself must be in a state that allows transaction log backups, otherwise the VLFs transition directly into their reusable state once all transactions within them have committed and been checkpointed. To allow transaction log backups, the database must have the Truncate Log on Checkpoint option turned off, and at least one full backup must have been executed.

`DBCC LogInfo` allows one to see the state of VLFs within the transaction log. A sample of the output of `DBCC LogInfo` follows:

```
FileId FileSize  StartOffset FSeqNo Status Parity CreateLSN
------ --------- ----------- ------ ------ ------ -------------
2      253952    8192        3      0      64     0
2      253952    262144      5      2      64     0
2      270336    516096      4      0      64   3000000045800005

(3 row(s) affected)

DBCC execution completed. If DBCC printed error messages,
contact your system administrator.
```

The status column in the above output shows which VLFs are active. The status of two is active. If the transaction logs will not grow any smaller when truncated, `DBCC LogInfo` can be used to determine if the problem is an active VLF at the end of the log file. An active VLF at the end of the log file will prevent any reduction in size, since VLFs can be removed only from the end of the file. If a problem active VLF exists at the end of the log file, the `DBCC OpenTran` can be used to locate which transaction is keeping the VLF active, and the stored procedure `sp_who` can be used to find out what connection is associated with that transaction. The user can then kill the connection and create enough additional transactions to fill the last VLF (if it's not already full). The user should then issue the `Checkpoint` command and try again to truncate the transaction log.

SQLMaint

The `SQLMaint` utility is an operating system command used to run many of the common maintenance functions for databases. Many of the parameters for `SQLMaint` perform the same tasks performed with DBCC. If the Database Maintenance Plan Wizard is run, the wizard will create jobs, all of which run the `SQLMaint` operating system command with a variety of parameters.

The `SQLMaint` command is not in the operating system path by default. The directory should be changed to \Program Files\Microsoft SQL Server\MSSQL\Binn or a similar appropriate directory for the instance of MSDE in use. In addition to being an operating system command, `SQLMaint` can be run from within a SQL script by using the `xp_sqlmaint` extended stored procedure.

The parameters used by `SQLMaint` fall into several categories:

✦ **Connection parameters**—specify the security context in which the maintenance will be performed.

✦ **Database parameters**—specify which database(s) will be the target of the maintenance activities.

✦ **Maintenance Task specifiers**—indicate which tasks should be performed.

✦ **Backup specifiers**—indicate the `SQLMaint` should perform a backup of the target database.

The parameters used to specify the connection to the database server are as follows:

✦ **-S**—allows one to specify the name of the MSDE server and instance on which to perform maintenance.

✦ **-U**—allows a user to specify the login ID that will be used to connect an established security context to the MSDE.

✦ **-P**—allows a user to specify the password for the security context in which maintenance will be performed.

The parameters that specify the database on which to perform the maintenance are as follows:

✦ **-D** — allows a user to specify the database name in which to perform maintenance.

✦ **-PlanName** — is used by the Database Maintenance Plan Wizard to specify plan, which is a list of database names to be maintained.

✦ **-PlanID** — is used by the Database Maintenance Plan Wizard to specify a GUID that identifies the planned list of databases to be maintained.

The parameters used to indicate the maintenance tasks to be performed are as follows:

✦ **-RmUnusedSpace** — requires threshold size and free percent as arguments. This argument will shrink the database, removing unused space. It is a synonym for `DBCC ShrinkFile`. This command will attempt to shrink the target database if the target database is larger than the threshold size. When it shrinks the database, it leaves free space in the database in accordance with the free percent argument.

✦ **-CkDB** — is a synonym for `DBCC CheckDB`. It performs a thorough analysis of the database verifying allocations and checking the store order and reasonableness of the contents of indexes and tables.

✦ **-CkAl** — is a synonym for `DBCC CheckAlloc`. It performs a subset of the `Check DB` command, verifying all allocations in the database.

✦ **-CkCat** — is a synonym for `DBCC CheckCatalog`. It verifies that all tables in use in the database have at least one defined column and that all data types used in column definitions are properly defined in the system table systypes.

✦ **-UpdSts** — is a synonym for the command `UPDATE STATISTICS`. It recalculates the selectivity and distribution statistics kept with every index in the database. It is necessary to run this command only if the automatic updating of statistics is turned off.

✦ **-UpdOptiSts** — is a synonym for the command `UPDATE STATISTICS` and accepts an argument that specifies the sampling rate. This command will run faster than `-UpdSts`, which examines every row in a table to generate the statistics rather than sampling a percentage of the roots. The results of this command will be slightly less accurate because every row is not examined.

✦ **-RebldIdx** — is a synonym for `DBCC DBReindex`. It rebuilds all of the indexes in the database. Confusingly, this command accepts as its parameter the percentage of free space that should be left in index pages at the completion of the rebuild, whereas `DBCC DBReindex` uses fill factor as a parameter, which is the amount of space in each page to be filled. This command is not the optimal way to rebuild indexes if there are clustered indexes on tables. `DBCC IndexDefrag` or `Create Index With Drop_Existing` is preferred for index maintenance.

The parameters that specify a backup operation to be performed are as follows:

✦ **-BkUpDB** — indicates a backup should be performed on the data portion of the target database. A data path can be specified as the argument for this parameter. The data path can specify either an up file system path and filename or a device name for tape.

✦ **-BkUpLog** — indicates a backup should be performed on the transaction log portion of the target database. A data path can be specified as the argument for this parameter. The data path can specify either an up file system path and filename or a device name for tape.

✦ **-BkUpOnlyIfClean** — indicates the backup should be performed only if no errors were found in any other tests performed by the `SQLMaint` command.

✦ **-VrfyBackup** — causes the backup system to verify the contents of the backup device after completing the backup.

✦ **-BkUpMedia** — is used to specify either disk or tape. The next three parameters are used only if the backup media parameter is set to disk.

✦ **-DelBkUps** — accepts a time period as an argument. Any backup files older than the time period are deleted automatically.

✦ **-CrBkSubDir** — automatically creates a new subdirectory in the specified path. The new subdirectory will be named according to the name of the target database.

✦ **-UseDefDir** — causes the backups to be saved into the default backup directory path to find the server. This parameter overrides any path specified in the backup data or backup log parameter arguments.

The parameters that specify how to handle output are as follows:

✦ **-Rpt** — writes a text output report file to the specified filename and path. `SQLMaint` appends an underscore and the date and time to the specified filename.

✦ **-DelTxtRpt** — requires a time period as an argument. Any text output files older than the time period will be deleted.

✦ **-HtmlRpt** — writes an HTML output report file to the specified filename and path. `SQLMaint` appends an underscore and the date and time to the specified filename.

✦ **-DelHtmlRpt** — requires a time period as an argument. Any HTML output files older than the time period will be deleted.

✦ **-To** — requires a valid SQL Server Agent operator as an argument. It sends the output report to the specified operator.

✦ **-WriteHistory** — creates a history entry in the msdb database in the sysdbmaintplan_history system table.

The following example performs a full integrity check on the pubs database and writes the results in the file C:\CheckDB _200006091523.Rpt (the date and time are appended to the specified filename). The command wraps to two lines here, but should be typed as a single continuous command:

```
SQLMaint -S Okh2h -U "sa" -P "" -D "pubs" -CkDB -Rpt
"c:\CheckDB.Rpt"
```

There must be a space after each parameter and before each argument, and any arguments must be enclosed in double quotes. The output, which is sent to the screen and the output file, is as follows:

```
Microsoft (R) SQLMaint Utility (Unicode), Version Logged on to
SQL Server 'OKH2H' as 'sa' (non-trusted)
Starting maintenance of database 'pubs' on Fri Jun 09 15:24:07
2000

[1] Database pubs: Check Data and Index Linkage...

    ** Execution Time: 0 hrs, 0 mins, 2 secs **

End of maintenance for database 'pubs' on Fri Jun 09 15:24:09
2000

SQLMAINT.EXE Process Exit Code: 0 (Success)
```

The following sample rebuilds the indexes for the pubs database. By specifying 0 percent free space, the original fill factor is preserved. The output is shown with the command:

```
C:\Program Files\Microsoft SQL Server\MSSQL\Binn>sqlmaint -S
dcwi7500 -U "sa" -P "" -D "pubs" -HtmlRpt "c:\rebuild.htm" -
RebldIdx 0

Microsoft (R) SQLMaint Utility (Unicode), Version 8.00.100
Copyright (C) Microsoft Corporation, 1995 - 1998

Logged on to SQL Server 'DCWI7500' as 'sa' (non-trusted)
Starting maintenance of database 'pubs' on 6/9/2000 3:42:17 PM
[1] Database pubs: Index Rebuild (leaving original % free
space)...

    Rebuilding indexes for table 'authors'
    Rebuilding indexes for table 'employee'
    Rebuilding indexes for table 'jobs'
    Rebuilding indexes for table 'pub_info'
    Rebuilding indexes for table 'publishers'
    Rebuilding indexes for table 'roysched'
    Rebuilding indexes for table 'sales'
    Rebuilding indexes for table 'stores'
    Rebuilding indexes for table 'titleauthor'
```

```
    Rebuilding indexes for table 'titles'

    ** Execution Time: 0 hrs, 0 mins, 1 secs **

End of maintenance for database 'pubs' on 6/9/2000 3:42:18 PM
SQLMAINT.EXE Process Exit Code: 0 (Success)
```

The following example shows how to run SQLMaint using the extended stored procedure xp_sqlmaint. The name of the backup is automatically created and written to the path specified as the argument for -BkUpDB. This example was run from Query Analyzer.

```
use master
exec xp_sqlmaint '-D "pubs" -BkUpMedia DISK -BkUpDB
"c:\backup"'

Output of sqlmaint.exe
---------------------------------------------------------------
Microsoft (R) SQLMaint Utility (Unicode), Version 8.00.100
Copyright (C) Microsoft Corporation, 1995 - 1998

Logged on to SQL Server 'DCWI7500\SQL2K' as 'sa' (non-trusted)

Starting maintenance of database 'pubs' on 6/9/2000 4:02:11 PM
[1] Database pubs: Database Backup...
    Destination: [c:\backup\pubs_db_200006091602.BAK]

    ** Execution Time: 0 hrs, 0 mins, 1 secs **

End of maintenance for database 'pubs' on 6/9/2000 4:02:11 PM
SQLMAINT.EXE Process Exit Code: 0 (Success)

(13 row(s) affected)
```

Summary

DBCC and the related SQLMaint command provide a wide variety of maintenance tasks that can be performed on a database server. The database can be checked for both structural integrity and integrity of user data. Various levels of automatic repair can be performed if any integrity violations are found.

DBCC can also be used to examine the database in a variety of ways. The ConcurrencyViolation parameter is specifically designed to help plan for upgrading from MSDE to the standard version of SQL Server. The Page parameter allows users to take a look at the contents of any page in the database. The OpenTran and LogInfo parameters allow users to retrieve detailed information about the state of the transaction log.

✦ ✦ ✦

Improving the Performance of Data Access

In This Chapter

Managing index fragmentation

Managing index statistics

Creating maintenance plans

Using the Index Tuning Wizard

MSDE provides a number of mechanisms for improving the performance of database access. One of the most important and effective of these is the index. In order for indexes to give the best possible performance, the right set of indexes must be created, maintained, and used properly. Programmers, developers, and administrators must understand how they work and when they are used in order to write efficient queries.

Chapter 9 described the basic structure and function of indexes. This chapter will examine the factors affecting the performance of indexes and the tools used to maintain them. Issues about the way indexes perform in various environments will also be addressed.

Maintaining Indexes

When an index is created, it operates in the most efficient way possible. All of the data in the index is stored in contiguous pages of the database, and the statistics that reflect the nature of the data in the index are highly accurate. As data is added to, deleted from, and modified in the table, the index becomes less contiguous (more fragmented), and thus, the statistics are likely to be less reflective of the data in the index, reducing performance.

Another aspect of index maintenance is verifying that the existing indexes meet the needs of the user community. It is usually the case that at the time a database application is designed and implemented, the exact profile of user access is not known. Without knowing which columns in which tables will be accessed in what way and how much, it is not possible to design a perfect set of indexes. To this end, Microsoft has provided an Index Tuning Wizard that analyzes user activities and recommends changes to index configuration that can improve performance.

Index fragmentation

Several primary characteristics of the index fragmentation affect performance. These include the amount of data stored on a single page, the internal fragmentation of pages, and the external fragmentation of pages with regard to extents. The effect that the amount of empty space in pages has on performance depends heavily on the kind of access that is typical of the database.

Several scenarios are described below to explain when fragmentation will occur and the effect it will have on performance. The `DBCC ShowContig` command is used to examine the level of fragmentation. `DBCC ShowContig` excepts a table name and optionally an index number as parameters. If no index number is provided, the resulting report will be generated with data from the base table, which will be index 0 if the table is a heap, and 1 if the table is a clustered index. The following example shows the execution of `DBCC ShowContig` and explains the output.

```
DBCC ShowContig([order details])

DBCC SHOWCONTIG scanning 'Order Details' table...
Table: 'Order Details' (325576198); index ID: 1, database ID: 6
TABLE level scan performed.
- Pages Scanned................................: 9
- Extents Scanned..............................: 6
- Extent Switches..............................: 5
- Avg. Pages per Extent........................: 1.5
- Scan Density [Best Count:Actual Count].......: 33.33% [2:6]
- Logical Scan Fragmentation ..................: 0.00%
- Extent Scan Fragmentation ...................: 16.67%
- Avg. Bytes Free per Page.....................: 673.2
- Avg. Page Density (full).....................: 91.68%
```

In this case, the Order Details table from the Northwind database has been analyzed without specifying the index. The second line of the output indicates index ID 1, which means the table is a clustered index. The object ID for the table is displayed, along with the database ID. The third line indicates a table level scan, as opposed to the leaf level scan that would occur for a non-clustered index.

Pages and extents scanned

The `Pages Scanned` shows how many pages are in the table. The `Extents Scanned` shows the number of extents used to contain those pages. In this case, nine pages are contained in six extents. Remembering that an extent is composed of eight pages, these pages are somewhat spread out throughout the database. Since the first nine pages of a table are stored in mixed extents, this is not unusual for a table of this size.

Extent switches

The `Extent Switches` shows how many times DBCC has to switch from one extent to another as it reads all of the pages of the table in order. Since there are five extents in this table, it is necessary to switch extents at least five times. Having the minimum possible number of extent switches indicates that the pages in this table are in order with respect to the extents they occupy, meaning DBCC does not have to read an extent for one page and later come back to the same extent to read another page from further down in the table.

Pages per extent

The `Avg. Pages Per Extent` is derived by dividing the first two values. This value can go no higher than 8, and is usually slightly below that even for a very large table, due to the mixed extents used for the first nine pages. As explained above, a table that is as small as Order Details or smaller frequently has a low number of pages per extent.

Scan density

The `Scan Density` is also derived from the first two values. It shows the ratio of the smallest possible number of extents that a table could occupy to the number of extents actually occupied. Because Order Details has nine pages, and an extent can hold eight, the minimum number of extents for this table is two. The fewer extents occupied by the table, the less I/O necessary to read that table, and therefore, the better the performance for queries. This number rarely reaches 100 percent, but a high percentage is beneficial, particularly for large tables.

Logical scan fragmentation

The `Logical Scan Fragmentation` is another view of the layout of the pages on disk. It is increased by pages that are out of order, or pages in a table that are not contiguous with one another. The value is derived by comparing the Index Allocation Map (IAM) with pages in the table as they appear on disk. The IAM is a bitmap of all the pages in the database, with the bits turned on for pages that belong to the table (or index) in question. So, if the 16th, 21st, and 25th bits in the IAM are turned on, then the 16th, 21st, and 25th pages in the database are allocated to the table that owns the IAM. If, as the pages are scanned in index order, they are read from the disk 16, 21, 25, then the logical scan fragmentation is 0. If they are read in some other order, the logical scan fragmentation increases. This measure equates to how much the disk head must jump back and forth across the disk as opposed to always jumping ahead. Always jumping ahead (a low logical scan fragmentation) yields better performance. The logical scan fragmentation of 0 shown for the Order Details indicates that although the pages for the table are somewhat spread out among extents, they are in order relative to one another.

Extent scan fragmentation

The `Extent Scan Fragmentation` number shows how contiguous the extents containing pages from the table are. In the case of the Order Details table, the extent scan fragmentation shows how closely clustered those extents are (pretty closely). Since the fragmentation is 17 percent, then about one in six of the extents is not located immediately contiguous with the extent that contains the next or previous pages from the table. The lower this number, the more contiguous the extents, and the better the query performance will be.

Bytes free per page and page density

`Bytes Free per Page` and `Page Density` are self-explanatory. The average amount of free space for each page in the Order Details table is 673 bytes, which equates to pages that are about 92 percent full. This number will rarely reach 100 percent, even if desired, because the rows in the tables will rarely be divided exactly evenly into the size of the page. This number should roughly reflect the fill-factor used when creating or rebuilding the index. Monitoring this number over time will help to determine the optimal fillfactor to use. For example, if the page density stabilizes at 75 percent in a table due to the number of inserts and deletes, then 75 percent would work well as the fillfactor when maintaining the indexes. If the fillfactor is set much higher than the stable page density, MSDE must work harder splitting pages until the page density lowers to the stable value. If the fillfactor is set much lower than the stable page density, then disk space is wasted, and the system reads more pages than necessary (including the unused space those pages contain) to read enough rows to satisfy queries.

Read-only tables

When reading data, more empty space on pages means more disk access. If pages are only half full, then twice as many pages must be read from disk compared to completely full pages when reading the same number of rows. The amount of I/O performed during a table scan is directly proportional to the percentage of empty space on the pages in the table. If a table is used only for selects, and data is only bulk loaded into that table, but otherwise never inserted or updated, using a fillfactor of 100 is a wise choice and will provide the best performance.

Read and insert on a heap

If a table is used for read access, but rows are also inserted in the normal course of operations, then having the pages completely full may have a detrimental effect on performance. The result of inserts into a table with completely full pages depends upon whether or not there is a clustered index on the table. If there is no clustered index, then new rows will be added wherever they fit. Pages will never have to be split because the system will never have to make room in a particular place for a row. The row can be added in any available free space, or a new page can be allocated to the table and used to store the row.

For example, here is a simple table with an integer column:

```
CREATE TABLE Heap
(RandomNum INT)
```

This example inserts 30,000 rows with random values:

```
DECLARE @cnt INT
WHILE @cnt < 30000
    BEGIN
    INSERT Heap VALUES (CONVERT (INT, RAND() * 30000))
    SET @cnt = @cnt + 1
    END
```

`DBCC ShowContig` will produce results similar to the following after the inserts:

```
DBCC SHOWCONTIG scanning 'Heap' table...
Table: 'Heap' (533576939); index ID: 0, database ID: 7
TABLE level scan performed.
- Pages Scanned................................: 51
- Extents Scanned..............................: 8
- Extent Switches..............................: 7
- Avg. Pages per Extent........................: 6.4
- Scan Density [Best Count:Actual Count].......: 87.50% [7:8]
- Extent Scan Fragmentation ...................: 12.50%
- Avg. Bytes Free per Page.....................: 448.9
- Avg. Page Density (full).....................: 94.45%
```

The pages are nearly full (94 percent), and they are packed nicely into their extents, as shown by the high scan density. The extent scan fragmentation number should be disregarded since this table is a heap. As a table gets larger, the scan density will continue to get better. It is thrown off a little by the first eight pages that exist in mixed extents. As many more inserts as desired may be performed, and the conditions in the table will remain relatively stable. The example above uses random numbers for the inserts, but the behavior will not alter based on patterns in the inserted rows (unlike with a clustered index).

Because there is no intrinsic order to a heap and the pages will be nearly filled, the read performance on a heap will remain reasonably constant in the face of many inserts. The high page density means that more rows will be accessible for each page that is read from disk.

Read and insert on a clustered index

When inserts are performed on a clustered index, the characteristics of the inserts will be determined by the column on which the clustered index is created. If the clustered index is created on some monotonically incrementing value, like order number, then inserts will always fall at the end of the table. If an insert means a new order, and a new order always gets the next higher number after the last most recent order, then the location for the new row is never in question; it is on the last page of the table. If the last page of the table has insufficient space for the new row, then a new page is allocated for the new row. This behavior is much like inserts into a heap because page splits are not required. In this environment, a fillfactor of 100 percent will probably yield the best performance because it provides for the greatest density of data but does not risk fragmentation.

To demonstrate an example of the effect of inserts into a clustered index with a key that increments with every new row, the following table is created with a clustered index on an integer column. Making the column a primary key will create an index and is typical of many production tables. This column would often have the identity property in production, but for the sake of later examples, increasing values will be created in code, and the column will remain available for user-supplied data entry:

```
CREATE TABLE RIClustered
(IncrNum INT PRIMARY KEY CLUSTERED)
```

The following rows are inserted with incrementally increasing values (leaving some gaps in the values for the next example):

```
DECLARE @cnt INT
SET @cnt = 0
WHILE @cnt < 300000
    BEGIN
    INSERT RIClustered VALUES (@cnt)
    SET @cnt = @cnt + 10
    END
```

`DBCC ShowContig` will show values similar to heap index results:

```
DBCC ShowContig

DBCC SHOWCONTIG scanning 'RIClustered' table...
Table: 'RIClustered' (597577167); index ID: 1, database ID: 7
TABLE level scan performed.
- Pages Scanned................................: 49
- Extents Scanned..............................: 8
- Extent Switches..............................: 7
- Avg. Pages per Extent........................: 6.1
- Scan Density [Best Count:Actual Count].......: 87.50% [7:8]
- Logical Scan Fragmentation ..................: 8.16%
- Extent Scan Fragmentation ...................: 0.00%
- Avg. Bytes Free per Page.....................: 136.8
- Avg. Page Density (full).....................: 98.31%
```

Since this is a clustered index, the order of the pages is important, but the scan fragmentation is low because each new value was added to the end of the table.

If reads and inserts are performed on a table with a clustered index that has been created on a column not related to the order of inserts, then a lower fillfactor is required. For example, if the clustered index has been created on last name, it is unlikely that all new records will be added with last names that fall further toward the end of the alphabet than all existing rows. When a new row is added in this case, the system must find the correct page location for the row and insert it there if there is sufficient free space. If there is insufficient free space, then a 50/50 pages split is performed. A new page is allocated and half of the rows are moved to the new page from the full page (at which point both pages are 50 percent full, hence the name). The new row can now be added to the appropriate location, guaranteed of sufficient space.

Using the table created and populated in the previous example and adding a new value in the gap left between each previous value (the counter is started at 5 this time) demonstrates page splitting behavior:

```
DECLARE @cnt INT
SET @cnt = 5
WHILE @cnt < 300000
    BEGIN
    INSERT RIClustered  VALUES (@cnt)
    SET @cnt = @cnt + 10
    END
```

This operation affects the fragmentation in the following way:

```
DBCC ShowContig (RIClustered)

DBCC SHOWCONTIG scanning 'RIClustered' table...
Table: 'RIClusetered' (597577167); index ID: 1, database ID: 7
TABLE level scan performed.
- Pages Scanned................................: 97
- Extents Scanned..............................: 14
- Extent Switches..............................: 96
- Avg. Pages per Extent........................: 6.9
- Scan Density [Best Count:Actual Count].......: 13.40% [13:97]
- Logical Scan Fragmentation ..................: 49.48%
- Extent Scan Fragmentation ...................: 0.00%
- Avg. Bytes Free per Page.....................: 54.8
- Avg. Page Density (full).....................: 99.32%
```

The scan density has dropped from 88 percent to 13 percent, which means that almost no pages with contiguous values are located contiguously in the extents. The logical scan fragmentation has fallen to 50 percent, since the number of pages was doubled and the new pages interleave with old pages in such a way that to read them in order, DBCC must jump ahead half of the time and back half of the time. The extent scan fragmentation has not risen because the new space allocations were performed in an ordered fashion and without intervening allocations for other objects. To summarize the state of this table after the inserts: there are two groups of contiguous extents containing pages that, when followed in order, jump back and forth between the two groups with every other page, but are otherwise in order.

A slightly more realistic test involves mixing activity from other tables. A second table similar to the one we have been working with follows:

```
CREATE TABLE RIClustered2
(IncrNum INT PRIMARY KEY CLUSTERED)
```

An initial set of rows is added in the same way the first rows were added to the RIClustered table.

```
DECLARE @cnt INT
SET @cnt = 0
WHILE @cnt < 300000
    BEGIN
    INSERT RIClustered2 VALUES (@cnt)
    SET @cnt = @cnt + 10
    END
```

The loop must be modified slightly to rows alternately to one table and then the other. The initial value of the counter is now four, so that the new rows will interleave into both tables. As new rows are added in the midst of both tables, MSDE will have to allocate new extents alternately to each table, unlike the previous scripts, in which the extents were all added to the same table one after another.

```
DECLARE @cnt INT
SET @cnt = 4
WHILE @cnt < 300000
    BEGIN
    INSERT RIClustered VALUES (@cnt)
    INSERT RIClustered2 VALUES (@cnt)
    @cnt = @cnt + 10
    END
```

Fragmentation statistics follow.

```
DBCC ShowContig (RIClustered)

DBCC SHOWCONTIG scanning 'RIClustered' table...
Table: 'RIClustered' (597577167); index ID: 1, database ID: 7
TABLE level scan performed.
- Pages Scanned................................: 193
- Extents Scanned..............................: 26
- Extent Switches..............................: 192
- Avg. Pages per Extent........................: 7.4
- Scan Density [Best Count:Actual Count].......: 12.95%
[25:193]
- Logical Scan Fragmentation ..................: 49.74%
```

```
- Extent Scan Fragmentation ...................: 26.92%
- Avg. Bytes Free per Page.....................: 2033.8
- Avg. Page Density (full).....................: 74.87%
```

The pages per extent continues to inch up as the proportion of uniform extents to mixed extents increases. The scan density remains poor. The logical scan fragmentation has not moved much. It will not change if the characteristics of the added data are unchanged. That is, each script that has run so far has been adding rows at evenly spaced intervals, starting at the beginning of the table and running to the end, so the overall pattern of relative positions remains the same.

With this script, the extent scan fragmentation has suddenly jumped from 0 to 27 percent. This change is expected because the inserts, and therefore the page splits and new allocations, were divided evenly between two tables. One can be reasonably certain that the newly allocated extents alternate ownership from one to the next.

The page density has suddenly fallen from the high 90s to the mid 70s. This change in free space on the pages has nothing to do with adding the second table to the script. If each page has 10 slots, when the table is initially populated, the first page is filled like this:

```
0
10
20
30
40
50
60
70
80
90
```

When the second script, that adds numbers ending in 5, is run, the first page is split into two pages, and half of the values are moved to the new page (the values that existed before the page split are marked in bold). The new values are then inserted, filling both pages like this:

0 **50**
5 55
10 **60**
15 65
20 **70**
25 75
30 **80**
35 85
40 **90**
45 95

When the third script is run adding numbers ending in 4, the two previous pages are both split, giving four pages, each half full (once again the bold represents rows that existed before the split). When the new values are inserted after the splits, they fill the pages as follows, leaving some empty slots on each page:

```
0    24   50   74
4    25   54   75
5    30   55   80
10   34   60   84
14   35   64   85
15   40   65   90
20   44   70   94
--   45   --   95
--   --   --   --
--   --   --   --
```

The example pages are, on average, 75 percent full, the same as the reported value for the RIClustered table.

In practice, inserts into the midst of a clustered index are not so neat. They tend to fall somewhat randomly throughout the table. Nevertheless, this example helps to show why tables that only have records added and not deleted still have some free space over long periods of time.

Effects of page splits

Page splits have several important side effects, some of which immediately impact performance, others of which save their impact for later. Splitting the page has immediate impact on performance. The free space in the split pages is significantly altered, and the newly allocated page is non-contiguous in the extent with the other pages with similar key values in the index.

Increased system load

The act of splitting a page causes some immediate performance degradation. The system cannot complete the transaction that caused the page split until it has found and allocated a new page, moved data to the new page, fixed any pointers to the page, added the new record, and fixed pointers in the non-leaf levels of the index, which may also cause page splits. While this work is happening, the transaction that caused it waits, load is put on the system to perform this work, and locks are placed during the work, possibly causing contention.

Page free space

Each of the two pages that result from the split is left with close to 50 percent free space. This is good for future inserts, since there is now plenty of space. It is bad for future reads since the data density is cut in half, so the number of reads required for the same number of rows has doubled.

Fragmentation

When a page has been allocated as the result of a page split, it will almost never be located immediately contiguously with the page that was split. In general, the new page will be on a different extent. Having pages with contiguous clustered index keys located on different extents slows future read performance because the Read Ahead Manager cannot work as efficiently. Even when a small table is allocated in only two or three extents, the order of the pages with respect to the extents is important.

Frequent updates on a heap

If updates are frequently made on a table with no clustered index (a heap), then it may behoove one to have some unused space available on the pages, particularly if the updates often cause the rows to grow in size. When an updated row in a heap grows in size, the system will attempt to keep the row on the same page by utilizing any available empty space on that page. If there is insufficient space on the page to allow the row to grow, the row will be moved to a different page, and a forwarding pointer that points to the new page will be added to the original page. The update itself does not require an extraordinary amount of I/O, but in future reads, two pages must be available: the one with the forwarding pointer and the one with the rest of the row. Having to access two pages will, of course, increase I/O and slow overall performance.

Tables used primarily for writes

All of the previous discussion has centered around the effects of data modifications on reading tables from the database. Some tables, however, are not used only or primarily for receiving changes, and are read either infrequently, or only during batch transfers to other systems. For such tables, fragmentation is not a problem. If there are no queries that request ranges of data or multiple rows, then it does not matter if the Read Ahead Manager cannot bring in multiple pages at one time.

In a table used primarily for writes, a clustered index probably does not make sense. Having a clustered index will open the possibility of page splits. Even though the fragmentation caused by page splits will not hurt performance, increased system load during the page split will still be an issue. If there is extremely high insert load, a clustered index may help to reduce the contention in area of the database, but the row locking mechanism in MSDE is quite efficient, so this is rarely an issue for a database that would be hosted on MSDE (as opposed to the Standard or Enterprise Editions of the SQL Server).

The mixing of inserts and deletes in a heap can be just as efficient, because the free space on pages will be reused immediately, spreading some of the insert load throughout the table. Finding the free space puts only a very small load on the system because of the clever system of bitmaps used to track free space.

Defragmenting Indexes

If tables are used for reading as well as writing, they should be periodically defragmented to improve the performance of the reads.

There are three methods of defragmenting, each of which has benefits and drawbacks: DBCC IndexDefrag, DBCC DBReindex, and Create Index With Drop_Existing.

DBCC IndexDefrag

DBCC IndexDefrag reorganizes the rows and pages within the table to reduce the level of logical scan fragmentation, to increase the scan density, and to reset the original fillfactor. In short, DBCC IndexDefrag does all the things that make reads faster. This command requires three parameters: the database name, the table name, and the index ID.

DBCC IndexDefrag moves rows within pages and pages within extents. It does not move or reallocate extents. DBCC DBReindex or Create Index With Drop_Existing should be used to improve the extent scan fragmentation.

DBCC IndexDefrag resets the fillfactor to its original value. If no value was specified for fillfactor when the table or index was created, it will have been set to the default value. If the default value is 0, then DBCC IndexDefrag will not compact the rows on the pages; the page density will remain unchanged.

Unlike DBCC DBReindex and Create Index With Drop_Existing, DBCC IndexDefrag does not lock users completely out of the table while it works. It places highly granular locks and uses short transactions to perform its work, so users can continue to access the data. The number of transactions it uses is related to the amount of fragmentation in the table or index, so if it is run frequently, it runs very quickly. Conversely, if it is run infrequently so that the table has the opportunity to become highly fragmented, it can take a very long time and use a large amount of space in the transaction log.

The following example shows the effect of DBCC IndexDefrag on a table. Running DBCC IndexDefrag on the RIClustered table as it existed at the end of the examples in the section above yields the following results:

```
DBCC IndexDefrag (Patient, RIClustered, 1)

Pages Scanned Pages Moved Pages Removed
------------- ----------- -------------
186           182          0

(1 row(s) affected)
```

The statistics after the defragmentation look like this:

```
DBCC ShowContig

DBCC SHOWCONTIG scanning 'RIClustered' table...
Table: 'RIClustered' (597577167); index ID: 1, database ID: 7
TABLE level scan performed.
- Pages Scanned................................: 193
- Extents Scanned..............................: 26
- Extent Switches..............................: 36
- Avg. Pages per Extent........................: 7.4
- Scan Density [Best Count:Actual Count].......: 67.57% [25:37]
- Logical Scan Fragmentation ..................: 3.63%
- Extent Scan Fragmentation ...................: 26.92%
- Avg. Bytes Free per Page.....................: 2033.8
- Avg. Page Density (full).....................: 74.87%
```

The scan density has improved by a reasonable amount from 13 percent (it had to switch extents after reading each page) to 68 percent (switching extents on average after having read about 5.4 pages). The improved scan density means that fewer I/Os are necessary to read the entire table, or any range within the table that includes more than a page.

The logical scan fragmentation has decreased to almost nothing, down from approximately 50 percent. The extent scan fragmentation has not changed at all because the IndexDefrag was only able to shuffle rows and pages in place. It did not reallocate any extents, and the extents allocated to RIClustered are intermingled with the extents allocated to RIClustered2. To reduce the logical scan fragmentation, a user would need to rebuild the index with `DBCC DBReIndex` or `Create Index with Drop_Existing`.

The page density has remained unchanged because the table was originally created without specifying a fillfactor. The default fillfactor at the time of table creation was 0. The difference occurring when a fillfactor is specified can be seen by creating a new table with a specific fillfactor, for example, 90 fillfactor.

```
CREATE TABLE test
(col1 int primary key clustered with fillfactor=90)
```

The table below is filled with rows to create fragmentation and the free space within pages. The following script is a slight modification of the scripts run above. It executes the outer loop three times, each time decrementing the starting value of the counter, so the single script will generate the same amount of fragmentation and free space.

```
DECLARE @startval INT
DECLARE @cnt INT
SET @startval = 3
```

```
WHILE @startval > 0
    BEGIN
    SET @cnt = @startval
    WHILE @cnt < 300000
        BEGIN
        INSERT test VALUES (@cnt)
        SET @cnt = @cnt + 10
        END
    SET @startval = @startval - 1
    END
```

When the script is finished, the statistics on the table should be similar to the following:

```
DBCC ShowContig (Test)

DBCC SHOWCONTIG scanning 'test' table...
Table: 'test' (757577737); index ID: 1, database ID: 7
TABLE level scan performed.
- Pages Scanned................................: 193
- Extents Scanned..............................: 26
- Extent Switches..............................: 191
- Avg. Pages per Extent........................: 7.4
- Scan Density [Best Count:Actual Count].......: 13.02%
[25:192]
- Logical Scan Fragmentation ..................: 49.74%
- Extent Scan Fragmentation ...................: 3.85%
- Avg. Bytes Free per Page.....................: 2033.8
- Avg. Page Density (full).....................: 74.87%
```

The numbers are similar to the last example, except that the extent scan fragmentation is much lower, because the extent allocation for the Test table was uninterrupted by allocations for any other object. The lack of interruption means that the extents for Test are contiguous with one another.

This time, when `DBCC IndexDefrag` is run, some pages are removed.

```
DBCC IndexDefrag (Patient, Test, 1)

Pages Scanned Pages Moved Pages Removed
------------- ----------- -------------
186           154         32

(1 row(s) affected)
```

The pages are removed because the rows are reorganized to leave free space in accordance with the original fillfactor. The 32 pages left over and unused at the end of the process are discarded. Examining the statistics for the table shows:

```
DBCC ShowContig (Test)

DBCC SHOWCONTIG scanning 'test' table...
Table: 'test' (757577737); index ID: 1, database ID: 7
TABLE level scan performed.
- Pages Scanned................................: 161
- Extents Scanned..............................: 22
- Extent Switches..............................: 32
- Avg. Pages per Extent........................: 7.3
- Scan Density [Best Count:Actual Count].......: 63.64% [21:33]
- Logical Scan Fragmentation ..................: 3.73%
- Extent Scan Fragmentation ...................: 9.09%
- Avg. Bytes Free per Page.....................: 828.9
- Avg. Page Density (full).....................: 89.76%
```

The scan density has been increased, the logical scan fragmentation has been decreased, and the page density has been increased to close to 90 percent. The number of extents has dropped from 26 to 22 because of the removal of the unused pages. The extent scan fragmentation has actually increased slightly because the ratio of the mixed extents at the beginning of the file to uniform extents has increased. The mixed extents are also the reason that the scan density has not increased more than it has.

If a table is highly fragmented, using `DBCC DBReindex` or `Create Index With Drop_Existing` can be more efficient and faster than `DBCC IndexDefrag`. In addition, those two commands don't run the risk of overflowing the transaction log.

DBCC DBReindex

`DBCC DBReindex` rebuilds (drops and re-creates) the indexes on a table. When indexes are rebuilt, the fillfactor can be reset to any value, the density is increased, and the fragmentation is reduced. Microsoft recommends the use of `Create Index With Drop_Existing` instead. Primarily, `Create Index` is superior because it defers the rebuild of non-clustered indexes until the clustered index has been completely rebuilt.

Create Index With Drop_Existing

Indexes, including the clustered index, can be rebuilt by issuing the `Create Index` command and using the `With Drop_Existing` parameter. When the `Create Index` command is used on a clustered index, the `With Drop_Existing` parameter causes MSDE to defer the rebuild of the non-clustered indexes. Non-clustered indexes use the clustered key as the row pointer when there is a clustered index on the table. When there is no clustered index on a table, the non-clustered indexes use the row ID as a row pointer. This means that, when a clustered index is dropped, all non-clustered indexes are automatically dropped and re-created to load the appropriate row ID's. When a clustered index is re-created, all of the non-clustered indexes are also, once again, dropped and rebuilt to replace the row IDs with clustered keys. Using the `With Drop_Existing` parameter prevents the first rebuild of non-clustered indexes.

When `Create Index` is used to rebuild indexes that have been created as part of a constraint, such as a primary key or a unique constraint, the `Create Index` command must re-create the index with the same properties that were used when it was initially created.

The following example shows the full effects of `Create Index`. It uses the two-table scenario used earlier in the chapter.

Two tables are created, each having a clustered index. The tables are filled at the same time, in a way that creates fragmentation, free space in the pages, and interleaved extents on the disk.

```
CREATE TABLE Test1
(col1 int primary key clustered with fillfactor=100)
CREATE TABLE Test2
(col1 int primary key clustered with fillfactor=100)

DECLARE @startval INT
DECLARE @cnt INT
SET @startval = 3
WHILE @startval > 0
    BEGIN
    SET @cnt = @startval
    WHILE @cnt < 300000
        BEGIN
        INSERT Test1 VALUES (@cnt)
        INSERT Test2 VALUES (@cnt)
        SET @cnt = @cnt + 10
        END
    SET @startval = @startval - 1
    END
```

The table statistics follow:

```
DBCC ShowContig (Test1)

DBCC SHOWCONTIG scanning 'Test1' table...
Table: 'Test1' (789577851); index ID: 1, database ID: 7
TABLE level scan performed.
- Pages Scanned................................: 193
- Extents Scanned..............................: 27
- Extent Switches..............................: 191
- Avg. Pages per Extent........................: 7.1
- Scan Density [Best Count:Actual Count].......: 13.02% [25:192]
- Logical Scan Fragmentation ..................: 49.74%
- Extent Scan Fragmentation ...................: 92.59%
```

```
- Avg. Bytes Free per Page.....................: 2033.8
- Avg. Page Density (full).....................: 74.87%
```

The clustered index must be re-created (the name assigned to the clustered index when the primary key was created will need to be looked up):

```
CREATE UNIQUE CLUSTERED INDEX PK__Test1__30F848ED
ON Test1(col1) WITH DROP_EXISTING
```

The statistics should be rechecked:

```
DBCC ShowContig (Test1)

DBCC SHOWCONTIG scanning 'Test1' table...
Table: 'Test1' (789577851); index ID: 1, database ID: 7
TABLE level scan performed.
- Pages Scanned................................: 146
- Extents Scanned..............................: 19
- Extent Switches..............................: 18
- Avg. Pages per Extent........................: 7.7
- Scan Density [Best Count:Actual Count].......: 100.00% [19:19]
- Logical Scan Fragmentation ..................: 0.00%
- Extent Scan Fragmentation ...................: 0.00%
- Avg. Bytes Free per Page.....................: 82.3
- Avg. Page Density (full).....................: 98.98%
```

The table now has an optimal configuration, including the extent scan fragmentation. In this case, the scan density has increased to 100 percent. As explained before, it is normal if the scan density goes close to, but does not reach 100 percent, because of the way the first eight pages are allocated in mixed extents. When the table was rebuilt in the previous example, all mixed extents were full, so a new mixed extent was allocated, and that mixed extent was immediately filled.

Updating statistics

For the query processor to make sound decisions about which indexes to use, it must have access to good statistics. For example, if a student wanted to find an occurrence of the word *antidisestablishmentarianism* in a book, he or she would probably look in the index defined page on which the word was located. On other hand, if he or she wanted to find an occurrence of the word *the*, he or she would most likely not look in the index, but simply open the book to the first page, or indeed any page. He or she knew to use the index in one case and not the other because he or she had implicit knowledge about the distribution of words in a typical text. When query is run on MSDE, the query processor is faced with the same decision, but it has no implicit knowledge. It must rely on the statistics specifically gathered about the values in tables to know whether it's likely to find many occurrences or few of a specific value.

As modifications are made to data in the database over a period of time, even the best statistics will become out of date. Automatic update and Manual update are mechanisms that can be used to update statistics. The administrator of the database must decide which of these two mechanisms will be more effective in his particular environment. If the statistics are updated automatically, they are always reasonably reflective of the reality that exists in tables. They are sampled, which means that not every row is examined in detail. The statistics are not 100 percent accurate, but are usually close enough. The drawback to automatic updating is that the statistics are gathered when users submit the query. The system decides upon receiving the query that enough data has changed in the table to make the current statistics unreliable. The system immediately starts the process of updating the statistics. While this happens, the user's query waits. The alternative is to use manually updated statistics, which allows administrators to choose when the process should happen and thus makes it less intrusive to users. The sampling rate can also be selected, a choice that involves a trade-off between the accuracy of the statistics and the time it will take to re-gather the statistics. You must be careful, however, not to let the statistics get too old. If statistics are generated without sampling, the system will examine every row in the table, and the statistics will be 100 percent accurate when created. However, as soon as the first row is modified in the table, the statistics are no longer 100 percent accurate. As more modifications are made, the statistics are likely to become less and less accurate.

In most environments that run MSDE, automatically updating statistics provides the best choice. To verify that statistics are updated automatically, the database option can be checked. If manually updating statistics is employed, the `Update Statistics` command can be used.

The statistics on a column can be viewed with the DBCC `Show_Statistics` command. This command takes two parameters: the table name and the index name.

If the database option Auto Create Statistics is turned on, MSDE will automatically create statistics for some columns that do not have indexes. These statistics collections assist the query processor with creating the most efficient possible execution plan for a query. Statistics in an automatically created statistics collection can be viewed in the same way as statistics for a normal index.

Running the Maintenance Plan Wizard

Performing regular maintenance on the indexes and statistics in a database will keep performance at its optimal level. Indexes must be defragmented on a regular basis, and occasionally rebuilt entirely. The statistics can be maintained automatically by MSDE, but, as explained above, there may be environments in which automatic updating of statistics is detrimental to overall performance.

The Maintenance Plan Wizard in Enterprise Manager can assist in creating jobs that will automatically perform maintenance on indexes and statistics. It will also automate database backups.

To access this Wizard in Enterprise Manager:

1. Click the server in the left pane, and choose Wizards from the Tools menu. The Select Wizard dialog box is displayed.
2. Expand Management, and select Database Maintenance Plan Wizard. The first screen is a banner, and the second screen allows the selection of the database(s) on which to perform maintenance.
3. The third screen, shown in Figure 30-1, controls whether to rebuild the indexes, or to update the statistics on them. These two choices are mutually exclusive. This screen can also be used to shrink the database.

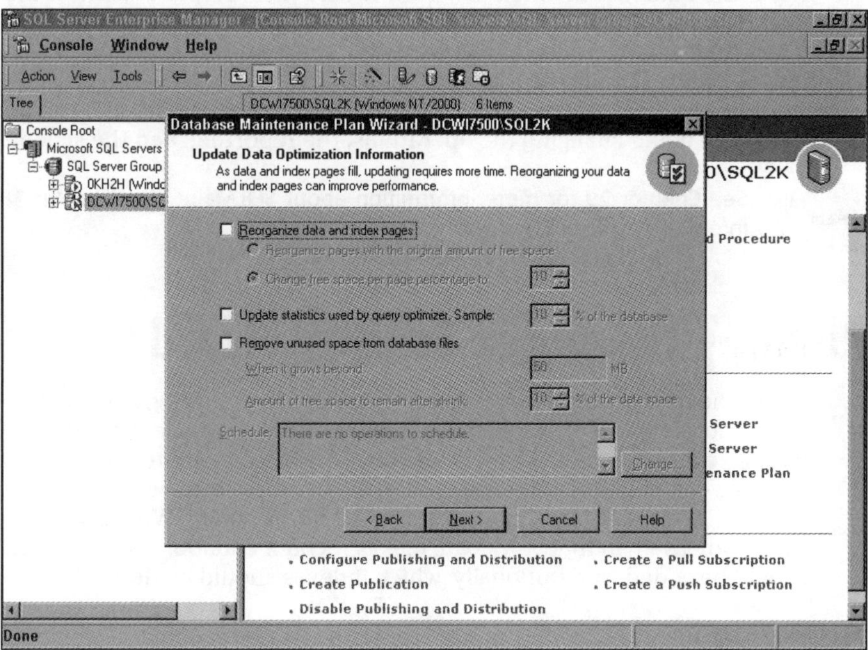

Figure 30-1: Database Maintenance Plan Wizard

Choosing to rebuild indexes by selecting "Reorganize data and index pages," also requires specifying how to handle the fillfactor. The options are to restore the original fillfactor ("Reorganize page with the original amount of free space"), or clicking "Change free space percentage to" and enter a value for free space. The number entered is the inverse of fillfactor and is the percentage of free space rather than the percentage of filled space.

If the administrator chooses to update the statistics, the sampling percentage can be entered. When the statistics are updated, they are updated based on reading a percentage of the rows in the table, e.g. choosing a 10 percent sampling rate would base the statistics on the values in every tenth row of the database. The higher the sampling rate, the more accurate the statistics, but the longer the update will take.

The rest of the screen in the Database Maintenance Plan Wizard allows other maintenance options to be chosen. Integrity checks can be performed on the database (including or excluding indexes), and the data files and the transaction log file can be backed up. For each page in the Wizard, a schedule can be set. For example, the index maintenance could be performed twice per day, while the integrity checks could be done once per week.

When the Database Maintenance Plan Wizard has completed, one or more SQL Agent jobs are created. These jobs run the `xp_sqlmaint` extended stored procedure. If the administrator chose to rebuild the indexes, `xp_sqlmaint` is run with the –RebldIdx parameter. If update statistics was selected, `xp_sqlmaint` is run with the –UpdOptiStats parameter. These jobs can be modified by an administrator, including changing the operations, the reporting, and the schedules.

See Chapter 29 for more information about SQLMaint. See Chapter 26 for more information about SQL Agent jobs.

Running the Index Tuning Wizard

To get the best possible performance from MSDE, indexes should match the usage of the database as closely as possible. Unfortunately, because the internal algorithms used by the query processor are so complex, it is difficult to know what the best possible combination of indexes would be. In order to solve this problem, Microsoft has provided the Index Tuning Wizard. The Index Tuning Wizard analyzes a workload, and based on that workload, makes recommendations about which indexes should be added, and optionally, which indexes should be deleted.

Before running the Index Tuning Wizard, the workload must be created and stored. The Profiler, which was described in Chapter 28, is used to capture and store workloads. The default trace settings can be used in the Profiler, and users will be able to access the database in their normal fashion. The Profiler saves all of the database activity to either a final or any database table.

The Index Tuning Wizard can be run from the Wizard's dialog box, available from the Tools menu in Enterprise Manager. The first screen in this Wizard is a greeting. The second screen, shown in Figure 30-2, allows the specification of the server and database to be analyzed. A selection is also available to control whether or not the

Index Tuning Wizard should recommend to delete any indexes by selecting or clearing the "Keep all existing indexes" check box.

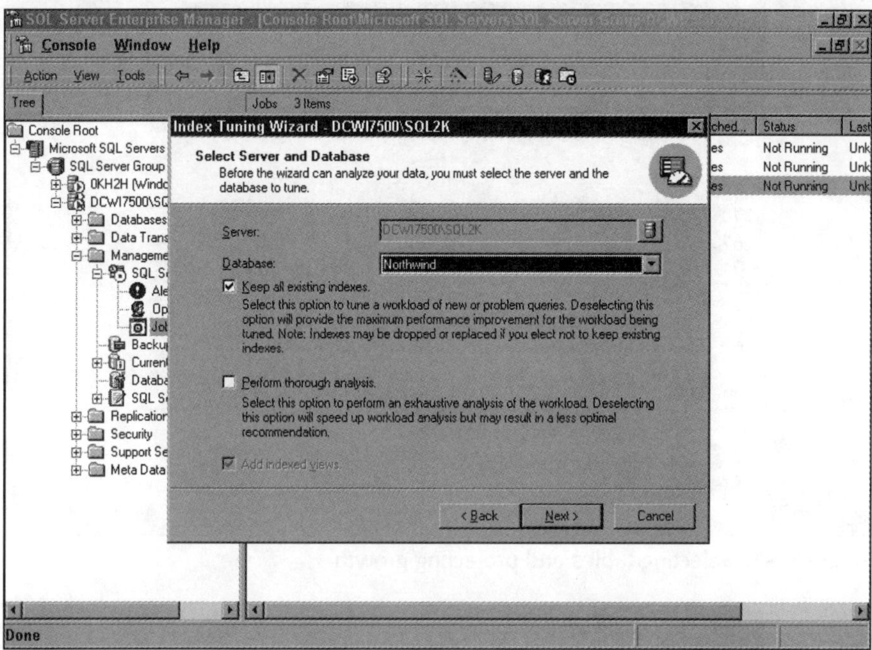

Figure 30-2: Selecting a database

A large number of possible combinations of indexes can be created on even a small table. An index can be created on any column in the table. Each index can either be a clustered index or a non-clustered index. And indexes can be created on every combination of columns and tables. Because there are so many possible alternatives, the user has the option of whether the Index Tuning Wizard should perform an exhaustive analysis or a greedy analysis. The default is a greedy analysis, leaving the "Perform a thorough analysis" check box blank. The Wizard will examine the most likely combinations of indexes to produce a performance gain, rather than examine every possible combination of indexes.

After selecting the server and database, the workload source, which can be either a table or a file, must be specified. Additionally, the tables within the database that are to be analyzed must be selected. The screen allowing table selection is shown in Figure 30-3. For each table, the Wizard shows the number of rows that currently exist in the table. A projected number of rows can be entered, which the Wizard will take into consideration when it performs its analysis.

After the tables have been selected, the projected growth has been entered, and Next has been clicked, the Wizard will perform the analysis. When it has finished its analysis, the Index Recommendations screen, shown in Figure 30-4, is displayed.

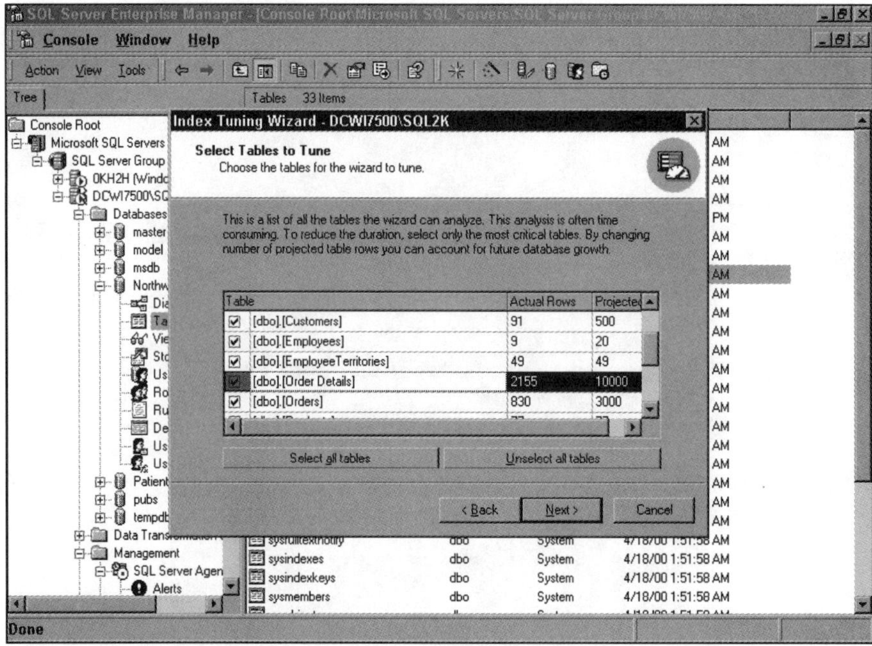

Figure 30-3: Selecting tables and projecting growth

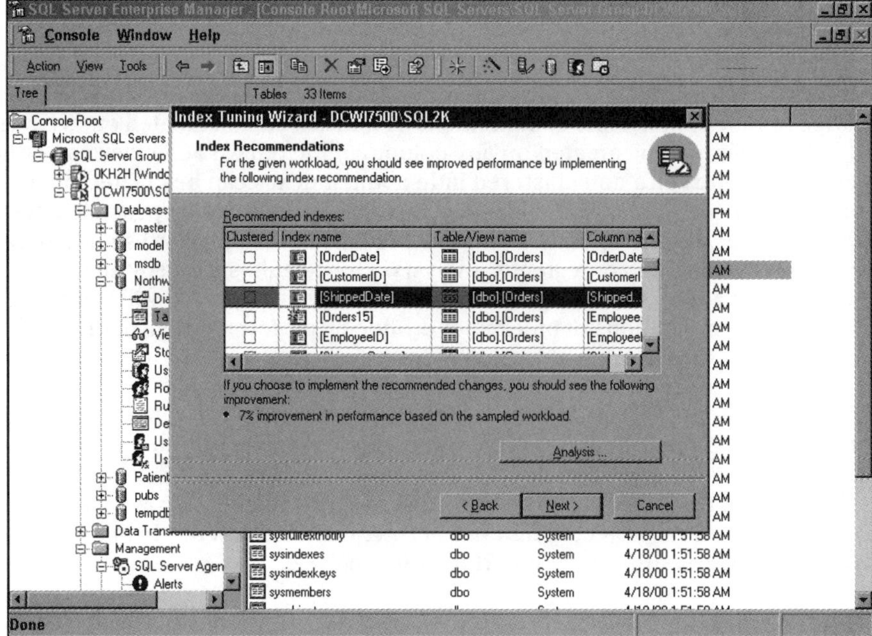

Figure 30-4: The Index Recommendations screen

The Index Recommendations screen shows a list of all indexes, including recommended new indexes, which are indicated with a slightly different icon. An estimation of the improvement in performance is shown at the bottom of the screen. The Analysis button at the bottom left of the screen allows the user to examine a number of detailed reports that show current and recommended configurations of the database and all of the usage statistics used to arrive at the recommendation.

Summary

MSDE is dependent upon the proper use of indexes to provide reasonable performance in a production environment. Different types of database usage call for different configurations of indexes. The way an index performs is dependent on whether the table is used primarily for reading data, writing data, or some combination of the two. It makes a big difference if there is a clustered index, and on which column a clustered index is created. There is also significant interaction between clustered indexes and the type of modifications performed on the table.

In most environments, indexes must be maintained on a regular basis to deliver a consistently high level of performance. As modifications are made to tables, indexes become fragmented, are scattered among extents on the desk, and gain or lose free space in the pages. Understanding the effects of the symptoms in database operations is crucial to developing a proper maintenance plan for defragmenting or rebuilding indexes.

In addition to defragmenting and rebuilding indexes, the index statistics must also be maintained. The database administrator must decide whether to allow MSDE to automatically update statistics on the fly, or to create an automated maintenance job that fulfills a function. The Database Maintenance Plan Wizard can make it easier to create SQL Server Agent jobs to perform both kinds of index maintenance.

Over time, the usage of a database will vary, and database administrators must be aware that the best combination on indexes may change. The Index Tuning Wizard can make this difficult process possible, and even (almost) easy.

✦ ✦ ✦

P A R T

VIII

Database Deployment

This part explains the ways MSDE can be deployed to users and, further, how MSDE can be deployed with Access projects and with Visual Studio projects.

In This Part

CHAPTER 31

MSDE Deployment Overview

In This Chapter

The Windows Installer

Installation packages

Merge modules

The MSDE setup program

Attaching a database

MSDE can be deployed to users in one of two ways: by running the setup program or by merging into a Windows Installer package. The setup program itself uses the Windows Installer internally. However, it can be launched like any other executable. In order to merge MSDE into a Windows Installer package, software that is compatible with the Windows Installer must be available.

The Windows Installer

The Windows Installer is a set of relatively new technologies that provides operating system components to coordinate installations of any application software. Using the Windows Installer to deploy software has several advantages:

- A single installation package can be used on a wide variety of computer configurations.
- The software setup can be designed to be more resilient than a classical setup. If any files for application are damaged, the operating system will be able to invoke the Windows Installer and automatically repair those files.
- Installer packages can be deployed to users in a Windows 2000 environment using a Group Policy Object (GPO). There are numerous benefits to using GPOs, including the ability to specifically target software to individual user's computers, to have software installed on demand, and to perform upgrades and uninstalls without having to visit the user's computer.

- Using a Windows Installer package provides more information to the host operating system, which helps alleviate the problems of having shared components inadvertently uninstalled when they are still needed or having them fail to uninstall when they are no longer needed.
- The Windows Installer supports the concept of a package rollback. During installation, a record is made of all changes that are made to this system, in case these changes need to be undone at a later time.

The Windows Installer itself is a component of, or an add-on to, the operating system. In order to use it, additional software to create the installation packages is necessary. A number of third-party packages exist that can create the msi files required for the Windows Installer. Some of this third-party software falls into the category of software repackagers, while some of it is intended to be used by software developers who need to create sophisticated setup programs.

The Visual Studio Installer is a Microsoft product that can be used to create the installation packages. Developers can also write programs that will create these packages by directly manipulating the Windows Installer API.

Operating system support

The Windows Installer is an integral part of the Windows 2000 operating system. It can also be installed on Windows 95, Windows 98, and Windows NT. The non-Windows 2000 versions of the Windows Installer do not have the full capabilities that are available with Windows 2000.

Windows 2000

The Windows Installer runs as a service on Windows 2000 clients. In addition to providing a standardized and flexible installation environment, it also integrates with GPOs when used in a network that supports Active Directory.

For software to use the Windows 2000 compatible logo, it must support the Windows Installer installation process.

Windows 95, 98, and NT 4.0

Windows 95, 98, and NT 4.0 were introduced before Windows Installer became available. A Windows Installer package will detect whether or not the Windows Installer has already been installed on computers running one of these operating systems. If it has not been installed, the installation process for Windows Installer itself will be initiated automatically.

Installer modules

Software packages that use the Windows Installer installation mechanism create one of two types of files used during installation: an installation package (msi) or a merge module (msm).

Installation packages

Installation packages are completely self-contained databases. They are identified by the .msi file extension. An msi file contains all the information needed to install the software package. That information includes all files and directory structures that will be created or modified. It also includes any information that must be added to or changed in the Registry.

A user can double-click an msi file to initiate installation of the software contents — assuming that Windows 2000 is running or that Windows Installer has been previously installed.

Microsoft Office 2000 uses the Windows Installer. Any computer that has had Office 2000 installed has also had the Windows Installer installed.

Merge modules

A merge module contains information about a piece of software that is intended to be installed as a subcomponent of some other piece of software. Merge modules are identified by the .msm file extension.

Software components that will be shared by more than one other piece of software are frequently set up in merge modules. A merge module for a shared component that is included in multiple packages allows the operating system to install the package only once and uninstall it only when it is no longer used by any software.

MSDE Setup Program

If MSDE is going to be deployed without the capability of having the merge modules in an installation package, the setup executable that comes with the MSDE can be used.

For example, if an Access 2000 project is being deployed, the Package and Deployment Wizard does not directly support the use of Installer packages. If a user is using the Package and Deployment Wizard in Access 2000, they can add the setup command itself or a batch file that runs the setup command to the end of the installation program.

Directory contents

When using the setup program, the following files must be added to the subdirectory from which the setup program will eventually be run:

- **setup.exe** — This executable will initiate the installation process for MSDE.
- **sqlrun.cab** — This cabinet file contains compressed copies of all the files that are necessary for the installation.
- **setup.ini** — This file contains the parameters that control the configuration of the install. The parameters are described below.
- **sqlrun01.msi through sqlrun09.msi** — Nine separate msi files are provided on the CD with MSDE. One of these files must be in the subdirectory with the setup executable. If more than one instance of MSDE is installed on the computer, then a different sqlrun0x.msi file must be used for each instance. These files are functionally identical except that they are used to individually identify each instance of MSDE to the Windows Installer and the operating system.
- **instmsi.exe** — This executable is necessary only if the Windows Installer has not previously been installed on the client computer. The setup program will automatically run it if it detects that the Installer has not previously been installed. Running this program may require a reboot of the computer.

Calling the setup program

The setup program has one required parameter, `/i`, which is used to specify the msi file that identifies this instance of MSDE. Other command line parameters can be used to specify an ini file that will contain the configuration for the installation. Alternatively, the configuration can be completely specified with command line parameters.

Command line parameters

The setup program for MSDE identifies parameters with a forward slash and uses a space between the parameter name and the value that is supplied with it. The command line parameters available for the MSDE setup program are as follows:

- **/?** — This parameter prints out a list of all the available command line parameters. It would not be used in a production deployment.
- **/i** — This parameter is used to specify the Installer package file. It is a required parameter.
- **/settings** — This parameter specifies the ini file containing the configuration for the installation. The possible ini file settings are described in the next section.

- **configuration parameters**—As an alternative to using the `/settings` parameter and a file containing the configuration settings, any of the configuration parameters described in the next section can be specified directly on the command line. Configuration parameters used on the command line cannot be used in combination with a settings file.
- **/x**—This parameter is used to uninstall MSDE. The name of the Installer package file that was used to install the instance that should be removed must be specified with this parameter. For example, if an instance of MSDE was installed with the following command line:

  ```
  setup /i sqlrun05.msi
  ```

  it must be uninstalled with this command line:

  ```
  setup /x sqlrun05.msi
  ```

Ini file

The ini file (or the `/settings` parameter) can accept any of the following parameters:

- **TARGETDIR**—This parameter specifies the directory in which the executable portion of MSDE will be stored. If this parameter is not supplied, the default directory will be used: c:\program files\Microsoft SQL Server\MSSQL
- **DATADIR**—This parameter specifies the directory in which the user databases will be stored. If this parameter is not specified, the default directory will be used: c:\program files\Microsoft SQL Server\MSSQL\Data
- **INSTANCENAME**—This parameter specifies a name that will be used to identify the instance of MSDE. This name is appended to the service name for the instance (if an instance name is set to Customers, the service name will be MSSQL$Customers). The instance name is also used when connecting to the databases. Connecting to the Customers instance would require you to specify *servername*\Customers.
- **COLLATION**—This parameter specifies the default collation for the server. The collation specifies the character set and sort order that will be used by default in each database on the server. If this parameter is not specified, the default collation will be used: `Latin1_General`.
- **SECURITYMODE**—This parameter accepts the value `SQL` to set the security mode to enable SQL authentication. By default, SQL authentication is enabled on Windows 98 and Me, and it is disabled on Windows NT and 2000.

Note

Books Online documents the parameters `USEDEFAULTSAPWD` and `SAPASSWORD`. These parameters are not used by the MSDE installation program, and any values supplied will be ignored.

MSDE Merge Modules

If a user has access to a program that will allow them to create an Installer package, then they can add the merge modules that come with MSDE CD into the installation package they are creating. For example, if a user is working with the Visual Studio Installer, they can specify these merge modules during the creation of the installation package. The merge modules are stored in the SQLMSDE\MSM subdirectory on the CD.

Required modules

The following modules are required to be added to the installation package for a successful installation of MSDE:

- atl.msm
- connect.msm
- dev_scm.msm
- dtc.msm
- dts.msm
- dts-1033.msm
- mfc42.msm
- msstkprp.msm
- msvcirt.msm
- msvcrt.msm
- sem.msm
- sem-1033.msm
- shared.msm
- sqlagent.msm
- sqlagent-1033.msm
- sqlbase.msm
- sqlsvr.msm
- sqlsvr-1033.msm
- tools.msm
- tools-1033.msm

Optional modules

The following modules are not required for a successful installation of MSDE. Omitting them will leave the server installation without the corresponding functionality.

The following two modules support replication functionality. If these modules are omitted, the instance of MSDE cannot take part in replication of any kind:

- ✦ Repl.msm
- ✦ Repl-1033.msm

The following two modules support the DMO functionality. Without these modules, programs and scripts that use DMO to manage MSDE will not function:

- ✦ Dmo.msm
- ✦ Dmo-1033.msm

Attaching a Database

Once MSDE has been successfully installed, the application database must be created. The easiest way to create an application database is to have a copy of the database file available with the installation, start the SQL Server service, and attach the database file.

See Chapter 22 for details on the many different ways to start and stop the MSDE services.

The database file can be attached with a stored procedure or by using DMO, which is usually more easily added to installation procedure using a scripting language.

The following script detaches the customer database in preparation for deploying it to a user's computer:

```
dim oMSDEserver
dim rstring
set oMSDEserver = CreateObject("SQLDMO.SQLServer")

oMSDEserver.connect "Okh2h\de","sa",""
rstring = oMSDEserver.detachDB ("Customer")

msgbox rstring
oMSDEserver.disconnect
```

You can find this code on the CD-ROM in the file named `Ch 31\detachdb.vbs`.

This script presents a message box that will display a status message indicating if the detach was successful.

After the database has been detached and moved to a computer with a freshly installed instance of MSDE, it can be reattached.

The following script attaches a database named "Customer" (note that the line that calls the `AttachDBWithSingleFile` method wraps):

```
dim oMSDEserver
dim rstring
set oMSDEserver = CreateObject("SQLDMO.SQLServer")

oMSDEserver.connect "Okh2h\de","sa",""

rstring = oMSDEserver.AttachDBWithSingleFile ("Customer",
"c:\program files\microsoft sql
server\mssql$de\data\cust_data.mdf")

msgbox rstring
oMSDEserver.disconnect
```

You can find this code on the CD-ROM in the file named `Ch 31\attachdb.vbs`.

This script presents a message box with an OK button—if all goes well. It will also display any error during the attachment.

Summary

MSDE uses a different installation mechanism than other editions of SQL Server. It is designed to be used as part of the setup for an application. The CD contains merge modules that can be added to an installation package if the application supports the Windows Installer. If a user is distributing a package that does not support Windows Installer merge modules (for example, Access 2000 Package and Deployment Wizard), the setup program on the CD can be run. Whichever way is chosen to deploy MSDE, a mechanism to start the SQL Server service and attach (or create) the database that will be used by the application must also be provided.

✦ ✦ ✦

CHAPTER 32

Deploying MSDE with Access Projects

✦ ✦ ✦ ✦

In This Chapter

Analyzing the user environment

Preparing to deploy a database application

Distributing Access applications

Distributing MSDE

Using the Office 2000 Package and Deployment Wizard

✦ ✦ ✦ ✦

A common use for MSDE is to provide a back end for applications developed in Access 2000. There are several ways of deploying Access applications to users. Understanding the desired configuration for MSDE and the ultimate software configuration for the users' computers will enable developers and administrators to make choices about how to deploy the applications.

End User Scenarios

The two primary questions that must be answered about users are the following: Will the user have a full copy of Access 2000 installed on the user's computer, and will an instance of MSDE be installed on the user's computer or on another computer?

Deploying a project to a user with Access 2000

If a user has Access 2000 installed on his or her computer, there are several options for deploying an application to that user. The application can be saved as an .adp file and then copied to the user's computer. The user can then open the project, and if the user has a properly configured connection to the database server, the project will be immediately available for use.

Even if the user has a full copy of Access 2000, the Package and Deployment Wizard can still be used to create a deployment package. A deployment package can simplify the distribution and installation of software. It also provides a number of additional functions. For example, the deployment package can include PE files that are necessary to install MSDE and can also initiate the installation program for MSDE after the Access application has been installed.

Deploying the Access 2000 runtime

If a user does not have a copy of Access 2000, then the Package and Deployment Wizard must be used to create a deployment package that includes the Access runtime engine. The Access runtime engine can be distributed only with the Microsoft Office Developer edition.

There are some advantages to deploying the Access runtime engine rather than installing Access on every user's computer. Much of the complexity of the product is hidden from the user, exposing only the interface that was developed specifically for the users. Hiding unnecessary complexity is an effective way of improving user productivity. Users will be unable to modify (and possibly diminish the effectiveness of) the design of the application, and users will not be confused by the additional functionality available in the full version of Access.

Deploying MSDE to a user

Once it has been ascertained that the users will be using the Access runtime engine, a decision must be made as to where MSDE will be located. For some applications, it makes sense to locate MSDE directly on the user's machine. For example, users with laptops who spend considerable time out of the office, perhaps at customer sites, may find it advantageous to have the database installed directly on their computer. This kind of scenario lends itself well to using merge replication in order to unify the data of the entire company.

In other situations, it may make more sense to install a single instance of MSDE on a single computer and have several users connect to it. If there are few users all working from computers that do not move from the location, this method provides a simpler way of administering the data because no replication is required.

In yet other situations, MSDE may be deployed to every user's computer requiring the application. If the application does not involve data that needs to be shared among users, and there is not an enormous amount of data, then a local copy of the database will provide the best performance for each user.

If MSDE must be distributed to many users, then the MSDE setup process should be chained to the end of the setup process for the Access application. This can be done by creating a subdirectory that contains the appropriate files for the MSDE setup, including the subdirectory in the Package and Deployment Wizard and including the setup command with the appropriate parameters as a command to execute after the installation is finished.

Figure 32-1 shows the connection properties dialog box for an Access project. The connection properties for a project can be accessed from the File ➪ Connection menu. The dialog box shown in Figure 32-1 is configured for a connection to a local instance of MSDE called DE. When an Access project is connected to an instance that is installed on the same computer, the server can be referred to as (local).

By using the (local) designation, a single project can be created that can be distributed to any number of computers, assuming that MSDE is also installed on the computer. (local) can be used alone to indicate the default instance of MSDE, or it can be used with a backslash and the name of an instance, as shown in Figure 32-1.

The security context that users will use to connect to MSDE can present some difficulty when distributing to many users. Figure 32-1 shows a connection that is configured to use the sa login with no password. If the information stored in the database requires no security, this can be a viable option. However, most environments require at least a minimal level of security. Remember that the sa login has complete administrative privilege on the server. sa does have the advantage of existing on every installation of MSDE.

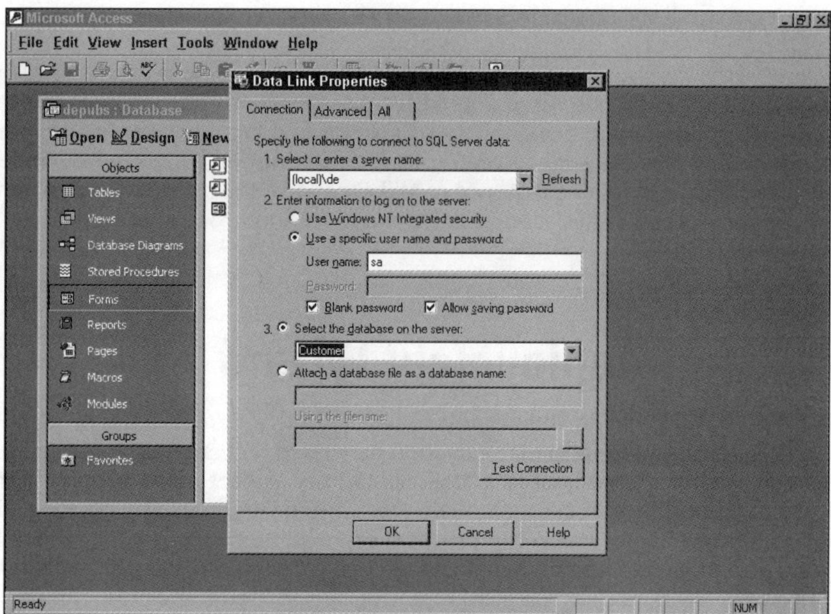

Figure 32-1: Access Connection Properties dialog box

If physical security cannot be guaranteed (as in most business environments), additional measures must be taken. While placing a password on the sa login helps to alleviate some of the security issues, it is often desirable to place additional limits on the access of the primary user. An additional login must be created on the server by writing code that connects to the server as the sa login and creates the user. The Access project must be configured to connect as this user. Using NT's integrated security can make the task of creating logins easier. The custom code can detect the name of the currently logged on user, connect to the server as the sa login, and create an NT login for the current user of the computer. In this case, the Access project connection can be configured to use Windows NT Integrated security. Using NT security is usually the most secure configuration.

Connecting a user to an existing MSDE

Distributing an Access project to multiple users that will connect to the same instance of MSDE requires a specific naming of the computer and instance in the connection properties of the project, rather than using the (local) designation. Specifying the server name means that the project must be customized for each server installation so that it includes the name of the computer on which MSDE is installed. Using this methodology makes the Access project somewhat less scalable than using a local instance; a local instance that gets installed as part of the setup can distribute to projects without concern for the names of the computers, the number of computers, or whether or not they are on the same network.

The name of the computer on which MSDE will be installed must be known. This computer will act as the server and must receive a custom setup that also installs MSDE (unless that part of the installation is performed manually or through some other automated process such as SMS software distribution). All other computers that will connect to the same instance of MSDE can use the same setup program that will install the Access project containing the connection properties configured with the server's name.

Package and Deployment Wizard

Access 2000 has a Package and Deployment Wizard that can ease the process of distributing an application to many users. The wizard will create a setup program that can be run by users to automatically install the project on their computers. If the users do not have Access installed, the setup program can be configured to install a runtime engine. The setup program can also be configured to run another program or batch file after the Access project is installed. This program or batch file can install MSDE and/or run a custom program written to perform initial setup on the database server, such as creating appropriate logins and attaching a database file.

Visual Basic for applications environment

The Package and Deployment Wizard can be run only from the Visual Basic (VB) environment within Access. The Visual Basic environment provides the capability to write highly complex and customized functionality in an Access project. Even if no VB code has been written, the environment must still be entered to access the Package and Deployment Wizard. To access the VB environment, your Access project must be opened and Tools ➪ Macro ➪ Visual Basic Editor should be chosen from the menu.

The Package and Deployment add-in

The Package and Deployment Wizard is an add-in not loaded by default. It must be loaded by choosing Add-Ins ➪ Add-In Manager from the menu within the Visual Basic environment. The Add-In Manager should show a list of available add-ins, as shown in Figure 32-2. If the Package and Deployment Wizard does not show up in this list, the Office Developer, which comes on a separate CD with the Developers' Edition of Office 2000, may need to be installed.

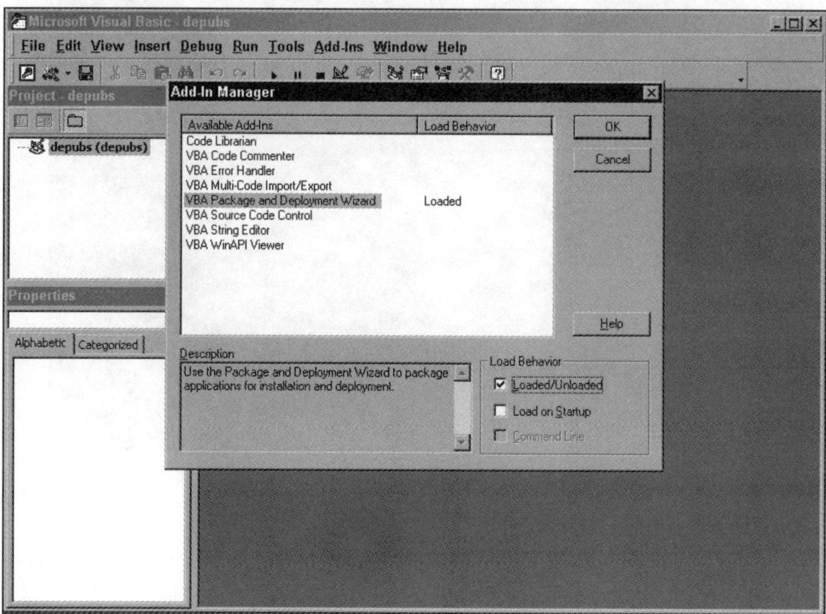

Figure 32-2: The Add-In Manager

Select Package and Deployment Wizard from the list and then select the Loaded/ Unloaded checkbox. The word *Loaded* should be displayed next to the wizard, as shown in the figure. If this wizard is used often, the Load at Startup checkbox can also be selected so that manually reloading the wizard each time Access is restarted is not necessary.

After the wizard is loaded, the Add-In manager can be closed. The Add-Ins menu now shows an option to start the wizard, and project packaging can now begin.

Figure 32-3 shows the main menu of the Package and Deployment Wizard. From this menu, a user can proceed to create the setup package for the user's project, deploy that package to a network directory or Web page, and manage previously created deployment packages.

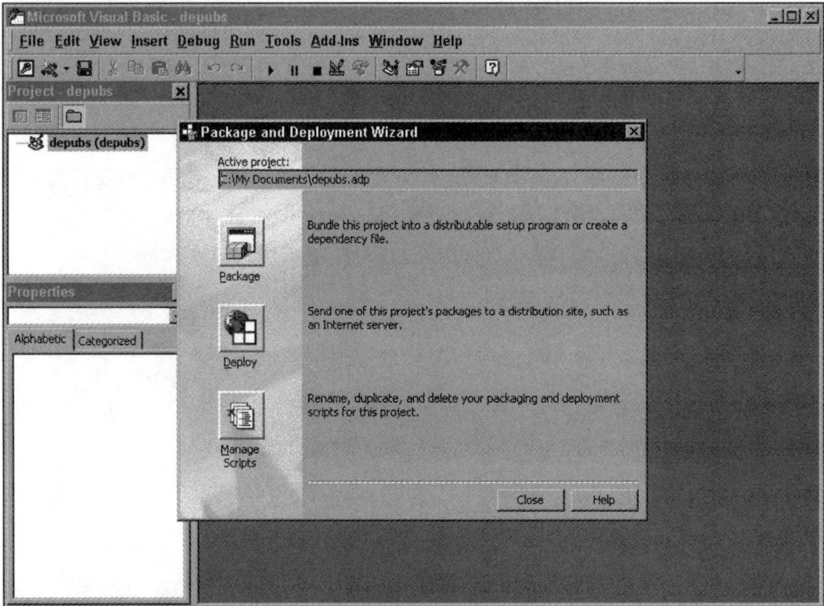

Figure 32-3: Package and Deployment Wizard main menu

Packaging the project

When choosing to create a package, a user is presented with the screen shown in Figure 32-4. This screen enables the user to choose whether to create a standard setup package or a dependency file.

The standard setup package will create a setup executable along with all necessary files, compressed into a cab file, to perform an automated setup of the Access project. This option is the one that is normally used when preparing to distribute applications to users.

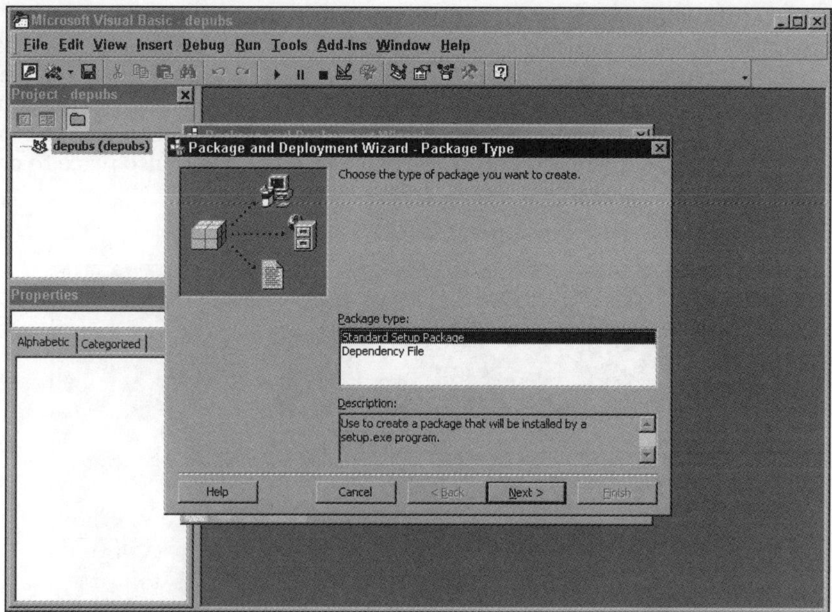

Figure 32-4: Choosing the package type

The dependency file lists all of the dependencies that the setup program would have if it were created. The dependencies include all files that will be added to the cab file, as well as any other files that those files may depend on. For example, dynamic link libraries (DLLs) may sometimes depend upon having other DLLs available to perform their functions properly. Creating a dependency file enables a user to record and possibly modify the list of all dependencies. Creating this file can be most helpful if the setup package will be rebuilt multiple times and dependencies not detected by the wizard must be recorded. Access applications rarely require a specific dependency file.

After running the Package and Deployment Wizard the first time, a script is created in a standard setup package or a dependency file. The script can be used in the future when building additional setup packages. The script can also be manually modified and will automatically create a reference to the dependency file if one was created. In this way, dependencies can be manually created so that the other files will automatically be included with the package anytime it is rebuilt. If any scripts exist, a script selection screen will be displayed prior to the screen prompt to create a setup package or a dependency file. A user can choose to use any existing script or none.

After having chosen a package type, a screen is displayed allowing the user to choose a subdirectory in which the package will be assembled. An existing subdirectory can be used, or a new subdirectory can be created. Using a single subdirectory for each package will reduce administrative overhead for maintenance.

Figure 32-5 shows the dialog box that appears after a working subdirectory is selected. This dialog box shows a list of the files that the wizard has automatically detected for inclusion in the package. Any of these files can be deselected if desired, although that is rarely necessary. A user can also add additional files to the setup package. If the user is going to include an installation of MSDE along with the installation of the Access application, this is the place to do it; this is also place to choose to include the Access runtime.

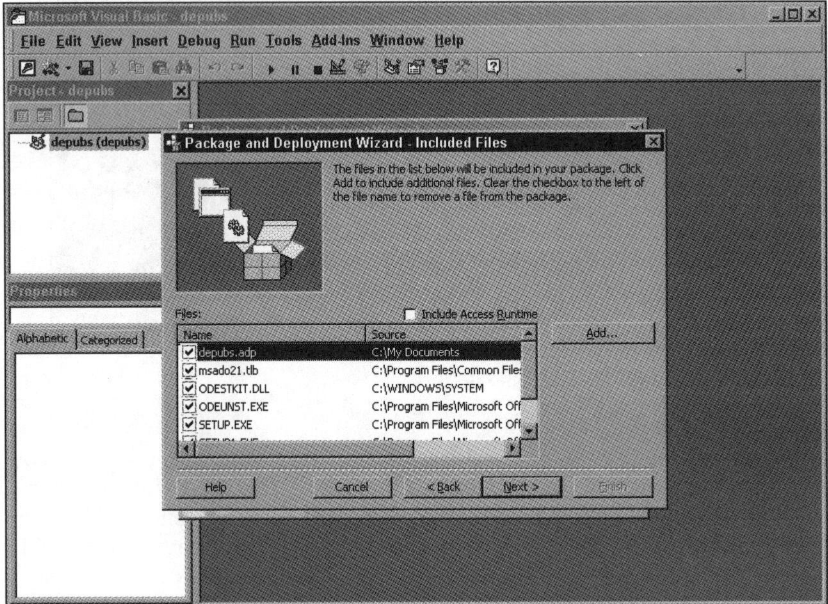

Figure 32-5: Including files

The Access runtime engine may not have been installed on the hard drive, in which case the Office Developer CD must be inserted so that the wizard can load the runtime engine into the setup package. The runtime engine should be copied into a subdirectory if packages will be created on a regular basis. The runtime engine is located on the CD in the directory ODETools\v9\AccessRT. If the contents of that directory are copied to the hard drive in Program Files\Microsoft Office\ODETools\v9\Runtime, the wizard will find them automatically.

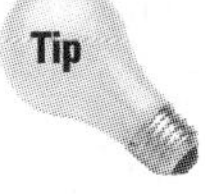

The files for the installation of MSDE cannot be added directly to the Access setup package because they both use files named setup.exe. One way to work around this is to put all of the files needed for MSDE setup into a self-extracting zip file and then include that file in the Access setup package.

After selecting all files to be included in the setup package, a dialog box is presented allowing the user to choose whether the package should be saved in a single file or in multiple 1.44MB files. The latter choice enables the package to be distributed on floppy disks.

Figure 32-6 shows the dialog box that follows the choice of cab files. In this dialog box, a user can select an installation title to be displayed during the setup process. An additional command, such as the one that starts the MSDE setup, can be selected to run at the conclusion of the setup. If all of the necessary files for the MSDE setup are included in a self-extracting zip file, the user can include a batch file at this point that will extract all the files from the zip and initiate the MSDE setup. This batch file must be on the list of included files so that it is available at the time setup is run.

In Figure 32-6, a batch file, InstDE.bat, has been added to run at the conclusion of the Access application installation. The batch file in the scenario mentioned above would unpack the MSDE setup files, start the MSDE setup, and perhaps perform any cleanup required at the end of the process. A batch file was used in the figure only as an example. There are many ways to initiate that install. A VBScript could be written, or if the Windows Scripting Host was installed on the destination computers, a program could be written and compiled into an executable using any programming language, such as Visual Basic or Visual C++.

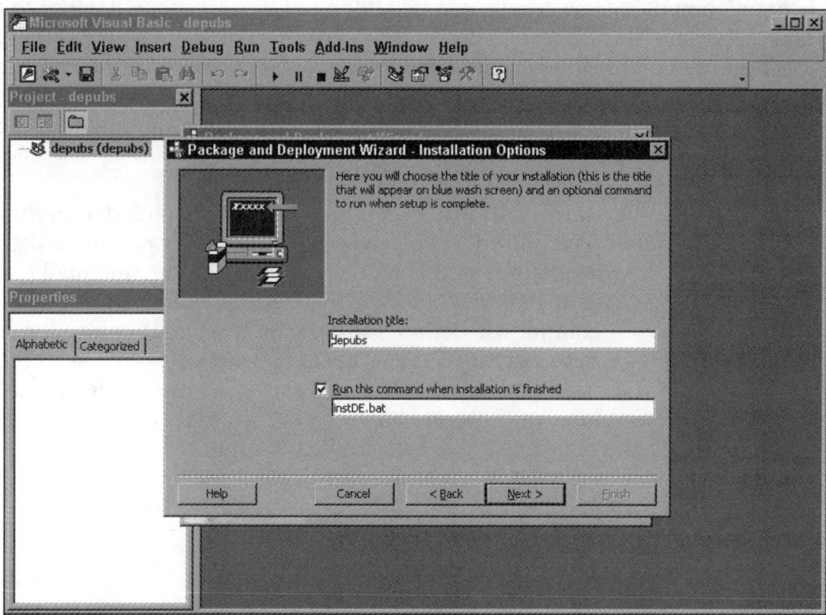

Figure 32-6: Adding additional commands

It is not necessary to initiate the MSDE setup from the same package used to distribute the Access application, even if that package was used to distribute the MSDE files to the target computer. Any of the following methods can be used to initiate the setup:

✦ A software distribution mechanism, such as that provided in Microsoft's SMS product or Novell's ZENWorks. These mechanisms can also provide a way to move files to a target computer, so careful evaluation of how to put the whole package together should be considered. It may not make sense to compress the MSDE setup files (which are compressed in a cab file to start) into a self-extracting zip, compressed into the Access application cab file, and so on.

✦ Use the Windows 2000 Active Directory GPO. GPOs can run logon scripts that can initiate the setup.

✦ Send an attachment through e-mail and let the user run it when it is convenient. The setup files must be on the user's computer at the time the attachment is run.

✦ Deliver a batch file or executable to the target computer in the Access application setup package, but allow the user to initiate the setup.

Figure 32-7 shows the screen that follows the screen shown in Figure 32-6. It provides a mechanism for having the Access application setup program modify the Start menu on the target computer. New groups can be added to the Start menu itself or to the Programs submenu. New items can be added to either menu or to a new submenu. With this tool, an icon for the Access application can be presented at any appropriate location on the Start menu. After any actions that should be applied to the Start menu have been specified, the locations in which the various components will be installed can be selected.

Figure 32-8 shows the Install Locations screen. Any of the files included in the setup package that are not required to be in a specific directory can be assigned to a directory that the user defines in this screen. All files that are manually added to the package appear in this window. The locations must be assigned carefully in order not to conflict with other software on the target computer and to support the follow-on setup of MSDE. Several special values can be selected from a drop-down list on this screen, or literal values can be used. The special values can also be combined with literal values, as shown in the last line in Figure 32-8, in which the Ssde.exe file is assigned to $(AppPath)\SSDE. In this example, Ssde.exe will be placed in a subdirectory called SSDE that will be created in the directory specified by the user for the installation of the Access application.

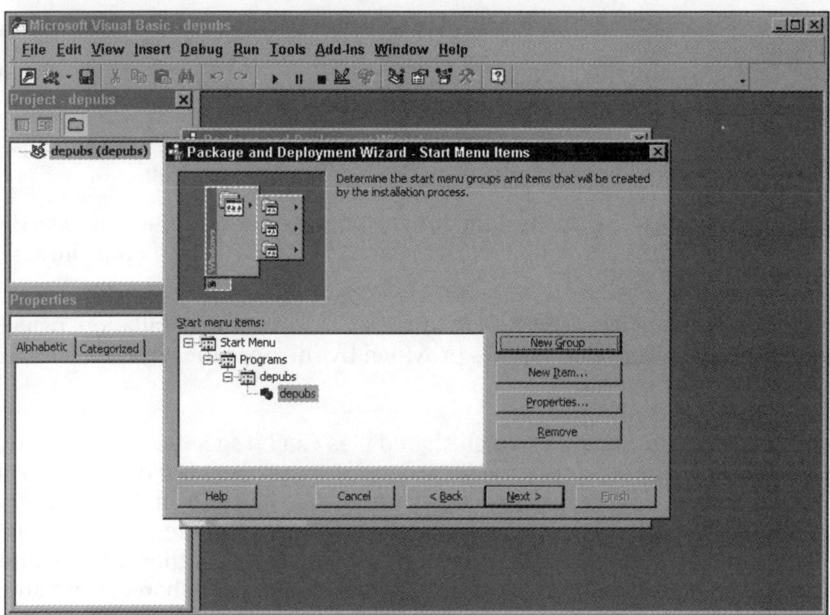

Figure 32-7: Modifying the Start menu

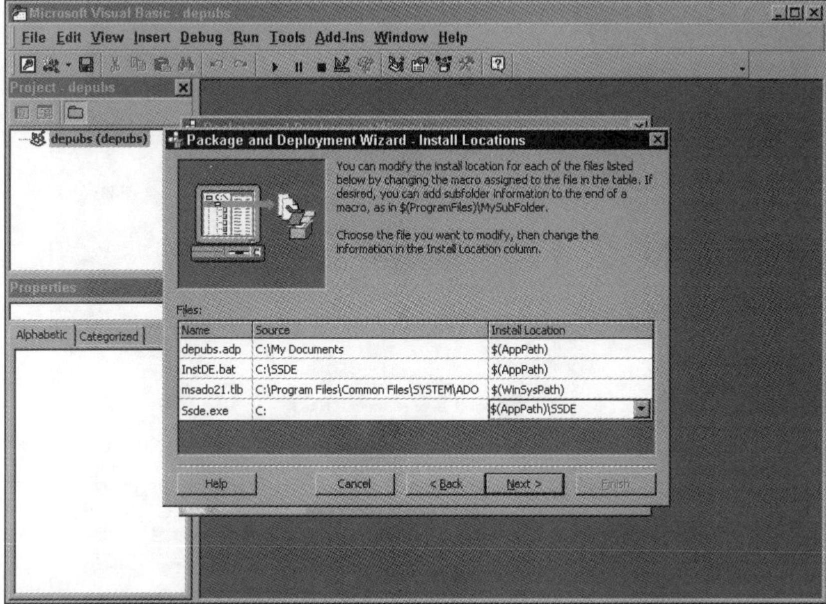

Figure 32-8: Install Locations screen

The most common special values used are the following:

- **$(AppPath)** — is the installation directory for the Access application that the user may choose during installation.
- **$(WinPath)** — is the directory in which Windows is installed. This value is provided by the operating system based on its initial installation.
- **$(WinSysPath)** — is the System directory located within the Windows directory. This value is provided by the operating system based on its initial installation.
- **$(ProgramFiles)** — is the default location for software installation, usually C:\Program Files. This value is provided by the operating system based on its initial installation.

Figure 32-9 shows the screen in which shared files can be specified. Windows tracks any files that are installed as shared files to make sure it does not delete them prematurely. For example, several programs may use the file mapi.dll, and each program may attempt to add that file when it is installed. When one of these programs is uninstalled, the uninstall process should delete the mapi.dll only if there are no other programs using that file. When programs indicate that a file is shared, a counter is kept in the Registry for the number of installed programs that reference the file. When any program that references the file is uninstalled, the counter is decremented by one. When a program decrements the counter to zero, the shared file can be removed safely.

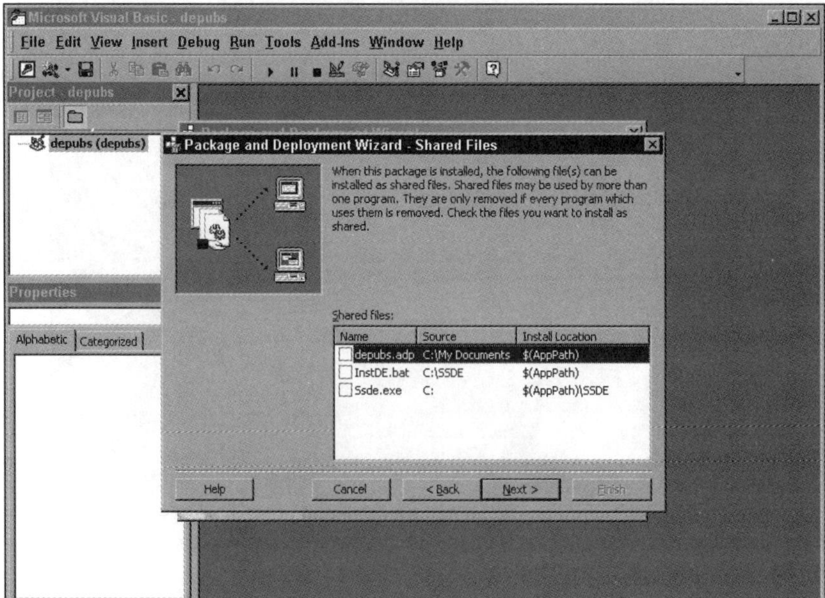

Figure 32-9: Shared Files screen

None of the files shown in Figure 32-9 is a good candidate for being shared. The adp file is the Access application, and it is unlikely that any other program would use it. The batch file and the executable are both used in the process of installing MSDE, and even though MSDE itself may be shared, the components that install it are not. These components may even be deleted immediately after MSDE is installed.

The last screen used in creating a package provides an opportunity for naming the script that the wizard creates. The script saves all of the configuration settings that were specified while running the wizard (for example, the additional files that you added to the package). The script can be reused when creating other packages in the future to speed the process.

When a user clicks Finish, the wizard creates a cab file containing all files necessary for the installation, a setup.exe that can be used to initiate the installation, and a setup.lst used to contain instructions for the setup executable. These three files are placed in the directory specified earlier in the wizard. There will also be a Support subdirectory created containing all the files from the cab and a batch file that can recreate the cab.

Deploying the project

If a user has created a project using the Package and Employment Wizard, the user can use the Employment part of the wizard to move the appropriate files to a location accessible to the target computers. The location can be on a network share, on a Web site, or on floppy disks. Using deployment can be particularly useful if a package will be deployed multiple times (for example, to floppy disks) or if numerous packages will be deployed to similar locations (for example, a Web site).

The first screen in the deployment part of the wizard allows the user to choose the package that the user wishes to deploy.

The second screen, shown in Figure 32-10, enables the user to choose the mechanism for distribution. The user can choose to deploy to a folder, which would allow the user to copy the distribution files to a network share or floppy disks. The user can also choose Web Publishing, which will enable the user to save the distribution files to a Web site.

Whichever method of deployment is chosen, the user is given the opportunity to select the files to be copied to the deployment location. Figure 32-11 shows the screen that enables this selection. By default, the files listed and selected in this window are the setup.lst file, the setup executable, and the cab file(s).

If deployment takes place using Web Publishing, the next screen, shown in Figure 32-12, enables the user to add additional files to the distribution location. This is a viable alternative to including the MSDE setup files in the package itself. Two setup executables will still be required, one for the Access application setup and one for the MSDE setup.

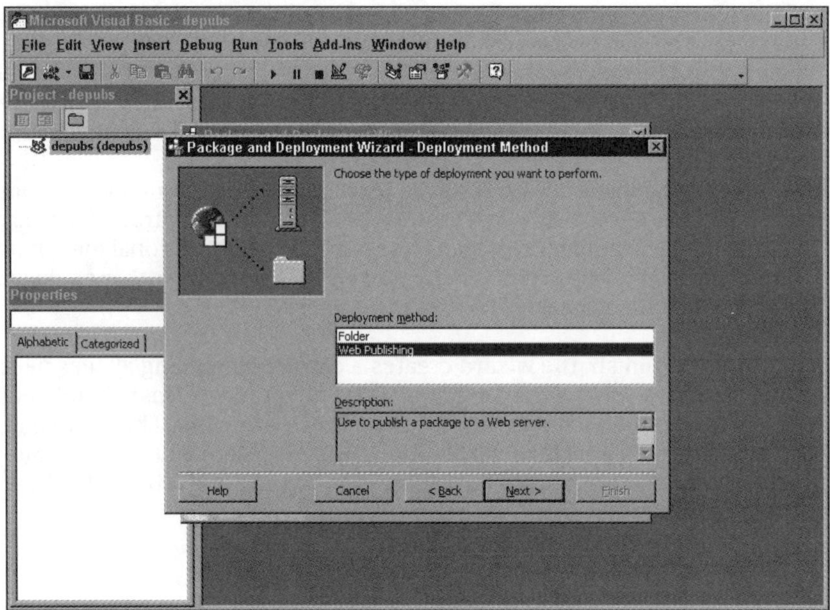

Figure 32-10: Choosing the deployment method

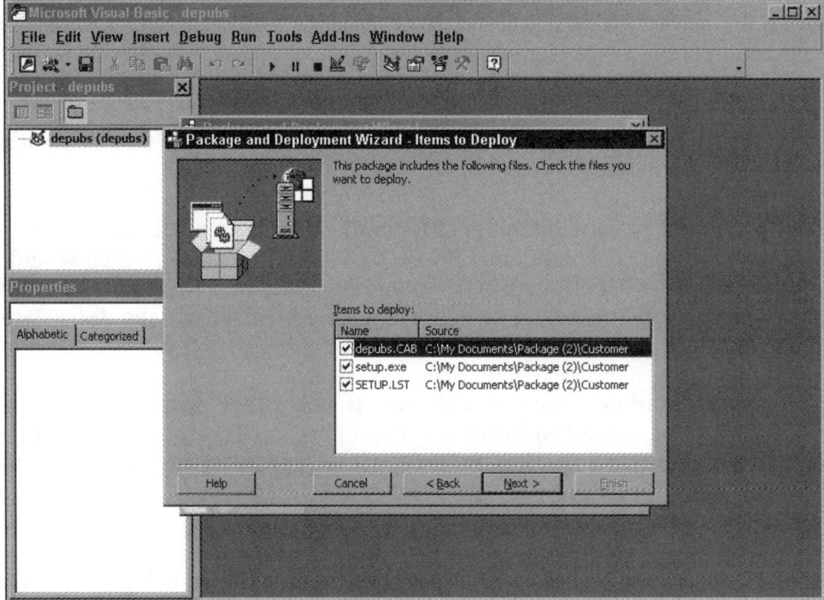

Figure 32-11: Selecting files to deploy

After selecting the files to be deployed and adding any additional files, the user will have the opportunity to specify the location for the deployment. If the deployment method is to a folder, the user can specify the folder. If Web deployment is chosen, the user is presented with the screen shown in Figure 32-13. This screen permits specification of the URL for distribution. The figure shows an example of a default home directory on a server called 0kh2h, but any valid URL path can be used.

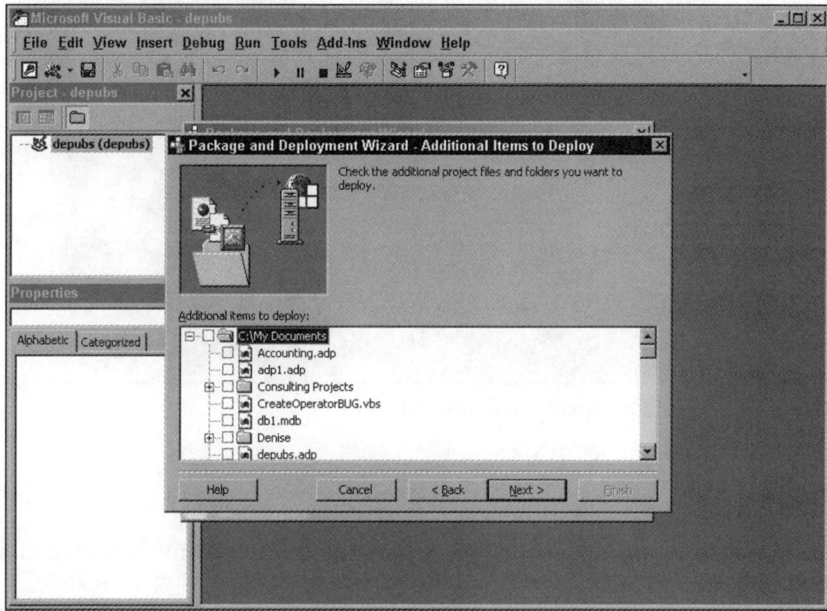

Figure 32-12: Adding files to a Web deployment

This screen also enables a user to choose the protocol to be followed to copy the files to the Web site. The Web server must be configured to accept the protocol selected, which can be either FTP or HTTP Post. If the protocol is FTP, then the files will be copied into an FTP directory. They can then be accessed with FTP, or if the FTP directory is also the directory used for a Web page, a user with HTTP can access them. If the protocol is HTTP Post, then the destination location will be a Web page.

When a user leaves this screen, a prompt will ask if the user wants the URL to be verified and saved to the Registry. If so, it will be available in the drop-down list for future deployments.

The deployment process for the wizard ends with a prompt requesting a name to associate with the script that is created and by copying the files to the deployment location.

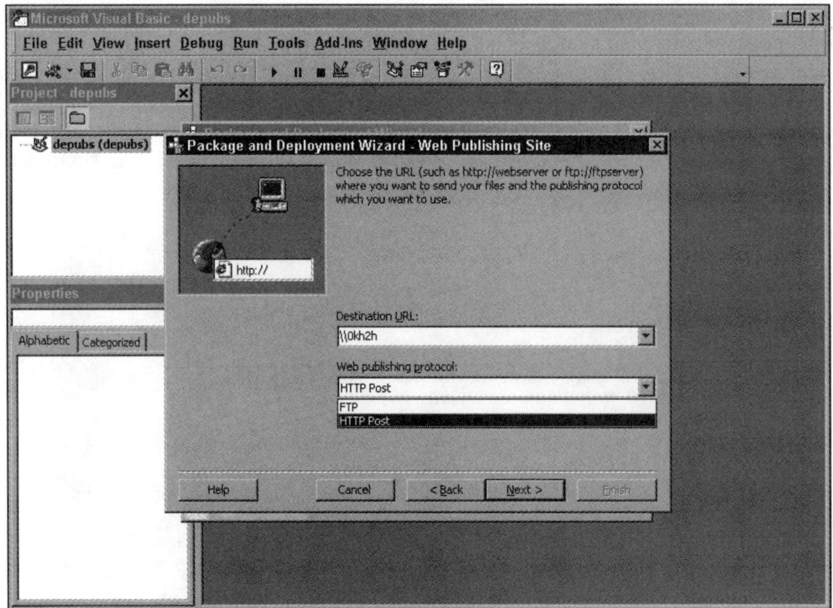

Figure 32-13: Web deployment configuration

Managing scripts

The third option in the main menu of the Package and Deployment Wizard enables a user to manage the scripts created while creating or deploying a package.

Figure 32-14 shows the interface for managing scripts. There are two tabs at the top that enable the user to choose the scripts that were created along with packages or those that were created during package deployment. The scripts save all of the settings chosen during either process, and enable the user to accept those settings again as defaults, although each value can be individually overridden. Saving and reusing a script can speed the process of recreating a package or creating multiple versions of the same package.

In the Manage Scripts dialog box, a user can rename, copy, and delete scripts. Names for the scripts should be as descriptive as possible. Scripts that will not be needed in the future should be deleted. Scripts increase productivity only if they can be easily found when needed.

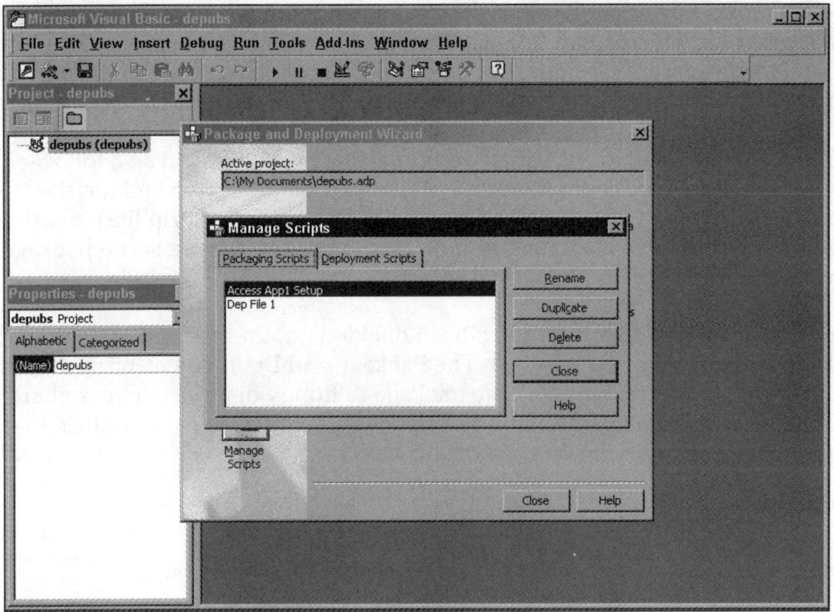

Figure 32-14: Managing scripts

Summary

Before deployment of MSDE with an Access application begins, the environment into which they will be deployed must be analyzed. A decision must be made as to whether each user will have a copy of MSDE installed locally or shared across the network. Security needs for the database must be understood, and customized setup programs to configure the security should be considered. The configuration of the database connection in the Access project must be compatible with the security solution employed.

An administrator must also decide how to deploy the Access project and MSDE to the computers on which they will reside. They can be deployed together with a single mechanism or with multiple mechanisms to suit the environment. Access projects can be copied to users' computers if those users have full versions of Access. If the users do not have full versions of Access, then the Access runtime engine must be distributed.

The Office 2000 Developer Edition of Access' Package and Deployment Wizard can be used to create a setup program that will install the application and a cab file containing all of the necessary files and, optionally, the Access runtime. The wizard can also be used to initiate another process when it finishes installing the Access application.

MSDE can be included in an Access setup package and installed as a follow-on process after the Access application installation completes. To include the MSDE setup files, they must be added to a single file (for example, a zip file) in order to avoid file-naming conflicts, because both MSDE and the Access setup package use a file called setup.exe.

After the package configuration has been decided on, the method of deploying the package to users must be selected. The Package and Deployment Wizard can help automate the process of moving the package to floppy disks, a network share, or a Web site. Other mechanisms, such as SMS, can also be used to move files to users' computers and initiate the installation process.

✦ ✦ ✦

CHAPTER 33

Deploying MSDE with Visual Studio Projects

✦ ✦ ✦ ✦

In This Chapter

Using the Visual Studio Installer

Creating Installer packages

Creating merge modules

Adding MSDE to an Installer package

Deploying a Visual Studio Installer package

Using the Package and Deployment Wizard with Visual Studio

✦ ✦ ✦ ✦

Visual Studio supports two primary methods for packaging and deploying projects: the Package and Deployment Wizard and the Visual Studio Installer. The SQL Server MSDE can be packaged and deployed along with a Visual Studio project using either method; it is much easier, however, when using the Visual Studio Installer. The Installer is a more recently developed software component and is not included on the original Visual Studio CDs. The Visual Studio Installer integrates with the Windows Installer and offers additional functionality relative to the Package and Deployment Wizard.

Visual Studio Installer

The Visual Studio Installer was developed after the release of Visual Studio 6.0. It is available to registered owners of Visual Studio by download or by ordering a CD. Both the download and the CD order form are on the Microsoft Web site at the following URL:

```
http://msdn.microsoft.com/vstudio/downloads/
vsi/default.asp
```

Features of the Visual Studio Installer

The Visual Studio Installer is a program that can assemble packages compatible with the Windows Installer. The packages contain all of the files and information necessary to install the software application under the control of the Windows Installer. Creating an installation package that is compatible with the Windows Installer gains several advantages over a stand-alone installation package:

✦ The installation package can contain software components that were developed in multiple languages within Visual Studio. For example, there could be component written in Visual Basic, as well as components written in Visual C++.

✦ The Visual Studio Installer contains templates that make it easy to create an installation package from a Visual Studio project.

✦ Modifications to the destination system are easily configured using the graphical interface.

✦ Applications can be configured to be self-healing. If a file required for the application becomes damaged or is accidentally deleted, the file can be automatically replaced by the operating system.

✦ Installer supports rollback as an alternative to a simple uninstall. During installation, information is recorded about all changes that are made to the computer so that all changes can be reversed to their previous state. This technology makes uninstalling software much safer that it has previously been.

When the Visual Studio Installer is installed, a new project type can be created within Visual Studio (VS). For any language other than Visual Basic (which uses a slightly different development environment), an Installer project can be added to the solution. For a program written in Visual Basic, a user can start the VS Installer from the Microsoft Visual Studio ➪ Visual Studio Enterprise Tools group in the Start menu and then be able to create a new Installer project. An application program project should be completely written, tested, and compiled before an Installer package is created.

VS Installer project types

Figure 33-1 is displayed when an Installer project is created. The Installer project template can be selected from the three choices shown in the dialog box.

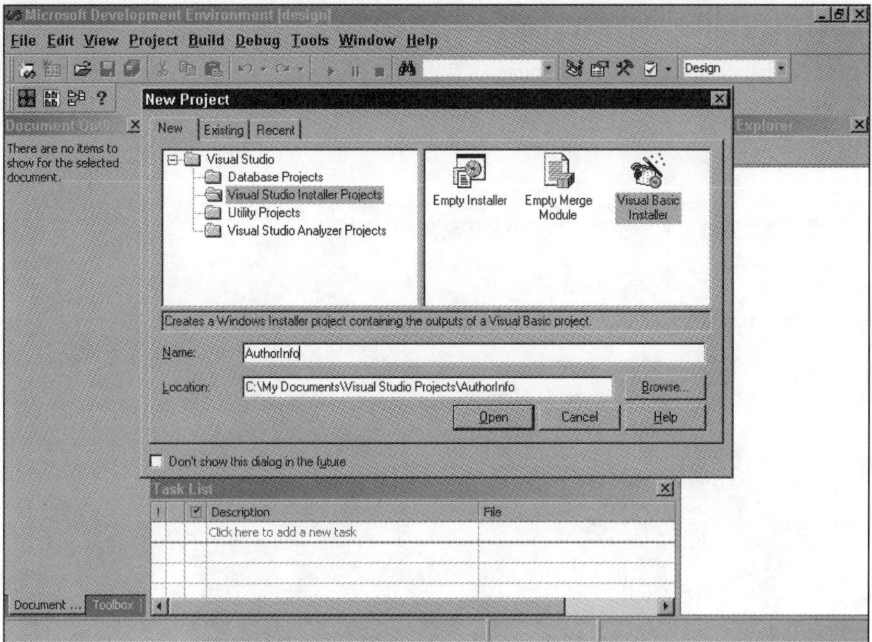

Figure 33-1: VS Installer project types

Empty Installer

An Empty Installer package enables the user to specify all of the contents of a complete Installer package. The resulting package can be installed on any computer that is running the Windows Installer.

Empty Merge Module

An Empty Merge Module enables the user to completely specify all of the contents of a merge module. A merge module cannot be installed as it stands; it must first be merged into a standard Installer package. Merge modules are often used for software components that will be shared by more than one application.

Visual Basic Installer

A Visual Basic Installer package contains some predefined logic to make it easier to create an Installer package from a Visual Basic project. Once the Visual Basic project is added, the user has complete control over the contents of the package. The resulting package can be installed on any computer running the Windows Installer.

Configuring an Installer package

Most of the configuration process is the same for each of the three Installer project templates. If a user chooses to create a Visual Basic Installer project, the screen shown in Figure 33-2 prompts the user to select a Visual Basic project.

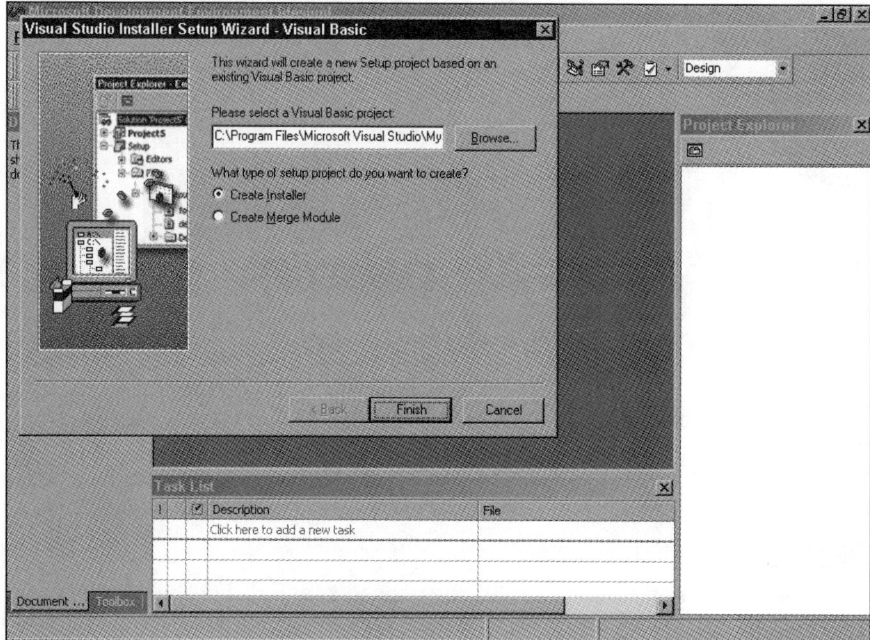

Figure 33-2: Selecting a Visual Basic project

Adding application program projects to an Installer package

A user can choose to make a Visual Basic project into an Installer package or a merge module. The package will be scanned, and all of the files necessary for the VB program will be added to the package. Settings will also be preset for the file system, user interface, Registry, and associations portions of the Installer package in accordance with the demands of the program.

The VS Installer can also be commanded to scan a Visual Basic project after the Installer project has been created by right-clicking the Installer project in the Project Explorer window and choosing Add ➪ Visual Basic Project Outputs. The outputs from multiple Visual Basic projects can be added to a single Installer package.

The outputs from J++ Visual Studio projects that are compiled as executables or COM DLLs can also be added by right-clicking the Installer project and choosing Add ➪ Project from the menu. Other types of J++ projects and all C++ projects can be added by individually adding the files associated with the projects.

Working with project files and dependencies

Figure 33-3 shows the Installer project immediately after a Visual Basic project has been scanned and its components added. The Project Explorer on the right side of the screen shows the containers for each aspect of the Installer package. At the bottom of the Project Explorer window, the Files container is expanded to show the files that have been added to the package as a result of scanning the Visual Basic project. In this case, there is a single executable, AuthorInfo.exe, and five dependencies. A Visual Basic program typically depends on having access to certain Dynamic Link Libraries (DLLs). The VS Installer automatically adds merge modules for standard DLLs to the Installer package. The merge modules contain all of the information and files necessary to install the DLLs on the destination computer.

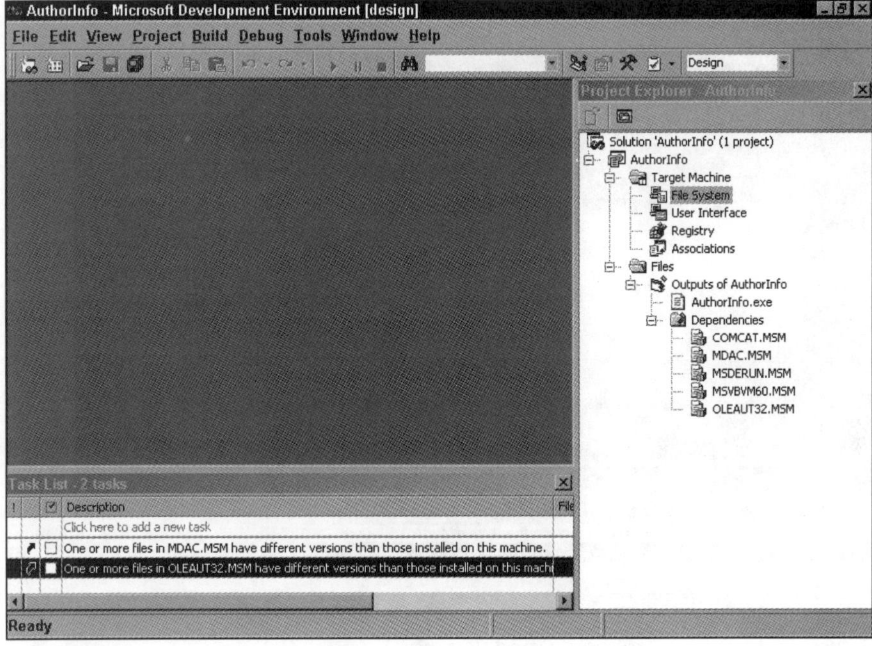

Figure 33-3: A Visual Basic Installer project

If all computers on which the Installer package will be deployed are known to already have the Visual Basic run time, MSVBMV60.MS can be removed from the dependencies list. This will make the package slightly smaller and the installation slightly faster. A deleted dependency still appears in the list, but with a dimmed icon. Deleted dependencies can be restored from the right-click menu.

The Installer also examines the versions of the DLLs in the merge modules and compares them with the versions installed on the computer on which it is run. The computer on which the VS Installer is run is usually the same computer on which the application program was originally developed and tested. It may be problematic if different versions of the DLLs are distributed with the project. Any version discrepancies are noted in the task list. There are two discrepancies shown in Figure 33-3. Particular attention should be paid to the associated DLLs during testing of the package.

Figure 33-4 shows the dialog box where search paths used to find merge modules can be changed. A user can change this path to update a merge module to add the correct version of a DLL to a package. This dialog box is accessed by right-clicking the project in the Project Explorer window, choosing Properties, and clicking the Merge Module Search Path tab. The check box at the bottom of this dialog box allows the DLL version checking to be turned off.

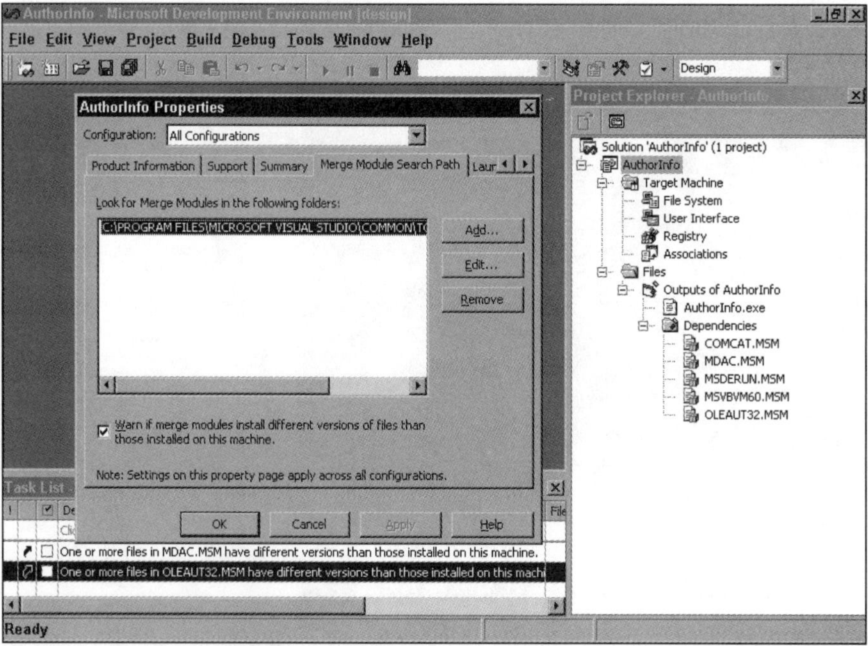

Figure 33-4: Setting the merge module path

Setting the project properties

Figure 33-5 displays another important dialog box from the project properties, the Build tab.

The Installer project Build properties dialog box allows a user to specify the name of the package file and the directory in which it will be stored. It also enables the user to configure several other aspects of the final package.

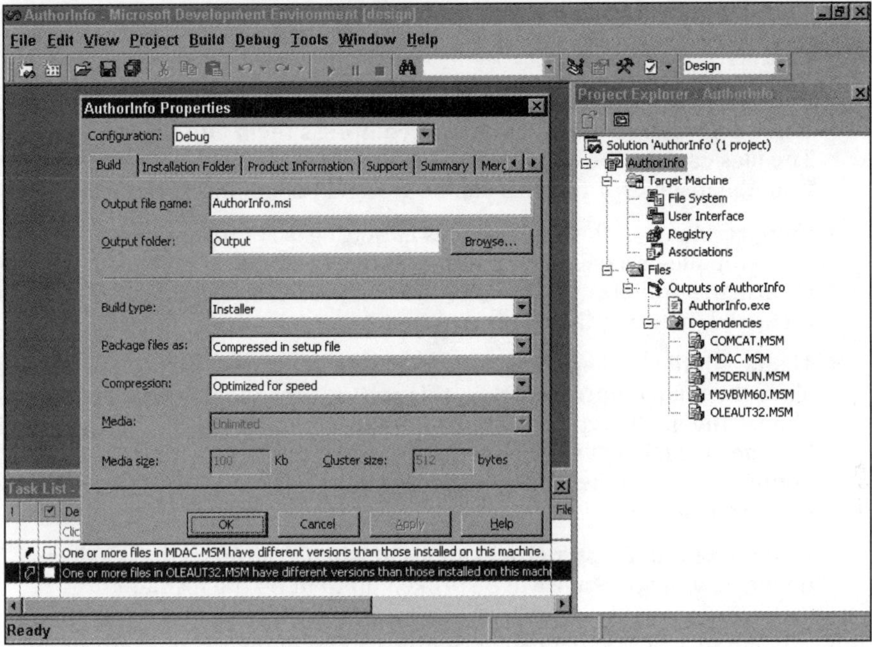

Figure 33-5: Installer project Build properties

The Build type drop-down list has three possible choices:

✦ **Installer**—creates an Installer package that can be installed on any computer that already has the Windows Installer set up and running.

✦ **Installer with Windows Installer Loader**—creates a setup executable that checks the destination computer for the presence of the Windows Installer, and if it is not present, will install it. This would not be necessary for any computers running Windows 2000, but would make the package more foolproof (and larger) for Windows 95, 98, or NT. Several additional files are added to the subdirectory when this option is used. These files are the msi file, which contains the package; the setup executable, which will run a detection process before starting the installation; setup.ini, which contains information for the setup executable; and instmsiw.exe and instmsia.exe, which are setup programs for the Windows Installer on Windows NT and Windows 95/98, respectively.

✦ **Merge Module**—changes the output into a merge module that must be merged into an Installer package before being deployed.

There are also some choices in this dialog box that control the compression and storage of the files that are part of the package:

- **Package files as**—enables a user to specify how the files used in the installation will be stored. The default is to compress them into the setup file itself. The files can also be compressed into a single cab file, which will be distinct from the msi file, or the files can be stored in uncompressed format.
- **Compression**—if the Package files as setting is set to compress the files in the setup file or a cab file, then this setting is enabled. It enables the user to choose the optimization used for the compression. The default is to optimize for speed, but to optimize for size or not to compress are also valid choices.
- **Media**—if the Package files as setting is set to store files in a cab file or to leave them uncompressed, then this setting is enabled. It enables the user to choose the media type on which to distribute the package. Choosing unlimited means no limits will be placed on the size of the package. Choosing CD, floppy, or custom means the package will be broken up into pieces that will fit on the chosen media.
- **Media size and Cluster size**—are used when custom media is selected. They define how the package will be broken up to fit on the media.

Other project properties that can be set by accessing the various tabs in the dialog box are as follows:

- **Installation folder**—specifies where, on the destination computer, the application will be installed.
- **Product information**—assigns a Global Unique Identifier (GUID) to the application being deployed and to the specific version of the application. The product code should be set to a new value for each new version of the software deployed. The upgrade code should remain the same so that the Windows Installer is capable of identifying whether or not there is an existing version on the computer and is capable of upgrading it appropriately. A human-readable version number in the form 1.0.0.0 can also be specified.
- **Support and summary**—provides information for users to identify the application and to contact support personnel.
- **Launch conditions**—perform conditional logic that will determine whether or not the application should be installed. For example, a user can test the version of the operating system to ensure that it will properly support the application. The conditions specified must evaluate to true on the destination computer, or the package will not install and will return an error message to the user.

File System settings

Figure 33-6 shows the File System window, which enables a user to specify any changes that will be made to the file system of the computer on which the package will be installed. This window can be accessed by double-clicking File System in the Project Explorer window.

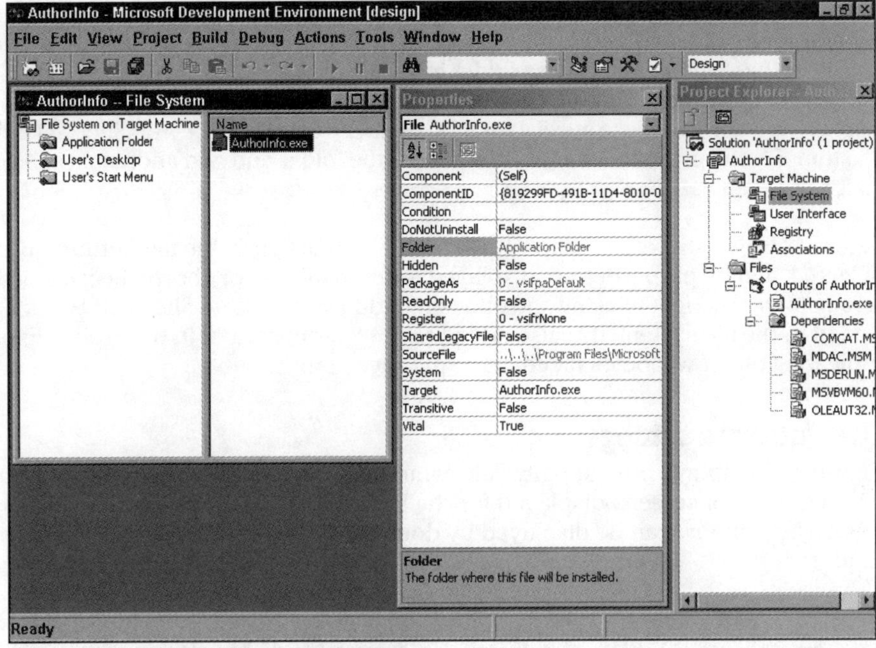

Figure 33-6: Configuring the File System

By default, three folders are shown in the File System window: the Application Folder, the User's Desktop, and the User's Start Menu. Additional folders can be displayed by right-clicking in the File System window and choosing Add Special Folder. This menu item enables the user to configure changes for any of the following folders on the target computer:

- Windows Folder
- Windows System Folder
- Common Files Folder
- User's Favorites Folder
- User's Application Data Folder
- User's Personal Data Folder
- User's Send To Menu
- User's Template Folder
- Font Folder

All of these folders are defined by the operating system on the target computer. Files or shortcuts can be added to any of these folders. New subfolders can also be added to any of these by right-clicking a folder in the File System window and choosing Add Folder from the menu. To add a new folder to the target computer that is not contained within one of these special folders, right-click and choose Add Special Folder ➪ Custom. The user can then enter the name of the folder and add additional subfolders to it as desired.

Figure 33-6 also shows the Properties window. In this figure, the file AuthorInfo.exe is selected, and its properties are displayed. Additional files or shortcuts can be added to any folder by right-clicking and choosing Add File or Create Shortcut. When a file is added to the file system, it is also added to the Files container in the Project Explorer, indicating that it will be included in the package.

User Interface settings

Figure 33-7 displays the User Interface window, which enables the user to control the sequence of screens displayed for the user during the package installation process. This window can be displayed by double-clicking User Interface in the Project Explorer.

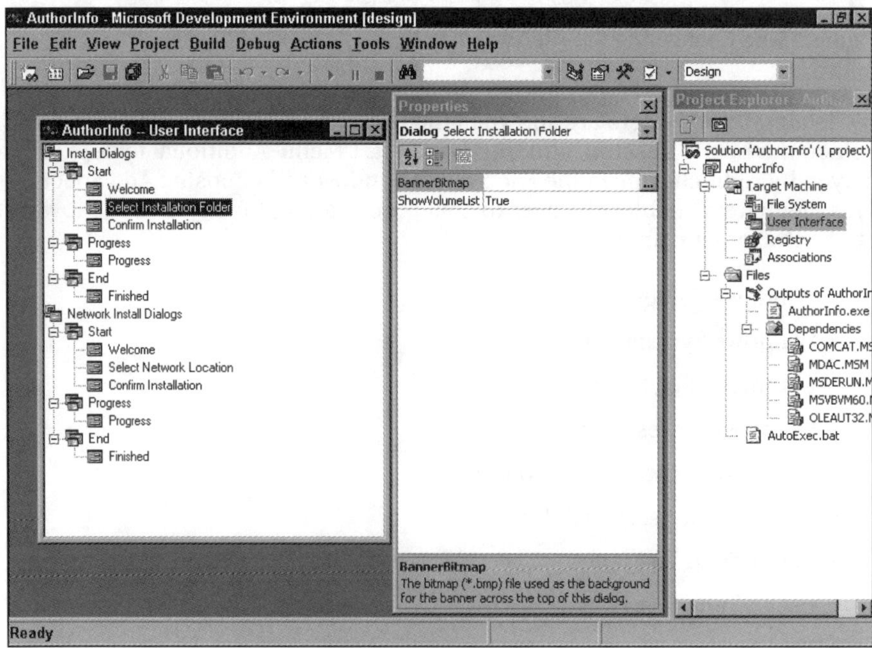

Figure 33-7: Configuring the User Interface

In addition to the dialogs shown in Figure 33-7, more dialogs can be added by right-clicking one of the nodes under Install Dialogs and choosing Add Dialog. The dialogs available to add are as follows:

- ✦ Register User
- ✦ Read Me
- ✦ Customer Information
- ✦ License Agreement
- ✦ Splash

Each dialog has a few properties. All dialogs enable the user to choose a banner bitmap that is representative of the application being installed. Some dialogs have their own specific properties, such as the Select Installation Folder, shown in Figure 33-7, which enables the user to choose whether or not a volume list control should be displayed.

Registry settings

Figure 33-8 shows the Registry window, which enables the user to configure any changes that the package should make on target computers during installation. This window can be displayed by double-clicking Registry in the Project Explorer.

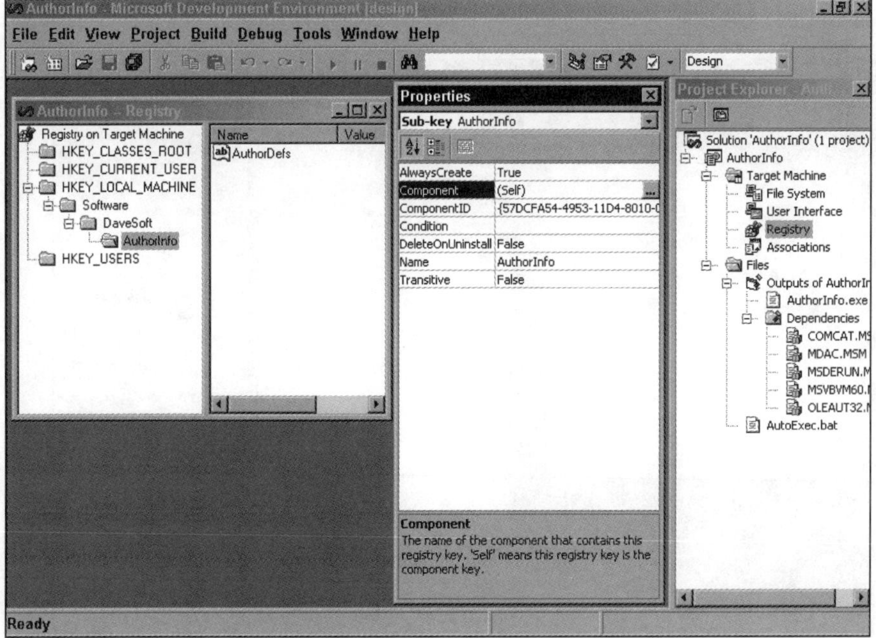

Figure 33-8: Configuring the Registry

By default, the Registry window shows four hives (hives are the top-level structure in the Registry) from the Registry: HKEY_CLASSES_ROOT, HKEY_CURRENT_USER, HKEY_LOCAL_MACHINE, and HKEY_USERS. To specify modifications that should be added to the Registry on the target computer:

1. Right-click on the appropriate hive.
2. From the menu, choose New ➪ Key.
3. Type the appropriate name in the new key and repeat the process until reaching the point in the Registry hierarchy at which new values should be added.
4. Right-click on the key that is to contain the value, choose Add from the menu, and select the type of value that is to be added: String, Binary, or DWORD.
5. Data can then be added to the value.

Both keys and values have properties. Figure 33-8 shows the properties associated with a key. A user can specify whether the key should be deleted if the application is ever uninstalled. A user can also specify a condition that must exist for the Installer to add the key to the Registry.

Associations settings

Figure 33-9 displays the Associations window, which enables the user to configure the associations that will be created on the target computer. Double-clicking Associations in the Project Explorer displays this window.

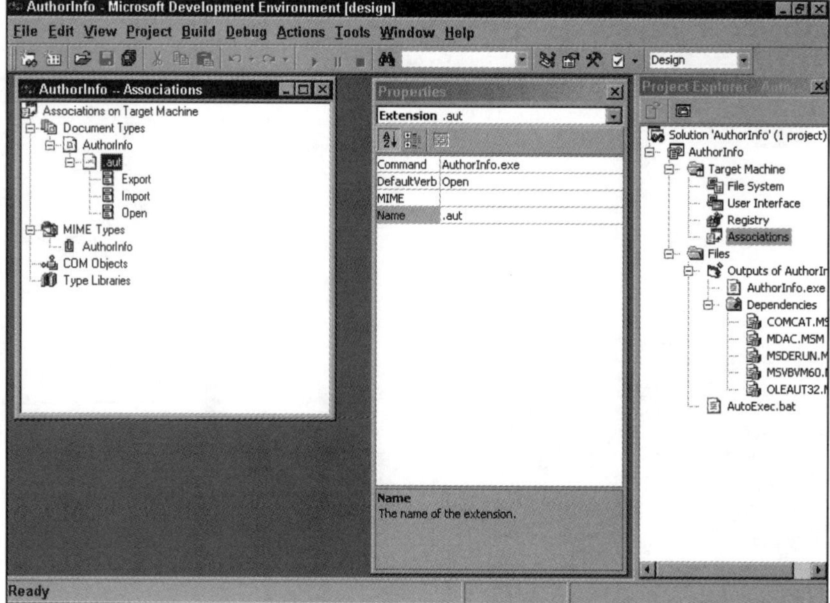

Figure 33-9: Configuring Associations

Four types of associations are available: document types, MIME types, COM objects, and Type libraries. Figure 33-9 shows a document type called AuthorInfo. Every document type must have at least one file extension that identifies it, as does AuthorInfo, but additional file extensions can be added if necessary. The properties of the file extension define the name of the extension, the command and MIME type that are associated with it, and a default verb. Any number of verbs may be associated with the file type; they are displayed when a file of that type is right-clicked in Windows Explorer. The verbs must all have defined meanings for the command associated with the file type.

MIME types can be added to associate an application with a MIME object. Doing so allows e-mail attachments to invoke the application. COM objects and type libraries can be added to allow the Windows Installer to perform the registration, rather than using self-registering objects. Enabling the Installer to perform the registration provides all of the advantages of the Installer for COM objects as well as application programs. The Installer can provide advertising for the objects, that is, the information about the object can be added to the target computer, but the actual installation of the object occurs only when it is first accessed. The Installer can also provide self-healing and rollback capabilities for the COM objects.

Building and deploying the package

When all of the settings have been configured for the file system, user interface, Registry, associations, files, dependencies, and project properties, the package can be built and deployed. Building the project compiles all of the components together into a package according to the specifications in the package properties. A user can initiate a build from the Build menu, or the package can be automatically built when deployed. Deploying copies the package to one or more locations.

By default, VS Installer will deploy the package to the local computer. A new deployment target can be added from the Project menu, by choosing New Deployment Target as shown in Figure 33-10. From the dialog box shown in the figure a user can select an Installer project and enter a URL to a Web server that is configured to receive HTTP posts. When a deployment location has been entered, it is displayed in the Deployment Explorer, as seen on the right side of Figure 33-10. As many deployment targets as are needed can be entered. The package can be deployed to any individual target or to all targets, either through the Project menu or by right-clicking in the Deployment Explorer.

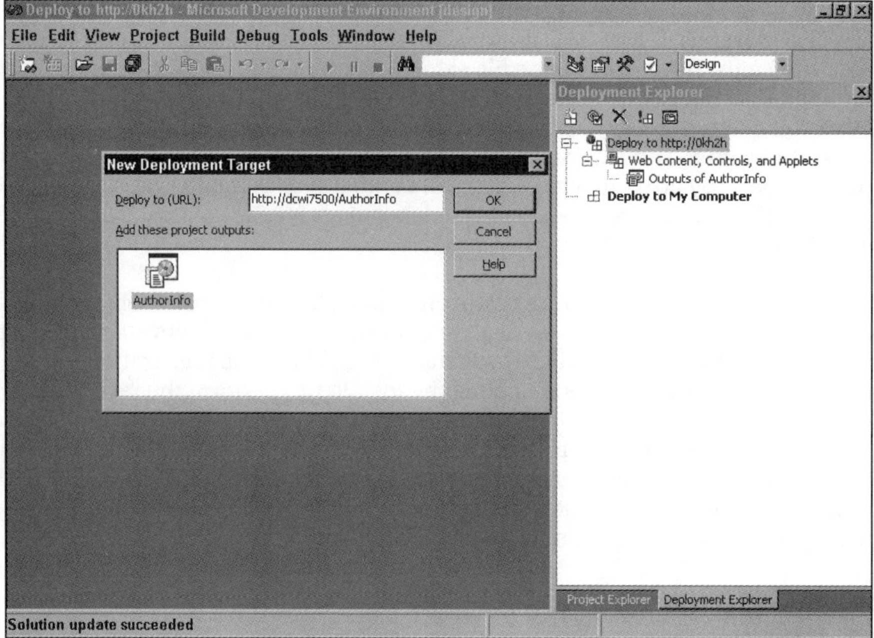

Figure 33-10: Deploying the package

Merging MSDE modules with your project

Two steps are required to add MSDE to an Installer package: add the merge modules into the package and add the configuration information to the package ini file.

To add the merge modules to the package:

1. Right-click anywhere in the Project Explorer and choose Add ⇨ Merge Modules.
2. Browse to the location of the merge modules, which on the SQL Server CD is \MSDE\MSM. Add all of the files in this directory.
3. Add the files in the appropriate localized subdirectory contained within the merge module directory. The subdirectory contains the localized, language-specific files. For U.S. English, the localized directory is Msm\1033.

After the merge modules are added project properties can be set as described above, and the project can be built. If a single msi file is built, MSDE will be installed with all default settings. The settings can be modified (for example, the instance name or install directory) by building an Installer package with Windows Installer Loader. A file called setup.ini will be placed in the output directory. This file must be opened to add a section called [Options] and to set any of the ini parameters for the MSDE setup (see Chapter 31).

Testing the Installer package

Because of the resilient features of Installer packages, special procedures must be followed to properly test the package. Whenever a package is installed on a computer, a copy of the msi file is cached on the computer. The cached copy allows the package to be repaired or reinstalled at any time. However, the cached copy is run preferentially. To test a new version of a package, the cached copy of the package msi file must be removed.

If an Installer package is run from within the Visual Studio Installer environment, the cached copy is automatically deleted. The package can be run from the Visual Studio Installer environment by right-clicking the package in the Project Explorer Window and choosing Launch Installer from the menu.

The cached copy of the msi file can also be removed by right-clicking the msi file itself and choosing Uninstall. The uninstall process will remove the cached copy as well as the entire application.

Distributing the Installer package

After an Installer package has been created and tested, it must be distributed to the target computers and installed. There are several methods for distribution. The choice of method is dependent on the environment in which a user is working.

Getting the file to the user

There are many methods for distributing packages to users. The method that will be used to integrate the distribution method with the installation process should be considered. Visual Studio Installer can distribute the package to a directory on a network share or to a Web site. Users can then initiate the installation process from their computers. Running the installation program can be automated by using a login script, sending a script to users (perhaps through e-mail), by using a software distribution mechanism such as SMS, or by using Group Policy.

Installing the Installer

When planning software distribution, a user must consider the operating systems that will be used. Windows 2000 comes with the Installer preinstalled as part of the operating system; Windows 95, 98, and NT do not. If the operating system does not have the Installer, the user must create a package that will install the Installer service as well as the application.

Using Group Policy in Windows 2000 Active Directory

Windows 2000 Active Directory provides a built-in mechanism for distributing and installing software. The mechanism is called Group Policy (it has other uses as well). It enables software to be published or advertised to a user or computer.

When the software has been published or advertised, it becomes available to the user, but is only fully installed when first used or when the user specifically installs it in Control Panel.

Package and Deployment Wizard

The Package and Deployment Wizard is an integral part of Visual Studio 6.0. It uses technology similar to the Package and Deployment Wizard available with Access 2000, which is discussed in detail in Chapter 32. The biggest difference between the two wizards, with regard to deploying MSDE, is that the Visual Studio wizard does not have support in the GUI for automatically starting a process at the conclusion of the primary installation.

To use the Package and Deployment Wizard to distribute MSDE along with the application, the setup1 executable must be modified. Setup1 is a component of the output of the Package and Deployment Wizard that is always run during setup. The source code for this project is provided by default in the directory \Program Files\Microsoft Visual Studio\VB98\Wizards\PDWizard\Setup1.

Summary

There are two primary methods for distributing projects created in Visual Studio: the Package and Deployment Wizard and the Visual Studio Installer. MSDE can be distributed with an application by using either method.

To distribute MSDE with the Package and Deployment Wizard requires the user to modify the code of the setup1 executable that the wizard uses as part of the package. It is a manual operation and does not integrate with the Windows Installer. Packages deployed with this method do not have self-healing or rollback capability.

To distribute MSDE with the Visual Studio Installer requires a user to add the merge modules to the project and, optionally, to add configuration commands to the ini file. Packages distributed this way integrate with the Windows Installer and Active Directory Group Policy. They support advertising, publishing, rollback, and self-healing.

✦ ✦ ✦

APPENDIX A

What's On the CD-ROM

✦ ✦ ✦ ✦

The CD that accompanies this book contains a complete copy of the text of the book in electronic (pdf) format. The Acrobat Reader software is also included to allow the viewing of any pdf file.

All the VBScript and Visual Basic code examples from the text are included on the CD. These programs have all been tested and are free of typographical errors. For the most part, only the server name in the code examples will need to be changed when they are run. The code files have been organized by chapter and named according to the function they perform. For example, the file createdb.vbs contains the code necessary to create a database. It will be found in the Ch 6 subdirectory, since it was presented in Chapter 6. All the code presented in the book also contains "On the CD-ROM" callouts that refer to the file on the CD for easy reference.

Most of the code samples are succinct to make them easy to understand and easy to reuse. This code can be used as a starting point in one's own software development. This book is intended to be used as a tool that will make developing applications that use MSDE easier, and the code we present is an important part of the package.

✦ ✦ ✦

Index

C

Continued

Continued

E

Continued

G

H

I

J

O

P

T

Continued

X

IDG Books Worldwide, Inc. End-User License Agreement

READ THIS. You should carefully read these terms and conditions before opening the software packet(s) included with this book ("Book"). This is a license agreement ("Agreement") between you and IDG Books Worldwide, Inc. ("IDGB"). By opening the accompanying software packet(s), you acknowledge that you have read and accept the following terms and conditions. If you do not agree and do not want to be bound by such terms and conditions, promptly return the Book and the unopened software packet(s) to the place you obtained them for a full refund.

1. **License Grant.** IDGB grants to you (either an individual or entity) a nonexclusive license to use one copy of the enclosed software program(s) (collectively, the "Software") solely for your own personal or business purposes on a single computer (whether a standard computer or a workstation component of a multiuser network). The Software is in use on a computer when it is loaded into temporary memory (RAM) or installed into permanent memory (hard disk, CD-ROM, or other storage device). IDGB reserves all rights not expressly granted herein.

2. **Ownership.** IDGB is the owner of all right, title, and interest, including copyright, in and to the compilation of the Software recorded on the disk(s) or CD-ROM ("Software Media"). Copyright to the individual programs recorded on the Software Media is owned by the author or other authorized copyright owner of each program. Ownership of the Software and all proprietary rights relating thereto remain with IDGB and its licensers.

3. **Restrictions On Use and Transfer.**

   (a) You may only (i) make one copy of the Software for backup or archival purposes, or (ii) transfer the Software to a single hard disk, provided that you keep the original for backup or archival purposes. You may not (i) rent or lease the Software, (ii) copy or reproduce the Software through a LAN or other network system or through any computer subscriber system or bulletin-board system, or (iii) modify, adapt, or create derivative works based on the Software.

   (b) You may not reverse engineer, decompile, or disassemble the Software. You may transfer the Software and user documentation on a permanent basis, provided that the transferee agrees to accept the terms and conditions of this Agreement and you retain no copies. If the Software is an update or has been updated, any transfer must include the most recent update and all prior versions.

4. **Restrictions on Use of Individual Programs.** You must follow the individual requirements and restrictions detailed for each individual program in the *What's on the CD-ROM* appendix of this Book. These limitations are also

contained in the individual license agreements recorded on the Software Media. These limitations may include a requirement that after using the program for a specified period of time, the user must pay a registration fee or discontinue use. By opening the Software packet(s), you will be agreeing to abide by the licenses and restrictions for these individual programs that are detailed in the *What's on the CD-ROM* appendix and on the Software Media. None of the material on this Software Media or listed in this Book may ever be redistributed, in original or modified form, for commercial purposes.

5. Limited Warranty.

(a) IDGB warrants that the Software and Software Media are free from defects in materials and workmanship under normal use for a period of sixty (60) days from the date of purchase of this Book. If IDGB receives notification within the warranty period of defects in materials or workmanship, IDGB will replace the defective Software Media.

(b) IDGB AND THE AUTHORS OF THE BOOK DISCLAIM ALL OTHER WARRANTIES, EXPRESS OR IMPLIED, INCLUDING WITHOUT LIMITATION IMPLIED WARRANTIES OF MERCHANTABILITY AND FITNESS FOR A PARTICULAR PURPOSE, WITH RESPECT TO THE SOFTWARE, THE PROGRAMS, THE SOURCE CODE CONTAINED THEREIN, AND/OR THE TECHNIQUES DESCRIBED IN THIS BOOK. IDGB DOES NOT WARRANT THAT THE FUNCTIONS CONTAINED IN THE SOFTWARE WILL MEET YOUR REQUIREMENTS OR THAT THE OPERATION OF THE SOFTWARE WILL BE ERROR FREE.

(c) This limited warranty gives you specific legal rights, and you may have other rights that vary from jurisdiction to jurisdiction.

6. Remedies.

(a) IDGB's entire liability and your exclusive remedy for defects in materials and workmanship shall be limited to replacement of the Software Media, which may be returned to IDGB with a copy of your receipt at the following address: Software Media Fulfillment Department, Attn.: *MSDE Bible*, IDG Books Worldwide, Inc., 10475 Crosspoint Blvd., Indianapolis, IN 46256, or call 1-800-762-2974. Please allow three to four weeks for delivery. This Limited Warranty is void if failure of the Software Media has resulted from accident, abuse, or misapplication. Any replacement Software Media will be warranted for the remainder of the original warranty period or thirty (30) days, whichever is longer.

(b) In no event shall IDGB or the authors be liable for any damages whatsoever (including without limitation damages for loss of business profits, business interruption, loss of business information, or any other pecuniary loss) arising from the use of or inability to use the Book or the Software, even if IDGB has been advised of the possibility of such damages.

(c) Because some jurisdictions do not allow the exclusion or limitation of liability for consequential or incidental damages, the above limitation or exclusion may not apply to you.

7. **U.S. Government Restricted Rights.** Use, duplication, or disclosure of the Software by the U.S. Government is subject to restrictions stated in paragraph (c)(1)(ii) of the Rights in Technical Data and Computer Software clause of DFARS 252.227-7013, and in subparagraphs (a) through (d) of the Commercial Computer—Restricted Rights clause at FAR 52.227-19, and in similar clauses in the NASA FAR supplement, when applicable.

8. **General.** This Agreement constitutes the entire understanding of the parties and revokes and supersedes all prior agreements, oral or written, between them and may not be modified or amended except in a writing signed by both parties hereto that specifically refers to this Agreement. This Agreement shall take precedence over any other documents that may be in conflict herewith. If any one or more provisions contained in this Agreement are held by any court or tribunal to be invalid, illegal, or otherwise unenforceable, each and every other provision shall remain in full force and effect.

my2cents.idgbooks.com

Register This Book — And Win!

Visit **http://my2cents.idgbooks.com** to register this book and we'll automatically enter you in our fantastic monthly prize giveaway. It's also your opportunity to give us feedback: let us know what you thought of this book and how you would like to see other topics covered.

Discover IDG Books Online!

The IDG Books Online Web site is your online resource for tackling technology — at home and at the office. Frequently updated, the IDG Books Online Web site features exclusive software, insider information, online books, and live events!

10 Productive & Career-Enhancing Things You Can Do at www.idgbooks.com

- Nab source code for your own programming projects.
- Download software.
- Read Web exclusives: special articles and book excerpts by IDG Books Worldwide authors.
- Take advantage of resources to help you advance your career as a Novell or Microsoft professional.
- Buy IDG Books Worldwide titles or find a convenient bookstore that carries them.
- Register your book and win a prize.
- Chat live online with authors.
- Sign up for regular e-mail updates about our latest books.
- Suggest a book you'd like to read or write.
- Give us your 2¢ about our books and about our Web site.

You say you're not on the Web yet? It's easy to get started with IDG Books' *Discover the Internet,* available at local retailers everywhere.

CD-ROM Installation Instructions

Each software item on the *MSDE Bible* CD-ROM is located in its own folder. To install a particular piece of software, open its folder with My Computer or Internet Explorer. What you do next depends on what you find in the software's folder:

1. First, look for a `ReadMe.txt` file or a `.doc` or `.htm` document. If this is present, it should contain installation instructions and other useful information.
2. If the folder contains an executable (`.exe`) file, this is usually an installation program. Often it will be called `Setup.exe` or `Install.exe`, but in some cases the filename reflects an abbreviated version of the software's name and version number. Run the `.exe` file to start the installation process.

The `ReadMe.txt` file in the CD-ROM's root directory may contain additional installation information, so be sure to check it.

For a listing of the software on the CD-ROM, see the Appendix.